INSTRUCTOR'S MANUAL

to accompany

THE ART
OF PUBLIC SPEAKING

Eighth Edition

STEPHEN E. LUCAS
University of Wisconsin—Madison

Mc
Graw
Hill

Boston   Burr Ridge, IL   Dubuque, IA   Madison, WI   New York   San Francisco   St. Louis
Bangkok   Bogotá   Caracas   Kuala Lumpur   Lisbon   London   Madrid   Mexico City
Milan   Montreal   New Delhi   Santiago   Seoul   Singapore   Sydney   Taipei   Toronto

Instructor's Manual to accompany
THE ART OF PUBLIC SPEAKING
Stephen E. Lucas

1 2 3 4 5 6 7 8 9 0 CUS/CUS 0 9 8 7 6 5 4 3

ISBN 0-07-256410-5

www.mhhe.com

Contents

Evaluation and Instructional Forms

Analyses of Speeches from *The Art of Public Speaking*

Preface

This manual is a guide to teaching from *The Art of Public Speaking*. It is intended primarily for the benefit of new and less experienced instructors, but I hope you will find it valuable even if you have been teaching public speaking for many years.

The first part of the manual presents course outlines based on *The Art of Public Speaking* for both the semester and quarter systems. Part II explains the speech assignments included in the course outlines and offers alternative assignments as well. Part III discusses evaluation and grading and includes several forms for evaluating student speeches.

Part IV is a chapter-by-chapter guide to *The Art of Public Speaking*. For each chapter of the book it provides a statement of objectives, a chapter outline, discussions of the application exercises presented in the book, additional suggestions for exercises and classroom activities, and a fully updated bibliography of supplementary learning and teaching resources.

In addition to the exercises in the book and in this manual, instructors will find more than 350 speech assignments and classroom activities in the five anthologies of selections from *The Speech Communication Teacher* that accompany this edition of *The Art of Public Speaking*. Written by teachers for teachers, these articles offer a wealth of practical ideas for classroom use.

Part V of this manual contains speeches for analysis and evaluation. They supplement the speeches in the appendix that follows Chapter 18 of the textbook, and each is followed by a brief guide for classroom discussion.

The Art of Public Speaking also includes an Annotated Instructor's Edition, which provides a wealth of teaching aids for each chapter in the book. These aids include instructional strategies, class activities, discussion questions, speech assignments, and related readings. The Annotated Instructor's Edition is designed to complement the *Instructor's Manual*, and it is cross-referenced with the *Manual* as well as with all the other supplements that accompany *The Art of Public Speaking*.

To help instructors prepare examinations, I have prepared a separate volume titled *Test Bank to Accompany The Art of Public Speaking*. The *Test Bank* contains more than 1,900 true-false, multiple-choice, short-answer, and essay questions—all of which are also available on disk for computerized test construction. In addition, the *Test Bank* provides two preconstructed quizzes for each chapter, as well as three sample final examinations. As a special feature, it also includes a guest essay by Anita Vangelisti of the University of Texas on test construction and assessment.

This manual has once again been printed on 8½ x 11 tear-out pages, so instructors can easily reproduce exercises, speeches, and evaluation forms for use in the classroom. Finally, to facilitate classroom discussion, many exercises from the manual are included in the binder of 120 overhead transparencies that accompanies this edition of *The Art of Public Speaking*.

In preparing this manual, my aim has been to provide the most helpful resource of its kind available with any public speaking textbook. If you have questions about the manual, or suggestions for improving it, please contact me at the Department of Communication Arts, University of Wisconsin, Madison, WI 53706. You can also reach me by e-mail at selucas@wisc.edu.

A Guide to Instructional Resources
for *The Art of Public Speaking*

Every aspect of the textbook, the print supplements, the Student CD-ROM, the video program, and *The Art of Public Speaking* Online Learning Center have been carefully developed to ensure that they work together as an integrated teaching and learning system. Each element of the system is explained below. By summarizing them here, my aim is to provide a clear sense of the teaching and learning resources available with *The Art of Pubic Speaking*, so individual instructors can determine which are best suited to meeting the needs of their students.

Student CD-ROM

Introduced with the 7th edition and fully revised for the current edition, the Student CD-ROM seeks to bring public speaking to life by bridging the gap between the printed page and the spoken word. Specially marked icons in the margins of the book direct readers to the appropriate resources on the CD. Those resources have been carefully designed to help students master the skills, concepts, and principles discussed in the text.

The CD was designed to be used by students, on their own, as they read the book, prepare their speeches, and study for exams. Many instructors, however, have integrated it with their reading assignments and classroom discussions—either by requiring that students view the appropriate section of the CD in preparation for class or by using the CD directly in the classroom. Instructors in distance-learning and online courses have found the CD to be especially valuable because it gives their students the kind of help they need to succeed outside the traditional classroom.

The CD contains 10 components: speech videos, study questions, speech outliner, outline exercises, bibliography formats, speech preparation checklists, glossary of key terms, key-term flashcards, notepad, and a link to the Online Learning Center with PowerWeb. Let me say a word about each.

Speech Videos

The CD contains 58 video clips that demonstrate the principles of public speaking in action. As students read the book, icons in the margins guide them to the appropriate video clips. Each clip has been chosen to illustrate a specific aspect of speechmaking, and each is fully coordinated with the book. So, for example, in the section of Chapter 9 that deals with preview statements, students can click on the CD and see how the preview statements they are reading in the book were delivered by the original speakers. The same is true of subjects from ethics to visual aids, supporting materials to extemporaneous delivery, introductions and conclusions to language use and audience adaptation.

Running in length from twenty seconds to a minute and a half, the video clips are distributed throughout the book. To help students prepare their classroom speeches, three-fourths are from student presentations. The remainder are from public figures and include such models of rhetorical excellence as Winston Churchill, Martin Luther King, Ronald Reagan, Mary Fisher, Jesse Jackson, and Elizabeth Dole. In addition to helping students develop their skills, these clips give them an opportunity to experience some of the finest and most important speeches of recent time.

In response to requests from users of the 7th edition, a second CD presents 11 full student speeches for analysis and discussion. Included are ice breaker speeches, informative speeches, persuasive speeches, and commemorative speeches. Together, the excerpts and full speeches provide students with approximately two hours of video.

Interactive Study Questions

To reinforce key principles and ideas, the CD contains a comprehensive set of study questions for each chapter. These questions are fully interactive, use a variety of formats, and systematically cover all the major concepts discussed in the book. Entirely different from items in the *Test Bank,* the questions have been written both to quiz students and to help them learn. After students enter their answer for each question, they receive not just an indication of whether the answer is right or wrong, but *feedback* that explains the correct answer.

Speech Outliner

In addition to video clips and study questions, the CD includes a speech outliner that guides students systematically through the process of organizing and outlining their speeches. Fully revised and updated from the speech outliner that accompanied the 7th edition, the new speech outliner is more powerful than its predecessor and provides a unique tool for speech preparation.

As students use the outliner, they move step by step through each element of the speech from title through bibliography. Tutorial screens explain the organizational methods involved in composing each part of the speech, and the outliner automatically formats the speech in accordance with proper outlining principles. It also allows students to save, revise, and print their work, as well as to export it to their own word processors.

Outline Exercises

New to the 8th edition, five interactive outlining exercises give students additional help in developing their skills of speech organization. These exercises present scrambled outlines that students can rearrange in the correct order by using standard drag-and-drop procedures. As in other parts of the CD, the aim of these exercises is to put the resources provided by computer technology to the best possible pedagogical use. The exercises can also be used in the classroom to facilitate the discussion of outlining principles.

Bibliography Formats

To help students prepare their speech bibliographies, the CD presents a comprehensive set of sample citations for both the Modern Language Association (MLA) and American Psychological Association (APA) formats. Covering more than 30 types of source material —from books, essays, and newspaper articles to government publications, personal interviews, television programs, and Internet documents—these sample citations have been fully updated for the current edition.

Speech Preparation Checklists

A dozen checklists help students keep on track as they prepare their speeches. Included are checklists for ethical public speaking, for framing the specific purpose and central idea, for phrasing and organizing main points, for creating the preparation outline, for composing introductions and conclusions, for using supporting materials, and for preparing and presenting visual aids.

Glossary of Key Terms

Throughout the book, key terms are defined in the margin as they appear in the text. Those key terms are reproduced on the CD, where they can be accessed either by chapter or via a master glossary arranged in alphabetical order. Whether students are reviewing for exams or working with the study questions on the CD, they can instantly check the meaning of any key term at the click of a mouse.

Key-Term Flashcards

Developed especially for this edition of *The Art of Public Speaking*, a set of electronic flashcards for each chapter provides another resource for studying key terms. In addition to being fully interactive, the flashcards include an audio option for students who are aural learners.

Notepad

New to this edition, the Notepad feature allows students to take notes as they are using the CD and to save those notes as a .txt file on their computer's hard drive.

Online Learning Center with PowerWeb

The CD contains a link to the *Art of Public Speaking* Online Learning Center, where students will find http://www.mhhe.com/lucas80 a wealth of additional resources that supplement the textbook. Among those resources is the Top 100 American Speeches of the 20th Century. Based on a nationwide survey of 137 communication scholars I conducted at the end of 1999 with Professor Martin Medhurst, the top 100 speeches were rated on two criteria: rhetorical artistry and historical impact.

The Online Learning Center includes at least one link to a website with a transcript of each speech. Many of the links also furnish historical background about the speech and/or links to additional sites with information about the speaker, speech, or occasion. Whenever possible, a link has been provided to a site that contains a full or partial audio presentation of the original speech.

My aim in developing the Top 100 website was to provide a readily accessible way for students to learn more about the rich history of public speaking. One way to incorporate the site into class is to have each student give an informative presentation about one of the Top 100 speeches. Students often find this a fascinating assignment that broadens their horizons beyond the boundaries of their classroom.

The Online Learning center also includes practice quizzes, worksheets, speech evaluation forms, and key-term crossword puzzles—as well as overviews, outlines, and learning objectives for each chapter of the book. Also available at the Online Learning Center are step-by-step tutorials for PowerPoint 2000 and PowerPoint 2002. These tutorials were created for students who need more guidance on the technical details of PowerPoint than can be covered in the textbook. The tutorials can be accessed at www.mhhe.com/lucaspowerpoint.

Finally, the Online Learning Center provides access to McGraw-Hill's Public Speaking PowerWeb, which keeps students up to date and helps them find topics for their presentations by reprinting recent speeches of public interest, as well as news and journal articles related to current issues and to public speaking in general. The PowerWeb also provides weekly updates, links to *New York Times* articles, and a powerful search capability. As with the CD, icons in the margins of the book guide readers to specific elements of the Online Learning Center.

Annotated Instructor's Edition

The *Annotated Instructor's Edition* provides a wealth of teaching aids for each chapter in the book. These aids include instructional strategies, class activities, discussion questions, speech assignments, and related readings. The *Annotated Instructor's Edition* is also cross-referenced with the *Instructor's Manual* and the other supplements that accompany *The Art of Public Speaking*. In preparing the annotations, I have focused primarily on the needs of new and beginning instructors, but I hope the annotations will prove helpful for more experienced instructors as well.

Instructor's Manual

Running to more than 500 pages, the *Instructor's Manual* is a comprehensive guide to teaching from *The Art of Public Speaking*. It contains outlines for each chapter of the book; discusses the end-of-chapter exercises; furnishes supplementary exercises, speeches, and classroom activities; offers suggested course outlines and speaking assignments; and provides 28 additional speeches for analysis and discussion.

Test Bank

The *Test Bank* furnishes more than 1,900 examination questions based on *The Art of Public Speaking*. Approximately 200 of those questions are new to this edition. As a special feature, the *Test Bank* also offers two preconstructed quizzes for each chapter in the book, as well as three complete final examinations. In addition to a print version, an electronic version is available for computerized test construction.

Selections from the Communication Teacher

This edition marks the fifth volume of selections from the *Communication Teacher* (formerly the *Speech Communication Teacher*) that I have compiled to accompany *The Art of Public Speaking*. Like its predecessors, the new collection covers a host of topics related to the teaching of public speaking, including audience analysis, critical thinking, diversity and multiculturalism, ethics, organization and outlining, speech anxiety, persuasion, testing and evaluation, and general instructional methods. All five volumes are available with this edition of the book. Taken together, they reprint almost 350 brief articles that offer a wealth of practical ideas for classroom use.

Videos

There are several videotapes of student presentations that accompany *The Art of Public Speaking*, including a new tape that offers 17 speeches, eight of which are new to this edition. Here is a listing of the speeches. Those marked with an asterisk are printed in the book; the others are printed in this manual.

*The Rare Phobia (Self-Introduction)

My Eye on the World (Self-Introduction)

A Mile in My Shoes (Self-Introduction)

*Steady and True (Introducing a Classmate)

*Questions of Culture (Commemorative)

*The Massachusetts 54th (Commemorative)

James "Cool Papa" Bell (Commemorative)

Feng Shui (Informative)

*Cryonics (Informative)

*Dying to Be Thin (Informative)

Sign Language (Informative: Demonstration)

CPR (Informative: Demonstration)

*The Great Wall of China (Informative: PowerPoint)

*Multicultural, Multilingual (Persuasive)

*Self-Defense on Campus (Persuasive: Monroe's)

*The Ultimate Gift (Persuasive: Monroe's)

To Save a Child (Persuasive: Monroe's)

Except for "Questions of Culture," which was presented at the University of Richmond commencement exercises, and "The Great Wall of China," which was developed especially to illustrate the use of PowerPoint, all the speeches were originally delivered in the classroom and were retaped in the studio. Additional student speeches are available on the videotapes developed in conjunction with previous editions of *The Art of Public Speaking*.

Instructors who adopt *The Art of Public Speaking* can also select from 20 Great Speeches videotapes that accompany the book. Among the selections on these tapes are Martin Luther King's "I Have a Dream," Barbara Bush's 1990 commencement speech at Wellesley College, and Mary Fisher's "A Whisper of AIDS"—all of which are reprinted in the book.

Two other videos—*Be Prepared to Speak* and *Speaking Effectively to 1 or 1,000*—introduce students to the public speaking process and provide helpful advice on dealing with stage fright. Both tapes are entertaining as well as informative, and either can be shown early in the course to help prepare students for their ice breaker speeches.

Overhead Transparencies

The 8th edition of *The Art of Public Speaking* comes with a binder of 120 overhead transparencies. Created to be of maximum value for lecture presentations and classroom discussions, they include a wide range of graphics, illustrations, and exercises from the textbook, as well as additional exercises and classroom activities from the *Instructor's Manual*.

PowerPoint Slides with Video Clips

There is also a collection of more than 400 slides for instructors who use PowerPoint in their lectures and discussions. Instructors can use these slides just as they are, or they can modify the slides to fit the special needs of individual classes. As a new feature, 50 slides include video speech clips as well as text. The PowerPoint slides can be found on the Instructor's Resource CD-ROM described below.

Teaching Public Speaking

Teaching Public Speaking reprints my essay of the same title from *Teaching Communication: Theory, Research, and Methods* (Lawrence Erlbaum Associates). The essay presents an overview of the pedagogical philosophy behind *The Art of Public Speaking* and discusses a number of practical classroom issues. It is available on the Instructor's Resource CD-ROM described below.

Teaching Public Speaking Online

This superb new pamphlet provides a wealth of practical guidance for instructors who are adapting *The Art of Public Speaking* for use in an online environment. Written by Professor Jennifer Cochrane of Indiana University-Purdue University at Indianapolis, it draws upon her experience with online instruction to explore how one can teach an intellectually rich, practically rewarding public speaking course via the Web.

Pamphlets for Teachers of Non-Native Speakers of English

Developed for instructors who have ESL students in their public speaking classes, this 60-page handbook focuses on the central issues that should be considered when working with students from different linguistic and cultural backgrounds. It is available in both print and electronic versions.

Instructor's Resource CD-ROM

For the convenience of instructors, a number of the resources discussed above are available on a single CD. These resources include electronic versions of the *Instructor's Manual*, *Test Bank*, *Selections from the Communication Teacher*, *Teaching Public Speaking*, *Teaching Public Speaking Online*, and the *Pamphlet for Instructors of Non-Native Teachers of English*. This CD also contains the instructor's PowerPoint slides (with videos), as well as files of the overhead transparencies. Like the other computerized resources that accompany *The Art of Public Speaking*, the Instructor's Resource CD is available in both Mac and Windows versions.

From Oratory to Public Speaking

Reprinted from my essay on "Public Speaking" in the *Encyclopedia of Rhetoric* (Oxford University Press), this pamphlet is a new supplement to the 8th edition of *The Art of Public Speaking*. It presents a synoptic view of major developments in the practice and teaching of public speaking during the 20th century, and it illuminates the role of public speaking as a powerful historical force. The pamphlet is brief enough to be assigned to students, but it is also designed to provide insight into the nature and importance of public speaking for graduate assistants and other instructors who may be new to the subject.

Online Resources

Instructors and students alike can take advantage of several outstanding online resources in conjunction with this edition, including the Online Learning Center with PowerWeb, which we discussed earlier. In addition, instructors using *The Art of Public Speaking* have full access to McGraw-Hill's PageOut, which allows teachers to create personal course websites by using a template provided by McGraw Hill. Special features of PageOut include an interactive course syllabus, an online grade book, online testing, and capability for posting personal files and discussions.

All online content for *The Art of Public Speaking* is supported by Web CT, Blackboard, and eCollege.com. For more details, check with a McGraw-Hill representative or visit www.mhhe.com.pageout.

Part One

SUGGESTED

COURSE OUTLINES

Introduction to Part One

The Art of Public Speaking is easily adapted to a wide variety of class schedules and teaching methods. The following class outlines reflect one approach to the course. They take students through a series of reading, application, and speaking assignments that build systematically upon one another. They are also designed to allow students to undertake their first graded speaking assignment without having to read practically the whole book. Reading assignments are structured to give students adequate preparation time for each speech.

The first part of the syllabus culminates in the informative speech and focuses on such basic matters as analyzing the audience, choosing a topic and specific purpose, and organizing the speech. The second part culminates in the persuasive speech and focuses on more complex matters such as the target audience, building credibility, and using evidence and reasoning. The third part culminates in the commemorative speech and focuses on the effective use of language. By the fourth part, which culminates in the final speech, students have been exposed to all the major skills of speechmaking discussed in the textbook. Now the instructor can concentrate on strengthening students' command of those skills.

The course outlines presented here are for a class of roughly twenty students. If you have an appreciably higher enrollment, you will probably have to reduce the length of the speeches or increase the number of class sessions devoted to the presentation of student speeches.

Finally, although these outlines include suggestions for classroom discussion based on the Exercises for Critical Thinking in *The Art of Public Speaking*, there are many more exercises in the Annotated Instructor's Edition of the book, in this manual, and in the five anthologies of selections from *The Speech Communication Teacher* that accompany the book. You should have no trouble choosing exercises that best fit your teaching emphases and the needs of your students.

The speaking assignments indicated in the course outlines are explained in Part Two of this manual.

OUTLINE FOR A 15-WEEK, 45-HOUR SEMESTER

Class Meeting	Topic—Activity	Reading
1	**Course Overview** Introduce yourself; hand out syllabi; explain grading and attendance policies. Assign introductory speeches.	
2	**Basic Principles of Speech Communication** Focus class discussion on selected exercises, text pp. 29-30, or additional exercises from pp. 67-72 of this manual. Explain introductory speeches; show "The Rare Phobia," "My Eye on the World," and "Steady and True" from the videotape of student speeches that accompanies this edition of *The Art of Public Speaking*.	Chapter 1 and "Giving Your First Speech" (pp. 73-83)
3	**Ethics and Public Speaking** Focus class discussion on exercises 1 and 3, text pp. 51-52. Have students develop a code of ethical speaking for their classroom as explained in additional exercise 1 on p. 94 of this manual.	Chapter 2
4	**Introductory Speeches**	
5	**Introductory Speeches**	
6	**Speaking to Inform** Assign informative speeches. Focus class discussion on kinds of informative speeches and guidelines for informative speaking. Show "Cryonics," "Dying to Be Thin," or "Feng Shui" from the videotape of student speeches that accompanies this edition of *The Art of Public Speaking*.	Chapter 14

Class Meeting	Topic—Activity	Reading
7	**Choosing Topics and Purposes** Focus class discussion on exercises 2-4, text pp. 105-106, and Applying the Power of Public Speaking, text p. 107.	Chapter 4
8	**Analyzing the Audience** Focus class discussion on exercises 2 and 4, text p. 134, and Applying the Power of Public Speaking, text p. 135. Use additional exercise 1 on pp. 145-146 of this manual as a classroom activity.	Chapter 5
9	**Organizing the Body of the Speech** Focus class discussion on exercises 1-3 and Applying the Power of Public Speaking, text pp. 220-221. Use additional exercises as needed from pp. 198-201 of this manual.	Chapter 8
10	**Introductions and Conclusions** Focus class discussion on exercise 1 and Applying the Power of Public Speaking, text pp. 244-245. Use additional exercise 1 or 2 on pp. 210-212 of this manual as a classroom activity.	Chapter 9
11	**Outlining the Speech** Focus class discussion on exercise 1, text pp. 261-262, and Applying the Power of Public Speaking, text pp. 262-263. Have students do the interactive outlining exercises on the CD-ROM as a homework assignment; discuss the results in class.	Chapter 10
12	**Delivering the Speech** Focus class discussion on principles of effective delivery. Select from exercises 1-3, text pp. 317-318, or the additional exercises on pp. 260-267 of this manual.	Chapter 12

Class Meeting	Topic—Activity	Reading
13	**Using Visual Aids** Focus class discussion on exercise 2, text p. 341. Use additional exercise 1 on p. 283 of this manual as a classroom activity. If students are using PowerPoint in their speeches, assign "Using PowerPoint," text pp. 343-362. Show "CPR," "Sign Language," or "The Great Wall of China" from the videotape of student speeches that accompanies this edition of the textbook.	Chapter 13
14	**Informative Speeches**	
15	**Informative Speeches**	
16	**Informative Speeches**	
17	**Informative Speeches**	
18	**Introduction to Persuasive Speaking** Assign persuasive speeches. Focus class discussion on selected exercises and Applying the Power of Public Speaking, text pp. 423-424.	Chapter 15
19	**Gathering Materials** Take library tour—see additional exercise 1 on p. 166 of this manual. Assign selected exercises from text pp. 170-171.	Chapter 6
20	**Using Supporting Materials** Focus class discussion on exercises 1-2, text p. 198. Assign Applying the Power of Public Speaking, text p. 198, as a homework assignment.	Chapter 7

Class Meeting	Topic—Activity	Reading
21	**Methods of Persuasion** Focus class discussion on selected exercises and Applying the Power of Public Speaking, text pp. 458-460. Use additional exercise 1 on pp. 340-343 of this manual as a classroom activity. Show "Self-Defense on Campus" from the videotape of student speeches that accompanies this edition of *The Art of Public Speaking*. For an analysis of the speech, see pp. 343-346 of this manual.	Chapter 16
22	**Analysis of Persuasive Speeches** Have students prepare brief analyses of the assigned speech or speeches. Good candidates for analysis include Mary Fisher, "A Whisper of AIDS," Jennifer Conard, "The Ultimate Gift," and Renee Varghese, "Multicultural, Multilingual." All these speeches are analyzed in this manual; check the Table of Contents for page numbers.	Selections from "Speeches for Analysis and Discussion," pp. A1-A20
23	**Listening to Speeches** Focus class discussion on exercise 2, text p. 71. (The Listening Self-Evaluation Form is available on p. 113 of this manual, as well as on textbook p. 63.) Choose from additional exercises on pp. 114-116 of this manual for classroom activities.	Chapter 3
24	**Persuasive Speeches**	
25	**Persuasive Speeches**	
26	**Persuasive Speeches**	
27	**Persuasive Speeches**	

Class Meeting	Topic—Activity	Reading
28	**Midterm Examination**	
29	**Commemorative Speaking** Assign commemorative speech. Focus class discussion on exercise 3, text p. 477. Show "The Massachusetts 54th" from the videotape of student speeches that accompanies this edition of *The Art of Public Speaking*. Select from additional commemorative speeches in Part Five of this manual.	Chapter 17, especially pp. 469-472
30	**Return and Review Midterm Examinations**	
31	**Using Language Effectively** Focus class discussion on selections from exercises 1-3, text pp. 289-290; Applying the Power of Public Speaking, text p. 290; and additional exercises on pp. 238-244 of this manual.	Chapter 11
32	**Using Language Effectively** Have students prepare a brief analysis of King's speech as directed in exercise 4, text p. 290. Show the videotape of "I Have a Dream" in class and focus discussion on King's use of language.	Martin Luther King, "I Have a Dream," pp. A7-A10
33	**Commemorative Speeches**	
34	**Commemorative Speeches**	
35	**Commemorative Speeches**	

Class Meeting	Topic—Activity	Reading
36	**The Final Speech** Assign final speeches and begin review of elements students most need to work on in preparing the final speech. Major items usually are supporting materials, organization and outlining, and delivery.	
37	**Preparing for the Final Speech: Supporting Materials** Focus class discussion on selected exercises from Chapter 7 of the text, or on analyzing speeches from pp. A1-A20 of the text or from Part Five of this manual.	Review Chapter 7
38	**Preparing for the Final Speech: Organization and Outlining** Focus class discussion on selected exercises from Chapters 8-10 and additional exercises from this manual.	Review Chapters 8-10
39	**Preparing for the Final Speech: Delivery** By this point in the course, many students are ready to work on polishing their delivery skills. Choose from among the exercises in Chapter 12 of the text, the additional exercises on pp. 260-267 of this manual, and the entries under "Delivery" in the five volumes of *Selections from the Speech Communication Teacher* that accompany *The Art of Public Speaking*.	Review Chapter 12
40	**Final Speeches**	
41	**Final Speeches**	
42	**Final Speeches**	
43	**Final Speeches**	

Class Meeting	Topic—Activity	Reading
44	**Final Speeches**	
45	**Summary and Review for Final Examination**	

OUTLINE FOR A ONE-SEMESTER COURSE
WITH A UNIT ON GROUP DISCUSSION

Class Meeting	Topic—Activity	Reading
1	**Course Overview** Introduce yourself; hand out syllabi; explain grading and attendance policies. Assign introductory speeches.	
2	**Basic Principles of Speech Communication** Focus class discussion on selected exercises, text pp. 29-30, or additional exercises from pp. 67-72 of this manual. Explain introductory speeches; show "The Rare Phobia," "My Eye on the World," and "Steady and True" from the videotape of student speeches that accompanies this edition of *The Art of Public Speaking*.	Chapter 1 and "Giving Your First Speech" (pp. 73-83)
3	**Ethics and Public Speaking** Focus class discussion on exercises 1 and 3, text pp. 51-52. Have students develop a code of ethical speaking for their classroom as explained in additional exercise 1 on p. 94 of this manual.	Chapter 2
4	**Introductory Speeches**	
5	**Introductory Speeches**	
6	**Speaking to Inform** Assign informative speeches. Focus class discussion on kinds of informative speeches and guidelines for informative speaking. Show "Cryonics," "Dying to Be Thin," or "Feng Shui" from the videotape of student speeches that accompanies this edition of *The Art of Public Speaking*.	Chapter 14

Class Meeting	Topic—Activity	Reading
7	**Choosing Topics and Purposes** Focus class discussion on exercises 2-4, text pp. 105-106, and Applying the Power of Public Speaking, text p. 107.	Chapter 4
8	**Analyzing the Audience** Focus class discussion on exercises 2 and 4, text p. 134, and Applying the Power of Public Speaking, text p. 135. Use additional exercise 1 on pp. 145-146 of this manual as a classroom activity.	Chapter 5
9	**Organizing the Body of the Speech** Focus class discussion on exercises 1-3 and Applying the Power of Public Speaking, text pp. 220-221. Use additional exercises as needed from pp. 198-201 of this manual.	Chapter 8
10	**Introductions and Conclusions** Focus class discussion on exercise 1 and Applying the Power of Public Speaking, text pp. 244-245. Use additional exercise 1 or 2 on pp. 210-212 of this manual as a classroom activity.	Chapter 9
11	**Outlining the Speech** Focus class discussion on exercise 1, text pp. 261-262, and Applying the Power of Public Speaking, text pp. 262-263. Have students do the interactive outlining exercises on the CD-ROM as a homework assignment; discuss the results in class.	Chapter 10

Class Meeting	Topic—Activity	Reading
12	**Delivering the Speech** Focus class discussion on principles of effective delivery. Select from exercises 1-3, text pp. 317-318, or the additional exercises on pp. 260-267 of this manual.	Chapter 12
13	**Using Visual Aids** Focus class discussion on exercise 2, text p. 341. Use additional exercise 1 on p. 283 of this manual as a classroom activity. If students are using PowerPoint in their speeches, assign "Using PowerPoint," text pp. 343-362. Show "CPR," "Sign Language," or "The Great Wall of China" from the videotape of student speeches that accompanies this edition of the textbook.	Chapter 13
14	**Informative Speeches**	
15	**Informative Speeches**	
16	**Informative Speeches**	
17	**Informative Speeches**	
18	**Introduction to Persuasive Speaking** Assign persuasive speeches. Focus class discussion on selected exercises and Applying the Power of Public Speaking, text pp. 423-424.	Chapter 15
19	**Gathering Materials** Take library tour—see additional exercise 1 on p. 166 of this manual. Assign selected exercises from text pp. 170-171.	Chapter 6

Class Meeting	Topic—Activity	Reading
20	**Using Supporting Materials** Focus class discussion on exercises 1-2, text p. 198. Assign Applying the Power of Public Speaking, text p. 198, as a homework assignment.	Chapter 7
21	**Methods of Persuasion** Focus class discussion on selected exercises and Applying the Power of Public Speaking, text pp. 458-460. Use additional exercise 1 on pp. 340-343 of this manual as a classroom activity. Show "Self-Defense on Campus" from the videotape of student speeches that accompanies this edition of *The Art of Public Speaking*. For an analysis of the speech, see pp. 343-346 of this manual.	Chapter 16
22	**Analysis of Persuasive Speeches** Have students prepare brief analyses of the assigned speech or speeches. Good candidates for analysis include Mary Fisher, "A Whisper of AIDS," Jennifer Conard, "The Ultimate Gift," and Renee Varghese, "Multicultural, Multilingual." All these speeches are analyzed in this manual; check the Table of Contents for page numbers.	Selections from "Speeches for Analysis and Discussion," pp. A1-A20
23	**Listening to Speeches** Focus class discussion on exercise 2, text p. 71. (The Listening Self-Evaluation Form is available on p. 113 of this manual, as well as on textbook p. 63.) Choose from additional exercises on pp. 114-116 of this manual for classroom activities.	Chapter 3
24	**Persuasive Speeches**	
25	**Persuasive Speeches**	

Class Meeting	Topic—Activity	Reading
26	**Persuasive Speeches**	
27	**Persuasive Speeches**	
28	**Midterm Examination**	
29	**Commemorative Speaking** Assign commemorative speech. Focus class discussion on exercise 3, text p. 450. Show "The Massachusetts 54th" from the videotape of student speeches that accompanies this edition of *The Art of Public Speaking*. Select from additional commemorative speeches in Part Five of this manual.	Chapter 17, especially pp. 469-472
30	**Return and Review Midterm Examinations**	
31	**Using Language Effectively** Focus class discussion on selections from exercises 1-3, text pp. 289-290; Applying the Power of Public Speaking, text p. 290; and additional exercises on pp. 238-244 of this manual.	Chapter 11
32	**Using Language Effectively** Have students prepare a brief analysis of King's speech as directed in exercise 4, text p. 290. Show the videotape of "I Have a Dream" in class and focus discussion on King's use of language.	Martin Luther King, "I Have a Dream," pp. A7-A10
33	**Commemorative Speeches**	
34	**Commemorative Speeches**	

Class Meeting	Topic—Activity	Reading
35	**Commemorative Speeches**	
36	**Introduction to Small-Group Discussion** Assign group discussion projects. Discuss Chapter 18, with special emphasis on pp. 479-490.	Chapter 18, especially pp. 479-490
37	**Problem Solving in Small Groups** Focus class discussion on the reflective-thinking method; use exercises 1 and 3, text pp. 498-499.	Chapter 18 especially pp. 490-500
38	**Decision-Making Processes in Small Groups** Do "Lost on the Moon" or "Hostages" activity from pp. 370-378 of this manual.	
39	**Group Project Work** Have groups work on their projects in class. This will give you a chance to meet briefly with each group to assess its progress and to offer guidance.	
40	**Group Presentations**	
41	**Group Presentations**	
42	**Group Presentations**	
43	**Group Presentations**	

44	**Group Presentations**	
45	**Summary and Review for Final Examinations**	

OUTLINE FOR A 10-WEEK, 30-HOUR QUARTER
OR
A 15-WEEK, 30-HOUR SEMESTER

Class Meeting	Topic—Activity	Reading
1	**Course Overview** Introduce yourself; hand out syllabi; explain grading and attendance policies. Assign introductory speeches.	
2	**Basic Principles of Speech Communication** Focus class discussion on selected exercises, text pp. 29-30, or additional exercises from pp. 67-72 of this manual. Explain introductory speeches; show "The Rare Phobia," "My Eye on the World," and "Steady and True" from the videotape of student speeches that accompanies this edition of *The Art of Public Speaking*.	Chapter 1 and "Giving Your First Speech" (pp. 73-83)
3	**Ethics and Public Speaking** Focus class discussion on exercises 1 and 3, text pp. 51-52. Have students develop a code of ethical speaking for their classroom as explained in additional exercise 1 on p. 94 of this manual.	Chapter 2
4	**Introductory Speeches**	
5	**Introductory Speeches**	
6	**Speaking to Inform** Assign informative speeches. Focus class discussion on kinds of informative speeches and guidelines for informative speaking. Show "Cryonics," "Dying to Be Thin," or "Feng Shui" from the videotape of student speeches that accompanies this edition of *The Art of Public Speaking*.	Chapter 14

Class Meeting	Topic—Activity	Reading
7	**Choosing Topics and Purposes** Focus class discussion on exercises 2-4, text pp. 105-106, and Applying the Power of Public Speaking, text p. 107.	Chapter 4
8	**Analyzing the Audience** Focus class discussion on exercises 2 and 4, text p. 134, and Applying the Power of Public Speaking, text p. 135. Use additional exercise 1 on pp. 145-146 of this manual as a classroom activity.	Chapter 5
9	**Organizing the Speech** Focus class discussion on exercises 1-3 and Applying the Power of Public Speaking, text pp. 220-221, and exercise 1, text p. 244. Use additional exercises as needed from pp. 198-201 and 210-212 of this manual.	Chapters 8-9
10	**Outlining the Speech** Focus class discussion on exercise 1, text pp. 261-262, and Applying the Power of Public Speaking, text pp. 262-263. Have students do the interactive outlining exercises on the CD-ROM as a homework assignment; discuss the results in class.	Chapter 10
11	**Delivering the Speech and Using Visual Aids** Select from exercises 1-3, text pp. 317-318, or the additional exercises on pp. 260-267 of this manual. If visual aids are required for the informative speech, discuss exercise 2, text p. 341. Use additional exercise 1 on p. 283 of this manual as a classroom activity. If students are using PowerPoint in their speeches, assign "Using PowerPoint," text pp. 343-362. Show "CPR," "Sign Language," or "The Great Wall of China" from the videotape of student speeches that accompanies this edition of the textbook.	Chapters 12-13

Class Meeting	Topic—Activity	Reading
12	**Informative Speeches**	
13	**Informative Speeches**	
14	**Informative Speeches**	
15	**Introduction to Persuasive Speaking** Assign persuasive speeches. Focus class discussion on selected exercises and Applying the Power of Public Speaking, text pp. 423-424.	Chapter 15
16	**Gathering Materials** Take library tour—see additional exercise 1 on p. 166 of this manual. Assign selected exercises from text pp. 170-171.	Chapter 6
17	**Using Supporting Materials** Focus class discussion on exercises 1-2, text p. 198. Assign Applying the Power of Public Speaking, text p. 198, as a homework assignment.	Chapter 7
18	**Methods of Persuasion** Focus class discussion on selected exercises and Applying the Power of Public Speaking, text pp. 458-460. Use additional exercise 1 on pp. 340-343 of this manual as a classroom activity. Show "Self-Defense on Campus" from the videotape of student speeches that accompanies this edition of *The Art of Public Speaking*. For an analysis of the speech, see pp. 343-346 of this manual.	Chapter 16

Class Meeting	Topic—Activity	Reading
19	**Listening to Speeches** Focus class discussion on exercise 2, text p. 71. (The Listening Self-Evaluation Form is available on p. 113 of this manual, as well as on textbook p. 63.) Choose from additional exercises on pp. 114-116 of this manual for classroom activities.	Chapter 3
20	**Persuasive Speeches**	
21	**Persuasive Speeches**	
22	**Persuasive Speeches**	
23	**Persuasive Speeches**	
24	**Commemorative Speaking** Assign commemorative speech. Focus class discussion on exercise 3, text p. 450. Show "The Massachusetts 54th" from the videotape of student speeches that accompanies this edition of *The Art of Public Speaking*. Select from additional commemorative speeches in Part Five of this manual.	Chapter 17, especially pp. 469-472
25	**Using Language Effectively** Focus class discussion on selections from exercises 1-3, text pp. 289-290; Applying the Power of Public Speaking, text p. 290; and additional exercises on pp. 238-244 of this manual.	Chapter 11

Class Meeting	Topic—Activity	Reading
26	**Using Language Effectively** Have students prepare a brief analysis of King's speech as directed in exercise 4, text p. 290. Show the videotape of "I Have a Dream" in class and focus discussion on King's use of language.	Martin Luther King, "I Have a Dream," pp. A7-A10
27	**Commemorative Speeches**	
28	**Commemorative Speeches**	
29	**Commemorative Speeches**	
30	**Summary and Review for Final Examination**	

OUTLINE FOR A 10-WEEK, 40-HOUR QUARTER

Class Meeting	Topic—Activity	Reading
1	**Course Overview** Introduce yourself; hand out syllabi; explain grading and attendance policies. Assign introductory speeches.	
2	**Basic Principles of Speech Communication** Focus class discussion on selected exercises, text pp. 29-30, or additional exercises from pp. 67-72 of this manual. Explain introductory speeches; show "The Rare Phobia," "My Eye on the World," and "Steady and True" from the videotape of student speeches that accompanies this edition of *The Art of Public Speaking*.	Chapter 1 and "Giving Your First Speech" (pp. 73-83)
3	**Ethics and Public Speaking** Focus class discussion on exercises 1 and 3, text pp. 51-52. Have students develop a code of ethical speaking for their classroom as explained in additional exercise 1 on p. 94 of this manual.	Chapter 2
4	**Introductory Speeches**	
5	**Introductory Speeches**	
6	**Speaking to Inform** Assign informative speeches. Focus class discussion on kinds of informative speeches and guidelines for informative speaking. Show "Cryonics," "Dying to Be Thin," or "Feng Shui" from the videotape of student speeches that accompanies this edition of *The Art of Public Speaking*.	Chapter 14

Class Meeting	Topic—Activity	Reading
7	**Choosing Topics and Purposes** Focus class discussion on exercises 2-4, text pp. 105-106, and Applying the Power of Public Speaking, text p. 107.	Chapter 4
8	**Analyzing the Audience** Focus class discussion on exercises 2 and 4, text p. 134, and Applying the Power of Public Speaking, text p. 135. Use additional exercise 1 on pp. 145-146 of this manual as a classroom activity.	Chapter 5
9	**Organizing the Speech** Focus class discussion on exercises 1-3 and Applying the Power of Public Speaking, text pp. 220-221, and exercise 1, text p. 244. Use additional exercises as needed from pp. 198-201 and 210-212 of this manual.	Chapters 8-9
10	**Outlining the Speech** Focus class discussion on exercise 1, text pp. 261-262, and Applying the Power of Public Speaking, text pp. 262-263. Have students do the interactive outlining exercises on the CD-ROM as a homework assignment; discuss the results in class.	Chapter 10
11	**Delivering the Speech and Using Visual Aids** Select from exercises 1-3, text pp. 317-318, or the additional exercises on pp. 260-267 of this manual. If visual aids are required for the informative speech, discuss exercise 2, text p. 341. Use additional exercise 1 on p. 283 of this manual as a classroom activity. If students are using PowerPoint in their speeches, assign "Using PowerPoint," text pp. 343-362. Show "CPR," "Sign Language," or "The Great Wall of China" from the videotape of student speeches that accompanies this edition of the textbook.	Chapters 12-13

Class Meeting	Topic—Activity	Reading
13	**Informative Speeches**	
14	**Informative Speeches**	
15	**Informative Speeches**	
16	**Introduction to Persuasive Speaking** Assign persuasive speeches. Focus class discussion on selected exercises and Applying the Power of Public Speaking, text pp. 423-424.	Chapter 15
17	**Gathering Materials** Take library tour—see additional exercise 1 on p. 166 of this manual. Assign selected exercises from text pp. 170-171.	Chapter 6
18	**Using Supporting Materials** Focus class discussion on exercises 1-2, text p. 198. Assign Applying the Power of Public Speaking, text p. 198, as a homework assignment.	Chapter 7
19	**Methods of Persuasion** Focus class discussion on selected exercises and Applying the Power of Public Speaking, text pp. 458-460. Use additional exercise 1 on pp. 340-343 of this manual as a classroom activity. Show "Self-Defense on Campus" from the videotape of student speeches that accompanies this edition of *The Art of Public Speaking*. For an analysis of the speech, see pp. 343-346 of this manual.	Chapter 16

Class Meeting	Topic—Activity	Reading
20	**Listening to Speeches** Focus class discussion on exercise 2, text p. 71. (The Listening Self-Evaluation Form is available on p. 113 of this manual, as well as on textbook p. 113.). Choose from additional exercises on pp. 114-116 of this manual for classroom activities.	Chapter 3
21	**Persuasive Speeches**	
22	**Persuasive Speeches**	
23	**Persuasive Speeches**	
24	**Persuasive Speeches**	
25	**Midterm Examination**	
26	**Commemorative Speaking** Assign commemorative speech. Focus class discussion on exercise 3, text p. 450. Show "The Massachusetts 54th" from the videotape of student speeches that accompanies this edition of *The Art of Public Speaking*. Select from additional commemorative speeches in Part Five of this manual.	Chapter 17, especially pp. 469-472
27	**Using Language Effectively** Focus class discussion on selections from exercises 1-3, text pp. 289-290; Applying the Power of Public Speaking, text p. 290; and additional exercises on pp. 238-244 of this manual.	Chapter 11

Class Meeting	Topic—Activity	Reading
28	**Using Language Effectively** Have students prepare a brief analysis of King's speech as directed in exercise 4, text p. 290. Show the videotape of "I Have a Dream" in class and focus discussion on King's use of language.	Martin Luther King, "I Have a Dream," pp. A7-A10
29	**Commemorative Speeches**	
30	**Commemorative Speeches**	
31	**Commemorative Speeches**	
32	**The Final Speech** Assign final speeches and begin review of elements students most need to concentrate on in preparing the final speech. Major items usually are supporting materials, organization and outlining, and delivery.	
33	**Preparing for the Final Speech: Supporting Materials** Focus class discussion on selected exercises from Chapter 7, or on analyzing speeches from pp. A1-A20 of the text or from Part Five of this manual.	Review Chapter 7
34	**Preparing for the Final Speech: Organization and Outlining** Focus class discussion on selected exercises from Chapters 8-10 and additional exercises from this manual.	Review Chapters 8-10

Class Meeting	Topic—Activity	Reading
35	**Preparing for the Final Speech: Delivery** By this point in the course, many students are ready to work on polishing their delivery skills. Choose from among the exercises in Chapter 12 of the text, the additional exercises on pp. 260-267 of this manual, and the entries under "Delivery" in the five volumes of *Selections from the Speech Communication Teacher* that accompany *The Art of Public Speaking*.	Review Chapter 12
36	**Final Speeches**	
37	**Final Speeches**	
38	**Final Speeches**	
39	**Final Speeches**	
40	**Summary and Review for Final Examination**	

Part Two

SPEAKING

ASSIGNMENTS

Introduction to Part Two

There are many kinds of speaking assignments that can be used in conjunction with *The Art of Public Speaking*. Most of those described below are keyed to the course outlines presented in Part One of this manual. When there are two or more options offered for a round of speeches (Option A, Option B, etc.), you should select one option, so the entire class is performing the same assignment during that round of speeches.

In addition to the formal speaking assignments presented here, the Exercises for Critical Thinking in the book and the Additional Exercises and Activities in Part Four of this manual contain a number of suggestions for speaking activities. So also do the five volumes of selections from *The Speech Communication Teacher* that are part of the *Instructional Resource Program* for this edition of *The Art of Public Speaking*. A listing of the speech assignments in these volumes is presented on pages 39-42 of this manual.

Introductory Speeches

Option A: A Two-Minute Speech Introducing a Classmate

The speech should be delivered extemporaneously from brief notes that occupy no more than one side of a single 4 x 6 index card. Stress that students are not to read their speeches and should use as much eye contact as possible.

In preparation for the speech, have students pair off and interview one another. The interviewing can be done in the last 15 to 20 minutes of the first class meeting. The assignment usually works better, however, if students conduct their interviews out of class. This gives them time to prepare questions for the interviews and allows for longer, more flexible interviews.

In their speeches, students will need to provide basic information such as the name of the person they are introducing, his or her home town, academic major, personal interests, hobbies, aspirations, and the like. But the speech need not be a routine recitation of biographical data. Encourage students to be creative in their interview questions and in their speeches.

Since the purpose of this speech is to give students a brief, initial exposure to speaking in front of an audience in a low-risk situation, many instructors do not affix a grade to it. Others, having found that students take the speech more seriously if they know they are being graded, weight it very lightly—in some cases, the same as a graded homework assignment, and in no circumstances more than 3 to 5 percent of the total grade for the class.

Option B: A Two-Minute Speech Introducing a Classmate

The speech should be delivered extemporaneously from brief notes that occupy no more than one side of a single 4 x 6 index card. Stress that students are not to read their speeches and should use as much eye contact as possible.

Unlike Option A above, this speech focuses specifically on the cultural background of the student being introduced to the class. Possible topics might include social customs, family traditions, holidays, clothing, food, religious traditions, sporting activities, and the like.

As in Option A, have students pair off and interview one another. The interviewing can be done in the last 15 to 20 minutes of the first class meeting. The assignment usually works better, however, if students conduct their interviews out of class. This gives them time to prepare questions for the interviews and allows for longer, more flexible interviews. If there is significant cultural diversity in your class, arrange the interview pairs so students interview someone whose cultural background is markedly different from their own.

Because this speech, like Option A, is designed to give students a brief, initial exposure to speaking in front of an audience in a low-risk situation, many instructors do not affix a grade to it. Others, having found that students take the speech more seriously if they know they are being graded, weight it very lightly—in some cases, the same as a graded homework assignment, and not more than 3 to 5 percent of the total class grade in any circumstance.

Option C: A Two-Minute Speech of Self-Introduction

The speech should be delivered extemporaneously from brief notes that occupy no more than one side of a single 4 x 6 index card. Stress that students are not to read their speeches and should use as much eye contact as possible.

In their speeches, students should begin by telling their name, home town, year in school, and academic major. They may focus the remainder of the speech however they wish—on describing an unusual or significant personal experience, on expressing an important personal belief or pet peeve, on explaining a favorite hobby or interest, on discussing someone who has been particularly influential in the speaker's life, etc. The purpose of the speech is not to persuade the audience to share the speaker's views, but to give the audience insight into the speaker's background, personality, attitudes, or aspirations.

Since the purpose of this speech is to give students a brief, initial exposure to speaking in front of an audience in a situation of minimal risk, many instructors do not affix a grade to it. Others weight it very lightly—in some cases, the same as a graded homework assignment, and in no circumstances more than 3 to 5 percent of the total grade for the class.

Option D: A Two-Minute Speech of Self-Introduction

The speech should be delivered extemporaneously from brief notes that occupy no more than one side of a single 4 x 6 index card. Stress that students are not to read their speeches and should use as much eye contact as possible.

In their speeches, students explain a significant aspect of their cultural background and how it has made a difference in their lives. Possible topics might include social customs, family traditions, holidays, clothing, food, religious traditions, sporting activities, etc. Encourage students to be creative in preparing their speeches and in finding ways to illustrate how the aspect of their culture they choose to explain relates to their personal lives.

Like the other options for introductory speeches, this speech is meant to give students a brief, initial exposure to speaking in front of an audience in a low-risk situation. Therefore, many instructors do not affix a grade to it. Others weight it very lightly—in some cases, the same as a graded homework assignment, and in no circumstances more than 3 to 5 percent of the total grade for the class. However you approach the grading of this speech, it works especially well as an ice-breaker in classes with substantial cultural diversity.

Option E: A Two-Minute Speech of Self-Introduction Based on a Newspaper or Magazine Article

The speech should be delivered extemporaneously from brief notes that occupy no more than one side of a single 4 x 6 index card. Stress that students are not to read their speeches and should use as much eye contact as possible.

To prepare for the speech, each student should go to the library and read through a newspaper from the day they were born or a magazine such as *Time* or *Newsweek* from the week they were born. They should then select an item—article, advertisement, photograph, editorial, etc.—from the newspaper or magazine that relates to the speaker's life in some meaningful way. Using that item as a point of departure, the student should construct a speech that explains some aspect of her or his personality, background, beliefs, or aspirations.

This assignment usually produces fairly interesting and creative speeches of self-introduction. It also gets students into the library right at the start of the course and provides them some insight into the state of the world when they were born. Indeed, many students find this aspect of the assignment so interesting that they spend a fair amount of time just reading through the magazine or newspaper they have chosen.

A good ice-breaking assignment, this speech is designed to give students a brief, initial exposure to speaking in front of an audience in a situation of minimal risk. Many instructors do not affix a grade to it. Others, having found that students take the speech more seriously if they know they are being graded, weight it very lightly—in some cases, the same as a graded homework assignment, and not more than 3 to 5 percent of the total class grade in any circumstance.

Option F: A Two-Minute Speech of Self-Introduction Based on a Personal Object

The speech should be delivered extemporaneously from brief notes that occupy no more than one side of a single 4 x 6 index card. Stress that students are not to read their speeches and should use as much eye contact as possible.

In preparation for this speech, have students select an object that represents a significant aspect of their background, personality, values, ambitions, etc. Using the chosen object as a point of departure, each student should develop a speech that explains how it relates to her or his life. For example, a journalism major might select a newspaper as a way to explain her or his professional goals. A new father might select a diaper as a vehicle for discussing his experiences as a parent. An avid tennis player might settle on a tennis racket to illustrate her passion about the sport.

If possible, students should bring the object of their speech to class on the day of their presentation. If this is not possible because the object is too large, too rare, or too valuable, the student should bring in a model, drawing, or photograph of the object. The purpose of this speech is not to explain the object in detail, but to use it as a vehicle for the speaker to introduce herself or himself to the class.

Like Option E, this assignment usually produces interesting and creative speeches of self-introduction. Since it is designed to give students a brief, initial exposure to speaking in front of an audience in a low-risk situation, many instructors do not affix a grade to it. Others weight it very lightly—in some cases, the same as a graded homework assignment, and in no circumstances more than 3 to 5 percent of the total grade for the class.

Informative Speeches

Option A: A Speech of 5 to 6 Minutes Informing the Audience About Some Object, Process, Concept, or Event

If desired, the assignment can be narrowed to concentrate specifically on a particular aspect of information-giving, such as definition, demonstration, or explanation. Encourage students to select topics that are useful and interesting. Students should turn in a complete preparation outline, but the speech itself should be delivered extemporaneously from a brief speaking outline.

Because this is the first graded speech, evaluation should focus on such basic matters as establishing eye contact, avoiding distracting mannerisms, formulating a sharp specific purpose statement, fulfilling the functions of an introduction and conclusion, limiting main points and arranging them properly, and employing connectives effectively.

Option B: A Speech of 5 to 6 Minutes Informing the Audience About Some Object, Process, Concept, or Event

Use of a visual aid is required. Students should turn in a complete preparation outline, but the speech itself should be delivered extemporaneously from a brief speaking outline.

This assignment is the same as Option A above, except for the stipulation that the speaker use a visual aid. Requiring a speech with visual aids gives students experience in a kind of speaking that is common in business and professional situations. Requiring such a speech early in the course usually increases student interest in the speeches, reduces the speakers' nervousness, and encourages them to rely less on their notes.

Urge students to be creative in selecting their visual aids and conscientious in following the guidelines for using them presented in Chapter 13. Decide whether you will impose any restrictions on the kinds of visual aids students can use and, if possible, provide an easel on which speakers can display their graphs, charts, and drawings if they are not using PowerPoint. If they are using PowerPoint, remind them to follow the guidelines discussed in the appendix on using PowerPoint, on pages 343-363 of the textbook.

**Option C: A Speech of 5 to 6 Minutes Demonstrating the Steps of a
Process or How to Perform the Steps of a Process**

As in Option B above, use of a visual aid is required. Students should turn in a complete preparation outline, but the speech itself should be delivered extemporaneously from a brief speaking outline.

Students should make sure they present the steps of their process clearly and systematically, leaving out none of the essential steps along the way. In all but a few cases, these speeches will fall naturally into chronological order. Be sure students follow the guidelines for visual aids discussed in Chapter 13, and have them pay special attention to the section on speeches about processes in Chapter 14. If students are using PowerPoint, remind them to follow the guidelines for PowerPoint explained on pages 343-363 of the textbook.

**Option D: A Speech of 5 to 6 Minutes in Which Students Explain a
Significant Aspect of a Culture Different From Their Own**

Possible topics include social customs, family traditions, holidays, clothing, food, religious traditions, sporting activities, and the like. Students should turn in a preparation outline, but the speech itself should be delivered extemporaneously from a brief speaking outline.

Research is required for this speech. If students have had direct contact with a different culture, they should be encouraged to supplement their library research with their personal experience, but the speech is not to be a travelogue or a presentation on "My Summer in Europe" or "My Year as an Exchange Student in Brazil." On the other hand, a speech on how Europeans spend their summer vacations or on the educational system of Brazil would be fine.

Because students are sometimes resistant when they are required to speak about a different culture, it can be helpful to present this as the "World Travel Agency" speech. If you take this approach, tell students that the class is going to travel around the world via their speeches. They will "visit" as many different countries as there are students in the class.

To help students choose topics as quickly as possible, prepare two sets of 3 x 5 index cards. Write the name of a different country on each card in the first set. Then write two or three cultural features on each card in the second set. Put each set of cards in a separate bag and have students randomly pick a card from each bag. When they are finished, they will have a country card (for instance, Italy) and a topic card (including, for example, sports, family traditions, and politics). The student will then speak on one of those three aspects of Italian life.

However students choose their topics, they should be encouraged to be imaginative in composing their speeches. It is not enough to summarize basic information from an encyclopedia or the Internet about the country on which they are speaking. As in any informative speech, students need to explain ideas clearly and to think about ways to relate the topic to the audience. Some instructors require a visual aid for this speech. Others encourage the use of a visual aid but do not require it.

Persuasive Speeches

Option A: A Speech of 7 to 8 Minutes Designed to Persuade the Audience For or Against a Question of Policy

Speakers may seek either passive agreement or immediate action from the audience, though they should be encouraged to seek the latter if there is appropriate action for the audience to take. In either case, students should be sure to deal with all three basic issues of policy speeches—need, plan, and practicality. A complete preparation outline should be submitted. Delivery of the speech is to be extemporaneous.

This speech will require considerable research and skillful use of the methods of persuasion. Special emphasis should be given to evidence and reasoning. This is also an excellent assignment for stressing audience analysis and adaptation. You may wish to have students prepare an audience analysis questionnaire similar to that discussed in Chapter 5 to help them identify with and adapt to their target audience.

Option B: A Speech of 7 to 8 Minutes Designed to Persuade the Audience on Either a Question of Fact or a Question of Value

A complete preparation outline should be submitted. Delivery of the speech is to be extemporaneous.

As with Option A above, this speech will require considerable research and skillful handling of the methods of persuasion. Also as with Option A, this is an excellent assignment for stressing audience analysis and adaptation. Students who speak on a question of fact will need to give special attention to evidence and reasoning. Students who speak on a question of value must be sure to identify their standards for judgment and to justify their value judgment in light of those standards.

Commemorative Speech

A Speech of 4 to 5 Minutes Paying Tribute to a Person, a Group of People, an Institution, or an Idea

The subject may be historical or contemporary, famous or obscure. A preparation outline is not required. This speech should be written out and delivered from manuscript. Students should hand in their manuscripts after their speeches.

This assignment calls for a less didactic speech than the informative and persuasive speeches. It focuses particularly on the use of language, and it gives students experience in speaking from a manuscript. Encourage students to use language imaginatively and to experiment with the devices for enhancing clarity and vividness discussed in Chapter 11. Also stress that students must rehearse their speeches thoroughly, so as to present them with strong eye contact and dynamic vocal variety.

After-Dinner Speech

A Speech of 4 to 5 Minutes Designed to Entertain

A preparation outline is not required. This speech should be written out and delivered from manuscript, and it should be thoroughly rehearsed so it can be presented with maximum eye contact and strong vocal variety. Students should hand in their manuscripts after their speeches.

This assignment demands considerable creativity on the part of students. It calls for a clever speech that makes a thoughtful point even as it approaches the topic in a light-hearted, diverting manner. Encourage students to choose topics based on their own experience and with which most members of the audience can easily identify—family interactions, job matters, school activities, travel adventures, and the like. Stress that the speech is not to be simply a string of jokes and that any humor must be in good taste.

Like the commemorative speech, this assignment also offers a special opportunity to focus on the use of language. Encourage students to use language imaginatively and to experiment with the stylistic devices discussed in Chapter 11.

Final Speeches

Option A: A Speech of 8 to 10 Minutes That May Be Either Informative or Persuasive

A complete preparation outline should be required. Delivery of the speech is to be extemporaneous.

You can allow students to choose individually whether to give an informative speech or a persuasive speech. Usually, however, it is best to assign the entire class one or the other kind of speech. Whichever kind you assign, let students know that this speech is particularly important. Criteria for evaluation include all major aspects of speech preparation and delivery covered since the first day of class.

Option B: A Speech of 8 to 10 Minutes That Is to Be a Major Revision of an Informative or Persuasive Speech Given Earlier in the Term

A complete preparation outline should be required. Delivery of the speech is to be extemporaneous.

Because time is often cramped at the end of the term, this assignment provides for a full-length speech without requiring that students start from scratch in choosing and researching an entirely new topic. It also gives students an opportunity to learn more about the revision process, which is essential to speeches outside the classroom.

If this assignment is to succeed, you must tell each student which previous speech he or she is to revise, must be quite specific in identifying for each student the kinds of revisions that are necessary, and must make clear that major revisions—including additional research—

are required if the speech is to receive a grade of B or better. Otherwise, you are likely to get little more than warmed-over rehashes of speeches you have already heard. Criteria for evaluation include all major aspects of speech preparation and delivery covered since the first day of class.

Option C: A Speech of 8 to 10 Minutes Informing the Audience About a Prominent Public Speaker

A complete preparation outline should be required. Delivery of the speech is to be extemporaneous.

Students can choose either a historical figure or a contemporary speaker for this assignment. In either case, students should deal with the following points in their speeches, though not necessarily in this order: (a) biographical background about the speaker; (b) the importance of public speaking in her or his career; (c) major ideas of her or his speeches; (d) analysis of the speaker's techniques, including organization, language, and delivery.

Complex and challenging, this speech requires substantial library research and allows students to apply the principles learned in class to established public speakers. Although it usually works best in more advanced classes, it can succeed in the introductory course as well.

Make the assignment early in the course so students can work on it throughout the term. In addition, give students a list of speakers from which they can choose. Helpful sources in this regard are *American Orators before 1900* and *American Orators of the Twentieth Century*, both edited by Bernard K. Duffy and Halford R. Ryan; *Women's Voices in Our Time*, edited by Victoria L. DeFrancisco and Marvin D. Jensen; *We Shall Be Heard: Women Speakers in America*, edited by Patricia Scileppi Kennedy and Gloria Hartmann O'Shields; and *Voices of Multicultural America: Notable Speeches Delivered by African, Asian, Hispanic, and Native Americans, 1790-1995*, edited by Deborah Gillan Straub.

Encourage students to do all they can to make the speeches creative and interesting by following the guidelines for informative speaking discussed in Chapter 14. Students who choose historical speakers may be able to use photographs or slides as visual aids; those who speak on current figures might consider showing videotapes of their subject in action. In either case, students should review Chapter 13 to make sure they use their visual aids properly and integrate them smoothly into the speech. Students who use PowerPoint should be reminded to follow the guidelines presented on pages 343-363 of the textbook.

Impromptu Speech

A Two-Minute Speech to Be Delivered Impromptu

The focus of the speech may be informative, persuasive, or entertaining.

Create a set of topics such as my family, my home town, my best friend, my favorite sport, my most embarrassing moment, my worst class, my biggest thrill, my biggest complaint, etc. Have students draw three topics and choose one to speak about. Give each speaker a few minutes to gather his or her thoughts before beginning to speak. You can do this by having the first three or four speakers choose their topics at the beginning of class. Then, as each speaker finishes, have a new student select his or her topic. Give the speakers time signals when they have one minute to go and then again when they have 30 seconds left.

This can be used as a regular, graded assignment or as an informal, non-graded speaking experience. In either case, try to keep the atmosphere low-key, since students are often particularly apprehensive about speaking impromptu.

For further discussion of approaches to impromptu speaking, see Additional Exercise/Activity 4 on pages 263-265 of this manual.

Problem-Solving Group Discussion with Symposium

Divide the class into small groups of four to six members. First, each group will be responsible for a problem-solving project in which they investigate a question of policy and recommend solutions to it. In their deliberations, the group should follow the reflective-thinking method of decision-making explained in Chapter 18. Members of the group should understand that this project will require research and group meetings outside of class.

Second, the group will be responsible for organizing and conducting a symposium in which the group presents its report to the class. One way to structure the symposium is to allow each speaker 4 to 5 minutes to explain the work of the group at each stage of the reflective-thinking process. Another approach is to have each speaker spend 4 to 5 minutes detailing some aspect of the group's recommended solutions. If time allows, follow the symposium with a question-and-answer session or general class discussion.

You can either assign topics to the groups or allow each group to choose its own topic. Students should be graded both on the quality of the group's presentation and on their individual contributions to the group.

For other approaches to this assignment, see Additional Exercises/Activities 3 and 4 on pages 378-380 of this manual.

Additional Speech Assignments

When preparing the instructional supplements to the fourth edition of *The Art of Public Speaking*, I compiled an anthology of 92 articles related to the public speaking course from *The Speech Communication Teacher*. Entitled *Selections from the Speech Communication Teacher, 1986-1991*, the anthology was so well received that I have put together four more collections: *Selections from the Speech Communication Teacher, 1991-1994*; *Selections from the Speech Communication Teacher, 1994-1996*; *Selections from the Speech Communication Teacher, 1996-1999*; and *Selections from the Communication Teacher, 1999-2002*. All five volumes are available to instructors as part of the *Instructional Resource Program* that accompanies the current edition of *The Art of Public Speaking*.

Included in these five volumes are a number of articles describing speech assignments, many of which are highly creative and offer excellent alternatives to the assignments described earlier in this section of the *Instructor's Manual*. To give you a sense of the variety of assignments presented, the relevant articles are listed below. You can locate individual articles in the volume of *Selections* indicated by the dates in parentheses after the title of each article.

Introductory Speeches

Bia Bernum, "A Drawing Speech of Introduction" (1999-2002).

Merry C. Buchanan, "Public Speaking Ice Breaker: Any Old Bag Will Do" (1996-1999).

Catherine A. Dobris, "Breaking the Ice Gently: A Student-Centered Application for Public Speaking" (1996-1999).

Ken Hawkinson, "Performing Personal Narratives" (1994-1996).

Chris R. Kasch, "'I Knew that I Was at My Best' Public Speaking Assignment" (1996-1999).

Helen Meldrum, "Using *Vital Speeches of the Day* in the Introductory Speech Classroom" (1986-1991).

Gloria Nicosia, "Public Speaking: Reducing Anxiety and Revealing a Process" (1996-1999).

Sean Raftis, "Brush with Greatness" (1986-1991).

Timothy B. Rumbough, "52 Ways to Break the Ice" (1999-2002).

Andrew Sachs, "Incorporating Ancient Roman Pedagogy into the Contemporary Persuasive Speaking Class: A Fable" (1996-1999).

Valerie L. Schneider, "The Personal Experience Speech in Public Speaking" (1986-1991).

Scott Smithson, "Interviewing: A Triadic Exercise" (1986-1991).

Debbie Ayres Sonandré and Joe Ayres, "Practice Makes Perfect" (1996-1999).

Willard A. Underwood, "Using Condensed Interviews to Improve Classroom Interaction" (1991-1994).

Lynne Webb, "The Analogy Speech" (1986-1991).

Susan R. Wilson, "The Little Speech that Could" (1996-1999).

Informative Speeches

Barbara Adler, "A Speech About a Great American Speech" (1986-1991).

J. Jeffrey Auer, "Creating an Extra and 'Real Life' Public Speaking Assignment" (1986-1991).

A. Anne Bowers, Jr., "Happy Birthday to Me" (1994-1996).

A. Anne Bowers, Jr., "The Telephone Interview" (1991-1994).

James Corey, "International Bazaar" (1986-1991).

Laura L. Gschwend, "Creating Confidence with the Popular Recording Speech" (1994-1996).

Katherine Rowan, "The Speech to Explain Difficult Ideas" (1986-1991).

Persuasive Speeches

C. Darrell Langley, "The Heckling Speech" (1986-1991).

John V. Modaff, "The Radio Commentary Speech" (1996-1999).

Raed A. Mohsen, "Out on Campus: A Challenging Public Speaking Experience" (1991-1994).

Kimberly A. Powell, "Debate as the Key to Teaching Persuasion Skills" (1994-1996).

Charlynn Ross, "The Challenging Audience Exercise" (1986-1991).

Impromptu Speeches

Lindsley F. Armstrong and Peter M. Kellett, "Teaching Public Speaking Principles Through Impromptu Speaking" (1994-1996).

Kathleen Beauchene, "Using Quotations as Impromptu Speech Topics" (1986-1991).

Randall Bytwerk, "The 'Just a Minute' Impromptu Exercise" (1986-1991).

Heather Crandall, "Practicing Impromptu Speeches" (1996-1999).

Diane Grainer, "Creativity vs. 'My Speech Is About Avocados'" (1986-1991).

James J. Kimble, "The Big Mouth Speakoff" (1994-1996).

Reed Markham, "Power Minutes" (1986-1991).

Wilma McClarty, "Impromptu Speaking Options" (1996-1999).

Wilma McClarty, "Nomination Speech: The Ideal Date" (1986-1991).

Bruce C. McKinney, "The 'Jeopardy' of Impromptu Speaking" (1986-1991).

Terilyn Goins Phillips, "Who's Who: Off-the-Cuff Character Assessments" (1994-1996).

Ed Purdy, "Painless Impromptu Speaking" (1986-1991).

Timothy B. Rumbough, "The 'Um . . . Uh . . .' Impromptu Speech Contest" (1996-1999).

Kara Schultz, "MTV Impromptu" (1994-1996).

Michael G. Stahl and Lori Adams, "Two Takes on Impromptu Speaking Topics: Retiring the Hat" (1991-1994).

Naomi Sugimoto, "Impromptu Fortune-Telling Exercise" (1991-1994).

Gwendolyn F. Sullivan, "Improving Delivery Skills: The Practice Impromptu" (1996-1999).

Jeanette Wall, "Me? Give an Impromptu Speech? No Way!" (1986-1991).

Dorothy Wilks, "Two Birds with One Stone" (1986-1991).

Speeches for Special Occasions

Martin Lamansky, "Getting to Know My Hero: The Speech of Tribute" (1991-1994).

Randall E. Majors, "Practical Ceremonial Speaking: Three Speech Activities" (1986-1991).

Barry Cole Poyner, "Adding a Ceremonial Touch" (1991-1994).

Lynn Rinehart, "Here's a Toast" (1996-1999).

Shirley Sikes, "Introducing the Speaker" (1991-1994).

Suzanne Walter, "Introduction of a Speaker: Multipurpose and Multicultural" (1991-1994).

General

Rhonda Ehrler, "Extemporizing Through Humor and Repetition" (1986-1991).

Steven E. Martin, "Stock Issues-Based Policy Speech Small Group Exercise" (1999-2002).

Loren O. Murfield, "Generating Interest and Community Involvement in Student Speeches" (1996-1999).

Scott A. Myers, "The Extempu Speech" (1994-1996).

Kathy Norris, "The Speech Shopping Channel" (1991-1994).

Lawrence Rifkind, "The Outstanding Speaker Contest" (1991-1994).

Henry L. Roubicek, "Presenting a Personal Narrative" (1999-2002).

Ray-Lynn Snowden, "Meet the Great Speakers: Let Me Introduce You to . . ." (1999-2002).

Charmaine E. Wilson, "Ending the Public Speaking Class on a Positive Note" (1999-2002).

Part Three

EVALUATION

AND GRADING

Introduction to Part Three

Evaluating student work and assigning grades are among the most difficult tasks facing any teacher. Students take their grades very seriously, and if they believe they are being assessed unfairly, they will quickly develop a negative view of the teacher and, perhaps, of the course in general. Moreover, the self-confidence that is essential for beginning speakers can be seriously damaged if the teacher is insensitive to their need for encouragement and positive reinforcement.

Yet instructors also have an obligation to assess students objectively on the quality of the work they produce. You cannot give students higher grades than they deserve just to maintain good feelings in the class. Striking a balance between the psychological needs of the students and the integrity of the grading system is one of the most difficult challenges facing a teacher of public speaking.

There are two major considerations in meeting this challenge. The first is assessing student work fairly, objectively, and consistently. The second is explaining your assessment to students so they accept it as fair, objective, and consistent. The former revolves around your grading criteria and how you apply them. The latter depends on your ability to communicate effectively with students about your assessment of their work, and is every bit as important as the assessment itself. As this section of the manual proceeds, we shall address both of these aspects of grading and evaluation.

Criteria, Exams, and Grading Scales

When grading speeches, do all you can to let students know when and how they will be evaluated. Explain speech assignments clearly and notify students of their speaking dates well in advance. Tell students the objectives of each assignment so they will know what to concentrate on in preparing their speeches. Also, be as specific as possible about your criteria for grading speeches. You may find it helpful to give students, on the first day of class, a sheet similar to the one on page 48, listing your basic criteria for grading speeches.

Although there is no substitute for experience when it comes to grading speeches, there are some steps you can take, if you are a new instructor, to sharpen your evaluative skills. One is to talk about grading with experienced instructors who are willing to share their philosophy, methods, and criteria. Another is to view a number of student speeches—either on videotape or in other sections—and see how your assessments of them stack up against those of veteran teachers. Yet another is to have a more seasoned instructor visit your class on a day when students are giving speeches. By comparing the grades you assigned with those the other instructor would have assigned had it been his or her class, you can get a good sense of whether you need to make any adjustments in either your criteria or your methods of evaluation.

Whereas the speeches indicate how well students have mastered the skills of speechmaking, written examinations gauge how well students understand the principles underlying those skills. There are many approaches to written examinations in public speaking classes. Some instructors give one or two major examinations. Others supplement major examinations with periodic brief quizzes. Still others rely solely on a series of quizzes. Some instructors prefer objective questions; others essay questions; others a mixture of question types. To help you construct examinations, the *Test Bank* that accompanies *The Art of Public Speaking* contains more than 1,900 true-false, multiple-choice, short-answer, and essay questions. In addition, it offers two preconstructed quizzes for each chapter of the book, as well as three complete sample final examinations that illustrate different approaches to testing and evaluation. Finally, the *Test Bank* includes a guest essay by Anita Vangelisti of the University of Texas on test construction and assessment.

There are a number of ways to weight individual assignments and determine final grades. Below is one system based on the assignments in the course outlines presented in Part One of this manual. It can be adjusted easily to reflect your assignments and your approach to determining final grades.

Assignment	Proportion of Final Grade
informative speech	10 percent
persuasive speech	20 percent
commemorative speech or after-dinner speech	15 percent
final speech	20 percent
examinations	25 percent
class participation and miscellaneous assignments	10 percent

To maintain the integrity of your grading system, you will need a firm attendance policy. Public speaking is a participation course. It also runs on a very tight schedule. If students habitually skip class when they are assigned to speak, the syllabus will be thrown off very quickly. Many instructors assign an automatic grade penalty to any student who fails to deliver a speech on the specified day because of an unexcused absence. Many also limit students to a maximum of two or three unexcused absences for the entire course. Excessive absences result in a reduction of the student's final grade. Whatever policy you adopt, be sure to write it on your syllabus so students will be aware of it from the very beginning of the course.

Evaluation Forms

No matter how grades are assigned, it is important that students receive written evaluations of their speeches. Because such evaluations are usually the major channel of feedback from the instructor about the speeches, they need to be handled with great care. Evaluation forms should indicate clearly the elements of the speech on which the student is being assessed. They should also allow room for written comments.

Pages 49 to 55 of this manual contain seven speech evaluation forms. The first three are suitable for almost any kind of speech. The fourth is designed for persuasive speeches on questions of policy, the fifth for speeches using Monroe's motivated sequence, the sixth for commemorative speeches, and the seventh for after-dinner speeches. The last four are included to suggest how evaluation forms can be adapted to the specific requirements of particular speech assignments.

In addition to varying slightly in content, each form has a somewhat different format. You may wish to use these forms as they are, or you may prefer to create your own by experimenting with formats and evaluation items. Regardless of which form you use, if you give your students a copy at the beginning of each speech assignment, they can use it as a checklist when preparing their speeches.

Strategies of Evaluation

The most difficult task when evaluating speeches is to maintain a positive, encouraging tone while at the same time being candid with students about the shortcomings of their speeches. Evaluations should be realistic in appraising the speech, but they should be offered in a kind, optimistic tone that provides hope and encouragement for future speeches.

Whether you are preparing a written evaluation, discussing speeches in class, or meeting individually with students in a post-speech conference, it is usually a good idea to adopt the "good news/bad news" strategy of evaluation. That is, focus first on what the student did well in her or his speech. Be sure to find some positive comments, even if nothing more than "Excellent choice of topic," "Nice job of meeting the time limits," or "You certainly have a strong speaking voice." In most cases, you will have a fair number of substantive positive comments to make.

Once you have provided the "good news," you can turn to the "bad news"—that is, comments about the weaknesses of the speech. There is no need, in composing these comments, to construct a high-powered rhetorical analysis. Your objective is to help students grow as speakers by letting them know exactly what they need to correct and what steps they can take to improve. Try to give each speaker a few specific items to work on in the next speech. This will focus your students' energies and give them a concrete sense of your expectations.

Evaluations by Students

It is also useful to have students fill out evaluation forms on their peers' speeches. One way to do this is to assign each student a partner who is responsible for providing a detailed, constructive evaluation of their partner's speech. Another approach is to assign a group of students as critics for each day's speeches. These students should fill out an evaluation form for each speech delivered that day. By the end of the unit, each student will have served as a critic for one day.

There are several schools of thought about dealing with student evaluations. Some instructors read the evaluations and grade them to encourage thorough, helpful, encouraging critiques. Whether or not you assign a grade to the evaluations, you should always look them over before giving them to the speaker to make sure they are sufficiently detailed and do not contain any destructive comments.

How much weight should be put on student evaluations in determining the speaker's grade? There are obvious dangers in having a student's grade hinge in any formal way on the responses of his or her classmates. In my own experience, student evaluations are most helpful as a way to encourage students to listen carefully to their classmates' speeches and to provide additional feedback to speakers.

In most cases, the students' judgments on such basic matters as organization and delivery will reflect fairly closely those of the instructor. There is always the possibility, however, that you will rate highly a speech to which students give low ratings, or vice versa. In such circumstances, you should double check your evaluation to make sure you are satisfied with it. If, after doing so, you are convinced that your original assessment is correct, you should write a note to the speaker on your evaluation form noting that her or his classmates appear to have overestimated (or underestimated) the speech and that the grade reflects your judgment rather than that of the student evaluators.

If your evaluation of the speech is higher than that of the speaker's classmates, the speaker will gladly defer to your wisdom and insight. If your evaluation is lower than that of the speaker's classmates, the speaker may challenge your wisdom and insight. In such circumstances, you should explain exactly what was wrong with the speech and how the speaker can improve next time. You should not allow students to browbeat you into changing your evaluation.

Finally, it is important to recognize that, no matter what you do, you cannot please all students when it comes to evaluation and grading. Even the most experienced, most effective teachers have students who are disgruntled over their grades. All you can do is assess your students fairly and seek to communicate that assessment clearly, concisely, and constructively. The rest is up to your students.

Criteria Used for Evaluating Speeches

The *average speech* (grade C) should meet the following criteria:

1. Conform to the kind of speech assigned—informative, persuasive, etc.

2. Be ready for presentation on the assigned date

3. Conform to the time limit

4. Fulfill any special requirements of the assignment—preparing an outline, using visual aids, conducting an interview, etc.

5. Have a clear specific purpose and central idea

6. Have an identifiable introduction, body, and conclusion

7. Show reasonable directness and competence in delivery

8. Be free of serious errors in grammar, pronunciation, and word usage

The *above average speech* (grade B) should meet the preceding criteria and also:

1. Deal with a challenging topic

2. Fulfill all major functions of a speech introduction and conclusion

3. Display clear organization of main points and supporting materials

4. Support main points with evidence that meets the tests of accuracy, relevance, objectivity, and sufficiency

5. Exhibit proficient use of connectives—transitions, internal previews, internal summaries, and signposts

6. Be delivered skillfully enough so as not to distract attention from the speaker's message

The *superior speech* (grade A) should meet all the preceding criteria and also:

1. Constitute a genuine contribution by the speaker to the knowledge or beliefs of the audience

2. Sustain positive interest, feeling, and/or commitment among the audience

3. Contain elements of vividness and special interest in the use of language

4. Be delivered in a fluent, polished manner that strengthens the impact of the speaker's message

The *below average speech* (grade D or F) is seriously deficient in the criteria required for the C speech.

Speech Evaluation Form

Speaker _____

Topic _____

Rate the speaker on each point: E-*excellent*   G-*good*   A-*average*   F-*fair*   P-*poor*

COMMENTS

INTRODUCTION

Gained attention and interest	E	G	A	F	P
Introduced topic clearly	E	G	A	F	P
Established credibility	E	G	A	F	P
Previewed body of speech	E	G	A	F	P
Related to audience	E	G	A	F	P

BODY

Main points clear	E	G	A	F	P
Main points fully supported	E	G	A	F	P
Organization well planned	E	G	A	F	P
Language accurate	E	G	A	F	P
Language clear, concise	E	G	A	F	P
Language appropriate	E	G	A	F	P
Connectives effective	E	G	A	F	P

CONCLUSION

Prepared audience for ending	E	G	A	F	P
Reinforced central idea	E	G	A	F	P

DELIVERY

Maintained eye contact	E	G	A	F	P
Used voice effectively	E	G	A	F	P
Used physical action effectively	E	G	A	F	P
Presented visual aids well	E	G	A	F	P

OVERALL EVALUATION

Topic challenging	E	G	A	F	P
Specific purpose well chosen	E	G	A	F	P
Speech adapted to audience	E	G	A	F	P
Speech completed in time limit	E	G	A	F	P

Speech Evaluation Form

Speaker _____

Topic _____

Rate the speaker on each point: *E-excellent*   *G-good*   *A-average*   *F-fair*   *P-poor*

INTRODUCTION

Gained attention and interest	E G A F P
Introduced topic clearly	E G A F P
Related topic to audience	E G A F P
Established credibility	E G A F P
Previewed body of speech	E G A F P

BODY

Main points clear	E G A F P
Main points fully supported	E G A F P
Organization well planned	E G A F P
Language accurate	E G A F P
Language clear	E G A F P
Language appropriate	E G A F P
Connectives effective	E G A F P

CONCLUSION

Prepared audience for ending	E G A F P
Reinforced central idea	E G A F P
Vivid ending	E G A F P

DELIVERY

Began speech without rushing	E G A F P
Maintained strong eye contact	E G A F P
Avoided distracting mannerisms	E G A F P
Articulated words clearly	E G A F P
Used pauses effectively	E G A F P
Used vocal variety to add impact	E G A F P
Presented visual aids well	E G A F P
Communicated enthusiasm for topic	E G A F P
Departed from lectern without rushing	E G A F P

OVERALL EVALUATION

Met assignment	E G A F P
Topic challenging	E G A F P
Specific purpose well chosen	E G A F P
Message adapted to audience	E G A F P
Speech completed within time limit	E G A F P
Held interest of audience	E G A F P

What did the speaker do most effectively? _____

_____

What should the speaker pay special attention to next time? _____

_____

General Comments _____

_____

_____

Speech Evaluation Form

Speaker _____

Topic _____

Rate the speaker on each point: *E-excellent*   *G-good*   *A-average*   *F-fair*   *P-poor*

What was the speaker's specific purpose? _____

_____

Introduction gained attention	E	G	A	F	P
Introduction revealed the topic clearly	E	G	A	F	P
Introduction related topic to the audience	E	G	A	F	P
Introduction established credibility	E	G	A	F	P
Introduction previewed the body of the speech	E	G	A	F	P

List the main points of the speech. On the line at right note the kinds of supporting materials used for each: *S-statistics*   *E-examples*   *T-testimony*

I. _____

II. _____

III. _____

IV. _____

V. _____

What pattern of organization did the speaker use? _____

_____

Conclusion reinforced the central idea	E	G	A	F	P
Conclusion ended on a strong note	E	G	A	F	P
Speaker's language was clear	E	G	A	F	P
Speaker's language was vivid	E	G	A	F	P
Speaker's language was appropriate	E	G	A	F	P
Speaker maintained strong eye contact	E	G	A	F	P
Speaker had sufficient vocal variety	E	G	A	F	P
Speaker articulated words clearly	E	G	A	F	P
Speaker seemed poised and confident	E	G	A	F	P
Speaker communicated enthusiasm for the topic	E	G	A	F	P
Overall evaluation of the speech	E	G	A	F	P

Policy Speech Evaluation Form

Speaker _____

Topic _____

Rate the speaker on each point: *E-excellent*   *G-good*   *A-average*   *F-fair*   *P-poor*

		E	G	A	F	P
1.	Introduction gained attention and interest	E	G	A	F	P
2.	Main points clearly organized and easy to follow	E	G	A	F	P
3.	Main points supported with sufficient evidence	E	G	A	F	P
4.	Evidence from qualified sources	E	G	A	F	P
5.	Reasoning clear and sound	E	G	A	F	P
6.	Need issue dealt with convincingly	E	G	A	F	P
7.	Speaker's plan clearly explained	E	G	A	F	P
8.	Practicality of plan demonstrated	E	G	A	F	P
9.	Connectives used effectively	E	G	A	F	P
10.	Language clear and concise	E	G	A	F	P
11.	Conclusion reinforced the central idea	E	G	A	F	P
12.	Sufficient eye contact	E	G	A	F	P
13.	Voice used to add impact	E	G	A	F	P
14.	Physical action effective	E	G	A	F	P
15.	Speech well adapted to the audience	E	G	A	F	P
16.	Overall evaluation of the speech	E	G	A	F	P

Comments: _____

_____

_____

_____

_____

_____

Monroe's Motivated Sequence Evaluation Form

Speaker _____

Topic _____

Rate the speaker on each point: *E-excellent*   *G-good*   *A-average*   *F-fair*   *P-poor*

COMMENTS

ATTENTION STEP

Gained attention of listeners	E	G	A	F	P
Introduced topic clearly	E	G	A	F	P
Showed importance of topic to this audience	E	G	A	F	P

NEED STEP

Need clearly explained	E	G	A	F	P
Need demonstrated with evidence	E	G	A	F	P
Need related to audience	E	G	A	F	P

SATISFACTION STEP

Plan clearly explained	E	G	A	F	P
Plan well thought out	E	G	A	F	P

VISUALIZATION STEP

Practicality of plan shown	E	G	A	F	P
Benefits of plan related to audience	E	G	A	F	P

ACTION STEP

Call for specific action by audience	E	G	A	F	P
Vivid concluding appeal	E	G	A	F	P

DELIVERY

Maintained eye contact	E	G	A	F	P
Extemporaneous and conversational	E	G	A	F	P
Poised, confident presentation	E	G	A	F	P
Words articulated clearly	E	G	A	F	P
Physical action effective	E	G	A	F	P
Communicated enthusiasm for topic	E	G	A	F	P

OVERALL EVALUATION

Language clear, concise	E	G	A	F	P
Connectives effective	E	G	A	F	P
Completed in time limit	E	G	A	F	P
Speaker's purpose achieved	E	G	A	F	P

Commemorative Speech Evaluation Form

Speaker _____

Topic _____

Rate the speaker on each point: *E-excellent*   *G-good*   *A-average*   *F-fair*   *P-poor*

	E	G	A	F	P
Introduction gained attention	E	G	A	F	P
Subject introduced clearly	E	G	A	F	P
Main ideas easily followed	E	G	A	F	P
Language clear	E	G	A	F	P
Language vivid	E	G	A	F	P
Topic dealt with creatively	E	G	A	F	P
Speech adapted to audience	E	G	A	F	P
Sufficient eye contact	E	G	A	F	P
Voice used effectively	E	G	A	F	P
Physical action effective	E	G	A	F	P
General evaluation of the speech	E	G	A	F	P

Comments

After-Dinner Speech Evaluation Form

Speaker _____

Topic _____

Rate the speaker on each point: *E-excellent*   *G-good*   *A-average*   *F-fair*   *P-poor*

Topic appropriate	E	G	A	F	P
Introduction gained attention	E	G	A	F	P
Subject introduced clearly	E	G	A	F	P
Main ideas easily followed	E	G	A	F	P
Topic dealt with creatively	E	G	A	F	P
Language clear, concrete	E	G	A	F	P
Language vivid, colorful	E	G	A	F	P
Supporting materials entertaining	E	G	A	F	P
Humor tasteful	E	G	A	F	P
Strong eye contact	E	G	A	F	P
Voice used expressively	E	G	A	F	P
Speech adapted to audience	E	G	A	F	P
Overall evaluation of speech	E	G	A	F	P

Comments

Part Four

CHAPTER-BY-CHAPTER

GUIDE TO

THE ART OF PUBLIC SPEAKING

Chapter 1 Speaking in Public

Chapter Objectives

After reading this chapter, students should be able to:

1. Explain the value of a course in public speaking.

2. Discuss the long tradition of studying public speaking.

3. Identify the major similarities and differences between public speaking and everyday conversation.

4. Explain why a certain amount of nervousness is normal—even desirable—for a public speaker.

5. Discuss methods of controlling nervousness and of making it work for, rather than against, a speaker.

6. Identify the basic elements of the speech communication process.

7. Explain how the cultural diversity of today's world can influence public speaking situations.

8. Define ethnocentrism and explain why public speakers need to avoid it when addressing audiences of diverse racial, ethnic, or cultural background.

Chapter Outline

I.   Public speaking is a vital means of communication (*text pages 4-6*).
    A.   During modern times, men and women around the globe have used public speaking to spread their ideas and influence.
        1.   In the U.S., the list would include Franklin Roosevelt, Billy Graham, Cesar Chavez, Martin Luther King, Barbara Jordan, Ronald Reagan, and Elizabeth Dole.
        2.   In other countries, it includes people such as Margaret Thatcher, Nelson Mandela, Rigoberta Menchu, and Aung San Suu Kyi.
    B.   The need for public speaking will touch almost every person at some time in her or his life.
        1.   Public speaking helps people succeed in nearly all professions.
        2.   Public speaking is a vital means of civic engagement.
        3.   Public speaking is a form of empowerment.

II.   Public speaking has been taught and studied around the globe for thousands of years (*text page 6*).
    A.   The importance of effective public speaking has been recognized for millennia in many cultures.
        1.   The oldest known handbook on effective speech was written on papyrus in Egypt some 4,500 years ago.
        2.   Eloquence was highly prized in ancient India, Africa, and China, as well as among the Aztecs and other pre-European cultures of North and South America.
    B.   In classical Greece and Rome, public speaking played a central role in education and civic life and was studied extensively.
        1.   Aristotle's *Rhetoric* is still considered the most important work on its subject.
        2.   The Roman leader Cicero used his speeches to defend liberty and wrote several works about oratory in general.
    C.   Over the centuries, many notable thinkers have dealt with issues of rhetoric, speech, and language.
        1.   These thinkers include the Roman educator Quintilian, the Christian preacher St. Augustine, the medieval writer Christine de Pizan, the British philosopher Francis Bacon, and the American critic Kenneth Burke.
        2.   In recent years, communication researchers have provided an increasingly scientific basis for understanding the methods and strategies of effective speech.
    D.   The aim of a public speaking course is to help students apply those methods and strategies.
        1.   As students read this book, they should keep in mind that the principles of public speaking are derived from a long tradition and have been confirmed by a substantial body of research.

2.   The more students know about those principles, the more effective they will be in their own speeches, as well as in listening to the speeches of other people.

III.   Public speaking and everyday conversation have a number of similarities and require similar skills (*text pages 6-8*).
A.   In both, people organize their thoughts logically.
B.   In both, people tailor their message to the audience.
C.   In both, people tell a story for maximum impact.
D.   In both, people adapt to feedback from listeners.

IV.   There are three key differences between public speaking and everyday conversation (*text page 9*).
A.   Public speaking is more highly structured than ordinary conversation.
1.   There are usually time limits on the length of a speech.
2.   In most situations listeners do not interrupt a public speaker to voice questions or comments.
B.   Public speaking requires more formal language than ordinary conversation.
1.   Listeners usually react negatively to slang, jargon, and bad grammar in public speeches.
2.   Because a public speech is supposed to be "special," most successful speakers elevate and polish their language when addressing an audience.
C.   Public speaking requires a different method of delivery from ordinary conversation.
1.   When conversing informally, most people talk quietly, interject stock phrases such "you know," "like," and "really," adopt a casual posture, and the like.
2.   Effective public speakers adopt a more formal manner of delivery and avoid distracting mannerisms and verbal habits.
D.   With study and practice, most people are able to master these differences and expand their conversational skills into speechmaking.

V.   One of the major concerns of students in any speech class is stage fright (*text pages 9-16*).
A.   It is entirely normal to feel nervous about the prospect of giving a public speech.
B.   Even experienced public speakers have stage fright before their presentations.
C.   There are six major steps students can take to control their nervousness and make it a positive force in their speeches.
1.   One is to take a speech class in which they will learn about speechmaking and gain speaking experience.
2.   Another is to be thoroughly prepared for every speech they present.
a.   It is difficult to be confident of success when one stands up to speak without knowing what to say or how to say it.

          b.   Most people find that their confidence increases dramatically when they practice a speech until they have full command of the ideas and the delivery.

    3.   It is also crucial that speakers think positively about themselves and the speech experience.

          a.   Confidence is largely the well-known power of positive thinking.

          b.   Speakers who think negatively about themselves and the speech experience are much more likely to be overcome by stage fright than are speakers who think positively.

          c.   For each negative thought about their speeches, students should counter with at least five positive ones.

    4.   Using the power of visualization is another excellent way to combat stage fright.

          a.   Visualization is used by athletes, musicians, actors, speakers, and others to enhance their performance in stressful situations.

          b.   The key to visualization is creating a mental blueprint in which one presents a successful speech.

    5.   Most speakers are also helped by knowing that their nervousness is usually not visible to the audience.

    6.   It is also important not to expect perfection when delivering a speech.

          a.   Even accomplished speakers make mistakes, but most of the time no one besides the speaker notices.

          b.   Speechmaking should be seen as an act of communication rather than as a kind of performance in which absolute perfection is required.

          c.   Speech audiences are not looking for a virtuoso performance, but for a well-thought-out address that communicates the speaker's ideas clearly and directly.

  D.   In addition, there are a number of specific tips that can help students deal with nervousness.

    1.   Be at your physical and mental best when speaking.

    2.   Quietly tighten and relax hand or leg muscles while waiting to speak.

    3.   Take a few slow, deep breaths before starting to speak.

    4.   Work especially hard on your introduction.

    5.   Make eye contact with people in the audience.

    6.   Concentrate on communicating with the audience rather than on worrying about your nervousness.

    7.   Use visual aids to help occupy the attention of the audience.

VI.   Public speaking helps people develop critical thinking skills (*text pages 16-17*).

  A.   Critical thinking involves a number of skills.

    1.   Critical thinking involves being able to assess the strengths and weaknesses of an argument.

    2.   Critical thinking involves distinguishing fact from opinion.

    3.   Critical thinking involves judging the credibility of sources.

   4. Critical thinking involves assessing the quality of evidence.

   5. Critical thinking involves discerning the relationships among ideas.

  B. These—and other—critical thinking skills are enriched by a public speaking class.

   1. As students organize their speeches, their ideas will become more clear and cohesive.

   2. As students work on expressing their ideas accurately, their thinking will become more precise.

   3. As students learn about the role of reasoning and evidence in speeches, they will become better able to assess reasoning and evidence in all types of situations.

VII. There are seven elements of the speech communication process (*text pages 17-22*).

  A. Speech communication begins with a speaker.

   1. The speaker is the person who presents the message.

   2. Successful speakers combine technical skill with personal enthusiasm.

  B. The message is whatever a speaker communicates to someone else.

   1. The goal of a speaker is to have the intended message be the message that is actually communicated.

   2. Achieving this depends both on what the speaker says (the verbal message) and how the speaker says it (the nonverbal message).

  C. The channel is the means by which a message is communicated.

   1. Public speakers may use one or more of several channels—microphone, radio, television, etc.

   2. In speech class, the channel is the most direct because listeners see and hear the speaker without any media or electronic intervention.

  D. The listener is the person who receives the communicated message.

   1. Everything a speaker says is filtered through a listener's frame of reference.

    a. A listener's frame of reference is the sum total of his or her knowledge, experience, goals, values, and attitudes.

    b. Because a speaker and listener are different people, they can never have exactly the same frame of reference.

   2. Because people have different frames of reference, a public speaker must take care to adapt the message to the particular audience being addressed.

  E. Feedback consists of messages sent from the listener to the speaker.

   1. Most communication situations involve two-way communication, in which the speaker can see how the audience is responding.

   2. Successful public speakers learn to interpret the feedback sent by listeners and to adjust their messages in response to the feedback.

  F. Interference is anything that impedes the communication of a message.

   1. Interference can be either external or internal.

    a. External interference comes from outside the audience—such as a ringing telephone, the noise of traffic, or static in a microphone.

        b.   Internal interference comes from within the audience—such as poor listening skills or lack of concentration.

   2.   Successful public speakers work to hold their listeners' attention despite interference.

G.   The situation is the time and place in which speech communication occurs.

   1.   Speech communication always takes place in a particular situation.

        a.   A conversation might occur over a candlelight dinner or in a noisy tavern.

        b.   A public speech might be presented in a small classroom, in a large auditorium, or at outdoor graduation ceremonies.

   2.   Successful public speakers are alert to the situation and adjust their remarks to it.

VIII. Public speakers need to be aware of and responsive to today's multicultural world (*text pages 22-27*).

A.   The United States has become the most diverse society on the face of the earth.

   1.   For more than a century, European immigrants and African Americans made the U.S. the "melting pot" of the world.

   2.   Today another great wave of immigration—mostly from Asia and Latin America—is making the U.S. a multicultural society of unparalleled diversity.

B.   Cultural diversity is more than a U.S. phenomenon.

   1.   We are living in an age of international multiculturalism.

   2.   Air travel, immigration, and electronic communication are making all nations and cultures part of a vast "global village."

C.   Diversity and multiculturalism are such basic facts of life in today's world that they affect many public speaking situations.

   1.   Because of the growing diversity of modern life, audiences often include people of different cultural, racial, and ethnic backgrounds.

   2.   Speechmaking becomes more complex as cultural diversity increases.

   3.   To be successful, public speakers need to take account of cultural differences between themselves and their listeners.

D.   It is especially important for public speakers to avoid ethnocentrism.

   1.   Ethnocentrism is the belief that one's own culture or group is superior to all others.

        a.   Ethnocentrism can play a positive role in creating group pride and loyalty.

        b.   Ethnocentrism can be destructive when it leads to prejudice and hostility.

   2.   Speakers can avoid ethnocentrism by respecting diverse cultural values.

        a.   They should remember that all societies have special beliefs and customs.

   b.   Although speakers do not have to agree with the beliefs and customs of all people, they will not be successful unless they show respect for the cultures of the people they address.
3.   Speakers can also take specific steps to adapt to listeners of diverse cultural, racial, and ethnic backgrounds.
   a.   When preparing the speech, they should put themselves in the place of listeners from different backgrounds to make sure the speech is clear and appropriate.
   b.   They should use examples, comparisons, and other supporting materials that can clarify ideas for a wide range of listeners.
   c.   They should consider using visual aids to bridge gaps in language or cultural background.
   d.   When presenting the speech, they should be alert to feedback that might indicate the audience is having difficulty understanding.
E.   Listeners also need to avoid ethnocentrism.
1.   Audiences have a responsibility to listen courteously and attentively to speakers of all cultural backgrounds.
2.   They need to be on guard against the temptation to reject speakers from different backgrounds on the basis of accent, personal appearance, or manner of delivery.

Exercises for Critical Thinking *(from text page 29)*

1.   Think back on an important conversation you had recently in which you wanted to achieve a particular result. (*Examples*: Asking your employer to change your work schedule; explaining to a friend how to change the oil and filter in a car; attempting to talk your spouse or partner into buying the computer you like rather than the one he or she prefers.) Work up a brief analysis of the conversation.

   In your analysis, explain the following: (1) your purpose in the conversation and the message strategy you chose to achieve your purpose; (2) the communication channels used during the conversation and how they affected the outcome; (3) the interference—internal or external—you encountered during the conversation; (4) the steps you took to adjust to feedback; (5) the strategic changes you would make in preparing for and carrying out the conversation if you had it to do over again.

   Discussion: This exercise can be a very effective vehicle for class discussion about the basic elements of the speech communication process and how they interact. By stressing the strategic aspects of everyday conversation, this exercise also points to the similarities between conversation and public speaking. Students should find that much of the strategic thinking that goes into preparing a speech is quite similar to the strategic thinking they often put into ordinary conversation.

2.   Divide a sheet of paper into two columns. Label one column "Characteristics of an Effective Public Speaker." Label the other column "Characteristics of an Ineffective Public Speaker." In the columns, list and briefly explain what you believe to be the five most important characteristics of effective and ineffective speakers. Be prepared to discuss your ideas in class.

> **Discussion:** When this exercise is discussed in class, it provides the basis for generating a set of criteria for effective speechmaking that is agreed upon by the entire class. You, of course, should know ahead of time the criteria you want to stress, so you can direct the class discussion in that direction.

3.   On the basis of the lists you developed for Exercise 2, candidly evaluate your own strengths and weaknesses as a speaker. Identify the three primary aspects of speechmaking you most want to improve.

> **Discussion:** This exercise encourages students to set specific goals for improving their public speaking. At various times in the term, you and the student can weigh her or his progress against the goals. Some teachers have students reassess their goals every few weeks. At the end of the course, you may want students to judge how well they have met their goals and to reassess their strengths and weaknesses as speakers in light of what they have learned in the course.

Applying the Power of Public Speaking *(from text pages 29-30)*

It has been three years since you finished college. After gaining experience as an administrative assistant at a major publishing company, you have just been promoted to marketing manager for a children's book series. Though you have occasionally given brief reports to other members of your work team, you are now facing your first speech to a large audience. At your company's annual sales meeting, you will address the sales force about the company's new books and how to sell them to wholesalers and retail bookstores.

You're pleased to have this opportunity, and you know it shows the company's faith in your abilities. Yet the closer you get to the day of the speech, the harder it is to control the butterflies in your stomach. There will be 150 people in your audience, including all the senior editors and regional managers, in addition to the sales force. All eyes will be on you. It's important that you come across as confident and well informed, but you're afraid your stage fright will send the opposite message. What strategies will you use to control your nerves and make them work for you?

Discussion: Like the other Applying the Power of Public Speaking scenarios throughout the book, this one is intended to show how public speaking is used in everyday life and to challenge students to apply their critical-thinking skills to a wide range of practical situations. Some of the scenarios have definite correct answers; others, like this one, allow for a wide range of responses and are designed to provide a spur for class discussion. In this case, you can anticipate that students will mention the major strategies discussed in the chapter for controlling stage fright—being fully prepared for the speech, thinking positively, using the power of visualization, recognizing that most nervousness is not visible to the audience, and not expecting perfection—but you should encourage them to come up with others as well.

Additional Exercises and Activities

1.   On the first day of class have students fill out and return the questionnaire on page 68 of this manual. This will give you a pretty clear early picture of the background and needs of the students enrolled in your class.

2.   Show students the videotape "Be Prepared to Speak," which is part of the videotape supplement to *The Art of Public Speaking*. Afterward, discuss the tape and highlight its main points about speech preparation and presentation.

> **Discussion:** "Be Prepared to Speak" is a 27-minute videotape that presents a dramatized overview of the entire public speaking process from choosing a topic to delivering the final presentation. Entertaining as well as informative, it shows students how to organize their ideas, develop an introduction and conclusion, rehearse the speech, overcome nervousness, and adapt to the audience and speaking occasion. The tape works especially well if shown early in the term—before the introductory speeches are presented. By giving students a concise introduction to all the steps of speech development and delivery, it prepares students for their initial speech without first having to read several chapters in the book.

3.   As an alternative to the preceding activity, show students "Speaking Effectively to 1 or 1,000," which is available as a videotape supplement to *The Art of Public Speaking*. Afterward, discuss the tape's message about preparation, nervousness, and other aspects of the speechmaking process.

> **Discussion:** Like "Be Prepared to Speak," "Speaking Effectively to 1 or 1,000" is an excellent videotape to show students early in the term as they are preparing for their ice-breaker speeches. Entertaining and well-produced, it is 21 minutes long and deals especially well with such issues as the importance of public speaking and how to deal with stage fright.

STUDENT INTRODUCTION QUESTIONNAIRE

Name _____   *Year* _____

Major _____

What reason(s) do you have for taking this class?

Do you have any specific goals for improving your speaking? What are they? (What would you like to learn how to do? What particular problems would you like to overcome?)

What classes in speech and related fields (such as journalism or English composition) have you had here or at other schools?

What kinds of speaking experiences have you had in your classes, jobs, religious organizations, extra-curricular activities, etc.?

When did you give your last speech? What was the topic?

What are your career plans? Will public speaking be important to your career? How so?

4.   Give students the following assignment: Think of a situation in which you sought to understand the message of, or to convey your own message to, someone from a different culture. The situation might have involved interpersonal communication, public speaking, or a mass media message such as a film or a television program. Write a brief analysis in which you explain (a) the participants in the communication situation, (b) the message that was meant to be communicated, (c) the difficulty you had communicating—or understanding—the message, (d) the outcome of the situation, and (e) what the situation reveals about the complexity of communicating with people of different cultural backgrounds. Be prepared to present your analysis in class.

> **Discussion:**   This exercise works best in classes in which a fair proportion of students have had personal communication with people from different cultures. It can provide an excellent vehicle for discussing ethnocentrism and the barriers it poses to intercultural communication. Because students are dealing with their own experiences, the exercise helps make the abstract concept of ethnocentrism more immediate and personal.

5.   Over the years a number of metaphors have been used to describe the mix of cultures in the United States. Best known is the melting pot metaphor, which originated in 1908 with *The Melting-Pot*, a play by Israel Zangwill, an English writer of Russian-Jewish heritage. According to this metaphor, the United States is like the kind of huge container used to melt and mix steel and other metals. As immigrants come to the United States, they blend together into one assimilated culture that is stronger than the individual cultures of which it is composed.

A second metaphor compares the U.S. to a set of streams or rivers each of which is composed of many people from different cultures. The streams or rivers flow separately, maintaining their unique identity until at some point they come together to form a mighty watershed in which the individual streams and rivers are combined into one.

In a third metaphor the U.S. is compared to a garden salad in which different cultures, like the different ingredients in a salad, are combined and tossed to create the final product without losing their individual texture and flavor.

A fourth metaphor likens the U.S. to a giant quilt or tapestry in which people of different cultural backgrounds, like the individual threads and patterns of a tapestry, are woven together to produce the overall design. Like the salad metaphor, in which the various ingredients retain their own texture and flavor, the tapestry metaphor stresses the uniqueness and importance of the individual threads, patterns, and colors out of which the whole fabric is constructed.

After presenting these metaphors to the class, conduct a class discussion in which students consider the strengths and weaknesses of each metaphor for describing the cultural diversity of life in the United States.

Discussion: This exercise can be conducted in small groups or with the class as a whole. In either case, it is an excellent vehicle for prompting reflection about cultural diversity in the U.S. Here are some issues to consider:

First, although the melting pot metaphor was widely employed through most of the twentieth century, it has fallen into some disfavor in recent years because it does not stress the capacity of cultural groups to maintain their individual identities as they "melt" into a single American culture. Second, the comparison of the U.S. to a set of streams or rivers that combine to form a single body of water allows for the uniqueness of individual cultures until the point at which they merge into a common current. But this metaphor also implies that the streams and rivers are inferior to or less consequential than the great body of water they form when brought together.

Third, in both the salad and tapestry metaphors, individual elements of the whole retain their identity and uniqueness even as they are combined to create a larger entity. Comparing the U.S. to a tapestry, however, suggests that at some point U.S. culture as a whole is an inert, finished product, when in fact it is constantly changing and evolving. The salad metaphor, on the other hand, captures both the dynamic quality of cultural diversity in the U.S. and the distinctiveness of individual cultural groups. For fuller analysis of these metaphors, see Myron W. Lustig and Jolene Koester, *Intercultural Competence: Interpersonal Communication Across Cultures*, 4th ed. (Boston: Allyn and Bacon, 2003), pp. 56-58, from which this discussion is adapted.

6. If your class has a fair number of international students, conduct a class discussion in which the international students compare and contrast common nonverbal signals in their countries with those in the United States.

Discussion: Depending on the composition of your class, this can be an excellent way to generate discussion of the nonverbal dimension of intercultural communication. The exercise also sensitizes U.S. students to the communication customs of students from abroad and to the adaptations international students have to make to communicate effectively in the U.S. If you begin the discussion with such basic signals as those for "hello," "goodbye," "come here," "okay," and the like, it will usually move naturally to more complex signals. Given the nature of college students, the discussion will also probably turn at some point to obscene gestures unless you declare that subject off limits.

For instructors who wish to know more about nonverbal communication among different cultures prior to discussion, Roger Axtell's *Gestures: The Do's and Taboos of Body Language Around the World*, rev. ed. (New York: Wiley, 1998), provides a highly readable, illustrated treatment. For an excellent general guide to teaching international students, see Karen E. Johnson and Paula Golombek, *Public Speaking for Non-Native Speakers: A Handbook for Instructors* (New York: McGraw-Hill, 1996), which is available as an instructional supplement to *The Art of Public Speaking*.

7. Assign a two-minute speech of self-introduction in which students explain a significant aspect of their cultural background and how it has made a difference in their lives. Possible topics might include social customs, family traditions, holidays, clothing, food, religious traditions, sporting activities, and the like. Encourage students to be creative in preparing their speeches and in finding ways to illustrate how the aspect of their culture they choose to explain relates to their personal lives.

> **Discussion:** This assignment accomplishes three goals at once. First, it fulfills the need for an introductory, ungraded speech in which students can begin the process of feeling comfortable in front of an audience. Second, it allows everyone in the class to learn something about their fellow students, which is an important step in creating a supportive, cooperative classroom atmosphere. Third, by focusing on the different cultural backgrounds of people in the class, it creates opportunities to discuss cultural diversity and its impact on public speaking in general. For more details on this assignment, see Introductory Speech, Option D, on pages 31-32 of this manual.

8. Assign a two-minute speech in which students introduce one of their classmates to the rest of the class. The speech should focus on some aspect of the cultural background of the person being introduced—social customs, family traditions, holidays, clothing, food, religious traditions, sporting activities, and the like. Encourage students to be creative in preparing their speeches and in talking about their classmates.

> **Discussion:** This assignment offers an alternative to Additional Exercise/Activity 7 above and accomplishes the same objectives. In preparation for the speech have students pair off and interview one another. If there is great cultural diversity in your class, arrange the interview pairs so that students interview someone with a substantially different cultural background from their own. Although the interviewing can be done in the last 15 to 20 minutes of the first class meeting, the assignment usually works better if students conduct their interviews out of class. This provides time for longer interviews and gives students a better chance to get to know one another. If this assignment is used for the introductory ice-breaker speech, it should not be graded. For more details, see Introductory Speech, Option B, on pages 30-31 of this manual.

9. Assign an informative speech of five to six minutes in which students explain a significant aspect of a culture different from their own—social customs, family traditions, holidays, clothing, religious traditions, music, sporting activities, educational systems, etc. Research is required for this speech. If students have had direct contact with a foreign culture, they should be encouraged to supplement their research with their personal experience, but the speech is not to be a travelogue or a presentation on "My Summer in Europe" or "My Year as an Exchange Student in Brazil." However, a speech on how Europeans spend their summer vacations, or on the educational system of Brazil, would be fine.

Discussion: Unlike Additional Exercises/Activities 7 and 8, this assignment involves a full-length, graded speech. The objectives with respect to cultural diversity, however, are much the same. Because students are sometimes resistant when they are required to speak on a different culture, it can be helpful to present this as the "World Travel Agency" speech. If you take this approach, tell students that the class is going to travel around the world via their speeches. They will "visit" as many different countries as there are students in the class.

To help students choose topics as quickly as possible, prepare two sets of 3 x 5 index cards. Write the name of a different country on each card in the first set. Then write two or three cultural features on each card in the second set (choose from the features listed at the start of this exercise, or, better yet, add some of your own devising). Put each set of cards in a separate bag and have students randomly pick a card from each bag. When they are finished, they will have a country card (for instance, Italy) and a topic card (including, for example, sports, family traditions, and politics). The student will then speak on one of those three aspects of Italian life.

However students choose their topics, they should be encouraged to be imaginative in composing their speeches. It is not enough to summarize basic information from an encyclopedia or the Internet about the country on which they are speaking. As in any informative speech, students need to explain ideas clearly and to think about ways to relate the topic to the audience. They also need to consider using visual aids. Indeed, many teachers require a visual aid for this speech. For further details on this assignment, see Informative Speech, Option D, on page 34 of this manual.

Extra Teaching and Learning Resources

General

Campbell, John Angus. "Oratory, Democracy, and the Classroom." In Roger Sader (ed.), *Democracy, Education, and the Schools*. San Francisco: Jossey Bass, 1995, pp. 211-243.

Carrell, Lori J., and Menzel, Kent E. "Variations in Learning, Motivation, and Perceived Immediacy between Live and Distance Education Classrooms." *Communication Education*, 50 (2001), 230-240.

Cohen, Jodi R. "The Relevance of a Course in Public Speaking." In Stephen E. Lucas (ed.), *Selections from the Speech Communication Teacher, 1986-1991*. New York: McGraw-Hill, 1992, pp. 2-3.

Clark, Ruth A., and Jones, David. "A Comparison of Traditional and Online Formats in a Public Speaking Course." *Communication Education*, 50 (2001), 109-124.

Darling, Ann L., and Dannels, Deanna P. "Practicing Engineers Talk About the Importance of Talk: A Report on the Role of Oral Communication in the Workplace." *Communication Education*, 52 (2003), 1-16.

Eberly, Rosa A. "Rhetoric and the Anti-Logos Doughball: Teaching Deliberating Bodies the Practices of Deliberatory Democracy." *Rhetoric and Public Affairs*, 5 (2002), pp. 287-300.

Ford, Wendy S. Zabava, and Wolvin, Andrew D. "The Differential Impact of a Basic Communication Course on Perceived Competencies in Class, Work, and Social Contexts." *Communication Education*, 42 (1993), 215-223.

Greene, John O.; Sassi, Marianne S.; Malek-Madani, Terri L.; and Edwards, Christopher N. "Adult Acquisition of Message-Production Skill." *Communication Monographs*, 64 (1997), 181-200.

Hart, Roderick P. "Why Communication? Why Education? Toward a Politics of Teaching." *Communication Education*, 42 (1993), 97-105.

Haynes, Lance W. "Public Speaking Pedagogy in the Media Age." *Communication Education*, 39 (1990), 89-102.

Lane, Derek R., and Shelton, Michael W. "The Centrality of Communication Education in Classroom Computer-Mediated-Communication: Toward a Practical and Evaluative Pedagogy." *Communication Education*, 50 (2001), 241-255.

Menzel, Kent E., and Carrell, Lori J. "The Relationship Between Preparation and Performance in Public Speaking." *Communication Education*, 43 (1994), 17-26.

Powers, John H. "On the Intellectual Structure of the Human Communication Discipline." *Communication Education*, 44 (1995), 191-222.

Rubin, Rebecca B; and Graham, Elizabeth E. "Communication Correlates of College Success: An Exploratory Investigation." *Communication Education*, 37 (1988), 14-27.

Shedletsky, Leonard J., and Aitken, Joan E. "The Paradoxes of Online Academic Work." *Communication Education*, 50 (2001), 206-217.

Shelton, Michael W.; Lane, Derek R.; and Waldhart, Enid S. "A Review and Assessment of National Educational Trends in Communication Instruction." *Communication Education*, 48 (1999), 228-237.

The Tradition of Public Speaking

Bizzell, Patricia, and Herzberg, Bruce (eds.). *The Rhetorical Tradition: Readings from Classical Times to the Present*, 2nd ed. New York: Bedford/St. Martin, 2001.

Cohen, David. "Oratory." In Thomas O. Sloane (ed.). *Encyclopedia of Rhetoric*. New York: Oxford University Press, 2001, pp. 538-547.

Copeland, Lewis; Lamm, Lawrence W.; and McKenna, Stephen J. (eds.). *The World's Great Speeches*, 4th ed. Mineola, NY: Dover Publications, 1999.

Corbett, Edward P. J., and Connors, Robert J. *Classical Rhetoric for the Modern Student*, 4th ed. New York: Oxford University Press, 1999.

Gill, Ann. *Rhetoric and Human Understanding*. Prospect Heights, IL: Waveland Press, 1994.

Greene, Richard (ed.). *Words That Shook the World: One Hundred Years of Unforgettable Speeches and Events*. New York: Penguin Putnam, 2002.

Herrick, James A. *The History and Theory of Rhetoric: An Introduction*, 2nd ed. Boston: Allyn and Bacon, 2000.

Kennedy, George A. *Comparative Rhetoric: An Historical and Cross-Cultural Introduction*. New York: Oxford University Press, 1998.

Kimball, Bruce A. *Orators and Philosophers: A History of the Idea of Liberal Education*, rev. ed. New York: College Entrance Examination Board, 1995.

Lucas, Stephen E. "Public Speaking." In Thomas O. Sloane (ed.). *Encyclopedia of Rhetoric*. New York: Oxford University Press, 2001, pp. 640-647.

MacArthur, Brian (ed.). *The Penguin Book of Historic Speeches*. London: Penguin, 1996.

Nix, S. Michele. *Women at the Podium: Memorable Speeches in History*. New York: HarperCollins, 2000.

Rohler, Lloyd, and Cook, Roger (eds.). *Great Speeches for Analysis and Criticism*, 4th ed. Greenwood, IN: Alistair Press, 2001.

Safire, William (ed.). *Lend Me Your Ears: Great Speeches in History*. New York: Norton, 1992.

Sloane, Thomas O. (ed.). *Encyclopedia of Rhetoric*. New York: Oxford University Press, 2001.

Smith, Craig R. *Rhetoric and Human Consciousness*, 2nd ed. Prospect Heights, IL: Waveland Press, 2003.

Straub, Deborah Gillan (ed.). *Voices of Multicultural America: Notable Speeches Delivered by African, Asian, Hispanic, and Native Americans, 1790-1995*. Detroit, MI: Gale, 1996.

Speech Anxiety

Adams, Lori. "Speech Anxiety Simulation." In Stephen E. Lucas (ed.), *Selections from the Speech Communication Teacher, 1991-1994*. New York: McGraw-Hill, 1995, p. 49.

Allen, Mike; Berkowitz, Sandra; Hunt, Steve; and Louden, Allen. "A Meta-Analysis of the Impact of Forensics and Communication Education on Critical Thinking." *Communication Education*, 48 (1999), 18-30.

Allen, Mike, and Bourhis, John. "The Relationship of Communication Apprehension to Communication Behavior: A Meta-Analysis." *Communication Quarterly*, 44 (1996), 214-226.

Ayres, Joe. "Comparing Self-Constructed Visualization Scripts with Guided Visualization." *Communication Reports*, 8 (1995), 193-199.

Ayres, Joe. "Reducing Public Speaking Apprehension through Speech Preparation." In Stephen E. Lucas (ed.), *Selections from the Speech Communication Teacher, 1996-1999*. New York: McGraw-Hill, 2001, p. 80.

Ayres, Joe. "Speech Preparation Processes and Speech Apprehension." *Communication Education*, 45 (1996), 228-235.

Ayres, Joe, and Heuett, Brian L. "The Relationship Between Visual Imagery and Public Speaking Apprehension." *Communication Reports*, 10 (1997), 87-94.

Ayres, Joe, and Hopf, Tim. *Coping with Speech Anxiety*. Norwood, NJ: Ablex, 1993.

Behnke, Ralph R., and Sawyer, Chris R. "Anticipatory Anxiety Patterns for Male and Female Public Speakers." *Communication Education*, 49 (2000), 187-195.

Bippus, Amy M., and Daly, John A. "What Do People Think Causes Stage Fright?: Naive Attributions About the Reasons for Public Speaking Anxiety." *Communication Education*, 48 (1999), 62-72.

Burk, John. "Communication Apprehension among Master's of Business Administration Students: Investigating a Gap in Communication Education." *Communication Education*, 50 (2001), 51-58.

Burleson, Brant B., and Planalp, Sally. "Producing Emotion(al) Messages." *Communication Theory*, 10 (2000), 221-250.

Byers, Peggy Yuhas, and Weber, Carolyn Secord. "The Timing of Speech Anxiety Reduction Treatments in the Public Speaking Classroom." *Southern Communication Journal*, 60 (1995), 246-256.

Cronin, Michael W.; Grice, George L.; and Olsen, Richard K., Jr. "The Effects of Interactive Video Instruction in Coping with Speech Fright." *Communication Education*, 43 (1994), 42-53.

Daly, John A.; McCroskey, James C.; Ayres, Joe; Hopf, Tim; and Ayres, Debbie M. (eds.). *Avoiding Communication: Shyness, Reticence, and Communication Apprehension*, 2nd ed. Cresskill, NJ: Hampton Press, 1997.

Daly, John A.; Vangelisti, Anita L.; and Weber, David J. "Speech Anxiety Affects How People Prepare Speeches: A Protocol Analysis of the Preparation Processes of Speakers." *Communication Monographs*, 62 (1995), 383-397.

Desberg, Peter, and Marsh, George D. *No More Butterflies: Overcoming Stagefright, Shyness, Interview Anxiety, and Fear of Public Speaking*. Oakland, CA: New Harbinger, 1996.

Dwyer, Karen Kangas. *Conquer Your Speechfright*. Fort Worth, TX: Harcourt Brace, 1998.

Hahner, Jeffrey C.; Sokoloff, Martin A.; and Salisch, Sandra L. *Speaking Clearly: Improving Voice and Diction*, 6th ed. New York: McGraw-Hill, 2002.

Hinton, J.S., and Kramer, Michael W. "The Impact of Self-Directed Video-Taped Feedback on Students' Self-Reported Levels of Communication Competence and Apprehension." *Communication Education*, 47 (1998), 151-161.

Isaacson, Zelda. "Paradoxical Intention: A Strategy to Alleviate the Anxiety Associated with Public Speaking." In Stephen E. Lucas (ed.), *Selections from the Speech Communication Teacher, 1991-1994*. New York: McGraw-Hill, 1995, pp. 49-50.

Langdon, Harry. "A Course on Stage Fright." In Stephen E. Lucas (ed.), *Selections from the Speech Communication Teacher, 1986-1991*. New York: McGraw-Hill, 1992, pp. 63-64.

MacIntyre, Peter, and Thivierge, Kimly A. "The Effects of Audience Pleasantness, Audience Familiarity and Speaking Contexts on Public Speaking Anxiety and Willingness to Speak." *Communication Quarterly*, 43 (1995), 456-466.

MacIntyre, Peter D.; Thivierge, Kimly A.; and MacDonald, Renee J. "The Effect of Audience Interest, Responsiveness, and Evaluation on Public Speaking Anxiety and Related Variables." *Communication Research Reports*, 14 (1997), 157-168.

Mandeville, Mary Y. "Positive Messages." In Stephen E. Lucas (ed.), *Selections from the Speech Communication Teacher, 1996-1999*. New York: McGraw-Hill, 2001, pp. 80-81.

McGuire, John; Stauble, Cherise; Abbott, David; and Fisher, Randy. "Ethical Issues in the Treatment of Communication Apprehension: A Survey of Communication Professionals." *Communication Education*, 44 (1995), 98-109.

Menzel, Kent E., and Carrell, Lori J. "The Relationship Between Preparation and Performance in Public Speaking." *Communication Education*, 43 (1994), 17-26.

Messman, Susan J., and Jones-Corley, Jennifer. "Effects of Communication Environment, Immediacy, and Communication Apprehension on Cognitive and Affective Learning." *Communication Monographs*, 68 (2001), 184-200.

Mino, Mary. "Building Confidence Through Oral Interpretation." In Stephen E. Lucas (ed.), *Selections from the Speech Communication Teacher, 1991-1994*. New York: McGraw-Hill, 1995, pp. 50-51.

Motley, Michael T. *Overcoming Your Fear of Public Speaking: A Proven Method*. Boston: Houghton Mifflin, 1998.

Proctor, Russell F. II; Douglas, Annamae T.; Garera-Izquierdo, Teresa; and Wartman, Stephanie L. "Approach, Avoidance, and Apprehension: Talking With High-CA Students About Getting Help." *Communication Education*, 43 (1994), 312-321.

Richmond, Virginia P., and McCroskey, James C. *Communication: Apprehension, Avoidance, and Effectiveness*, 5th ed. Boston: Allyn and Bacon, 1998.

Robinson II, Thomas E. "Communication Apprehension and the Basic Public Speaking Course: A National Survey of In-Class Treatment Techniques." *Communication Education*, 46 (1997), 188-197.

Rose, Heidi M.; Rancer, Andrew S.; and Crannell, Kenneth C. "The Impact of a Basic Course in Oral Interpretation and Public Speaking on Communication Apprehension." *Communication Reports*, 6 (1993), 54-60.

Rubin, Rebecca B.; Rubin, Alan M.; and Jordan, Felicia F. "Effects of Instruction on Communication Apprehension and Communication Competence." *Communication Education*, 46 (1997), 104-114.

Stowell, Jessica. "Free Writing to Deal with Speech Anxiety." In Stephen E. Lucas (ed.), *Selections from the Speech Communication Teacher, 1991-1994*. New York: McGraw-Hill, 1995, pp. 51-52.

Tillson, Lou Davidson. "Building Community and Reducing Communication Apprehension: A Case Study Approach." In Stephen E. Lucas (ed.), *Selections from the Speech Communication Teacher, 1994-1996*. New York: McGraw-Hill, 1998, pp. 66-67.

Ungerleider, Steven. *Mental Training for Peak Performance*. Emmaus, PA: Rodale Press, 1996.

Critical Thinking

Allen, Mike; Berkowitz, Sandra; Hunt, Steve; and Louden, Allen. "A Meta-Analysis of the Impact of Forensics and Communication Education on Critical Thinking." *Communication Education*, 48 (1999), 18-30.

Beall, Melissa L. "Thinking about Thinking." In Stephen E. Lucas (ed.), *Selections from the Speech Communication Teacher, 1986-1991*. New York: McGraw-Hill, 1992, pp. 19-20.

Beyer, Barry K. *Critical Thinking*. Bloomington, IN: Phi Delta Kappa Educational Foundation, 1995.

Bozik, Mary. "Fact or Opinion?" In Stephen E. Lucas (ed.), *Selections from the Speech Communication Teacher, 1996-1999*. New York: McGraw-Hill, 2001, pp. 18-19.

Browne, M. Neil, and Keeley, Stuart M. *Asking the Right Questions: A Guide to Critical Thinking*, 6th ed. Upper Saddle River, NJ: Prentice Hall, 2001.

Diestler, Sherry. *Becoming a Critical Thinker: A User Friendly Manual*. 3rd ed. Upper Saddle River, NJ: Prentice Hall, 2001.

Eldred, Jean Parker. "A Procedure for Teaching Criteria Generation." In Stephen E. Lucas (ed.), *Selections from the Speech Communication Teacher, 1994-1996*. New York: McGraw-Hill, 1998, pp. 11-12.

Fritz, Paul A., and Weaver, Richard L., II. "Teaching Critical Thinking in the Basic Speaking Course: A Liberal Arts Perspective." *Communication Education*, 35 (1986), 174-182.

Garside, Colleen. "Look Who's Talking: A Comparison of Lecture and Group Discussion Teaching Strategies in Developing Critical Thinking Skills." *Communication Education*, 45 (1996), 212-227.

Hamlet, Janice D. "Editorial Sessions: A Different Approach to Teaching Argumentation." In Stephen E. Lucas (ed.), *Selections from the Speech Communication Teacher, 1994-1996*. New York: McGraw-Hill, 1998, p. 5.

Koehler, Carol. "Using Collaborative Controversy in the Critical Thinking Classroom." In Stephen E. Lucas (ed.), *Selections from the Speech Communication Teacher, 1996-1999*. New York: McGraw-Hill, 2001, pp. 19-20.

Meltzer, Marilyn, and Palau, Susan Marcus. *Acquiring Critical Thinking Skills*. Philadelphia: W.B. Saunders, 1996.

Newburger, Craig. "Testing Students' Ability to Distinguish Facts from Inferences." In Stephen E. Lucas (ed.), *Selections from the Speech Communication Teacher, 1991-1994*. New York: McGraw-Hill, 1995, pp. 20-21.

O'Keefe, Virginia. *Developing Critical Thinking: The Speaking/Listening Connection*. Portsmouth, NH: Boynton/Cook, 2000.

Proctor, Russell F., II. "Using Feature Films to Teach Critical Thinking: Multiple Morals to the Stories." In Stephen E. Lucas (ed.), *Selections from the Speech Communication Teacher, 1991-1994*. New York: McGraw-Hill, 1995, pp. 21-22.

Sanders, Judith A., Wiseman, Richard L., and Gass, Robert H. "Does Teaching Argumentation Facilitate Students' Critical Thinking?" *Communication Reports*, 7 (1994), 27-35.

Schumer, Allison. "Speech Communication via Critical Thinking." In Stephen E. Lucas (ed.), *Selections from the Speech Communication Teacher, 1986-1991*. New York: McGraw-Hill, 1992, pp. 21-22.

Spicer, Karin-Leigh, and Hanks, William E. "Critical Thinking Activities for Public Speaking Textbooks." In Stephen E. Lucas (ed.), *Selections from the Speech Communication Teacher, 1991-1994*. New York: McGraw-Hill, 1995, pp. 22-23.

The Speech Communication Process

Burgoon, Michael; Hunsaker, Frank G.; and Dawson, Edwin J. *Human Communication*, 3rd ed. Thousand Oaks, CA: Sage, 1994.

Griffin, Em. *A First Look at Communication Theory*, 5th ed. New York: McGraw-Hill, 2003.

Heath, Robert L., and Bryant, Jennings. *Human Communication Theory and Research*, 2nd ed. Mahwah, NJ: Lawrence Erlbaum, 2000.

Krivanek, Patricia Scileppi. *How Then Shall We Live? Values for Interpersonal Communication*. New York: McGraw-Hill, 2000.

Lippert, Lance, and Paynton, Scott T. "Send, Receive, and Draw." In Stephen E. Lucas (ed.), *Selections from the Speech Communication Teacher, 1996-1999*. New York: McGraw-Hill, 2001, pp. 98-100.

Liska, Jo. "Bee Dances, Bird Songs, Monkey Calls, and Cetacean Sonar: Is Speech Unique?" *Western Journal of Communication*, 57 (1993), 1-26.

Littlejohn, Stephen W. *Theories of Human Communication*, 7th ed. Belmont, CA: Wadsworth, 2002.

Phillips, Terilyn Goins. "Name That Analogy: The Communication Game." In Stephen E. Lucas (ed.), *Selections from the Speech Communication Teacher, 1994-1996*. New York: McGraw-Hill, 1998, pp. 87-88.

Ruben, Brent D., and Stewart, Lea P. *Communication and Human Behavior*, 4th ed. Boston: Allyn and Bacon, 1998.

Tubbs, Stewart L., and Moss, Sylvia. *Human Communication*, 9th ed. New York: McGraw-Hill, 2003.

West, Richard, and Turner, Lynn H. *Introducing Communication Theory: Analysis and Application*. Mountain View, CA: Mayfield, 2000.

Public Speaking in a Multicultural World

Axtell, Roger E. *Gestures: The Do's and Taboos of Body Language Around the World*, rev. ed. New York: Wiley, 1998.

Baldwin, John R. "Intercultural Pals: A Focused Journal." In Stephen E. Lucas (ed.), *Selections from the Communication Teacher, 1999-2002*. New York: McGraw-Hill, 2004, pp. 23-24.

Barone, Michael. *The New Americans: How the Melting Pot Can Work Again*. New York: Regnery, 2001.

Beamer, Linda, and Varner, Iris. *Intercultural Communication in the Global Workplace*, 2nd ed. New York: McGraw-Hill, 2001.

Bollinger, Lee, and Sandarg, Jana. "Dare Go Where Others Fear to Tread." In Stephen E. Lucas (ed.), *Selections from the Speech Communication Teacher, 1996-1999*. New York: McGraw-Hill, 2001, pp. 27-28.

Bradford, Lisa, and Uecker, Deborah. "Intercultural Simulations: Enhancing Their Pedagogical Value." In Stephen E. Lucas (ed.), *Selections from the Speech Communication Teacher, 1996-1999*. New York: McGraw-Hill, 2001, pp. 28-34.

Brice, Lynn M. "Cultural Bingo." In Stephen E. Lucas (ed.), *Selections from the Speech Communication Teacher, 1994-1996*. New York: McGraw-Hill, 1998, pp. 17-18.

Brunson, Deborah A. "A Perceptual Awareness Exercise in Interracial Communication." In Stephen E. Lucas (ed.), *Selections from the Speech Communication Teacher, 1994-1996*. New York: McGraw-Hill, 1998, pp. 18-19.

Brunson, Deborah A. "Talking About Race by Talking About Whiteness." In Stephen E. Lucas (ed.), *Selections from the Communication Teacher, 1999-2002*. New York: McGraw-Hill, 2004, pp. 24-26.

Corey, James. "International Bazaar." In Stephen E. Lucas (ed.), *Selections from the Speech Communication Teacher, 1986-1991*. New York: McGraw-Hill, 1992, p. 73.

Cushner, Kenneth, and Brislin, Richard W. *Intercultural Interactions: A Practical Guide*, 2nd ed. Thousand Oaks, CA: Sage, 1996.

Dellinger-Pate, Charlene. "A Model for Guiding Intercultural Discussions." In Stephen E. Lucas (ed.), *Selections from the Speech Communication Teacher, 1996-1999*. New York: McGraw-Hill, 2001, pp. 34-35.

Dillon, Randy K. "The Diversity Board." In Stephen E. Lucas (ed.), *Selections from the Speech Communication Teacher, 1996-1999*. New York: McGraw-Hill, 2001, pp. 35-37.

Dinnerstein, Leonard; Nichols, Roger L.; and Reimers, David M. *Natives and Strangers: A Multicultural History of Americans*, 4th ed. New York: Oxford University Press, 2003.

Ekachi, Daradirek. "Diversity Icebreaker." In Stephen E. Lucas (ed.), *Selections from the Speech Communication Teacher, 1994-1996*. New York: McGraw-Hill, 1998, pp. 21-22.

Fuller, Rex M. "Discovering Cultural Diversity Through Literature." In Stephen E. Lucas (ed.), *Selections from the Speech Communication Teacher, 1996-1999*. New York: McGraw-Hill, 2001, pp. 37-38.

Garbowitz, Fred. "Changing Classroom Populations Call for Increased Diversity." In Stephen E. Lucas (ed.), *Selections from the Speech Communication Teacher, 1986-1991*. New York: McGraw-Hill, 1992, pp. 26-27.

Gitterman, Martin R. "Improving Performance by Maximizing Feedback for Native and Non-Native Speakers of English." In Stephen E. Lucas (ed.), *Selections from the Speech Communication Teacher, 1986-1991*. New York: McGraw-Hill, 1992, pp. 27-28.

Gudykunst, William B., and Moody, Bella (eds.). *Handbook of International and Inter-cultural Communication*, 2nd ed. Thousand Oaks, CA: Sage, 2002.

Gudykunst, William B., and Young, Yun Kim. *Communicating with Strangers: An Approach to Intercultural Communication*, 4th ed. New York: McGraw-Hill, 2003.

Harvey, Vickie L. "Cultural Musical Chairs." In Stephen E. Lucas (ed.), *Selections from the Communication Teacher, 1999-2002*. New York: McGraw-Hill, 2004, pp. 27-28.

Hastings, Sally O. "Increasing Intercultural Empathy: From Principle to Practice." In Stephen E. Lucas (ed.), *Selections from the Speech Communication Teacher, 1996-1999*. New York: McGraw-Hill, 2001, pp. 38-40.

Hawkinson, Ken. "Two Exercises on Diversity and Gender." In Stephen E. Lucas (ed.), *Selections from the Speech Communication Teacher, 1991-1994*. New York: McGraw-Hill, 1995, pp. 24-25.

Hochel, Sandra. "Analyzing How Others See the Dominant U.S. Culture." In Stephen E. Lucas (ed.), *Selections from the Communication Teacher, 1999-2002*. New York: McGraw-Hill, 2004, pp. 29-31.

Hochel, Sandra. "An Exercise in Understanding Ethnocentrism." In Stephen E. Lucas (ed.), *Selections from the Speech Communication Teacher, 1994-1996*. New York: McGraw-Hill, 1998, pp. 23-24.

Jandt, Fred E. *Intercultural Communication: An Introduction*, 3rd ed. Thousand Oaks, CA: Sage, 2001.

Johnson, Karen E., and Golombek, Paula. *Public Speaking for Non-Native Speakers: A Handbook for Instructors*. New York: McGraw-Hill, 1996.

Johnson, Scott D. "Exploring the Influences of Culture on Small Groups." In Stephen E. Lucas (ed.), *Selections from the Speech Communication Teacher, 1994-1996*. New York: McGraw-Hill, 1998, pp. 25-26.

Johnson, Scott D., and Miller, Ann N. "A Cross-Cultural Study of Immediacy, Credibility, and Learning in the U.S. and Kenya." *Communication Education*, 51 (2002), 280-292.

Jones, Enid B. "A Look at the Pedagogy of Teaching Immigrant English-Speaking Students." In Stephen E. Lucas (ed.), *Selections from the Communication Teacher, 1999-2002*. New York: McGraw-Hill, 2004, pp. 31-33.

Kim, Min-Sun. *Non-Western Perspectives on Human Communication*. Thousand Oaks, CA: Sage, 2002.

Kinser, Amber E. "Diversity Scrapbook." In Stephen E. Lucas (ed.), *Selections from the Communication Teacher, 1999-2002*. New York: McGraw-Hill, 2004, pp. 33-35.

Kirby, Erika L., and Harter, Lynn M. "Examining Images of Organizational Diversity in Popular Culture." In Stephen E. Lucas (ed.), *Selections from the Communication Teacher, 1999-2002*. New York: McGraw-Hill, 2004, pp. 35-37.

Kurtz, Patricia L. *The Global Speaker: An English Speaker's Guide to Making Presentations Around the World*. New York: Amacom, 1995.

Lustig, Myron W., and Koester, Jolene. *Intercultural Competence: Interpersonal Communication Across Cultures*. 4th ed. Boston: Allyn and Bacon, 2003.

Martin, Judith N.; Nakayama, Thomas K.; and Flores, Lisa A. *Readings in Intercultural Communication: Experiences and Contexts*, 2nd ed. New York: McGraw-Hill, 2002.

McCroskey, James C.; Sallinen, Aino; Fayer, Joan M.; Richmond, Virginia P.; and Barraclough, Robert A. "Nonverbal Immediacy and Cognitive Learning: A Cross-Cultural Investigation." *Communication Education*, 45 (1996), 200-211.

Miller, Ann N. "An Exploration of Kenyan Public Speaking Patterns with Implications for the American Introductory Public Speaking Course." *Communication Education*, 51 (2002), 168-182.

Miller, Ann Neville. "Cultural Partners: Diversity and Intercultural Communication Beyond the Classroom." In Stephen E. Lucas (ed.), *Selections from the Speech Communication Teacher, 1996-1999*. New York: McGraw-Hill, 2001, pp. 40-41.

Naylor, Larry L. (ed.). *Cultural Diversity in the United States*. Westport, CT: Bergin and Garvey, 1997.

Pennington, Dorothy L. "A Culture-Based Approach to Teaching African-American Public Address." In Stephen E. Lucas (ed.), *Selections from the Speech Communication Teacher, 1996-1999*. New York: McGraw-Hill, 2001, pp. 41-42.

Rivers, Mary J. "For Better or Worse? Let's Make It Better." In Stephen E. Lucas (ed.), *Selections from the Communication Teacher, 1999-2002*. New York: McGraw-Hill, 2004, pp. 38-39.

Ross, Charlynn. "Suggestions for Teaching International Students." In Stephen E. Lucas (ed.), *Selections from the Speech Communication Teacher, 1986-1991*. New York: McGraw-Hill, 1992, pp. 28-29.

Rumbough, Timothy B. "Intercultural Communication via the Internet." In Stephen E. Lucas (ed.), *Selections from the Speech Communication Teacher, 1996-1999*. New York: McGraw-Hill, 2001, pp. 42-44.

Samovar, Larry A., and Porter, Richard E. *Communication Between Cultures*, 4th ed. Belmont, CA: Wadsworth, 2001.

Samovar, Larry A., and Porter, Richard E. (eds.). *Intercultural Communication: A Reader*, 7th ed. Belmont, CA: Wadsworth, 1999.

Sanger, Kerran L., and Netzhammer, Emile C. "Magazine Day: Minorities and the Media." In Stephen E. Lucas (ed.), *Selections from the Communication Teacher, 1999-2002*. New York: McGraw-Hill, 2004, pp. 40-41.

Schrader, Stuart M. "Increasing Cultural Awareness: Importance of Story Telling in Speech Making." In Stephen E. Lucas (ed.), *Selections from the Speech Communication Teacher, 1996-1999*. New York: McGraw-Hill, 2001, pp. 44-45.

Schumer, Allison. "Helping International Students Adapt to American Communication Norms." In Stephen E. Lucas (ed.), *Selections from the Speech Communication Teacher, 1986-1991*. New York: McGraw-Hill, 1992, p. 30.

Simonds, Cheri J. "Pennies from Heaven." In Stephen E. Lucas (ed.), *Selections from the Communication Teacher, 1999-2002*. New York: McGraw-Hill, 2004, pp. 41-42.

Souza, Tasha J. "Framing Equity: Examining Approaches to Diversity." In Stephen E. Lucas (ed.), *Selections from the Communication Teacher, 1999-2002*. New York: McGraw-Hill, 2004, pp. 43-44.

Takaki, Ronald. *A Different Mirror: A History of Multicultural America*. Boston: Little, Brown, 1993.

Walter, Suzanne. "Experiences in Intercultural Communication." In Stephen E. Lucas (ed.), *Selections from the Speech Communication Teacher, 1994-1996*. New York: McGraw-Hill, 1998, pp. 29-30.

Walter, Suzanne. "Introduction of a Speaker: Multipurpose and Multicultural." In Stephen E. Lucas (ed.), *Selections from the Speech Communication Teacher, 1991-1994*. New York: McGraw-Hill, 1995, pp. 60-61.

Wood, Julia. "Diversity and Commonality: Sustaining Their Tension in Communication Courses." *Western Journal of Communication*, 57 (1993), 367-380.

Yook, Eunkyong Lee. "An Experiential Approach to Diversity Education." In Stephen E. Lucas (ed.), *Selections from the Speech Communication Teacher, 1996-1999*. New York: McGraw-Hill, 2001, pp. 45-46.

Yook, Eunkyong Lee. "Students Creating Intercultural Sensitizers: Storytelling and Attribution." In Stephen E. Lucas (ed.), *Selections from the Speech Communication Teacher, 1994-1996*. New York: McGraw-Hill, 1998, pp. 26-27.

Zimmerman, Stephanie. "Perceptions of Intercultural Communication Competence and International Student Adaptation to an American Campus." *Communication Education*, 44 (1995), 321-335.

Films and Videos

"Anxiety." Insight Media (1997). 30 minutes.

"Basic Speech." Insight Media (2002). 28 minutes.

"Bravo! What a Presentation!" CRM Films (1995). 18 minutes.

"Communication." Insight Media (2001). 23 minutes.

"Communication Skills for the Workplace." Insight Media (2000). 30 minutes.

"Communication Skills in a Multicultural World." Insight Media (1994). 20 minutes.

"Communication Skills That Build Winning Relationships." Insight Media (2002). 22 minutes.

"Communication: The Number One Job Skill." Insight Media (1999). 26 minutes.

"Conquer Your Fear of Public Speaking." Insight Media (1992). 70 minutes.

"Critical Thinking." Insight Media (1999). 30 minutes.

"Cross-Cultural Communication." Insight Media (2002). 24 minutes.

"Cross-Cultural Communication in Diverse Settings." Insight Media (1992). 60 minutes.

"The Cross-Cultural Conference Room." Insight Media (2002). 35 minutes.

"Cross-Cultural Understanding." Insight Media (1999). 45 minutes.

"Developing Cultural Sensitivity." Insight Media (1992). 30 minutes.

"disAbility Awareness." Insight Media (1999). 19 minutes.

"Diversity Series." Quality Media Resources (1993). Four-module set; 20 minutes per module.

"Diversity Through Character." CRM Films (1996). 17 minutes.

"Doing Business Internationally." CRM Films (1992). 43 minutes.

"Great American Speeches: 80 Years of Political Oratory." Films for the Humanities and Sciences (1995). Six volumes; 275 minutes.

"Having Something to Say When You Have Something to Say." Insight Media (1997). Two volumes; 137 minutes.

"The Hidden Dimension in International Business Communication." Insight Media (1996). 62 minutes.

"How to Speak Without Fear." Insight Media (1997). Three volumes; 180 minutes.

"Human Communications Theory." Insight Media (1998). 24 minutes.

"I'm Normal, You're Weird: Understanding Other Cultures." Insight Media (1997). 23 minutes.

"Information Age." Insight Media (2002). 20 minutes.

"Intercultural Communicating." Insight Media (1999) 41 minutes.

"Intercultural Communication." Insight Media (1997). 30 minutes.

"Interpersonal Relationships in a Multicultural World." Insight Media (1994). 22 minutes.

"Introduction to Public Speaking." Insight Media (1997). 30 minutes.

"Keys to Effective Speaking." Insight Media (1994). 20 minutes.

"Making Your Presentation." Films for the Humanities and Sciences (1997). 21 minutes.

"Managing Across Cultures." Insight Media (1992). 30 minutes.

"Managing Diversity." CRM Films (1991). 22 minutes.

"Negotiating Cultural Communication." Insight Media (2001). 60 minutes.

"A Peacock in the Land of Penguins." CRM Films (1995). 10 minutes.

"Perfect Communication." Insight Media (2001). 23 minutes.

Peters, Tom. "Ten Vital Rules for Giving Incredible Speeches and Why They're Irrelevant." Video Publishing House (1990). 32 minutes.

"The Power of Speech." Films for the Humanities and Sciences (1994). 30 minutes.

"Public Speaking: Time to Stand." Films for the Humanities and Sciences (2000). 27 minutes.

"Reasoning, Critical Thinking, and Creativity." Insight Media (1993). 60 minutes.

"Sell Yourself: Successful Job Interviewing." Insight Media (1999). 23 minutes.

"Speaking Effectively to 1 or 1,000," revised edition. CRM Films (1992). 21 minutes.

"Speaking for Success." Insight Media (1999). 40 minutes.

"Speaking with Confidence: Critical Thinking." Insight Media (1997). 30 minutes.

"The Speeches of Martin Luther King, Jr." Insight Media (1998). 60 minutes.

"A Tale of 'O,'" revised edition. CRM Films (1993). 18 minutes.

"Talk, Talk, Talk: Opinion or Fact?" Films for the Humanities and Sciences (1995). 28 minutes.

"Top 10½ Tips for Thinking Critically." Insight Media (1999). 15 minutes.

"The Unbiased Mind: Obstacles to Clear Thinking." Insight Media (1994). 23 minutes.

"Unraveling the Mysteries of Critical Thinking." Insight Media (1999). 30 minutes.

"Valuing Diversity: Multicultural Communication." Insight Media (1994). 49 minutes.

"Voices of Experience: Cross-Cultural Communication." Insight Media (1999). 36 minutes.

"Workplace Communication in Action." Insight Media (2000). 101 minutes.

"A World of Diversity." Insight Media (1996). Two volumes; 45 minutes.

"A World of Gestures." University of California Extension Center for Media and Independent Learning (1991). 28 minutes.

Chapter 2 Ethics and Public Speaking

Chapter Objectives

After reading this chapter, students should be able to:

1. Explain why a strong sense of ethical responsibility is vital for public speakers.

2. Discuss the five guidelines for ethical speechmaking presented in the chapter.

3. Define the differences among global plagiarism, patchwork plagiarism, and incremental plagiarism, and explain why each type of plagiarism is unethical.

4. Identify the three basic guidelines for ethical listening discussed in the chapter.

Chapter Outline

I.   Questions of ethics are central to the art of public speaking *(text pages 34-36)*.
     A. Ethics is the branch of philosophy that deals with issues of right and wrong in human affairs.
     B. Ethical issues arise when we ask whether a course of action is moral or immoral, fair or unfair, just or unjust, honest or dishonest.
     C. Questions of ethics come into play whenever a public speaker faces an audience.
         1. Because speechmaking is a form of power, it carries heavy ethical responsibilities.
         2. Public speakers face ethical issues at every stage of the speechmaking process.

D. As stated by the Roman rhetorician Quintilian, the ideal of commendable speechmaking is the good person speaking well.

II. As there are guidelines for ethical behavior in other areas of life, so are there guidelines for ethical behavior in public speaking *(text pages 36-41)*.

A. Public speakers should make sure their goals are ethically sound.
1. As history demonstrates, public speaking can be used for either worthy or unworthy goals.
2. Although there can be legitimate disagreements when it comes to assessing a speaker's goals, this is not a reason to avoid asking ethical questions.
3. Responsible public speakers take care to assess the ethical soundness of their goals.

B. Public speakers should be fully prepared for each speech.
1. Being fully prepared is vital to delivering an effective speech, but it is also important ethically.
2. Unprepared speakers waste the collective time of their listeners.
3. Unprepared speakers may give the audience erroneous information or faulty advice that can lead to grievous consequences.

C. Public speakers should be honest in what they say.
1. Nothing is more important to ethical speechmaking than honesty.
2. Ethical public speakers avoid blatant forms of dishonesty such as telling outright lies.
3. They also avoid more subtle forms of dishonesty such as juggling statistics, quoting out of context, painting tentative findings as firm conclusions, citing unusual cases as typical examples, and the like.

D. Public speakers should avoid name-calling and other forms of abusive language.
1. Name-calling is the use of language to demean other individuals or groups.
2. Whether based on race, religion, ethnicity, sexual orientation, or gender, name-calling degrades the personal dignity of the people being attacked.
   a. It conveys negative, stereotyped, and misleading information about those people.
   b. It implies that they are inferior and do not deserve to be treated with the same respect as other members of society.
3. Name-calling also creates problems in public speaking when it is used to silence opposing voices.
   a. In the U.S. all citizens have the right to voice their ideas on issues of public consequence.
   b. Public speakers have an ethical obligation to help preserve that right by avoiding tactics such as name-calling that automatically impugn the accuracy or respectability of statements made by groups or individuals who disagree with the speaker.

E. Public speakers should put ethical principles into practice.
1. Being ethical means behaving ethically all the time, not only when it is convenient.

      2.   Public speakers need to take their ethical responsibilities as seriously as their strategic objectives.

      3.   They should do their best to follow the guidelines for ethical speechmaking whenever they address an audience.

III.   Plagiarism is one of the most serious ethical lapses a public speaker can commit *(text pages 42-47)*.

    A.   Plagiarism is presenting another person's language or ideas as one's own.

    B.   Plagiarism is a serious offense.

      1.   In the classroom, it can be punished with a failing grade or even expulsion from school.

      2.   Outside the classroom, it can damage a speaker's reputation or career.

    C.   There are three types of plagiarism.

      1.   Global plagiarism is taking an entire speech from a single source and passing it off as one's own.

      2.   Patchwork plagiarism occurs when a speaker patches a speech together by copying verbatim from two or three sources.

         a.   Copying word for word from a few sources is no less plagiarism than is copying from a single source.

         b.   Giving a speech is just like putting one's name on a paper in an English class.

         c.   The speaker warrants that the speech represents his or her own thinking, beliefs, and language.

      3.   Incremental plagiarism occurs when a speaker fails to give credit for specific parts—increments—of the speech that are borrowed from other people.

         a.   One form of incremental plagiarism is quoting someone verbatim without attributing the words to that person.

         b.   A second form of incremental plagiarism is paraphrasing an author without citing the author.

    D.   Just as one needs to credit the authors of print books and articles, so one needs to credit the authors of documents found online.

      1.   Taking careful research notes is imperative when working with Internet documents.

      2.   Internet sources need to be identified both in the speech bibliography and when the speech is presented orally.

IV.   Listeners, as well as speakers, have ethical obligations *(text pages 47-50)*.

    A.   Listeners should be courteous and attentive during the speech.

      1.   This responsibility is a matter of civility in any situation.

      2.   It is especially important in a speech classroom because novice speakers need encouraging and supportive audiences.

    B.   Listeners should avoid prejudging the speaker.

      1.   In addition to being a major cause of poor listening, jumping to conclusions about a speaker's ideas has serious ethical implications.

    2.   Just as speakers have an obligation to prepare fully and conscientiously, listeners have a responsibility to hear a speaker out before deciding to accept or reject the speaker's message.

C.   Listeners should maintain the free and open expression of ideas.

    1.   A free society depends on the right of individual citizens to speak their minds on public issues.

    2.   Just as speakers need to avoid name-calling and other tactics that can undermine free speech, so listeners have an obligation to maintain the right of speakers to be heard.

    3.   Listeners can disagree entirely with a message but still support the speaker's right to express it.

Exercises for Critical Thinking *(from text pages 51-52)*

1.   Look back at the story of Felicia Robinson on page 35 of the textbook. Evaluate her dilemma in light of the guidelines for ethical speechmaking presented in this chapter. Explain what you believe would be the most ethical course of action in her case.

> **Discussion:** This exercise is designed to have students apply the guidelines for ethical public speaking discussed in the chapter. The best way to conduct the exercise is to discuss each guideline individually and then apply it to the case of Felicia Robinson. The case study approach used in this exercise is the preferred method of teaching ethics today, and it works exceedingly well in conveying the nature of ethical judgment and its application to public speakers. If students prepare this exercise before coming to class, it should generate a fruitful discussion.

2.   The issue of insulting and abusive speech—especially slurs directed against people on the basis of race, religion, gender, or sexual orientation—is extremely controversial. Do you believe society should punish such speech with criminal penalties? To what degree are colleges and universities justified in trying to discipline students who engage in such speech? Do you feel it is proper to place any boundaries on free expression in order to prohibit insulting and abusive speech? Why or why not? Be prepared to explain your ideas in class.

> **Discussion:** Few issues have generated more heat on college campuses—and in American society at large—in recent years than abusive language and how to deal with it. Most controversial is the question of whether schools can justifiably impose restrictions on "hate speech" against racial or religious minorities, women, gays, lesbians, and people with physical disabilities. Defensible arguments can be made on both sides of the question. The purpose of this exercise is not to have students reach the "right" answer, but to spark intelligent discussion. For an excellent overview of these issues, see Thomas L. Tedford and Dale A. Herbeck, *Freedom of Speech in the United States*, 4th ed. (State College, PA: Strata, 2001), pp. 174-180, which is reprinted on pages 97-104 of this manual.

3.   All the following situations could arise in your speech class. Identify the ethical issues in each and explain what, as a responsible speaker or listener, your course of action would be.

   a.   You are speaking on the topic of prison reform. In your research, you run across two public opinion polls. One of them, an independent survey by the Gallup Organization, shows that a majority of people in your state oppose your position. The other poll, suspect in its methods and conducted by a partisan organization, says a majority of people in your state support your position. Which poll do you cite in your speech? If you cite the second poll, do you point out its shortcomings?

   Discussion: Like the other two scenarios in this exercise, this one is designed to relate ethical questions directly to situations students will face in their classroom speeches. In this scenario, of course, the most ethical decision would be to use the Gallup poll rather than the partisan poll, even though the latter supports the speaker's position. It would be especially unethical to use the partisan poll without indicating its weaknesses to the audience. This would clearly violate the speaker's obligation to be honest in presenting facts and figures.

   b.   When listening to an informative speech by one of your classmates, you realize that much of it is plagiarized from a magazine article you read a couple weeks earlier. What do you do? Do you say something when your instructor asks for comments about the speech? Do you mention your concern to the instructor after class? Do you talk with the speaker? Do you remain silent?

   Discussion: This case raises interesting questions about plagiarism and the ethical obligations of listeners. If faced with this situation in real life, most students would doubtless remain silent—not because they approved of the speaker's behavior, but because they would not want to "tell on" the speaker. Some might argue that even though plagiarism is wrong, students are under no ethical obligation to report someone who commits plagiarism in a speech. Because this is a complex issue, few classes are likely to reach agreement on it. They can, however, reach agreement on the fact that plagiarism is ethically wrong and that students who commit it should face stiff penalties if they are detected.

   c.   While researching your persuasive speech, you find a quotation from an article by a highly respected expert that will nail down one of your most important points. But as you read the rest of the article, you realize the author does not in fact support the policy you are advocating. Should you still include the quotation in your speech?

Discussion: This scenario gets at a fairly subtle point about ethics and public speaking. Yet it is a point worth discussing, for it shows that being an ethical speaker is not just a matter of "big" obligations such as having ethically sound goals and avoiding plagiarism. It also shows that one needs to consider the facts of a situation carefully in making ethical judgments.

In the scenario at hand, at least three defensible ethical positions can be advanced: (1) That the speaker should not quote the expert in support of any point if the expert does not support the speaker's policy; (2) That the speaker can ethically quote the expert on one aspect of the topic (the existence of a problem, for example) as long as the speaker does not state or imply that the expert supports the speaker's position in general; (3) That the speaker cannot ethically quote the expert on any aspect of the topic unless the speaker states explicitly that the expert does not support the policy advocated by the speaker. The purpose of class discussion on this scenario is not to reach unanimous agreement on one of these three positions, but to make students aware of the ethical issues involved and, in the process, to heighten their sensitivity to the wide range of ethical issues faced by public speakers.

Applying the Power of Public Speaking *(from text page 52)*

Having graduated with a degree in public administration and hoping to pursue a career in politics, you have been fortunate to receive a staff position with one of the leading senators in your state legislature. Since your arrival two months ago, you have answered phones, ordered lunch, made copies, stapled mailings, and stuffed envelopes. Finally you have been asked to look over a speech the senator will deliver at your alma mater. Surely, you think, this will be the first of many important assignments once your value is recognized.

After reading the speech, however, your enthusiasm is dampened. You agree wholeheartedly with its support of a bill to fund scholarships for low-income students, but you're dismayed by its attack on opponents of the bill as "elitist bigots who would deny a college education to those who need it most." You haven't been asked to comment on the ethics of the speech, and you certainly don't want to jeopardize your position on the senator's staff. At the same time, you think his use of name-calling may actually arouse sympathy for the opposition. The senator would like your comments in two hours. What will you tell him?

Discussion: Like many of the other Applying the Power of Public Speaking scenarios throughout the book, this one does not admit of an unequivocal right-or-wrong answer. Recognizing the ethical problem with the senator's speech is one thing; pointing out the problem to the senator is another. In most circumstances, a new staff member would not find it prudent to confront his or her employer on a matter of rhetorical ethics. It might be more prudent to raise the practical question of whether the senator's attack on "elitist bigots" is likely to create a backlash against the senator's position, but even this would need to be approached tactfully. On the other hand, if the senator did not want an opinion, he probably would not have asked. Apart from the ethical implications of remaining silent, there are potential practical pitfalls in this course of action as well. As your students discuss the scenario, remind them that the kinds of issues raised by it are not limited to politics and could occur in a wide range of rhetorical situations.

Additional Exercises and Activities

1.   Lead a class discussion in which students develop a code of ethical speaking for their classroom. The final product of the discussion will be a list titled "Ethical Speaking for Our Speech Class." By the end of the discussion, the entire class should not only agree on the content of the list, but should pledge themselves to follow it throughout the term.

> **Discussion:**   This exercise works extremely well in promoting dialogue about the ethics of public speaking. It also relates abstract issues of ethics to the situation in which students will be giving speeches for the next several months. By developing their own rules for ethical speechmaking, students will be more committed to following those rules.
>
> Don't be surprised if much of the discussion turns on questions related to plagiarism. This is probably the most pressing ethical issue facing students in a speech classroom, and many do not have a clear understanding of what constitutes plagiarism and what does not.
>
> As students develop their code, encourage them to be specific in their criteria. For example, rather than saying "We will not plagiarize our speeches," they should try to develop more precise statements such as "We will not copy our speeches from the work of current or previous students," or "We will always cite the sources of ideas or supporting materials that we use in our speeches."

2.   Lead a class discussion in which students develop a code of ethical listening for their speech classroom. The final product of the discussion will be a list titled "Ethical Listening for Our Speech Class." By the end of the discussion, the entire class should not only agree on the content of the list, but should pledge themselves to follow it throughout the term.

> **Discussion:** A companion to Additional Exercise/Activity 1 above, this is an excellent way to get students thinking about the ethical obligations of listeners. Like Exercise 1, it relates ethical issues directly to the speech classroom and gives those issues more immediacy than might otherwise be the case. Also like Exercise 1, it allows

students to formulate their own ethical criteria, thereby increasing the likelihood that they will feel committed to following those criteria.

As with Exercise 1, encourage students to be specific as they develop their code. Rather than saying "We will listen courteously and attentively," for instance, they should work for statements such as "We will not do work for other classes while listening to our classmates' speeches," or "Even if we disagree with a speaker's position at the start of a speech, we will listen with an open mind to the entire speech before making a judgment about it." One way to generate criteria is to ask students what kinds of attitudes and behavior they would like to see in listeners to their own speeches.

3. Give each student the following assignment: Identify a situation in your life in which an issue related to speech ethics was involved. The issue could have affected you either as a speaker or as a listener. Work up a brief analysis in which you explain the situation and the ethical issue (or issues) involved.

    Discussion: This exercise can work very well to promote class discussion about ethical issues in public speaking. Because it deals with issues that are related to the experience of each student, the exercise often gives the discussion more immediacy than dealing with hypothetical ethical scenarios. It usually works best when given as a homework assignment so students have plenty of time to develop their analyses.

4. If your class meets during a presidential election year, ethical issues are bound to arise in relation to the candidates' campaign rhetoric. Such issues might include the use of negative campaigning, the distortion of evidence in campaign speeches and advertisements, the use of name-calling to denigrate the opposing candidate or party, and the tendency of candidates to say different things to different groups of voters. Set aside time periodically during the term to deal with such issues—especially when they achieve prominence in press coverage of the campaign.

    Discussion: Because presidential campaigns usually generate fairly intense reactions, they provide an excellent vehicle for getting students interested in questions of communication ethics. They also have a tendency to provoke heated discussion—especially among students who are fiercely partisan to one candidate or another. The challenge for instructors is to keep discussion focused on ethical issues rather than on the general merits and policies of each candidate. It is important that students learn to separate their feelings for and against the candidates from their reasoned judgments about the ethics of the candidates' rhetoric.

    The aims of this exercise can be achieved either through informal class discussion or through more formal assignments in which students—working individually or in groups—prepare systematic analyses for presentation in class. The same kind of exercise can also be used during local or state elections.

5.   Have students create "Speech Ethics" scrapbooks in which they keep magazine and newspaper articles that deal with ethical issues in public speaking. Articles can touch on any aspect of speech ethics, including consideration of a speaker's goals, preparation, truthfulness, evidence, reasoning, language, emotional appeal, or impact on audiences. Articles can also deal with the ethics of listening. Students should be sure to record the source and date of each article. Collect the scrapbooks near the end of the term.

> **Discussion:** Once students start thinking about ethical issues and looking for articles that deal with them, it is astounding how many they can find. Although some instructors use this exercise as a required assignment, others use it as an extra-credit opportunity. In either case, if done properly it can be of considerable benefit for the students. Not only does it help sensitize them to the range, complexity, and importance of ethical issues in public speaking, but it often gets them to reading newspapers and magazines more regularly than they would otherwise.

6.   Students often ask about ghostwriting when dealing with the issue of plagiarism. Why, they ask, is it ethical for politicians, business leaders, and other public figures to have ghostwriters and unethical for students to have someone else write their speeches? If students raise this issue, be prepared to conduct a class discussion on the relationship between plagiarism and ghostwriting.

> **Discussion:** Scholars and popular commentators alike have spent a great deal of time on the subject of ghostwriting. Most regard it as ethically acceptable among politicians, business leaders, and other public figures as long as (1) the speaker does not deceive the audience by claiming to have written a speech when in fact it is ghostwritten, and (2) the speaker takes full responsibility for what he or she says regardless of who may have written the actual words of the speech.
>
> Speeches given in the classroom, however, are quite different. Students are in a learning situation. They cannot learn the skills of speech preparation by having someone else compose their speeches for them. Nor can their performance in class be fairly evaluated if they do not do their own work. As noted in the chapter, when students stand up to deliver a speech, it is just like putting their name on a paper in their English class—they are declaring that the speech represents their own work, their own thinking, their own language.

* * *

Words that Wound: Abusive and Threatening Language[*]
Thomas L. Tedford

Several years ago, a black architecture student returned some merchandise to a store and requested a refund. In order to get the refund, he was required to sign a form upon which an employee of the store had written, "Arrogant Nigger refuses exchange—says he doesn't like products." The student sued for damages but lost the case because the court found such language not "sufficiently severe" to merit damages. In the late 1980s, on the campus of the University of Wisconsin, minority students vigorously protested a mock slave auction. And at Tufts University in 1990, a male student was suspended for selling T-shirts stating "15 reasons why beer is better than women at Tufts." The fighting-words rule, with its focus on words spoken in a face-to-face confrontation between individuals, has little application to the types of nonconfrontational expression illustrated by these examples.

Society's concern with abusive speech and expressions of hatred is not new. In 1952 the U.S. Supreme Court upheld the constitutionality of the Illinois group libel law that made it a crime to portray persons of any "race, color, creed or religion" as depraved, criminal, or unchaste. Although Illinois later dropped the group libel law from its criminal code, the concept is still alive and is proposed from time to time in various legislative bodies as a way of dealing with hate messages. Other cases relating to the issue include the 1976-1977 controversy about permitting neo-Nazis to parade on the city streets of Skokie, Illinois, and the efforts by some feminists to permit suits against those who disseminate pornography perceived as demeaning to women. In order to analyze this issue in an organized way, we will first look at the problem as it concerns society at large. We will then examine what a number of institutions of higher education have done in recent years about "words that wound."

Abusive Speech in Society at Large

The U.S. Supreme Court has so narrowed the fighting-words doctrine and the law of defamation that much insulting or threatening expression is not actionable under either criminal or tort law. This development has called forth arguments for change. For instance, Kent Greenawalt, professor of law at Columbia University, asserts that four harms result from abusive speech: (1) the threat of immediate violence, (2) offensiveness of the language to those who hear it, (3) psychological hurt to individuals, and (4) the long-term

---

[*]From Thomas L. Tedford and Dale A. Herbeck, *Freedom of Speech in the United States*, 4th ed. (State College, PA: Strata Publishing, 2001), pp. 174-180. Reprinted with permission of Thomas L. Tedford and Strata Publishing.

reinforcement of negative social attitudes (such as racism, sexism, and homophobia) that result from such expression. He recommends that suits for damages be allowed in some instances and that criminal action be permitted in others. Let us look further at what proponents of civil and criminal action have to say about "words that wound."

Civil Remedies for Abusive Speech

One approach to abusive and threatening speech is to make it a crime. Proponents of this approach argue that messages of hate should not be protected by the First Amendment, and that specific types of hate speech should be criminalized. Criminalization could be attempted by reviving the concept of group libel. In her essay "Group Libel Revisited," Ruth McGaffey summarizes the arguments of those who favor group libel laws and provides an example of such a law that was recommended to the city of Milwaukee in 1975. The proposed ordinance criminalized expression that portrayed "depravity, criminality, unchastity or lack of virtue of a class of citizens, or any race, color, creed or religion," or that exposed these groups to "contempt, derision or obloquy . . . which is productive of breach of the peace or riots." Although this proposal was not enacted into law, it does illustrate the group libel approach.

Another proposal is to make *racist* speech a specific crime. In the late 1980s—before the Supreme Court's *R.A.V.* decision, discussed further below—this approach was supported by a number of legal scholars, including Mari Matsuda, a professor of law. Matsuda sets out her "narrow definition" of punishable racist expression as that which is "so historically untenable, so dangerous, and so tied to perpetuation of violence and degradation" of minorities that it is "outside the realm of protected discourse." Such "racist hate messages" have three identifying characteristics, she adds, all three of which must be present for a criminal action to take place: (1) the message must be one of "racial inferiority"; (2) it must be "directed against a historically oppressed group"; and (3) it must be "persecutorial, hateful, and degrading." She cites as a real-life example the placing of swastikas near the desks of racial minorities employed in a newly integrated fire department.

The proposal of Matsuda and others to criminalize hate speech was strongly rebuffed by the U.S. Supreme Court in the 1992 case of *R.A.V. v. St. Paul*. The case began in 1990 when a group of white teenagers in St. Paul, Minnesota, burned a cross in the yard of a black family that had moved into an all-white neighborhood. The teenagers were charged with violating the St. Paul Bias-Motivated Crime Ordinance, which made it a misdemeanor to place on public or private property "a symbol, object, appellation, characterization or graffiti, including, but not limited to, a burning cross or Nazi swastika, which one knows or has reasonable grounds to know arouses anger, alarm, or resentment in others on the basis of race, color, creed, religion, or gender . . . ." (The Court noted that there were other laws that could have been used in this case, including Minnesota's statutes against terroristic threats, arson, and criminal damage to property; however, these were rejected by the prosecution in favor of the St. Paul Ordinance.) Although the trial court dismissed the case on First Amendment grounds, stating that the ordinance was overbroad and impermissibly content-based, the Minnesota Supreme Court reversed the trial court and upheld the constitutionality of the ordinance, ruling that it was narrowly drawn to reach only "fighting words."

The U.S. Supreme Court unanimously reversed the court below, even though the justices disagreed about the reason for the reversal. A majority of five justices, led by Justice Scalia, stated a content-discrimination argument, observing that the St. Paul ordinance did not prohibit fighting words in general, but only specific types of fighting words, such as those based on race, color, or religion. (To illustrate, the ordinance did not include hostile speech based on political views, union membership, or homosexuality.) This amounts to content discrimination, Justice Scalia concluded, which is "precisely what the First Amendment forbids."

Justice White filed a concurring opinion (joined by Justices Blackman and O'Connor, and in part by Justice Stevens) agreeing to the judgment but arguing that the reasoning of the majority was flawed. Justice White objected to Justice Scalia's content-discrimination argument, pointing out that it departed from precedent by stating a new doctrine of "underbreadth." He characterized this new doctrine as "folly," arguing that all the Court needed to do was follow precedent by declaring the St. Paul ordinance void for *overbreadth*. Regardless of the opinion one prefers, the unanimity of the judgment has cooled efforts to make racist speech a crime. Professor Greenawalt summarizes well the effect of this case: "*R.A.V.* seems to foreclose for the near future the possibility of any broad law against hate speech—one that reaches beyond fighting words."

A year later, in the case of *Wisconsin v. Mitchell*, the issue of penalty enhancement for criminal conduct motivated by bigotry was considered by the U.S. Supreme Court. Here, a young black man, Todd Mitchell, had been convicted of aggravated battery for leading a group of blacks to attack a white youth. Based on comments made by Mitchell before the attack ("Do you all feel hyped up to move on some white people? . . . There goes a white boy; go get him."), the jury had found that the attack was racially motivated. Consequently, the trial court had added two years to the maximum sentence for aggravated battery under a Wisconsin law that provided an extra penalty for crimes motivated by bigotry. As Franklyn S. Haiman points out, the issue of free speech is implicated in such cases because "the only way to identify group hatred as the motivation is by statements the perpetrator has made or by other symbolic behavior engaged in before, during or after the commission of the crime." What followed on appeal—first to the Wisconsin Supreme Court, and then to the U.S. Supreme Court—illustrates well the contrasting positions that judges can take on the key issues involved.

The Wisconsin Supreme Court declared the penalty-enhancement provision unconstitutional, primarily on the grounds of free speech and overbreadth. Relying on the U.S. Supreme Court's decision in *R.A.V. v. St. Paul*, the Wisconsin justices held that the statute "violates the First Amendment directly by punishing what the legislature has deemed to be offensive thought." In addition, the Wisconsin Supreme Court ruled that the statute in question was "unconstitutionally overbroad," for it would require in many cases that state prosecutors introduce evidence of constitutionally protected statements made by a defendant prior to the commission of the crime in question. The Court observed that this "evidentiary use of protected speech . . . would have a 'chilling effect' on those who feared the possibility of prosecution for offenses subject to penalty enhancement."

The justices of the U.S. Supreme Court unanimously disagreed with the decision of the court below, declaring the penalty-enhancement law constitutional. In his opinion of the Court, Chief Justice Rehnquist distinguished this case from *R.A.V. v. St. Paul* by noting that "the ordinance struck down in *R.A.V.* was explicitly directed at expression" whereas "the statute in this case is aimed at *conduct* unprotected by the First Amendment." [Emphasis added.] Furthermore, the conduct being inspired by bias "is thought to inflict greater individual and societal harm." Thus, the "State's desire to redress these perceived harms provides an adequate explanation for its penalty-enhancement provision over and above mere disagreement with offenders' beliefs or biases." In addition, the Chief Justice rejected the overbreadth argument, stating that it is too "speculative a hypothesis" to assume that a citizen would suppress bigoted beliefs "for fear that evidence of such beliefs will be introduced against him at trial if he commits a more serious offense against person or property." Thus, the Chief Justice concluded, the possibility of the statute's "chilling effect" on expression is too remote to violate the Constitution.

Civil Remedies for Abusive Speech

Because of the Supreme Court's ruling in *R.A.V. v. St. Paul*, those who wish to punish abusive speech have turned to the civil remedies of tort law, particularly the tort of intentional infliction of emotional distress. Although "emotional distress" is not as well established or as clearly defined as are defamation and invasion of privacy, some plaintiffs using the tort in racial harassment suits have won their cases. Delgado summarizes three such cases: one in which a black truck driver was called a "goddam nigger" and was fired from his job; a second in which a native of East India was called "a black nigger" and "member of an inferior race" by his job supervisor; and a third in which a waitress called a customer a "black son-of-a-bitch" and a "nigger."

The emotional distress approach is argued in detail by Shawna H. Yen in an article published a year after the St. Paul case. Yen recognizes that *R.A.V.* "has the potential to invalidate many, if not all," hate crime laws. She proposes that the response to hate speech—racist speech in particular—should be use of the "tort of intentional infliction of emotional distress" because it is "an already-existing means by which victims of racist epithets could recover for their injuries without violating the First Amendment." She explains further:

> Racist speech should be the basis of a cause of action under the tort of intentional infliction of emotional distress so long as the plaintiff alleges the four elements generally required for that tort: (1) that the defendant engaged in extreme and outrageous conduct, (2) that the defendant intended or acted recklessly to cause the emotional harm, (3) that the plaintiff suffered severe

and extreme emotional distress as a result of defendant's actions, and (4) that the defendant proximately caused the emotional injury to the plaintiff . . . . [O]nce the plaintiff has alleged these four elements, a court should let the case go to the jury to determine whether or not the evidence supports recovery for the plaintiff.

Finally, a related approach is to create a *new* tort which permits suits for class-based insults and epithets. Greenawalt, for example, proposes that when extreme emotional distress cannot be shown, suits be allowed for speech that has the "intent to demean" or to inflict "grave humiliations" on persons. With proposals such as these being argued in law schools and in legal journals, students of the First Amendment should be alert to developments. Meanwhile, on many college campuses in recent years, proponents of punishment for insulting and harassing speech have received a sympathetic ear. A number of schools developed policies for "correct" campus speech which, in a number of instances, generated legal challenges based on the First Amendment. Let us examine this issue in more detail.

Abusive Speech on the Campus

In December of 1987, at the University of Connecticut, eight Asian-American students on their way to a dance were harassed for almost an hour by a group of football players who spat on them, called them "Oriental faggots," and challenged them to a fight. In the spring of 1989, at the University of Arizona in Tempe, a number of white fraternity members harassed a black student who was walking past some fraternity houses by chanting "Coon," "Nigger," and "Porchmonkey." A fight developed and police were required to restore order. In response to incidents of this type, a number of American colleges and universities have adopted codes of conduct prohibiting such harassment. Typically, the codes address insulting or threatening speech directed at racial or religious minorities, women, handicapped persons, and homosexuals. Punishment for violators ranges from a reprimand to expulsion from the institution. The discussion below first examines how the courts have responded to several controversies that have resulted from campus rules against abusive expression. This is followed by a summary of the position of a leading civil liberties organization—the American Civil Liberties Union—on the issue of abusive expression on the college campus.

Campus-Speech Rules and the Courts

The initial response of a number of institutions of higher learning to abusive speech was to develop broad rules and regulations against abusive expression. These broad regulations covered a variety of forms of expression. For example, the University of Connecticut approved a rule that punished students for the use of "derogatory names, inappropriately directed laughter, inconsiderate jokes, and conspicuous exclusion [of another student] from conversation." The rule developed by the University of Pennsylvania prohibits language that "stigmatizes or victimizes individuals" as well as expression that "creates an intimidating or offensive environment." In 1991 a student who shouted racial epithets was permanently expelled from Brown University under school policy that prohibits "subjection of another person, group, or class of persons, to inappropriate, abusive, threatening, or demeaning actions, based on race, religion, gender, handicap, ethnicity, national origin, or sexual orientation."

One of the broadest regulations was developed at the University of Michigan. Entitled the "Policy on Discrimination and Discriminatory Harassment of Students in the University Environment," Michigan's rule was adopted by the board of regents in 1988. Although it excluded campus publications, such as the *Michigan Daily*—evidently on First Amendment grounds—it did cover university housing and "educational and academic centers, such as classroom buildings, libraries, research laboratories, recreation and study centers." Its provisions include punishment for:

> Any behavior, verbal or physical, that stigmatizes or victimizes an individual on the basis of race, ethnicity, religion, sex, sexual orientation, creed, national origin, ancestry, age, marital status, handicap or Vietnam-era veteran status. . . . Sexual advances, requests for sexual favors, and verbal or physical conduct that stigmatizes or victimizes an individual on the basis of sex or sexual orientation where such behavior . . . [c]reates an intimidating, hostile, or demeaning environment for educational pursuits, employment or participation in University sponsored extra-curricular activities.

The policy was challenged in federal court by a University of Michigan graduate student in psychology who was concerned that the rule would prevent free academic discussion of a variety of controversial theories in his field, especially those claiming "biologically-based differences between sexes and races." The U.S. district court ruled for the student, declaring the policy unconstitutional both on First Amendment grounds and on the due process grounds of vagueness.

First, the court found the language of the policy so *overbroad* that it swept within its scope a significant amount of expression that was protected by the First Amendment. Second, the court found the policy vague—especially its use of terms such as "stigmatize" and "victimize." Such terms are not clear, as evidenced by the fact that even the counsel for the university could not explain what they meant when asked to do so by the judge during the hearings. Consequently, the court observed, students "of common understanding were necessarily forced to guess at whether a comment about a controversial issue would later be found to be sanctionable under the policy."

Two years after the Michigan decision, a U.S. district court in Wisconsin declared unconstitutional a similar hate-speech rule from the University of Wisconsin. The Wisconsin regulation, which was a part of the student conduct code, authorized disciplinary action against students in nonacademic situations for racist or discriminatory expression directed at an individual that demeaned "the race, sex, religion, color, creed, disability, sexual orientation, national origin, ancestry or age of the individual or individuals" or for expression that created a "hostile or demeaning environment" in educational activity. The district court rejected the university's *Chaplinsky*-based arguments in support of the regulation, announcing that the rule in question was unconstitutional for both overbreadth and vagueness. Concerning overbreadth, the Court noted that *Chaplinsky* was limited to words spoken in direct confrontation that were likely to cause an immediate breach of the peace. The university rule exceeded the scope of this requirement, for it is not limited to direct confrontation and imminent breach of the peace. Second, the Court said that the rule was vague "because it does not make clear whether the prohibited speech must actually create a hostile educational environment or whether the speaker must merely intend to create such an environment." For these reasons, said the district court, the Wisconsin regulation violates the Constitution.

After considering the decision of the U.S. Supreme Court in *R.A.V. v. St. Paul* together with lower court decisions such as those from Michigan and Wisconsin summarized above, many legal authorities have concluded that campus speech codes in public colleges and universities are likely to be struck down as unconstitutional. These authorities include Robert Sedler, an attorney in the case of *John Doe v. University of Michigan*. Consequently, alternative approaches to the issue of campus hate speech have received considerable attention. Let us now examine an alternative proposal that was set out a year after the district court decision in the Michigan case.

Campus-Speech Rules and Civil Liberties

In 1990 the American Civil Liberties Union (ACLU), one of the nation's leading defenders of constitutional rights, formulated a position on the issue of abusive speech on the campus. Entitled "Free Speech and Bias on College Campuses," the ACLU policy statement begins by recognizing the problem of racist, sexist, and homophobic bias on the campus, and by proposing that, instead of restricting speech, colleges take constructive steps to combat the problem. The policy emphasizes the necessity for "freedom of thought and expression" in the field of education, and asserts that all members of "the academic community have the right to hold and to express views that others may find repugnant, offensive, or emotionally distressing." Consequently, the policy continues, the ACLU "opposes all campus regulations which interfere with the freedom of professors, students and administrators to teach, learn, discuss and debate or to express ideas, opinions or feelings" in the classroom and in public or private discourse.

After affirming its opposition to disciplinary codes that "reach beyond permissible boundaries into the realm of protected speech," the policy adds that the ACLU is not opposed to disciplinary codes "aimed at restricting acts of intimidation and invasion of privacy." The ACLU recognizes that the terms "harassment," "intimidation," and "invasion of privacy" are imprecise, and warns against applying them in an overbroad manner. The policy emphasizes that the terms are used here to describe *conduct* directed at a specific person or persons that is intended to "frighten, coerce, or unreasonably harry or intrude upon its target." A threatening phone call to a minority student's dormitory room is given as an example of such punishable conduct. The ACLU policy continues: "The fact that words may be used in connection with otherwise actionable conduct does not immunize such conduct from appropriate regulation." In addition to intimidating phone calls, examples of unprotected conduct that include elements of expression are threats of attack, extortion, and blackmail.

Finally, the ACLU policy lists a number of steps that colleges can take to address bigotry without offending First Amendment freedoms. These recommendations include the following: having the administration, faculty, and students undertake an organized effort to publicize the school's commitment to understanding and tolerance; conducting workshops, programs, and counseling on the subject of bias in its various forms; formulating a comprehensive plan for responding promptly to incidents of harassment and discrimination; working actively to attract more minorities to the administration, faculty, and the student body; and offering courses of study in various manifestations of prejudice.

* * *

Extra Teaching and Learning Resources

General

Arnett, Ronald C. "The Practical Philosophy of Communication Ethics and Free Speech as the Foundation for Speech Communication." *Communication Quarterly*, 38 (1990), 208-217.

Bickford, Susan. *The Dissonance of Democracy: Listening, Conflict, and Citizenship.* Ithaca, NY: Cornell University Press, 1996.

Bollinger, Lee C., and Stone, Geoffrey R. (eds.). *Eternally Vigilant: Free Speech in the Modern Era*. Chicago: University of Chicago Press, 2002.

Christians, Clifford C., and Lambeth, Edmund B. "The State-of-the-Art in Teaching Communication Ethics." *Communication Education*, 45 (1996), 236-243.

Cooper, David E. *Ethics: The Classic Readings*. Oxford: Blackwell, 1998.

Crossen, Cynthia. *Tainted Truth: The Manipulation of Fact in America*. New York: Simon and Schuster, 1995.

Day, Louis A. *Ethics in Media Communication: Cases and Controversies*, 3rd ed. Belmont, CA: Wadsworth, 2000.

Denton, Robert E. (ed.). *Ethical Dimensions of Political Communication*. New York: Praeger, 1991.

Ekman, Paul. *Telling Lies: Clues to Deceit in the Marketplace, Politics, and Marriage.* New York: Norton, 1992.

Golding, Martin P. *Free Speech on Campus*. New York: Rowman and Littlefield, 2000.

Greenberg, Karen Joy (ed.). *Conversations on Communication Ethics*. Norwood, NJ: Ablex, 1991.

Haiman, Franklyn S. *"Speech Acts" and the First Amendment*. Carbondale, IL: Southern Illinois University Press, 1994.

Harris, Robert A. *The Plagiarism Handbook: Strategies for Preventing, Detecting, and Dealing with Plagiarism*. Los Angeles: Pyrczak Publishing, 2001.

Herrick, James A. "Rhetoric, Ethics, and Virtue." *Communication Studies*, 43 (1992), 133-149.

Jaska, James A., and Pritchard, Michael A. *Responsible Communication: Ethical Issues in Business, Industry, and the Professions*. Cresskill, NJ: Hampton Press, 1997.

Johannesen, Richard L. *Ethics in Human Communication*, 5th ed. Prospect Heights, IL: Waveland Press, 2002.

Johannesen, Richard L. "The Ethics of Plagiarism Reconsidered: The Oratory of Martin Luther King, Jr." *Southern Communication Journal*, 60 (1995), 185-194.

Kennedy, Sheila Suess (ed.). *Free Expression in America: A Documentary History*. Westport, CT: Greenwood Publishing, 1999.

Lederer, Laura, and Delgado, Richard (eds.). *The Price We Pay: The Case Against Racist Speech, Hate Propaganda, and Pornography*. New York: Hill and Wang, 1995.

Luper, Steven. *A Guide to Ethics*. New York: McGraw-Hill, 2002.

MacEdo, Stephen (ed.). *Deliberative Politics: Essays on Democracy and Disagreement*. New York: Oxford University Press, 1999.

Makau, Josina M., and Arnett, Ronald C. (eds.). *Communication Ethics in an Age of Diversity*. Urbana: University of Illinois Press, 1997.

Mallon, Thomas. *Stolen Words: Forays into the Origins and Ravages of Plagiarism*, updated ed. New York: Harvest Books, 2001.

Nyberg, David. *The Varnished Truth: Truth Telling and Deceiving in Ordinary Life*. Chicago: University of Chicago Press, 1994.

Rachels, James (ed.). *Ethical Theory*. New York: Oxford University Press, 1998.

Ruggiero, Vincent Ryan. *Thinking Critically About Ethical Issues*, 5th ed. New York: McGraw-Hill, 2001.

Singer, Peter. *How Are We to Live? Ethics in an Age of Self-Interest*. Amherst, NY: Prometheus Books, 1995.

Smolla, Rodney M. *Free Speech in an Open Society*. New York: Random House, 1992.

Sunstein, Cass R. *Democracy and the Problem of Free Speech*. New York: Free Press, 1993.

Tedford, Thomas L, and Herbeck, Dale A. *Freedom of Speech in the United States*, 4th ed. State College PA: Strata Publishing, 2001.

Tsesis, Alexander. *Destructive Messages: How Hate Speech Paves the Way for Harmful Social Movements*. New York: New York University Press, 2002.

Walker, Samuel. *Hate Speech: The History of an American Controversy*. Lincoln, NE: University of Nebraska Press, 1994.

Wolfson, Nicholas. *Hate Speech, Sex Speech, Free Speech*. Westport, CT: Praeger, 1997.

Classroom Activities and Assignments

Jensen, Marvin D. "Developing Ways to Confront Hateful Speech." In Stephen E. Lucas, (ed.), *Selections from the Speech Communication Teacher, 1991-1994*. New York: McGraw-Hill, 1995, p. 26.

Jensen, Marvin D. "Speeches of Resignation as Lessons in Ethics." In Stephen E. Lucas (ed.), *Selections from the Speech Communication Teacher, 1996-1999*. New York: McGraw-Hill, 2001, pp. 47-48.

Mello, Bradford. "Ethics Speech Assignment." In Stephen E. Lucas (ed.), *Selections from the Speech Communication Teacher, 1996-1999*. New York: McGraw-Hill, 2001, pp. 48-49.

Thameling, Carl L. "Ethical Communication in Interpersonal Relationships." In Stephen E. Lucas (ed.), *Selections from the Communication Teacher, 1999-2002*. New York: McGraw-Hill, 2004, pp. 45-47.

Films and Videos

"Amendment 1: Freedom of Religion, Speech, Press, Assembly, and Petition." Insight Media (1998). 20 minutes.

"Communication Skills in a Multicultural World." Insight Media (1994). 20 minutes.

"Crediting Your Sources." RMI Media Productions (1991). 30 minutes.

"Developing Cultural Sensitivity." Insight Media (1992). 30 minutes.

"Diversity Series." Quality Media Resources (1993). Four-module set; 20 minutes per module.

"Diversity Through Character." CRM Films (1996). 17 minutes.

"Free Speech, Politics, and the Web." Films for the Humanities and Sciences (1998). 30 minutes.

"For Goodness Sake!" CRM Films (1993). 24 minutes.

"Hate and the Internet: Web Sites and the Issue of Free Speech." Films for the Humanities and Sciences (1998). 22 minutes.

"Media Ethics." Films for the Humanities and Sciences (1997). 28 minutes.

"A Peacock in the Land of Penguins." CRM Films (1995). 10 minutes.

"Speaking with Confidence: Ethics." Insight Media (1997). 30 minutes.

"A Tale of 'O,'" revised edition. CRM Films (1993). 18 minutes.

"The Truth About Lying." Films for the Humanities and Sciences (2001). 21 minutes.

"Valuing Diversity: Multicultural Communication." Insight Media (1994). 49 minutes.

"Watch What You Say: Free Speech in Times of National Crisis." Films for the Humanities and Sciences (2001). 38 minutes.

"You Can't Say That! 'Politically Correct' Free Speech." Films for the Humanities and Sciences (2000). 43 minutes.

Chapter 3 Listening

Chapter Objectives

After reading this chapter, students should be able to:

1. Explain the difference between hearing and listening.

2. Define the four different kinds of listening and explain their relationship to critical thinking.

3. Explain why good listening is important to effective speechmaking.

4. Identify the four major causes of poor listening.

5. Discuss the seven ways to become a better listener presented in the text.

Chapter Outline

I. Listening is an important skill to master *(text pages 56-57)*.
   A. Hearing and listening are different processes.
      1. Hearing is a physiological process that involves the vibration of sound waves on the eardrums and the firing of electrochemical impulses from the inner ear to the brain.
      2. Listening is a mental process that involves paying close attention to, and making sense of, what is heard.
   B. Most people are poor listeners.
      1. Researchers find that most people only understand about half of what they hear.
      2. After 24 hours most people remember only 10 percent of the original message.

C.   In our communication-oriented age, listening is more important than ever.

    1.   Listening is an important job skill.

        a.   Effective listeners hold higher positions and are promoted more often than poor listeners.

        b.   Business managers rank listening as the communication skill most crucial to their jobs.

        c.   A survey of Fortune 500 companies showed that more than half provide listening training for their employees.

    2.   Effective listening is useful in all aspects of life, including academics.

        a.   Close to 90 percent of class time in American colleges and universities is spent listening.

        b.   Students with the highest grades are usually those with the strongest listening skills.

D.   Listening is also an excellent way to improve one's speaking skills.

    1.   Speakers get many of their ideas by listening to lectures, television, radio, etc.

    2.   Listening attentively to good speeches is an excellent way to improve one's own speaking skills.

II.   Listening skills are closely linked to critical thinking *(text pages 57-58)*.

A.   There are four types of listening.

    1.   Appreciative listening is listening for pleasure or enjoyment.

        a.   Listening to music is one example of appreciative listening.

        b.   Listening to a comedy routine is another example of appreciative listening.

    2.   Empathic listening is listening to provide emotional support for the speaker.

        a.   A counselor practices empathic listening.

        b.   Friends practice empathic listening when they discuss something with a person in distress.

    3.   Comprehensive listening focuses on understanding the speaker's message.

        a.   Listening to classroom lectures is one example of comprehensive listening.

        b.   Getting directions to a friend's house is another instance of comprehensive listening.

    4.   Critical listening involves evaluating a message either to accept it or reject it.

        a.   Listening to a sales pitch is an opportunity for critical listening.

        b.   Listening to a campaign speech is another opportunity to listen critically.

B.   Because comprehensive and critical listening are closely tied to critical thinking, they are most important for public speaking.

    1.   Several critical thinking skills are central to comprehensive listening.

        a.   One such skill is the ability to summarize information.

        b.   Another is the ability to recall facts.

        c.   A third is the ability to distinguish main points from minor points.

2. Several critical thinking skills are important to critical listening.
   a. Separating fact from opinion is one.
   b. Spotting weaknesses in reasoning is another.
   c. Judging the quality of evidence is yet another.
3. Listening and critical thinking are so closely allied that training in listening is really training in thinking.

III. There are four main causes of poor listening *(text pages 58-62)*.
   A. Not concentrating is one cause of poor listening.
      1. Because the human brain processes information very efficiently, it is easy for listeners to become distracted.
         a. The human brain can process from 400 to 800 words a minute.
         b. This efficiency leaves people with a great deal of extra brain time to think about other things than what a speaker is saying.
      2. Because of this, listeners must force themselves to concentrate on a speaker's message.
   B. Listening too hard can also interfere with effective listening.
      1. Listening too hard involves trying to remember every detail of a message.
      2. When listeners focus on every detail, they often miss the speaker's main points.
   C. Jumping to conclusions also prevents listeners from hearing messages accurately.
      1. One way we jump to conclusions is by assuming we know what someone is going to say before that person actually speaks.
      2. Another way we jump to conclusions is by prematurely rejecting a speaker's ideas as boring or misguided without hearing the entire message.
   D. Focusing on delivery and personal appearance instead of listening to a speaker's message is another cause of poor listening.
      1. Some people are so put off by personal appearance, accents, or unusual vocal mannerisms that they do not bother to listen.
      2. This type of emotional censorship is deadly to communication.

IV. There are seven ways to improve one's listening skills *(text pages 62-70)*.
   A. The first step in improving listening skills is to take listening seriously.
      1. Good listening is a skill that demands practice and self-discipline.
      2. One can become a better listener by working to improve listening skills.
   B. A second way to improve listening skills is to become an active listener.
      1. Active listeners give their undivided attention to the speaker in a genuine effort to understand her or his point of view.
      2. When listening to a speech, they do not allow themselves to be distracted by internal or external interference, and they do not prejudge the speaker.

C.   A third way to improve listening skills is to resist distractions.
  1.   Effective listeners make a conscious effort keep their minds on what the speaker is saying.
  2.   When they find their minds wandering, they force their attention back to the speech.
D.   A fourth way to improve listening skills is not to be diverted by appearance or delivery.
  1.   Effective listeners set aside preconceived negative judgments about a speaker's looks or manner of speech.
  2.   They also guard against being beguiled by a speaker's attractive appearance or hypnotic delivery skills.
E.   A fifth way to improve listening skills is to suspend judgment until hearing a speaker's full message.
  1.   Effective listeners realize they will hear things with which they disagree, but they make an effort not to reject a speaker out of hand.
  2.   They assess a speaker's evidence and reasoning before making a judgment.
F.   A sixth way to improve listening skills is to focus one's listening.
  1.   Effective listeners focus on a speaker's main points.
  2.   Effective listeners focus on the quality of a speaker's evidence.
    a.   They seek to assess whether the evidence is accurate.
    b.   They try to determine whether the evidence comes from objective sources.
    c.   They ask whether the evidence is relevant to the speaker's claims.
    d.   They gauge whether there is sufficient evidence to support the speaker's claims.
  3.   Effective listeners also focus on speaking techniques they can use in their own speeches.
    a.   They analyze the effectiveness of the introduction.
    b.   They assess the organization of the speech.
    c.   They study the speaker's use of language.
    d.   They diagnose the speaker's delivery.
G.   A seventh way to improve listening skills is to develop strong note-taking skills.
  1.   There is substantial research to show that note taking enhances listening.
  2.   Unfortunately, many people suffer from one or another of two weaknesses in note taking.
    a.   The first weakness is attempting to write down a speaker's every word.
    b.   The second weakness is concentrating only on fascinating tidbits of information.
  3.   Efficient note takers develop two good habits, both of which lead to stronger listening skills.
    a.   They learn to concentrate on a speaker's main ideas and supporting materials.
    b.   They use key-word outlines to summarize the speaker's message.

Exercises for Critical Thinking *(from text page 71)*

1. Which of the four causes of poor listening do you consider the most important? Choose a specific case of poor listening in which you were involved. Explain what went wrong.

    Discussion: This exercise is designed to have students think about the causes of poor listening in terms of their personal experience. If the students prepare this exercise before coming to class, it should generate a rich variety of examples for class discussion.

2. Using the Listening Self-Evaluation form on page 63 of the textbook, undertake a candid evaluation of your major strengths and weaknesses as a listener. Explain what steps you need to take to become a better listener.

    Discussion: This should be handled much like the third Exercise for Critical Thinking in Chapter 1. At the end of the course, students can be asked to assess their progress both as speakers and as listeners. For instructors who wish to distribute the Listening Self-Evaluation form in class, it is reprinted on the next page of this manual.

3. Watch the lead story this week on "60 Minutes," "20/20," or another news magazine program. Using the key-word method of note taking, record the main ideas of the story.

    Discussion: This can be a good diagnostic tool to gauge which students take notes effectively and which do not. Because the lead story on "60 Minutes" is usually somewhat controversial, this exercise can also illustrate how a person's listening is affected by his or her attitudes on the speaker's topic. For an alternative to this exercise, see items 3 and 4 under Additional Exercises/Activities for this chapter.

4. Choose a lecture in one of your other classes. Analyze what the lecturer does most effectively. Identify three things the lecturer could do better to help students keep track of the lecture.

    Discussion: The objective of this exercise is to focus attention on things a speaker can do to help listeners gain hold of the speaker's ideas. Usually students will produce a number of excellent suggestions—such as making sure the speech is well organized, previewing main points in the introduction, using internal summaries and transitions, employing visual aids, avoiding technical language, and the like. You can then urge that students be sure to follow these suggestions in their own speeches.

LISTENING SELF-EVALUATION

How often do you indulge in the following 10 bad listening habits? Check yourself carefully on each one:

HABIT	FREQUENCY					SCORE
	Almost always	Usually	Some-times	Seldom	Almost never	
1. Giving in to mental distractions	____	____	____	____	____	
2. Giving in to physical distractions	____	____	____	____	____	
3. Trying to recall everything a speaker says	____	____	____	____	____	
4. Rejecting a topic as uninteresting before hearing the speaker	____	____	____	____	____	
5. Faking paying attention	____	____	____	____	____	
6. Jumping to conclusions about a speaker's meaning	____	____	____	____	____	
7. Deciding a speaker is wrong before hearing everything she or he has to say	____	____	____	____	____	
8. Judging a speaker on personal appearance	____	____	____	____	____	
9. Not paying attention to a speaker's evidence	____	____	____	____	____	
10. Focusing on delivery rather than on what the speaker says	____	____	____	____	____	

TOTAL ____

How to score:

For every "almost always" checked, give yourself a score of	2
For every "usually" checked, give yourself a score of	4
For every "sometimes" checked, give yourself a score of	6
For every "seldom" checked, give yourself a score of	8
For every "almost never" checked, give yourself a score of	10

Total score interpretation:

Below 70	You need lots of training in listening.
From 71-90	You listen well.
Above 90	You listen exceptionally well.

Additional Exercises and Activities

1.   Lead a class discussion in which students develop a code of listening behavior for their speech classroom. The final product of this discussion will be a list entitled "Listening Behavior for Our Speech Class." By the end of the discussion, the entire class should not only agree on the content of the list, but should also pledge themselves to follow it throughout the term.

> **Discussion:** This activity is especially helpful for relating general issues about listening directly to the classroom situation. As students create their listening code, encourage them to be specific in their criteria. For example, rather than saying "Pay attention to what the speaker is saying," they should try to develop more precise statements such as "Write down the speaker's main points," "Look attentive and interested while other students are speaking," and "Do not read the newspaper or work on other assignments during speeches."
>
> This exercise works well when the class is divided into groups of 4 to 5 students. Give each group 10 to 15 minutes to come up with a list of 8 to 10 items to guide listening behavior in the class. Then, working from the group lists, conduct a general discussion which eventuates in a listening code that is agreed upon by the entire class. Another approach is to have each student create her or his own list as part of a homework assignment. You can then move immediately to a general class discussion rather than first dividing the class into small groups.

2.   Have one student step outside of the classroom with you. Give her or him a written copy of the following message: "To get to Lou's place, turn left at the first traffic light and go two blocks until you see a yellow house." Leaving the written copy with you, the student should return to the classroom and whisper the message to the person in the next seat. This person should then whisper the message to the person sitting next to him or her, and so on until the message has been relayed through the entire class. Have the last student to receive the message write it down on a sheet of paper and read it to the entire class. Then have the student to whom you gave the original message read that message to the class. There will almost always be an enormous variation between the original message and the message received by the last student.

> **Discussion:** This exercise takes only a few minutes to complete. It illustrates dramatically—and often humorously—the great distortion that can take place between what a speaker says and what a listener hears. You can, of course, substitute any message you wish for that given in the exercise.

3.   Bring two short editorials to class. Read one of the editorials to your students. Have them take notes and try to identify the main points and evidence of the editorial. Check the results in the class discussion, and give pointers for listening and taking notes more effectively. Then read the second editorial and give students a chance to apply those pointers. Again, check the results in a class discussion.

> **Discussion:** Although this exercise takes much of a class session, it can be very helpful because it prepares students for listening to speeches. Because many students do poorly on the first editorial, the exercise also serves the useful function of illustrating to students how poorly they listen and how much they need to work to improve their note taking. For an alternative, see the next Additional Exercise/ Activity.

4.   Show your class one of the selections from the videotapes of student speeches that accompany *The Art of Public Speaking*. Have them take notes in which they try to demarcate where the introduction of the speech ends, to list the main points and subpoints in the body, and to identify where the conclusion begins. Check the results in a class discussion and give pointers for listening and taking notes more effectively. Then play another speech and see if students do a better job of note taking. Again, check the results in a class discussion.

> **Discussion:** Because the student speeches on the videotapes are 6 to 8 minutes long, this activity takes a whole class session, but it is extremely helpful for students. It can be made even more helpful by selecting speeches for viewing that are connected with whatever speech assignment is coming up in class. That is, if you use this exercise as students are preparing the informative speech, show two informative speeches. Not only will this help students with their listening skills, but it will give them additional exposure to the principles of informative speaking.

5.   For each round of speeches, assign students specific listening tasks. For example, you might have a particular group of students (or all students) take notes on their classmates' speeches in an effort to identify the speakers' main points and evidence. After each speech, make a quick check of two or three listeners to see what they recorded.

> **Discussion:** This is one way to help students improve their listening and note-taking skills throughout the course. An added benefit of the exercise is that as students try to take notes on their classmates' speeches, they discover how helpful it is when the speaker follows a clear method of organization, previews the main points at the end of the introduction, uses connectives to help listeners keep track of main points, recaps the speech in the conclusion, avoids distracting nonverbal mannerisms, and uses her or his voice to emphasize ideas. This helps students learn what they need to do as speakers to help listeners take good notes.

6. For at least one round of speeches, have students prepare evaluations of their peers' speeches using the evaluation form on page 51 of this manual.

    > **Discussion:** This is an excellent alternative to Additional Exercise/ Activity 5 above. In addition to including the usual items for speech evaluation, the form on page 51 is designed to gauge students' listening skills by requiring them to state the speaker's specific purpose, main points, pattern of organization, and types of supporting materials. Some teachers use the form for every speech, and they report that it helps considerably to improve students' listening skills by the end of the term.

7. Have students keep a personal journal of their listening activities for a full day. The journal should include brief descriptions of all the listening situations each student experienced during that day. It should also include the student's analysis of how well he or she listened in each situation and of why he or she did (or did not) listen effectively in each situation. At the end of the day, the student should fill out the Listening Self-Evaluation form on page 63 of the textbook. Finally, the journal should conclude with the student's honest assessment of her or his strengths and weaknesses as a listener and an explanation of what specific steps the student should take to become a better listener.

    > **Discussion:** This is a useful alternative to the second Exercise for Critical Thinking on page 71 of the textbook. Like that exercise, it is a way to get students to think about their personal listening habits and how to improve them. Some teachers have students complete a listening journal two or three times during the course, as a way for students to keep track of their progress (or lack of progress) in strengthening their listening skills.

Extra Teaching and Learning Resources

General

Barker, Larry, and Watson, Kittie. *Listen Up*. New York: St. Martin's Griffin, 2000.

Bonet, Diana. *The Business of Listening: A Practical Guide to Effective Listening*, 3rd ed. MenloPark, CA: Crisp Publications, 2001.

Borisoff, Deborah, and Purdy, Michael (eds.). *Listening in Everyday Life: A Personal and Professional Approach*, 2nd ed. Lanham, MD: University Press of America, 1997.

Burley-Allen, Madelyn. *Listening: The Forgotten Skill*. New York: Wiley, 1995.

Nichols, Michael P. *The Lost Art of Listening*. New York: Guilford, 1995.

O'Keefe, Virginia. *Developing Critical Thinking: The Speaking/Listening Connection*. Portsmouth, NH: Boynton/Cook, 1999.

Robertson, Arthur K. *Listen for Success: A Guide to Effective Listening*. Burr Ridge, IL: Irwin, 1994.

Shafir, Rebecca Z. *The Zen of Listening: Mindful Communication in an Age of Distractions*. Wheaton, IL: Quest Books, 2000.

Titsworth, B. Scott. "The Effects of Teacher Immediacy, Use of Organizational Lecture Cues and Students' Notetaking on Cognitive Learning." *Communication Education*, 50 (2001), 283-297.

Wakefield, Norm. *The Art of Perceptive Listening*. Grand Rapids, MI: Fleming H. Revell, 2002.

Wolff, Florence I., and Marsnik, Nadine C. *Perceptive Listening*, 2nd ed. Fort Worth, TX: Harcourt Brace Jovanovich, 1992.

Wolvin, Andrew, and Coakley, Carolyn Gwynn. *Listening*, 5th ed. Dubuque, IA: Brown and Benchmark, 1995.

Wolvin, Andrew D., and Coakley, Carolyn Gwynn (eds.). *Perspectives on Listening*. Norwood, NJ: Ablex, 1993.

Wolvin, Andrew D., and Coakley, Carolyn Gwynn. "A Survey of the Status of Listening Training in Some Fortune 500 Corporations." *Communication Education*, 40 (1991), 152-164.

Classroom Activities and Assignments

Bohlken, Bob. "Learning to Listen and You Listen to Learn." In Stephen E. Lucas (ed.), *Selections from the Speech Communication Teacher, 1991-1994*. New York: McGraw-Hill, 1995, pp. 40-41.

Bohlken, Bob. "Think About Listening." In Stephen E. Lucas (ed.), *Selections from the Speech Communication Teacher, 1994-1996*. New York: McGraw-Hill, 1997, pp. 46-47.

Forestieri, Mary C. "Listening Instruction." In Stephen E. Lucas (ed.), *Selections from the Speech Communication Teacher, 1986-1991*. New York: McGraw-Hill, 1992, pp. 44-45.

Hyde, Richard Bruce. "Council: Using a Talking Stick to Teach Listening." In Stephen E. Lucas (ed.), *Selections from the Speech Communication Teacher, 1991-1994*. New York: McGraw-Hill, 1995, pp. 41-42.

Lynch, Christopher. "Speech Listening Compared to Heart Monitor." In Stephen E. Lucas (ed.), *Selections from the Speech Communication Teacher, 1994-1996*. New York: McGraw-Hill, 1997, pp. 47-48.

Mallard, Kina S. "The Listening Box." In Stephen E. Lucas (ed.), *Selections from the Speech Communication Teacher, 1996-1999*. New York: McGraw-Hill, 2001, p. 69.

McPeak, Judith L. "Listening Activities." In Stephen E. Lucas (ed.), *Selections from the Speech Communication Teacher, 1994-1996*. New York: McGraw-Hill, 1997, pp. 48-49.

Mino, Mary, "Creating Listening Rules." In Stephen E. Lucas (ed.), *Selections from the Speech Communication Teacher, 1996-1999*. New York: McGraw-Hill, 2001, pp. 6970.

Portnoy, Enid. "Activities to Promote Students' Speaking and Listening Abilities." In Stephen E. Lucas (ed.), *Selections from the Speech Communication Teacher, 1986-1991*. New York: McGraw-Hill, 1992, pp. 45-46.

Ross, Roseanna. "What Is In the Shoe Box?" In Stephen E. Lucas (ed.), *Selections from the Speech Communication Teacher, 1986-1991*. New York: McGraw-Hill, 1992, pp. 46-47.

Schneider, Valerie L. "A Three-Step Process for Better Speaking and Listening." In Stephen E. Lucas (ed.), *Selections from the Speech Communication Teacher, 1986-1991*. New York: McGraw-Hill, 1992, pp. 47-48.

Films and Videos

"The Art of Listening." Insight Media (1992). 27 minutes.

"Critical Listening." Insight Media (1999). 20 minutes.

"Extreme Listening: Hearing and Listening." Insight Media (1998). 60 minutes.

"I Never Learned Anything by Talking: Effective Listening Skills." Insight Media (1999). 43 minutes.

"Listen Up: Hear What's Really Being Said." Insight Media (1998). 60 minutes.

"Now Hear This: Anatomy of the Ears." Insight Media (1994). 25 minutes.

"The Six Essentials of Effective Listening." Insight Media (1997). 24 minutes.

"Speaking with Confidence: Listening." Insight Media (1997). 30 minutes.

Appendix

Giving Your First Speech

Appendix Objectives

After reading this appendix, students should be able to:

1. Explain the major factors involved in developing and organizing their first classroom speech.

2. Explain the nature of extemporaneous delivery and how they can work on speaking extemporaneously as they rehearse their first classroom speech.

3. Explain the elements discussed in the textbook with regard to delivering the first classroom speech.

Appendix Outline

I. The first speech assignment is often called an ice breaker speech because it is designed to "break the ice" by getting students up in front of the class as soon as possible (*text page 74*).
   A. There are many options for this assignment.
      1. Some teachers assign a speech of self-introduction.
      2. Some assign a speech introducing a classmate.
      3. Some assign a "brush with greatness" speech.
      4. Some assign a speech with multicultural dimensions.
   B. Whatever the assignment, the speech is usually brief and is often ungraded.

II. The initial step in giving the first speech is deciding on a topic, identifying main points, and developing those points creatively (*text pages 74-75*).
   A. Students should make sure their topic is appropriate for the time limit.
   B. Once students have a speech topic, they should be creative in developing it.
      1. They can think of ways to make the speech mysterious or suspenseful.
      2. They can talk about dangerous situations, adventure, or drama.
      3. They can use colorful, descriptive language.
      4. They can use humor as long as it is in good taste and grows naturally out of the speech content.

III. The second step in giving the first speech is organizing the content (*text pages 75-77*).
   A. The introduction should get the audience's attention and reveal the topic of the speech.
   B. The body can be organized in a number of ways, including chronological order and topical order.
      1. No matter which method of organization is used, there should be no more than two or three main points.
      2. Each main point should focus on a single aspect of the topic.
      3. Each main point should be introduced with a transition statement.
   C. The conclusion should signal the end of the speech, reinforce the major theme, and, if possible, end on a dramatic or thought-provoking note.

IV. The third step in giving the first speech is working on delivery (*text pages 78-81*).
   A. Most experts recommend speaking extemporaneously, which involves planning main points and supporting materials but not memorizing the speech.
      1. Extemporaneous speakers should be familiar with the substance of their speech so they need only a brief set of speaking notes.
      2. When speaking extemporaneously, students should try to feel as comfortable in front of the class as they do conversing with friends.
   B. Effective extemporaneous delivery requires a great deal of rehearsal.
      1. During their initial rehearsals, speakers should focus on gaining control of the ideas rather than learning the speech word for word.
      2. The speech should be practiced out loud.
      3. When rehearsing, it is important to time the speech so it is neither too long nor too short.
   C. There are several things to concentrate on when presenting the speech in class.
      1. Before beginning, speakers should take a moment to arrange their notes, set their body in an upright but relaxed posture, and smile at the audience.
      2. During the speech, they should gesture naturally, avoid distracting movements, maintain eye contact with the audience, and speak expressively.
      3. Speakers should also remember that nervousness is natural and that the anxiety they feel inside is usually not visible to the audience.

Chapter 4 Selecting a Topic and a Purpose

Chapter Objectives

After reading this chapter, students should be able to:

1. Explain four methods they can use to brainstorm for a speech topic.

2. Identify the difference between a general and a specific purpose.

3. Distinguish between the specific purpose and the central idea of a speech.

4. Formulate a specific purpose statement and a central idea in accordance with the guidelines presented in the text.

Chapter Outline

I. The first step in speechmaking is choosing a topic *(text pages 86-93)*.
    A. Topics for speeches outside the classroom are usually determined by the occasion, the audience, and the speaker's qualifications.
    B. There are several sources for topics for classroom speeches.
        1. Topics for classroom speeches can come from subjects about which students already know a great deal.
        2. Topics for classroom speeches can come from subjects about which a student is interested and wants to learn more.
        3. Topics for classroom speeches can come from issues about which students hold strong opinions and beliefs.

    4.   Students can use several brainstorming procedures to help select a topic.
        a.   They can make an inventory of interests, skills, experiences, and the like.
        b.   They can cluster possible topics into categories such as people, places, events, processes, plans and policies, and so forth.
        c.   They can browse through encyclopedias, dictionaries, or other reference materials in search of a topic.
        d.   They can use a subject-based search engine such as Yahoo to help find a topic via the Internet.
    5.   Whatever method students use, they should settle on a topic as early as possible.

II.   After choosing a topic, speakers need to determine the general purpose of the speech *(text page 93)*.
    A.   There are usually two general purposes for classroom speeches—to inform or to persuade.
    B.   When the general purpose is to inform, speakers act as teachers.
        1.   Their goal is to communicate information clearly, accurately, and interestingly.
        2.   They seek to enhance the knowledge and understanding of their listeners.
    C.   When the general purpose is to persuade, speakers act as advocates.
        1.   Their goal is to change the attitudes or actions of their audience.
        2.   They seek to get their listeners to believe something or to do something.

III.   Once the general purpose is clear, the next step is narrowing to the specific purpose *(text pages 93-100)*.
    A.   The specific purpose should indicate precisely what the speaker wants the audience to know or believe after the speech.
        1.   It should focus on a clearly defined aspect of the topic.
        2.   It should be expressed as a single infinitive phrase that includes the audience.
    B.   There are five tips for forming a good specific purpose statement.
        1.   It should be a full infinitive phrase, not a fragment.
        2.   It should be phrased as a statement, not a question.
        3.   It should avoid figurative language.
        4.   It should be limited to one distinct idea.
        5.   It should not be too vague or general.
    C.   Once students have a specific purpose statement, they should ask themselves the following questions:
        1.   Does the specific purpose meet the assignment?
        2.   Can this specific purpose be accomplished effectively in the time allotted?
        3.   Is the specific purpose relevant to the audience?
        4.   Is the specific purpose too trivial for the audience?
        5.   Is the specific purpose too technical for the audience?

IV.   The central idea further refines and sharpens the specific purpose statement *(text pages 100-104)*.
    A.   The central idea is a concise statement of what the speaker expects to say in the speech.
        1.   It is more precise than the topic or the specific purpose statement.

      2.   It sums up the speech in a single statement.

B.   Often called a thesis statement, the central idea encapsulates the main points to be developed in the body of the speech.

      1.   It is what the speaker wants the audience to remember when they have forgotten everything else about the speech.

      2.   It reveals more about the content of the speech than does the specific purpose statement.

C.   Unlike the specific purpose statement, the central idea usually crystallizes late in the process of preparing a speech.

D.   A well-worded central idea should meet four criteria.

      1.   It should be expressed in a full sentence.

      2.   It should not be in the form of a question.

      3.   It should avoid figurative language.

      4.   It should not be too vague or general.

Exercises for Critical Thinking *(from text pages 105-106)*

1.   Using one of the four brainstorming methods described in this chapter, come up with three topics you might like to deal with in your next classroom speech. For each topic, devise two possible specific purpose statements suitable for the speech assignment. Make sure the specific purpose statements fit the guidelines discussed in the chapter.

> **Discussion:** This exercise gives students an opportunity to practice brainstorming, to begin the process of selecting a topic for their next speech, and to work on framing specific purpose statements. In class discussion, you can assess not only the suitability of the students' topics, but also how effectively the students have phrased their specific purposes.

2.   At the bottom of page 105 of the textbook is a list of nine topics. Choose three, and for each of the three compose two specific purpose statements—one suitable for an informative speech and one suitable for a persuasive speech.

education	technology	crime
sports	politics	prejudice
science	music	health

> **Discussion:** This exercise works well to clarify the differences between specific purpose statements for informative speeches and specific purpose statements for persuasive speeches. Start with the first topic, and have one or two students share their specific purpose statements with the class. Discuss those statements briefly with the class, and then repeat the procedure with the next topic.

3.   Here are several specific purpose statements for classroom speeches. Identify the problem with each, and rewrite the statement to correct the problem.

    a.   To inform my audience how to make perfect popcorn every time.

        Discussion: Although Orville Redenbacher would find how to make popcorn a consequential topic, this specific purpose is too trivial for most classroom speeches.

    b.   To inform my audience about the growth of credit card fraud and the methods of sound financial planning.

        Discussion: This specific purpose statement contains two separate ideas. A more effective statement would be "To inform my audience about the growth of credit card fraud." Or "To inform my audience about the methods of sound financial planning." Or even "To inform my audience how to manage their use of credit cards in a manner consistent with sound financial planning."

    c.   What is obsessive compulsive disorder?

        Discussion: This specific purpose statement is phrased as a question. A more effective statement would be "To inform my audience about the symptoms, causes, and treatment of obsessive compulsive disorder."

    d.   To inform my audience why square grooves are superior to U-shaped grooves on golf clubs.

        Discussion: This specific purpose statement is too technical—and perhaps too trivial—for an audience not composed of golf enthusiasts. A more effective specific purpose statement for a classroom speech on golf might be "To inform my audience about the development of golf as a popular sport." Or "To inform my audience about the different kinds of clubs used in playing golf."

    e.   To inform my audience about Thailand.

        Discussion: This specific purpose statement is too broad. A more effective statement would be "To inform my audience about the major customs of everyday life in Thailand."

    f.   Donate blood.

        Discussion: This specific purpose statement is written as a fragment. A more effective statement would be "To persuade my audience to contribute to the next campus blood drive."

    g.   To persuade my audience that something has to be done about the problem of antibiotic-resistant bacteria.

        Discussion: This specific purpose statement is too broad; it does not specify what should be done about the problem of antibiotic-resistant bacteria. A more effective specific purpose statement would be "To persuade my audience that the federal government should increase research to deal with the alarming growth of antibiotic-resistant bacteria."

4. Below are three sets of main points for speeches. For each set supply the general purpose, specific purpose, and central idea.

General Purpose: To inform

Specific Purpose: To inform my audience about the four major steps in making pottery.

Central Idea: The four major steps in making pottery are preparing the clay, shaping the clay, decorating and glazing the clay, and firing the finished product.

Main Points:
I. The first step in making pottery is preparing the clay until it is soft and smooth.
II. The second step in making pottery is shaping the clay to the desired form.
III. The third step in making pottery is decorating and glazing the shaped clay.
IV. The fourth step in making pottery is firing the finished product to make it hard and strong.

General Purpose: To persuade

Specific Purpose: To persuade my audience to volunteer as a literacy tutor.

Central Idea: You should volunteer as a literacy tutor because it helps children, strengthens the community, and is personally rewarding.

Main Points:
I. You should volunteer as a literacy tutor because it helps children.
II. You should volunteer as a literacy tutor because it strengthens the community.
III. You should volunteer as a literacy tutor because it is personally rewarding.

General Purpose: To inform

Specific Purpose: To inform my audience about the accomplishments of Leonardo da Vinci.

Central Idea: Leonardo da Vinci was an accomplished painter, inventor, and astronomer.

Main Points:
I. As a painter, Leonardo da Vinci produced *The Last Supper*, the *Mona Lisa*, and other masterpieces.
II. As an inventor, Leonardo da Vinci drew plans for such devices as a parachute and a flying machine.
III. As an astronomer, Leonardo da Vinci concluded that the earth revolves around the sun.

Discussion: The virtue of this exercise is that it clarifies the relationships among the specific purpose, the central idea, and the main points. It looks easy, but quite a few students have trouble with it. To facilitate class discussion, this exercise is also available in the binder of full-color overhead transparencies that accompanies *The Art of Public Speaking*. (For variations, see Additional Exercises/ Activities 1 and 2 on pages 128-132 of this manual.)

Applying the Power of Public Speaking *(from text page 107)*

Your chemistry degree and excellent communication skills have helped you land a job in the Office of Public Information in your state's Department of Health. With a particularly dangerous strain of type-A influenza moving through your state, a news briefing has been scheduled to inform residents about the disease. You are selected to present the briefing.

After gathering information from your agency's medical personnel, you plan what you will say in the briefing. You decide that you will (1) report the symptoms of the disease, (2) identify the people—young children, the elderly, and others—who are most at-risk to catch the disease, (3) explain preventive measures to avoid getting the disease, and (4) relate how to treat the disease if one does come down with it.

Following the format used in this chapter, state the general purpose, specific purpose, main points, and central idea of your speech.

Discussion: As with the other Applying the Power of Public Speaking exercises throughout the book, this one is intended to illustrate how one might apply the principles discussed in the book to situations outside the classroom. The purpose is less to have students come up with the "right" answer than to get them thinking about the practical applications of what they are reading and studying in class. Here is what a reasonable answer to the questions posed in this scenario might look like:

General Purpose:	To inform
Specific Purpose:	To inform my audience about the symptoms, at-risk groups, preventive measures, and treatment of the type-A influenza threatening our state.
Central Idea:	Because the type-A influenza threatening our state is extremely dangerous, people need to know its symptoms, who is most at-risk to contract it, how to prevent it, and methods of treating it.

Main Points:

I.   Symptoms of type-A influenza include nausea, headaches, muscle pain, high fever, delirium, and potentially death.

II. Although type-A influenza can strike anyone, young children, the elderly, and people with immune-system disorders are especially at risk.

III. There are several preventive measures one can take to reduce the risk of contracting type-A influenza.

IV. If one does come down with the disease, it is vital to seek prompt, professional medical treatment.

Additional Exercises and Activities

1. Below are two central ideas for speeches. For each central idea provide the general purpose, specific purpose, and main points of the speech.

General Purpose:

Specific Purpose:

Central Idea: The four stages of alcoholism are the warning stage, the danger stage, the crucial stage, and the chronic stage.

Main Points: I.

II.

III.

IV.

General Purpose:

Specific Purpose:

Central Idea: You should join a sorority or fraternity because of the social, academic, and economic benefits.

Main Points: I.

                       II.

                       III.

Discussion: This complements Exercise 4 on page 106 of the textbook and gives students additional work in understanding the relationships among the general purpose, specific purpose, central idea, and main points of the speech. For another exercise along these lines, see Additional Exercise/Activity 2 on pages 130-132 of this manual. Here are the answers to the present exercise. To facilitate class discussion, the answers are also available in the binder of full-color overhead transparencies that accompanies *The Art of Public Speaking.*

General Purpose: To inform

Specific Purpose: To inform my audience of the four stages of alcoholism.

Central Idea: The four stages of alcoholism are the warning stage, the danger stage, the crucial stage, and the chronic stage.

Main Points: I.   The first stage of alcoholism is the warning stage.
                       II.   The second stage of alcoholism is the danger stage.
                       III. The third stage of alcoholism is the crucial stage.
                       IV.   The fourth stage of alcoholism is the chronic stage.

General Purpose: To persuade

Specific Purpose: To persuade my audience to join a sorority or a fraternity.

Central Idea: You should join a sorority or fraternity because of the social, academic, and economic benefits.

Main Points:
I.   You should join a sorority or fraternity because of the social benefits.
II. You should join a sorority or fraternity because of the academic benefits.
III. You should join a sorority or fraternity because of the economic benefits.

2. Below are two central ideas for speeches. For each central idea provide the general purpose, specific purpose, and main points of the speech.

General Purpose:

Specific Purpose:

Central Idea: The pyramids of ancient Egypt had three major uses—as tombs for the burial of monarchs, as temples for worshipping the gods, and as observatories for studying the stars.

Main Points:

General Purpose:

Specific Purpose:

Central Idea: Handwriting analysts try to determine personality traits by examining the consistency, angularity, and size of a person's writing.

Main Points:

Discussion: By not providing the number of main points, this exercise is somewhat more difficult than the previous one. It provides additional work for students who are having trouble with the relationships among the general purpose, specific purpose, central idea, and main points. Here is what the exercise should look like when all the blanks are filled in. To facilitate class discussion, the answers are also available in the binder of full-color overhead transparencies that accompanies *The Art of Public Speaking*.

General Purpose: To inform

Specific Purpose: To inform my audience of the three major uses of the pyramids of ancient Egypt.

Central Idea: The pyramids of ancient Egypt had three major uses—as tombs for the burial of monarchs, as temples for worshipping the gods, and as observatories for studying the stars and the planets.

Main Points:
    I.   The first major use of the pyramids of ancient Egypt was as tombs for the burial of monarchs.
    II. The second major use of the pyramids of ancient Egypt was as temples for worshipping the gods.
    III. The third major use of the pyramids of ancient Egypt was as observatories for studying the stars and the planets.

General Purpose: To inform

Specific Purpose: To inform my audience how handwriting analysts try to determine personality traits by examining a person's handwriting.

Central Idea: Handwriting analysts try to determine personality traits by examining the consistency, angularity, and size of a person's handwriting.

Main Points: I.   Handwriting analysts try to determine personality traits by examining the consistency of a person's handwriting.
                        II.   Handwriting analysts try to determine personality traits by examining the angularity of a person's handwriting.
                        III. Handwriting analysts try to determine personality traits by examining the size of a person's handwriting.

3. Once students start to work on each speech assignment, set aside part of a class session to discuss the students' topics. Ask each student to reveal her or his topic and specific purpose. Ask other classmates to indicate whether they find the topic interesting and what suggestions they have for the speaker's approach to it.

> **Discussion:** In some classes this works very well. In other classes—when the students are not well prepared or are reluctant to share their opinions—it is less effective. Some teachers use this activity quite successfully to help students focus their topics and adjust them to their classmates.

4. Divide the class into groups of 5 to 6 students each. Assign each group one of the following resources to investigate for possible speech topics: (a) an issue of a magazine such as *Time*, *Newsweek*, or *U.S. News and World Report*; (b) the Sunday edition of the leading local newspaper; (c) any issue of a major national newspaper—*New York Times*, *Los Angeles Times*, *Washington Post*, *Christian Science Monitor*—that is available at the college library; (d) an hour of news broadcasting on CNN; (e) two nights of the evening news telecast on ABC, NBC, or CBS. On the basis of these resources, each group is responsible for bringing into class five speech topics and specific purpose statements for each of those topics. Conduct a class discussion on the kinds and quality of topics and specific purpose statements generated by each group.

> **Discussion:** This exercise requires a fair amount of time outside of class and works especially well in courses that include a unit on group discussion. An added benefit of the exercise is that it often leads several students to topics that they eventually use in one or more of their speeches during the term.

Extra Teaching and Learning Resources

General

Ayan, Jordan E. *Aha! 10 Ways to Free Your Creative Spirit and Find Your Great Ideas.* New York: Crown, 1997.

Barron, Frank; Montuori, Alfonso; and Barron, Anthea (eds.). *Creators on Creating: Awakening and Cultivating the Imaginative Mind.* New York: Putnam's, 1997.

Browne, M. Neil, and Keeley, Stuart M. *Asking the Right Questions: A Guide to Critical Thinking,* 6th ed. Upper Saddle River, NJ: Prentice Hall, 2001.

Csikszentmihalyi, Mihaly. *Creativity: Flow and the Psychology of Discovery and Invention.* New York: HarperCollins, 1996.

Diestler, Sherry. *Becoming a Critical Thinker: A User Friendly Manual.* 3rd ed. Upper Saddle River, NJ: Prentice Hall, 2001.

Gelb, Michael. *How to Think Like Leonardo da Vinci: Seven Steps to Genius Every Day.* New York: Dell Books, 2000.

McCoy, Charles W. *Why Didn't I Think of That? Think the Unthinkable and Achieve Creative Greatness.* Upper Saddle River, NJ: Prentice-Hall, 2002.

Michalko, Michael. *Cracking Creativity: The Secrets of Creative Genius.* Berkeley, CA: Ten Speed Press, 1998.

Rowan, Katherine E. "A New Pedagogy For Explanatory Public Speaking: Why Arrangement Should Not Substitute for Invention." *Communication Education*, 44 (1995), 236-250.

Sternberg, Robert J. (ed.). *Handbook of Creativity.* Cambridge: Cambridge University Press, 1999.

Thorp, Scott. *How to Think Like Einstein: Simple Ways to Break the Rules and Discover Your Hidden Genius.* Naperville, IL: Sourcebooks, 2000.

Classroom Activities and Assignments

Avadian, Brenda, and Thanos, Marilyn. "Speechmapping: The Road Through Speech Preparation and Delivery." In Stephen E. Lucas (ed.), *Selections from the Speech Communication Teacher, 1986-1991.* New York: McGraw-Hill, 1992, pp. 51-52.

Duffy, Susan. "Using Magazines to Stimulate Topic Choices for Speeches." In Stephen E. Lucas (ed.), *Selections from the Speech Communication Teacher, 1986-1991*. New York: McGraw-Hill, 1992, pp. 16-17.

Garrett, Roger L. "Helping Students Discover Interviewing Skills." In Stephen E. Lucas (ed.), *Selections from the Speech Communication Teacher, 1986-1991*. New York: McGraw-Hill, 1992, pp. 37-38.

Glaser, Hollis F. "Focusing the Students on Three Speech Topics." In Stephen E. Lucas (ed.), *Selections from the Speech Communication Teacher, 1996-1999*. New York: McGraw-Hill, 2001, p. 17.

Grainer, Diane. "Creativity vs. My Speech Is About Avocados." In Stephen E. Lucas (ed.), *Selections from the Speech Communication Teacher, 1986-1991*. New York: McGraw-Hill, 1992, p. 74.

Hugenberg, Lawrence W., and O'Neill, Daniel J. "Speaking on Critical Issue Topics in the Public Speaking Course." In Stephen E. Lucas (ed.), *Selections from the Speech Communication Teacher, 1986-1991*. New York: McGraw-Hill, 1992, pp. 17-18.

Smith, Robert E. "Clustering: A Way to Discover Speech Topics." In Stephen E. Lucas (ed.), *Selections from the Speech Communication Teacher, 1991-1994*. New York: McGraw-Hill, 1995, pp. 13-14.

Woodside, Daria. "Choosing Topics for Speeches: A Breath of Fresh Air (Earth, Water, and Fire)." In Stephen E. Lucas (ed.), *Selections from the Speech Communication Teacher, 1991-1994*. New York: McGraw-Hill, 1995, pp. 14-15.

Films and Videos

"The Green Movie: Empowerment Within a Framework." CRM Films (1995). 15 minutes.

"How to Think Creatively." Insight Media (1997). Two volumes; 104 minutes.

"Ideas Into Action." CRM Films (1993). 10 minutes.

"Reasoning, Critical Thinking, and Creativity." Insight Media (1993). 60 minutes.

"Selecting a Topic." Insight Media (1997). 30 minutes.

"Top 10½ Tips for Thinking Critically." Insight Media (1999). 15 minutes.

"Why Didn't I Think of That?" Insight Media (1990). 28 minutes.

Chapter 5 Analyzing the Audience

Chapter Objectives

After reading this chapter, students should be able to:

1.   Explain why public speakers must be audience centered.

2.   Explain what it means to say that audiences are egocentric.

3.   Identify the major demographic traits of audiences.

4.   Identify the major situational traits of audiences.

5.   Use a questionnaire as a method of audience analysis for classroom speeches.

6.   Explain how a speaker can adapt to the audience while preparing the speech and while delivering the speech.

Chapter Outline

I.   Good speakers are audience-centered *(text pages 110-112)*.
    A.   They understand that the primary purpose of public speaking is to gain a desired response from their listeners.
    B.   They keep three questions in mind as they prepare their speeches:
        1.   To whom am I speaking?
        2.   What do I want the audience to know, believe, or do as a result of my speech?

        3.   How can I most effectively compose and present my speech to accomplish that aim?

    C.   They seek to create a bond—what communication scholars call identification—with listeners by emphasizing common values, goals, and experiences.

II.   It is important for student speakers to approach their classmates as a real audience *(text pages 112-113)*.

    A.   Because the classroom seems like an artificial speaking situation, it is easy for students to lose sight of their classmates as an authentic audience.

    B.   The best student speakers take their audience seriously and treat their classmates as worthy of their best effort.

III.   Good speakers understand the psychology of audiences *(text pages 113-114)*.

    A.   A speaker's task is to make the audience want to pay attention to her or his message.

    B.   The auditory perception of audiences is always selective.

        1.   Everything a speaker says is filtered through a listener's frame of reference.

        2.   Every speech contains two messages—that sent by the speaker and that received by the audience.

    C.   Audiences are egocentric.

        1.   They pay closest attention to messages that affect them directly.

        2.   They typically approach speeches by asking, "Why is this important to me?"

    D.   These psychological principles have two important implications for speakers.

        1.   Listeners will judge a speech on the basis of what they already know and believe.

        2.   Speakers must take care to relate their messages to an audience's existing knowledge and beliefs.

IV.   The first stage of audience analysis is examining demographic traits of the audience and how they might affect reception of the speech *(text pages 114-121)*.

    A.   Demographic audience analysis is a useful tool in understanding audiences, but it needs to be used properly.

        1.   When analyzing demographic information about the audience, it is essential to avoid stereotyping.

        2.   Demographic audience analysis should always be combined with situational audience analysis.

    B.   Few things affect a person's outlook more than her or his age.

        1.   Each generation has more-or-less common experiences and values.

        2.   Effective speakers adapt to these experiences and values when addressing an audience.

    C.   Gender issues can have a strong impact on how an audience responds to a speech.

        1.   Women and men in the United States share a broader range of experiences than was the case a few decades ago.

        2.   The composition of audiences has also changed.

            a.   Many audiences that were once predominantly male now include large numbers of women.

        b.   Many audiences that were once predominantly female now include a substantial number of men.

   3.   To be effective in today's world, public speakers must avoid outdated gender stereotypes and be responsive to *both* the similarities and the differences between men and women.

D.   It is important to adapt to the audience on the basis of sexual orientation.

   1.   Audience-centered speakers avoid words and phrases that demean people on the basis of sexual orientation.

   2.   They also avoid examples and other supporting materials that may unintentionally exclude listeners with same-sex partners.

E.   It is also important to consider the racial, ethnic, or cultural background of audience members.

   1.   Audience-centered speakers are sensitive to the fact that most Americans support racial, ethnic, and cultural diversity as a fundamental element in today's globalized world.

   2.   Audience-centered speakers are also sensitive to the ways racial, ethnic, and cultural differences among audience members might affect reactions to a speech.

F.   The religious views of the audience need to be considered.

   1.   A speaker cannot assume that her or his religious views, whatever they may be, will be shared by all members of the audience.

   2.   As the United States becomes more diverse culturally, it is also becoming more diverse religiously.

   3.   Failure to consider the religious views of the audience can seriously weaken a speech.

G.   The group membership of an audience is another important factor to consider.

   1.   There are thousands of national, state, and local voluntary associations in the U.S.

   2.   The group affiliations of audience members can provide valuable clues about their interests and attitudes.

H.   There are also a number of other potentially important demographic variables.

   1.   They include occupation, economic position, education, intelligence, and place of residence.

   2.   Special demographic variables for classroom speeches might include year in school, major, extracurricular activities, job aspirations, and living arrangements.

   3.   Anything characteristic of a given audience is potentially important to a speaker trying to gauge how listeners will respond to her or his speech.

V.   Another stage of audience analysis is examining features of the audience unique to the speaking situation at hand *(text pages 121-126)*.

   A.   The first factor to consider is the size of the audience.

      1.   Larger audiences usually require more formal presentations.

      2.   Audience size may also affect a speaker's language, choice of appeals, and use of visual aids.

B.   The second factor to consider is the physical setting of the speech.
  1.   The receptivity of listeners is frequently influenced by physical conditions such as the size, seating, and temperature of the room.
  2.   Speakers should do what they can to control the influence of physical setting on the audience.
C.   The third factor to consider is the audience's disposition toward the topic.
  1.   A speaker needs to assess the audience's interest in the topic.
    a.   Outside the classroom, people seldom expend the time and effort to attend a speech unless they are interested in the topic.
    b.   For classroom speeches, it is usually necessary to take special measures to get the audience involved.
  2.   A speaker needs to assess the audience's knowledge about the topic.
    a.   If the audience knows little about the topic, the speaker will have to talk at a more elementary level.
    b.   If the audience knows a lot about the topic, the speaker can take a more advanced approach.
  3.   A speaker needs to assess the audience's attitude toward the topic.
    a.   If the audience is skeptical about or hostile toward the speaker's views on the topic, the speaker will have to adapt to that skepticism or hostility.
    b.   If the audience is favorably disposed toward the speaker's view of the topic, the speaker will usually have an easier task.
D.   The fourth factor to consider is the audience's disposition toward the speaker.
  1.   An audience's response to a message is invariably colored by their perceptions of the speaker.
  2.   The more credible and competent listeners believe a speaker to be, the more likely they are to accept what the speaker says.
E.   The fifth factor to consider is the audience's disposition toward the occasion.
  1.   The occasion will often determine the audience's expectations about the length and content of the speech.
  2.   Speakers who seriously violate these expectations risk alienating the audience.

VI.   There are several ways to get demographic and situational information about the audience *(text pages 127-130)*.
  A.   For speeches outside the classroom, speakers often make informal inquiries about their audience.
    1.   They may ask the person who invites them to speak to explain the group's history and purpose.
    2.   They may sound out someone else who has addressed the same group.
  B.   For classroom speeches, students often use audience-analysis questionnaires.
    1.   There are three basic types of questions for such questionnaires.
      a.   Fixed-alternative questions offer a choice between two or more specific responses.
      b.   Scale questions allow for a continuum of answers.
      c.   Open-ended questions give maximum leeway in responding.

2.   There are four guidelines for effective audience-analysis questionnaires.
   a.   They should be carefully planned to elicit the necessary information.
   b.   They should use all three types of questions to get specific and detailed information.
   c.   They should be clear and unambiguous.
   d.   They should be relatively brief.

VII.   Once speakers complete their audience analysis, they use that analysis to adapt their speech to their listeners *(text pages 130-132)*.
   A.   Most of the work of audience adaptation takes place before the speech as part of the preparation process.
      1.   A speaker should keep the audience in mind at every stage of speech preparation.
      2.   A speaker should keep the following questions constantly in mind while preparing the speech.
         a.   How is the audience likely to respond to what I will say?
         b.   How can I adjust my message to make it as clear and convincing as possible?
      3.   Adjusting the message to the audience requires two things of a speaker during the process of speech preparation.
         a.   The speaker must anticipate how listeners will respond to the speech.
         b.   The speaker must be creative in thinking of ways to adapt the speech to listeners.
   B.   Audience adaptation also takes place during the presentation of the speech.
      1.   No matter how hard a speaker works ahead of time, things do not always go smoothly on the day of the speech.
         a.   Physical circumstances might be different than anticipated.
         b.   The audience might respond differently than anticipated.
      2.   Skillful speakers learn to adapt to these kinds of changes.
         a.   They modify whatever aspect of their speech is necessary to take account of changed physical circumstances.
         b.   They keep an eye out for audience feedback and adjust their remarks accordingly.

Exercises for Critical Thinking *(from text page 134)*

1.   Advertisers are usually very conscious of their audience. Choose an issue of a popular magazine such as *Time, Newsweek, Sports Illustrated, Cosmopolitan,* or the like. From that issue select five advertisements to analyze. Try to determine the audience being appealed to in each advertisement, and analyze the appeals (verbal and visual) used to persuade buyers. How might the appeals differ if the ads were designed to persuade a different audience?

Discussion: Because the audience appeal of most magazine advertisements is quite obvious, this exercise usually promotes vigorous class discussion on the principles of audience analysis and adaptation. In addition, it almost always provokes questions about the ethics of audience adaptation. If you use this exercise, be sure to have students bring a copy of their advertisements to class.

2.   Below are three general speech topics and, for each, two hypothetical audiences to which a speech might be delivered. For each topic, write a brief paragraph explaining how you might adjust your specific purpose and message according to the demographic characteristics of the audience.

   a.   Topic: "Superconductivity"

   Audience #1:   50% physics majors, 30% engineering majors, 20% music majors

   Audience #2:   40% English majors, 40% business majors, 20% physics majors

   Discussion: Audience #1 will likely be more interested in and knowledgeable about the topic than will audience #2. The speaker addressing audience #2 will have to give special attention to gaining attention, to relating the topic to the audience, and to avoiding technical language.

   b.   Topic: "Sexual Assault: The Biggest Campus Crime"

   Audience #1:   80% female, 20% male

   Audience #2:   80% male, 20% female

   Discussion: Although sexual assault is a topic of great interest to both male and female students, the orientations of each toward the topic are usually different. Because women face the threat of sexual assault on a daily basis, a speech to audience #1 might stress steps that women can take to avoid becoming victims of sexual assault. Because men do not face the same personal threat of sexual assault, a speech to audience #2 might seek to sensitize male listeners to the seriousness of the problem, demonstrate that men are not immune from the problem because their wives, sisters, mothers or girlfriends could become victims of sexual assault, and explain steps men can take to make campus a safer place for women students.

c. Topic: "The 1986 *Challenger* Explosion"

    Audience #1:   Day class: 70% age 18 to 22, 30% age 23 and over

    Audience #2:   Evening class: 50% age 35 and over, 30% age 23 to 34, 20% age 18 to 22

> **Discussion:** The space shuttle *Challenger* exploded on January 28, 1986, only 70 seconds after liftoff from Cape Canaveral, Florida, killing all seven crew members and stunning the nation. In addition to being a setback for the U.S. space program and a personal tragedy for the astronauts and their families, the explosion was viewed live in elementary schools across the United States because one of the crew members, Christa McAuliffe, was a teacher who had been chosen especially for this flight.
>
> Although most members of audience #1 have probably seen television footage of the explosion, they are too young to have a firsthand recollection of it or the emotional shock it generated. A speech to this group would have to provide substantial historical information about the explosion and its consequences. Nor can a speaker addressing audience #1 assume that most of his or her listeners will necessarily be interested in the topic.
>
> On the other hand, a speaker addressing audience #2 can assume that most listeners have a fair stock of knowledge about the *Challenger* explosion. Much of the audience lived through the disaster and may recall it rather vividly. They are more likely to be interested in it than audience #1, and they probably will not need a great deal of historical background about it. Finally, the speaker will have to take some account of the 20 percent of this audience who are too young to know much about the crisis.

3. For your next speech, design and circulate among your classmates an audience analysis questionnaire like that discussed on pages 127-130 of the textbook. Use all three kinds of questions explained in the text: fixed-alternative questions, scale questions, and open-ended questions. After you have tabulated the results of the questionnaire, write an analysis explaining what the questionnaire reveals about your audience and what steps you must take to adapt your speech to the audience.

> **Discussion:** Although speakers outside the classroom seldom use questionnaires, this exercise is extremely useful because it requires students to engage in systematic audience analysis. It also requires them to conceive of their classmates as a genuine audience.
>
> This exercise works best in conjunction with the first persuasive speech. You can set aside 5 to 10 minutes at the start of several class meetings to allow students to respond to questionnaires, or you can have students fill in the questionnaires at home and return them at the next class meeting. Finally, I would recommend having students turn in the analyses of their questionnaires at the time they turn in their preparation outlines.

4.   Read Barbara Bush's "Choices and Change" in the appendix of sample speeches following Chapter 18. Focus on how Bush adapts her message to her audience in light of the controversy that preceded her speech. Be prepared to discuss your ideas in class.

> **Discussion:** Barbara Bush's commencement speech at Wellesley College is an excellent study in audience analysis and adaptation. As the discussion at the start of this chapter explains, the choice of Bush as speaker touched off a protest among roughly one-quarter of Wellesley's graduating seniors. The protest in turn sparked a national controversy involving students, educators, politicians, and newspaper editorialists. When Bush rose to speak, she faced an immediate audience that had been polarized by the controversy and many members of which were skeptical, some even hostile, to her appearance at Wellesley.
>
> Instead of pretending there was no controversy, Bush acknowledged it and turned it to her advantage with a deft blend of humor and goodwill. She did not abandon her own views on the issues facing women in American society, but neither did she disparage listeners who held different views. The result is a speech that students find interesting both for its approach to audience adaptation and for its message about the role of women in the United States. Expect a lively discussion on both aspects of the speech.
>
> Have students prepare their analysis based on the transcript of the speech in the textbook. Then, before discussing the speech in class, show students the videotape of the speech from "Commencement Speeches at Wellesley College, June 1, 1990," which is part of the videotape supplement to *The Art of Public Speaking*. If you show the videotape, take advantage of the opportunity to discuss how Bush's delivery helps or hinders the presentation of her message to the audience at Wellesley. Here is a synopsis of the speech:
>
> Introduction: The introduction consists of paragraph 1, in which Bush acknowledges other dignitaries as well as members of her audience. Christine Bicknell, whom Bush calls her "new best friend" was the student speaker who had preceded her on the podium.
>
> Body: The body runs from paragraph 2 through paragraph 17 and contains two main points. The first is developed in paragraphs 2-7. In this section of the speech, Bush praises Wellesley's commitment to diversity, but she does not define diversity in racial, ethnic, or sexual terms. Rather, she characterizes it in general terms as requiring the effort "to learn about and respect difference, to be compassionate with one another, to cherish our own identity, and to accept unconditionally the same in others" (paragraph 7). This is a crucial move, for it allows Bush to identify with a value shared by most of her listeners while at the same time implying that the people opposed to her appearance have not been acting in the true spirit of diversity.

Any potential conflict over this move, however, is quickly dissipated by Bush's good-natured treatment, in paragraph 8, of the fact that Alice Walker had been the senior class' first choice for commencement speaker. In the second half of paragraph 8, Bush introduces her second main point—that Wellesley's seniors will have crucial choices to make as they begin the journey for their own true colors.

As Bush develops this point in paragraphs 9-17, she urges her listeners to make three choices—to get involved in major social issues (paragraph 10), to keep in mind that life is supposed to be fun (paragraphs 11-12), and to cherish their human relationships with family and friends (paragraphs 13-16). Bush spends most of her time on the third choice, and in doing so presents a number of lines that were widely quoted afterward by commentators on the speech.

Paragraph 17 brings the second main point to a close and contains the best known line of the speech, in which Bush says: "Somewhere out in this audience may even be someone who will one day follow in my footsteps, and preside over the White House as the president's spouse. And I wish him well!" Although Bush had used this line in previous speeches, it was new to the audience at Wellesley, and they responded with cheering and prolonged applause. Paragraph 17 is also noteworthy for the way it links the two main points of the speech by referring back to the story in main point one about where the mermaids stand.

Conclusion: The conclusion consists of paragraph 18, in which Bush states that the controversy over her appearance is over but that the conversation on women's issues is only beginning. After thanking the seniors for the "courtesy and honor" of addressing them, Bush closes by saying to the seniors, "may your future be worthy of your dreams."

Applying the Power of Public Speaking *(from text page 135)*

As a university professor, your research, writing, and teaching in the area of gender communication has attracted media attention. It seems that nearly everyone is interested in the differences between the communication styles of men and women. You have been asked to address the managers of a large local manufacturing company on the topic of gender communication in the workplace.

To prepare for your speech, you have scheduled a meeting with the company's human resource director who contacted you. Having taken a public speaking class in college, you know how important it is to analyze the audience you will be addressing. List (1) the three most important questions you want to ask the resource director about the demographics of your audience, and (2) the three most important questions you want to ask about the situational traits of your audience. Be specific in your questions, and be prepared, if necessary, to explain your choice of questions.

Discussion: There is no right or wrong answer to this scenario. Its purpose is to have students see how the principles of audience analysis discussed in the chapter can be applied in real-life situations outside the classroom. As far as demographic audience analysis is concerned, most people would agree that gender is the paramount factor in this scenario. An audience of men may have a different set of attitudes on the subject of gender in the workplace than will an audience of women. Students may also identify age as an important demographic variable. A younger audience is more likely to be "up to date" in its attitudes toward women in the workplace than is an older audience.

Although all the situational factors discussed in the chapter could conceivably come into play in the scenario, the most important is probably the attitude of the audience toward the topic. If the audience has a negative attitude toward the topic (or the fact that they have to divert time from their workday to deal with it), the speaker will need to find ways to allay that negativity and to establish common ground with the audience.

In addition, it would be very helpful to know the size of the audience and the physical setting for the speech. With a small audience, it would be possible to take an informal, interactive approach that would make it easier to communicate with audience members on a personal basis. Physical setting is always something a speaker should inquire about regardless of the other situational or demographic variables. The time of day, the size and configuration of the room, the kinds of facilities for visual aids, and the like will have an impact on almost any speech.

Additional Exercises and Activities

1. Below are six specific purpose statements for classroom speeches. For each specific purpose statement, lead a class discussion that seeks to answer the question: "What steps would a speaker with this specific purpose statement need to take to adapt her or his speech to the interests, knowledge, and attitudes of this class?"

    a.   To inform my audience how they can protect their apartment or dorm room against burglaries.

    b.   To inform my audience about the principles of aerodynamics that allow an airplane to fly.

    c.   To inform my audience about the causes, symptoms, and treatment of eating disorders.

    d.   To persuade my audience that the Social Security system should be modified with a national system of individual retirement accounts.

e.   To persuade my audience that capital punishment should be abolished in all parts of the United States.

f.   To persuade my audience to participate in intramural sports.

> **Discussion:** This is an excellent alternative (or supplement) to Exercise 2 on page 134 of the textbook. While that exercise asks students to generalize about hypothetical listeners, this exercise gets them thinking about a specific real audience—their speech class. As a result, it has two benefits. One, of course, is to expand their understanding of the factors involved in audience analysis and adaptation in general. The second is to give them insight into the audience they will be addressing in their classroom speeches.
>
> This exercise can be conducted entirely in class or, to save time, it can be given to students as a homework assignment. To facilitate classroom discussion, the six specific purpose statements are included in the binder of full-color overhead transparencies that accompanies *The Art of Public Speaking*.

2.   You may wish to have your students prepare a formal demographic analysis of the class. One method is to lead a class discussion in which students create the items for a demographic audience analysis questionnaire. Another method is to give students a questionnaire format such as that on the next page.

> **Discussion:** Although the demographic questionnaire is not as useful for students as creating a situational audience analysis questionnaire, it is a good way to begin to get them attuned to the process of audience analysis. You should be aware, however, that some schools have deemed demographic questionnaires to be an invasion of students' privacy. If you have any doubts about the situation at your school, be sure to check before distributing the questionnaire.

3.   Have students prepare an Audience Analysis and Adaptation Worksheet (see pages 148-149) in conjunction with one or more of their speeches. Hand out the worksheets early, so students can use them throughout the speech preparation process. You can have the students turn in their worksheets at the same time as their initial preparation outlines, or you can require that they be turned in on the day of each student's speech.

> **Discussion:** This is a relatively detailed worksheet, but if students use it conscientiously, it will help them become much more aware of the factors involved in audience analysis and adaptation. To help ensure that students take the worksheet seriously, you should probably make it a graded assignment. Some teachers simply include the worksheet as part of the overall grade for the speech; others assign a separate grade for the worksheet.

Questionnaire for Demographic Audience Analysis

1. Age _____

2. Sex: Male _____   Female_____

3. Relationship status: Married _____   Single _____

                                  Divorced _____   Engaged _____

                                  Widowed _____   Partnered _____

4. Religion _____

5. Race/Ethnic Background _____

6. Year in school: Freshman _____   Sophomore _____

                             Junior _____   Senior _____

7. Major (declared or anticipated) _____

8. Home town _____

    Population _____

9. Campus organizations to which you belong _____

    _____

10. Off-campus organizations to which you belong _____

    _____

    _____

11. Jobs you have held _____

    _____

    _____

    _____

Audience Analysis and Adaptation Worksheet
Part I

Speaker _____   **Topic** _____

What is the audience for this speech? _____

_____

What is the specific purpose of this speech? _____

_____

In choosing a specific purpose, how can you narrow the topic so it will be appropriate to this audience?

_____

_____

Demographic audience analysis: What special adaptation is necessary in the speech because of the audience's

age _____

gender _____

sexual orientation _____

religion _____

racial, ethnic, and cultural background _____

group membership _____

other (specify) _____

Situational audience analysis: What special adaptation is necessary in the speech because of the audience's

size _____

response to the physical setting _____

knowledge about the topic _____

interest level in the topic _____

attitude toward the topic _____

disposition toward the speaker _____

disposition toward the occasion _____

(continued in Part II)

Audience Analysis and Adaptation Worksheet
Part II

Speaker _____   **Topic** _____

Adaptation in the speech: Answer each of the following questions.

What device(s) did you use in the introduction to gain attention from this audience?

_____

_____

What steps did you take to relate the topic directly to this audience in the introduction?

_____

_____

What are the main points of the speech? Why did you develop these particular main points for this audience?

_____

_____

What decisions did you make in choosing supporting materials for this audience?

_____

_____

What steps did you take to make your language clear and appropriate to this audience?

_____

_____

What adjustments did you make in delivery—rate of speech, volume, tone of voice, gestures, and the like—to communicate your ideas to this audience?

_____

_____

_____

Extra Teaching and Learning Resources

General

Barone, Michael. *The New Americans: How the Melting Pot Can Work Again*. New York: Regnery, 2001.

Beamer, Linda, and Varner, Iris. *Intercultural Communication in the Global Workplace*, 2nd ed. New York: McGraw-Hill, 2001.

Borisoff, Deborah, and Merrill, Lisa. *The Power to Communicate: Gender Differences as Barriers*. Prospect Heights, IL: Waveland, 1998.

Brunson, Deborah A. "Talking About Race by Talking About Whiteness." In Stephen E. Lucas (ed.), *Selections from the Communication Teacher, 1999-2002*. New York: McGraw-Hill, 2004, pp. 24-26.

Bucher, Richard D. *Diversity Consciousness: Opening Our Minds to People, Cultures, and Opportunities*. Englewood Cliffs, NJ: Prentice-Hall, 1999.

Deaux, Kay, and LaFrance, Marianne. "Gender." In Gilbert, Daniel T.; Fiske, Susan T.; and Lindzey, Gardner (eds.), *Handbook of Social Psychology*, 4th ed. New York: McGraw-Hill, 1998, Vol. I, pp. 788-828.

Dillard, James Price, and Pfau, Michael (eds.). *The Persuasion Handbook: Developments in Theory and Practice*. Thousand Oaks, CA: Sage, 2002.

Dinnerstein, Leonard; Nichols, Roger L.; and Reimers, David M. *Natives and Strangers: A Multicultural History of Americans*, 4th ed. New York: Oxford University Press, 2003.

Doniger, Wendy (ed.). *Merriam-Webster's Encyclopedia of World Religions*. Springfield, MA: Merriam-Webster, 1999.

Eagly, Alice H., and Chaiken, Shelly. *The Psychology of Attitudes*. Fort Worth, TX: Harcourt Brace Jovanovich, 1993.

Eberly, Rosa A. "Rhetoric and the Anti-Logos Doughball: Teaching Deliberating Bodies the Practices of Deliberatory Democracy." *Rhetoric and Public Affairs*, 5 (2002), pp. 287-300.

Eck, Diana L. *A New Religious America*. New York: HarperCollins, 2001.

Gudykunst, William B., and Moody, Bella (eds.). *Handbook of International and Intercultural Communication*, 2nd ed. Thousand Oaks, CA: Sage, 2002.

Gudykunst, William B., and Young, Yun Kim. *Communicating with Strangers: An Approach to Intercultural Communication*, 4th ed. New York: McGraw-Hill, 2003.

Ivy, Diana K., and Backlund, Phil. *Exploring GenderSpeak: Personal Effectiveness in Gender Communication*, 2nd ed. New York: McGraw-Hill, 2000.

Kurtz, Patricia L. *The Global Speaker: An English Speaker's Guide to Making Presentations Around the World*. New York: Amacom, 1995.

Lustig, Myron W., and Koester, Jolene. *Intercultural Competence: Interpersonal Communication Across Cultures*, 4th ed. Boston: Allyn and Bacon, 2003.

Melton, J. Gordon (ed.). *Encyclopedia of American Religions*, 6th ed. Detroit: Gale, 1998.

Melzer, Arthur M.; Weinberger, J.; and Zinman, Richard M. (eds.). *Multiculturalism and American Democracy*. Lawrence: University Press of Kansas, 1998.

Naylor, Larry (ed.). *Cultural Diversity in the United States*. Westport, CT: Bergin & Garvey, 1997.

O'Keefe, Daniel. J. *Persuasion: Theory and Research*, 2nd ed. Thousand Oaks, CA: Sage, 2002.

Perloff, Richard M. *The Dynamics of Persuasion*. Mahwah, NJ: Lawrence Erlbaum, 2003.

Petty, Richard E., and Wegener, Duane T. "Attitude Change: Multiple Roles for Persuasion Variables." In Gilbert, Daniel T.; Fiske, Susan T.; and Lindzey, Gardner (eds.), *Handbook of Social Psychology*, 4th ed. New York: McGraw-Hill, 1998, Vol. I, pp. 323-390.

Prothero, Stephen R.; Shattuck, H. Gardiner; and Queen, Edward L., III (eds.). *Encyclopedia of American Religious History*. New York: Facts on File, 1996.

Romaine, Suzanne. *Communicating Gender*. Mahwah, NJ: Lawrence Erlbaum, 1999.

Samovar, Larry A., and Porter, Richard E. *Communication Between Cultures*, 4th ed. Belmont, CA: Wadsworth, 2001.

Simons, Herbert W. *Persuasion in Society*. Thousand Oaks, CA: Sage, 2001.

Sitaram, K.S., and Prosser, Michael S. (eds.). *Civic Discourse: Multiculturalism, Cultural Diversity, and Global Communication*. Norwood, NJ: Ablex, 1999.

Sonnenschein, William, and Bell, Arthur H. *The Diversity Toolkit: How You Can Build and Benefit from a Diverse Workforce*. Lincolnwood, IL: Contemporary Books, 1999.

Thau, Richard D., and Heflin, Jay S. (eds.). *Generations Apart: Xers Vs. Boomers Vs. the Elderly*. Amherst, NY: Prometheus Books, 1997.

Valentine, Kristin B.; Hecht, Michael L.; Corey, Frederick; and Jacobsen, Janet L. "Two Measures of Audience Response to Performance." *Communication Reports*, 8 (1995), 170-177.

Wood, Julia T. *Gendered Lives: Communication, Gender, and Culture*, 5th ed. Belmont, CA: Wadsworth, 2003.

Zemke, Ron; Raines, Claire; and Filipczak, Bob. *Generations at Work: Managing the Clash of Veterans, Boomers, Xers, and Nexters in Your Workplace*. New York: Amacom, 1999.

Classroom Activities and Assignments

Bowers, A. Anne, Jr. "When We Become They: Teaching Audience Awareness Skills." In Stephen E. Lucas (ed.), *Selections from the Speech Communication Teacher, 1994-1996*. New York: McGraw-Hill, 1997, pp. 7-8.

Bradford, Lisa, and Uecker, Deborah. "Intercultural Simulations: Enhancing Their Pedagogical Value." In Stephen E. Lucas (ed.), *Selections from the Speech Communication Teacher, 1996-1999*. New York: McGraw-Hill, 2001, pp. 28-34.

Brunson, Deborah A. "A Perceptual Awareness Exercise in Interracial Communication." In Stephen E. Lucas (ed.), *Selections from the Speech Communication Teacher, 1994-1996*. New York: McGraw-Hill, 1997, pp. 18-19.

Dellinger-Pate, Charlene. "A Model for Guiding Intercultural Discussions." In Stephen E. Lucas (ed.), *Selections from the Speech Communication Teacher, 1996-1999*. New York: McGraw-Hill, 2001, pp. 34-35.

Dillon, Randy K. "The Diversity Board." In Stephen E. Lucas (ed.), *Selections from the Speech Communication Teacher, 1996-1999*. New York: McGraw-Hill, 2001, pp. 35-37.

Downey, Sharon D. "Audience Analysis Exercise." In Stephen E. Lucas (ed.), *Selections from the Speech Communication Teacher, 1986-1991*. New York: McGraw-Hill, 1992, pp. 12-13.

Fuller, Linda K. "Participatory Audience Analysis: A Research Technique that Teaches About the Community." In Stephen E. Lucas (ed.), *Selections from the Speech Communication Teacher, 1994-1996*. New York: McGraw-Hill, 1997, pp. 8-9.

Garbowitz, Fred. "Changing Classroom Populations Call for Increased Diversity." In Stephen E. Lucas (ed.), *Selections from the Speech Communication Teacher, 1986-1991*. New York: McGraw-Hill, 1992, pp. 26-27.

Geyerman, Chris B. "Interpretation and the Social Construction of Gender Differences." In Stephen E. Lucas (ed.), *Selections from the Speech Communication Teacher, 1994-1996*. New York: McGraw-Hill, 1997, pp. 22-23.

Hart, Joy L.; Walker, Kandi; and Morgan, Melanie. "Tom Green and MTV: The Cancer Special." In Stephen E. Lucas (ed.), *Selections from the Communication Teacher, 1999-2002*. New York: McGraw-Hill, 2004, pp. 19-20.

Hastings, Sally O. "Increasing Intercultural Empathy: From Principle to Practice." In Stephen E. Lucas (ed.), *Selections from the Speech Communication Teacher, 1996-1999*. New York: McGraw-Hill, 2001, pp. 38-40.

Hawkinson, Ken. "Two Exercises on Diversity and Gender." In Stephen E. Lucas (ed.), *Selections from the Speech Communication Teacher, 1991-1994*. New York: McGraw-Hill, 1995, pp. 24-25.

Langley, Darrell C. "The Heckling Speech." In Stephen E. Lucas (ed.), *Selections from the Speech Communication Teacher, 1986-1991*. New York: McGraw-Hill, 1992, p. 67.

McClarty, Wilma. "Audience Analysis: Go and Tell." In Stephen E. Lucas (ed.), *Selections from the Speech Communication Teacher, 1991-1994*. New York: McGraw-Hill, 1995, p. 12.

McKinney, Bruce C. "Audience Analysis Exercise." In Stephen E. Lucas (ed.), *Selections from the Speech Communication Teacher, 1986-1991*. New York: McGraw-Hill, 1992, p. 13.

Miller, Ann Neville. "Cultural Partners: Diversity and Intercultural Communication Beyond the Classroom." In Stephen E. Lucas (ed.), *Selections from the Speech Communication Teacher, 1996-1999*. New York: McGraw-Hill, 2001, pp. 40-41.

Mohsen, Raed A. "Out on Campus: A Challenging Public Speaking Experience." In Stephen E. Lucas (ed.), *Selections from the Speech Communication Teacher, 1991-1994*. New York: McGraw-Hill, 1995, pp. 56-57.

Neumann, David. "Selecting Messages: An Exercise in Audience Analysis." In Stephen E. Lucas (ed.), *Selections from the Speech Communication Teacher, 1986-1991*. New York: McGraw-Hill, 1992, p. 14.

Pennington, Dorothy L. "A Culture-Based Approach to Teaching African-American Public Address." In Stephen E. Lucas (ed.), *Selections from the Speech Communication Teacher, 1996-1999*. New York: McGraw-Hill, 2001, pp. 41-42.

Portnoy, Enid J. "Gender Communication Scavenger Hunt." In Stephen E. Lucas (ed.), *Selections from the Speech Communication Teacher, 1994-1996*. New York: McGraw-Hill, 1997, pp. 9-10.

Portnoy, Enid J. "Teaching Gender and Communication." In Stephen E. Lucas (ed.), *Selections from the Speech Communication Teacher, 1994-1996*. New York: McGraw-Hill, 1997, pp. 27-28.

Ross, Charlynn. "The Challenging Audience Exercise." In Stephen E. Lucas (ed.), *Selections from the Speech Communication Teacher, 1986-1991*. New York: McGraw-Hill, 1992, p. 69.

Ross, Charlynn. "Suggestions for Teaching International Students." In Stephen E. Lucas (ed.), *Selections from the Speech Communication Teacher, 1986-1991*. New York: McGraw-Hill, 1992, pp. 28-29.

Rowan, Katherine. "The Speech to Explain Difficult Ideas." In Stephen E. Lucas (ed.), *Selections from the Speech Communication Teacher, 1986-1991*. New York: McGraw-Hill, 1992, pp. 69-71.

Schrader, Stuart M. "Increasing Cultural Awareness: Importance of Story Telling in Speech Making." In Stephen E. Lucas (ed.), *Selections from the Speech Communication Teacher, 1996-1999*. New York: McGraw-Hill, 2001, pp. 44-45.

Schumer, Allison. "Helping International Students Adapt to American Communication Norms." In Stephen E. Lucas (ed.), *Selections from the Speech Communication Teacher, 1986-1991*. New York: McGraw-Hill, 1992, p. 30.

Smith, Donald C. "Look Who's Listening: The Importance of Sub-Audiences in Public Speaking." In Stephen E. Lucas (ed.), *Selections from the Speech Communication Teacher, 1994-1996*. New York: McGraw-Hill, 1997, p. 10.

Stern, Rick. "Audience Spinouts." In Stephen E. Lucas (ed.), *Selections from the Speech Communication Teacher, 1986-1991*. New York: McGraw-Hill, 1992, pp. 14-15.

Yook, Eunkyong Lee. "An Experiential Approach to Diversity Education." In Stephen E. Lucas (ed.), *Selections from the Speech Communication Teacher, 1996-1999*. New York: McGraw-Hill, 2001, pp. 45-46.

Films and Videos

"The Audience." Insight Media (1997). 30 minutes.

"Communication Skills in a Multicultural World." Insight Media (1994). 20 minutes.

"Cross-Cultural Communication." Insight Media (2002). 24 minutes.

"Cross-Cultural Communication in Diverse Settings." Insight Media (1992). 60 minutes.

"The Cross-Cultural Conference Room." Insight Media (2002). 35 minutes.

"Cross-Cultural Understanding." Insight Media (1999). 45 minutes.

"Developing Cultural Sensitivity." Insight Media (1992). 30 minutes.

"disAbility Awareness." Insight Media (1999). 19 minutes.

"Diversity Series." Quality Media Resources (1993). Four-module set; 20 minutes per module.

"Diversity Through Character." CRM Films (1996). 17 minutes.

"Doing Business Internationally." CRM Films (1992). 43 minutes.

"Gender and Communication: She Talks, He Talks." Insight Media (1994). 22 minutes.

"He Said, She Said: Gender, Language, and Communication." Insight Media (2001). 50 minutes.

"Intercultural Communicating." Insight Media (1999). 41 minutes.

"Intercultural Communication." Insight Media (1997). 30 minutes.

"Invisible Rules: Men, Women, and Teams." CRM Films (1996). 34 minutes.

"Managing Across Cultures." Insight Media (1992). 30 minutes.

"Managing Diversity." CRM Films (1991). 22 minutes.

"Negotiating Cultural Communication." Insight Media (2001). 60 minutes.

"A Peacock in the Land of Penguins." CRM Films (1995). 10 minutes.

"The Power Dead-Even Rule and Other Gender Differences in the Workplace." CRM Films (1996), 36 minutes.

"A Tale of 'O,'" revised edition. CRM Films (1993). 18 minutes.

"Valuing Diversity: Multicultural Communication." Insight Media (1994). 49 minutes.

"A World of Diversity." Insight Media (1996). Two volumes; 45 minutes.

"A World of Gestures." University of California Extension Center for Media and Independent Learning (1991). 28 minutes.

Chapter 6 Gathering Materials

Chapter Objectives

After reading this chapter, students should be able to:

1. Explain how drawing on their own knowledge and experience can enrich their speeches.

2. Explain the major resources available for researching speeches in the library.

3. Explain how to use the Internet for speech research efficiently and responsibly.

4. Delineate the three stages of interviewing and explain the responsibilities of the interviewer at each stage.

5. Follow the five tips for doing research discussed in the chapter.

Chapter Outline

I.   A speaker's own knowledge and experience can be a valuable resource for information on a speech topic *(text pages 138-139)*.
   A. We usually speak best about topics with which we are familiar.
   B. Supplementing facts and figures from books with personal experience can add color and emotion to a speech.

II. Library research is an important source of material for speeches *(text pages 139-147)*.
   A. Librarians are an excellent resource.
      1. They can help locate specific information.
      2. They can also identify specialized research sources.

B. The catalog lists all the books, periodicals, and other resources owned by the library.
   1. Most catalogues allow users to search by author, title, subject, or keyword.
   2. The key to finding a book on the shelves is the call number.
C. Periodical databases are indispensable for finding articles in magazines and journals.
   1. Depending on the database, users may be able to call up the full text of articles.
   2. Most databases provide an abstract that summarizes the content of each article.
   3. There are two major types of periodical databases: special and general.
D. Newspapers are invaluable for research on many topics.
   1. Local newspapers can usually be found in the periodicals room.
   2. Articles from national and international newspapers can be found on databases such as ProQuest Newspapers, LexisNexis Academic Universe, and Global NewsBank.
   3. Another excellent resource is *Editorials on File*, which reprints editorials from hundreds of U.S. newspapers.
E. Reference works contain a wealth of information about almost any topic.
   1. Encyclopedias provide accurate, objective information on a wide range of subjects.
      a. General encyclopedias offer articles about all branches of human knowledge.
      b. Special encyclopedias are devoted to specific subjects and are more detailed than general encyclopedias.
   2. Yearbooks are annual publications that are invaluable for current information.
      a. The *Statistical Abstract* is the standard source for numerical information on life in the United States.
      b. The *World Almanac and Book of Facts* includes data from international sources.
      c. *Facts on File* covers national and international news events.
   3. Dictionaries offer a wide range of information about language.
      a. Some dictionaries, such as *Webster's*, define words currently in use.
      b. Others, such as the *Oxford English Dictionary*, provide histories of words or phrases.
   4. Quotation books can be useful, especially for introductions and conclusions.
      a. The best-known quotation book is *Bartlett's Familiar Quotations*.
      b. There are also many specialized quotation books.
   5. Biographical aids provide information about people in the news.
      a. Works such as *International Who's Who* and *Who's Who of American Women* contain brief life and career facts.
      b. *Current Biography* provides more detailed information.
   6. Atlases and gazetteers provide geographical information.
      a. Atlases contain maps, charts, and tables about all parts of the world.

        b.   Gazetteers follow the same alphabetical format as dictionaries, but all the entries deal with geographical topics.

III.   When used responsibly and efficiently, the Internet can be a powerful tool for speech research *(text pages 147-157)*.

    A.   There are three major kinds of search aids for locating information on the Web.

        1.   Search engines index Web pages and comb through them to find what a researcher wants.

            a.   Each search engine works a little differently and indexes different pages.

            b.   Researchers may need to use more than one search engine to find what they need.

        2.   Metasearch engines send a researcher's request to several search engines at the same time.

            a.   Metasearch engines allow researchers to cast a broader net than with a single search engine.

            b.   Metasearch engines are especially useful when looking for something very obscure.

        3.   Virtual libraries combine Internet technology with traditional library methods of cataloguing and assessing data.

            a.   Virtual libraries have been established by librarians and other information professionals.

            b.   Though much smaller than commercial search engines, virtual libraries are the best tools for locating reliable, high-quality Web resources.

    B.   Regardless of the kind of search aid one chooses, it should be used systematically and efficiently.

        1.   One approach is to conduct a keyword search.

            a.   Each search engine has its own procedures for efficient keyword searches.

            b.   Following those procedures is especially important for searches involving multiple words.

        2.   Another approach is to conduct a subject search.

            a.   Searching by subject is often more efficient than conducting a keyword search.

            b.   The most popular subject-based search engine is Yahoo.

    C.   Whether one researches by subject or by keyword, it is vital to have a method of keeping track of useful looking sources.

        1.   Each Web site is identified by its URL (Uniform Resource Locator).

        2.   The URL can be recorded either by hand or by bookmarking it electronically.

    D.   The Internet also contains many specialized resources for researching a speech.

        1.   It provides handy access to government documents and publications.

        2.   It has a number of sites for basic reference information.

        3.   It contains many sites for information about news and current events.

        4.   It is a rich source of material on topics with multicultural dimensions.

    E.   There are three primary criteria for evaluating the quality of documents found on the Internet.

        1.   If possible, one should assess the objectivity and expertise of a document's author.

        2.   If there is no identifiable author, one should assess the sponsoring organization that produced the document.

        3.   Regardless of authorship or sponsorship, it is important to check the recency of the document.

    F.   Research materials found on the Internet need to be cited both in the speech bibliography and in the speech itself.

        1.   Bibliography citations should include the author, title, date of publication, URL, and date the document was accessed.

           a.   One format for bibliographical citation is taken from the American Psychological Association (APA).

           b.   Another format is taken from the Modern Language Association (MLA).

        2.   Citing Internet sources in the speech is just as important as citing print sources.

           a.   It would take too much time to include all the information included on the bibliographic citation.

           b.   On the other hand, a speaker should not simply say, "As I found on the Internet."

           c.   Oral citations should identify the author or sponsoring organization, as well as the Web site on which the information was found.

IV.   Interviewing people with specialized knowledge is another way to gather materials for a speech *(text pages 158-162)*.

    A.   The first stage in the interviewing process takes place before the interview.

        1.   The interview process begins when a speaker formulates a purpose for the interview.

        2.   Once the purpose of the interview is clear, a speaker must decide whom to interview and set up an appointment with that person.

        3.   Next the speaker needs to decide whether or not to record the interview.

           a.   The major advantage of recording an interview is that recording makes it easy to check for direct quotes and important facts.

           b.   Even when a recorder is used, the interviewer should take notes in case the recorder malfunctions.

           c.   It is unethical to record an interview without the knowledge or consent of the person being interviewed.

        4.   The most important task before the interview is preparing the questions to be asked.

           a.   Avoid leading questions, hostile questions, and questions that can be answered without the interview.

           b.   Phrase tough questions as neutrally as possible and save them until near the end of the interview.

           c.   Arrange questions in the order they are to be asked and go to the interview with a list of questions.

B.   The second stage of the interview process takes place during the interview itself.
    1.   It is important to dress appropriately and to show up on time.
    2.   It is a good idea at the outset to restate the purpose of the interview so as to refresh the interviewee's memory.
    3.   If the interviewee consents to having the interview recorded, the equipment should be set up quickly and inconspicuously.
    4.   The most important part of the interview is asking the questions.
        a.   Effective interviewers keep on track by making sure they cover the questions on their prearranged list.
        b.   At the same time, they take advantage of opportunities to ask follow-up questions or to pursue new information.
    5.   In addition to asking good questions, the interviewer must listen carefully to the answers.
        a.   Effective interviewers will ask for clarification if an answer is unclear.
        b.   They will also double check if they have questions about a quotation.
    6.   Finally, the interviewer should try not to exceed the stipulated time period for the interview.

C.   The third stage of the interview process takes place after the interview.
    1.   While the interview is still fresh, the researcher should review her or his notes.
        a.   Effective interviewers try to discover the main points that emerged during the interview.
        b.   They also try to identify specific information that may be useful in the speech.
        c.   If anything is unclear, the interviewer should call the interviewee to check the facts.
    2.   As soon as possible after the interview, the researcher should transcribe ideas and information from the interview into the same format as the rest of her or his research notes.

V.   Regardless of which resources speakers rely on in gathering speech materials, there are several ways to make their research more productive *(text pages 163-168)*.
  A.   It is imperative that speakers begin their research early.
    1.   Starting early helps ensure that there will be adequate time to conduct thorough research.
    2.   Starting early also allows the speaker time to think about and organize materials gathered during the research process.
  B.   Speakers should create a preliminary bibliography of research sources.
    1.   A preliminary bibliography lists every source that looks as if it might be helpful in preparing the speech.
    2.   It is longer than the final bibliography, which lists only those sources that are actually used in the speech.
  C.   Speakers can save time and energy by taking research notes efficiently.
    1.   They should take plenty of notes.
    2.   They should record notes in a consistent format and make a subject heading for each note.

3. They should make a separate entry for each note.
4. They should distinguish among direct quotations, paraphrases, and their own ideas.
5. They should use index cards if they record notes by hand.

D. The research process is most productive when speakers think about their materials as they research.
1. Doing research is more than a mechanical routine.
2. It involves creativity to find interesting information.
3. It involves critical thinking in assessing research materials and their relationship to the speech topic.

Exercises for Critical Thinking *(from text pages 170-171)*

1. Using one of the general periodical databases discussed on pages 140-141 of the textbook, find three magazine or journal articles on the topic of your next speech. Prepare a preliminary bibliography entry for each article. Read the full text of the articles and assess their value for your speech.

> **Discussion:** It is astounding how many college students have never used a general periodical database such as the *Readers' Guide Full Text*, *ProQuest Research Library*, or *Academic Search*. This exercise is meant to remedy that situation and to help students get started on researching their next speech.

2. Using one of the news databases discussed on pages 143-144 of the textbook, find three magazine or journal articles on the topic of your next speech. Prepare a preliminary bibliography entry for each article. Read the full text of the articles and assess their value for your speech.

> **Discussion:** Newspapers can be great sources for speech information—especially on topics that deal with current events. This exercise gives students an opportunity to familiarize themselves with the newspaper resources available in the library.

3. Using the procedures for keyword searches explained on page 150 of the textbook, find three Internet documents on the topic of your next speech and prepare a preliminary bibliography entry for each document. Assess all three documents in light of the criteria discussed on pages 155-157 of the textbook for evaluating Internet documents. Be specific.

> **Discussion:** It is vital that students think critically about their research materials, and this is particularly true of materials found on the Internet. As explained on pages 155-157 of the textbook, it is imperative to evaluate the authorship, sponsorship, and recency of Web documents. If you have students do this exercise as a homework assignment, you can use the class discussion to clarify how to conduct research on the Web efficiently and responsibly.

4.   Plan to conduct an interview for one of your classroom speeches. Be sure to follow the guidelines presented in this chapter for effective interviewing. Afterward, evaluate the interview. Did you prepare for it adequately? Did you get the information you needed? What would you do differently if you could conduct the interview again?

> **Discussion:** This exercise is most applicable if you assign students to conduct a research interview for one of their speeches. Having students write evaluations of their interviews requires them to think systematically about the interview process.

5.   This exercise is designed to give you firsthand experience with some of the major reference works discussed on pages 144-147 of the textbook. Your task is to answer each of the following questions. Some of the questions indicate where you will find the answer, and some do not. If necessary, look back through the chapter to see in which reference works you are most likely to find the answers. For each question, record both your answer and where you found it.

a.   According to the *Oxford English Dictionary*, what are the origins of "terrorism" as a political term?

> ("Terrorism" as a political term was first applied to the Jacobins and their agents and partisans in the French Revolution, especially to those connected with the revolutionary tribunals during the "Reign of Terror." *Oxford English Dictionary*, 2nd ed., Vol. 17, pp. 820-821.)

b.   What is the opening quotation by Jordan's Queen Rania in the article about her in the 2001 *Current Biography Yearbook*?

> (The opening quotation is: "I am an Arab through and through, but I am also one who speaks the international language." *Current Biography Yearbook 2001*, p. 434.)

c.   How many U.S. towns or cities are named Paris, and in which states are they located?

> (There are eight U.S. towns or cities named Paris. They are located in Arkansas, Idaho, Illinois, Kentucky, Maine, Missouri, Tennessee, and Texas. *Merriam-Webster's Geographical Dictionary*, 3rd ed., p. 905.)

d.   As explained in the *Encyclopedia of Computer Science*, where and when were the first e-mail messages sent?

   (The first e-mail messages were sent in 1971 during an experiment by Ray Tomlinson in a Bolt Beranen and Newman laboratory. *Encyclopedia of Computer Science*, 4th ed., p. 640.)

e.   What does the *Latino Encyclopedia* identify as the origins of El Día de la Raza?

   (El Día de la Raza, or "The Day of the Race," was the name given to Columbus Day in Latin America as part of the Hispanidad movement that began in 1892. The *Latino Encyclopedia*, Vol. 2, p. 475.)

f.   According to the 2001 *Statistical Abstract of the United States*, what percentage of people 18 to 34 years old had Internet access at home or at work in 2000? What was the percentage for people 55 years old and over?

   (During the year 2000, 37.9 percent of people 18-34 years old had Internet access at home or work. In contrast, only 16.2 percent of people 55 years old and over had Internet access at home or work. *Statistical Abstract of the United States: 2001*, p. 719.)

g.   What were listed in *Facts on File* as the three top-rated prime-time U.S. television programs for the period April 29 to June 2, 2002?

   (The three top-rated television programs for the period April 29– June 2, 2002, were *Friends*, *ER*, and *CSI: Crime Scene Investigation*. *Facts on File*, June 6, 2002, p. 428.)

h.   As explained in the *Asian American Encyclopedia*, what is the global Hmong population, and how many Hmong clans are there?

   (There are 6 million Hmong worldwide, and there are 23 Hmong clans. *The Asian American Encyclopedia*, Vol. 2, p. 593.)

i.   What is the definition of "fog" in the *McGraw-Hill Encyclopedia of Science and Technology*?

(Fog is defined as "A cloud comprising waterdroplets or (less commonly) ice crystals formed near the ground and resulting in visibility to below 0.6 mi (1km)." *McGraw-Hill Encyclopedia of Science and Technology*, 7th ed., Vol. 7, p. 235.)

Discussion: This is an excellent way to acquaint students with reference sources they otherwise might not employ. Under ideal circumstances, each student would complete the exercise working alone. Practically, however, this is seldom possible. One alternative is to divide the class into groups and have each group be responsible for tracking down answers. This can be followed by a class discussion comparing the groups' answers. Another alternative is to assign each student two or three specific questions to answer. Whichever method you use, you will probably need more than the nine questions included in the textbook. Therefore, two more sets of questions are included among the Additional Exercises/Activities below.

If you assign this exercise, it is probably a good idea to alert the librarians in the reference section a few days ahead of time. They may also appreciate receiving a copy of the exercise. This will allow them to make whatever special preparations may be necessary to help your students.

Applying the Power of Public Speaking *(from text page 171)*

Your eight-year-old daughter has recently been diagnosed as being allergic to latex, making her one of the growing number of people nationwide with this serious condition. After speaking with other parents in your daughter's school, you discover there are several other children with latex allergies. For the last year an informal group has been meeting to exchange ideas on balancing treatment plans and preventive strategies while maintaining regular family life. Now you have volunteered to do research on whether there is a national support network for people with latex allergies and how you can contact them about setting up for your own formal organization.

Find the information you need by conducting a subject search through the Librarians' Index to the Internet.

Discussion: The purpose of this scenario is to help students see how the skills of Internet research discussed in the chapter can be applied in real-life situations outside the classroom. I specify searching through the Librarians' Index to the Internet so as to give students a chance to become acquainted with a search aid other than one of the commercial search engines.

At the time this edition went to press, the path to the information specified in the scenario was as follows: (1) Access the Librarians' Index to the Internet homepage at http://lii.org and click on Health and Medicine, followed by Diseases and Conditions. (2) Select Allergy on the resulting screen. (3) When the next screen appears, click on AllAllergy.net, for a directory of links to allergy-related resources. (4) When the AllAllergy screen comes up, click Overview and choose Support Groups from the menu on the subsequent screen. (6) Then click on ALERT Latex Allergy Support Groups for the American Latex Allergy Association homepage. (7) When the page appears, select Nationwide Support for a list of local support contacts.

Of course, using a search aid other than the Librarian's Index to the Internet would result in a different path to the desired information. For an interesting variation on this exercise, assign different search aids to different students. Have each student keep track of the path he or she follows to find the required information. Focus class discussion on the differences in ease and quality of results from search aid to search aid.

Additional Exercises and Activities

1.   Arrange for your students to take a tour of the campus library. Students should read Chapter 6 before the tour, and they should be assigned application exercises from the chapter after the tour.

Discussion: Because so many students do not know how to use the library efficiently, this activity is extremely beneficial. Not only are most libraries pleased to conduct such a tour, but they are quite adept at orienting it to the specific needs of individual classes. Arrange the tour two or three weeks in advance. Then contact the library a few days before the tour to indicate whether your students are mostly freshmen, sophomores, juniors, or seniors; what research tasks they will face in preparing their speeches; and any special features of the library you wish to have stressed on the tour. Students usually find the tour so helpful that, at the end of the term, they often rank it—and the development of their research skills— among the most valuable aspects of their speech class.

2.   Answer each of the following questions. Some of the questions indicate where the answer can be found, and some do not. If necessary, recheck Chapter 6 of the textbook to see in which reference sources you are most likely to find the answers. For each question, record both your answer and where you found it, following the format on page 170 of the textbook.

a.   As stated in *My Soul Looks Back, 'Less I Forget*, who said, "Education is a ladder"?

b.   According to an editorial from *The Union Leader* dated December 6, 2002, and reprinted in *Editorials on File*, the Department of Homeland Security's surveillance and information collecting responsibilities may result in an increased risk of what type of crime against Americans?

c.   What is the e-mail address of Russian politician Vladimir Aleksandrovich Ryzhkov?

d.   According to the 2001 *Statistical Abstract of the United States*, how many new cases of breast cancer were estimated to occur in 2001?

e.   As stated in the *Guinness Encyclopedia of Popular Music,* what did former *Rolling Stone* critic Jon Landau say about Bruce Springsteen in 1974?

f.   According to the *2003 World Almanac and Book of Facts,* what were the three best-selling U.S. magazines as of 2001?

g.   As stated in the *Dictionary of Hispanic Biography*, how many times did Ellen Ochoa, the first Mexican-American astronaut, change her major as a college student?

h.   According to the *McGraw-Hill Encyclopedia of Science and Technology*, what is the most active month for tornadoes, and what percentage of the annual number of tornadoes occurs during this month?

i.   What is the first entry under "Rome" in *Merriam Webster's Geographical Dictionary*?

j.   According to the *Encyclopedia of World Crime*, Edward Tinker was the first person in the United States to commit what crime?

Answers to Additional Exercise 2:

a.   As stated in *My Soul Looks Back, 'Less I Forget*, who said, "Education is a ladder"?

> (The statement "Education is a ladder" was uttered by Manuelito of the Navahos in a speech given to Congress in 1865. *My Soul Looks Back, 'Less I Forget: A Collection of Quotations by People of Color*, page 111.)

b.   According to an editorial from *The Union Leader* dated December 6, 2002, and reprinted in *Editorials on File*, the Department of Homeland Security's surveillance and information collecting responsibilities may result in an increased risk of what type of crime against Americans?

> (According to *The Union Leader*, the Department of Homeland Security's surveillance and information collecting responsibilities may result in an increased risk of identity theft against Americans. *Editorials on File*, Volume 33, page 1429.)

c.   What is the e-mail address of Russian politician Vladimir Aleksandrovich Ryzhkov?

> (Vladimir Aleksandrovich Ryzhkov's e-mail address is ryzhkov@duma.gov.ru. *International Who's Who, 2002*, page 1339.)

d.   According to the 2001 *Statistical Abstract of the United States*, how many new cases of breast cancer were estimated to occur in 2001?

> (It was estimated that 194,000 new cases of breast cancer would occur in 2001. *Statistical Abstract of the United States, 2001*, page 125.)

e.   As stated in the *Guinness Encyclopedia of Popular Music*, what did former *Rolling Stone* critic Jon Landau say about Bruce Springsteen in 1974?

> (In 1974 Jon Landau said, "I saw rock 'n' roll future, and its name is Bruce Springsteen." *Guinness Encyclopedia of Popular Music*, 2nd edition, Volume 5, page 3919.)

f.   According to the *2003 World Almanac and Book of Facts*, what were the three best-selling U.S. magazines as of 2001?

> (The three best-selling U.S. magazines as of 2001 were *Reader's Digest, TV Guide,* and *Better Homes and Gardens. 2003 World Almanac and Book of Facts,* page 275.)

g.   As stated in the *Dictionary of Hispanic Biography*, how many times did Ellen Ochoa, the first Mexican-American astronaut, change her major as a college student?

> (Ellen Ochoa changed her major five times. *Dictionary of Hispanic Biography,* page 618.)

h.   According to the *McGraw-Hill Encyclopedia of Science and Technology*, what is the most active month for tornadoes, and what percentage of the annual number of tornadoes occurs during this month?

> (May is the most active month, with 20 percent of the annual number of tornadoes. *McGraw-Hill Encyclopedia of Science and Technology,* 7th edition, Volume 18, page 438.)

i.   What is the first entry under "Rome" in *Merriam Webster's Geographical Dictionary*?

> (The first entry under "Rome" is for the city of Rome in Floyd County, Georgia. *Merriam Webster's Geographical Dictionary,* 3rd ed., page 1001.)

j.   According to the *Encyclopedia of World Crime*, Edward Tinker was the first person in the United States to commit what crime?

> (Edward Tinker was the first U.S. ship captain to attempt insurance fraud by sinking his ship. *Encyclopedia of World Crime,* Volume 4, page 2956.)

3.   Answer each of the following questions. Some of the questions indicate where the answer can be found, and some do not. If necessary, recheck Chapter 6 of the textbook to see in which reference sources you are most likely to find the answers. For each question, record both your answer and where you found it, following the format on page 170 of the textbook.

a.   As listed in volume 33 of the *Alternative Press Index*, where can you find an article titled "Is Your Bathtub a Toxic Dump? Fluoride in the Bath Water"?

b.   The right to privacy is limited by competing rights. Name two of the competing rights identified in the *Routledge Encyclopedia of Philosophy*.

c.   According to the *Dictionary of Feminist Theory*, the phrase "first wave" usually refers to what?

d.   Who said, "We must not confuse dissent with disloyalty"—and in what year?

e.   According to the 2003 edition of the *World Almanac and Book of Facts*, what percentage of U.S. households had cellular phones in 2001?

f.   What does *International Who's Who* list as the birth date and occupation of Jerzy Duda-Gracz?

g.   As noted in the article on Korean-American women in *The Asian-American Encyclopedia*, when did the first wave of Korean immigration to the U.S. occur?

h.   What is the final theory identified in the *Morris Dictionary of Word and Phrase Origins* for the genesis of the phrase "knock on wood"?

i.   According to *Native American Women: A Biographical Dictionary*, where does Laura Tohe live and what is the rough translation of her Navajo name?

j.   There is an Orange County in eight U.S. states. Which states are they?

Answers to Additional Exercise 3:

a.   As listed in volume 33 of the *Alternative Press Index*, where can you find an article titled "Is Your Bathtub a Toxic Dump? Fluoride in the Bath Water"?

   ("Is Your Bathtub a Toxic Dump? Fluoride in the Bath Water" was published in the Summer 2001 issue of *Earth Island Journal*. *Alternative Press Index*, Volume 33, page 677.)

b.   The right to privacy is limited by competing rights. Name two of the competing rights identified in the *Routledge Encyclopedia of Philosophy*.

   (The right to privacy is limited by freedom of speech and freedom of the press. *Routledge Encyclopedia of Philosophy*, Volume 7, page 691.)

c.   According to the *Dictionary of Feminist Theory*, the phrase "first wave" usually refers to what?

   (The phrase "first wave" usually refers to the mobilization of the suffrage movement in America and England between 1880 and 1920. *Dictionary of Feminist Theory*, 2nd edition, page 98.)

d.   Who said, "We must not confuse dissent with disloyalty"—and in what year?

   (Broadcaster Edward R. Murrow said, "We must not confuse dissent with disloyalty" in 1954. *Bartlett's Familiar Quotations*, 15th edition, page 872.)

e.   According to the 2003 edition of the *World Almanac and Book of Facts*, what percentage of U.S. households had cellular phones in 2001?

   (Sixty-six percent of U.S. households had cellular phones in 2001. *2003 World Almanac and Book of Facts*, page 231.)

f.   What does *International Who's Who* list as the birth date and occupation of Jerzy Duda-Gracz?

(The birth date of Polish painter Jerzy Duda-Gracz is March 20, 1941. *International Who's Who*, 2002, page 421.)

g.   As noted in the article on Korean-American women in *The Asian-American Encyclopedia*, when did the first wave of Korean immigration to the U.S. occur?

(The first wave of Korean immigration to the U.S. occurred during the years 1903-1910. *The Asian-American Encyclopedia*, Volume 3, page 868.)

h.   What is the final theory identified in the *Morris Dictionary of Word and Phrase Origins* for the genesis of the phrase "knock on wood"?

(The final theory in the *Morris Dictionary of Word and Phrase Origins* for the genesis of "knock on wood" traces the phrase to the Spanish Inquisition of the 1490s: "During that time Jews were in flight and since temples and synagogues were built of wood, they evolved a code to use in knocking on doors to gain admission. Since this resulted in lives being saved, it became commonplace to *knock on wood* for good luck." *Morris Dictionary of Word and Phrase Origins*, 2nd edition, pages 336-337.)

i.   According to *Native American Women: A Biographical Dictionary*, where does Laura Tohe live and what is the rough translation of her Navajo name?

(Laura Tohe lives in Omaha, Nebraska, and her Navajo name translates roughly to Woman Among Warriors. *Native American Women: A Biographical Dictionary*, page 262.)

j.   There is an Orange County in eight U.S. states. Which states are they?

(California, Florida, Indiana, New York, North Carolina, Texas, Vermont, and Virginia all have an Orange County. *Merriam Webster's Geographical Dictionary*, 3rd edition, page 873.)

Extra Teaching and Learning Resources

General

Alexander, Janet E., and Tate, Marsha Ann. *Web Wisdom: How to Evaluate and Create Information Quality on the Web*. Mahwah, NJ: Lawrence Erlbaum, 1999.

Berkman, Robert I. *Find It Fast: How to Uncover Expert Information on Any Subject Online or in Print*. New York: Harper Resource, 2000.

Booth, Wayne; Colomb Gregory G.; and Williams, Joseph M. *The Craft of Research*. Chicago: University of Chicago Press, 1995.

Callahan, Christopher. *A Journalist's Guide to the Internet*, 2nd ed. Boston: Allyn and Bacon, 2002.

Gibaldi, Joseph. *MLA Handbook for Writers of Research Papers*, 5th ed. New York: Modern Language Association, 1999.

Harnack, Andrew, and Kleppinger, Eugene. *Online! A Reference Guide to Using Internet Sources*. New York: St. Martins, 2001.

Hock, Randolph. *The Extreme Searcher's Guide to Web Search Engines: A Handbook for the Serious Researcher*, 2nd ed. Medford, NJ: Information Today, 2001.

Katz, William A. *Introduction to Reference Work*, 8th ed. New York: McGraw-Hill, 2001.

Mann, Thomas. *The Oxford Guide to Library Research*. New York: Oxford University Press, 1998.

McGuire, Mary; Stillborne, Linda; McAdams, Melinda; and Hyatt, Laurel. *The Internet Handbook for Writers, Researchers, and Journalists, 2002/2003 Edition*. New York: Guilford, 2002.

Metter, Ellen. *Facts in a Flash: A Research Guide for Writers*. Cincinnati: Writer's Digest Books, 1999.

Metzler, Ken. *Creative Interviewing: The Writer's Guide to Gathering Information by Asking Questions*, 3rd ed. Boston: Allyn and Bacon, 1997.

Publication Manual of the American Psychological Association, 5th ed. Washington, D.C.: American Psychological Association, 2001.

Schlein, Alan M. *Find It Online: The Complete Guide to Online Research*. Tempe, AZ: Facts on Demand Press, 2001.

Sherman, Chris, and Price, Gary. *The Invisible Web: Uncovering Information Sources Search Engines Can't See*. Medford, NJ: Information Today, 2001.

Stewart, Charles J. "Teaching Interviewing." In Vangelisti, Anita L.; Daly, John A.; and Friedrich, Gustav W. (eds.), *Teaching Communication: Theory, Research, and Methods*, 2nd ed. Mahwah, NJ: Lawrence Erlbaum, 1999, pp. 181-193.

Stewart, Charles J., and Cash, William B., Jr. *Interviewing: Principles and Practices*, 10th ed. New York: McGraw-Hill, 2003.

Weiss, Robert S. *Learning from Strangers: The Art and Method of Qualitative Interview Studies*. New York: Free Press, 1995.

Wells, Amy Tracy; Calcari, Susan; and Koplow, Travis. *The Amazing Internet Challenge: How Leading Projects Use Library Skills to Organize the Web*. Chicago: American Library Association, 1999.

Classroom Activities and Assignments

Boatman, Sara A. "Introducing Communication Resources." In Stephen E. Lucas (ed.), *Selections from the Speech Communication Teacher, 1994-1996*. New York: McGraw-Hill, 1997, pp. 60-61.

DeHart, Joan. "Self-Contained Library Tour." In Stephen E. Lucas (ed.), *Selections from the Speech Communication Teacher, 1994-1996*. New York: McGraw-Hill, 1997, p. 61.

Garrett, Roger L. "Helping Students Discover Interviewing Skills." In Stephen E. Lucas (ed.), *Selections from the Speech Communication Teacher, 1986-1991*. New York: McGraw-Hill, 1992, pp. 37-38.

Gellis, Mark. "Teaching Research, Teaching Speech." In Stephen E. Lucas (ed.), *Selections from the Communication Teacher, 1999-2002*. New York: McGraw-Hill, 2004, pp. 65-67.

Hankins, Gail. "Gathering Materials: A Three-Course Solution to a One-Course Problem." In Stephen E. Lucas (ed.), *Selections from the Speech Communication Teacher, 1991-1994*. New York: McGraw-Hill, 1995, p. 47.

Herzog, Robert L. "Library Research Assignment." In Stephen E. Lucas (ed.), *Selections from the Speech Communication Teacher, 1994-1996*. New York: McGraw-Hill, 1997, pp. 61-62.

Holton, Susan A. "Who Am I? A Personalized Introduction to Research." In Stephen E. Lucas (ed.), *Selections from the Speech Communication Teacher, 1994-1996*. New York: McGraw-Hill, 1997, pp. 62-63.

Hugenberg, Lawrence W., and O'Neill, Daniel J. "Researching National Issues Forum Topics." In Stephen E. Lucas (ed.), *Selections from the Speech Communication Teacher, 1991-1994*. New York: McGraw-Hill, 1995, pp. 47-48.

Kent, Michael L. "Getting the Most from Your Search Engine." In Stephen E. Lucas (ed.), *Selections from the Communication Teacher, 1999-2002*. New York: McGraw-Hill, 2004, pp.68-70.

Kent, Michael L. "How to Evaluate Web Site Validity and Reliability." In Stephen E. Lucas (ed.), *Selections from the Speech Communication Teacher, 1996-1999*. New York: McGraw-Hill, 2001, pp. 78-79.

Sellnow, Timothy L. "An Oral History Exercise for the Self-Evaluation of Interview Skills." In Stephen E. Lucas (ed.), *Selections from the Speech Communication Teacher, 1991-1994*. New York: McGraw-Hill, 1995, pp. 24-25.

Wright, Mark H., and Wilson, Susan R. "An Interview Analysis Project for Public Speaking Classes." In Stephen E. Lucas (ed.), *Selections from the Speech Communication Teacher, 1991-1994*. New York: McGraw-Hill, 1995, pp. 35-36.

Films and Videos

"Crediting Your Sources." RMI Media Productions (1991). 30 minutes.

"Doing Great Research." Insight Media (1996). 16 minutes.

"Finding Information." Insight Media (1997). 30 minutes.

"Getting Facts from Interviews." Films for the Humanities and Sciences (1992). 15 minutes.

"Hate and the Internet: Web Sites and the Issue of Free Speech." Films for the Humanities and Sciences (1998). 22 minutes.

"Research Basics on the Internet." Films for the Humanities and Sciences (1999). 19 minutes.

"The Top 10½ Tips for Thinking Critically." Insight Media (1999). 15 minutes.

Chapter 7 Supporting Your Ideas

Chapter Objectives

After reading this chapter, students should be able to:

1. Explain why speakers need strong supporting materials for their ideas.

2. Distinguish among extended examples, brief examples, and hypothetical examples.

3. Explain how to use examples effectively in a speech.

4. Identify three questions for judging the reliability of statistics.

5. Discuss how to use statistics effectively in a speech.

6. Distinguish between peer testimony and expert testimony and explain the proper use of testimony in a speech.

Chapter Outline

I. Speeches need strong supporting materials to bolster the speaker's point of view *(text pages 174-175)*.
   A. A speech composed of unsupported assertions may leave an audience skeptical and unconvinced.
   B. Specific and credible details are more convincing than are unsupported generalizations.

II.   The use of supporting materials is closely related to critical thinking *(text page 175)*.
    A.   Choosing the supporting materials for a speech requires critical thinking.
        1.   Speakers must determine which ideas need to be supported given the audience, topic, and purpose.
        2.   Speakers must do research to find materials that will support their ideas clearly and creatively.
        3.   Speakers must evaluate their supporting materials to make sure they really do back up their ideas.
    B.   Assessing the quality of supporting materials in a speech requires critical thinking.
        1.   Speakers must make sure their supporting materials are accurate.
        2.   Speakers must make sure their supporting materials are relevant.
        3.   Speakers must make sure their supporting materials come from reliable sources.

III.   Examples are the first major kind of supporting material *(text pages 175-180)*.
    A.   Examples are an excellent way to get an audience involved with a speech.
        1.   They provide concrete details that make ideas specific, personal, and lively.
        2.   Researchers have found that examples have more impact on an audience's beliefs than any other kind of supporting material.
    B.   There are three types of examples—brief, extended, and hypothetical.
        1.   Brief examples are specific instances that a speaker refers to in passing.
            a.   They are often employed when a speaker wants to quickly illustrate a point.
            b.   They are sometimes used when a speaker is introducing a topic.
            c.   They are also effective when stacked up to reinforce a speaker's point.
        2.   Extended examples are longer and more detailed than brief examples.
            a.   They are often called illustrations, narratives, or anecdotes.
            b.   Because they tell a story vividly and dramatically, they are an excellent way to pull listeners into a speech.
        3.   Hypothetical examples describe an imaginary situation.
            a.   They are especially effective for relating a general principle directly to the audience.
            b.   Whenever a speaker uses a hypothetical example, it should be supplemented with statistics or testimony to show that the example could really occur.
    C.   There are several tips for using examples effectively.
        1.   A speaker should use examples to clarify ideas.
        2.   A speaker should use examples to reinforce ideas.
        3.   A speaker should use examples to personalize ideas.
        4.   A speaker should use extended examples that are vivid and richly textured.
        5.   A speaker should practice delivery to enhance the impact of extended examples.

IV.   Statistics are the second major kind of supporting material *(text pages 180-189)*.
    A.   When used properly, statistics are an effective way to support a speaker's ideas.
        1.   Like brief examples, statistics can be cited in passing to clarify or strengthen a speaker's points.
        2.   Statistics can also be used in combination to show the magnitude or seriousness of an issue.
    B.   Because statistics can be easily manipulated and distorted, speakers should evaluate their statistics carefully.
        1.   Speakers need to make sure their statistics are representative of what they claim to measure.
        2.   Speakers need to understand the differences among basic statistical measures such as the mean, the median, and the mode.
            a.   The mean—popularly called the average—is determined by summing all the items in a group and dividing by the number of items.
            b.   The median is the middle figure in a group once the figures are put in order from highest to lowest.
            c.   The mode is the number that occurs most frequently in a group of numbers.
        3.   Speakers need to determine whether their statistics come from reliable sources.
    C.   There are several tips for using statistics effectively.
        1.   Statistics should be used to quantify ideas.
            a.   The main value of statistics is to give ideas numerical precision.
            b.   Research has shown that statistics can greatly enhance the impact of examples by quantifying the speaker's point.
        2.   Statistics should be used sparingly.
            a.   Cluttering a speech with too many numbers can make it dull and uninteresting.
            b.   Effective speakers include statistics only when they are needed.
        3.   The source of statistics should be identified in the speech.
            a.   Critical listeners understand that statistics can easily be manipulated.
            b.   Research indicates that speakers are more persuasive to careful listeners when they identify the sources of their statistics.
        4.   Statistics should be explained and made meaningful to the audience.
            a.   Statistics don't speak for themselves.
            b.   They need to be interpreted and related to the audience.
            c.   This is especially important when dealing with large figures that may be remote from the audience's frame of reference.
        5.   Complicated statistics should be rounded off.
            a.   Detailed figures can be too lengthy and involved to be readily understood by listeners.
            b.   Unless there is a strong reason to give exact numbers, lengthy figures should be rounded off for the audience.
        6.   Statistical trends should be clarified with visual aids.
            a.   It is often difficult for listeners to grasp the meaning of statistical trends when they are presented verbally.

b.   Effective speakers frequently use graphs and other visual aids to make their statistics easier to comprehend.

D.   Statistics can be found in many sources.

1.   Newspapers, magazines, and scholarly journals, are good sources of statistics.

2.   Works such as *Statistical Abstract* and *Statistical Yearbook* are devoted exclusively to statistics.

3.   There are also many sources of statistics on the World Wide Web.

V.   Testimony is the third basic kind of supporting material *(text pages 189-194)*.

A.   Testimony can be highly effective when used in a speech.

1.   Listeners are often influenced by people who have special knowledge or experience on a topic.

2.   By quoting or paraphrasing such people, speakers can give their ideas greater strength and impact.

B.   There are two kinds of testimony—expert testimony and peer testimony.

1.   Expert testimony comes from people who are acknowledged authorities in their fields.

a.   This type of testimony provides credibility when the speaker is not an expert on the speech topic.

b.   Expert testimony is especially important when the topic is controversial or when the audience is skeptical about the speaker's point of view.

2.   Peer testimony comes from ordinary people who have firsthand experience with a topic.

a.   This type of testimony gives a more personal viewpoint than can be gained by expert testimony.

b.   It usually has much greater authenticity and emotional impact than does expert testimony.

C.   Testimony can be presented by quoting or by paraphrasing.

1.   One way to present testimony is by quoting word for word.

a.   Quotations are most effective when they are brief.

b.   Quotations are most effective when they convey the speaker's meaning better than the speaker's own words.

c.   Quotations are most effective when they are eloquent, witty, or compelling.

2.   Another way to present testimony is by paraphrasing.

a.   Paraphrasing is preferable when the wording of a quotation is obscure or awkward.

b.   Paraphrasing is preferable when the quotation is longer than two or three sentences.

D.   There are several tips for using testimony effectively.

1.   Speakers should quote or paraphrase accurately.

2.   Speakers should use testimony from qualified sources.

3.   Speakers should use testimony from unbiased sources.

4.   Speakers should identify the people being quoted or paraphrased.

Exercises for Critical Thinking *(from text page 198)*

1.   Each of the following statements violates at least one of the criteria for effective supporting materials discussed in the chapter. Identify the flaw (or flaws) in each statement.

a.   In a random survey last month of 470 members of the Sierra Club, 98 percent of those interviewed opposed drilling for oil in the Alaskan wilderness. Clearly, then, the American people oppose such drilling.

> **Discussion:** As a lobbying group, the Sierra Club opposes drilling for oil in the Alaskan Wilderness and encourages its members to do the same. A random survey of 470 Sierra Club members is too small, too restricted, and too preconceived in its attitudes to be considered representative of the opinion of "the American people." Yet another problem is that the source of the "random survey" is not identified.

b.   In the words of one expert, "Mainstream medical care is not meeting the needs of many Americans. I encourage people to pursue alternative treatments such as acupuncture, chiropractic, and massage therapy."

> **Discussion:** The speaker does not identify "one expert" or present the expert's credentials as an authority on the topic.

c.   Statistics compiled by the National Education Association show that the median salary for teachers in our state is $48,835. This shows that teachers average almost $49,000 a year in salary.

> **Discussion:** The speaker is confusing the median salary with the mean, which is popularly called the average. The median is the middle figure in a group once the numbers are arranged from highest to lowest and may differ considerably from the average.

d.   According to a survey conducted for Verizon Wireless, most people prefer Verizon's cellular service to that of Cingular, Nextel, or Sprint PCS.

> **Discussion:** Because Verizon is a competitor of Cingular, Nextel, and Sprint, it can hardly be considered an objective source of polling data on the question of whose cellular service most people prefer. Although it is possible that Verizon could hire a research firm that would conduct a scientifically valid survey, a survey conducted by an independent consumer group would be a more credible source in this case.

e.   There's no reason insurance companies should charge higher rates for drivers under the age of 25. All my friends drive a lot and almost none of them have been in car accidents.

> **Discussion:** The example cited here may well be unrepresentative of drivers under the age of 25. The experience of the speaker and his or her friends is not a sufficient basis for reaching a sweeping conclusion about the accident rates for people under the age of 25 in general.

f.   According to *The New York Times Almanac*, San Francisco has the highest per capita annual income of any U.S. city—$57,414. The lowest per capita annual income belongs to McAllen-Edinburg-Mission, Texas, at $13,344. The average per capita annual income for all U.S. metropolitan areas is $31,332.

> **Discussion:** This is an instructive set of statistics from a reliable source, but the speaker should round off the numbers. There is no reason to give exact figures down to the dollar. In fact, by not rounding off, the speaker actually dilutes the impact of the figures. It would be more effective to say that the average per capita income in San Francisco is "more than $57,000 a year," that the per capita income in McAllen-Edinburg-Mission, Texas, is "roughly $13,000," and that the average per capita annual income for all U.S. metropolitan areas is "in excess of $31,000."

g.   As Sean Penn noted in a recent interview, the United States needs to change its foreign policy in the Middle East. Otherwise, Penn said, it will be impossible to bring about lasting peace in the region.

> **Discussion:** Although a concerned citizen, Sean Penn is not a highly qualified source on the Middle East. The speaker would be better off citing someone who is an authority in the area.

2.   Analyze Renee Varghese's "Multicultural, Multilingual," in the appendix of sample speeches following Chapter 18 of the textbook. Identify the main points of the speech and the supporting materials used for each. Evaluate the speaker's use of supporting materials in light of the criteria discussed in this chapter.

> **Discussion:** By analyzing the use of supporting materials in a speech, students often get a better idea of how to use them in their own speeches. "Multicultural, Multilingual" has a variety of supporting materials and illustrates how they can be employed to clarify and bolster a speaker's ideas. It also provides an opportunity for students to discuss how the speaker could have employed supporting materials more effectively. In addition to having students read the speech, you may want to show the videotape of it, which is available as part of the instructional

supplement to *The Art of Public Speaking*. Here is a synopsis of the speech:

Specific Purpose: To persuade my audience that foreign language instruction should be mandatory in all U.S. elementary schools.

Central Idea: Mandatory foreign language instruction in all U.S. elementary schools will help prepare today's students for interaction in the global economy and in the increasingly multicultural context of the United States itself.

Method of Organization: Problem-Solution

Introduction: The introduction consists of paragraphs 1-4. Posing the opening question in Spanish is an excellent attention-getter. In paragraph 2 the speaker relates the question to her audience, and in paragraph 3 she mentions the results of her audience-analysis questionnaire, which showed that the great bulk of her classmates concurred that current foreign language instruction at the high-school level is insufficient to provide a working knowledge of a language. Paragraph 4 provides a clear overview of the speech and reinforces the speaker's credibility.

Body: There are two main points in the body of this speech. The first explains why knowledge of a second language is vital for the world today and is developed in paragraphs 5-9. The speaker begins by demonstrating that being able to communicate in a foreign tongue is a great advantage in the global economy (paragraphs 5-6). After an excellent transition in paragraph 7, she then shows that the United States itself is growing more multilingual day by day (paragraphs 8-9).

The second main point presents the speaker's solution and runs from paragraph 10 through paragraph 17. In paragraphs 10-11 the speaker introduces her policy of mandatory foreign language instruction in all U.S. elementary schools. Paragraphs 12-17 are devoted to discussing the policy's practicality. The speaker notes that a similar policy is already working in a few U.S. states (paragraph 12) and has worked in other countries for years (paragraph 13). She also shows that foreign language instruction is most effective when begun at an early age (paragraphs 14-15), that it has no adverse effects on the learning of other subjects (paragraph 16), and that it can help students become more tolerant in dealing with people outside their own culture (paragraph 17).

Conclusion: The conclusion consists of paragraphs 18-21. In paragraph 18 the speaker gives a sense of psychological unity to the speech and subtly lets the audience know that it is coming to an end by echoing the introduction with another question posed in Spanish. Paragraphs 19-20 reinforce the central idea by summarizing the speaker's main points, while paragraph 22 ends the speech with a strong closing line.

Supporting Materials: The speaker uses a number of brief examples to reinforce her ideas. One example appears in the problem section when the speaker observes that some accountants at firms such as Chase Manhattan Bank and National City Bank need a second language to better serve the banks' international clients (paragraph 6). This example is especially effective because most people would assume that accounting is a technical subject that does not require knowledge of a foreign language.

The heaviest concentration of brief examples in this speech occurs in the solution section, and especially in the paragraphs devoted to showing the practicality of the speaker's policy. In paragraph 12 she cites several states that have successfully instituted a program similar to the one she recommends. In paragraph 13 she mentions that European and Asian nations have long begun foreign language instruction in the early grades, and in the same paragraph she specifies Australia as an example of an English-speaking nation that requires extensive foreign language training in elementary school. In paragraph 16 she points to the experience of public schools in New York, Minnesota, and Pennsylvania to show that studying a foreign language can actually enhance performance in other subjects.

The speaker does not present any extended examples. Although it is easy to envision how one or two might have helped reinforce her argument, it is difficult to point to anything currently in the speech that could easily be deleted so as to make room for an extended example or two. The key to using supporting materials effectively is to choose those that will best strengthen the speaker's ideas given the topic, purpose, audience, and length of the speech. In this case, the speaker appears to have chosen wisely for the most part.

This can be seen as well in her use of statistics. In paragraph 3 she cites the results of her class survey to show that 92 percent of her classmates agree that they would have been better served by starting foreign language instruction earlier in their education. In paragraph 6 she presents figures from the *Foreign Language Annals* about the growth of international business. In the same paragraph she draws from a survey in the *Journal of Education for Business* to note that 51 percent of the responding firms would give hiring preferences to accounting and business majors skilled in a foreign language. As in other parts of the speech, her figures here are drawn from credible, clearly identified sources.

Statistics are also important to the speaker's argument about the increasingly multilingual nature of U.S. society. In the first sentence of paragraph 8 she references Table 57 in the *Statistical Abstract of the United States* to document the fact that 9 percent of the U.S. population was born in another country. In the next sentence she presents figures from the *Population Bulletin* about the 32 million people in the U.S. that speak a language other than English at home. She then translates that figure into more meaningful terms for her audience by showing that it is larger than the populations of New York, Pennsylvania, and Colorado combined and is six times greater than the population of Wisconsin, where the speech was presented. Finally, in paragraph 9 the speaker cites statistics from the Census Bureau showing that 17 million people in the U.S. speak Spanish as their primary language.

It is worth noting that all of the speaker's statistics occur in the need section of the speech, while most of her examples occur in the practicality section. This is not unusual in a persuasive speech on a question of policy. When demonstrating the need for a change from current policy, a speaker will typically seek to quantify the extent of the problem that needs solving. When showing that his or her policy will solve the problem, a speaker will most often turn to examples that illustrate how the policy, or something close to it, has worked when implemented in other circumstances.

Some students will identify the speaker's citations in paragraph 6 of the *Foreign Policy Annals, Career World*, and the *Journal of Education for Business* as instances of testimony. In each of these cases, however, the speaker is citing a source either for statistics or for brief examples. Testimony, in the strict sense of the term, refers to the expression of opinion and can come from either an expert source or a peer source. Although it is easy to think of cases in which the lines among testimony, examples, and statistics can begin to blur, students usually find it helpful when the distinctions among them are clearly established. Problematic cases can then be dealt with on an individual basis as they arise.

There are a number of clear cases of testimony in this speech. In paragraph 9 the speaker presents a quotation from Kathy Lemmons, chairwoman of the foreign language department at Fayetteville High School about the need for knowledge of Spanish among doctors, lawyers, and business people. Although the speaker does not say so explicitly, this quotation is especially important because Arkansas is not usually thought of as a state with a large Spanish-speaking population. If there is a need for knowledge of Spanish in Arkansas, that need is doubtless many times greater in states like California, Texas, Florida, and Arizona.

Testimony also figures prominently in the solution section of the speech. In paragraph 11 the speaker presents a quotation from Olwen Bell, a French teacher who has worked with the FLES program that the speaker advocates. In paragraphs 14 and 16 she paraphrases two books—the first about the effectiveness of foreign language instruction for children of young ages, the second to show that early foreign language instruction does not interfere with learning in other subjects. Paragraph 15 contains what is probably the most effective piece of testimony in the entire speech— a quotation from John Silber underscoring the point that early instruction is the best way for a child to acquire fluency in a second language.

The only point in the speech that is not documented occurs in paragraph 17, where the speaker asserts that studying a foreign language helps students become more tolerant and more understanding of people outside their own culture. While this point would appear more or less self-evident, it certainly would have carried more force had it been backed up by testimony or some other kind of evidence. All in all, however, the speech provides an instructive example of how students can increase both the clarity and persuasiveness of their ideas by the skillful use of supporting materials.

Applying the Power of Public Speaking *(from text pages 198-199)*

While driving home from Thanksgiving dinner with your family, you are blindsided by a drunk driver. Miraculously, everyone involved is uninjured, but you know the outcome could easily have been different. Shaken by the experience, you have become committed to working for tougher legal and judicial action against drunk driving.

Your state ranks among the lowest in the fight against drunk drivers, but you know a bill will be introduced in the next session of the state senate to change that. To build support for the bill, you will be speaking to several local service organizations. You will tell them about your personal experience and provide testimony in support of the new legislation, but you will also need to support your speech with national and state drunk-driving statistics. Because your accident occurred on Thanksgiving, you also want to know if anyone has compiled figures that correlate drunk-driving accidents with specific holidays throughout the year.

As part of your research, you decide to check the website of Mothers Against Drunk Driving (www.madd.org/). What do you find that will help you in your speech? Be specific.

> **Discussion:**   Locating statistics is often a major challenge for students. As this scenario is meant to suggest, that challenge will not disappear once students finish their speech class or graduate from college. Public speakers need strong, credible, up-to-date facts and figures whether they are addressing their classmates or a business meeting, the state senate or a local community group, a jury or the school board.
>
> Respected public-interest groups such as Mothers Against Drunk Driving are often excellent sources for statistical information. At the time this edition of *The Art of Public Speaking* went to press, one of the menu items on the MADD homepage was Stats & Resources. Clicking on Stats & Resources will bring up a screen with five options: Statistics, Laws, Drunk Driving Research, Underage Drinking Research, and Links. Choosing Statistics will result in a screen with multiple options that include By State, which provides annual totals for alcohol-related deaths divided by state, and By Holiday, which provides annual crash fatalities divided by state. All told, the MADD site provides a remarkably detailed set of figures on every aspect of drunk driving. Indeed one benefit of this exercise is that it can provide a springboard for discussing the different kinds of statistics a speaker might use. In class discussion, encourage students to note the array of statistics offered by MADD and to explore ways in which a speaker might use one set of statistics or another depending on the audience and purpose of the speech.

Additional Exercises and Activities

1.   Have students prepare and present a one-point speech in which they state their point, support it with three pieces of supporting material, and then summarize the point. The speech should be 1 to 2 minutes in length and should be accorded the same weight in grading as a homework assignment.

> **Discussion:**   If done properly, this can be an excellent way to give students an extra oral performance while at the same time helping them learn to use supporting materials effectively. Students should be allowed—indeed, encouraged—to use materials from the major speech assignment on which they are currently working. For example, if you deal with Chapter 7 during the unit on persuasive speaking, urge students to develop their one-point speech using materials that will appear in their persuasive speech. Some teachers require that students use all three kinds of supporting materials in the speech; others require that they use at least two. In most cases, the entire class will be able to present their speeches in a single session.

2.   Evaluate the use of supporting materials in the following speech excerpt. Be sure to deal with all the supporting materials in each paragraph, and be specific in assessing their strengths and weaknesses.

According to emergency medicine specialist Dr. Randall Sword, emergency rooms will handle more than 160 million cases this year alone. This means that one out of every 16 Americans will spend time in an emergency room this year. Unfortunately, the National Academy of Sciences states that "emergency medical care is one of the weakest links in the delivery of health care in the nation." In fact, medical researchers estimate that 5,000 deaths annually from poisoning, drowning, and drug overdoses, as well as 20 percent of all deaths from automobile accidents, would not have happened if the victims had received prompt and proper emergency room care.

One cause of this problem is that many doctors are not properly trained in emergency care. According to *U.S. News and World Report*, fewer than 50 percent of emergency room physicians have completed special emergency training courses. A survey by Frey and Mangold found that untrained emergency room physicians felt they were unsure how to diagnose or treat many of the extreme abdomen, chest, and cardiac disorders that often appear in hospital emergency rooms.

Another cause of the problem is that precious time is often wasted on useless paperwork before vital emergency treatment begins. Several years ago, a man driving by an elementary school in my hometown had a heart attack and crashed into a schoolyard. Seven children were taken to the emergency room three blocks away, but the real tragedy had not yet begun. Once in the emergency room, the children were denied treatment until their parents were contacted and the admitting forms were filled out. By the time the forms were completed, two of the children had died.

Discussion: This speech excerpt is brief enough to be used as a classroom activity. One approach is to divide the class into groups of four to five students each. Give each group ten minutes to read and analyze the excerpt, and then have each group make a two-minute report to the class assessing the strengths and weaknesses of the supporting materials in the excerpt. Another approach, of course, is to give the excerpt to each student individually. In either case, you should be able to generate an effective class discussion. Here is a brief analysis of the excerpt:

Paragraph One: The statistic in sentence 1 comes from a credible source. In sentence 2 the speaker does a nice job of showing what the statistic means for the U.S. public in general, though she might also have related it directly to her audience by stating how many of them would probably require emergency care during the year. The quotation from the National Academy of Sciences is excellent, and it is followed by statistics showing the seriousness of the problem. The statistics, however, should have been attributed to a specific source, rather than to unidentified "medical researchers."

Paragraph Two: The supporting materials in this paragraph are certainly relevant to the speaker's claim that doctors are not properly trained in emergency care. The statistics in sentence 2 are from a credible source, and the source is clearly identified. Unfortunately, in sentence 3 the speaker does not identify Frey and Mangold or their qualifications with respect to the topic.

Paragraph Three: While the extended example in this paragraph is dramatic, vivid, and relevant to the speaker's point, the speaker should have provided statistics or testimony to show that the example is not atypical.

3.   Have students analyze the speech in Part Five of this manual by Dawn Follendorf ("To Save a Child") or Rob Goeckel ("Boxing: The Most Dangerous Sport"). Have students focus their analysis on the speaker's use of supporting materials.

Discussion: "To Save a Child" and "Boxing: The Most Dangerous Sport" are both persuasive speeches on a question of policy. They provide excellent vehicles for giving students additional work analyzing the use—and occasional misuse—of supporting materials. For full discussion of the speeches see pages 445-449 and pages 461-466 of this manual.

Extra Teaching and Learning Resources

General

Allen, M.; Bruflat, R.; Fucilla, R.; Kramer, M.; McKellips, S.; Ryan, D.J.; and Spiegelhoff, M. "Testing the Persuasiveness of Evidence: Combining Narrative and Statistical Forms." *Communication Research Reports*, 17 (2000), pp. 331-336.

Allen, Mike, and Preiss, Raymond W. "Comparing the Persuasiveness of Narrative and Statistical Evidence Using Meta-Analysis." *Communication Research Reports*, 14 (1997), 123-131.

Berger, Charles R. "Evidence? For What?" *Western Journal of Communication*, 58 (1994), 11-19.

Best, Joel. *Damned Lies and Statistics: Untangling Numbers from the Media, Politicians, and Activists*. Berkeley: University of California Press, 2001.

Crossen, Cynthia. *Tainted Truth: The Manipulation of Fact in America*. New York: Simon & Schuster, 1994.

Crossen, Cynthia. *Tainted Truth: The Manipulation of Fact in America*. New York: Simon & Schuster, 1994.

Gigerenzer, Gerd. *Calculated Risks: How to Know When the Numbers Deceive You*. New York: Simon and Schuster, 2002.

Harris, Robert A. *Using Sources Effectively: Strengthening Your Writing and Avoiding Plagiarism*. Los Angeles: Pyrczak Publishing, 2002.

Herrick, James A. *Argumentation: Understanding and Shaping Arguments*. Scottsdale, AZ: Gorsuch Scarisbrick, 1995.

Kazoleas, Dean C. "A Comparison of the Persuasive Effectiveness of Qualitative versus Quantitative Evidence: A Test of Explanatory Hypotheses." *Communication Quarterly*, 41 (1993), 40-50.

O'Keefe, Daniel J. *Persuasion: Theory and Research*, 2nd ed. Thousand Oaks, CA: Sage, 2002.

Paulos, John Allen. *A Mathematician Reads the Newspaper*. New York: Basic Books, 1995.

Perloff, Richard M. *The Dynamics of Persuasion*, 2nd ed. Mahwah, NJ: Lawrence Erlbaum, 2003.

Reinard, John C. "The Empirical Study of the Persuasive Effects of Evidence: The Status after Fifty Years of Research." *Human Communication Research*, 15 (1988), 3-59.

Reynolds, Rodney A., and Reynolds, Lynn J. "Evidence." In James Price Dillard and Michael Pfau (eds.). *The Persuasion Handbook: Developments in Theory and Practice*. Thousand Oaks, CA: Sage, 2002, pp. 427-444.

Rieke, Richard D., and Sillars, Malcolm O. *Argumentation and Critical Decision Making*, 5th ed. New York: Addison Wesley, 2000.

Rosteck, Thomas. "Narrative in Martin Luther King's *I've Been to the Mountaintop*." *Southern Communication Journal*, 58 (1992), 22-32.

Slan, Joanna. *Using Stories and Humor*. Boston: Allyn and Bacon, 1998.

Stuckey, Mary E. "Anecdotes and Conversations: The Narrational and Dialogic Styles of Modern Presidential Communication." *Communication Quarterly*, 40 (1992), 45-55.

Wang, Chamont. *Sense and Nonsense of Statistical Inference: Controversy, Misuse, and Subtlety*. New York: Marcel Dekker, 1993.

Classroom Activities and Assignments

Dittus, James K. "Grade Begging as an Exercise in Argumentation." In Stephen E. Lucas (ed.), *Selections from the Speech Communication Teacher, 1991-1994*. New York: McGraw-Hill, 1995, pp. 16-17.

Kauffman, James. "Collecting and Evaluating Evidence." In Stephen E. Lucas (ed.) *Selections from the Speech Communication Teacher, 1991-1994*. New York: McGraw-Hill, 1995, pp. 18-19.

Newburger, Craig. "Testing Students' Ability to Distinguish Facts from Inferences." In Stephen E. Lucas (ed.), *Selections from the Speech Communication Teacher, 1991-1994*. New York: McGraw-Hill, 1995, pp. 20-21.

Films and Videos

"Crediting Your Sources." RMI Media Productions (1991). 30 minutes.

"Critical Thinking." Insight Media (1999). 30 minutes.

"How Numbers Lie: Media Truth or Fiction." Insight Media (1996). 23 minutes.

"Presenting an Argument." Films for the Humanities and Sciences (1992). 20 minutes.

"Reasoning, Critical Thinking, and Creativity." Insight Media (1993). 60 minutes.

"Shared Visions: The Art of Storytelling." Insight Media (1999). 24 minutes.

"The Statistician Strikes Back." Films for the Humanities and Sciences (1993). 24 minutes.

"Statistics." Insight Media (1989). 3 volumes; 360 minutes.

"Top 10½ Tips for Thinking Critically." Insight Media (1999). 15 minutes.

"Unraveling the Mysteries of Critical Thinking." Insight Media (1999). 30 minutes.

Chapter 8 Organizing the Body of the Speech

Chapter Objectives

After reading this chapter, students should be able to:

1. Explain why it is important to organize speeches clearly and coherently.

2. Identify the five major patterns of organizing main points in a speech.

3. Discuss the guidelines given in the text for organizing main points.

4. Explain the four kinds of speech connectives and their roles in a speech.

Chapter Outline

I. The ability to organize one's ideas clearly and coherently is a vital skill *(text pages 202-203)*.
    A. Clear organization is essential to effective public speaking.
        1. Research shows that well-organized speeches are easier for listeners to comprehend.
            a. Listeners demand coherence from speakers.
            b. Because listeners get only one chance to grasp the ideas in a speech, it is crucial that those ideas be clearly structured.
        2. Research shows that listeners find speakers who give well-organized speeches more competent and trustworthy.

B.   Clear organization is also connected to critical thinking.
1.   Organizing speeches helps students understand the relationships between ideas.
2.   The skills of critical thinking used in organizing speeches will benefit students in many aspects of their lives.

II.   The main points are the most important element in organizing the body of a speech *(text pages 203-213)*.
A.   Because main points are the central features in the body of a speech, they should be selected carefully.
1.   Sometimes the main points are evident from a speaker's specific purpose statement.
2.   Often they emerge as the speaker researches the topic.
B.   Speeches should have a limited number of main points.
1.   Most speeches contain from two to five main points.
a.   Students do not have time in classroom speeches to develop more than five main points.
b.   No matter how long a speech may be, it should have a limited number of main points or the audience will have trouble sorting them out.
2.   If a speaker discovers that she or he has too many main points, the points should be condensed into a few broad categories.
C.   Main points should be organized strategically to achieve the speaker's purpose.
1.   When arranged chronologically, main points follow a time sequence.
a.   Chronological order is used when a speaker recounts a series of historical events in the order they happened.
b.   Chronological order is also effective for speeches that explain a process or that demonstrate how to do something.
2.   When arranged spatially, main points follow a directional pattern.
a.   Main points in spatial order proceed from top to bottom, right to left, east to west, or some other route.
b.   Like chronological order, spatial order is used most often in informative speeches.
3.   When arranged causally, main points show a cause-and-effect relationship.
a.   Speeches with causal organization have two main points.
(1)   One main point deals with the causes of an event.
(2)   The other main point deals with the effects of an event.
b.   Causal order is flexible enough to be used for informative and persuasive speeches alike.
4.   Main points can also be organized in problem-solution order.
a.   The first point main point of a problem-solution speech shows the existence of a problem.
b.   The second main point presents a solution to the problem.
c.   Problem-solution order is most effective for persuasive speeches.

5.   Main points are most often arranged in topical order.
    a.   Speeches that follow topical order break the speech topic into its constituent parts.
        (1)   A speech on fireworks might focus on four different kinds of fireworks.
        (2)   A speech on Babe Didrikson might focus on the three major sports in which she excelled.
    b.   The main points should divide the topic logically and consistently.
    c.   Topical order works equally well for informative and persuasive speeches.

D.   There are three tips for preparing effective main points.
    1.   Speakers should keep their main points separate and distinct.
        a.   Each main point should focus on a single idea.
        b.   Each main point should be worded clearly.
    2.   Speakers should try to use parallel wording in their main points.
        a.   Parallel wording makes main points easier to understand.
        b.   Parallel wording makes main points stand out from the details of the speech.
    3.   Speakers should balance the amount of time devoted to each main point.
        a.   Each main point needs to receive enough emphasis to be clear and convincing.
        b.   The time devoted to each main point does not need to be equal, but it should usually be roughly balanced.

III.   Once the main points of a speech are in strategic order, a speaker must make sure that the supporting materials are effectively organized *(text pages 213-215)*.
    A.   It is crucial that supporting materials be well organized because misplaced supporting materials are confusing to listeners.
    B.   Details and evidence need to be directly relevant to the main points they support.

IV.   Speakers should use connectives to strengthen their organization in the body of the speech *(text pages 215-218)*.
    A.   Connectives are words or phrases that join one thought to another and indicate the relationship between them.
        1.   Connectives are like ligaments and tendons in the human body.
        2.   They hold the speech together, making it unified and coherent.
    B.   There are four types of connectives.
        1.   Transitions indicate when a speaker has completed one thought and is moving on to another.
            a.   Technically, transitions state *both* the thought a speaker has completed and the thought she or he is about to develop.
            b.   Without transitions, a speech will seem disjointed and uncoordinated.

2. Internal previews let the audience know what the speaker will take up next.
   a. Internal previews are more detailed than transitions.
   b. They are rarely necessary for every main point.
3. Internal summaries remind listeners of what they have just heard.
   a. Internal summaries are especially useful when a speaker finishes a complex or important point.
   b. They clarify and reinforce the speaker's ideas.
4. Signposts are brief statements that indicate exactly where a speaker is in the speech or that focus attention on key ideas.
   a. Signposts can be numerical ("First," "Second," "Third," etc.).
   b. Questions also work well as signposts.
   c. So do phrases such as "Be sure to keep this in mind," "Above all, you need to know," and the like.

Exercises for Critical Thinking *(from text pages 220-221)*

1. Identify the organizational method used in each of the following sets of main points.

   I. Cesar Chavez is best known for his efforts to protect the rights of Hispanic farmworkers in California.

   II. Cesar Chavez was also a tireless advocate for Hispanic racial and cultural pride in general.

   (topical)

   I. The game we know as golf originated in Scotland during the 15th century.

   II. Most of golf's rules and traditions developed during the 19th century.

   III. Professional golf tours for men and women emerged during the 20th century.

   IV. Today golf is at a peak of popularity among everyday players and as a spectator sport.

   (chronological)

   I. Caused by the bite of infected mosquitos, West Nile virus is spreading throughout the United States.

   II. The effects of West Nile virus include flu-like symptoms, convulsions, swelling of the brain, and, in some cases, death.

   (causal)

I.   The outer layer of the skin, the epidermis, is about as thick as a sheet of paper.

II. The middle layer of the skin, the dermis, is 15-40 times thicker than the epidermis.

III. The innermost layer of the skin, the subcutaneous tissue, is by far the thickest layer.

(spatial)

I.   Childhood obesity has reached crisis proportions in the United States.

II. Solving the problem will require changes in attitudes, eating habits, and exercise.

(problem-solution)

2.   What organizational method (or methods) might you use to arrange main points for speeches with the following specific purpose statements?

To inform my audience about the major events in the development of the civil rights movement from 1955 to 1970.

To inform my audience of the causes and effects of the erosion of America's seacoasts.

To inform my audience about the nonviolent philosophy of Mahatma Gandhi.

To inform my audience about the geographical regions of the Philippines.

To persuade my audience that our state legislature should enact tougher laws to deal with the problem of motorists who run red lights.

To inform my audience about the major kinds of symbols used in traditional Native American art.

Discussion: Here are suggestions for organizational methods that could be used for each of these specific purpose statements:

To inform my audience about the major events in the development of the civil rights movement from 1955 to 1970.

(The most obvious choice for a speech with this specific purpose would be chronological order, but it could also be arranged topically.)

To inform my audience of the causes and effects of the erosion of America's seacoasts.

> (A speech with this specific purpose would probably be structured in causal order.)

To inform my audience about the nonviolent philosophy of Mahatma Gandhi.

> (A speech with this specific purpose would most likely be organized topically, with each main point dealing with a different aspect of Gandhi's philosophy of nonviolence.)

To inform my audience about the geographical regions of the Philippines.

> (A speech with this specific purpose would probably be organized spatially, though it could also be structured topically.)

To persuade my audience that our state legislature should enact tougher laws to deal with the problem of motorists who run red lights.

> (Based on the methods of organization discussed in this chapter, a speech with this specific purpose would most likely be arranged in problem-solution order. In Chapter 15, we shall discuss more specialized methods for organizing persuasive speeches.)

To inform my audience about the major kinds of symbols used in traditional Native American art.

> (Although a speech with this specific purpose would probably be arranged in topical order, it might be organized chronologically if the speaker were to deal with the changes in Native American art symbols over the years.)

3. Turn to the outline of main points and supporting materials for the speech about hypnosis on pages 213-214 of the textbook. Create appropriate transitions, internal previews, internal summaries, and signposts for the speech.

> **Discussion:** The purpose of this exercise is to give students practice in thinking about where connectives are needed in a speech and in creating the appropriate connectives. The exercise seems to work best when used as an in-class activity. Divide the class into groups, and have each group perform the exercise. Follow this with a class discussion in which each group presents its handiwork.

Applying the Power of Public Speaking   *(from text page 221)*

After working for two other firms, you have spent the last several years at a Fortune 500 company that, as part of its operations, is a major manufacturer of lawn care equipment. The company has recently acquired three specialized European businesses that produce similar products. With your engineering degree and experience as part of the fast-growing Product Quality Group, you were the logical candidate to visit the newly acquired companies and evaluate their products for safety, quality, and emissions controls.

You have just returned from a weeklong trip to the three sites in Scotland, France, and Germany. You will deliver your findings and recommendations to the management group for new acquisitions, but you're unsure how best to organize your speech. Your major choices are chronological order, spatial order, and topical order. What might be the main points of your speech in each of these methods of organization? Explain which method you think would be most effective for your presentation.

Discussion: The purpose of this scenario is to have students see how the principles of speech organization discussed in the chapter can arise in real-life situations outside the classroom. Begin class discussion by focusing on the first question posed at the end of the scenario. Students should have little difficulty understanding that chronological order would result in a speech that narrates the events of the trip in the order they occurred. Students should also pick up quickly on the fact that spatial order would discuss the sites by starting in, say, Scotland and working one's way south, or perhaps by starting in France and proceeding from there toward the north.

The most difficult method of organization for students to grasp is topical order. One option, if the speech were arranged topically, would be to devote each main point to a different company without regard to its geographical location or to where it fell in the time sequence of the trip. Another option would be to focus each main point on one of the three major issues dealt with during the trip—safety, quality, and emissions controls. In this case, information about the specific companies would appear, where relevant, as subpoints under each of the main points.

Once students understand the different methods of organization, you can turn to the question of which method would be most effective for the presentation to the management group. There is no right or wrong answer to this question, since any of the three methods could work effectively depending on the specific ideas the speaker wanted to communicate in her or his presentation. The important thing is to explore the strategic factors that might go into a decision to use one or another method of speech organization—both in this scenario and in general.

Additional Exercises and Activities

1.   Below is a speech outline with 12 main points. Reorganize the outline so as to reduce the original 12 main points to three main points, each with three subpoints. Use the new main points and subpoints to fill in the blank outline at the bottom of this page. Be sure to use parallel wording when stating the main points.

I.   The first part of preparing for a backpacking trip is plotting the course.

II.   Choose a course that is suitable for everyone in the hiking group.

III.   Check detailed maps so you can identify obstacles on your course.

IV.   Consider the climate of the hiking area when plotting your course.

V.   Preparing your food is also important.

VI.   Work out a menu that covers all meals you will eat on the trip.

VII.   Shop for the food you will need.

VIII. Carefully pack the food in waterproof bags.

IX.   Good equipment is a necessity as well.

X.   You will need a tent that is lightweight yet spacious.

XI.   You will need strong, comfortable hiking boots.

XII.   You will need proper clothing for the terrain and climate.

I.

    A.

    B.

    C.

II.

    A.

    B.

    C.

III.

    A.

    B.

    C.

Discussion: When reorganized, the outline should look similar to the one printed below. Although the main points need not be stated exactly as written here, they should use parallel wording. The most important matter, however, is that students see how the 12 original points can be regrouped into three main points with three subpoints each. To facilitate class discussion, this answer is included with the overhead transparencies that accompany *The Art of Public Speaking*.

I.   The first part of preparing for a backpacking trip is plotting the course.

    A.   Choose a course that is suitable for everyone in the hiking group.

    B.   Check up-to-date maps so you can identify obstacles on your course.

    C.   Consider the climate of the hiking area when plotting your course.

II.   The second part of preparing for a backpacking trip is getting the food.

    A.   Work out a menu that covers all meals you will eat on the trip.

    B.   Shop for the food you will need.

    C.   Pack the food in waterproof bags.

III.   The third part of planning a backpacking trip is choosing the equipment.

    A.   Pick a tent that is lightweight yet spacious.

    B.   Look for strong, comfortable hiking boots.

    C.   Get proper clothing for the terrain and climate.

2.   Have students read Jennifer Conard, "The Ultimate Gift," in the appendix of sample speeches that follows Chapter 18 in the textbook. Assign students three tasks: (1) Pick out the main points of the speech; (2) Locate places where it uses connectives; (3) In each case, identify the kind of connective used—transition, internal preview, internal summary, or signpost.

Discussion: This exercise can be done with almost any of the speeches in the appendix of the book or in Part Five of this manual. I recommend "The Ultimate Gift" because, of all the speeches printed in the book, it is the richest in its use of connectives. Other excellent choices are "The Dangers of Chewing Tobacco," "The Thrilling World of Roller Coasters," and "Seatbelts: A Habit That Can Save Your Life," all of which appear in

Part Five of this manual and can readily be copied for distribution to students.

Regardless of the speech you assign, this exercise usually works best when it is given as a homework assignment followed by a class discussion. Be sure, in the discussion, to ask students to assess how well the speaker uses connectives and to identify places where additional connectives would have enhanced the clarity or coherence of the speech.

3.   Identify the organizational method used in each of the following sets of main points.

I.   Early people did not have money, but used a system of exchange based on the barter of goods and services.
II.   Coin money was invented in ancient Turkey, China, and India before the birth of Christ.
III. Paper money began in China about 600 A.D. but did not become popular in the West until the 1600s.
IV.   Today almost every country has an official currency tied to the international rate of exchange.

I.   Genetic engineering is producing new plant hybrids that will vastly increase world agricultural production.
II.   Genetic engineering is producing breakthroughs in medicine that will allow people to live healthier lives.
III. Genetic engineering is producing bacteria that will help clean up industrial pollutants.

I.   Gambling addiction is an increasingly serious problem throughout the United States.
II.   The problem of gambling addiction can best be solved by a combination of education and rehabilitation.

I.   There are several causes for the destruction of the rain forests in South America.
II.   If the destruction of the rain forests continues, the effects will have global impact.

I.   The top layer of the earth is a rocky "skin" called the crust.
II.   Beneath the crust is a thick layer of rock called the mantle.
III. The next lower section is a mass of melted rock called the outer core.
IV.   At the center of the earth is a solid mass called the inner core.

Discussion: This complements Exercise 1 on page 220 of the textbook and gives students additional work in understanding the methods of organization discussed in this chapter. To facilitate class discussion, this exercise is included in the binder of overhead transparencies that accompanies *The Art of Public Speaking*. Here are answers to the exercise.

I. Early people did not have money, but used a system of exchange based on the barter of goods and services.

II. Coin money was invented in ancient Turkey, China, and India before the birth of Christ.

III. Paper money began in China about 600 A.D. but did not become popular in the West until the 1600s.

IV. Today almost every country has an official currency tied to the international rate of exchange.

(chronological)

I. Genetic engineering is producing new plant hybrids that will vastly increase world agricultural production.

II. Genetic engineering is producing breakthroughs in medicine that will allow people to live healthier lives.

III. Genetic engineering is producing bacteria that will help clean up industrial pollutants.

(topical)

I. Gambling addiction is an increasingly serious problem throughout the United States.

II. The problem of gambling addiction can best be solved by a combination of education and rehabilitation.

(problem-solution)

I. There are several causes for the destruction of the rain forests in South America.

II. If the destruction of the rain forests continues, the effects will have global impact.

(causal)

I. The top layer of the earth is a rocky "skin" called the crust.

II. Beneath the crust is a thick layer of rock called the mantle.

III. The next lower section is a mass of melted rock called the outer core.

IV. At the center of the earth is a solid mass called the inner core.

(spatial)

Extra Teaching and Learning Resources

General

Chesebro, Joseph L., and McCroskey, James C. "The Relationship of Teacher Clarity and Immediacy with Student State Receiver Apprehension, Affect, and Cognitive Learning." *Communication Education*, 50 (2001), 59-68.

Corbett, Edward P.J., and Connors, Robert J. *Classical Rhetoric for the Modern Student*, 4th ed. New York: Oxford University Press, 1999, Chapter 3.

D'Arcy, Jan. *Technically Speaking: Proven Ways to Make Your Next Presentation a Success*. New York: American Management Association, 1992, Chapter 11.

Dowis, Richard. *The Lost Art of the Great Speech*. New York: Amacom, 1999, Chapter 4.

Hauser, Margaret Fitch. "Message Structure, Inference Making, and Recall." In Robert N. Bostrom (ed.), *Communication Yearbook 8*. Beverly Hills, CA: Sage, 1984, pp. 278-292.

Hoffman, Regina M. "Temporal Organization as a Rhetorical Resource." *Southern Communication Journal*, 57 (1992), 194-204.

Leech, Thomas. *How to Prepare, Stage, and Deliver Winning Presentations*, rev. ed. New York: Amacom, 1993, Chapter 6.

Titsworth, B. Scott. "The Effects of Teacher Immediacy, Use of Organizational Lecture Cues, and Students' Notetaking on Cognitive Learning." *Communication Education*, 50 (2001), 283-297.

Classroom Activities and Assignments

Avadian, Brenda, and Thanos, Marilyn. "Speechmapping: The Road Through Speech Preparation and Delivery." In Stephen E. Lucas (ed.), *Selections from the Speech Communication Teacher, 1986-1991*. New York: McGraw-Hill, 1992, pp. 51-52.

Blom, Patricia. "Using Group Activities in Basic Public Speaking." In Stephen E. Lucas (ed.), *Selections from the Speech Communication Teacher, 1986-1991*. New York: McGraw-Hill, 1992, pp. 52-53.

Brown, Kevin James. "'Spidergrams': An Aid for Teaching Outlining and Organization." In Stephen E. Lucas (ed.), *Selections from the Speech Communication Teacher, 1986-1991*. New York: McGraw-Hill, 1992, pp. 53-54.

Ensign, Russell L. "The 'Arrow through Ass's Ribs' Outline: A Teaching Aid for the Basic Course." *Speech Communication Teacher* (Fall 1993), 10-11.

Hufman, Melody. "The Maze as an Instrument for Public Speaking." *Communication Education*, 34 (1985), 63-68.

McClish, Glen. "The 'Authorial Conversion' Structure in Oral Argument." In Stephen E. Lucas (ed.), *Selections from the Speech Communication Teacher, 1991-1994*. New York: McGraw-Hill, 1995, pp. 19-20.

Mino, Mary. "Structuring: An Alternate Approach for Developing Clear Organization." In Stephen E. Lucas (ed.), *Selections from the Speech Communication Teacher, 1986-1991*. New York: McGraw-Hill, 1992, pp. 55-56.

Muir, Star A. "Organizing and Critiquing Ideas." In Stephen E. Lucas (ed.), *Selections from the Speech Communication Teacher, 1994-1996*. New York: McGraw-Hill, 1997, pp. 53-54.

Schnell, Jim. "The Developmental Speech Sequence Model (DSSM)." In Stephen E. Lucas (ed.), *Selections from the Speech Communication Teacher, 1986-1991*. New York: McGraw-Hill, 1992, p. 56.

Films and Videos

"Be Prepared to Speak." Kantola-Skeie Productions (1985). 27 minutes.

"Organizing and Outlining." Insight Media (1997). 30 minutes.

Chapter **9** Beginning and Ending the Speech

Chapter Objectives

After reading this chapter, students should be able to:

1. Identify the four objectives of a speech introduction.

2. Explain seven methods that can be used to gain attention in an introduction.

3. Identify the major functions of a speech conclusion.

4. Explain the methods a speaker can use to fulfill the functions of a conclusion.

Chapter Outline

I.   Speeches need effective introductions and conclusions *(text page 224)*.
    A.   An effective introduction gets the speaker off on the right foot.
        1.   It creates a favorable first impression with the audience.
        2.   It boosts a speaker's self-confidence for the rest of the speech.
    B.   An effective conclusion ends the speech on a strong note.
        1.   It gives the speaker one last chance to emphasize his or her main points.
        2.   It creates a favorable final impression.

II. There are four objectives of a speech introduction *(text pages 224-236)*.
    A.   The first objective is to gain the attention and interest of the audience.
        1.   One method of gaining attention is to relate the topic to the audience.
            a.   People pay attention to things that affect them directly.

        b.   No matter what other interest-arousing lures a speaker uses, she or he should *always* relate the topic to the audience.

   2.   A second method of gaining attention is to state the importance of the topic.

        a.   An audience is not likely to be interested in a topic they regard as unimportant.

        b.   Whenever a speaker discusses a topic whose importance may not be clear to the audience, the speaker should think about ways to demonstrate its importance in the introduction.

   3.   A third method of gaining attention is to startle the audience.

        a.   This method can be highly effective.

        b.   It is important, however, that the startling material be directly related to the speech.

   4.   A fourth method of gaining attention is to arouse the curiosity of the audience.

        a.   People are curious.

        b.   Their interest can be engaged with a series of statements that whet their curiosity about the subject of the speech.

   5.   A fifth method of gaining attention is to question the audience.

        a.   A speaker can use either a single question or a series of questions.

        b.   The question or questions should be firmly related to the content of the speech.

   6.   A sixth method of gaining attention is to begin with a quotation.

        a.   A well-chosen quotation can add depth, human interest, or humor to an introduction.

        b.   The quotation will be most effective if it is no longer than a sentence or two.

   7.   A seventh method of gaining attention is to tell a story.

        a.   Because most people enjoy stories, this may be the most effective method of beginning a speech.

        b.   For this method to work, the story must be delivered well.

   8.   Other methods of gaining attention include referring to the occasion, inviting audience participation, using audio equipment or visual aids, relating to a previous speaker, and beginning with humor.

        a.   All of these methods can be effective depending on the audience, the topic, and the occasion.

        b.   Unlike the first seven methods of gaining attention, these additional methods are used more frequently in speeches outside the classroom than in the classroom.

B.   The second objective of a speech introduction is to reveal the topic of the speech.

   1.   An effective introduction clearly states the speech topic to avoid confusing the audience.

   2.   Even if the audience already knows the topic, a speaker should usually restate it during the introduction.

   C.   The third objective of a speech introduction is to establish the credibility and
         goodwill of the speaker.
         1.   Credibility is a matter of being perceived by the audience as qualified to
               speak on a particular topic.
               a.   Credibility can be based on research or firsthand experience.
               b.   Whatever the source of a speaker's credibility, she or he should let
                     the audience know.
         2.   Establishing goodwill is a matter of showing that the speaker has the
               audience's best interests in mind.
               a.   Creating good will is especially crucial for speakers outside the
                     classroom who may be identified with causes that arouse hostility
                     among the audience.
               b.   Creating good will can also be a concern for students who advocate
                     highly unpopular positions in their classroom speeches.
   D.   The fourth objective of a speech introduction is to preview the body of the speech.
         1.   A preview statement tells an audience what to listen for in the rest of the
               speech.
         2.   Because they generally come at the end of the introduction, preview
               statements provide a smooth lead-in to the body of the speech.
         3.   Previews are also an opportunity to present special information, such as
               definitions of terms, that the audience will need to understand the rest of
               speech.

III.   There are five tips for preparing an effective introduction *(text page 237)*.
   A.   The introduction should usually be relatively brief.
   B.   Speakers should keep an eye out for potential introductory material as they
         research the speech.
   C.   Speakers should be creative when devising their introductions.
   D.   Speakers should not be concerned with the exact wording of the introduction
         until the body of the speech is finished.
   E.   The introduction should be worked out in detail so it can be delivered effectively.

IV.   A speech conclusion has two primary functions *(text pages 237-242)*.
   A.   The first function is to signal the end of the speech.
         1.   Abrupt endings leave listeners surprised and unfulfilled.
         2.   One way to signal the end of a speech is with a brief verbal cue such as
               "In conclusion" or "One last thought."
         3.   Another way to signal the end is by the speaker's manner of delivery.
               a.   In a crescendo ending, the speech builds in force until it reaches a
                     zenith of power and intensity.
               b.   In a dissolve ending, the final words fade like a spotlight on a
                     concert singer, bringing the speech to an emotional close.
   B.   The second function of a conclusion is to reinforce the audience's under-
         standing of or commitment to the central idea of the speech.
         1.   There are four methods of accomplishing this.
               a.   One method is to summarize the main points of the speech.

    b. A second method is to conclude with a quotation.

    c. A third method is to end with a dramatic statement.

    d. A fourth method is to refer back to the introduction of the speech.

  2. These methods can be used separately or in combination to create an effective conclusion.

V. There are four tips for preparing an effective conclusion *(text page 243)*.

 A. Speakers should keep an eye out for potential concluding materials as they research the speech.

 B. Speakers should conclude with a bang instead of a whimper.

 C. Speakers should not be long-winded in the conclusion.

 D. Speakers should prepare the content and delivery of their conclusions with special care.

Exercises for Critical Thinking *(from text page 244)*

1. Here are six speech topics. Explain how you might relate each to your classmates in the introduction of a speech.

Social Security	laughter
illiteracy	steroids
soap operas	blood donation

Discussion: Students often have great difficulty deciding how to relate their speech topics directly to their classmates. This exercise is designed to give them some practice, and it works equally well as a homework assignment, as a group activity in class, or simply as the basis for a general class discussion. After the class deals with each item, you may want to read your students the following excerpts from the introductions of student speeches on each of the six topics.

Social
Security: Many of you may think, "What does Social Security have to do with me? I'm young, healthy, and nowhere near retirement age."

  But Social Security has a lot to do with you. If you don't have a job today, you will in a couple of years. And when you do, you will pay Social Security taxes. How much will you pay? That depends on how much you earn. If you earn $40,000, you will pay more than $3,000 a year in Social Security taxes. At present tax rates, that comes to more than $125,000 in the course of your working career. You should know where your money goes and whether you will ever benefit from it.

illiteracy: Imagine that you are in France visiting some friends. Because your friends are busy, you offer to go to the grocery store—even though you don't know a word of French. At the store, you look for what you need, but none of the cans or boxes have pictures on them. You come out of the store thinking you have bought a box of cereal and a can of soup, but when you get to your friends' house, you discover that you have a box of laundry detergent and a can of dog food.

Although this scenario is admittedly far-fetched, it should give you some idea of how frustrating it is to look at a bunch of letters and not know what they mean. This is the same frustration that millions of adults in the United States experience every day because they are functionally illiterate.

soap operas: Are you an addict? Do you need a daily fix to keep going? Are you hooked on one of the modern college students' most popular escapes from reality?

I'm talking, of course, about soap operas. According to Newsweek magazine, students across the land are watching soap operas in record numbers. I don't know about you, but in my experience, getting a front-row seat for "The Young and the Restless" in the dorms or the union is just as tough as getting a seat on the fifty-yard line for football or at center court for basketball!

laughter: The neural circuits in your brain begin to reverberate. Chemical and electrical impulses start flowing rapidly through your body. Your pituitary gland is stimulated. Hormones and endorphins race through your blood.

Your body temperature rises by half a degree. Your pulse and blood pressure increase. Your arteries and chest muscles contract, your vocal chords quiver, and your face contorts. Pressure builds in your lungs. Your lower jaw suddenly becomes uncontrollable and breath bursts from your mouth at seventy miles per hour.

This is surely no laughing matter. Or is it? It is! This is a medical description of what happens in your body during a burst of laughter. It sounds dreadful, but we all know it feels great.

steroids: Imagine that you're one of an elite group of students fighting for a spot at the top of your class. You're fully aware of the implications of an upcoming exam. If you blow it, you lose your rank. However, a good grade virtually assures you of prestige and a comfortable job.

So you look for that extra edge—a little something to push your already strained mind further. If there were a pill that would increase your mental sharpness for a short period of time and ensure you a high score on the exam, chances are many of you would consider taking it.

Amateur and professional athletes are faced with a similar dilemma every day of their competitive lives. In the never-ending search for the extra edge in sports, many athletes have given in to the lure of anabolic steroids.

blood
donation: Picture this: You're walking home from class with your best friend. You begin to cross College Avenue. All of a sudden, out of nowhere comes a car that doesn't stop for the red light. Your friend is hit. It happened so fast that all you know is your friend is down and can't move.

The ambulance arrives and takes your friend to the hospital. At the hospital you find out your friend has serious internal bleeding and desperately needs blood. One major problem—at this time there is no blood available in your friend's blood type. Your throat tightens up. You naturally thought there was always enough blood. Now you find out there isn't.

Even though this situation is hypothetical, it is far from impossible. A poster from the Red Cross sums this up well: "Blood is like a parachute. If it's not there when you need it, chances are you'll never need it again."

2.   Think of a speech topic (preferably one for your next speech in class). Create an introduction for a speech dealing with any aspect of the topic you wish. In your introduction be sure to gain the attention of the audience, to reveal the topic and relate it to the audience, to establish your credibility, and to preview the body of the speech.

Discussion: This exercise is designed to give students practice developing a complete introduction. For an alternative activity, see the first entry under Additional Exercises/Activities in this chapter.

3.   Using the same topic as in Exercise 2, create a speech conclusion. Be sure to let your audience know the speech is ending, to reinforce the central idea, and to make the conclusion vivid and memorable.

Discussion: This exercise is designed to give students practice in developing a complete conclusion. For an alternative activity, see the first entry under Additional Exercises/Activities in this chapter.

Applying the Power of Public Speaking (from text page 245)

Since leaving college with a degree in education, you have been a classroom teacher, high-school principal, and now assistant superintendent in a large urban school district—the same district in which you, yourself, attended high school. Because of your excellent public speaking skills, you have been chosen to represent the district at a meeting of parents, alumni, and neighborhood residents called to protest the closing of the city's oldest high school. With 1,200 current students and thousands of graduates still in the city, the school has produced many top scholars, as well as championship athletic teams.

At the meeting, you will need to explain the decision to close the school and to demolish the 1907 building. Architects, engineers, and city planners agree that renovation of the old structure is impractical and that the city's changing population requires construction of a new school in a new location.

As a graduate of the high school, you understand the feelings of people who want it to remain open. As a member of the school district administration, you understand why it must be closed. You also know that if your speech is to be persuasive, you must use the introduction to establish your credibility and goodwill so the audience will be willing to listen receptively to what you say in the body.

Write a draft of your introduction. In it, be sure to address all four functions of a speech introduction discussed in this chapter.

> **Discussion:** As with most of the other Applying the Power of Public Speaking scenarios throughout the book, there is no single correct answer to this one. Its purpose is to get students thinking about the functions of speech introductions and to illustrate how those functions are just as important for speeches outside the classroom as for those in the classroom. The best way to handle this exercise is to divide the class into groups and give each 15 to 20 minutes of class time to compose an introduction. Have one member from each group present its introduction to the class, and follow with a general discussion about all of the groups' introductions.

Additional Exercises and Activities

1.   Divide the class into groups of 3 to 5 students. Assign each group a topic on which it must prepare a complete introduction and conclusion. Give the groups 20 minutes to work on their introductions and conclusions. Each group should pick one of its members to deliver its introduction and conclusion to the class.

> **Discussion:** This is an effective alternative to Exercises 2 and 3 on page 244 of the textbook. By working in groups, students can use brainstorming to devise more creative introductions and conclusions. Presenting the introductions and conclusions orally allows the whole class to participate in a discussion about the strengths and weaknesses of each group's results.

2.   Here are four complete introductions from classroom speeches. Each has at least one flaw that keeps it from fulfilling all the functions of a good introduction. In each case identify the flaw (or flaws) and make specific suggestions for improving the introduction.

   a.   What tiny crystal fortified the coffers of many ancient empires and laid waste to others? What mineral has the power to create and the power to destroy? What is "good as gold" when scarce and "cheap as dirt" when abundant?

   The answer to all of these questions is salt, the spice of life. Today I would like to look at the importance of salt in history, at how we spice up our lives with salt today, and at the role salt will probably play in the future.

   b.   We have so much unused human potential. By improving the use of your time, you can have much more time for social activities. You can use your mental processes more fully, thereby improving your grades. You can also increase your physical stamina and improve your health. We must learn to know our bodies.

   c.   A six-year-old collie lay battered and helpless by the side of the road. The car that hit her had broken her pelvis, dislocated her hip, and smashed her jaw. It had also blinded her, and she whimpered in pain and fear.

   Unfortunately, this true story happens much too frequently because of the growing problem of pet overpopulation. Having grown up on a farm with animals of all kinds, I care deeply about their welfare, and I have become aware through my veterinary courses of how serious the problem of pet overpopulation is.

   d.   Every problem has at least two sides. When one side is right, and the other side is wrong, the problem is easy to solve. But what if both sides have merit in their arguments? How do you solve these problems?

   Balancing the rights of everyone in an adoption is one of these problems. The parents who give up the child have a right that all the information they disclose be kept confidential, while the adopted child has a right to know about the identity of his or her natural parents.

   Today I'd like to explore this problem with you and look at one approach to solving it.

   Discussion: This is an excellent exercise because it gets students to focus on all four objectives of a speech introduction. Here is a brief analysis of each of the introductions in the exercise.

   a.   This introduction uses a series of questions to get attention, introduces the topic clearly, and has a concise preview statement. Its most obvious flaw is a lack of material establishing the speaker's credibility. It might also be improved by relating the topic of salt directly to the audience at the outset.

b.   By relating to the audience, this introduction does a fair job of capturing attention—but that is all. It does not reveal the topic of the speech, establish the credibility of the speaker, or preview the main points of the speech.

c.   This introduction does an excellent job of gaining attention, of introducing the topic of pet overpopulation, and of establishing the speaker's credibility. It is flawed, however, by its lack of a preview statement. As with the introduction on salt, it also could be strengthened if it related the topic directly to the audience.

d.   This introduction does a good job of revealing the topic and previewing the main points of the speech. It does nothing to establish the speaker's credibility, and it is weak as an attention-getter.

3.   Have the class pay special attention to their classmates' introductions and conclusions during the next round of speeches. Afterward, have the class select the three most effective introductions and the three most effective conclusions.

> **Discussion:** This is a good way to review the principles of effective introductions and conclusions. Surprisingly, students usually tend to agree about the most effective introductions and conclusions. To avoid hurt feelings, though, it is a good idea not to rank-order the three top choices.

Extra Teaching and Learning Resources

General

Dowis, Richard. *The Lost Art of the Great Speech*. New York: Amacom, 1999, Chapters 5 and 13.

Ehrilch, Henry. *Writing Effective Speeches*. New York: Paragon House, 1992, Chapters 10-11.

McCroskey, James C., and Teven, Jason J. "Credibility: A Reexamination of the Construct and Its Measurement." *Communication Monographs*, 66 (1999), 90-103.

Wilder, Claudyne. *The Presentations Kit: Ten Steps for Selling Your Ideas*, rev. ed. New York: Wiley, 1994, Chapter 7.

Zinsser, William. *On Writing Well*, 25th ann. New York: HarperCollins, 2001, Chapter 9.

Classroom Activities and Assignments

Avadian, Brenda, and Thanos, Marilyn. "Speechmapping: The Road Through Speech Preparation and Delivery." In Stephen E. Lucas (ed.), *Selections from the Speech Communication Teacher, 1986-1991*. New York: McGraw-Hill, 1992, pp. 51-52.

Hibben, Jean. "Eliminating the 'My Speech Is About' Introduction." In Stephen E. Lucas (ed.) *Selections from the Speech Communication Teacher, 1991-1994*. New York: McGraw-Hill, 1995, p. 37.

Overton, Julia. "Introductions and Conclusions: Helping Public Speaking Students Write Effective Beginnings and Endings." In Stephen E. Lucas (ed.), *Selections from the Speech Communication Teacher, 1994-1996*. New York: McGraw-Hill, 1997, pp. 40-41.

Schnell, Jim. "The Developmental Speech Sequence Model (DSSM)." In Stephen E. Lucas (ed.), *Selections from the Speech Communication Teacher, 1986-1991*. New York: McGraw-Hill, 1992, p. 56.

Films and Videos

"Be Prepared to Speak." Kantola-Skeie Productions (1985). 27 minutes.

"Great Openings and Closings." Insight Media (1998). Two volumes; 112 minutes.

"Introductions and Conclusions." Insight Media (1997). 30 minutes.

Chapter 10 Outlining the Speech

Chapter Objectives

After reading this chapter, students should be able to:

1. Explain why it is important to outline speeches.

2. Explain the differences between a preparation outline and a speaking outline.

3. Construct a preparation outline following the guidelines presented in the book.

4. Construct a speaking outline following the guidelines presented in the book.

Chapter Outline

I.   Outlines are essential to effective speeches *(text page 248)*.
    A.   An outline helps a speaker see the full scope and content of the speech at a glance.
    B.   An outline helps a speaker judge whether each part of the speech is fully developed.
    C.   An outline helps create a coherent structure for the speech.

II. Creating a preparation outline is a vital step in putting a speech together *(text pages 248-253)*.
    A.   A preparation outline is a detailed outline used to plan a speech.

B.   The process of writing a preparation outline requires that a speaker bring together all the major elements of the speech.

      1.   One element is what will be said in the introduction.

      2.   Another is how main points will be stated and supported.

      3.   Yet another is what will be said in the conclusion.

C.   There are eight guidelines for effective preparation outlines.

      1.   The preparation outline should include the speaker's specific purpose statement.

          a.   The specific purpose statement should be written before the text of the outline itself.

          b.   Including the specific purpose statement makes it easier to judge how well the speech accomplishes the speaker's aim.

      2.   The preparation outline should include the speaker's central idea.

          a.   The central idea can follow the specific purpose as an independent element of the outline.

          b.   It can also be identified in the body of the outline.

      3.   The preparation outline should clearly label the introduction, body, and conclusion of the speech.

          a.   This ensures that the speech indeed has an introduction, body, and conclusion.

          b.   It also helps guarantee that each part of the speech meets its objectives.

          c.   Labels for the introduction, body, and conclusion are stated separately from the system of symbolization used in the outline.

      4.   The preparation outline should have a consistent pattern of symbolization and indentation.

          a.   In the most common system of outlining, main points are identified by Roman numerals and are indented equally.

          b.   Subpoints are identified with capital letters and are indented equally.

          c.   There may also be sub-subpoints and even sub-sub-subpoints.

          d.   Using a consistent pattern of symbolization and indentation provides a clear visual framework that shows the relationships among the ideas in the speech.

      5.   The preparation outline should state main points and subpoints in full sentences.

          a.   Using full sentences clearly identifies the content of each point.

          b.   Using full sentences helps ensure that a speaker has thought out the points fully.

      6.   The preparation outline should label transitions, internal summaries, and internal previews.

          a.   This helps make sure that the speech has sufficient transitions, internal summaries, and internal previews.

          b.   Labels for these elements are not included in the system of symbolization of the outline.

      7.   The preparation outline should include a bibliography.

          a.   The bibliography is a list of all the sources used in preparing the speech.

       b.   Students should check with their teacher to see if they must follow a specific format for the bibliography.

   8.   The preparation outline may also include a title for the speech.

       a.   Students should check with their teacher to see if a title is required.

       b.   If a title is required, it should be brief, attract the attention of the audience, and encapsulate the main thrust of the speech.

III.   Once the preparation outline is completed, a speaking outline can be drawn up *(text pages 256-259)*.

   A.   A speaking outline is a brief outline used to deliver a speech.

   B.   The primary purpose of a speaking outline is to help a speaker remember what to say.

      1.   It includes key words and phrases from the preparation outline.

      2.   It includes essential statistics and quotations the speaker does not want to forget.

      3.   It includes cues to direct and sharpen a speaker's delivery.

   C.   Speaking outlines are especially effective for extemporaneous speeches.

      1.   An extemporaneous speech is thoroughly prepared and practiced in advance.

      2.   The specific wording, however, is selected as the speech is being delivered.

      3.   Most classroom speeches are delivered extemporaneously.

   D.   There are four guidelines for effective speaking outlines.

      1.   The speaking outline should follow the same visual framework used in the preparation outline.

         a.   Using the same symbolization and indentation as in the preparation outline makes the speaking outline easier to prepare.

         b.   It also makes it easier for the speaker to see where she or he is in the speech at any given moment.

      2.   The speaking outline should be plainly legible.

         a.   A speaking outline is worthless unless it is instantly readable at a distance.

         b.   Using dark ink, large letters, and leaving extra space helps make the speaking outline more readable.

      3.   The speaking outline should be as brief as possible.

         a.   Detailed notes often prevent a speaker from maintaining eye contact with the audience.

         b.   The best rule is that a speaking outline should contain the minimum necessary to jog a speaker's memory and keep him or her on track.

      4.   The speaking outline should include cues for delivering the speech.

         a.   One technique is to highlight key ideas that require special vocal emphasis.

         b.   Another is to jot down prompts for delivery such as "slow down," "pause," and "louder."

Exercises for Critical Thinking *(from text pages 261-262)*

1.   In the left-hand column below is a partially blank outline from a speech about sleep deprivation. In the right-hand column, arranged in random order, are the subpoints to fill in the outline. Choose the appropriate subpoint for each blank in the outline.

<table>
<tr><th>Outline</th><th>Subpoints</th></tr>
<tr><td>I.   Sleep deprivation is a major cause of traffic accidents and deaths.</td><td>Sleep deprivation has been linked to a number of specific disorders.</td></tr>
<tr><td>A.</td><td>The *Times* also blames falling asleep at the wheel for 6,500 U.S. traffic deaths each year.</td></tr>
<tr><td>1.</td><td>Second, it increases the risk of heart disease.</td></tr>
<tr><td>2.</td><td>The statistics linking sleep deprivation to traffic accidents and deaths are alarming.</td></tr>
<tr><td>B.</td><td>First, it weakens the immune system.</td></tr>
<tr><td>II. Sleep deprivation also contributes to poor personal health.</td><td>Sleep deprivation is second only to alcohol as the leading cause of traffic accidents and deaths.</td></tr>
<tr><td>A.</td><td>*Newsweek* reports that "sleep deprivation has become one of the most pervasive health problems facing the U.S."</td></tr>
<tr><td>B.</td><td>Third, it contributes to gastrointestinal illness.</td></tr>
<tr><td>1.</td><td>The *Los Angeles Times* reports that drowsiness causes 200,000 auto accidents each year.</td></tr>
<tr><td>2.</td><td></td></tr>
<tr><td>3.</td><td></td></tr>
</table>

Discussion: This is an excellent exercise to help students develop outlining skills. In case you wish to assign more than one such exercise, there are two scrambled outlines among the Additional Exercises/Activities (pages 224-227), and two more among the essay exam questions in Chapter 10 of the *Test Bank*.

When filled in, the outline on sleep deprivation should look like the following. To facilitate class discussion, the outline is included in the binder of full-color overhead transparencies that accompanies *The Art of Public Speaking*.

I.   Sleep deprivation is a major cause of traffic accidents and deaths.

    A.   The statistics linking sleep deprivation to traffic accidents and deaths are alarming.

        1.   The *Los Angeles Times* reports that drowsiness causes 200,000 auto accidents each year.

        2.   The *Times* also blames falling asleep at the wheel for 6,500 U.S. traffic deaths each year.

    B.   Sleep deprivation is second only to alcohol as the leading cause of traffic accidents and deaths.

II.   Sleep deprivation also contributes to poor personal health.

    A.   *Newsweek* reports that "sleep deprivation has become one of the most pervasive health problems facing the U.S."

    B.   Sleep deprivation has been linked to a number of specific disorders.

        1.   First, it weakens the immune system.

        2.   Second, it increases the risk of heart disease.

        3.   Third, it contributes to gastrointestinal illness.

2.   Following the format used in the sample preparation outline on pages 253-255 of the textbook, outline "Cryonics," the sample speech at the end of Chapter 14. Be sure to include a specific purpose statement, to identify the central idea, to label the introduction, body and conclusion, to use a consistent pattern of symbolization and indentation, to state the main points and subpoints in full sentences, and to label transitions and internal summaries.

Discussion: This exercise serves two purposes. First, it gives students a chance to practice using the outline format explained in the book. As a result, it usually improves the quality of the students' initial preparation outlines. Second, this exercise is a capstone to Chapters 8 to 10. It requires students to work with all of the organizational elements discussed in the last three chapters—to delineate the introduction, body, and conclusion; to distinguish main points from supporting materials; to identify connectives; and the like. By analyzing how these elements work in a single speech, students should get a better sense of how to construct their own speeches.

This exercise works best when it is assigned to students to complete at home in preparation for class discussion. Allow at least 30 minutes to discuss the outline in class. Go through the speech step by step, asking students what they identified as the specific purpose, central idea, introduction, main points, connectives, etc. Expect a lively discussion and plenty of questions.

A complete preparation outline of the speech follows. To facilitate class discussion, the outline is included in the binder of full-color overhead transparencies that accompanies *The Art of Public Speaking*. To help students see the relationship among main points, subpoints, and so forth, the outline consists of several color-coded transparencies that cumulatively present the different elements in the outline.

"Cryonics"

Specific Purpose: To inform my audience about the history, methods, and future of cryonics.

Central Idea: Although cryonics has moved in recent years from science fiction to scientific reality, it is still far from foolproof.

Introduction

I.   Imagine the following scenes.
   A.   Your mother or father has suffered a heart attack.
   B.   Your grandmother or grandfather lie near death in their nursing home.
   C.   Your best friend is in the hospital with a massive system-wide infection.

II.   For most people, these circumstances would herald the end of life.

III.   But all of you may be able to meet again in the future through the process of cryonics.

IV.   Cryonics is the process of freezing people in the hope that medical science will be able to revive them in the future.

V.   Intrigued by the subject, I have read dozens of newspaper and magazine articles about it.

VI.   I would like to give you a brief overview of the history, methods, and future of cryonics.

(*Transition:* Let's start with the development of cryonics.)

Body

I.   Cryonics has a very interesting history.
    A.   The notion of preserving people after death is age-old.
        1.   In the 1770s Ben Franklin wrote that he wanted to be "immersed in a cask of Madeira wine, 'til that time when he could be recalled to life."
        2.   Cryonics has been featured in science fiction novels, movies, and magazine and newspaper articles.
    B.   Cryonics remained firmly in the realm of science fiction until 1964.
        1.   In that year Robert Ettinger's *The Prospect of Immortality* claimed that cryonics was indeed possible.
        2.   On January 12, 1967, James H. Bedford became the first human being to be cryonically frozen.
    C.   Since then cryonics has steadily increased in popularity.
        1.   There are currently four cryonics institutions in the United States.
        2.   So far 80 people from around the world have been cryonically frozen.
        3.   Another 800 people have signed up to be frozen when they die.

(*Transition*: You're probably wondering how will they do it? How does cryonics work?)

II.   When a person who has signed up to be cryonically frozen dies, a specific procedure must be carried out.
    A.   The person must decide whether to freeze the entire body or just the head.
    B.   If the whole body will be frozen, it must be preserved.
        1.   Immediately after death, the patient is connected to a heart-lung machine.
        2.   Chemicals are circulated through the blood to minimize freezing damage.
        3.   Cold packs are used to reduce the patient's internal temperature.
    C.   If only the head will be frozen, a different procedure is followed.
        1.   The head is surgically detached from the body and preserved in a separate container.
        2.   Why would someone preserve only their head?
            a.   With some diseases the body is in very poor condition.
            b.   The head is preserved in hopes that science can create a healthy new body to go with it in the future.

D. Once the head or body is ready for freezing, the rest of the process takes place.
    1. Cryoprotectants are circulated through the body or head to reduce cell damage.
    2. Over a 20-day period, the body or head is cooled to negative 320 degrees Fahrenheit.
        a. The patient is then stored in a steel cylinder of liquid nitrogen.
        b. According to *Omni* magazine, "At this temperature, biological function ceases and the patient will remain unchanged for hundreds of years."

(Transition: Now that we have explored the development of cryonics and how the freezing process works, you may wonder how much it costs and whether the people that are frozen can be rethawed.)

III. Two major issues in the future of cryonics are its high cost and the need to perfect the freezing and rethawing process.
    A. The cost of cryonic suspension ranges from $60,000 to $125,000.
        1. In some cases, this can be paid for with one's life insurance policy.
        2. As one cryonics member states, "Facing my own mortality turned out to be much harder than coming up with the cash to pay for life insurance premiums."
    B. The details involved in freezing and rethawing have yet to be fully worked out.
        1. As explained in *New Scientist*, the freezing process inflicts a crippling amount of cellular damage.
            a. So far, only a few types of human tissue can be successfully thawed once they are frozen.
            b. It is not yet possible to freeze and rethaw complicated organs, not to mention a complete body or brain.
        2. Scientists are working on ways to reduce the damage caused by the freezing process.
            a. They are researching better cryoprotectants to control cell damage.
            b. They are also developing microscopic machines to repair cells at the molecular level.

Conclusion

I. Cryonics has become much more than a plot in a science fiction novel.
    A. Eighty people have already been frozen and hundreds more have signed up.
    B. If scientists can figure out how to rethaw people successfully, cryonics will become much more popular.

II. So think again of your mother or father suffering a heart attack, your grandmother or grandfather dying of pneumonia, or your close friend being stricken with AIDS.

A. If they choose to be buried or cremated in traditional fashion, their physical minds and bodies will be destroyed.

B. In contrast, being cryonically frozen offers some small chance that they might be revived in the future.

C. Even if that chance is small, it's more than no chance at all.

3. From the preparation outline you constructed in Exercise 2, create a speaking outline that you might use in delivering the speech. Follow the guidelines for a speaking outline discussed in this chapter.

> **Discussion:** This exercise helps clarify the differences between a preparation outline and a speaking outline and gives students practice in creating a speaking outline. Whether or not you have students complete this exercise at home, you can follow class discussion of the preparation outline for "Cryonics" by discussing what a speaking outline for the same speech might include.

Applying the Power of Public Speaking *(from text pages 262-263)*

As the defense attorney in a car theft case, you need to prepare your closing argument to the jury before it begins its deliberations. After reviewing evidence from the trial, you decide to stress the following points to demonstrate the innocence of your client:

a. The stolen car was found abandoned three hours after the theft with the engine still warm; at the time the car was found, your client was at the airport to meet the flight of a friend who was flying into town.

b. Lab analysis of muddy shoe prints on the floor mat of the car indicates that the prints came from a size 13 shoe; your client wears a size 10.

c. Lab analysis shows the presence of cigarette smoke in the car, but your client does not smoke.

d. The only eyewitness to the crime, who was 50 feet from the car, said the thief "looked like" your client; yet the eyewitness admitted that at the time of the theft she was not wearing her corrective lenses, which had been prescribed for improving distance vision.

e.   The car was stolen at about 1 P.M.; your client testified that he was in a small town 175 miles away at 11 A.M.

f.   In a statement to police, the eyewitness described the thief as blond; your client has red hair.

As you work on the outline of your speech, you see that these points can be organized into three main points, each with two supporting points. Compose an outline that organizes the points in this manner.

Discussion: As with the other Applying the Power of Public Speaking scenarios throughout the book, this one is meant to illustrate that the principles of effective speechmaking are applied in a wide range of situations outside the classroom. In dealing with this scenario, students should construct an outline whose three main points deal with lab analysis, with the timeline of events, and with eyewitness testimony. Once the six points stated in the scenario are reorganized as subpoints under the lab analysis, timeline, and eyewitness main points, the outline will look as follows (allowing, of course, for differences in the exact wording of main points and in the order of some subpoints). The answer is included in the binder of full-color overhead transparencies that accompanies *The Art of Public Speaking*.

I.   Lab analysis does not support a guilty verdict.
    A.   Lab analysis of muddy shoe prints on the floor mat of the car indicates that the prints came from a size 13 shoe; the defendant wears a size 10.
    B.   Lab analysis also shows the presence of cigarette smoke in the car, but the defendant does not smoke.

II.   The timeline of events in the case does not support a guilty verdict.
    A.   The stolen car was found abandoned three hours after the theft with the engine still warm; at the time the car was found, the defendant was at the airport to meet the flight of a friend who was flying into town.
    B.   The car was stolen at about 1 p.m.; the defendant testified that he was in a small town 175 miles away at 11 a.m.

III.   Eyewitness testimony does not support a guilty verdict.
    A.   The only eyewitness to the crime, who was fifty feet from the car, said the thief "looked like" the defendant; yet the eyewitness admitted that at the time of the theft she was not wearing her corrective lenses, which had been prescribed for improving distance vision.
    B.   In a statement to police, the eyewitness described the thief as blond; the defendant has red hair.

Additional Exercises and Activities

1.   In the left-hand column below is a partially blank outline from a speech about suicide among college students. In the right-hand column, arranged in random order, are the subpoints to fill in the outline. Choose the appropriate subpoint for each blank in the outline.

Outline	Subpoints

Outline

I.   Suicide among college students is a serious problem.

    A.

    B.

    C.

        1.

        2.

II.   We can help solve the problem by knowing how to identify potential suicide victims and whom to contact about helping them.

    A.

        1.

        2.

            a.

            b.

            c.

    B.

        1.

        2.

Subpoints

Even on our campus the rate of suicide and attempted suicide is quite high.

There are also more subtle warning signs that a person may try to commit suicide.

There are excellent services available on campus and in the community to help potential suicide victims.

In town students can go to the Suicide Prevention Center.

One warning sign is loss of appetite.

Identifying potential suicide victims is easier than you think.

Dean Howard also said that for every known suicide attempt, two or three more go unnoticed.

According to the National Institute of Mental Health, suicide is the fastest growing cause of death for people aged 17 to 24 nationwide.

In an interview with Roger Howard, associate dean of students, I learned that last year there were over 60 known suicide attempts on our campus.

A second warning sign is prolonged depression.

The National Institute of Mental Health says 80 percent of the people who commit suicide tell someone ahead of time that they are going to kill themselves.

A third warning sign is giving away one's possessions.

Last year 10,000 young Americans committed suicide.

On campus students can go to the University Counseling Service.

Discussion: When filled in, the outline should look like the one below. (The order of points IA and IB can be reversed without damaging the students' answers.) To facilitate class discussion, the outline is included in the binder of overhead transparencies that accompanies *The Art of Public Speaking.*

I.   Suicide among college students is a serious problem.

    A.   According to the National Institute of Mental Health, suicide is the fastest growing cause of death for people aged 17 to 24 nationwide.

    B.   Last year 10,000 young Americans committed suicide.

    C.   Even on our campus the rate of suicide and attempted suicide is quite high.

        1.   In an interview with Roger Howard, associate dean of students, I learned that last year there were over 60 known suicide attempts on our campus.

        2.   Dean Howard also said that for every known suicide attempt, two or three more go unnoticed.

II.   We can help to solve the problem by knowing how to identify potential suicide victims and whom to contact about helping them.

    A.   Identifying potential suicide victims is easier than you might think.

        1.   The National Institute of Mental Health says that 80 percent of the people who commit suicide tell someone ahead of time that they are going to kill themselves.

        2.   There are also more subtle warning signs that a person may try to commit suicide.

            a.   One warning sign is loss of appetite.

            b.   A second warning sign is prolonged depression.

            c.   A third warning sign is giving away one's possessions.

    B.   There are excellent services on campus and in the community to help potential suicide victims.

        1.   On campus students can go to the University Counseling Service.

        2.   In town students can go to the Suicide Prevention Center.

2.   In the left-hand column below is a blank outline from a speech about the achievements of Booker T. Washington. In the right-hand column, arranged in random order, are the main points and subpoints to fill in the outline. Choose the appropriate main point or subpoint for each blank in the outline.

Outline	**Main Points and Subpoints**
I.	All told, Washington delivered some 4,000 public speeches during his 30-year career as an orator.
A.	Some people praise the speech as a brilliant example of audience adaptation in a very difficult situation.
1.	Washington is also known as one of the ablest speakers in American history.
2.	When Washington founded Tuskegee Institute in 1881, the school had only one dilapidated building and an enrollment of 40 students.
B.	Today, Tuskegee Institute remains a leader in applied research and practical education.
	Washington's most famous speech is his "Atlanta Exposition Address" of 1895.
II.	The growth of Tuskegee Institute under Washington's guidance was nothing short of phenomenal.
A.	To this day, Washington's speech at Atlanta remains highly controversial.
B.	Booker T. Washington is best known for founding Tuskegee Institute in Alabama.
1.	By the time Washington died in 1915, Tuskegee Institute occupied 2,000 acres of land, enrolled 1,500 students, and boasted a faculty of 200 instructors.
2.	Other people condemn the speech for failing to denounce racial segregation and inequality.
a.	In the "Atlanta Exposition Address" Washington urged blacks to strive for economic advancement rather than to agitate for immediate social equality.
b.	

Discussion: When filled in, the outline should look the one below. To facilitate class discussion, the outline is included in the binder of overhead transparencies that accompanies *The Art of Public Speaking.*

I.   Booker T. Washington is best known for founding Tuskegee Institute in Alabama.

    A.   The growth of Tuskegee Institute under Washington's guidance was nothing short of phenomenal.

        1.   When Washington founded Tuskegee Institute in 1881, the school had only one dilapidated building and an enrollment of 40 students.

        2.   By the time Washington died in 1915, Tuskegee Institute occupied 2,000 acres of land, enrolled 1,500 students, and boasted a faculty of 200 instructors.

    B.   Today, Tuskegee Institute remains a leader in applied research and practical education.

II.   Booker T. Washington is also known as one of the ablest speakers in American history.

    A.   All told, Washington delivered some 4,000 public speeches during his 30-year career as an orator.

    B.   Washington's most famous speech is his "Atlanta Exposition Address" of 1895.

        1.   In the "Atlanta Exposition Address" Washington urged blacks to strive for economic advancement rather than to agitate for immediate social equality.

        2.   To this day, Washington's speech at Atlanta remains highly controversial.

            a.   Some people praise the speech as a brilliant example of audience adaptation in a very difficult situation.

            b.   Other people condemn the speech for failing to denounce racial segregation and inequality.

Extra Teaching and Learning Resources

Avadian, Brenda, and Thanos, Marilyn. "Speechmapping: The Road Through Speech Preparation and Delivery." In Stephen E. Lucas (ed.), *Selections from the Speech Communication Teacher, 1986-1991*. New York: McGraw-Hill, 1992, pp. 51-52.

Brown, Kevin James. "'Spidergrams': An Aid for Teaching Outlining and Organization." In Stephen E. Lucas (ed.), *Selections from the Speech Communication Teacher, 1986-1991*. New York: McGraw-Hill, 1992, pp. 53-54.

Ensign, Russell L. "The 'Arrow through Ass's Ribs' Outline: A Teaching Aid for the Basic Course." In Stephen E. Lucas (ed.), *Selections from the Speech Communication Teacher, 1986-1991*. New York: McGraw-Hill, 1992, pp. 53-54.

Gschwend, Laura L. "Outlining Relay." In Stephen E. Lucas (ed.), *Selections from the Speech Communication Teacher, 1994-1996*. New York: McGraw-Hill, 1997, pp. 52-53.

Gullickson-Tolman, Liz. "Creating Outlines." In Stephen E. Lucas (ed.), *Selections from the Speech Communication Teacher, 1996-1999*. New York: McGraw-Hill, 2001, pp. 72-73.

McClish, Glen. "The 'Authorial Conversion' Structure in Oral Argument." In Stephen E. Lucas (ed.), *Selections from the Speech Communication Teacher, 1991-1994*. New York: McGraw-Hill, 1995, pp. 19-20.

Mino, Mary. "Structuring: An Alternate Approach for Developing Clear Organization." In Stephen E. Lucas (ed.), *Selections from the Speech Communication Teacher, 1986-1991*. New York: McGraw-Hill, 1992, pp. 55-56.

Muir, Star A. "Organizing and Critiquing Ideas." In Stephen E. Lucas (ed.), *Selections from the Speech Communication Teacher, 1994-1996*. New York: McGraw-Hill, 1997, pp. 53-54.

Schnell, Jim. "The Developmental Speech Sequence Model (DSSM)." In Stephen E. Lucas (ed.), *Selections from the Speech Communication Teacher, 1986-1991*. New York: McGraw-Hill, 1992, p. 56.

West, Valerie Y. "Newspaper Outlines." In Stephen E. Lucas (ed.), *Selections from the Speech Communication Teacher, 1994-1996*. New York: McGraw-Hill, 1997, pp. 54-55.

Chapter 11 Using Language

Chapter Objectives

After reading this chapter, students should be able to:

1. Explain why the effective use of language is vital to a public speaker.

2. Explain the differences between denotative and connotative meaning.

3. Explain the importance of using language accurately in public speeches.

4. Identify three methods public speakers can use to help ensure that their language will be clear to listeners.

5. Explain how public speakers can use imagery and rhythm to help bring their ideas to life.

6. Explain why public speakers need to use inclusive language and identify five ways they can do so.

Chapter Outline

I. Language is important *(text pages 266-268)*.
   A. Contrary to popular belief, language does not simply mirror reality.
   B. Language helps create our sense of reality by giving meaning to events.
      1. Language is not neutral.
      2. The words we use to label an event determine to a great extent how we respond to it.
   C. Words are vital to thinking itself.
      1. Thought and language are closely linked.

       2.   On most occasions when we are looking for "just the right word," what we are really looking for is just the right idea.

    D.   Words are the tools of a speaker's craft.

       1.   Different words have different uses—just like the tools of any profession.

       2.   Public speakers must choose the right words for the job they want to do.

II.   Words have two kinds of meaning—denotative and connotative *(text pages 268-269)*.

    A.   Denotative meaning is precise, literal, and objective.

       1.   It describes the object, person, or idea referred to.

       2.   One way to think of a word's denotative meaning is as its dictionary definition.

    B.   Connotative meaning is more variable, figurative, and subjective.

       1.   It is what the word suggests or implies.

       2.   Connotative meaning includes all the ideas, feelings, and emotions associated with the word.

    C.   Choosing words skillfully for their denotative and connotative meanings is a crucial part of the speaker's art.

III.   Public speakers need to use language accurately *(text pages 269-270)*.

    A.   Using language accurately is as vital to a speaker as using numbers accurately is to an accountant.

       1.   Speakers need to be sensitive to the shades of meaning of different words.

       2.   Speakers should not use a word unless they are confident of its meaning.

    B.   Speakers who have serious aspirations should develop a systematic plan for improving their vocabulary.

IV.   Public speakers need to use language clearly *(text pages 271-276)*.

    A.   Because listeners cannot turn to a dictionary or reread a speaker's words to discover their meaning, a speaker's meaning must be immediately comprehensible.

    B.   One way to ensure that a speaker's meaning is clear is to use familiar words.

       1.   A major barrier to clear speech is using stuffy, unfamiliar words when ordinary, familiar ones will do the job better.

       2.   Familiar words allow a speaker's meaning to come across without forcing the audience to perform mental gymnastics.

       3.   Even when dealing with technical topics, effective speakers find ways to explain their ideas in language that is familiar to the audience.

    C.   A second way to ensure that a speaker's meaning is clear is to use concrete words.

       1.   Concrete words refer to tangible objects and are more specific than abstract words.

       2.   Listeners are more likely to be interested in and to remember concrete words.

    D.   A third way to ensure that a speaker's meaning is clear is to eliminate linguistic clutter.

       1.   "Clutter" refers to the habit of using many more words than is necessary to express a speaker's meaning.

        2.   Cluttered speech forces listeners to hack through a tangle of words to discover the speaker's meaning.

        3.   Clear speakers keep their language lean and lively, clean and crisp.

V.   Public speakers need to use language vividly *(text pages 276-282)*.

    A.   Effective speakers use imagery to express their ideas vividly.

        1.   One way to generate imagery is to use concrete words.

            a.   Because concrete words call up mental impression of sights, sounds, touch, smell, and taste, they are the key to effective imagery.

            b.   By using concrete words a speaker can create vivid images that pull listeners irresistibly into the speech.

        2.   A second way to generate imagery is through the use of simile.

            a.   Simile is an explicit comparison between things that are essentially different yet have something in common.

            b.   A simile always contains the words "like" or "as"—as in "Air pollution is eating away at the monuments in Washington, D.C., like a giant Alka-Seltzer tablet."

        3.   A third way to generate imagery is through the use of metaphor.

            a.   Metaphor is an implicit comparison between things that are essentially different yet have something in common.

            b.   Unlike simile, metaphor does not contain the words "like" or "as"—as in "America's cities are the windows through which the world looks at American society."

    B.   Effective speakers use rhythm to enhance the vividness of their discourse.

        1.   Language has a rhythm created by the choice and arrangement of words.

            a.   Speakers, like poets, sometimes seek to exploit the rhythm of language.

            b.   By catching listeners up in an arresting string of sounds, speakers can strengthen the impact of their words.

        2.   There are four basic stylistic devices for enhancing the rhythm of a speech.

            a.   The first device is parallelism—the similar arrangement of a pair or series of related words, phrases, or sentences.

            b.   The second device is repetition—repeating the same word or set of words at the beginning or end of successive clauses or sentences.

            c.   The third device is alliteration—repeating the initial consonant sound in close or adjoining words.

            d.   The fourth device is antithesis—juxtaposing contrasting ideas, usually in parallel structure.

VI.   Public speakers need to use language appropriately *(text pages 282-284)*.

    A.   A speaker's language should be appropriate to the occasion.

        1.   Language that is appropriate for some occasions may not be appropriate for others.

        2.   Effective speakers adjust their language to the formality and etiquette of the occasion.

B.   A speaker's language should be appropriate to the audience.
1.   Language that is appropriate for some audiences may not be appropriate for others.
a.   Technical language may be fine for an audience of specialists, but it would not be suitable for a general audience.
b.   Profanity or off-color language might be fine for a comedian in a nightclub, but most listeners would find it offensive in a formal public speech.
c.   Most listeners are also offended by name-calling and other forms of abusive language.
2.   As a general rule, speakers should bend over backward to avoid language that might confuse or offend their audience.
C.   A speaker's language should be appropriate to the topic.
1.   When speaking to inform, for example, straightforward, descriptive language is usually most appropriate.
2.   When speaking to commemorate, on the other hand, special language devices such as metaphor, antithesis, and alliteration would be quite suitable.
D.   A speaker's language should be appropriate to the speaker himself or herself.
1.   Every speaker has her or his own language style.
2.   Effective speakers develop their language styles over many years of trial, practice, and error.

VII.   Public speakers are more effective when they use inclusive language *(text pages 284-287)*.
A.   Audiences today expect public speakers to use inclusive language that is respectful of the different groups that make up American society.
1.   Inclusive language does not stereotype, demean, or patronize people on the basis of gender, race, religion, disability, sexual orientation, or other factors.
2.   Using inclusive language is important as a matter of ethics.
3.   Using inclusive language is important as a matter of accuracy.
4.   Using inclusive language is important to being an audience-centered public speaker.
B.   There are five principles for inclusive language that have become so widespread that no aspiring speaker can afford to ignore them.
1.   The first principle is to avoid the generic "he."
2.   The second principle is to avoid the use of "man" when referring to both men and women.
3.   The third principle is to avoid stereotyping jobs and social roles by gender.
4.   The fourth principle is to avoid identifying personal traits that are unrelated to the topic.
5.   The fifth principle is to use names that groups use to identify themselves.
C.   If speakers have questions about inclusive language, they should consult one of the many guidebooks on this subject.

Exercises for Critical Thinking *(from text pages 289-290)*

1. Arrange each of the sequences below in order, from the most abstract word to the most concrete word.

    a.   housing complex, building, dining room, structure, apartment

         (structure, building, housing complex, apartment, dining room)

    b.   *Mona Lisa*, art, painting, creative activity, portrait

         (creative activity, art, painting, portrait, *Mona Lisa*)

    c.   automobile, vehicle, Ferrari, transportation, sports car

         (transportation, vehicle, automobile, sports car, Ferrari)

2. Rewrite each of the following sentences using clear, familiar words.

    a.   My employment objective is to attain a position of maximum financial reward.

         (I want a job that pays well.)

    b.   All professors at this school are expected to achieve high standards of excellence in their instructional duties.

         (All professors here are expected to be good teachers.)

    c.   In the eventuality of a fire, it is imperative that all persons evacuate the building without undue delay.

         (In case of fire, get out of the building as quickly as possible.)

3. Each of the statements below uses one or more of the following stylistic devices: metaphor, simile, parallelism, repetition, alliteration, antithesis. Identify the device (or devices) used in each statement.

    a.   "We are a people in a quandary about the present. We are a people in search of our future. We are a people in search of a national community." (Barbara Jordan)

         (repetition and parallelism)

b.   "The vice presidency is the sand trap of American politics. It's near the prize, and designed to be limiting." (Howard Fineman)

(metaphor)

c.   "We should not demean our democracy with the politics of distraction, denial, and despair." (Al Gore)

(alliteration)

d.   "America is not like a blanket—one piece of unbroken cloth, the same color, the same texture, the same size. America is more like a quilt—many patches, many sizes, and woven and held together by a common thread." (Jesse Jackson)

(simile, repetition, parallelism)

4.   Analyze Martin Luther King's "I Have a Dream" in the appendix of sample speeches that follows Chapter 18 in the textbook. Identify the methods King uses to make his language clear, vivid, and appropriate. Look particularly at King's use of familiar words, concrete words, imagery, and rhythm.

> **Discussion:** King's speech usually works quite well for study in the classroom. Because it is so famous, students look forward to reading it; yet it is short enough for them to do a thorough job of analysis. Also, the speech is so rich in its use of language that students can readily identify the major techniques King uses to make his ideas clear and compelling.
>
> Have students prepare their analysis as a homework assignment based on the transcript of the speech in the textbook. Then, before discussing the speech in class, show students the videotape of the speech from Volume I of the *Great Speeches* series that accompanies *The Art of Public Speaking*. If you show the videotape, take advantage of the opportunity to discuss how King's masterful delivery reinforces the impact of his words. Here is a synopsis of the speech.
>
> Specific Purpose: To reinforce the commitment of the audience to the principles of the nonviolent civil rights movement.
>
> Central Idea: By continued nonviolent protest, African Americans will achieve their full citizenship rights.
>
> Method of Organization: Topical
>
> Introduction: The opening sentence constitutes the introduction of King's speech. Such a perfunctory introduction is unusual, but

it was appropriate in King's situation. The audience had been waiting all afternoon to hear King speak. He did not need any special devices to secure their attention or to build his credibility. The speech might have been improved by an explicit preview statement, but the opening paragraph implies that King will focus on the meaning and importance of "the greatest demonstration for freedom in the history of our nation."

Body: There are four main sections in the body of the speech. The first runs from paragraph 2 through paragraph 8. In this section King addresses the nation at large and develops two subpoints. In paragraphs 3-6 he bemoans the "shameful condition" of American blacks, who still face poverty, segregation, and discrimination 100 years after the Emancipation Proclamation. In paragraphs 7-8 King reminds the nation of "the fierce urgency of now" and warns that continued protest will "shake the foundations of our nation until the bright day of justice emerges."

The second section of the body consists of paragraphs 9-14, in which King speaks primarily to his followers. He develops four subpoints: (1) In paragraphs 9-10 he urges black Americans to maintain their commitment to nonviolent methods of protest. (2) In paragraph 11, which received more applause than any other part of the speech, King reaffirms the need for blacks and whites to work together for freedom and equality. (3) In paragraph 12 King again stresses that African Americans cannot be satisfied until their grievances are resolved. (4) In paragraphs 13-14 King acknowledges that many African Americans have suffered "trials and tribulations" in their quest for freedom, but he urges them to keep the faith that their situation "can and will be changed."

The third section of the body consists of paragraphs 15-21, in which King dramatizes his "dream" of all Americans living in freedom and brotherhood. This is the most famous section of the speech, but the ideas were not new. King had said much the same thing, including repetition of the phrase "I Have a Dream," in a speech at Detroit two months earlier.

The fourth section of the body consists of paragraphs 22-29. Here King reaffirms his belief that "we will be free one day." He recites the first verse of "My Country 'Tis of Thee," builds into the series of sentences beginning with "Let freedom ring," and then moves into the emotionally charged final paragraph.

Conclusion: "I Have a Dream" is one of those speeches in which it is almost impossible to identify a discrete conclusion. The speech builds steadily to the powerful closing lines without a discernible shift from body to conclusion. The important question when judging a speech is not "Does the speech have a conclusion?" but "Does the speech conclude effectively?" In King's case the answer to the latter question is unequivocally yes.

Language: The most important feature of King's language is his use of familiar, concrete words. From beginning to end, he relies on words and phrases that create sharp, vivid images— "flames of withering injustice," "manacles of segregation and chains of discrimination," "sunlit path of racial justice," "whirlwinds of revolt," "heightening Alleghenies of Pennsylvania." This kind of language helps King make tangible the abstract principles of liberty and equality.

This is best seen in the "dream" section (paragraphs 15-21). Dreams are visual phenomena, and King's "dream" is strikingly visual. Instead of talking in vague terms about the ideals of freedom and justice, he makes those ideals concrete. Listening to him, we can almost see the sons of former slaves and the sons of former slave owners sitting down together on the red hills of Georgia. We can feel the sweltering heat of Mississippi and the cool breezes of the oasis of freedom and justice it will become. We can picture little black boys and black girls joining hands in Alabama with little white boys and white girls. By making his "dream" so vivid, King communicates it much more effectively than he could have through abstract language.

King's speech is also notable for its heavy use of metaphor. Most obvious is the extended metaphor of the "promissory note" or "bad check" in paragraphs 4-6, but there are also a number of brief metaphors scattered throughout the speech (see especially paragraphs 2-3, 7-9, 13, and 22) as well as a brace of similes in paragraph 2.

It is important to note that most of the metaphors and similes occur in pairs and are arranged to emphasize progress from a negative condition to a positive condition. For example: "It came as a joyous daybreak to end the long night of their captivity" (paragraph 2); ". . . to rise from the dark and desolate valley of segregation to the sunlit path of racial justice" (paragraph 7); ". . . to lift our nation from the quicksands of racial injustice to the solid rock of brotherhood" (paragraph 7); "The whirlwinds of revolt will continue to shake the foundations of our nation until the bright day of justice emerges" (paragraph 8); ". . . transform the jangling discords of our nation into a beautiful symphony of brotherhood" (paragraph 22). These metaphors strengthen King's message that continued protest will change things for the better.

King also relies heavily on repetition and parallelism to reinforce his ideas and accent the cadence of his speech. There are eight major units of repetition and parallelism: (1) The "One hundred years later . . ." series in paragraph 3; (2) The "Now is the time . . ." series in paragraph 7; (3) The "We must . . ." and "We must not . . ." series in paragraphs 9 and 10; (4) The "We can never be satisfied . . ." and "We cannot be satisfied . . ." series in paragraph 12; (5) The "Go back to . . ." series in paragraph 14; (6) The "I have a dream . . ." series in paragraphs 15-21; (7) The "to . . . together" series in paragraph 22; (8) The "Let freedom ring . . ." series in paragraphs 24-28.

Finally, one can observe the heavy religious tone of King's speech. Not only are there a number of explicit religious references, but many of King's words and images are biblical in origin. For example, "It came as a joyous daybreak to end the long night of their captivity" (paragraph 2) brings forth images of the exodus of the Jews from ancient Egypt. The phrase "until justice rolls down like waters and righteousness like a mighty stream" (paragraph 12) echoes the words of the prophet Amos. Similarly, King's statement in paragraph 21 that "every valley shall be exalted, every hill and mountain shall be made low, the rough places will be made plane and the crooked places will be made straight, and the glory of the Lord shall be revealed, and all flesh shall see it together" is repeated almost verbatim from the Old Testament book of Isaiah.

Applying the Power of Public Speaking *(from text page 290)*

Since graduating from college, you have developed a successful business that is located near the campus. As part of its plan to involve more alumni and community members in college affairs, the school has asked you to speak with new students during registration week for the fall term. In the opening section of your speech, you want the audience to feel what you felt the first few days you were on campus as a new student. The best strategy, you decide, is to present two or three similes that complete the sentence, "Beginning college is like . . ." Write your similes.

Discussion: As with the other Applying the Power of Public Speaking Scenarios throughout the book, this one is designed to demonstrate how the skills of public speaking discussed in the chapter apply to situations outside the classroom. An excellent way to use this scenario is to divide the class into groups and give each group five minutes to come up with several similes that complete the sentence, "Beginning college is like . . ." Have one member from each group present its similes to the class, and follow with a general discussion about similes and other figures of speech.

Additional Exercises and Activities

1.   In each of the following sentences, select the most appropriate word to complete the statement:

    a.   insisted, persisted, urged, persevered

       I _____ her to treat her roommates more kindly.

       Though he tried to prove his innocence, the district attorney _____ in believing him guilty.

       Despite the difficulty of the job, she _____ until she completed it.

       He _____ that gun control legislation will do little to reduce crimes of violence.

    b.   guess, prediction, estimate, forecast

       I just read the *Wall Street Journal*'s _____ for the economy next year.

       Will you turn on the television and get the weather _____ for tomorrow?

       It's always a good idea to get a written _____ before taking your car in for repairs.

       Chien doesn't have the foggiest idea how many jelly beans are in the jar. He's just making a _____ .

    c.   snap, tap, clap, slap

       I knew someone was following me through the woods when I heard a twig _____ behind me.

       The insistent _____ of the flag against the pole increased the drama of the military funeral.

       Sheila walked with so much spring in her step you could hear her feet _____ on the sidewalk.

       All at once we heard a tremendous _____ of thunder.

    d.   necessary, compulsory, unavoidable, irresistible

       The final exam in this course is _____ .

       Milos tried to turn down the offer of a free Caribbean cruise, but in the end he found it simply _____ .

       Proper clothing is _____ to survival in the Arctic.

       Because Crystal's train was late, her failure to keep the appointment was really _____ .

Discussion: This is an enjoyable exercise that increases students' awareness of the importance of careful, accurate word choice. The correct answers follow. To facilitate class discussion, this exercise is included in the binder of overhead transparencies that accompanies *The Art of Public Speaking.*

a.   insisted, persisted, urged, persevered

I ___urged___ her to treat her roommates more kindly.

Though he tried to prove his innocence, the district attorney ___persisted___ in believing him guilty.

Despite the difficulty of the job, she ___persevered___ until she completed it.

He ___insisted___ that gun control legislation will do little to reduce crimes of violence.

b.   guess, prediction, estimate, forecast

I just read the *Wall Street Journal*'s ___prediction___ for the economy next year.

Will you turn on the television and get the weather ___forecast___ for tomorrow?

It's always a good idea to get a written ___estimate___ before taking your car in for repairs.

Chien doesn't have the foggiest idea how many jelly beans are in the jar. He's just making a ___guess___ .

c.   snap, tap, clap, slap

I knew someone was following me through the woods when I heard a twig ___snap___ behind me.

The insistent ___slap___ of the flag against the pole increased the drama of the military funeral.

Sheila walked with so much spring in her step you could hear her feet ___tap___ on the sidewalk.

All at once we heard a tremendous ___clap___ of thunder.

d.   necessary, compulsory, unavoidable, irresistible

The final exam in this course is ___compulsory___ .

Milos tried to turn down the offer of a free Caribbean cruise, but in the end he found it simply ___irresistible___ .

Proper clothing is ___necessary___ to survival in the Arctic.

Because Crystal's train was late, her failure to keep the appointment was really ___unavoidable___ .

2.   Have students analyze the speech by Keith Framnes in Chapter 17 of the textbook ("The Massachusetts 54th," pages 471-472). Students should focus their analysis on how Framnes utilizes imagery, parallelism, repetition, and other resources of language to enhance the impact of his ideas.

> **Discussion:**   "The Massachusetts 54th" is an excellent speech to study in conjunction with Chapter 11—especially if you do not deal with it as part of the section on commemorative speaking in Chapter 17. It is particularly valuable as a complement to Exercise 4 on page 290 of the textbook, in which students analyze Martin Luther King's "I Have a Dream."
>
> Although most students are fascinated by the stylistic brilliance of King's masterpiece, they are often so overwhelmed by it that they cannot envision themselves emulating King's use of language in their own speeches. "The Massachusetts 54th," however, is a classroom speech, and it shows how students can use the same devices as King to elevate and enliven their discourse. For analysis of "The Massachusetts 54th," see pages 357-358 of this manual. If you discuss the speech in class, you may also want to show the videotape of it, which is available as part of the instructional supplement to *The Art of Public Speaking*.

3.   Distribute copies of Andrea Besikof's "The Survivors" or James Davis' "Hail to the Heroes," which appear on pages 499-503 of this manual. Have students focus on how each speaker uses imagery, repetition, parallelism, and other resources of language to enhance the impact of his or her ideas.

> **Discussion:**   Both student commemorative speeches, "The Survivors" and "Hail to the Heroes," are rich texts to study for their use of language. As with Keith Framnes' "The Massachusetts 54th," (see the previous Additional Exercise/Activity), they illustrate how students can use the resources of language to elevate and polish their discourse. For a synopsis of the speeches, see pages 499-503 of this manual.

4.   Have students compose one page of prose in which they use all the resources of language discussed in the textbook—imagery, simile, metaphor, antithesis, alliteration, etc.—to describe a scene or to capture an emotion. Possible topics include:

the beach at sunset	my happiest moment
walking in the forest	my most fearful experience
a rainy night	my favorite person
life in the city	my most embarrassing moment
a boisterous party	my worst experience
any special location	my favorite childhood memory

Discussion: Encourage students to be as "literary" or "poetic" as they wish in this exercise. Some will go overboard and become excessively maudlin or melodramatic, but some will create surprisingly effective and moving prose. If you have students present orally what they have written, this exercise can also provide an additional brief speaking opportunity in class.

5. The following paragraph is filled with verbal clutter. Following the model on page 275 of the textbook, edit the paragraph so as to eliminate the unnecessary words. You should be able to find 50 to 60 such words. If you don't find that many, go back to the paragraph and edit it again.

Imagine the thought of burning up a priceless painting by Rembrandt just in order to stay warm for ten minutes. Sounds really crazy, doesn't it? But that is comparable to just what is happening right now in the Amazon rain forest of Brazil. The president of Brazil authorized a 14,000-mile network of highways to open up the vast area of the rain forest to settlement. Unfortunately, the project has been nothing but a disaster from the very beginning. Working in the hot, torrid, steamy jungle caused many fatal deaths among the workers. Soon a whole lot of foreign businesses began to get themselves involved in the project. Now the whole thing is utterly out of hand. Today there is a very real danger that the whole ecological balance of the rain forest will be irrevocably destroyed completely and altogether. This will have important and serious future implications in terms of what it means not only for Brazil, but for all of the rest of South America.

Discussion: This exercise is especially helpful if you have students prepare a manuscript speech. It works well as an in-class exercise, since it can be completed fairly quickly. To give students additional practice in clearing the underbrush out of their prose, this exercise can be supplemented with Additional Exercise/Activity 6 below. Here is what the paragraph looks like when it has been edited to eliminate the clutter. To facilitate class discussion, the edited paragraph is included in the binder of overhead transparencies that accompanies *The Art of Public Speaking*.

Imagine ~~the thought of~~ burning ~~up~~ a priceless painting by Rembrandt just ~~in order~~ to stay warm for ten minutes. Sounds ~~really~~ crazy, doesn't it? But that is comparable to ~~just~~ what is happening ~~right now~~ in the Amazon rain forest of Brazil. The president of Brazil authorized a 14,000-mile network of highways to open ~~up~~ the vast ~~area of the~~ rain forest to settlement. Unfortunately, the project has been ~~nothing but~~ a disaster from the ~~very~~ beginning. Working in the ~~hot, torrid, steamy~~ jungle caused many ~~fatal~~ deaths among the workers. Soon ~~a whole lot of~~ foreign businesses began to get ~~themselves~~ involved in the project. ~~Now the whole thing is utterly out of hand.~~ Today there is a ~~very real~~ danger that the ~~whole~~ ecological balance of the rain forest will be irrevocably destroyed ~~completely and altogether~~. This will have important ~~and serious future~~ implications ~~in terms of what it means~~ not only for Brazil, but for all of ~~the rest of~~ South America.

6.   The following paragraph is filled with verbal clutter. Following the model on page 275 of the textbook, edit the paragraph so as to eliminate the unnecessary words. You should be able to find 40 to 50 such words. If you don't find that many, go back to the paragraph and edit it again.

Rock music is such a big and important part of our lives today

that it is extremely difficult to imagine a time when people lived

without it. But there was once such a time. The early 1950s were

a time of bubble gum and soda pop—a pure and simple age. Then

a new kind of music started coming on the scene like a huge tidal

wave on a calm and quiet beach. A whole lot of young

performers were appearing who were revolutionizing the shape of

American popular music. Bill Haley, Chuck Berry, Elvis Presley,

Fats Domino, Little Richard, Jerry Lee Lewis—the list is a long

one that goes on and on. But one rock and roll performer stands

out above the rest as the most original and innovative of them all.

His name? Buddy Holly.

Discussion: Like the previous Additional Exercise/Activity, this works well as an in-class activity and is especially helpful if you have students prepare a manuscript speech. Here is what the paragraph looks like when it has been edited to eliminate the clutter. To facilitate class discussion, the edited paragraph is included in the binder of overhead transparencies that accompanies *The Art of Public Speaking*.

Rock music is such a big ~~and important~~ part of our lives ~~today~~

that it is ~~extremely~~ difficult to imagine a time when people lived

without it. But there was ~~once~~ such a time. The early 1950s were a

time of bubble gum and soda pop—a pure and simple age. Then a

new kind of music started ~~coming on the scene~~ like a ~~huge~~ tidal

wave on a ~~calm and~~ quiet beach. A ~~whole~~ lot of young performers

~~were appearing who~~ were revolutionizing ~~the shape of~~ American

popular music. Bill Haley, Chuck Berry, Elvis Presley, Fats

Domino, Little Richard, Jerry Lee Lewis—the list ~~is a long one that~~

goes on and on. But one ~~rock and roll~~ performer stands out ~~above~~

~~the rest~~ as the most ~~original and~~ innovative of ~~them~~ all. His name?

Buddy Holly.

Extra Teaching and Learning Resources

General

Black, Edwin. "Gettysburg and Silence." *Quarterly Journal of Speech*, 80 (1994), 21-36.

Bryson, Bill. *Made in America: An Informal History of the English Language in the United States*. New York: Avon Books, 1996.

Carpenter, Ronald H. *Choosing Powerful Words: Eloquence That Works*. Boston: Allyn and Bacon, 1999.

Fiske, Robert Hartwell, and Lederer, Richard. *The Dictionary of Concise Writing: 10,000 Alternatives to Wordy Phrases*. Oak Park, IL: Marion Street Press, 2002.

Graddol, David; Leith, Dick; and Swann, Joan (eds.). *English: History, Diversity, and Change*. London: Routledge, 1996.

Harris, Robert A. *Writing with Clarity and Style: A Guide to Rhetorical Devices for Contemporary Writers*. Los Angeles: Pyrczak Publishing, 2003.

Kane, Thomas S. *The New Oxford Guide to Writing*. New York: Oxford University Press, 1994.

Krauss, Robert M., and Chiu, Chi-Yue. "Language and Social Behavior." In Gilbert, Daniel T.; Fiske, Susan T.; and Lindzey, Gardner (eds.), *Handbook of Social Psychology*, 4th ed. New York: McGraw-Hill, 1998, Vol. II, pp. 41-188.

Lakoff, Robin Tolmach. *The Language War*. Berkeley: University of California Press, 2000.

Lederer, Richard. *The Miracle of Language*, rev. ed. New York: Pocket Books, 1999.

Lucas, Stephen E. "The Stylistic Artistry of the Declaration of Independence." *Prologue: Quarterly of the National Archives*, 22 (1990), 24-43.

Lutz, William. *Doublespeak Defined*. New York: HarperCollins, 1999.

McArthur, Tom (ed.). *The Oxford Companion to the English Language*. Oxford: Oxford University Press, 1992.

McCrone, John. *The Ape That Spoke: Language and the Evolution of the Human Mind*. New York: Morrow, 1991.

McWhorter, John. *The Power of Babel: A Natural History of Language*. New York: Henry Holt, 2001.

Pinker, Steven. *The Language Instinct: How the Mind Creates Language*. New York: HarperCollins, 1994.

Pinker, Steven. *Words and Rules: The Ingredients of Language*. New York: HarperCollins, 2000.

Rhodes, Richard. *How to Write: Advice and Reflections*. New York: Morrow, 1995.

Soukhanov, Anne H., and Flexner, Stuart B. (eds.). *Speaking Freely: A Guided Tour of American English from Plymouth Rock to Silicon Valley*. New York: Oxford University Press, 1997.

Williams, Joseph M. *Style: Ten Lessons in Clarity and Grace*, 7th ed. Chicago: University of Chicago Press, 2002.

Wilson, Paula. "The Rhythm of Rhetoric: Jesse Jackson at the 1988 Democratic National Convention." *Southern Communication Journal*, 61 (1996), 253-264.

Wolfram, Walt, and Schilling-Estes, Natalie. *American English: Dialects and Variation*. Oxford: Blackwell, 1998.

Zinsser, William. *On Writing Well*, 25th anniversary ed. New York: HarperCollins, 2001.

Figures of Speech

Baldick, Chris. *The Concise Oxford Dictionary of Literary Terms*. New York: Oxford University Press, 1992.

Corbett, Edward P. J., and Connors, Robert J. *Classical Rhetoric for the Modern Student*. 4th ed. New York: Oxford University Press, 1999, Chapter 4.

Fahnestock, Jeanne. *Rhetorical Figures in Science*. New York: Oxford University Press, 1999.

Lanham, Richard A. *A Handlist of Rhetorical Terms*, 2nd ed. Berkeley: University of California Press, 1992.

Quinn, Arthur. *Figures of Speech: Sixty Ways to Turn a Phrase*. Davis, CA: Hermagoras Press, 1993.

Sommer, Elyse, and Sommer, Mike. *Similes Dictionary*. Detroit: Visible Ink Press, 1998.

Sommer, Elyse, and Weiss, Dorrie. *Metaphors Dictionary*. Detroit: Visible Ink Press, 1996.

Sopory, Pradeep, and Dillard, James Price. "The Persuasive Effects of Metaphor: A Meta-Analysis." *Human Communication Research*, 28 (2002), pp. 282-419.

Inclusive Language

Cameron, Deborah (ed.). *The Feminist Critique of Language: A Reader*, 2nd ed. London: Routledge, 1998.

Herbst, Phillip H. *The Color of Words: An Encyclopaedic Dictionary of Ethnic Bias in the United States*. Yarmouth, ME: Intercultural Press, 1997.

Ivy, Diana K., and Backlund, Phil. *Exploring GenderSpeak: Personal Effectiveness in Gender Communication*, 2nd ed. New York: McGraw-Hill, 2000.

Maggio, Rosalie. *Talking About People: A Guide to Fair and Accurate Language*. Phoenix, AZ: Oryx Press, 1997.

Wood, Julia T. *Gendered Lives: Communication, Gender, and Culture*, 5th ed. Belmont, CA: Wadsworth, 2003.

Classroom Activities and Assignments

Adams, John C. "Earstorming." In Stephen E. Lucas (ed.), *Selections from the Speech Communication Teacher, 1991-1994*. New York: McGraw-Hill, 1995, p. 16.

Bozik, Mary, and Beall, Melissa. "Modeling Metaphorical Thinking." In Stephen E. Lucas (ed.), *Selections from the Speech Communication Teacher, 1991-1994*. New York: McGraw-Hill, 1995, pp. 38-39.

Gschwend, Laura L. "Acquiring the Artful Use of Antithesis." In Stephen E. Lucas (ed.), *Selections from the Speech Communication Teacher, 1994-1996*. New York: McGraw-Hill, 1997, pp. 42-43.

Hochel, Sandra. "Language Awareness and Assessment." In Stephen E. Lucas (ed.), *Selections from the Speech Communication Teacher, 1986-1991*. New York: McGraw-Hill, 1992, p. 39.

Jensen, Marvin D. "Revising Speech Style." In Stephen E. Lucas (ed.), *Selections from the Speech Communication Teacher, 1986-1991*. New York: McGraw-Hill, 1992, pp. 39-41.

Lamoureux, Edward Lee. "Practicing Creative Word Choice with Dialogic Listening." In Stephen E. Lucas (ed.), *Selections from the Speech Communication Teacher, 1986-1991*. New York: McGraw-Hill, 1992, pp. 41-42.

McGrath, Richard. "The Slang Game." In Stephen E. Lucas (ed.), *Selections from the Speech Communication Teacher, 1986-1991*. New York: McGraw-Hill, 1992, pp. 42-43.

Pendleton, Susan C. "Using Figurative Language in Persuasive Speeches." In Stephen E. Lucas (ed.), *Selections from the Speech Communication Teacher, 1996-1999*. New York: McGraw-Hill, 2001, pp. 64-65.

Phillips, Terilyn Goins. "Introducing Gender-Biased Language: Much Ado About Something." In Stephen E. Lucas (ed.), *Selections from the Speech Communication Teacher, 1996-1999*. New York: McGraw-Hill, 2001, pp. 65-66.

Ringer, R. Jeffrey. "Simply Jargon." In Stephen E. Lucas (ed.), *Selections from the Speech Communication Teacher, 1994-1996*. New York: McGraw-Hill, 1997, p. 43.

Rowley, Edwin N. "More Than Mere Words." In Stephen E. Lucas (ed.), *Selections from the Speech Communication Teacher, 1991-1994*. New York: McGraw-Hill, 1995, p. 39.

Shelton, Michael W. "The Meaning Exercise: A Focus on Denotation and Connotation." In Stephen E. Lucas (ed.), *Selections from the Speech Communication Teacher, 1996-1999*. New York: McGraw-Hill, 2001, pp. 67-68.

Siddens, Paul J., III. "Figures of Speech in Poetic and Everyday Discourse." In Stephen E. Lucas (ed.), *Selections from the Speech Communication Teacher, 1994-1996*. New York: McGraw-Hill, 1997, pp. 43-44.

Young, Kathryn Sue. "Proving the Importance of Inclusive Language in the Basic Course." In Stephen E. Lucas (ed.), *Selections from the Speech Communication Teacher, 1996-1999*. New York: McGraw-Hill, 2001, pp. 66-67.

Zizik, Catherine H. "Powerspeak: Avoiding Ambiguous Language." In Stephen E. Lucas (ed.), *Selections from the Speech Communication Teacher, 1994-1996*. New York: McGraw-Hill, 1997, pp. 44-45.

Films and Videos

"Abraham Lincoln on Communication." Insight Media (1995). 60 minutes.

"Acquiring the Human Language: 'Playing the Language Game.'" Film Library (1995). 55 minutes.

"Cognition and Language." Insight Media (2001). 30 minutes.

"Discovering the Human Language: 'Colorless Green Ideas.'" Film Library (1995). 55 minutes.

"The Ebonics Controversy." Insight Media (1998). 30 minutes.

"The Global Tongue: English." Films for the Humanities and Sciences (1997). 24 minutes.

"Great American Speeches: 80 Years of Political Oratory." Films for the Humanities and Sciences (1995). Six volumes; 275 minutes.

"He Said, She Said: Gender, Language, and Communication." Insight Media (2001). 50 minutes.

"The Human Language Evolves: With and Without Words." Film Library (1995). 55 minutes.

"Language and Mind." Insight Media (1998). 55 minutes.

"The Language of Leadership: The Winston Churchill Method." Films for the Humanities and Sciences (1993). 60 minutes.

"The Language of War." Insight Media (1990). 29 minutes.

"A Light History of the English Language." Insight Media (1997). 37 minutes.

"In Search of the First Language." Insight Media (1994). 54 minutes.

"Language." Films for the Humanities and Sciences (1999). 52 minutes.

"Language." Insight Media (1997). 30 minutes.

"A Light History of the English Language." Insight Media (1997). 37 minutes.

"Peggy Noonan: Creator of 'A Kinder, Gentler America.'" Films for the Humanities and Sciences (1990). 24 minutes.

"Sexism in Language." Films for the Humanities and Sciences (1993). 20 minutes.

"The Speeches of Martin Luther King, Jr." Insight Media (1998). 60 minutes.

"Technology: The Web and 'World English.'" Films for the Humanities and Sciences (2001). 52 minutes.

"Ted Sorenson: On Speechwriting." Insight Media (1995). 33 minutes.

"Unlocking Language." Films for the Humanities and Sciences (1998). 29 minutes.

"Verbal Communication: The Power of Words," revised edition. CRM Films (1992). 22 minutes.

"You Can't Say That! 'Politically Correct' Free Speech." Films for the Humanities and Sciences (2000). 43 minutes.

Chapter **12** Delivery

Chapter Objectives

After reading this chapter, students should be able to:

1. Explain why good delivery is important to successful speaking.

2. Explain the major characteristics of effective speech delivery.

3. Identify the four methods of delivering a speech.

4. Explain the eight aspects of voice usage that are crucial to public speaking.

5. Discuss the four aspects of physical action that are most important to a public speaker.

6. Explain the five-step method presented in the chapter for practicing extemporaneous speech delivery.

7. Identify the two stages in preparing for a question-and-answer session and explain six things a speaker should keep in mind when responding to questions during the session itself.

Chapter Outline

I. Good delivery can make the difference between a successful speech and an unsuccessful speech *(text pages 294-295)*.
   A. In addition to having something to say, a speaker must know *how* to say it.
      1. A wonderfully written speech can be destroyed by poor delivery.
      2. Even a mediocre speech will be more effective if it is delivered well.

3.   Speech delivery is based on nonverbal communication: the speaker's use of voice and body to convey the message expressed by words.

B.   Good delivery is an art.

1.   It conveys the speaker's message clearly, interestingly, and without distracting the audience.

2.   Most audiences prefer delivery that combines a certain degree of formality with the best attributes of good conversation—directness, vocal and facial expressiveness, and a lively sense of communication.

II.   There are four basic methods of delivering a speech *(text pages 295-299)*.

A.   Some speeches are read verbatim from a manuscript.

1.   Manuscript speeches are often used in situations that require absolute accuracy of wording or that impose strict time limits upon the speaker.

2.   Speakers should take several steps when speaking from a manuscript.

a.   They should rehearse the speech aloud to make sure it sounds natural.

b.   They should work on establishing eye contact with the audience.

c.   They should make sure the final copy of the manuscript is legible at a glance.

d.   They should concentrate on *talking with* the audience rather than *reading to* them.

B.   Some speeches are recited from memory.

1.   Nowadays it is customary to deliver only the shortest speeches from memory.

2.   When delivering a speech from memory, the speaker should learn it so thoroughly that she or he can concentrate on communicating with the audience rather than on remembering specific words.

C.   Some speeches are delivered impromptu.

1.   Impromptu speeches are presented with little or no immediate preparation.

2.   When speakers find themselves faced with an impromptu speaking situation, they should follow four simple steps to organize their thoughts quickly.

a.   First, they should state the point to which they are responding.

b.   Second, they should state the point they want to make.

c.   Third, they should use whatever support they have—examples, statistics, or testimony—to prove their point.

d.   Fourth, they should summarize their point.

3.   In addition, an impromptu speaker should consider the following suggestions.

a.   If there is sufficient time, quickly jot down brief a outline to remember what to say.

b.   Try to remain calm and assured regardless of how nervous you might be.

c.   Maintain strong eye contact with the audience.

d.   Concentrate on speaking at a clear, deliberate pace.

e.   Use signposts ("first," "second," etc.) to help the audience keep track of your ideas.

D.   Some speeches are delivered extemporaneously.

1.   Extemporaneous speeches are carefully prepared and practiced in advance.

2. They are presented from a set of notes, but the exact wording is chosen at the moment of delivery.
3. There are several advantages to extemporaneous delivery.
   a. It gives greater control over ideas and language than impromptu delivery.
   b. It allows for greater spontaneity and directness than memorized or manuscript delivery.
   c. It encourages conversational vocal qualities, natural gestures, and strong eye contact.
4. Most classroom speeches are delivered extemporaneously.
5. At the end of this chapter, students will find a five-step method for practicing extemporaneous delivery.

III. Effective speakers learn to control their voices to enhance the impact of their message *(text pages 299-306)*.
A. The volume of a speaker's voice is basic to effective delivery.
   1. If a speaker talks too softly, he or she will not be heard.
   2. If a speaker talks too loudly, he or she will be thought boorish.
   3. Whether speaking with or without a microphone, a speaker must adjust her or his volume to the acoustics of the room and the size of the audience.
B. The pitch of a speaker's voice has an impact on delivery.
   1. Pitch is the highness or lowness of a speaker's voice.
   2. Speakers who do not change their pitch speak in a monotone, which makes their voice flat and lifeless.
   3. Effective speakers vary their pitch to generate interest and to convey meaning and emotion.
C. The rate of a speaker's voice will affect the outcome of a speech.
   1. Rate refers to the speed at which a person speaks.
   2. Although most people in the United States speak at a rate between 120 and 150 words per minute, there is no uniform rate for effective speechmaking.
   3. The most appropriate rate depends on the speaker's voice, the mood the speaker is trying to create, the audience, and the occasion.
   4. Two obvious faults to avoid are speaking so slowly that listeners get bored or so fast that they lose track of the message.
D. Effective pauses can contribute greatly to a speaker's impact.
   1. Pauses can be used to signal the end of a thought unit, to give an idea time to sink in, or to lend dramatic impact to a statement.
   2. Novice speakers can develop their use of pauses by practice and by observing experienced speakers.
   3. Above all, a speaker should avoid vocalized pauses.
      a. Vocalized pauses include statements such as "like," "er," "uh," or "um."
      b. Research shows that too many vocalized pauses reduce a speaker's credibility and persuasiveness.
E. Vocal variety is one of the most important elements in effective delivery.
   1. Vocal variety refers to modulations in the rate, pitch, volume, and timing of a speaker's voice.

2. Speakers who lack vocal variety come across as flat, dull, and uncommunicative.

3. Speakers who possess strong vocal variety come across as lively, dynamic, and communicative.

F. Pronunciation is another vocal feature that influences the outcome of a speech.

1. Errors in pronunciation can reduce a speaker's credibility.

2. If a speaker has doubts about how to pronounce a word, she or he should check the pronunciation in a dictionary or with another person.

G. Articulation also has an impact on how a speech is received.

1. Articulation refers to how crisply and distinctly we form particular speech sounds.

2. Some errors in articulation are caused by physical problems such as a cleft palate, a misaligned jaw, or a poorly fitted dental plate.

3. Most errors in articulation are caused by laziness—by failing to produce speech sounds clearly and precisely.

4. Articulation errors caused by physical problems often require the aid of a certified speech therapist.

5. Articulation errors caused by laziness can be remedied by diagnosing the errors and working to correct them.

H. A speaker's dialect can influence how the speech is received.

1. Dialects are accents, grammatical patterns, and vocabulary distinctive to particular regions or ethnic groups.

2. Although no dialect is inherently superior or inferior to another, heavy use of dialect in public speaking can be troublesome if the audience does not share the dialect in question.

3. Regional or ethnic dialects usually do not pose a problem if listeners are familiar with the dialect and find it appropriate to the occasion.

IV. Effective speakers learn to use their body to enhance the impact of their message *(text pages 306-310)*.

A. Physical actions can play a major role in the outcome of a speech.

1. Researchers estimate that hundreds of thousands of messages are conveyed through physical actions.

2. Studies show that in some situations these actions account for much of the meaning communicated by a speaker.

B. Four aspects of physical action are especially important for public speakers.

1. The first aspect is personal appearance.

a. Listeners always see a speaker before they hear the speaker.

b. Just as speakers adapt to the audience and occasion in other respects, so should they take care to dress and groom appropriately.

2. The second aspect is movement.

a. Effective speakers avoid distracting movements such as fidgeting with notes, leaning on the lectern, and shifting weight from one foot to the other.

b. Effective speakers are also aware of their movements before and after the speech as well as during it.

    (1) Before the speech, they walk confidently to the lectern, establish eye contact with the audience, and look poised and confident regardless of how nervous they may be.

    (2) After the speech, they give their closing line a few moments to sink in, calmly gather up their notes, and maintain their confident demeanor while returning to their seat.

3. The third aspect is gestures.

    a. Some accomplished speakers gesture a great deal; others hardly at all.

    b. The cardinal rule is that whatever gestures a speaker does make should not draw attention to themselves or distract from the message of the speech.

    c. Gestures should appear natural and spontaneous, clarify or reinforce the speaker's ideas, and be appropriate to the audience and occasion.

4. The fourth aspect is eye contact.

    a. Audiences often look at a speaker's eyes for clues about the speaker's truthfulness, intelligence, and feelings.

    b. Although customs of eye contact in interpersonal communication vary from culture to culture, there is fairly wide agreement across cultures on the importance of eye contact in public speaking.

    c. Research shows that in the United States speakers who fail to establish eye contact are perceived as ill at ease and often as insincere or dishonest.

    d. Establishing eye contact is one of the quickest ways to establish a communicative bond with an audience.

        (1) Eye contact helps capture an audience's attention.

        (2) Eye contact helps establish the speaker's credibility.

        (3) Eye contact allows speakers to see and respond to feedback.

V. Speakers can improve their speech delivery by following a five-step method *(text pages 310-311)*.

A. First, the speaker should go over her or his preparation outline aloud.

    1. This allows the speaker to judge how the written outline translates into spoken discourse.

    2. It also gives the speaker a chance to clarify and revise the speech as necessary.

B. Second, the speaker should prepare a speaking outline.

    1. Preparing a speaking outline increases the speaker's familiarity with the speech.

    2. The speaking outline should conform to the guidelines presented in Chapter 10.

C. Third, the speaker should practice the speech aloud several times using only the speaking outline.

    1. At this stage, the speaker should not worry about getting everything in the speech just right.

      2.   The aim is to gain control of the ideas and structure of the speech, not to learn it word for word.

D.   Fourth, the speaker should polish and refine the delivery.
      1.   Practicing in front of a mirror is one way to check on nonverbal communication such as gestures and eye contact.
      2.   Tape recording the speech is an excellent way to gauge such things as rate, pauses, articulation, and vocal variety.
      3.   A few practice sessions in front of other people—friends, family, roommates, etc.—can be especially valuable.

E.   Fifth, the speaker should give the speech a dress rehearsal under conditions as close as possible to those he or she will face during the actual speech.
      1.   Some students like to try the speech in an empty classroom a day or two before the speech is due.
      2.   It is important that the dress rehearsal incorporate every aspect of the speech, including visual aids.

F.   In order for this method to be effective, speakers must start early.
      1.   A single practice session—no matter how long—is rarely enough.
      2.   Student speakers should give themselves *at least* a couple of days, preferably more, to gain command of the speech and its presentation.

VI.   Answering audience questions is often an important part of public speaking *(text pages 311-316)*.

A.   Many speeches include a question-and-answer session with the audience.
      1.   Depending on the situation, questioning may occur after the presentation or throughout the speech itself.
      2.   In either case, how a speaker handles questions can have as strong an impact on the audience as the speech itself.

B.   Thorough preparation is essential for a successful question-and-answer session.
      1.   The first step in preparing is to formulate answers to possible questions.
          a.   It is important to think about possible questions even as one is writing the speech.
          b.   Writing out answers in full helps ensure that the speaker has thought them out completely.
      2.   The second step in preparing is to practice delivering the answers.
          a.   Writing out answers and vocalizing them effectively under the pressure of a question period are two different things.
          b.   Since the answers will be presented orally, they should be rehearsed orally.

C.   Managing the question-and-answer session is an important skill in its own right.
      1.   If there is any doubt about whether questions will be handled during or after the speech, the speaker should clarify this at the outset.
      2.   It is vital to approach questions with a positive attitude.
          a.   Questions should be seen as a genuine effort by the audience to learn more about the topic of the speech.

  b.   If someone has misunderstood part of the speech, the question
        session is a perfect opportunity to clarify.

  c.   If hostile questions arise, the speaker should respond openly and
        calmly, rather than defensively or argumentatively.

3. Listening carefully to questions is vital to a successful question-and-
    answer session.

  a.   It's hard to answer a question well if a person doesn't listen
        carefully to it.

  b.   If a question is hard to understand, the speaker should ask the
        questioner to restate it.

4. Answers should be directed to the entire audience, not just to the questioner.

  a.   Speaking to the audience as a whole helps keep everyone interested.

  b.   When speaking to a large audience, it's important to restate each
        question after it is asked so the entire audience can hear it.

5. Questions should be answered honestly and straightforwardly.

  a.   If a speaker doesn't know the answer to a question, he or she should
        say so and offer to get it after the speech.

  b.   A speaker should not try to bluff his or her way through an answer.

6. Unless there is a moderator for the question period, the speaker is
    responsible for keeping it on track.

  a.   The best course is usually to allow one question and one follow-up
        from each person.

  b.   A speaker should avoid being diverted into a personal debate with
        any questioner.

  c.   When time for the question period is running down, the speaker
        should answer one or two final inquiries and wrap up by thanking
        the audience for its attention.

Exercises for Critical Thinking *(from text pages 317-318)*

1. An excellent way to improve your vocal variety is to read aloud selections from poetry
    that require emphasis and feeling. Choose one of your favorite poems that falls into this
    category, or find one by leafing through a poetry anthology. Practice reading the
    selection aloud. As you read, use your voice to make the poem come alive. Vary your
    volume, rate, and pitch. Find the appropriate places for pauses. Underline the key
    words or phrases you think should be stressed. Modulate your tone of voice; use
    inflections for emphasis and meaning.

    For this to work, you must overcome your fear of sounding affected or "dramatic."
    Most beginning speakers do better if they exaggerate changes in volume, rate, pitch,
    and expression. This will make you more aware of the many ways you can use your
    voice to express a wide range of moods and meanings. Besides, what sounds overly
    "dramatic" to you usually does not sound that way to an audience. By adding luster,

warmth, and enthusiasm to your voice, you will go a long way toward capturing and keeping the interest of your listeners.

If possible, practice reading the selection into a digital recorder. Listen to the playback. If you are not satisfied with what you hear, practice the selection some more and record it again.

> **Discussion:**   Beginning speakers are often much less animated delivering a speech than in ordinary conversation. This is due partly to inexperience, partly to nervousness, partly to fear of sounding affected. But whatever the cause, the result is dull and lifeless delivery.
>
> This exercise is designed to help students over this barrier. At the start of the course they are likely to feel more comfortable using their voices expressively when reciting poetry than when delivering a speech. As they work with their poems, they often become more accustomed to modulating their voices to enhance the meaning of the words. As a capstone to the exercise, have students present their poems orally in class.

2.   Watch a 10-minute segment of a television drama with the sound turned off. What do the characters say with their dress, gestures, facial expressions, and the like? Do the same with a television comedy. How do the nonverbal messages in the two shows differ? Be prepared to report your observations in class.

> **Discussion:**   This exercise attunes students to the dimensions and effects of nonverbal communication, and it usually generates a lively class discussion. It works best if you assign particular programs for the entire class to watch.

3.   Attend a speech on campus. You may choose either a presentation by a guest speaker from outside the college or a class session by a professor who has a reputation as a good lecturer. Prepare a brief report on the speaker's vocal and nonverbal communication.

In your report, first analyze the speaker's volume, pitch, rate, pauses, vocal variety, pronunciation, and articulation. Then evaluate the speaker's personal appearance, bodily action, gestures, and eye contact. Explain how the speaker's delivery added to or detracted from what the speaker said. Finally, note at least two techniques of delivery used by the speaker that you might want to try in your next speech.

> **Discussion:**   This exercise provides for an out-of-class speech observation. You may want to have students write a brief paper reporting their observations; you may prefer that they use an observation form such as the one provided on page 259.

Out-of-Class Speech Observation—Delivery

Your name _____ **Speaker** _____

Where was the speech presented? _____

What was the occasion for the speech? _____

VOCAL COMMUNICATION: *Record your observations about each of the following aspects of the speaker's voice.*

Volume _____

Pitch _____

Rate _____

Pauses _____

Vocal variety _____

Pronunciation _____

Articulation _____

PHYSICAL ACTION: *Record your observations about each of the following aspects of the speaker's physical action.*

Personal appearance _____

Movement _____

Gestures _____

Eye contact _____

OVERALL EVALUATION OF DELIVERY: *Explain how the speaker's delivery added to or detracted from the message.*

_____

_____

WHAT IT MEANS FOR ME: *Explain at least two techniques of delivery used by the speaker that you might want to try in your next speech.*

_____

_____

Applying the Power of Public Speaking *(from text page 318)*

Utilizing your business degree and computer savvy, you have made a success of the online marketing company you started after graduating from college. Now in its third year, the company has prepared a proposal to design the e-commerce site for a major sporting goods retailer. In your 30-minute presentation to the retailer's management team, you will review the home-page designs, site maps, and security protocols.

You notice on the agenda that another 30 minutes have been allotted after your presentation for questions and answers. Knowing from your previous experience with clients how important the Q&A session can be, you want to be sure you are ready for it. What steps will you take to prepare?

Discussion: Like the Applying the Power of Public Speaking scenarios in other chapters, this one is designed to show how the principles of public speaking discussed in the textbook are used in everyday life. In this case, you can anticipate that students will mention what the chapter identifies as the major steps in preparing for a question-and-answer session: formulating answers to possible questions and practicing the delivery of those answers. In class discussion, encourage students to be specific about the processes involved in both of these steps, and use the discussion as a springboard to exploring how to manage the question-and-answer session itself.

Additional Exercises and Activities

1. Lead a class discussion in which students develop a set of criteria for effective speech delivery. After the discussion, codify the criteria into an evaluation form that can be used by the class for the remainder of the term.

   Discussion: Although this exercise takes most of a class period, it can be quite helpful. At the start of the discussion, tell students that they should draw their criteria not only from the textbook, but also from their own experience. Although most of the class may not have much background as public speakers, they all have considerable experience as consumers of speeches (in classroom lectures, if nowhere else). As a result, they are already fairly expert in detecting delivery behaviors that enhance or inhibit effective communication.

   By combining what they have read in the textbook with what they have learned from experience, most classes put together an excellent set of criteria for speech delivery. Moreover, because they have generated the evaluation form themselves, students are more committed to it. For a more complete discussion of how this kind of exercise works in the classroom, see Lynne Webb, "A Student-Devised Evaluation Form," in Stephen E. Lucas (ed.), *Selections from the Speech Communication Teacher, 1986-1991,* pp. 88-89, which is part of the instructional supplement that accompanies *The Art of Public Speaking.*

2.   Show students one or more selections from the videotapes of student speeches that accompany *The Art of Public Speaking*. Use the videotapes to illustrate points about effective and ineffective speech delivery.

Discussion: It is extremely difficult to teach delivery from a textbook. Perhaps the greatest benefit of using videotapes in the speech classroom is that they help students see in action the principles of delivery discussed in the textbook. Any of the speeches on the videotapes that accompany *The Art of Public Speaking* can be used for this purpose, and you will want to choose speeches that illustrate most clearly the points you emphasize in your classes.

For the convenience of instructors, 10 of the student speeches available on videotape are printed in this edition of *The Art of Public Speaking*. These speeches include "The Rare Phobia" (pages 81-82), "Steady and True" (pages 82-83), "The Great Wall of China" (pages 361-362), "Cryonics" (pages 385-388), "Self-Defense on Campus" (pages 453-456), "The Massachusetts 54th" (pages 471-472), "Questions of Culture" (pages A2-A4), "Dying to Be Thin" (pages A10-A12), "The Ultimate Gift" (pages A15-A17), and "Multicultural, Multilingual" (pages A18-A20).

Of these speeches, the most remarkable in terms of delivery is Sajjid Zahir Chinoy's "Questions of Culture." Presented at the University of Richmond's commencement ceremonies in May 1996, Chinoy's address was given extemporaneously, without notes, to an audience of several thousand people. What follows is a synopsis of Chinoy's speech. For information on the other speeches, consult the synopses in this manual (see the Table of Contents for page numbers).

Introduction: As in many commemorative speeches, the introduction of Chinoy's speech is very brief. It comprises only the first paragraph and consists of his salutation. Although the speech could have profited from a brief reference to the occasion or a statement by Chinoy that he was privileged to be chosen as the student commencement speaker, the lack of further introductory remarks proved not to be a serious problem.

Body: The body of Chinoy's speech runs from paragraph 2 through paragraph 23 and is divided into three main sections. The first section deals with Chinoy's departure from Bombay, India, and the questions of culture he contemplated during his flight to the United States (paragraphs 2-8). In paragraphs 2-6 he deals with his personal questions of culture and whether he would fit in as one of only three Indian students at the University of Richmond. In paragraphs 7-8 he shifts to global questions of culture and ethnicity, noting that countries, like individuals, face the problem of bringing different cultures together in peace and harmony.

The second major section of the body runs from paragraph 9 through paragraph 17. In these paragraphs Chinoy explains how his personal questions of culture were answered in the affirmative by his experiences at the University of Richmond. Referring to his time at the university as "the four most spectacular years of his life," Chinoy focuses on four special moments of human interaction—his first Thanksgiving in America (paragraph 11), his first Christmas eve (paragraph 12), his talk with a friend before a calculus exam (paragraph 13), and his roommate's support when India was undergoing communal riots in Chinoy's home town (paragraph 14). As a result of these and other experiences, Chinoy says, he discovered that the commonality of the human experience far transcends superficial differences of culture, language, and background.

In the third section of the body Chinoy compares his positive experiences at the University of Richmond with the cultural conflicts ravaging people and countries around the world (paragraphs 18-23). After looking at tragic events in Bosnia, India, and Africa (paragraphs 19-21), he laments all the "madness" that has occurred because people have stressed their differences rather than their "inherent similarities." He ends the body in paragraph 23 with the statement: "Two similar questions of culture in 1992. Two diametrically opposite results in 1996."

Conclusion: The conclusion consists of paragraphs 24-26. After encouraging the graduating class to distinguish itself, Chinoy returns to his central theme in paragraph 25 by urging his listeners to remember that it is cultural understanding—or the lack of it—that "can mean the difference between complete despair for one young boy in Bosnia and remarkable hope for another young boy at Richmond." With these words, Chinoy brings the entire speech together and reinforces the connections between his personal questions of culture and the global questions of culture broached in the first section of the body.

Chinoy closes the speech in paragraph 26 with the simple words, "Thank you." Although a case can be made that a speaker should not, in normal circumstances, dilute the impact of his or her conclusion by adding "Thank you" at the end, in this case the words are entirely appropriate because they can be read not just as thanking the audience for listening, but also as thanking it for providing the positive cultural experience that made Chinoy's years at Richmond so rewarding.

All in all, this is an exceptional speech. Not only is it perfectly suited to the audience and occasion, but it is superbly developed, written, and structured. Chinoy moves with great skill between his personal experiences and the larger questions of culture confronting the world. Although one might cavil that Chinoy's solution to those questions is oversimplified, it is hard to dispute his point that the world needs much more cultural understanding if it is to avoid the "madness" that Chinoy so eloquently laments.

This speech is also noteworthy for its delivery. Although Chinoy had a written manuscript, he delivered the speech extemporaneously and without notes—an especially remarkable feat given the size of his audience and the importance of the occasion. The moral to be stressed for students, however, is not that they must give all their speeches without notes—after all, Chinoy was an accomplished speaker with a great deal of experience in competitive debate and forensics—but how important it is to speak fluently, sincerely, dynamically, and with strong eye contact, regardless of the amount of notes one uses.

3.   Show students a videotape of a speech. After a couple of minutes turn off the sound and have students concentrate on the cues sent by the speaker's appearance, bodily movement, gestures, and eye contact. After a couple of minutes turn the sound back on so students can concentrate on the interaction of the speaker's vocal and physical communication.

Discussion: This is an easy way to illustrate the wide range of nonverbal cues sent by a speaker. To their surprise, students can usually tell from physical action alone whether the speaker is intent on communicating with the audience or is simply going through the motions. To save time, try combining this activity with the preceding exercise.

4.   Assign one or more rounds of impromptu speeches. Speeches should be one and a half minutes to two minutes in length. Encourage students to follow the guidelines for impromptu speaking discussed on pages 296-298 of the textbook.

Discussion: When you announce this assignment, most students will act as if you had condemned them to a fate worse than death. Yet for most students, impromptu speeches, if handled properly by the instructor, can be an enormously valuable confidence builder.

One way to approach impromptu speeches is to assign two or three at various intervals throughout the term. Another approach is to devote as many as three consecutive days to impromptu speeches, with each student in the class giving a speech on each day. The latter approach works particularly well because it gives students a chance to become comfortable with the impromptu situation. With each succeeding day, students gain poise and confidence. By the third day, many are so relaxed—and are giving such good speeches—that they ask to do more impromptu presentations. Another benefit of this approach is that students get so used to speaking without notes that their skills of extemporaneous speaking also improve dramatically—especially with respect to eye contact, gestures, and vocal variety.

If you assign two or more consecutive days of impromptu speaking, try to schedule them about two-thirds of the way through the term. If you assign them too early, students will not have learned enough about speechmaking in general to have a solid foundation for giving impromptu speeches. In addition, impromptu speaking involves considerable psychological risk on the part of students. The more comfortable students are with their classmates, the more willing they are to take the necessary risk. If you assign a series of impromptu speeches too early in the semester, students may recoil from the assignment rather then benefiting from it.

Although impromptu speeches can be used as a graded assignment, most teachers use them as an informal, non-graded speaking experience. Because students are usually apprehensive about speaking impromptu—especially initially—you should do all you can to maintain a low-key, supportive atmosphere.

One of the major questions with respect to impromptu speaking is how to select topics. When faced with impromptu speaking situations outside the classroom, students will speak about issues of immediate concern to their job, their church, their community, and the like. One way to approximate this experience is to develop a topic for each student based on one of her or his previous classroom speeches.

For example, if a student has given an informative speech on the benefits of learning CPR, you might assign him or her the following topic: "Doesn't learning CPR take a lot of time and money? Besides, I have never come across a person having a heart attack or drowning. It all seems like a lot of bother for something most people will never use. Is it really that important to know CPR?"

Or if a student has given a persuasive speech urging the audience to help save the world's rain forests, you might give her or him this topic: "Of course, it would be nice to save the rain forests in South America, but who are we to tell South Americans what to do with their land? After all, the United States uses more natural resources per capita than any other country in the world. Aren't we being hypocritical in asking other people to save the rain forests while we continue our dependence on foreign oil?"

Now you have created a situation analogous to one people often face in real life—defending their position on a subject with which they are already familiar. Students should feel free to use material from their previous speech in the impromptu speech—indeed, they should be encouraged to do so.

If you conduct a second round of impromptu speeches, again give students a choice of topics that will allow them to draw on familiar ideas and experiences. Some possibilities include: (1) What is your favorite—or least favorite—hobby/academic subject/sport/time of year, etc.? Why? (2) What are two or three things that really annoy you? (3) What is the most—or least—favorite aspect of your college experience so far? (4) If you could change any single aspect of college life at this school, what would it be? (5) What do you think it means to be successful in life? (6) What is the most fulfilling or rewarding aspect of your life to date? These topics are so universal that students will have no difficulty finding one on which to speak.

If you hold a third round of speeches, you can use the same set of topics—just make sure each student chooses a different individual topic from the one he or she chose in the second round. You can also devise new topics of a similar nature for the third round. You might even require that each student supply one or two topics that can go into the pool of possible topics for the entire class. This works especially well when students have responded positively to the first two days of impromptu speeches.

Regardless of the kinds of topics you use, give each student a few minutes to prepare the speech. You can do this by having the first 3 to 4 speakers choose their topics at the beginning of class. Then, as each speaker finishes, have a new student select his or her topic. If the speeches are to be two minutes in length, give the speakers time signals when they have one minute to go and then again when they have 30 seconds left. If you have an especially large class, you may have to reduce the length of the speeches to ensure that all students have an opportunity to perform on each day of impromptu speeches.

For other approaches to impromptu speaking, see the articles on this subject in the five volumes of *Selections from the Speech Communication Teacher* that accompany *The Art of Public Speaking*.

5. Divide the class into groups of 3 to 5 students. Assign each group a short children's story to present at the next class session. In presenting the story, each group is to act as if its audience were a ward of small children at a local hospital. Tell the students they must exaggerate their voice, their gestures, their facial expressions, and their bodily actions just as they would if they were actually telling the story to a group of children. Presentations should be 5 to 7 minutes in length, and each group should get together for an hour or so the evening before the assignment is due to assign speaking parts and to rehearse its presentation.

> **Discussion:** This exercise can work very well to help students use their voices and bodies expressively to communicate with an audience. By role playing as if they were addressing an audience of small children, many students feel less inhibited than if they were "actually" addressing their peers. They also tend to feel less intimidated speaking as members of groups. Indeed, a side benefit of this exercise is that it can help break down barriers among members of the class—especially if it is assigned fairly early in the quarter or semester.
>
> Good candidates for children's stories include such time-honored classics as "The Three Little Pigs," "Little Red Riding Hood," "Goldilocks," and "The Gingerbread Man"—all of which contain vivid action and dramatic dialogue. There are also a number of more contemporary stories that work quite well, including "The Tawny Scrawny Lion," Charlotte Zolotow's "Mister Rabbit and the Lovely Present," Maurice Sendak's "Pierre" and "Where the Wild Things Are," and Dr. Seuss's "The Cat in the Hat" and "Horton the Elephant."

To help ensure that all students participate fully in this exercise, many teachers assign some sort of minor grade to each group's presentation.

6.   Arrange to videotape at least one round of informative or persuasive speeches. Meet individually with each student to review her or his tape. Stop the tape periodically to point out what the speaker does particularly well and to indicate where improvement is needed.

> **Discussion:** This can be extraordinarily valuable for students because it gives them a chance to hear and see themselves as others hear and see them. It also gives you a chance to give each student a constructive "blow-by-blow" critique of his or her speech. At first students are somewhat apprehensive about being videotaped. But once they see how valuable it is, they often request to have the next speech taped as well.

7.   As an alternative to the preceding exercise, have students use their videotapes to prepare written self-assessments of their speeches.

> **Discussion:** Given the size of many classes, it is often impractical for instructors to meet with each student individually to review her or his videotape. Another option is to have students review their own tapes and prepare self-assessments of them. Some instructors provide students a detailed evaluation form for this purpose. Others require students to answer a set of questions covering each major aspect of the speech from topic selection and audience adaptation to supporting materials, delivery, and visual aids. Still others make the assignment open-ended and ask students to produce a two-page typed self-assessment. If you choose this last option, make sure students understand that the self-assessment is to be thoughtfully composed and carefully proofread. Tell them to focus both on the major strengths of the speech and on areas they wish to improve upon in the next speech.
>
> In my experience, most students take this assignment seriously and do a fine job of assessing their performance. Nonetheless, I recommend making it a graded assignment, if for no other reason than to reward students who do an especially thorough job with it. I have also found an interesting dynamic in the assessments. On the one hand, students can be rather hard on themselves—especially with regard to small matters of delivery. On the other hand, they recognize the fact that they look much more confident on tape than they felt internally while they were presenting the speech.
>
> Regardless of the approach you take to the self-assessment, it can be exceptionally effective, for it is founded on the principles of self-teaching. It should not be used, however, as a replacement for a thorough assessment from the instructor. Usually, the two assessments will be remarkably close in their judgments. If there are major discrepancies in some cases, you might wish to schedule individual conferences to clarify your judgments about the speech and to make sure students have a clear sense of what they need to concentrate on in their next presentation.

8.   Radio and television announcers must have outstanding articulation. One way they develop it is by practicing tongue twisters such as those listed below. Give students the list so they can work on their articulation. Tell students to begin by saying the tongue twisters slowly and firmly, so that each sound is clearly formed. Once they have the sounds correct, they can gradually increase to a normal rate of speech.

   a.   Pure food for four pure mules.

   b.   Which wily wizard wished wicked wishes for Willy?

   c.   The sixth sick Sheik's sheep is sick.

   d.   Fetch me the finest French-fried freshest fish that Finney fries.

   e.   Shy Sarah saw six Swiss wristwatches.

   f.   One year we had a Christmas brunch with Merry Christmas mush to munch. But I don't think you'd care for such. We didn't like to munch mush much.

   g.   The view from the veranda gave forth a fine vista of waves and leafy foliage.

   h.   She sells seashells on the seashore.

   i.   While we waited for the whistle on the wharf, we whittled vigorously on the white weatherboards.

   j.   Grass grew green on the graves in Grace Gray's grandfather's graveyard.

   k.   Pete Briggs pats pigs.
         Briggs pats pink pigs.
         Briggs pats big pigs.
         Pete Briggs is a pink pig, big pig patter.

   l.   Amidst the mists and coldest frosts,
         With stoutest wrists and loudest boasts,
         He thrusts his fists against the posts,
         And still insists he sees the ghosts.

         Discussion: Try this as an in-class activity. It's enjoyable and it helps make students aware of the need for precise articulation. Students who want additional work on articulation should be encouraged to practice with the list outside of class.

Extra Teaching and Learning Resources

General

Burgoon, Judee K.; Buller, David B.; and Woodall, W. Gill. *Nonverbal Communication: The Unspoken Dialogue*, 2nd ed. New York: McGraw-Hill, 1996.

Cassidy, Frederic G., and Hall, Joan H. (eds.). *Dictionary of American Regional English*, 4 vols. to date. Cambridge, MA: Harvard University Press, 1985-2002.

Chamberlin, Carla R. "Nonverbal Behaviors and Initial Impressions of Trustworthiness in Teacher-Supervisor Relationships." *Communication Education*, 49 (2000), pp. 352-364.

DePaulo, Bella M., and Friedman, Howard S. "Nonverbal Communication." In Gilbert, Daniel T.; Fiske, Susan T.; and Lindzey, Gardner (eds.), *Handbook of Social Psychology*, 4th ed. New York: McGraw-Hill, 1998, Vol. II, pp. 3-40.

DiResta, Diane. *Knockout Presentations: How to Deliver Your Message with Power, Punch, and Pizzazz*. Worcester, MA: Chandler House Press, 1998.

Gottsman, Deb, and Mauro, Buzz. *Taking Center Stage: Masterful Public Speaking Using Acting Skills You Never Knew You Had*. New York: Berkley Books, 2001.

Guerrero, Laura K.; DeVito Joseph; and Hecht, Michael L. *The Nonverbal Communication Reader: Classic and Contemporary Readings*. 2nd ed. Prospect Heights, IL: Waveland Press, 1999.

Hillman, Ralph. *Delivering Dynamic Presentations: Using Your Voice and Body for Impact*. Boston: Allyn Bacon, 1999.

Johnson, Scott D., and Miller, Ann, N. "A Cross-Cultural Study of Immediacy, Credibility, and Learning in the U.S. and Kenya." *Communication Education*, 51 (2002), pp. 280-292.

Knapp, Mark L. "Teaching Nonverbal Communication." In Vangelisti, Anita L.; Daly, John A.; and Friedrich, Gustav W. (eds.), *Teaching Communication: Theory, Research, and Methods*, 2nd ed. Mahwah, NJ: Lawrence Erlbaum, 1999, pp. 157-170.

Knapp, Mark L., and Hall, Judith A. *Nonverbal Communication in Human Interaction*, 5th ed. Belmont, CA: Wadsworth, 2002.

Rogers, Natalie H. *The New Talk Power: The Mind-Body Way to Speak Without Fear*. Sterling, VA: Capital Books, 2000.

Witt, Paul L., and Wheeless, Lawrence R. "An Experimental Study of Teachers' Verbal and Nonverbal Immediacy and Students' Affective and Cognitive Learning." *Communication Education*, 50 (2001), 327-342.

The Speaker's Voice

Branham, Robert James, and Pearce, W. Barnett. "The Conversational Frame in Public Address." *Communication Quarterly*, 44 (1996), 423-439.

Crannell, Kenneth C. *Voice and Articulation*, 4th ed. Belmont, CA: Wadsworth, 2000.

Esarey, Gary R. *Pronunciation Exercises for English as a Second Language*, 2nd ed. Ann Arbor: University of Michigan Press, 1996.

Gill, Mary M. "Accents and Stereotypes: Their Effect on Perceptions of Teachers and Lecture Comprehension." *Journal of Applied Communication Research*, 22 (1994), 348-361.

Gitterman, Martin R. "Improving the Pronunciation of English as a Second Language (ESL) Students." In Stephen E. Lucas (ed.), *Selections from the Speech Communication Teacher, 1994-1996*. New York: McGraw-Hill, 1997, pp. 13-14.

Grant-Williams, Renee. *Voice Power: Using Your Voice to Captivate, Persuade, and Command Attention*. New York: Amacom, 2002.

Hahner, Jeffrey C.; Sokoloff, Martin A.; and Salisch, Sandra L. *Speaking Clearly: Improving Voice and Diction*, 6th ed. New York: McGraw-Hill, 2002.

Hewings, Martin, and Goldstein, Sharon. *Pronunciation Plus: Practice Through Interaction, North American English*. Cambridge: Cambridge University Press, 1999.

Jacobi, Jeffrey. *How to Say It with Your Voice*. Englewood Cliffs, NJ: Prentice Hall, 2000.

Johnson, Karen E., and Golombek, Paula. *Public Speaking for Non-Native Speakers: A Handbook for Instructors*. New York: McGraw-Hill, 1996.

Love, Roger, *Set Your Voice Free*. Boston: Little Brown, 1999.

Mayer, Lyle V. *Fundamentals of Voice and Articulation*, 12th ed. New York: McGraw-Hill, 1999.

McCallion, Michael. *The Voice Book*, rev. ed. New York: Theatre Arts Books, 1998.

McWhorter, John. *Word on the Street: Debunking the Muth of "Pure" Standard English*. Cambridge, MA: Perseus Publishing, 2001.

Mino, Mary. "The Relative Effects of Vocal Delivery During a Simulated Employment Interview." *Communication Research Reports*, 13 (1996), 225-238.

Silverstein, Bernard. *Perfecting the Sounds of American English*. Lincolnwood, IL: NTC Publishing Group, 1997.

Wilson, Joni. *The 3-Dimensional Voice*. San Diego: Blue Loon Press, 2000.

The Speaker's Body

Axtell, Roger E. *Gestures: The Do's and Taboos of Body Language Around the World*, rev. ed. New York: Wiley, 1998.

Bavelas, Janet Beavin; Coates, Linda; and Johnson, Trudy. "Listener Responses as a Collaborative Process: The Role of Gaze." *Journal of Communication*, 52 (2002), 566-580.

Burgoon, Judee K., and Le Poire, Beth A. "Nonverbal Cues and Interpersonal Judgments: Participant and Observer Perceptions of Intimacy, Dominance, Composure and Formality." *Communication Monographs*, 66 (June 1999), 105-124.

Chamberlin, Carla R. "Nonverbal Behaviors and Initial Impressions of Trustworthiness in Teacher-Supervisor Relationships." *Communication Education*, 49 (2000), 352-364.

Goldman, Ellen. *As Others See Us: Body Movement and the Art of Successful Communication*. Langhome, PA: Gordon and Branch, 1994.

Manusov, Valerie, and Trees, April R. "'Are You Kidding Me?': The Role of Nonverbal Cues in the Verbal Accounting Process." *Journal of Communication*, 52 (2002), 640-656.

McCroskey, James C.; Sallinen, Aino; Fayer, Joan M.; Richmond, Virginia P.; and Barraclough, Robert A. "Nonverbal Immediacy and Cognitive Learning: A Cross-Cultural Investigation." *Communication Education*, 45 (1996), 200-211.

Palmer, Mark T., and Simmons, Karl B. "Communicating Intentions through Nonverbal Behaviors." *Human Communication Research*, 22 (1995), 128-160.

Question-and-Answer Sessions

DiResta, Diane. *Knockout Presentations: How to Deliver Your Message with Power, Punch, and Pizzazz.* Worcester, MA: Chandler House Press, 1998, pp. 232-255.

Fry, Ron, *101 Great Answers to the Toughest Interview Questions.* 4th ed. Franklin Lakes, NJ: Career Press, 2000.

Mira, Thomas K. *Speak Smart.* New York: Random House, 1997, pp. 115-123.

Rogers, Natalie H. *The New Talk Power: The Mind-Body Way to Speak Without Fear.* Sterling, VA: Capital Books, 2000, pp. 195-211.

Wilder, Claudyne. *The Presentations Kit: 10 Steps for Selling Your Ideas*, rev. ed. New York: Wiley, 1994, pp. 207-225.

Woodall, Marian K. *Thinking on Your Feet: How to Communicate Under Pressure*, 2nd ed. Lake Oswego, OR: Professional Business Communications, 1996.

Classroom Activities and Assignments—General

Avdeyeva, Tatyana V. "Practicing Delivery Skills." In Stephen E. Lucas (ed.), *Selections from the Speech Communication Teacher, 1996-1999.* New York: McGraw-Hill, 2001, p. 21.

Bahti, Cynthia L. "At the Sound of the Beep . . . Utter Nonsense." In Stephen E. Lucas (ed.), *Selections from the Speech Communication Teacher, 1994-1996.* New York: McGraw-Hill, 1997, p. 13.

Gaulard, Joan M. "To Read, To Memorize, or To Speak." In Stephen E. Lucas (ed.), *Selections from the Speech Communication Teacher, 1986-1991.* New York: McGraw-Hill, 1992, pp. 23-24.

Hayward, Pamela. "Delivery Cards." In Stephen E. Lucas (ed.), *Selections from the Speech Communication Teacher, 1994-1996.* New York: McGraw-Hill, 1997, pp. 14-15.

Lattin, Bohn D. "Choral Oral Literacy." In Stephen E. Lucas (ed.), *Selections from the Speech Communication Teacher, 1996-1999.* New York: McGraw-Hill, 2001, pp. 22-23.

Mills, Daniel D. "Tag Team Championship: Improving Delivery Skills." In Stephen E. Lucas (ed.), *Selections from the Speech Communication Teacher, 1986-1991.* New York: McGraw-Hill, 1992, p. 24.

Murray, Patricia. "The Objective Game." In Stephen E. Lucas (ed.), *Selections from the Speech Communication Teacher, 1986-1991*. New York: McGraw-Hill, 1992, pp. 24-25.

Snyder, Lee. "Twenty-Five Speeches an Hour." In Stephen E. Lucas (ed.), *Selections from the Speech Communication Teacher, 1986-1991*. New York: McGraw-Hill, 1992, p. 25.

Sonandré, Debbie Ayres, and Ayres, Joe. "Practice Makes Perfect." In Stephen E. Lucas (ed.), *Selections from the Speech Communication Teacher, 1996-1999*. New York: McGraw-Hill, 2001, pp. 25-26.

Classroom Activities and Assignments—Nonverbal Communication

Carbone, Amy. "Helpful Hints for Public Speaking." In Stephen E. Lucas (ed.), *Selections from the Speech Communication Teacher, 1996-1999*. New York: McGraw-Hill, 2001, p. 22.

Johnson, Craig. "People's Court Comes to the Classroom." In Stephen E. Lucas (ed.), *Selections from the Speech Communication Teacher, 1986-1991*. New York: McGraw-Hill, 1992, p. 49.

May, Sarah T. "Proxemics: The Hula Hoop and Use of Personal Space." In Stephen E. Lucas (ed.), *Selections from the Communication Teacher, 1999-2002*. New York: McGraw-Hill, 2004, pp. 59-60.

Myers, Scott A. "Classroom by Design." In Stephen E. Lucas (ed.), *Selections from the Speech Communication Teacher, 1994-1996*. New York: McGraw-Hill, 1997, pp. 50-51.

O'Mara, Joan. "The Power of Proxemics." In Stephen E. Lucas (ed.), *Selections from the Speech Communication Teacher, 1996-1999*. New York: McGraw-Hill, 2001, p. 71.

Ratliff, Jeanne Nelson. "Wearing Sunglasses Can Promote Eye Contact." In Stephen E. Lucas (ed.), *Selections from the Speech Communication Teacher, 1994-1996*. New York: McGraw-Hill, 1997, pp. 15-16.

Roach, Thomas J., and Goodnight, Lisa J. "Eye Contact Shooting Gallery." In Stephen E. Lucas (ed.), *Selections from the Speech Communication Teacher, 1996-1999*. New York: McGraw-Hill, 2001, p. 23.

Rollman, Steven A. "Classroom Exercises for Teaching Nonverbal Communication." In Stephen E. Lucas (ed.), *Selections from the Speech Communication Teacher, 1986-1991*. New York: McGraw-Hill, 1992, pp. 49-50.

Schnell, James A. "Experiential Learning of Nonverbal Communication in Popular Magazine Advertising." In Stephen E. Lucas (ed.), *Selections from the Speech Communication Teacher, 1986-1991*. New York: McGraw-Hill, 1992, p. 50.

Valentine, Carol Ann, and Arnold, William E. "Nonverbal Scavenger Hunt." In Stephen E. Lucas (ed.), *Selections from the Speech Communication Teacher, 1991-1994*. New York: McGraw-Hill, 1995, pp. 43-44.

Classroom Activities and Assignments—Speech Anxiety

Adams, Lori. "Speech Anxiety Simulation." In Stephen E. Lucas (ed.), *Selections from the Speech Communication Teacher, 1991-1994*. New York: McGraw-Hill, 1995, p. 49.

Ayres, Joe. "Reducing Public Speaking Apprehension through Speech Preparation." In Stephen E. Lucas (ed.), *Selections from the Speech Communication Teacher, 1996-1999*. New York: McGraw-Hill, 2001, p. 80.

Ayres, Joe; Hopf, Theodore S.; and Ady, Jeff. "Coping with Speech Anxiety." In Stephen E. Lucas (ed.), *Selections from the Speech Communication Teacher, 1986-1991*. New York: McGraw-Hill, 1992, pp. 62-63.

Isaacson, Zelda. "Paradoxical Intention: A Strategy to Alleviate the Anxiety Associated with Public Speaking." In Stephen E. Lucas (ed.), *Selections from the Speech Communication Teacher, 1991-1994*. New York: McGraw-Hill, 1995, pp. 49-50.

Langdon, Harry. "A Course on Stage Fright." In Stephen E. Lucas (ed.), *Selections from the Speech Communication Teacher, 1986-1991*. New York: McGraw-Hill, 1992, pp. 63-64.

Mino, Mary. "Building Confidence Through Oral Interpretation." In Stephen E. Lucas (ed.), *Selections from the Speech Communication Teacher, 1991-1994*. New York: McGraw-Hill, 1995, pp. 50-51.

Stowell, Jessica. "Free Writing to Deal with Speech Anxiety." In Stephen E. Lucas (ed.), *Selections from the Speech Communication Teacher, 1991-1994*. New York: McGraw-Hill, 1995, pp. 51-52.

Classroom Activities and Assignments—Impromptu Speeches

Armstrong, Lindsley F., and Kellett, Peter M. "Teaching Public Speaking Principles Through Impromptu Speaking." In Stephen E. Lucas (ed.), *Selections from the Speech Communication Teacher, 1994-1996*. New York: McGraw-Hill, 1997, pp. 77-78.

Beauchene, Kathleen. "Using Quotations as Impromptu Speech Topics." In Stephen E. Lucas (ed.), *Selections from the Speech Communication Teacher, 1986-1991*. New York: McGraw-Hill, 1992, p. 72.

Bytwerk, Randall. "The 'Just a Minute' Impromptu Exercise." In Stephen E. Lucas (ed.), *Selections from the Speech Communication Teacher, 1986-1991*. New York: McGraw-Hill, 1992, pp. 72-73.

Crandall, Heather. "Practicing Impromptu Speeches." In Stephen E. Lucas (ed.), *Selections from the Speech Communication Teacher, 1996-1999*. New York: McGraw-Hill, 2001, p. 94.

Kimble, James J. "The Big Mouth Speakoff." In Stephen E. Lucas (ed.), *Selections from the Speech Communication Teacher, 1994-1996*. New York: McGraw-Hill, 1997, p. 79.

Markham, Reed. "Power Minutes." In Stephen E. Lucas (ed.), *Selections from the Speech Communication Teacher, 1986-1991*. New York: McGraw-Hill, 1992, pp. 74-75.

McClarty, Wilma, "Impromptu Speaking Options." In Stephen E. Lucas (ed.), *Selections from the Speech Communication Teacher, 1996-1999*. New York: McGraw-Hill, 2001, pp. 94-95.

McClarty, Wilma. "Nomination Speech: The Ideal Date." In Stephen E. Lucas (ed.), *Selections from the Speech Communication Teacher, 1986-1991*. New York: McGraw-Hill, 1992, pp. 75-76.

McKinney, Bruce C. "The 'Jeopardy' of Impromptu Speaking." In Stephen E. Lucas (ed.), *Selections from the Speech Communication Teacher, 1986-1991*. New York: McGraw-Hill, 1992, pp. 76-77.

Phillips, Terilyn Goins. "Who's Who: Off-the-Cuff Character Assessments." In Stephen E. Lucas (ed.), *Selections from the Speech Communication Teacher, 1994-1996*. New York: McGraw-Hill, 1997, pp. 80-81.

Purdy, Ed. "Painless Impromptu Speaking." In Stephen E. Lucas (ed.), *Selections from the Speech Communication Teacher, 1986-1991*. New York: McGraw-Hill, 1992, p. 77.

Rumbough, Timothy B. "The 'Um . . . Uh . . .' Impromptu Speech Contest." In Stephen E. Lucas (ed.), *Selections from the Speech Communication Teacher, 1996-1999*. New York: McGraw-Hill, 2001, p. 24.

Schumer, Allison. "Structure and Substance in a One-Minute Speech." In Stephen E. Lucas (ed.), *Selections from the Speech Communication Teacher, 1986-1991*. New York: McGraw-Hill, 1992, pp. 77-78.

Shultz, Kara. "MTV Impromptu." In Stephen E. Lucas (ed.), *Selections from the Speech Communication Teacher, 1994-1996*. New York: McGraw-Hill, 1997, pp. 81-82.

Stahl, Michael G., and Adams, Lori. "Two Takes on Impromptu Speaking Topics: Retiring the Hat." In Stephen E. Lucas (ed.), *Selections from the Speech Communication Teacher, 1991-1994*. New York: McGraw-Hill, 1995, pp. 62-63.

Sugimoto, Naomi. "Impromptu Fortune-Telling Exercise." In Stephen E. Lucas (ed.), *Selections from the Speech Communication Teacher, 1991-1994*. New York: McGraw-Hill, 1995, pp. 63-64.

Sullivan, Gwendolyn F. "Improving Delivery Skills: The Practice Impromptu." In Stephen E. Lucas (ed.), *Selections from the Speech Communication Teacher, 1996-1999*. New York: McGraw-Hill, 2001, pp. 95-96.

Wall, Jeanette. "Me? Give an Impromptu Speech? No Way!" In Stephen E. Lucas (ed.), *Selections from the Speech Communication Teacher, 1986-1991*. New York: McGraw-Hill, 1992, pp. 78-79.

Wilks, Dorothy. "Two Birds with One Stone." In Stephen E. Lucas (ed.), *Selections from the Speech Communication Teacher, 1986-1991*. New York: McGraw-Hill, 1992, p. 79.

Films and Videos

"The Accent Reduction Program: The Standard Edition." Insight Media (2001). 100 minutes.

"African-American English: An Introduction." Insight Media (1997). 64 minutes.

"Anxiety." Insight Media (1997). 30 minutes.

"Basic Speech." Insight Media (2002). 28 minutes.

"Body Language: An International View." Insight Media (1999). 25 minutes.

"Body Language: Introduction to Nonverbal Communication." Insight Media (1993). 30 minutes.

"Body Language Skills." Insight Media (2002). 47 minutes.

"Breaking the Accent Barrier." Insight Media (1991). 60 minutes.

"Charisma." Insight Media (1998). 30 minutes.

"Conquer Your Fear of Public Speaking." Insight Media (1992). 70 minutes.

"The Ebonics Controversy." Insight Media (1998). 30 minutes.

"The Language of the Body." Films for the Humanities and Sciences (1994). 50 minutes.

"Making Your Presentation." Films for the Humanities and Sciences (1997). 21 minutes.

"More Voice Skills." Insight Media (2002). 47 minutes.

"Nonverbal Codes." Insight Media (1997). 29 minutes.

"Nonverbal Communication." Insight Media (1996). 45 minutes.

"Oral Interpretation: How to Read Aloud." Insight Media (1998). 21 minutes.

"Oral Interpretation Made Easy." Insight Media (2000). 21 minutes.

"Perfect Communication." Insight Media (2001). 23 minutes.

"Perfect English Pronunciation." Insight Media (1991). Two volumes; 116 minutes.

"Public Speaking: Time to Stand." Films for the Humanities and Sciences (2000). 27 minutes.

"Reading People: The Unwritten Language of the Body." Insight Media (1997). 23 minutes.

"The Silent Language: Nonverbal Communication." Insight Media (1994). 20 minutes.

"The Speeches of Martin Luther King, Jr." Insight Media (1998). 60 minutes.

"Understanding Body Language." Insight Media (2000). 15 minutes.

"Vocal Awareness." Insight Media (1999). 99 minutes.

"Voice Skills." Insight Media (2002). 45 minutes.

"Voice Skills III." Insight Media (2002). 38 minutes.

"A World of Gestures." University of California Extension Center for Media and Independent Learning (1991). 28 minutes.

Chapter **13** Using Visual Aids

Chapter Objectives

After reading this chapter, students should be able to:

1.   Explain the major advantages of using visual aids in a speech.

2.   Identify the kinds of visual aids available for use in speeches.

3.   Apply the guidelines given in the chapter for preparing and presenting visual aids.

Chapter Outline

I.   Visual aids offer a speaker several advantages *(text pages 322-323)*.
  A.   Visual aids strengthen the clarity of a speaker's message.
  B.   Visual aids increase the interest of a speaker's information.
  C.   Visual aids make a speaker's message easier for listeners to retain.
  D.   Visual aids enhance a speaker's credibility.
  E.   Visual aids can improve a speaker's persuasiveness.
  F.   Visual aids can even help a speaker combat stage fright.

II.   There are many kinds of visual aids *(text pages 323-326)*.
  A.   Objects can work extremely well as visual aids.
    1.   Showing the object being discussed is a fine way to clarify a speaker's ideas and give them dramatic impact.
    2.   Unfortunately, many objects cannot be used in speeches because they are too large, too small, unavailable, etc.
  B.   Models provide an excellent alternative to objects.
    1.   One type is a life-size model.

        2.   Another type is a small-scale model of a large object.

        3.   A third type is a large-scale model of a small object.

C.   Photographs are another kind of visual aid.

        1.   Photographs can be of great advantage to a speaker.

        2.   To be effective, they must be significantly enlarged so the audience can see them.

        3.   Multimedia programs are excellent vehicles for incorporating photographs into a speech.

D.   Drawings can provide superb alternatives to photographs.

        1.   Drawings (including diagrams, sketches, and maps) offer the advantage of being inexpensive.

        2.   They can also be specifically designed for the speech so as to illustrate the speaker's points precisely.

E.   Graphs are a good way to clarify and simplify statistics.

        1.   Line graphs are best for illustrating statistical trends.

        2.   Pie graphs are well suited for demonstrating distribution patterns.

        3.   Bar graphs are effective for showing comparisons between two or more items.

F.   Charts are a good choice when a speaker needs to summarize large blocks of information.

        1.   They can be used to present a larger number of categories than can be shown on a bar graph.

        2.   They can be used to summarize the steps of a process.

        3.   They can be used to present information the audience may want to write down.

G.   Video can be extremely effective as a visual aid.

        1.   The detail, vividness, and immediacy of video are hard to match.

        2.   Video is effective only when it is edited skillfully and is integrated smoothly into the speech.

        3.   When using video, a speaker should practice with the playback equipment ahead of time so it will work flawlessly during the speech.

H.   Transparencies are an effective way to present a wide variety of visual aids.

        1.   Transparencies can be made from many types of visual aids, including photographs, drawings, graphs, and charges.

        2.   Transparencies are inexpensive, easy to produce, and provide a strong visual image.

        3.   When preparing transparencies, a speaker must make sure any writing is large enough to be seen clearly from the back of the room.

        4.   The speaker should use the overhead projector when rehearsing the speech to make sure the transparencies are well coordinated with the rest of the presentation.

I.   Multimedia presentations allow a speaker to combine charts, graphs, photographs, and video in the same talk.

        1.   When used properly, multimedia presentations can be highly effective.

2.   Yet they also have drawbacks, including the high cost of equipment, the time required for preparation and rehearsal, and the possibility of computer malfunction.

J.   Sometimes the speaker can use her or his own body as a visual aid.

1.   This occurs most often in speeches of demonstration, in which a speaker shows how to do something.

2.   Doing a demonstration well requires practice to coordinate the speaker's actions with his or her words.

III.   There are six basic guidelines to follow whether creating visual aids by hand or by computer *(text pages 332-336)*.

A.   Prepare visual aids in advance.

1.   Advance preparation provides time to devise a creative and attractive visual aid.

2.   It also allows the speaker to practice the speech with the visual aid.

B.   Keep visual aids simple.

1.   The purpose of a visual aid is to enhance communication, not to display one's artistic talent or computer wizardry.

2.   A visual aid should be clear, straightforward, and uncluttered.

3.   It should include only what is needed to make the speaker's point.

C.   Make sure visual aids are large enough.

1.   A visual aid is useless if the audience cannot see it.

2.   When preparing drawings, charts, graphs, or transparencies, speakers must guard against the tendency to write or draw too small.

3.   Speakers can check the visibility of their visual aids by getting as far away from them as the most distant listener will be sitting.

4.   When creating visual aids by computer, one should use 36-point type for titles, 24-point type for subtitles, and 18-point type for other text.

D.   Use fonts that are easy to read.

1.   Most decorative fonts are distracting and hard to read.

2.   When preparing visual aids, speakers should use basic fonts that are clear and easy to read from a distance.

E.   Use a limited number of fonts.

1.   Experts recommend using no more than two fonts in a single visual aid—one for the title or major headings, another for subtitles or text.

2.   Standard procedure is to use a block typeface for the title and a rounder typeface for subtitles and text.

F.   Use color effectively.

1.   When used effectively, color can dramatically increase the impact of a visual aid.

2.   There are several basic guidelines for using color effectively.

a.   Use contrasting colors that can be easily differentiated.

b.   Use a limited number of colors.

c.   Use colors consistently.

d.   Use color strategically to highlight key points.

IV. In addition to preparing visual aids effectively, speakers should follow seven guidelines when presenting visual aids during a speech *(text pages 336-340)*.

A. Speakers should avoid using the chalkboard for visual aids.
  1. Writing on the chalkboard has the disadvantage of requiring speakers to turn their backs to the audience.
  2. Even if visual aids are drawn on the chalkboard in advance, they usually lack the vividness or neatness of aids presented on poster board or a transparency.

B. Speakers should display visual aids where listeners can see them.
  1. Good speech preparation includes checking where a speaker will display her or his visual aids.
  2. Once the speaker has chosen a suitable location for the aid, the speaker must be sure to stand where all listeners can see the aid during the speech.

C. Speakers should avoid passing visual aids among the audience.
  1. Once visual aids get into the hands of the audience, people pay more attention to the visuals than to the speaker.
  2. This is also true of handouts, which can easily distract an audience's attention from the speaker.
  3. If a speaker wants the audience to have information to take home, it should be passed out after the speech.

D. Speakers should display visual aids only while discussing them.
  1. Visual aids become distracting when they are displayed throughout the speech.
  2. To avoid distracting the audience, a speaker should cover or remove visual aids when they are not in use.

E. Speakers should talk to their audience, not to their visual aid.
  1. It is easy to break eye contact with the audience when presenting a visual aid.
  2. Effective speakers glance periodically at their visual aids, but also keep eye contact with the audience to get feedback about how the aid is coming across.

F. Speakers should explain their visual aids clearly and concisely.
  1. A visual aid is only as useful as the explanation that goes with it.
  2. Unfortunately, speakers often rush over their visual aid too quickly.
  3. Instead, they should describe the major features of the aid and spell out its meaning for the audience.

G. Speakers should practice with their visual aids when rehearsing the speech.
  1. More than one speaker has ruined the effect of a visual aid by not practicing with it before the speech.
  2. Effective speakers work out in advance how they will set up, explain, and remove their visual aids so the speech flows smoothly.

Exercises for Critical Thinking *(from text pages 341-342)*

1.   Watch a "how-to" television program (a cooking or gardening show, for example) or the weather portion of a local newscast. Notice how the speaker uses visual aids to help communicate the message. What kinds of visual aids are used? How do they enhance the clarity, interest, and retainability of the speaker's message? What would the speaker have to do to communicate the message effectively without visual aids?

> **Discussion:** This exercise helps attune students to the advantages and logistics of using visual aids in a speech. It works best if you assign a single program for the entire class to watch, so there is a common basis for class discussion. As an alternative, you can videotape segments of several programs yourself and show them to the class.

2.   Consider how you might use visual aids to explain each of the following:

   a.   How to perform the Heimlich maneuver to help a choking victim.

   b.   The proportion of the electorate that votes in major national elections in the United States, France, Germany, England, and Japan, respectively.

   c.   Where to write for information about student loans.

   d.   The wing patterns of various species of butterflies.

   e.   The increase in the amount of money spent by Americans on health care since 1985.

   f.   How to change a bicycle tire.

   g.   The basic equipment and techniques of rock climbing.

> **Discussion:** This exercise is designed to get students thinking about how they might use visual aids in their classroom speeches. Handle the class discussion as a kind of brainstorming session and encourage students to be creative in their suggestions for visual aids. As the discussion progresses, you can also draw attention to the guidelines for using visual aids effectively.

3.   Plan to use visual aids in at least one of your classroom speeches. Be creative in devising your aids, and be sure to follow the guidelines discussed in the chapter for using them. After the speech, analyze how effectively you employed your visual aids, what you learned about the use of visual aids from your experience, and what changes you would make in using visual aids if you were to deliver the speech again.

Discussion: Some teachers assign a round of speeches—usually informative—in which students must use visual aids. Such an assignment has several advantages. First, it gives students practical experience in creating and using visual aids. Second, it often reduces nervousness—because the visual aid heightens audience interest, helps divert the gaze of listeners from the speaker, and makes the speaker feel less self-conscious. Third, it encourages students to get away from their notes and to speak extemporaneously while explaining the visual aid.

Applying the Power of Public Speaking *(from text page 342)*

As a veterinarian and owner of a small-animal practice, you work closely with your local humane society to help control a growing population of unwanted dogs and cats. You and your staff devote many hours annually in free and reduced-cost medical services to animals adopted from the society. Now you have been asked to speak to the city council in support of legislation proposed by the society for stronger enforcement of animal licensing and leash laws.

In your speech, you plan to include statistics that (1) compare estimates of the city's dog population with the number of licenses issued during the past five years and (2) show the small number of citations given by local law enforcement for unleashed pets during the same period of time. Knowing from your college public speaking class how valuable visual aids can be in presenting statistics, you decide to illustrate one set of statistics with a chart and the other with a graph.

For which set of statistics will a chart be more appropriate? For which set will a graph be more appropriate? Of the three kinds of graphs discussed in this chapter (bar, line, pie), which will work best for your statistics and why?

Discussion: As with other Applying the Power of Public Speaking scenarios throughout the book, this one is designed to give students a sense of the many kinds of public speaking situations they can encounter once they leave college. In this case, the scenario also aims to help students understand the differences between charts and graphs, as well as the differences among the three kinds of graphs discussed in the chapter.

The first set of statistics in the scenario—comparing estimates of the city's dog population with the number of dog licenses issued during the past five years—would be best illustrated with a graph. Although either a bar graph or a line graph could work effectively, the better choice would be a line graph, which is especially useful for showing statistical changes over time. It is conceivable that the second set of statistics—showing the small number of citations given by local law enforcement for unleashed pets during the past five years—could be represented with a line graph that contained only one line. But this would not be as effective as a chart that simply listed the figures for each year. Graphs are especially valuable for showing statistical trends or comparisons. Since that is not the primary purpose of the second set of statistics, a chart would be the better choice for them.

Additional Exercises and Activities

1.   Develop a file of old visual aids you can bring to class to demonstrate for students the characteristics of effective and ineffective visual aids. Have the students identify which aids work well, which do not, and why. Ask students for ways to improve the ineffective visual aids.

> **Discussion:** When it comes to teaching students about visual aids, a picture is truly worth a thousand words. Bringing old visual aids to class is an excellent teaching device you can use to help students understand how to use visual aids in their speeches. This allows them to see how large the print or drawing must be, how important it is to keep the aid clean and uncluttered, how using bright, contrasting colors brings aids to life, how visual aids don't explain themselves, etc. It also allows you to illustrate the proper techniques for setting up and displaying visual aids, for explaining the point made by an aid, for communicating directly with the audience while discussing an aid, and so forth.
>
> Developing a file of visual aids is not very difficult. Simply collect the aids from your students after their speeches. Keep the aids in your office, so they will be at hand when you need to use them. After a few classes, you'll find that you have more than enough aids to demonstrate just about any point you wish to make. Some course directors keep a central file of visual aids from which instructors can draw as the need arises.

Extra Teaching and Learning Resources

General

Anholt, Robert R. H. *Dazzle 'em with Style: The Art of Oral Scientific Presentation*. New York: W. H. Freeman, 1994.

Ayres, Joe. "Using Visual Aids to Reduce Speech Anxiety." *Communication Research Reports* (1991), 73-79.

Brown, Alan L. *Power Pitches: How to Produce Winning Presentations Using Charts, Slides, Video and Multimedia*. Chicago: Irwin, 1997.

Craig, Malcolm. *Thinking Visually: Business Applications of 14 Core Diagrams*. New York: Continuum Publishing Group, 2000.

Downing, Joe, and Garmon, Cecile. "Teaching Students in the Basic Course How to Use Presentation Software." *Communication Education*, 50 (2002), 218-229.

Harris, Robert L. *Information Graphics: A Comprehensive Illustrated Reference*. New York: Oxford University Press, 2000.

Hofstetter, Fred T. *Multimedia Literacy*, 3rd ed. New York: McGraw-Hill, 2001.

Joss, Molly W. *Looking Good in Presentations*, 3rd ed. Scottsdale, AZ: Paraglyph Press, 2002.

Mayer, Richard E., and Sims, Valerie K. "For Whom Is a Picture Worth a Thousand Words? Extensions of a Dual-Coding Theory of Multimedia Learning." *Journal of Educational Psychology*, 86 (1994), 389-401.

Morrisey, George L.; Sechrest, Thomas L.; and Warman, Wendy S. *Loud and Clear: How to Prepare and Deliver Effective Business and Technical Presentations*, 4th ed. Portland, OR: Perseus Press, 1997.

Rabb, Margaret. *The Presentation Design Book: Projecting a Good Image with Your Desktop Computer*, 2nd ed. Chapel Hill, NC: Ventana Press, 1999.

Robbins, Jo. *High-Impact Presentations: A Multimedia Approach*. New York: Wiley, 1997.

Rutledge, Patrice-Ann, and Mucciolo, Tom. *Special Edition Using Microsoft PowerPoint 2002*. Indianapolis, IN: Que, 2001.

Tufte, Edward R. *The Visual Display of Quantitative Information*, 2nd ed. Cheshire, CT: Graphics Press, 2001.

Wempen, Faithe. *Microsoft PowerPoint 2000 Bible*. New York: Hungry Minds, 1999.

Wilder, Claudyne, and Rotondo, Jennifer. *A Quick Guide to Brilliant Laptop Presentations*, rev. ed. San Francisco: Jossey-Bass, 2002.

Zelazny, Gene. *Say It with Presentations*. New York: McGraw-Hill, 2000.

Classroom Activities and Assignments

Danielson, Mary Ann. "A Critical Thinking Approach to the Use of Visual Aids." In Stephen E. Lucas (ed.), *Selections from the Speech Communication Teacher, 1994-1996*. New York: McGraw-Hill, 1997, pp. 64-65.

Gutgold, Nichola D. "Pointing Groups to PowerPoint." In Stephen E. Lucas (ed.), *Selections from the Speech Communication Teacher, 1996-1999*. New York: McGraw-Hill, 2001, p. 76.

Layng, Jacqueline M. "Developing Multimedia Presentations in a New Technology Communication Course." In Stephen E. Lucas (ed.), *Selections from the Speech Communication Teacher, 1996-1999*. New York: McGraw-Hill, 2001, pp. 76-77.

Wilks, Dorothy. "Two Birds with One Stone." In Stephen E. Lucas (ed.), *Selections from the Speech Communication Teacher, 1986-1991*. New York: McGraw-Hill, 1992, p. 79.

Films and Videos

"Multimedia Presentations." Insight Media (1998). 13 minutes.

"Presentational Aids." Insight Media (1997). 30 minutes.

Appendix

Using PowerPoint

Appendix Objectives

After reading this appendix, students should be able to:

1. Explain the pluses and minuses of using PowerPoint in a speech.

2. Discuss the importance of planning for the effective use of PowerPoint.

3. Identify the basic elements of PowerPoint screen elements, templates, and slide layouts.

4. Explain the major principles for the effective use of text, photographs, clip art, graphs, sounds, and video in a PowerPoint presentation.

5. Explain the major principles for the effective use of color, fonts, space, and animation when formatting PowerPoint slides.

6. Identify the major factors to consider when delivering a speech with PowerPoint.

7. Discuss the guidelines for fair use of copyrighted materials in PowerPoint slides.

Appendix Outline

I. PowerPoint is used in a wide range of speaking situations (*text page 344*).
    A. A survey of 300 professional speakers showed that 94 percent use PowerPoint during at least part of their talks.
    B. Another study revealed that 90 percent of the multimedia presentations in the United States are developed with PowerPoint.

II.   There are pluses and minuses to using PowerPoint in public speeches (*text page 344*).
    A.   When used well, PowerPoint is a great boon to communication.
        1.   It allows a speaker to use a variety of visual aids without having to juggle multiple pieces of equipment.
        2.   It allows a speaker to incorporate text, photographs, charts, graphs, sound, and video into the same presentation.
    B.   Unfortunately, PowerPoint is not always used well.
        1.   Some speakers allow PowerPoint technology to dominate their presentations and end up losing sight of their message.
        2.   Other speakers throw their presentations together carelessly and make little eye contact with listeners.
        3.   Still others use PowerPoint to illustrate every point of their talk.

III.   Using PowerPoint well requires a great deal of planning (*text pages 344-345*).
    A.   Speakers should have a clear idea of exactly why, how, and when they are going to use PowerPoint in their speeches.
    B.   Rather than using PowerPoint to illustrate every thought, effective speakers use it only when it genuinely enhances their message.

IV.   To get started in PowerPoint, a speaker needs to know its basic features (*text pages 345-348*).
    A.   Two important components of PowerPoint are slides and presentations.
        1.   A slide is a single frame in a PowerPoint presentation.
        2.   A presentation is a PowerPoint file that contains all the slides for a given speech.
    B.   There are several elements that appear when PowerPoint is first opened.
        1.   The menu bar helps users perform major functions such as opening and closing presentations, choosing fonts, inserting images, and viewing slides.
        2.   The upper tool bar provides shortcuts for such tasks as creating new slides, adding bold or italicized text, undoing a previous action, and saving work.
        3.   The tool bar at the bottom of the screen provides buttons for viewing the presentation as well as for adding text boxes, charts, clip art, and color.
        4.   The main part of the screen appears in Normal view.
            a.   The center area displays the current slide.
            b.   The left pane allows the user to switch between different views of his or her slides.
            c.   The right pane provides tools for creating new presentations and for formatting slides.
    C.   PowerPoint offers three methods for creating a presentation.
        1.   Designed primarily for business speakers, AutoContent Wizard provides templates with predetermined outlines and sample text.
        2.   Blank Presentation, which comes with no preset designs, is often preferred by experienced speakers.

       3.   Most students like to start with Design Templates, which generates a presentation in which all the slides are unified by a preselected combination of colors, fonts, and graphics.

    D.   Both the Blank Presentation and Design Template options provide more than two dozen slide layouts for arranging items on slides.

V.   PowerPoint allows a speaker to include such elements as text, photographs, clip art, graphs, sounds, and video (*text pages 348-351*).

    A.   Most PowerPoint slides contain some kind of text.

        1.   Text can be used by itself.

        2.   Text can also be used in conjunction with photographs, clip art, and other images.

    B.   One of the benefits of PowerPoint is the ease with which it allows a speaker to add photographs to a presentation.

        1.   PowerPoint can be used to display a speaker's personal photographs.

        2.   It can also be used to display photographs downloaded from the Web.

    C.   Clip art is composed of pictures and symbols that represent common objects, processes, and ideas.

        1.   Clip art can be humorous and entertaining, but it can also be distracting and inappropriate.

        2.   Speakers should use clip art sparingly and should make certain it conveys the same emotional tone as the speech.

    D.   Graphs are excellent for communicating statistical trends and patterns.

        1.   Speakers can create custom graphs using PowerPoint's graph program.

        2.   Speakers can also download graphs from the Internet for use with PowerPoint.

    E.   PowerPoint makes it easy for speakers to incorporate sounds into their presentations.

        1.   Sounds can be played from a CD, downloaded from the Web, or recorded by the speaker.

        2.   Whatever their source, sounds should be used only if they are essential for communicating the speaker's message.

    F.   Speakers can also use PowerPoint to add video to a presentation.

        1.   Video can come from a speaker's personal video files or from the Internet.

        2.   As with sounds, video should be used only when it is indispensable to the speaker's message.

VI.   PowerPoint slides should be formatted to communicate the speaker's message as effectively as possible (*text pages 352-355*).

    A.   There are several principles for the use of color.

        1.   Stick to a limited number of colors and use them consistently.

        2.   Use one color for background, one color for titles, and one color for other text.

3. Be aware that light text against a dark background provides the best contrast for LCD projection.

B. There are several principles for the use of fonts.
1. Choose fonts that are clear and easy to read.
2. Avoid using ALL CAPS.
3. Don't use more than two fonts on a single slide.
4. Use the same fonts on all your slides.
5. Use appropriate font sizes.

C. There are several principles for the use of space.
1. One of the biggest mistakes people make when using PowerPoint is putting too much on a single slide.
2. In addition to keeping slides uncluttered, speakers should achieve a pleasing sense of visual balance when arranging elements on slides.

D. There are several principles for the use of animation.
1. In PowerPoint, "animation" refers to the way objects enter and exit a slide.
2. Speakers should avoid animation effects that might distract the attention of listeners.
3. Speakers should stick with a limited number of animation effects and use them consistently from slide to slide.

VII. After creating slides, the next step is delivering the speech with PowerPoint (*text pages 355-359*).
A. Before rehearsing the speech, speakers should double check their slides to see if anything is missing, misplaced, or misspelled.
B. Speakers should make sure they know the major Slide Show commands.
C. Speakers should practice their speech with PowerPoint.
D. Speakers should display slides only when discussing them.
E. Speakers should check the room in which they will be speaking and the equipment they will use for the speech.
F. Speakers should develop a backup plan in case the PowerPoint equipment fails.

VIII. When using materials downloaded from the Internet, it is important to observe copyright laws (*text pages 359-360*).
A. Under copyright law, someone who wishes to use the original work of another person must obtain permission and often must pay a usage fee.
B. The fair use provision of copyright law permits students and educators to employ portions of copyrighted electronic materials for educational purposes.
1. They may use portions of copyrighted materials for a multimedia presentation created for a specific class.
2. They may not post copyrighted materials back to the Web without written permission from the copyright owner.
3. They may use up to three minutes or 10 percent, whichever is less, of a copyrighted film, video, or other motion media work without obtaining permission.

4. They may use up to 10 percent but no more than 30 seconds of music and lyrics from an individual musical work without obtaining permission.

5. They may use an entire photograph or illustration without obtaining permission, but they may use no more than 15 images or 10 percent, whichever is less, of a collection of works.

6. They must credit their sources and display the copyright symbol when using copyrighted materials in a PowerPoint presentation.

Chapter 14 Speaking to Inform

Chapter Objectives

After reading this chapter, students should be able to:

1. Explain the four kinds of informative speeches discussed in the chapter.

2. Apply the five guidelines for informative speaking offered in the chapter.

Chapter Outline

I. Speaking to inform is one of the most important skills a student can develop *(text pages 366-367)*.
   A. Informative speaking is vital to success in the workplace.
      1. In one survey, informative speaking was ranked as the most important speech skill in the workplace.
      2. In another survey, 62 percent of the respondents said they used informative speaking "almost constantly."
   B. Public speaking to inform occurs in a wide range of everyday situations.
      1. There are endless situations in which people need to inform others.
      2. The ability to convey knowledge and understanding will prove valuable to students throughout their lives.
   C. There are three criteria for effective informative speaking.
      1. The information should be communicated accurately.

      2.   The information should be communicated clearly.

      3.   The information should be made meaningful and interesting to the audience.

II.   Informative speeches can be classified into four types *(text pages 367-376)*.

    A.   Some informative speeches are about objects.

        1.   Speeches about objects describe something that is visible, tangible, and stable in form.

           a.   Objects may have moving parts or be alive.

           b.   They may include places, structures, animals, even people.

        2.   Speeches about objects need to be sharply focused.

           a.   A speaker cannot convey everything about an object in a brief speech.

           b.   It is important to choose a specific purpose that is not too broad to be achieved in the allotted time.

        3.   Speeches about objects can use a variety of organizational patterns.

           a.   A speech about the history or evolution of an object would be arranged in chronological order.

           b.   A speech about the main features of an object might be arranged in spatial order.

           c.   Most informative speeches about objects will fall into topical order.

    B.   Some informative speeches are about processes.

        1.   A process is a systematic series of actions that leads to a specific result or product.

        2.   Speeches about processes explain how something is made, describe how something is done, or convey how something works.

        3.   There are two kinds of informative speeches about processes.

           a.   One type explains a process so the audience will understand it better.

           b.   The other type explains a process so the audience will be able to perform the process themselves.

        4.   Speeches about processes often require visual aids.

           a.   Charts are an effective way to outline the steps of a process.

           b.   In some cases, the speaker will need to demonstrate the steps or techniques of the process.

        5.   Speeches about processes require careful organization.

           a.   Speeches that explain a process step by step are arranged in chronological order.

           b.   Speeches that focus on the major principles or techniques involved in performing the process are usually arranged in topical order.

           c.   Whichever method of organization is used, each step in the process must be clear and easy for listeners to follow.

    C.   Some informative speeches are about events.

        1.   Speeches about events can deal with any kind of happening or occurrence.

           a.   The occurrence may be historical in nature—such as the Battle of Little Big Horn or the civil rights movement.

          b.   The occurrence may be everyday in nature—such as modern dance or chronic fatigue syndrome.

     2.   There are many ways to organize a speech about an event.

          a.   Speeches that recount the history of an event are arranged in chronological order.

          b.   Speeches that analyze the causes and effects of an event are arranged in causal order.

          c.   Speeches that deal with particular elements of an event are usually arranged in topical order.

D.   Some informative speeches are about concepts.

     1.   Speeches about concepts convey information concerning beliefs, theories, principles, or other abstract subjects.

     2.   Speeches about concepts are usually arranged in topical order.

          a.   One common approach is to enumerate the main features or aspects of the concept.

          b.   A more complex approach is to define the concept, identify its major elements, and illustrate it with specific examples.

          c.   Yet another approach is to explain competing schools of thought about the concept.

     3.   Speeches about concepts are often more complex than other kinds of informative speeches.

          a.   When discussing concepts, a speaker should avoid technical language and define terms clearly.

          b.   A speaker should also use examples and comparisons to make concepts understandable to listeners.

E.   The lines dividing speeches about objects, processes, events, and concepts are not absolute.

     1.   Most topics can fit into more than one category depending on how the speech is developed.

     2.   The most important thing is that speakers decide how they want to handle a topic and then develop the speech accordingly.

III.   There are five guidelines for effective informative speaking *(text pages 376-384)*.

A.   Informative speakers should be wary of overestimating what the audience knows.

     1.   In most cases, the audience will be only vaguely knowledgeable about the speaker's topic.

     2.   The speaker cannot assume the audience will know what he or she means.

     3.   To avoid misunderstanding, the speaker must explain ideas thoroughly and clearly.

     4.   One way to do this is to consider whether the speech will be clear to someone who is hearing about the topic for the first time.

5.   Informative speakers should keep in mind the journalists' code: "Never *over*estimate the knowledge of your audience; never *under*estimate the intelligence of your audience."

B.   Informative speakers should find ways to relate the subject directly to the audience.

1.   Informative speakers must recognize that what is fascinating to them may not be fascinating to everybody.

2.   Effective informative speakers work to get the audience interested—and to keep them interested.

a.   They begin with a creative introduction that connects the topic with the interests and concerns of the audience.

b.   They find ways throughout the body of the speech to talk about the topic in terms of their listeners.

C.   Informative speakers should avoid being too technical.

1.   An informative speech may be overly technical because the subject matter is too specialized for the audience.

2.   An informative speech may also be overly technical because of the speaker's use of jargon or obscure language.

3.   Effective informative speakers select topics that are not too technical for the audience.

4.   Effective informative speakers recognize that language appropriate for an audience of specialists may well be confusing to a general audience.

D.   Informative speakers should avoid abstractions.

1.   Replacing tedious abstractions with specific details makes an informative speech more compelling.

2.   One way to avoid abstractions is through description.

a.   Colorful descriptions of external events can draw listeners into the speech.

b.   Description can also be used to communicate internal feelings vividly and engagingly.

3.   A second way to avoid abstractions is with comparisons.

a.   Comparisons allow a speaker to explain new ideas in concrete, familiar terms.

b.   Effective informative speakers are adept at using comparisons to draw listeners into the speech.

4.   A third way to avoid abstractions is with contrast.

a.   Like comparison, contrast can put abstractions into concrete terms.

b.   Contrast is also an excellent way to give listeners a sense of perspective on concepts and events.

E.   Informative speakers should personalize their ideas.

1.   Nothing enlivens an informative speech more than personal illustrations.

2.   Whenever possible, informative speakers should try to dramatize their ideas in human terms.

3.   The best way to accomplish this is with examples—real or hypothetical—that personalize the subject matter.

Exercises for Critical Thinking *(from text pages 389-390)*

1.   Below is a list of subjects for informative speeches. Your task is twofold: (a) Select four of the topics and prepare a specific purpose statement for an informative speech about each of the four. Make sure that your four specific purpose statements include at least one that deals with its topic as an object, one that deals with its topic as a process, one that deals with its topic as an event, and one that deals with its topic as a concept. (b) Explain what method of organization you would most likely use in structuring a speech about each of your specific purpose statements.

hobbies	sports
animals	music
science	cultural customs
education	technology
media	health

Discussion: This exercise gets students to work on developing specific purpose statements for informative speeches. It also leads them to apply what is said in the text about methods of organizing informative speeches. If you include Chapter 4, "Selecting a Topic and Purpose," or Chapter 8, "Organizing the Body of the Speech," in the unit on informative speaking, you may wish to forego this exercise in favor of the exercises in Chapters 4 and 8.

2.   Analyze Jennifer Breuer's "Dying to Be Thin" in the appendix of sample speeches that follows Chapter 18 of the textbook. Identify the specific purpose, central idea, main points, and method of organization. Evaluate the speech in light of the guidelines for informative speaking discussed in this chapter.

Discussion: Clear, well-supported, and sharply organized, "Dying to Be Thin" shows how students can apply the guidelines for informative speaking presented in the chapter. It is also available as part of the videotape supplement to *The Art of Public Speaking.* Here is a brief synopsis of the speech.

Specific Purpose: To inform my audience about the symptoms, causes, and treatment of anorexia.

Central Idea: A serious, potentially fatal disorder, anorexia has several major causes and no easy cure.

Method of Organization: Topical

Introduction: The introduction consists of paragraphs 1-4. The first two paragraphs gain attention and gradually reveal the topic of the speech. Paragraph 3 quantifies the problem of anorexia and relates it to a college-age audience. Paragraph 4 reinforces the speaker's credibility and previews the main points to be discussed in the body of the speech. All in all, this is a very effective introduction.

Body: Arranged in topical order, the body of the speech consists of three main points, the first of which explains the nature and symptoms of anorexia (paragraphs 5-7). After defining anorexia as a disorder of self-starvation, the speaker identifies the four major traits of all anorexics (paragraph 5). She then explains the physical consequences of anorexia, which range from dry skin and brittle hair to a decreased pulse rate and even death (paragraph 6). In paragraph 7 the speaker returns to the story of her friend Julie that she began in the introduction. In addition to illustrating the speaker's ideas, this story provides a unifying element to which the speaker will return throughout the speech.

A signpost at the beginning of paragraph 8 alerts the audience to the fact that the speaker is moving into her second main point, in which she explains why people become anorexic (paragraphs 8-11). The speaker identifies three major causes of anorexia: societal pressure to be thin (paragraph 8), individual personality traits (paragraph 9), and chemical reactions in the body that may make anorexia physically addictive (paragraph 10). She ends the second main point in paragraph 11 by once again talking of Julie, who tried to make herself perfect by losing weight.

In paragraph 12, the speaker uses another signpost to introduce her third main point, dealing with the treatment of anorexia (paragraphs 12-14). As in other parts of the speech, the speaker uses credible sources to support her ideas, and she identifies the sources for her audience. The quotation from Dr. Katherine Halmi in paragraph 12 dispels the notion that anorexia can be cured by personal will power, while the statistic in paragraph 14 reinforces the fact that, for many anorexics, there is no effective treatment.

Although the topic of anorexia is far from novel, the speaker does a good job of keeping the audience interested. She avoids technical language, explains ideas clearly, and uses a variety of supporting materials. By returning to the story of Julie at the end of each main point, she personalizes the topic and reinforces its tragic consequences.

Conclusion: The conclusion consists of the final paragraph. After restating her central idea, the speaker ends by completing the story of her friend Julie. The emotional appeal of this story is unusual for an informative speech, but it is extremely effective. When delivered in class, it had a powerful impact.

Applying the Power of Public Speaking *(from text page 390)*

As the manager for a local chain of coffeehouses, you have been asked to speak to a gourmet group about how to make genuine Italian cappuccino. As you write down ideas for your speech, you find that you have the following main points:

I.   First you must make the espresso.

II.   Grind the coffee beans so they are fine but not too fine.

III.   Place the ground coffee in the filter holder of the espresso machine.

IV.   Tamp the coffee once lightly to level the grind in the filter holder.

V.   Lock the filter holder onto the brew head of the espresso machine.

VI.   Activate the on switch to extract the espresso.

VII.   In addition to making the espresso, you must prepare frothed milk for cappuccino.

VIII.   Fill a steaming pitcher 1/3 full of very cold milk.

IX.   Place the steam vent of the espresso machine just below the surface of the milk in the pitcher.

X.   Fully open the steam vent.

XI.   Keeping the tip of the steam vent just below the surface of the milk, move the pitcher in a circular motion.

XII.   Be careful not to overheat or scald the milk, which will ruin the froth.

XIII.   Once you have the desired amount and consistency of froth, turn the steam vent off and remove it from the pitcher.

XIV.   Now you are ready to combine the espresso and frothed milk.

XV.   The normal proportions for cappuccino are 1/3 espresso to 2/3 frothed milk.

XVI.   Some people prefer to pour the espresso into the frothed milk in a cappuccino cup.

XVII.   Other people prefer to pour or spoon the frothed milk over the espresso.

Having taken a speech class in college, you know this is too many main points for an audience to keep track of. As you look over your list again, however, you realize that it can easily be reorganized into three main points, each with several subpoints. What are those main points and subpoints?

Discussion: Like the other Applying the Power of Public Speaking scenarios throughout the book, this one is designed to show students that the principles of effective public speaking are as applicable outside the classroom as in it. In this case, the speaker is presenting an informative speech about a process and needs to group the steps of the process into units so as to limit the number of main points.

This exercise is most effective when students work on it as a homework assignment and then share their ideas in a class discussion. Below is an outline of the main points and subpoints. For ease of classroom discussion, it is included in the binder of overhead transparencies that accompanies *The Art of Public Speaking.*

I.   The first step in making cappuccino is extracting the espresso.

    A.   Grind the coffee beans so they are fine but not too fine.

    B.   Place the ground coffee in the filter holder of the espresso machine.

    C.   Tamp the coffee once lightly to level the grind in the filter holder.

    D.   Lock the filter holder onto the brew head of the espresso machine.

    E.   Activate the on switch to extract the espresso.

II.   The second step in making cappuccino is preparing the frothed milk.

    A.   Fill a steaming pitcher 1/3 full of very cold milk.

    B.   Place the steam vent of the espresso machine just below the surface of the milk in the pitcher.

    C.   Fully open the steam vent.

    D.   Keeping the tip of the steam vent just below the surface of the milk, move the pitcher in a circular motion.

    E.   Be careful not to overheat or scald the milk, which will ruin the froth.

    F.   Once you have the desired amount and consistency of froth, turn the steam vent off and remove it from the pitcher.

III. The third step in making cappuccino is combining the espresso and frothed milk.

    A.   The normal proportions for cappuccino are 1/3 espresso to 2/3 frothed milk.

    B.   Some people prefer to pour the espresso into the frothed milk in a cappuccino cup.

    C.   Other people prefer to pour or spoon the frothed milk over the espresso.

Additional Exercises and Activities

1.   Show the class one or more informative speeches from the videotapes of student speeches that accompany *The Art of Public Speaking*. Use the videotapes to illustrate points about effective informative speaking.

>   **Discussion:**   There are several excellent student informative speeches on the videotape supplement to *The Art of Public Speaking*. Two of those speeches—"Cryonics" and "Dying to Be Thin"—are printed in the book. Also available on videotape are "Sign Language" and "CPR," both of which are excellent demonstration speeches; "The Thrilling World of Roller Coasters," which illustrates how to integrate video clips into an informative speech; and "Dandelions: The Uncommon Weed," which shows how even the most ordinary of topics can be turned into a creative and engaging presentation.

2.   Popular nonfiction writing often provides helpful models of informative discourse on technical topics. Have each student select an article of interest from the medicine, science, or business section of *Time* or *Newsweek*. The student should prepare a brief report on the article answering each of the following:

a.   How effectively does the author use definition, explanation, description, comparison, contrast, and examples to make the subject clear and interesting to ordinary readers? Identify two particular techniques used in the article that you might want to try in your next informative speech.

b.   Are there some points in the story that you don't fully understand? If so, what information might the author have supplied to make the points clear to you?

c.   Assume you will be giving a speech on the same topic as the article. What specific steps would you take to relate the topic directly to your classmates? To make it fully understandable to them? Consider not only what you might say in your speech, but also how you might use visual aids to enhance what you say.

>   **Discussion:**   This can be a very helpful exercise if you have students give more than one informative speech or if you are teaching an advanced public speaking class. Because of its complexity, it does not always work well when beginning speakers are preparing their first informative speech.

3. Divide the class into groups of three to four students each. Have each group select one of the topics listed below (or other topics of your choosing). Each group has 15 minutes to work out a two-minute explanation designed for an audience that knows absolutely nothing about the topic. Each group should select one of its members to present the explanation orally to the class.

    How to tie a shoe lace

    How to change a car tire

    The basic rules of baseball

    How to access the Internet

    How to program a VCR

    The basic rules of checkers

    Discussion: This exercise drives home the complexity of giving information to listeners who are not already familiar with the topic. Like the preceding activity, it is usually too demanding for novice speakers who are working on their first informative speech. It can work very well in an advanced public speaking class or in the later stages of an introductory class with very good students.

4. Distribute copies of "Sign Language," by Leah Pogoriler, which appears on pages 405-406 of this manual. Have students analyze the speech in light of the criteria for informative speaking presented in this chapter of the textbook.

    Discussion: One of several outstanding informative speeches printed in Part Five of this manual, "Sign Language" shows how one can work a demonstration into an informative presentation. For instructors who want to show the speech in class, it is available on the student speech videotape that accompanies this edition of *The Art of Public Speaking*. See pages 407-408 of this manual for an analysis of the speech.

5. Distribute copies of "Feng Shui," by Elizabeth Elegant, which appears on pages 400-402 of this manual. Have students analyze the speech in light of the criteria for informative speaking presented in this chapter of the textbook.

    Discussion: "Feng Shui" provides a fine example of an informative speech on a concept. For instructors who want to show the speech in class, it is available on the student speech videotape that accompanies this edition of *The Art of Public Speaking*. See pages 403-404 of this manual for an analysis of the speech.

6. Distribute copies of "Edible Insects," by Chinaka Steady, which appears on pages 426-427 of this manual. Have students analyze the speech in light of the criteria for informative speaking presented in this chapter of the textbook.

> **Discussion:**   Interesting, clearly organized, and superbly delivered, "Edible Insects" is a guaranteed crowd-pleaser that is also available on *Speeches for Analysis and Discussion: A Videotape Supplement to The Art of Public Speaking, Sixth Edition.* An analysis of the speech can be found on pages 428-429 of this manual.

7. Distribute copies of "CPR," by Margaret Fugate, which appears on pages 409-410 of this manual. Have students analyze the speech in light of the criteria for informative speaking presented in this chapter of the textbook.

> **Discussion:**   An excellent demonstration speech, "CPR" is especially valuable if you have students who are preparing this kind of speech for the informative round. Not only does the text of the speech fit well with the guidelines for informative speaking discussed in the book, but its delivery provides a fine model of how students can work their demonstration seamlessly into the speech as a whole. For instructors who want to show "CPR" in class, it is available on the videotape of student speeches that accompanies this edition of *The Art of Public Speaking.* For analysis of the speech, see pages 411-412 of this manual.

Extra Teaching and Learning Resources

General

Anholt, Robert R. H. *Dazzle 'em with Style: The Art of Oral Scientific Presentation.* New York: W. H. Freeman, 1994.

D'Arcy, Jan. *Technically Speaking: A Guide for Communicating Complex Information.* Piscataway, NJ: IEEE, 1998.

Davidson, Jeffrey P. "The Shortcomings of the Information Age." *Vital Speeches of the Day,* 62 (June 1, 1996), 495-502.

Hager, Peter J., and Scheiber, H.J. *Designing and Delivering Scientific, Technical, and Managerial Presentations.* New York: Wiley, 1997.

Paradis, James G., and Zimmerman, Muriel L. *The MIT Guide to Science and Engineering Communication.* Cambridge, MA: MIT Press, 1997.

Rowan, Katherine E. "A New Pedagogy for Explanatory Public Speaking: Why Arrangement Should Not Substitute for Invention." *Communication Education*, 44 (1995), 236-250.

Zinsser, William. *On Writing Well*, 25th ann. New York: HarperCollins, 2001.

Classroom Activities and Assignments

Adler, Barbara. "A Speech About a Great American Speech." In Stephen E. Lucas (ed.), *Selections from the Speech Communication Teacher, 1986-1991*. New York: McGraw-Hill, 1992, p. 65.

Bowers, Anne A. "Happy Birthday to Me." In Stephen E. Lucas (ed.), *Selections from the Speech Communication Teacher, 1994-1996*. New York: McGraw-Hill, 1997, p. 68.

Fregoe, David H. "Informative vs. Persuasive Speaking: The Objects Game." In Stephen E. Lucas (ed.), *Selections from the Speech Communication Teacher, 1986-1991*. New York: McGraw-Hill, 1992, pp. 57-58.

Gschwend, Laura L. "Creating Confidence with the Popular Recording Speech." In Stephen E. Lucas (ed.), *Selections from the Speech Communication Teacher, 1994-1996*. New York: McGraw-Hill, 1997, pp. 68-69.

Rowan, Katherine. "The Speech to Explain Difficult Ideas." In Stephen E. Lucas (ed.), *Selections from the Speech Communication Teacher, 1986-1991*. New York: McGraw-Hill, 1992, pp. 69-71.

Schumer, Allison. "Custom Comparison Speeches." In Stephen E. Lucas (ed.), *Selections from the Speech Communication Teacher, 1986-1991*. New York: McGraw-Hill, 1992, p. 71.

Films and Videos

"Finding Information." Insight Media (1997). 30 minutes.

"Information Age." Insight Media (2002). 20 minutes.

"Informative Speaking." Insight Media (1997). 30 minutes.

"Informative Speaking: Organization." Insight Media (1997). 30 minutes.

"Informative Speaking: Strategies." Insight Media (1997). 30 minutes.

"Making Your Presentation." Films for the Humanities and Sciences (1997). 21 minutes.

Chapter **15** Speaking to Persuade

Chapter Objectives

After reading this chapter, students should be able to:

1. Define persuasion and explain why it is an important subject.

2. Explain why meeting ethical obligations can be especially challenging in persuasive speaking and identify the ethical responsibilities of persuasive speakers.

3. Clarify the differences between an informative speech and a persuasive speech and explain why speaking to persuade is especially challenging.

4. Explain what it means to say that audiences engage in a mental dialogue with the speaker as they listen to a persuasive speech.

5. Discuss the concept of target audience and its role in persuasive speaking.

6. Define a question of fact and give an example of a specific purpose statement for a persuasive speech on a question of fact.

7. Define a question of value and give an example of a specific purpose statement for a persuasive speech on a question of value.

8. Define a question of policy and give an example of a specific purpose statement for a persuasive speech on a question of policy.

9.   Explain the difference between passive agreement and immediate action as goals for persuasive speeches on questions of policy.

10.   Explain the three basic issues of need, plan, and practicality and their importance in persuasive speeches on questions of policy.

11.   Discuss the four methods of organization used most often in persuasive speeches on questions of policy.

12.   Identify the five steps in Monroe's motivated sequence.

Chapter Outline

I.   Persuasion is the process of creating, reinforcing, or changing people's beliefs or actions *(text pages 394-395)*.
      A.   Most people do a certain amount of persuading everyday, even though they may not call it that.
      B.   The ability to speak persuasively is beneficial in everything from personal relationships to career aspirations, to civic deliberation.

II.   Meeting ethical obligations can be especially challenging when one is speaking to persuade *(text pages 395-396)*.
      A.   Persuasive speakers should keep in mind the guidelines for ethical speaking.
            1.   They should make sure their goals are ethically sound.
            2.   They should study the topic thoroughly so they won't mislead the audience.
            3.   They should learn about all sides of an issue and make sure they get the facts right.
            4.   They should be honest in what they say.
            5.   They should guard against subtle forms of dishonesty such as quoting out of context, portraying a few details as the whole story, and misrepresenting sources.
            6.   They should present evidence fairly and accurately.
      B.   Persuasive speakers should keep in mind the power of language and employ it responsibly.
            1.   They should respect the rights of free speech and expression.
            2.   They should avoid name-calling and other forms of abusive language.
            3.   If they use emotional appeal, they should make sure it is appropriate to the topic and is supported by facts and logic.

III. Persuasion is a psychological process *(text pages 396-400)*.
      A.   Of all the types of public speaking, persuasion is the most complex and the most challenging.
            1.   Persuasive speeches often deal with controversial topics that involve people's most basic attitudes, values, and beliefs.

2.   No matter how skilled a speaker may be, some listeners are so committed to their own ideas that they cannot be persuaded to the speaker's point of view.

3.   For this reason, persuasive speakers must enter a speech situation with realistic goals.

    a.   If listeners are not strongly committed one way or another on the speech topic, a speaker can realistically hope to move some of them toward her or his viewpoint.

    b.   If listeners are strongly opposed to a speaker's message, the speaker can consider the speech a success if it moves even a few to reexamine their views.

B.   When processing persuasive messages listeners engage in a mental give-and-take with the speaker.

1.   Listeners do not sit passively and soak in everything a speaker says.

    a.   As they listen, they assess the speaker's credibility, delivery, supporting materials, language, and the like.

    b.   They may argue, inside their own minds, with the speaker.

2.   Effective persuasive speakers regard their speeches as a kind of mental dialogue with the audience.

    a.   When preparing the speech, they try to put themselves in the place of the audience and imagine how they will respond.

    b.   Above all, they try to anticipate audience objections and to answer them in the speech.

C.   It is often helpful for persuasive speakers to think in terms of reaching their target audience.

1.   The target audience is the part of the whole audience a speaker most wants to reach with his or her message.

2.   In most situations, the target audience consists of uncommitted listeners, listeners who are inclining toward agreement with the speaker, and listeners who disagree with the speaker but who are open to persuasion.

3.   Once a speaker knows where the target audience stands, she or he can adapt the speech to fit the values and concerns of the target audience.

4.   Concentrating on the target audience, however, does not mean the speaker should exclude other listeners.

    a.   Targeting one portion of the audience does not give speakers license to ignore or insult the rest of their listeners.

    b.   A speaker must always keep in mind the ideas and feelings of the entire audience.

IV.   Some persuasive speeches deal with questions of fact *(text pages 400-403)*.

A.   Persuasive speeches on questions of fact seek to persuade an audience to accept the speaker's view of the facts on a particular issue.

1.   Some questions of fact can be answered with certainty—for example, how far is it from New York to Baghdad?

      2.   Other questions of fact cannot be answered with certainty—for example, will the economy be better or worse next year?

  B.   A persuasive speech on a question of fact is different from an informative speech.

      1.   The aim of an informative speech is to give information as impartially as possible, not to argue for a particular point of view.

      2.   Unlike speeches to inform, persuasive speeches on questions of fact take a partisan view of the information and try to persuade the audience to accept the speaker's view about that information.

          a.   The legal system is a good model for understanding persuasive speeches on questions of fact.

          b.   In a trial, the competing attorneys will try to persuade the jury that the facts of the case prove either the guilt or the innocence of the defendant.

  C.   Most persuasive speeches on questions of fact are organized topically.

      1.   In such speeches, each main point will present a reason why the audience should agree with the speaker.

      2.   As in other speeches using topical order, persuasive speeches on questions of fact should subdivide the topic logically and consistently.

V.   Some persuasive speeches deal with questions of value *(text pages 403-405)*.

  A.   Questions of value require judgments based on a person's beliefs about what is right or wrong, good or bad, moral or immoral, etc.

  B.   When dealing with a question of value, a speaker needs to justify her or his value judgment in light of a clearly defined set of standards.

      1.   The first step is to define the speaker's standards for value judgment.

      2.   The second step is to judge the subject of the speech against those standards.

  C.   Speeches on questions of value are usually organized topically.

      1.   The first main point establishes the standards for the speaker's value judgment.

      2.   The second main point applies those standards to the speech topic.

VI. Most persuasive speeches deal with questions of policy *(text pages 405-410)*.

  A.   Questions of policy deal with specific courses of action.

      1.   They inevitably involve questions of fact.

      2.   They may also involve questions of value.

      3.   But they always go beyond questions of fact or value to decide whether something should or should not be done.

  B.   There are two types of persuasive speeches on questions of policy.

      1.   One type seeks to gain passive agreement that a policy is desirable, necessary, and practical.

          a.   The speaker's aim is to affect the thinking of listeners.

          b.   The speaker does not try to get listeners to take action in support of the policy.

      2.   The second type seeks to motivate the audience to take immediate action.

          a.   The speaker's aim is to get the audience to do something in support of the policy.

       b.   When seeking immediate action, speakers should make their recommendations for action as specific as possible.

C.   Persuasive speeches on questions of policy must address three basic issues— need, plan, and practicality.

    1.   The first basic issue is need.

        a.   Speakers who advocate a change in policy must prove there is a need for the change.

        b.   Speakers who oppose a change in policy will try to show there is no need for change.

    2.   The second basic issue is plan.

        a.   After showing the need for change, a persuasive speaker must offer a specific plan—policy—that will solve the need.

        b.   The speaker should be as specific as time allows in identifying the major features of the plan.

    3.   The third basic issue is practicality.

        a.   Speakers who advocate a new policy must show their plan is workable and will solve the need without creating new problems.

        b.   Speakers who oppose a shift in policy will argue that a proposed plan is impractical and will create more problems than it will solve.

    4.   The amount of time devoted to need, plan, and practicality in any given speech will depend on the topic and the audience.

VII.   Four patterns of organization are especially effective for persuasive speeches on questions of policy *(text pages 410-417)*.

A.   The first pattern is problem-solution order.

    1.   Speeches that advocate a change in policy often fall naturally into problem-solution order.

        a.   The first main point shows the need for a new policy by proving the existence of a serious problem.

        b.   The second main point presents a plan for solving the problem and demonstrates its practicality.

    2.   Problem-solution order can also be used in speeches opposing a change in policy.

        a.   The first main point shows that there is *no* need for change.

        b.   The second main point shows that even if there were a need, the proposed new policy would not solve it and would create serious problems of its own.

B.   The second pattern is problem-cause-solution order.

    1.   Speeches following this method of organization have three main points.

        a.   The first main point shows the existence of a problem.

        b.   The second main point analyzes the causes of the problem.

        c.   The third main point presents a solution to the problem.

    2.   Problem-cause-solution order makes it easier to check whether the proposed solution will get at the causes of the problem, rather than merely controlling its symptoms.

C.   The third pattern is comparative advantages order.
1.   This pattern of organization is most effective when the audience already agrees there is a need for a new policy.
2.   Rather than dwelling on the need, the speaker devotes each main point to explaining why his or her plan is preferable to other solutions.

D.   The fourth pattern is Monroe's motivated sequence.
1.   The motivated sequence has five steps that follow the psychology of persuasion.
a.   The first step is to gain the attention of the audience.
b.   The second step is to show the need for a change.
c.   The third step is to satisfy the sense of need by presenting a plan that will remedy the need.
d.   The fourth step is to visualize the benefits and practicality of the plan.
e.   The fifth step is to urge the audience to take action in support of the plan.
2.   Because it is psychologically based, the motivated sequence is especially valuable for persuasive speeches that seek immediate action.

Exercises for Critical Thinking *(from text pages 423-424)*

1.   Look back at the story of Ramon Trujillo at the beginning of this chapter (page 394). Like Ramon, most people do a certain amount of persuading every day in normal conversation. Keep a journal of your communication activities for an entire day, making special note of all instances in which you tried to persuade someone else to your point of view. Choose one of those instances and prepare a brief analysis of it.

In your analysis, answer the following questions: (1) Who was the audience for your persuasive effort? (2) What were the "specific purpose" and the "central idea" of your persuasive message? (3) Did you rehearse your persuasive message ahead of time, or did it arise spontaneously from the situation? (4) Were you successful in achieving your specific purpose? (5) If you faced the same situation again, what strategic changes would you make in your persuasive effort?

Discussion: This exercise emphasizes the extent to which most people engage in persuasion as part of normal conversation. It also provides a good springboard for discussion about the similarities between the kind of informal persuasive "speeches" we all give every day and the formal persuasive speeches students will present in class. Students should find that the strategic thinking they put into planning a formal persuasive speech is similar in many ways to the strategic thinking they use when trying to persuade someone in ordinary conversation.

2.   Below are four specific purposes for persuasive speeches. In each case explain whether the speech associated with it concerns a question of fact, a question of value, or a question of policy. Then rewrite the specific purpose statement to make it appropriate for a speech about one of the other two kinds of questions. For instance, if the original purpose statement is about a question of policy, write a new specific purpose statement that deals with the same topic as either a question of fact or a question of value.

a.   To persuade my audience to donate time as a community volunteer.

b.   To persuade my audience that violence on television is a major cause of violent behavior in society.

c.   To persuade my audience that a national sales tax should be adopted to help pay off the national debt.

d.   To persuade my audience that it is unethical for businesses to use genetic testing in screening potential employees.

> **Discussion:**   This exercise works extremely well to help students understand the differences among questions of fact, value, and policy. Two possible variations follow each of the statements in the exercise.

> a.   To persuade my audience to donate time as a community volunteer. (question of policy)
>
> Question of fact: To persuade my audience that there is a serious shortage of community volunteers in our locality.
>
> Question of value: To persuade my audience that they have a moral obligation to help people less fortunate than themselves.

> b.   To persuade my audience that violence on television is a major cause of violent behavior in society. (question of fact)
>
> Question of value: To persuade my audience that the federal government has a moral duty to monitor the amount of violence in television programming.
>
> Question of policy: To persuade my audience that further reforms should be enacted to reduce the amount of violence on television programs designed for children.

c.   To persuade my audience that a national sales tax should be adopted to help pay off the national debt. (question of policy)

>   Question of fact: To persuade my audience that a major source of new revenue is needed to pay off the national debt.

>   Question of value: To persuade my audience that a national sales tax is an equitable way to help pay off the national debt.

d.   To persuade my audience that it is unethical for businesses to use genetic testing in screening potential employees. (question of value)

>   Question of fact: To persuade my audience that genetic testing is not always accurate in predicting whether people will contract particular diseases or come down with other medical conditions.

>   Question of policy: To persuade my audience that businesses should be prohibited from using genetic testing as a method of screening potential employees.

3.   Choose a topic for a persuasive speech on a question of policy. Create two specific purpose statements about that topic—one for a speech to gain passive agreement, another for a speech to motivate immediate action. Once you have the specific purpose statements, explain how the speech seeking immediate action would differ in structure and persuasive appeals from the speech seeking passive agreement. Be specific.

>   **Discussion:**   Understanding the distinction between seeking passive agreement and immediate action is crucial for effective persuasive speeches on questions of policy. This exercise helps students understand that distinction and the impact it has on the organization and strategy of a speech to persuade. The exercise works best when it is given as a homework assignment so students have plenty of time to work out their answers.
>
>   As an alternative, the exercise can also be used as the basis for a small-group activity in class. Divide the class into groups and have each come up with its own answers. Designate one person to present the result of each group's work to the class.
>
>   Here, as a general guide, is what the results might look like for a speech on the topic of cardiopulmonary resuscitation (CPR).
>
>   a.   Specific purpose statement for a speech seeking passive agreement: To persuade my audience that everyone should learn CPR.
>
>   b.   Specific purpose statement for a speech seeking immediate action: To persuade my audience to enroll in a CPR class at the Red Cross.
>
>   c.   Structure of the speech seeking passive agreement: This speech would most likely be organized either in topical order

(in which case each main point would explain a reason why everyone should learn CPR) or in problem-solution order (in which case the first main point would show why the lack of general CPR training is a problem and the second main point would present the speaker's plan to solve the problem).

d.   Structure of the speech seeking immediate action: This speech could be organized in problem-solution order, but if it were, the speaker would have to be sure to include a call to action as part of the solution. A more effective organizational pattern would be Monroe's motivated sequence, which is specifically designed for speeches that aim to motivate listeners to take immediate action.

e.   Persuasive appeals of the speech seeking passive agreement: This speech would focus on convincing the audience that it would be desirable for everyone to have training in CPR, but it would not try to persuade the audience to go out and learn CPR. As a result, the speaker could deal with the topic at a general level without having to confront the audience's objections to taking a CPR class themselves.

f.   Persuasive appeals of the speech seeking immediate action: A speaker cannot motivate an audience to immediate action without relating the topic directly to the audience and providing motivational appeals showing why they must change their behavior. It is also crucial that the speaker deal with the audience's potential reasons for not taking action—cost, lack of time, inconvenience, etc.

In the case of a speech on CPR, the speaker would need to show not just that there is a significant problem that can be solved by learning CPR, but also that it is necessary and practical for the listeners themselves to learn CPR. The speaker would have to anticipate the objections listeners might have to enrolling in a CPR class (too little time, not enough money, etc.) and answer those objections in the speech. The speaker might also rely more on emotional appeal in the speech seeking immediate action than in the speech seeking passive agreement. (See Chapter 16, pages 449-453, of the textbook for a discussion of emotional appeal in persuasive speaking.)

4.   Analyze the sample speech with commentary at the end of Chapter 15 of the textbook ("The Problem with Pennies," pages 418-420). Because this is a speech on a question of policy, pay special attention to how the speaker deals with the three basic issues of need, plan, and practicality. Does the speaker present a convincing case that a serious problem exists? Does she offer a clear plan to solve the problem? Does she demonstrate that the plan is practical?

Discussion: "The Problem with Pennies" is an excellent persuasive speech on a question of policy and provides an instructive model for students who are preparing their own speeches. The commentary that accompanies the speech on pages 418-420 of the textbook points out a number of its major features. Here is a synopsis that gives special attention to how the speaker deals with the issues of need, plan, and practicality.

Specific Purpose: To persuade my audience that pennies should be eliminated from the United States money supply.

Central Idea: Because pennies cause problems for individuals, businesses, and the economy as a whole, they should be eliminated from the U.S. money supply.

Method of Organization: Problem-solution.

Need: The speaker deals with the need for a change in the first main point of the body, which runs from paragraph 4 through paragraph 8. In paragraphs 4-5 she shows that pennies are such an annoyance that many people simply don't use them. After citing the results of her class survey, in which two-thirds of the class said they found pennies bothersome, the speaker presents a series of specific situations in which pennies are a nuisance. Her repeated use of "you" in paragraph 4 gives the speech a personal tone and relates it directly to the audience. So, too, does the story from writer Noel Gunther in paragraph 5 about his experience collecting pennies while in college.

In paragraph 6 the speaker claims that pennies are a nuisance for businesses as well as for individuals. She supports the claim with an arresting set of figures from *Fortune* magazine and the National Association of Convenience Stores. Here, as elsewhere, the speaker's evidence is from reliable sources which she identifies for the audience.

Paragraphs 7 and 8 present a combination of statistics and testimony to demonstrate the problems created for the nation as a whole by keeping pennies in circulation. The evidence in paragraph 8 is particularly strong and builds cumulatively to the statement, based on testimony from U.S. Treasury officials, that "it costs our society considerably more than a penny to transact a penny's worth of business." All in all, the need section of this speech is extremely well developed.

Plan: After a transition in paragraph 9, the speaker moves to her second main point, in which she presents her plan and demonstrates its practicality. The plan has four steps, which are presented in paragraphs 10-13. Each step is explained clearly and concisely so that listeners will understand exactly what the speaker is proposing. This is especially notable in paragraphs 10 and 11. Notice how much less effective the speech would have been if the speaker had failed in those paragraphs to explain the procedures by which purchases and sales taxes will be rounded off to the nearest nickel.

Practicality: The speaker demonstrates the practicality of her plan in paragraphs 14 and 15. Dealing with questions of practicality is especially crucial in a speech such as "The Problem with Pennies," in which listeners are likely to be skeptical about a speaker's plan. As discussed on pages 397-398 of the textbook, persuasive speakers must think of their speech as a kind of mental dialogue with the audience. The speaker must anticipate the possible objections listeners will raise to the speaker's point of view and answer those objections in the speech.

"The Problem with Pennies" provides an excellent example of how to do this. In paragraph 14 the speaker reasons analogically in showing that her plan is similar to that by which half-pennies were abolished during the nineteenth century. "None of us miss the half-cent," she explains, "and in a few years none of us will miss the penny." (For a discussion of analogical reasoning and its role in persuasive speaking, see Chapter 16, pages 444-445, of the textbook.)

In paragraph 15 the speaker deals with possible reservations about the feasibility of rounding off purchases to the nearest nickel by showing that most people already do exactly that when they use the "Take a Penny, Leave a Penny" containers at local convenience stores. It is also important to note how the speaker relates her ideas in paragraphs 14 and 15 directly to her audience by using words such as "us," "we," and "you." Because the speaker is trying to answer the objections of her immediate listeners, it only makes sense for her to bring her ideas home to those listeners in personal terms.

5. Select a television commercial that is organized according to Monroe's motivated sequence. Prepare a brief analysis in which you (a) identify the target audience for the commercial and (b) describe each step in the motivated sequence as it appears in the commercial.

Discussion: Although this exercise does not deal directly with public speaking, it is a splendid way to get students to think about Monroe's motivated sequence and the structure of persuasive messages in general, and it almost always produces a lively class discussion. It works best when given as a homework assignment, so students have plenty of time to think about and to analyze the commercials they select. When discussing the commercials in class, be sure to make connections between the organization of the commercials and the organization of a speech.

6.   Analyze Jennifer Conard's "The Ultimate Gift," in the appendix of sample speeches that follows Chapter 18 of the textbook. Because this speech is organized in Monroe's motivated sequence, pay special attention to how the speaker develops each step in the sequence—attention, need, satisfaction, visualization, action. Identify where each step of the sequence occurs in the speech and explain how the persuasive appeal of the speech builds from step to step.

Discussion: This exercise is especially helpful if you require that students use Monroe's motivated sequence in their persuasive speeches. "The Ultimate Gift" provides an excellent model of the sequence in action, and it is included on the videotape of student speeches that accompanies this edition of *The Art of Public Speaking*. For another model, have students analyze "Self-Defense on Campus," the sample speech with commentary at the end of Chapter 16 (text pages 453-456), which is also available on the student speech videotape. Here is a synopsis of "The Ultimate Gift" that focuses on its use of Monroe's motivated sequence.

Specific Purpose: To persuade my audience to become regular blood donors.

Central Idea: By becoming regular blood donors, college students can help save lives and replenish the shrinking U.S. blood supply.

Method of Organization: Monroe's motivated sequence

Attention: The attention section of the speech can be found in the introduction, which consists of paragraphs 1-3. The opening sequence of three rhetorical questions in paragraph 1 gets the audience involved right at the outset, while the first sentence of paragraph 2 moves from the opening questions to the topic of blood donation. After pulling the audience further into the speech by referring to her audience-analysis questionnaire, the speaker establishes her credibility by noting that she has been a regular blood donor for the past two years. A concise preview statement in paragraph 3 completes the introduction and provides a strong lead-in to the next section of the speech.

Need: The need section, which comprises the first main point in the body of the speech, runs from paragraph 4 through paragraph 7. In this section, the speaker supports her claim that the lack of participation by eligible blood donors is a serious problem. She begins in paragraph 4 by presenting statistics from the American Red Cross and by noting some of the medical conditions that require blood donations for treatment. In paragraphs 5-6 she presents an extended example of a three-year-old child named Brooke who requires massive amounts of blood for her cancer treatments. Paragraph 7 completes the need section by moving from the example of Brooke to additional quantitative evidence about the shortage of blood donors nationally.

Satisfaction: An excellent transition at the beginning of paragraph 8 moves the speaker from the need section to the satisfaction section, which constitutes the second main point in the body. After stating her policy in paragraph 8, the speaker devotes paragraphs 9-11 to explaining the process of donating blood. In doing so, she addresses three concerns that many of her classmates had mentioned on their audience-analysis questionnaires. First, she spells out the details of the process so people will know exactly what to expect when they go to donate blood. Second, she notes that all blood is drawn with sterile, nonreusable needles, so one need not fear contracting AIDS from donating. Third, she reassures listeners that despite many people's fear of needles, the process of donating blood is virtually painless.

Clear, crisp, and detailed, this section of the speech provides a model satisfaction section. One of the best ways to communicate this to students is to ask them to imagine the speech without paragraphs 9-11. Most will see at once how much weaker the speech would be if these paragraphs were not present. It is also worth noting how the speaker relates her ideas directly to the audience by talking in terms of "you" and "your" throughout paragraphs 9-11.

Visualization: After completing the satisfaction section, the speaker shifts to the visualization section with a transition at the start of paragraph 12. Consisting of paragraphs 12-13, this section comprises the third main point in the body. Here the speaker visualizes for her audience the benefits that will accrue if her policy is adopted.

She begins in paragraph 12 by explaining that because every unit of donated blood is divided three ways, it is possible to help as many as three people with a single donation. In paragraph 13 she builds upon this analysis by noting that since a person can donate blood six times annually, it is possible to help as many as 18 different people in a single year and up to 180 over ten years. The final sentence of paragraph 13 does an excellent job of relating these figures to the speaker's classmates by stating that their donations could benefit a friend, a family member, or even themselves.

Action: Another excellent transition, at the beginning of paragraph 14, marks the beginning of the action section, which constitutes the conclusion and runs through the end of the speech in paragraph 16. As with the other parts of the speech, this section is extremely well developed. Rather than cursorily stating that her classmates should start donating blood, the speaker steadily builds her call for action throughout paragraphs 14-16.

In paragraph 14 she appeals both to first-time blood donors and to people who have donated before. In paragraph 15 she uses emotional appeal by asking the audience to think of someone dear to them who might be denied blood when they urgently need it—just like the three-year-old girl discussed earlier in the speech. The speaker then tells her classmates exactly where they can go to donate blood, including the location of the next blood drive on campus. She ends in paragraph 16 with three sentences that become progressively shorter and more imperative in tone. As in the rest of the speech, she brings her ideas home to her classmates throughout the action section by addressing them directly as "you."

Applying the Power of Public Speaking *(from text page 424)*

As a local union leader, it is your job to present a contract offer made by management to your striking membership. Though the proposed offer falls short of meeting all your union's demands, you believe it is a good offer, and in your speech, you will recommend that the union members vote to accept it.

The contract issues have been hotly debated, so you have an idea how some of your 42 members will cast their ballots. One issue is that management has guaranteed to maintain full benefits for current workers but wants to reduce benefits for new workers. Though the proposed offer limits these reductions, you know of 12 members who will vote against any proposal that limits the benefits of future workers. Already with you, however, are the 8 members who voted not to strike at all and who will vote to accept any reasonable offer. Among the undecided voters are those who think that since the strike is only in its second week, a better contract may be offered if this proposal is rejected.

Who is the target audience for your speech? How will you persuade them to vote yes on the contract offer? Which of the following methods of organization will you use for your speech, and why: problem-solution, comparative advantages, Monroe's motivated sequence?

Discussion: Given the information provided in the scenario, the most obvious target audience would be those union members who are undecided on the contract. To persuade them to vote yes on the contract, the speaker will need to address their reasons for going on strike and their concerns about the specific provisions of the contract. Certainly, the speaker will need to make a persuasive case that remaining out on strike for a longer period of time will not result in a significantly better contract.

Although the speaker could use any of the methods of organization mentioned in the question, problem-solution order would probably be the least effective. Because the speaker is seeking immediate action, Monroe's motivated sequence would be more appropriate than problem-solution. Another possibility, of course, would be comparative advantages order, in which the speaker would systematically compare the advantages of accepting the contract with the disadvantages of not accepting it.

This exercise works well as a vehicle for class discussion on the target audience and its role in persuasive speaking. Divide the class into groups and give each a few minutes to come up with answers to the questions posed at the end of the scenario. Designate one person to present each group's answers to the class. Follow with a general class discussion.

Additional Exercises and Activities

1. Below are eight statements. Explain whether each statement deals *primarily* with a question of fact, a question of value, or a question of policy.

    a. President Franklin D. Roosevelt knew in advance about the Japanese plan to attack Pearl Harbor and allowed it to happen.

    b. If Franklin D. Roosevelt knew in advance about the Japanese plan to attack Pearl Harbor, he was wrong in allowing it to happen.

    c. Using lie detector tests as screening devices for jobs in private business is a violation of the employee's right to privacy.

    d. The use of lie detector tests for screening employees in private business should be banned by law.

    e. A federal law should be passed requiring that trunk safety releases be standard on all new cars sold in the United States.

    f. If trunk safety releases were standard equipment on all cars sold in the United States, we could save several hundred lives every year.

    g. Colorizing classic movies such as *Casablanca* violates the artistic integrity of such movies.

    h. Congress should protect the artistic integrity of movies such as *Casablanca* by passing a law prohibiting the colorization of classic American films.

Discussion: These statements are somewhat more complex than those in Exercise 2 on page 423 of the textbook. Dealing with them provides valuable extra work for students in distinguishing among questions of fact, value, and policy. It also helps demonstrate how one kind of question can have strong implications for a speech on one of the other types of questions. To facilitate class discussion, this exercise is included in the binder of overhead transparencies that accompanies *The Art of Public Speaking*.

a.   President Franklin D. Roosevelt knew in advance about the Japanese plan to attack Pearl Harbor and allowed it to happen.

(question of fact)

b.   If Franklin D. Roosevelt knew in advance about the Japanese plan to attack Pearl Harbor, he was wrong in allowing it to happen.

(question of value)

c.   Using lie detector tests as screening devices for jobs in private business is a violation of the employee's right to privacy.

(question of value)

d.   The use of lie detector tests for screening employees in private business should be banned by law.

(question of policy)

e.   A federal law should be passed requiring that trunk safety releases be standard on all new cars sold in the United States.

(question of policy)

f.   If trunk safety releases were standard on all cars sold in the United States, we could save several hundred lives every year.

(question of fact)

g.   Colorizing classic movies such as *Casablanca* violates the artistic integrity of such movies.

(question of value)

h.   Congress should protect the artistic integrity of movies such as *Casablanca* by passing a law prohibiting the colorization of classic American films.

(question of policy. Although defining "artistic integrity" and deciding what constitutes a "classic" film both involve value judgments, the statement is concerned primarily with advocating a congressional policy preventing colorization.)

2. Conduct a class discussion on the ethics of persuasive speaking. Among the issues to consider are: (1) Is it ethical for one person to try to persuade another? (2) What is the most ethical approach for a speaker to take when trying to persuade an audience? (3) To what extent should a persuasive speaker reveal her or his true motives to the audience? (4) Are there any situations in which it would be ethical for a speaker to distort the truth in order to persuade an audience? (5) Is it ethical for a speaker to use emotional appeal to sway listeners?

> **Discussion:** Questions of ethics can arise every time a speaker seeks to persuade an audience. By dealing with the issue at the start of the unit on persuasive speaking, instructors can emphasize to students the importance of keeping a firm ethical rudder in their speeches. It may be helpful to have students review Chapter 2 of the textbook ("Ethics and Public Speaking") in preparation for discussion.
>
> Although this exercise can work very well early in the unit on persuasion, some instructors prefer to discuss ethics in conjunction with the next chapter of the textbook, which contains a section devoted to the ethics of emotional appeal (text pages 448-453). For a similar exercise in Chapter 16, see page 459 of the textbook.

3. Bring to class a bag containing a half-dozen or so ordinary household items—rubber band, stapler, hairbrush, can of soda, etc. Also bring a bag containing an equal number of slips of paper on which you have identified potential speech audiences—retirees, college students, middle-class baby boomers, elementary-school students, etc. Divide the class into groups and have each group select an item from one bag and an audience from the other.

Give each group 10 minutes to compose a 1 to 2 minute speech designed to sell its object to the chosen audience. There are two special requirements. First, the group must come up with a completely new use for its item. For example, if the item is a can opener, the group must devise some use for it other than opening cans or bottles. Second, the speech must be organized according to Monroe's motivated sequence. Have one member from each group present its speech to the class. After each speech, ask the rest of the class if they can identify the target audience for the speech.

> **Discussion:** Not only do students enjoy this activity, but it provides an excellent vehicle for discussion of two central concepts discussed in this chapter—the target audience and Monroe's motivated sequence. Encourage students to be creative in their speeches and expect a lively session.

4. As an alternative to the preceding activity, divide the class into groups and have each group prepare a 1 to 2 minute speech with the specific purpose, "To persuade my audience that all students should take a course in public speaking." The speech must be organized according to Monroe's motivated sequence. Have one member from each group present the speech to the class.

> **Discussion:** There are an almost endless number of potential variations on this activity depending on the specific purpose you assign and the aspects of persuasive speaking you want to illustrate. It can also be adapted to provide a brief individual speech assignment rather than a group activity.

5.   Show the class one or more persuasive speeches from the videotapes of student speeches that accompany *The Art of Public Speaking*. Use the videotapes to illustrate points about effective persuasive speaking.

> **Discussion:** The videotape supplement to *The Art of Public Speaking* contains several student persuasive speeches that can be used for classroom analysis and discussion. Three of those speeches—"Self-Defense on Campus," "The Ultimate Gift," and "Multicultural, Multilingual"—are printed in the book. The others are available in Part Five of this manual.

6.   Distribute copies of "To Save a Child," by Dawn Follendorf, which appears on pages 445-447 of this manual. Have students analyze the speech in light of the criteria for persuasive speeches on questions of policy presented in the chapter.

> **Discussion:** A persuasive speech on a question of policy, "To Save a Child" is an excellent speech for analysis and discussion. Because it is organized according to Monroe's motivated sequence, it can be especially valuable for students who plan to use the motivated sequence in their own persuasive speeches. For full discussion of the speech, see pages 448-449 of this manual.

7.   Distribute copies of "Ghosts," by Ken Lonnquist, which is printed on pages 489-492 of this manual. Have students analyze the speech in light of the criteria for persuasive speeches on questions of value discussed in the chapter.

> **Discussion:** "Ghosts" is a persuasive speech on a question of value. Delivered in an introductory argumentation and debate class, it is considerably more complex than the typical classroom speech. The speaker's purpose was to convince his classmates that abortion is morally wrong, and he knew from his audience analysis that all but one of his listeners opposed his position.
>
>   Because the topic of the speech is so controversial, it invariably sparks a heated class discussion. If that discussion is to be most productive, however, it needs to focus primarily on the speaker's techniques rather than on his position regarding abortion. If you assign the speech, urge students to put aside their personal opinions about abortion and to analyze the speech in light of questions such as the following:

(1)   Is the introduction well suited to the speaker's task of gaining good will and establishing common ground with his audience?

(2)   What kind of reasoning does the speaker rely on most of all throughout the speech?

(3)   Although the speech deals with a question of value, its persuasiveness rests largely on the speaker's ability to convince his listeners about a question of fact. What is that question of fact? How effectively does the speaker deal with it given the opposition of his listeners?

(4)   How effectively does the speaker use the resources of language discussed in Chapter 11—imagery, metaphor, parallelism, repetition, etc.—to express his ideas? What are the "ghosts" to which he refers throughout the speech? Is this an appropriate image for the speech, or does it distract attention from the major issue?

For full commentary on the speech, see pages 493-494 of this manual.

Extra Teaching and Learning Resources

General

Allen, Mike, and Preiss, Ray W. (eds.). *Persuasion: Advances Through Meta-Analysis*. Cresskill, NJ: Hampton Press, 1997.

Cialdini, Robert B. *Influence: Science and Practice of Persuasion*, 4th ed. Boston: Allyn and Bacon, 2001.

Dillard, James Price, and Pfau, Michael (eds.). *The Persuasion Handbook: Developments in Theory and Practice*. Thousand Oaks, CA: Sage, 2002.

Griffin, Em. *A First Look at Communication Theory*, 5th ed. New York: McGraw-Hill, 2003.

Hogan, Kevin. *The Psychology of Persuasion: How to Persuade Others to Your Way of Thinking*. Gretna, LA: Pelican, 1998.

Johannesen, Richard L. *Ethics in Human Communication*, 5th ed. Prospect Heights, IL: Waveland Press, 2002.

Jowett, Garth, and O'Donnell, Victoria. *Propaganda and Persuasion*. 3rd ed. Walnut Creek, CA: Altamira Press, 1999.

Larson, Charles U. *Persuasion: Reception and Responsibility*, 9th ed. Belmont, CA: Wadsworth, 2001.

Lucas, Richard H., and McCoy, K. Byron. *The Winning Edge: Effective Communication and Persuasion Techniques for Lawyers*. Tucson, AZ: Lawyers and Judges Publishing Company, 1999.

Mills, Harry A. *Artful Persuasion: How to Command Attention, Change Minds, and Influence People*. New York: Amacom, 2000.

O'Keefe, Daniel J. *Persuasion: Theory and Research*, 2nd ed. Newbury Park, CA: Sage, 2002.

Perloff, Richard M. *The Dynamics of Persuasion: Communication and Attitudes in the 21st Century*, 2nd ed. Mahwah, NJ: Lawrence Erlbaum, 2003.

Petty, Richard E., and Wegener, Duane T. "Attitude Change: Multiple Roles for Persuasion Variables." In Gilbert, Daniel T.; Fiske, Susan T.; and Lindzey, Gardner (eds.), *Handbook of Social Psychology*, 4th ed. New York: McGraw-Hill, 1998, Vol. I, pp. 323-390.

Pratkanis, Anthony, and Aronson, Elliot. *Age of Propaganda: The Everyday Use and Abuse of Persuasion*, rev. ed. New York: W. H. Freeman, 2001.

Roskos-Ewoldsen, David R. "Implicit Theories of Persuasion." *Human Communication Theory*, 24 (1997), 31-63.

Simons, Herbert W. *Persuasion in Society*. Thousand Oaks, CA: Sage, 2001.

Wilkins, Fred. *Persuasive Jury Communication: Case Studies from Successful Trials*. Colorado Springs, CO: Shepard's, 2000.

Woodward, Gary C., Jr., and Denton, Robert E. *Persuasion and Influence in American Life*, 4th ed. Prospect Heights, IL: Waveland Press, 2000.

Classroom Activities and Assignments

Daughton, Suzanne M. "Aristotle Meets Gary Larson: Making Enthymemes Memorable." In Stephen E. Lucas (ed.), *Selections from the Speech Communication Teacher, 1996-1999*. New York: McGraw-Hill, 2001, pp. 74-75.

Fregoe, David H. "Informative vs. Persuasive Speaking." In Stephen E. Lucas (ed.), *Selections from the Speech Communication Teacher, 1986-1991*. New York: McGraw-Hill, 1992, pp. 57-58.

Garrett, Roger L. "The Premises of Persuasion." In Stephen E. Lucas (ed.), *Selections from the Speech Communication Teacher, 1986-1991*. New York: McGraw-Hill, 1992, pp. 58-59.

Langley, C. Darrell. "The Heckling Speech." In Stephen E. Lucas (ed.), *Selections from the Speech Communication Teacher, 1986-1991*. New York: McGraw-Hill, 1992, p. 67.

MacDonald, Madlyne A. "The Key to Persuasion." In Stephen E. Lucas (ed.), *Selections from the Speech Communication Teacher, 1986-1991*. New York: McGraw-Hill, 1992, pp. 59-60.

McKinney, Bruce C. "Audience Analysis Exercise." In Stephen E. Lucas (ed.), *Selections from the Speech Communication Teacher, 1986-1991*. New York: McGraw-Hill, 1992, p. 13.

Mohsen, Raed A. "Out on Campus: A Challenging Public Speaking Experience." In Stephen E. Lucas (ed.), *Selections from the Speech Communication Teacher, 1991-1994*. New York: McGraw-Hill, 1995, pp. 56-57.

Nelson, Lee Ann. "Sell Us Monroe's Motivated Sequence." In Stephen E. Lucas (ed.), *Selections from the Speech Communication Teacher, 1994-1996*. New York: McGraw-Hill, 1997, p. 57.

Powell, Kimberly A. "Debate as the Key to Teaching Persuasion Skills." In Stephen E. Lucas (ed.), *Selections from the Speech Communication Teacher, 1994-1996*. New York: McGraw-Hill, 1997, pp. 83-84.

Proctor, Russell F. "Using *Swing Kids* to Teach Theories of Persuasion." In Stephen E. Lucas (ed.), *Selections from the Communication Teacher, 1999-2002*. New York: McGraw-Hill, 2004, pp. 61-62.

Ross, Charlynn. "The Challenging Audience Exercise." In Stephen E. Lucas (ed.), *Selections from the Speech Communication Teacher, 1986-1991*. New York: McGraw-Hill, 1992, p. 69.

Schreier, Howard N. "Experiencing Persuasion and the Persuader." In Stephen E. Lucas (ed.), *Selections from the Communication Teacher, 1999-2002*. New York: McGraw-Hill, 2004, pp. 62-64.

Schreir, Howard N. "Analyzing Persuasive Tactics." In Stephen E. Lucas (ed.), *Selections from the Speech Communication Teacher, 1986-1991*. New York: McGraw-Hill, 1992, p. 61.

Smith, Robert E., Jr. "Persuasion Principles from Slick, Sticky, and Sloppy Ads." In Stephen E. Lucas (ed.), *Selections from the Speech Communication Teacher, 1996-1999*. New York: McGraw-Hill, 2001, p. 74.

Films and Videos

"The Language of Persuasion." Insight Media (1999). 20 minutes.

"Persuasion." Insight Media (1996). 26 minutes.

"Persuasion at Work." Insight Media (1998). 3 segments; 32 minutes total.

"Persuasive Language: Using and Understanding It." Insight Media (1998). 2 segments; 30 minutes total.

"Persuasive Speaking." Insight Media (1997). 30 minutes.

"Persuasive Speaking: Organization." Insight Media (1997). 30 minutes.

"Persuasive Speaking: Strategies." Insight Media (1997). 30 minutes.

"Propaganda." Films for the Humanities and Sciences (2000). 29 minutes.

"Psycho-Sell: Advertising and Persuasion." Insight Media (1991). 25 minutes.

"When You Buy: How Ads Persuade." Insight Media (1989). 33 minutes.

Chapter 16 Methods of Persuasion

Chapter Objectives

After reading this chapter, students should be able to:

1. Explain the role of speaker credibility in persuasive speaking.

2. Define the differences among initial credibility, derived credibility, and terminal credibility.

3. Discuss three ways a speaker can enhance her or his credibility during a persuasive speech.

4. Explain why it is important for persuasive speakers to use evidence in their speeches.

5. Discuss the four tips presented in the chapter for using evidence in persuasive speeches.

6. Define reasoning from specific instances and explain the guidelines given in the chapter for using this method of reasoning.

7. Define reasoning from principle and explain the guidelines a speaker should follow when employing reasoning from principle.

8. Define causal reasoning and explain the two common errors speakers need to avoid when using causal reasoning.

9. Define analogical reasoning and explain how to judge the validity of an analogy.

10. Identify the red herring, *ad hominem*, either-or, bandwagon, and slippery slope fallacies.

11. Explain the role of emotional appeal in persuasive speaking and discuss when it is ethical for a speaker to employ emotional appeal.

12. Identify three methods a speaker can use to generate emotional appeal when speaking to persuade.

Chapter Outline

I. There is a perpetual interest in the methods of persuasion *(text page 428)*.
    A. People have been studying the strategies and tactics of successful persuasion for thousands of years.
    B. Scholars generally agree that listeners are persuaded by a speaker for one or more of four reasons.
        1. Because they perceive the speaker as having high credibility.
        2. Because they are won over by the speaker's evidence.
        3. Because they are convinced by the speaker's reasoning.
        4. Because their emotions are touched by the speaker's ideas or language.

II. A speaker's credibility plays an important role in persuading the audience *(text pages 428-433)*.
    A. Credibility is the audience's attitude toward or perception of the speaker.
        1. The more favorably listeners view a speaker, the more likely they are to accept what the speaker says.
        2. A speaker's credibility will vary from audience to audience and topic to topic.
            a. The same speaker may have high credibility for one audience and low credibility for another.
            b. A speaker may also have high credibility on one topic and low credibility on another.
    B. A speaker's credibility is affected by two primary factors—competence and character.
        1. Competence refers to how an audience regards a speaker's intelligence, expertise, and knowledge of the subject.
        2. Character refers to how an audience regards a speaker's sincerity, trustworthiness, and concern for the well-being of the audience.
    C. There are three types of credibility.
        1. Initial credibility is the audience's perception of the speaker before the speech begins.

          2.   Derived credibility is produced by everything a speaker says and does during the speech.

          3.   Terminal credibility is the audience's perception of the speaker at the end of the speech.

    D.   There are three strategies speakers can use to enhance their credibility.

          1.   Speakers can enhance their credibility by explaining their competence.

              a.   They can stress their research on the speech topic.

              b.   They can stress special knowledge of the topic gained through personal experience.

          2.   Speakers can enhance their credibility by establishing common ground with the audience.

              a.   Establishing common ground means showing respect for and identifying with the audience's values and beliefs.

              b.   Establishing common ground is especially important in the introduction of a persuasive speech.

          3.   Speakers can enhance their credibility by delivering their speeches fluently, expressively, and with conviction.

              a.   There is substantial research showing that fluent, animated delivery greatly enhances a speaker's credibility.

              b.   Speaking with genuine conviction also does a great deal to strengthen a speaker's credibility.

III.   A speaker's use of evidence plays an important role in persuading the audience *(text pages 433-437)*.

    A.   Evidence consists of examples, statistics, and testimony used to prove or disprove something.

    B.   To be persuasive, speakers must support their views with evidence.

          1.   Careful listeners are skeptical of unsupported claims and generalizations.

          2.   Strong evidence is particularly important when the speaker is not recognized as an expert on the speech topic.

          3.   Strong evidence is also crucial when the target audience opposes the speaker's point of view.

              a.   Skeptical listeners will mentally create counterarguments to answer what the speaker says.

              b.   The speaker's success will depend partly on how well she or he anticipates these internal responses and gives evidence to refute them.

    C.   There are four tips persuasive speakers should follow to use evidence effectively.

          1.   Persuasive speakers should use specific evidence.

              a.   Research indicates that evidence is more persuasive when it is stated in specific rather than general terms.

              b.   Specific evidence also enhances a speaker's credibility by demonstrating his or her grasp of the topic.

          2.   Persuasive speakers should use novel evidence.

              a.   Studies show that evidence will be more persuasive when it is new to the audience.

      b.   Presenting an audience new facts and figures requires resourceful research, but it is well worth the effort.

   3.   Persuasive speakers should use evidence from credible sources.

      a.   There is a good deal of research indicating that listeners find evidence from competent, credible sources more persuasive than evidence from less qualified sources.

      b.   Listeners are especially skeptical about evidence from sources that appear to be biased or self-interested.

   4.   Persuasive speakers should make clear the point of their evidence.

      a.   Studies have shown that speakers cannot count on listeners to draw, on their own, the conclusion a speaker wants them to reach.

      b.   In most situations, persuasive speakers need to be sure to state the point they are trying to make with their evidence.

IV.   A speaker's reasoning plays an important role in persuading the audience *(text pages 437-448)*.

   A.   Reasoning is the process of drawing a conclusion based on evidence.

   B.   Public speakers have two major concerns with respect to reasoning.

     1.   The first is to make sure the speaker's reasoning is sound.

     2.   The second is to get listeners to agree with the speaker's reasoning.

   C.   Persuasive speakers often use reasoning from specific instances.

     1.   When speakers reason from specific instances, they progress from a number of particular facts to a general conclusion.

     2.   Speakers should follow three guidelines when reasoning from specific instances.

        a.   They need to beware of hasty generalizations based on insufficient evidence.

        b.   They need to be careful with their wording so as not to overstate the facts.

        c.   They need to reinforce their argument with statistics or testimony.

   D.   Persuasive speakers often use reasoning from principle.

     1.   When speakers reason from principle, they move from a general principle to a specific conclusion.

     2.   Speakers should follow two basic guidelines when reasoning from principle.

        a.   They need to make certain the audience will accept the general principle.

        b.   They also need to make sure the audience will accept the minor premise.

   E.   Persuasive speakers often use causal reasoning.

     1.   Causal reasoning tries to establish the relationship between causes and effects.

     2.   Speakers should follow two guidelines when using causal reasoning.

        a.   They should avoid the fallacy of false cause.

            (1)   This fallacy is often known by its Latin name, *post hoc, ergo propter hoc*, which means "after this, therefore because of this."

          (2)   Speakers who commit this fallacy assume that because one event comes after another, the first event must necessarily be the cause of the second.

      b.   Speakers should also avoid the fallacy of assuming that events have only one cause.

          (1)   Most events have several causes.

          (2)   Speakers need to be wary of oversimplifying complex causes or attributing a complex effect to a single cause.

F.   Persuasive speakers often use analogical reasoning.

    1.   Analogical reasoning compares two similar cases to draw the conclusion that what is true in one case will also be true in the other.

    2.   The most important guideline for speakers using analogical reasoning is to make sure the two cases being compared are essentially alike.

      a.   If the cases being compared are essentially alike, the analogy is valid.

      b.   If the cases being compared are not essentially alike, the analogy is invalid.

G.   Regardless of the method of reasoning they use, speakers must guard against logical fallacies in their presentations.

    1.   Three of those fallacies, as we saw earlier, are hasty generalization, false cause, and invalid analogy.

    2.   Five additional fallacies are discussed here.

      a.   The red herring fallacy introduces an irrelevant issue in order to divert attention from the subject under discussion.

      b.   The *ad hominem* fallacy substitutes an attack on the person for discussion of the real issue in dispute.

      c.   The either-or fallacy, sometimes referred to as a false dilemma, forces listeners to choose between two alternatives when more than two alternatives exist.

      d.   The bandwagon fallacy assumes that because something is popular, it is therefore good, correct, or desirable.

      e.   The slippery slope fallacy assumes that taking a first step will lead inevitably to a second step and so on down the slope to disaster.

V.   A speaker's emotional appeals play an important role in persuading the audience *(text pages 448-453)*.

    A.   Emotional appeals—often called motivational appeals—are intended to make listeners feel sad, angry, guilty, fearful, reverent, or the like.

    B.   Effective persuasion often requires emotional appeal.

      1.   Few people are moved to change their attitudes or take action when they are bored or complacent.

      2.   As George Campbell wrote in his *Philosophy of Rhetoric*, "When persuasion is the end, passion also must be engaged."

    C.   Speakers can generate emotional appeal in three ways.

      1.   One way to generate emotional appeal is with emotionally charged language.

        a.   Language can generate strong responses in an audience by evoking emotions attached to particular words and phrases.

      b. Speakers should be careful, however, of calling attention to their emotional appeals with a sudden barrage of emotional language that is inconsistent with the rest of the speech.

    2. A second way to generate emotional appeal is with vivid examples.

      a. Vivid, richly textured examples allow emotional appeal to grow naturally out of the content of the speech.

      b. Examples add impact, bring ideas home to listeners in personal terms, and make the speech more compelling.

    3. A third way to generate emotional appeal is to speak with sincerity and conviction.

      a. The strongest source of emotional appeal is the conviction and sincerity of the speaker.

      b. Speakers who feel the emotion themselves will communicate that emotion through everything they say and do in the speech.

D. Because emotional appeals have so much potential power, they need to be used with a strong sense of ethical responsibility.

    1. Emotional appeals can be abused by unscrupulous speakers for detestable causes.

    2. Emotional appeals can also be used by principled speakers for noble causes.

    3. Ethical speakers make sure their emotional appeals are appropriate to the speech topic.

      a. Emotional appeals are often necessary when a speaker is trying to persuade an audience to take action.

      b. Emotional appeals are usually inappropriate when a speaker is discussing a question of fact.

    4. Even when trying to move listeners to action, a speaker should never substitute emotional appeals for evidence and reasoning.

      a. Persuasive speeches should always be built on a firm foundation of facts and logic.

      b. Speakers need to develop a good case based on reason *and* kindle the emotions of the audience.

    5. When using emotional appeals, persuasive speakers should also keep in mind the guidelines for ethical speechmaking discussed in Chapter 2.

Exercises for Critical Thinking *(from text pages 458-459)*

1. Research has shown that a speaker's initial credibility can have great impact on how the speaker's ideas are received by listeners. Research has also shown that a speaker's credibility will vary from topic to topic and audience to audience. In the left-hand column below is a list of well-known public figures. In the right-hand column is a list of potential speech topics. Assume that each speaker will be addressing your speech class.

    For each speaker, identify the topic in the right-hand column on which she or he would have the highest initial credibility for your class. Then explain how the speaker's initial credibility might be affected if the speaker were discussing the topic in the right-hand column directly across from her or his name.

Speaker	*Topic*
Oprah Winfrey	Women in Politics
Jesse Jackson	Talk Shows: Their Role in Society
Steven Spielberg	The Perils of Broadcast Journalism
Hillary Clinton	African Americans: The Next Agenda
Peter Jennings	Movies in the 21st Century

Discussion: This exercise is almost certain to provoke a lively discussion and is a fine way to launch a class discussion on the importance of credibility in persuasive speaking. Here are some plausible responses to the questions about each of the speakers listed in the exercise:

Oprah Winfrey: Although Oprah Winfrey might be seen as a credible speaker on several of the topics listed in the right-hand column—especially "African Americans: The Next Agenda"—she would have the greatest credibility on "Talk Shows: Their Role in Society" Indeed, as one of the most highly respected talk-show hosts on television, this is a subject she has addressed on many occasions.

Jesse Jackson: Although Jackson could doubtless speak with insight on the merits of T.V. talk shows, as well as on the role of women in U.S. politics, the topic on which he would have the highest credibility is "African Americans: The Next Agenda." This would be true both for listeners who are strong backers of Jackson and for listeners who are not. His status as a spokesperson for African Americans is widely acknowledged across racial, social, and political lines.

Steven Spielberg: The director of such films as *Schindler's List, ET, Jurassic Park,* and *Raiders of the Lost Ark,* Spielberg would command a rapt audience on the subject of movies in the 21st century. Despite the fact that he works in the mass media and certainly knows something about television news, he would have much less credibility on the topic across from his name, "The Perils of Broadcast Journalism."

Hillary Clinton: As a woman and a major political figure, Clinton's credibility would be highest if she were speaking on "Women in Politics." Although the views of Peter Jennings and Jesse Jackson might be well regarded by some listeners, neither has Clinton's firsthand experience on this topic. If Clinton were speaking on the topic across from her name—"African Americans: The Next Agenda"—she would have some credibility (certainly more, for example, than Steven Spielberg), but nowhere near as much as Jesse Jackson.

Peter Jennings: With his years of experience covering politics and reporting the news, Jennings could probably speak credibly on any of the topics in this exercise with the exception of "Movies in the 21st Century." The one on which he would have the greatest credibility, however, would be "The Perils of Broadcast Journalism."

2.   Identify the kind of reasoning used in each of the following statements. What weaknesses, if any, can you find in the reasoning of each?

a.   According to a study by the American Medical Association, men with bald spots have three times the risk of heart attack as men with a full head of hair. Strange as it may seem, it looks as if baldness is a cause of heart attacks.

Discussion: This statement is an example of causal reasoning. It is flawed by the fallacy of false cause. The fact that men with bald spots have three times the risk of heart attack does not mean their baldness is a cause of their heart attacks. If there is any connection between baldness and heart attacks, it is that both are brought on by similar factors—stress, heredity, diet, etc.—but medical researchers do not yet have an answer to this question.

b.   Contrary to what the chemical industry argues, limiting pesticide use does not threaten the food supply. Sweden has cut back on pesticides by 50 percent over the last few years with almost no decrease in its harvest. The Campbell Soup Company uses no pesticides at all on tomatoes grown in Mexico, and they reap as much fruit as ever. Many California farmers who practice pesticide-free agriculture have actually experienced increases in their crop yields.

Discussion: This statement is an example of reasoning from specific instances. Whether it is flawed depends on whether the three specific instances mentioned in the statement are representative of what happens in most cases in which farmers reduce their use of pesticides. And that cannot be determined in the absence of further evidence. One way to provide that evidence would be to follow the three instances with expert testimony that limiting pesticide use does not threaten the food supply. Another way would be to offer statistics showing that in a wide number of cases farmers have reduced their use of pesticides without reducing their crop yields. Even then, however, a skeptical listener (or a representative of the pesticide industry) could argue that the testimony is not conclusive or that the statistics are not sufficient to prove the speaker's point beyond doubt.

c.   The United States Constitution guarantees all citizens the right to bear arms. Gun control legislation infringes on the right of citizens to bear arms. Therefore, gun control legislation is contrary to the Constitution.

> **Discussion:**   This statement is an example of reasoning from principle. The reasoning is valid in that the movement from the general principle (The U.S. Constitution guarantees all citizens the right to bear arms) to the minor premise (Gun control legislation infringes on the right of citizens to bear arms) to the conclusion (Therefore, gun control legislation is contrary to the Constitution) is logically valid.
>
> Logical validity, however, is judged by the form of an argument, not by its content. If the conclusion has been correctly inferred from the premises, the argument is valid regardless of whether or not the premises are true. It is possible to have a valid argument from principle that is patently unsound. For example:
>
> 1.   All movie stars live in Hollywood.
>
> 2.   Tommy Lee Jones is a movie star.
>
> 3.   Therefore, Tommy Lee Jones lives in Hollywood.
>
> This is a valid argument. If it is true that all movie stars live in Hollywood, and if it is also true that Tommy Lee Jones is a movie star, then it must be true that Tommy Lee Jones lives in Hollywood. In fact, however, it is not true that all movie stars live in Hollywood. Many live outside Hollywood; Tommy Lee Jones lives in Texas. Even though the argument is valid, it is not sound.
>
> A sound argument from principle is one in which the reasoning is valid and all of the premises are true. For example:
>
> 1.   To be elected President of the United States a person must be at least 35 years of age.
>
> 2.   George W. Bush was elected President of the United States.
>
> 3.   Therefore, George W. Bush is at least 35 years of age.
>
> In this case, the reasoning is valid and the premises are true. The conclusion is sound.
>
> What about the argument regarding gun control? Is it sound as well as valid? That depends upon how one interprets the meaning of the clause of the U.S. Constitution ensuring citizens the right to bear arms. If one interprets that clause as meaning that all citizens have the right to own any kind of gun they please, then gun control legislation would certainly be contrary to the Constitution. If one interprets the right to bear arms in an 18th-century context as meaning that all citizens have the right to maintain their own weapons so as to be able to serve in the militia—a situation that is

not relevant to U.S. life in the 21st century—then gun control legislation might not be contrary to the Constitution.

The persuasiveness of the argument in any given situation will depend on the ability of the speaker to convince the audience that he or she has the correct interpretation of the clause of the Constitution that guarantees citizens the right to bear arms. As with the example of reasoning from specific instances presented earlier, this case demonstrates that reasoning is not always a cut-and-dried matter.

d.   Almost every industrialized nation in the world except for the United States has a national curriculum and national tests to help ensure that schools throughout the country are meeting high standards of education. If such a system can work elsewhere, it can work in the United States as well.

Discussion: This statement is an example of analogical reasoning. Its validity depends upon whether the factors that allow a national curriculum and national testing to work successfully in most industrialized nations are also present in the United States. Advocates of nationalizing the educational system argue that the U.S. is similar enough to most other industrialized countries to conclude, on the basis of their experience, that a national curriculum and national tests would work successfully in the U.S. Opponents of nationalizing the educational system argue that U.S. society and its educational objectives are so unique that it is not possible to conclude, on the basis of other countries' experience, that a national curriculum and national testing can be successfully implemented in the U.S. In my opinion, the evidence is not yet conclusive enough to determine which side is correct. The important point is that students understand how one would judge the validity of the analogy.

3.   Over the years there has been much debate about the role of emotional appeal in public speaking. Do you believe it is ethical for public speakers to use emotional appeals when seeking to persuade an audience? Do you feel there are certain kinds of emotions to which an ethical speaker should not appeal? Why or why not? Be prepared to explain your ideas in class.

Discussion: Because so much has been written over the years about the ethics of emotional appeal in persuasion, it is often valuable to take some time in class to discuss the issue. The purpose of the discussion is not so much for students to come away with the "correct" answer as it is for them to develop their own thinking about the ethics of emotional appeal. Instructors who wish to learn more about this topic should consult the Extra Teaching and Learning Resources for this chapter of the manual.

4.   Analyze Mary Fisher's "A Whisper of AIDS" in the appendix of sample speeches that follows Chapter 18 of the textbook. In your analysis concentrate on how Fisher builds her credibility, employs evidence and reasoning, and generates emotional appeal. In addition, study how she uses the resources of language discussed in Chapter 11 to bring her message home to listeners.

Discussion: One of the most acclaimed public discourses of recent years, Mary Fisher's 1992 address to the Republican National Convention provides a masterful illustration of the art of public speaking. Not only does it utilize many of the methods of persuasion treated in this chapter, but it is strikingly eloquent in its use of the resources of language explored in Chapter 11. It also works well for discussion because it deals with one of the burning issues of our time yet is short enough that students can look closely at its rhetorical methods. The exercise usually works best if you have students prepare their analyses of the speech as a homework assignment, so they will be fully prepared to deal with the speech in class. Here is a synopsis of the speech.

Specific Purpose: To persuade my audience to adopt attitudes of awareness toward the AIDS epidemic and of compassion toward people who are HIV-positive.

Central Idea: Because AIDS can strike anyone at any time, we must do all we can to combat it and to be compassionate toward people who are HIV-positive.

Method of Organization: Topical

Introduction: The introduction of Fisher's speech consists of paragraphs 1-2, in which she succinctly states her aim to "lift the shroud of silence" that has covered the issue of HIV/AIDS in the Republican Party. Because her speech was preceded by a brief video that established her credentials as a traditional Republican despite her status as HIV-positive, she did not need a longer introduction.

Body: The body of the speech falls into four main sections, the first of which runs from paragraph 3 through paragraph 6. In these paragraphs Fisher discusses the seriousness of the AIDS crisis in an effort to convince Republicans that neither they—nor anyone else—is immune from the disease. After giving statistics on the extent of the epidemic, she notes that AIDS is not a political creature—it attacks people regardless of age, gender, race, political affiliation, or sexual orientation. And, she stresses, despite everything that has been done to combat AIDS, "it's the epidemic that is winning."

The second section of the body consists of paragraphs 7-10, in which Fisher issues a call to the Republican Party to treat AIDS victims with the compassion they deserve. People who are HIV-positive, she tells her audience, do not merit shame or condemnation. After praising President and Mrs. Bush for their personal compassion toward her, she urges the Party as a whole to act with similar compassion toward AIDS victims in general. It is not possible, she pointedly remarks, to "praise the American family but ignore a virus that destroys it."

In the third section of the body, paragraphs 11-14, Fisher issues a powerful plea to the nation for awareness. Reasoning analogically, she compares people who shrug their shoulders over AIDS to people who did not protest against Hitler's concentration camps in Nazi Germany. No matter what we may think, she warns, "There is no family or community, no race or religion, no place left in America that is safe." Until the U.S. comes to terms with this fact, she warns, it will continue to be a nation at risk.

The fourth—and longest—section of the body runs from paragraph 15 through paragraph 24. In this section Fisher moves back and forth between personal observations about her condition and her family and comments directed to various portions of her audience. After thanking her family in paragraph 15 for their support and compassion, she speaks in paragraphs 16-17 to HIV-positive people who lack support and compassion. It is not you who should feel shame, she says, but those of us who "tolerate ignorance and practice prejudice."

In paragraphs 18-19 Fisher speaks movingly of her two sons—how she hopes they will remember her and how she hopes they will act with courage and leadership when she is gone. Then Fisher urges her audience to act with courage and leadership as well. Turning in paragraph 20 to AIDS sufferers, she tells them that if they have courage, they will find comfort. In paragraph 21 she calls on people who do not have AIDS to exercise leadership by setting aside "prejudice and politics to make room for compassion and sound policy."

Bringing the speech to an emotional climax, Fisher returns to her children in paragraphs 22-23, addresses them by name, and expresses the hope that they will not suffer shame on her account. Then she moves back to her general audience and appeals one last time for awareness and compassion so "my children will not be afraid to say the word AIDS when I am gone."

Conclusion: If there is a clearly identifiable conclusion to Fisher's speech, it is the brief words of paragraph 25—"God bless the children, and God bless us all"—and even those words are so closely connected to the content of paragraph 24 that they can be considered an extension of that paragraph rather than a distinct conclusion. As with Martin Luther King's "I Have a Dream," the most meaningful question to ask about the end of Fisher's speech is not whether it has an explicit conclusion, but whether it concludes effectively—which it unquestionably does.

Credibility: Fisher faced two problems with respect to her credibility. The first was to be seen as someone with substantial enough Republican credentials to be taken seriously by the convention audience. Because of the repeated praise of "family values" and the negative tone toward people who are HIV-positive by previous speakers at the convention, there was no guarantee that Fisher's immediate audience would pay much heed to her message.

To boost Fisher's credibility as a Republican, her speech was preceded by a video stressing her family's long-time connections with the Republican Party, including her work as a staff assistant to President Ford and her father's activities as a Republican fund-raiser. During the speech itself, Fisher reminded the audience of her Republican credentials by mentioning her testimony before the platform committee three months earlier (paragraph 1), her family's close relationship with President and Mrs. Bush (paragraph 8), and her commitment to the President's cause (paragraph 10).

Fisher's second concern with respect to credibility was to be seen as a bona fide spokesperson for the AIDS community. The video before her speech helped, as it explained the circumstances by which she had become HIV-positive and projected a positive personal image of her as a mother and as an AIDS activist. Whatever positive impact the film had, however, could easily have been destroyed by a poor speech. As it turned out, everything Fisher said and did in her address boosted her terminal credibility far above her initial credibility. Perhaps most important in this regard were her lack of self-pity, her compassion and good will, her poignant emotional appeals, and her eloquent language.

Evidence and reasoning: Although Fisher does not employ a great deal of statistical evidence, she does present telling figures in paragraphs 3 and 6 about the extent of the AIDS epidemic. These figures are necessary to establish her point that AIDS is on the march in the United States and the world. However, had she presented too many statistics, she would have changed the tone of her speech and may have undermined its personal, emotional appeal.

Fisher's strongest use of testimony comes in paragraph 12, in which she quotes Pastor Niemoeller about the consequences of not protesting against the Nazi death camps during World War II. She then uses this quotation as the basis for the analogy, in paragraph 13, between the tragic results of ignoring the concentration camps and the tragic consequences of ignoring the explosive growth of the AIDS epidemic.

Fisher uses two extended examples in her speech. The first comes in paragraph 8 and describes the compassionate response she has received from President and Mrs. Bush. The moral, of course, is that Republicans in general should respond compassionately to all people who are HIV-positive. The second extended example occurs in paragraph 15, where Fisher explains the support she has received from her family. She then contrasts that support, in paragraphs 16-17, with the prejudice faced by many people who are HIV-positive.

As in both of these examples, most of the evidence in Fisher's speech comes from her personal experience. Not only is this appropriate given her status as HIV-positive, but it is sound rhetorical strategy. To be successful, Fisher had to move the AIDS debate beyond the level of statistics and experts and relate it to the lives of ordinary Americans. By drawing on her own experience, Fisher personalizes the issue and gives it an immediacy it had previously lacked for most of her audience.

Emotional appeal: Fisher's speech offers a splendid example of the power of emotional appeal in persuasive speaking. Much of her emotional appeal comes, of course, from the highly personal nature of the speech, which was reinforced by Fisher's direct, unaffected delivery. As we shall see shortly, the eloquence, simplicity, and genuine pathos of Fisher's language also contribute to her emotional appeal.

As the speech progresses, Fisher appeals primarily to two contrasting emotions—fear and compassion. The most notable fear appeals are in paragraphs 3-6 and 11-14, in which Fisher explains the brutal reality of the AIDS epidemic and seeks to convince her audience that no one is immune from it. The most extended appeals to compassion are in paragraphs 7-10, 15-17, and 21-25, but the need for compassion runs through the entire speech as a theme in a symphony.

Language: As effective as Fisher's speech is in other respects, it is distinguished above all by its use of language. Just as Martin Luther King's "I Have a Dream" stands out from the thousands of speeches delivered during the civil rights movement, so the artistry and eloquence of Fisher's address make it the most memorable public discourse to date of the struggle against AIDS.

As in most speeches noted for their eloquence, Fisher's language is clear, familiar, and concrete. She creates sharp visual images—often of great poignancy and emotional power, and often in combination with repetition and parallel structure. Examples of this occur in the affecting imagery of paragraphs 4-5, the "Because I was not . . ." series of paragraph 11, the uncompromising insistence of paragraphs

13-14, and the gentle compassion of paragraph 16. It is also worth noting how Fisher uses repetition and parallelism to build the cadence and power of her address as she builds to her conclusion in paragraphs 19-25.

Fisher also makes effective use of antithesis. Thematically she juxtaposes the contrasting impulses of fear and compassion, ignorance and awareness, silence and speech. This thematic antithesis is reinforced by the heavy use of stylistic antithesis. In paragraph 2, for example, Fisher says, "I bear a message of challenge, not self-congratulation. I want your attention, not your applause." In paragraph 6 she cautions that AIDS "is not a distant threat; it is a present danger." In paragraph 10 she counsels that "We cannot love justice and ignore prejudice, love our children and fear to teach them." In paragraph 13 she warns, "If you think you are safe, you are at risk." In paragraph 17 she tells AIDS victims, "It is not you who should feel shame; it is we." Indeed, antithesis occurs so frequently that one can find examples of it throughout the address.

Applying the Power of Public Speaking *(from text pages 459-460)*

As marketing director, you've helped your small company grow from ownership of one health club to nine in as many years. Now one of your less successful competitors is throwing in the towel and has announced plans to sell its seven clubs. Most members of your company's management team want to make an offer to purchase these clubs. However, some members, including yourself, believe the purchase would jeopardize your company's stability by nearly doubling its size overnight.

At a meeting of the management team, you listen as one of the advocates of purchasing the clubs makes his case. Among his points are the following: (1) The company must either purchase the clubs or abandon any thoughts of future growth; (2) If the company can successfully add clubs one at a time, as it has done in the past, then it should be able to add seven at once; and (3) Because a majority of the management team supports the purchase, it must be a good idea.

In your speech, you will point out the fallacy in each of these points. What are those fallacies?

Discussion: Like the other Applying the Power of Public Speaking scenarios throughout the book, this one is intended to show how public speaking is used in everyday life and to challenge students to apply their critical-thinking skills to a wide range of practical situations. If you assign the scenario as a homework exercise, you can go over the answers with students in a class discussion. The fallacies in the scenario are as follows:

(1) The claim that the company must either purchase the health clubs or abandon any thought of future growth is an instance of the either-or fallacy because it forces listeners to choose between two alternatives when more than two alternatives exist. There are numerous ways for the company to expand without purchasing all seven of the competitor's clubs at this moment.

(2) The claim that the company should be able to add seven clubs all at once because it has been able to add clubs one at a time in the past is an instance of invalid analogy because it incorrectly assumes that purchasing seven clubs is essentially the same as purchasing a single club. There are a host of factors that make adding seven clubs to the company in one fell swoop much more difficult than adding a single club.

(3) The claim that the purchase must be a good idea because it is supported by a majority of the company's management team is an instance of the bandwagon fallacy because it assumes that something is correct simply because it is popular. It may be that the management team's majority is correct in its opinion, but that should be decided on the basis of analyzing all the factors involved in the purchase, and not simply on the fact that most of the management team supports it.

To give your students more work on fallacies, distribute Additional Exercise 1 on pages 340-343 of this manual.

Additional Exercises and Activities

1.   Identify the fallacy in each of the following statements and, in each case, explain why the statement is fallacious.

   a.   I don't see any reason to wear a helmet when I ride a bike. Everyone bikes without a helmet.

   b.   It's ridiculous to worry about protecting America's national parks against pollution and overuse when innocent people are being endangered by terrorists.

   c.   There can be no doubt that the Great Depression was caused by Herbert Hoover. He became President in March 1929, and the stock market crashed just seven months later.

d.   If we allow the school board to spend money remodeling the gymnasium, next they will want to build a new school and give all the teachers a huge raise. Taxes will soar so high that businesses will leave and then there will be no jobs for anyone in this town.

e.   Raising a child is just like having a pet—you need to feed it, play with it, and everything will be fine.

f.   I can't support Representative Frey's proposal for campaign finance reform. After all, he was kicked out of law school for cheating on an exam.

g.   One nonsmoker, interviewed at a restaurant, said, "I can eat dinner just fine even though people around me are smoking." Another, responding to a *Los Angeles Times* survey, said, "I don't see what all the fuss is about. My wife has smoked for years and it has never bothered me." We can see, then, that secondhand smoke does not cause a problem for most nonsmokers.

h.   Our school must either increase tuition or cut back on library services for students.

   Discussion: This exercise gives students practice in identifying the eight fallacies discussed in the chapter and supplements the second Exercise for Critical Thinking on page 459 of the textbook. For ease of classroom discussion, this exercise is included in the binder of overhead transparencies that accompanies *The Art of Public Speaking*.

a.   I don't see any reason to wear a helmet when I ride a bike. Everyone bikes without a helmet.

   Discussion: This statement commits the bandwagon fallacy. Even if it were true that "Everyone bikes without a helmet," that does not mean it is a good idea to do so. It is fallacious to assume that an idea or course of action is correct just because it is popular.

b.   It's ridiculous to worry about protecting America's national parks against pollution and overuse when innocent people are being endangered by terrorists.

   Discussion: This statement commits the red herring fallacy. By introducing the issue of terrorism, which is irrelevant to the question of protecting America's national parks against pollution and overuse, the speaker hopes to divert attention from the issue at hand.

c.   There can be no doubt that the Great Depression was caused by Herbert Hoover. He became President in March 1929, and the stock market crashed just seven months later.

>   **Discussion:** This statement commits the fallacy of false cause: *post hoc, ergo propter hoc.* That the stock market crashed just seven months after Herbert Hoover became President does not mean that Hoover caused the Great Depression. The Depression was caused by a number of complex forces, most of which had been in motion well before Hoover became President.

d.   If we allow the school board to spend money remodeling the gymnasium, next they will want to build a new school and give all the teachers a huge raise. Taxes will soar so high that businesses will leave and then there will be no jobs for anyone in this town.

>   **Discussion:**   This statement commits the slippery slope fallacy. It assumes that taking a first step (remodeling the gymnasium) will lead inevitably to subsequent steps (building a new school and giving the teachers huge raises), and eventually to a disaster (people losing their jobs because of businesses leaving town to avoid high taxes). The fallacy does not result from claiming that the train of events will take place, but in assuming that it will without providing evidence or reasoning in support of the speaker's claim.

e.   Raising a child is just like having a pet—you need to feed it, play with it, and everything will be fine.

>   **Discussion:**   This statement commits the fallacy of invalid analogy. One does need to feed and play with a child—just as one needs to feed and play with a pet—but that does not mean that raising a child is just like having a pet. There is much more involved in raising a child than in owning a pet. The differences between the two situations far outweigh their similarities.

f.   I can't support Representative Frey's proposal for campaign finance reform. After all, he was kicked out of law school for cheating on an exam.

>   **Discussion:**   This statement commits the *ad hominem* fallacy. Instead of dealing with the substance of Representative Frey's proposal for campaign finance reform, the speaker rejects that proposal because Frey was kicked out of law school for cheating on an exam. Even if it is true that Frey was expelled from law school for cheating, that fact has no bearing on the merits of his proposal for campaign finance reform.

g.   One nonsmoker, interviewed at a restaurant, said, "I can eat dinner just fine even though people around me are smoking." Another, responding to a *Los Angeles Times* survey, said, "I don't see what all the fuss is about. My wife has smoked for years and it has never bothered me." We can see, then, that secondhand smoke does not cause a problem for most nonsmokers.

> **Discussion:**   This statement commits the fallacy of hasty generalization. Two examples are hardly enough to establish the claim that secondhand smoke does not cause a problem for most nonsmokers. Certainly it would be no problem for an opposing speaker to marshall the examples of two or more nonsmokers who are bothered by secondhand smoke.

h.   Our school must either increase tuition or cut back on library services for students.

> **Discussion:**   This statement commits the either-or fallacy. The speaker oversimplifies a complex issue by reducing it to a simple either-or choice. A critical listener might ask, "Is cutting library services for students the only alternative to increasing tuition? Why not reduce the amount of money spent on athletics? Why not cut back on spending by college administrators?"

2.   Have students analyze "Self-Defense on Campus," by Rebecca Hanson, which appears on pages 453-456 of the textbook. In their analyses, students should pay special attention to how the speaker uses the methods of persuasion discussed in the chapter.

> **Discussion:**   "Self-Defense on Campus" is an excellent speech that illustrates how students can utilize all the methods of persuasion discussed in the textbook. In is also available as part of the videotape supplement for this edition of *The Art of Public Speaking*. The commentary that accompanies the speech on pages 453-456 of the textbook points out a number of its major features. Here is a synopsis that focuses on how the speaker employs the methods of persuasion.
>
> Specific Purpose: To persuade my audience to enroll in a self-defense class.
>
> Central Idea: Enrolling in a self-defense class is an effective way for students to help protect themselves against the dangers of crime they face on campus and in society at large.
>
> Method of Organization: Monroe's motivated sequence
>
> Credibility: In keeping with the functions of a speech introduction discussed in Chapter 9 of the textbook, the speaker

establishes her credibility in paragraph 3 by noting that because she has taken a self-defense class, she feels more prepared to deal with potentially dangerous situations. The audience is more likely to listen carefully to the rest of the speech knowing that the speaker has firsthand experience on the topic.

The speaker turns to her experience again in paragraphs 10-11 when she presents an extended example showing how she learned to protect herself in her self-defense class. Although this example is used to demonstrate the practicality of the speaker's policy, it also reinforces her credibility and strengthens the persuasiveness of the entire speech. So, too, do the speaker's sincerity, command of the topic, and goodwill toward the audience—all of which are evident throughout her presentation.

Evidence: The speaker uses two extended examples to excellent effect. The hypothetical example that opens the speech gains attention and relates the topic to the audience. Its impact is reinforced by the statistics in paragraph 2 that connect the example directly to the college community in which the speech was delivered. In paragraphs 10-11 the speaker uses an extended example based on her own experience to demonstrate how taking a class in self-defense can increase one's confidence and ability to respond properly in a dangerous situation. These two examples are among the most memorable parts of the speech and are central to in its persuasive appeal.

The speaker is equally adept in her use of statistics. Those in paragraph 2 show that the hypothetical example presented in paragraph 1 is not far-fetched, while those in paragraph 4 reinforce the point that crime is a serious problem in American society. It should also be noted how, in paragraph 4, the speaker translates her numbers into terms that relate directly to her classmates by noting that, during the 50 minutes of their speech class, 187 people will have been the victims of a violent crime. In paragraph 6 the speaker presents figures that show the correlation between violent crimes and the use of alcohol and/or illegal drugs. Here, as elsewhere, the speaker's statistics come from reputable sources, and she identifies those sources for the audience.

As with examples and statistics, testimony plays an important role in this speech. The speaker uses testimony twice in paragraph 5 to underscore the importance of taking precautions against crime—first, when she paraphrases the book *Street Wisdom for Women*, and second, when she quotes the Wake Forest University Crime Prevention website. In paragraph 7 she cites the Security on Campus website to support her point that many college campuses are the highest crime areas in their communities. In paragraph 9 she presents expert testimony from Patrick

Lee, a self-defense instructor, and in paragraph 12 she employs peer testimony from a woman named Cindy who used her self-defense knowledge to scare off an assailant. Finally, in paragraph 14 the speaker concludes with a quotation from Patrick Lee asking, "Do you want to be the victim or the survivor?"

Reasoning: The primary method of reasoning in this speech is causal. The speaker does not claim that lack of training in self-defense causes crime, or that taking a self-defense class will produce a reduction in crime. Rather, she argues that lack of training in self-defense makes a person more vulnerable to crime and that taking a self-defense course will make a person more confident and more prepared to deal with potentially dangerous situations.

What makes the reasoning of this speech persuasive, however, is less the structure of the speaker's argument than the strength of her evidence. All of her main points are backed up with excellent supporting materials, and she does an especially good job in paragraphs 9-12 of demonstrating that taking a self-defense course will in fact produce the benefits she claims for it. Given the speaker's evidence, most listeners are prepared to accept her reasoning.

Emotional appeal: Although "Self-Defense on Campus" does not employ a great deal of overtly emotional language, it still generates fairly strong emotional appeal. One of the emotions it taps is the fear of becoming a crime victim. This is especially evident in the vivid hypothetical example that opens the speech, but it is reinforced by the speaker's statistics and testimony throughout the problem section (paragraphs 4-6). The speaker's use of fear appeals can also be seen in paragraph 10, in which she narrates her experience of being unable to fight off the padded attacker at the beginning of her self-defense class.

In addition to presenting fear appeals, the speaker provides a specific course of action through which her listeners can combat the source of fear. Research has demonstrated that this is the most effective way to use fear appeals in a persuasive speech. Having aroused the audience's concern about being able to protect themselves in a dangerous situation, the speaker then discusses the sense of security, confidence, and even happiness that come from receiving training in self-defense. In paragraph 11 she explains how she learned to thwart the padded attacker by the end of her self-defense class, and in paragraph 12 she quotes the feeling of "pure joy" described by one woman who used her self-defense training to scare off an assailant.

In all these cases, the emotional appeal grows naturally out of the speech content and is strengthened by the speaker's sincerity and conviction. It is also worth noting that there is a strongly gendered dimension to the emotional appeal in this speech. Although the speaker makes a concerted effort in several places to relate her subject to the men in her audience, there is no doubt that the fear of crime—and especially of personal assault—is greater among women than among men. It is also true that the speaker's extended examples—both the hypothetical example in paragraph 1 and the personal example in paragraphs 10-11—tend to resonate most powerfully with women. This is not a weakness in the speech, but it does provide an interesting point for discussion about the nature of emotional appeal and the manner in which it can vary from audience to audience.

3.   Distribute copies of "To Save a Child," by Dawn Follendorf, which appears on pages 445-447 of this manual. Have students analyze how the speaker employs the methods of persuasion discussed in the chapter.

> **Discussion:** A persuasive speech on a question of policy, "To Save a Child" provides an excellent model for class discussion. For instructors who wish to show it to their classes, it is available on the videotape of student speeches that accompanies this edition of *The Art of Public Speaking*. See pages 448-449 of this manual for full discussion of the speech. Additional persuasive speeches for analysis and discussion can be found in Part V of this manual.

4.   Distribute copies of "Ghosts," by Ken Lonnquist, which is printed on pages 489-492 of this manual. Have students analyze the speech in light of the methods of persuasion discussed in the chapter.

> **Discussion:**   "Ghosts" is a persuasive speech on a question of value. Delivered in an argumentation and debate class, it is considerably more complex than the typical classroom speech. The speaker's purpose was to convince his classmates that abortion is morally wrong, and he knew from his audience analysis that all but one of his listeners opposed his position.
>
> Because the topic of the speech is so controversial, it invariably sparks a heated class discussion. If that discussion is to be most productive, however, it needs to focus primarily on the speaker's techniques rather than on his position regarding abortion. If you assign the speech, urge students to put aside their personal opinions about abortion and to analyze the speech in light of questions such as the following:
>
> (1)   Is the introduction well suited to the speaker's task of gaining good will and establishing common ground with his audience?

(2)   Although the speech deals with a question of value, its persuasiveness rests largely on the speaker's ability to convince his listeners about a question of fact. What is that question of fact? How effectively does the speaker deal with it given the opposition of his listeners? Does the speaker provide sufficient evidence to establish his claim on the question of fact?

(3)   What kind of reasoning does the speaker rely on most of all throughout the speech? How well does his reasoning accord with the guidelines presented in the chapter?

(4)   How effective are the speaker's emotional appeals? Do they develop naturally from the content of the speech? Are they likely to be persuasive to listeners who do not already agree with the speaker's position?

(5)   How does the speaker use the resources of language discussed in Chapter 11—imagery, metaphor, parallelism, repetition, etc.—to express his ideas? What are the "ghosts" to which he refers throughout the speech? Is this an appropriate image for the speech, or does it distract attention from the major issue?

For full commentary on the speech, see pages 493-494 of this manual.

Extra Teaching and Learning Resources

General

Allen, Mike, and Preiss, Ray W. (eds.). *Persuasion: Advances Through Meta-Analysis*. Cresskill, NJ: Hampton Press, 1997.

Cannavo, S. *Think to Win: The Power of Logic in Everyday Life*. Amherst, NY: Prometheus Books, 1998.

Cialdini, Robert B. *Influence: Science and Practice of Persuasion*, 4th ed. Boston: Allyn and Bacon, 2001.

Corbett, Edward P. J., and Eberly, Rosa. *The Elements of Reasoning*, 2nd ed. New York: Longman, 2000.

Dillard, James Price, and Peck, Eugenia. "Persuasion and the Structure of Affect: Dual Systems and Discrete Emotions as Complimentary Models." *Human Communication Research*, 27 (2001), pp. 38-68.

Dillard, James Price, and Pfau, Michael (eds.). *The Persuasion Handbook: Developments in Theory and Practice*. Thousand Oaks, CA: Sage, 2002.

Engel, S. Morris. *With Good Reason: An Introduction to Informal Fallacies*, 6th ed. New York: St. Martin's, 2000.

Hogan, Kevin. *The Psychology of Persuasion: How to Persuade Others to Your Way of Thinking*. Gretna, LA: Pelican, 1998.

Johannesen, Richard L. *Ethics in Human Communication*, 5th ed. Prospect Heights, IL: Waveland Press, 2002.

Jowett, Garth, and O'Donnell, Victoria. *Propaganda and Persuasion*. 3rd ed. Walnut Creek, CA: Altamira Press, 1999.

Kahane, Howard, and Cavender, Nancy. *Logic and Contemporary Rhetoric: The Use of Reason in Everyday Life*, 9th ed. Belmont, CA: Wadsworth, 2002.

Kouzes, James M. *Credibility: How Leaders Gain and Lose It, Why People Demand It*. San Francisco: Jossey-Bass, 1995.

Lucas, Richard H., and McCoy, K. Byron. *The Winning Edge: Effective Communication and Persuasion Techniques for Lawyers*. Tucson, AZ: Lawyers and Judges Publishing Company, 1999.

McCroskey, James C., and Teven, Jason J. "Credibility: A Reexamination of the Construct and Its Measurement." *Communication Monographs*, 66 (1999), 90-103.

Mills, Harry A. *Artful Persuasion: How to Command Attention, Change Minds, and Influence People*. New York: Amacom, 2000.

O'Keefe, Daniel. *Persuasion: Theory and Research*, 2nd ed. Thousand Oaks, CA: Sage, 2002.

Perloff, Richard M. *The Dynamics of Persuasion: Communication and Attitudes in the 21st Century*, 2nd ed. Mahwah, NJ: Lawrence Erlbaum, 2003.

Petty, Richard E., and Wegener, Duane T. "Attitude Change: Multiple Roles for Persuasion Variables." In Gilbert, Daniel T.; Fiske, Susan T.; and Lindzey, Gardner (eds.), *Handbook of Social Psychology*, 4th ed. New York: McGraw-Hill, 1998, Vol. I, pp. 323-390.

Pfau, Michael; Szabo, Erin A.; Anderson, Jason; Morrill, Joshua; Zubric, Jessica; and Wan, Hua-Hsin. "The Role and Impact of Affect in the Process of Resistance to Persuasion." *Human Communication Research*, 27 (2001), 216-252.

Pratkanis, Anthony, and Aronson, Elliot. *Age of Propaganda: The Everyday Use and Abuse of Persuasion*, rev. ed. New York: W. H. Freeman, 2001.

Reinard, John C. "The Empirical Study of the Persuasive Effects of Evidence: The Status after Fifty Years of Research." *Human Communication Research*, 15 (1988), 3-59.

Rieke, Richard D., and Sillars, Malcolm O. *Argumentation and Critical Decision Making*, 5th ed. Boston: Addison Wesley, 2000.

Simons, Herbert W. *Persuasion in Society*. Thousand Oaks, CA: Sage, 2001.

Weston, Anthony. *A Rulebook for Arguments*, 3rd ed. Indianapolis, IN: Hackett, 2001.

Wilkins, Fred. *Persuasive Jury Communication: Case Studies from Successful Trials*. Colorado Springs, CO: Shepard's, 2000.

Witte, Kim, and Allen, Mike. "A Meta-Analysis of Fear Appeals: Implications for Effective Public Health Campaigns." *Health Education and Behavior*, 27 (2000), 608-632.

Zajonc, Robert B. "Emotions." In Gilbert, Daniel T.; Fiske, Susan T.; and Lindzey, Gardner (eds.), *Handbook of Social Psychology*, 4th ed. New York: McGraw-Hill, 1998, Vol. I, pp. 591-632.

Classroom Activities and Assignments

Daughton, Suzanne M. "Aristotle Meets Gary Larson: Making Enthymemes Memorable." In Stephen E. Lucas (ed.), *Selections from the Speech Communication Teacher, 1996-1999*. New York: McGraw-Hill, 2001, pp. 74-75.

Dittus, James K. "Grade Begging as an Exercise in Argumentation." In Stephen E. Lucas (ed.), *Selections from the Speech Communication Teacher, 1991-1994*. New York: McGraw-Hill, 1995, pp. 16-17.

Garrett, Roger L. "The Premises of Persuasion." In Stephen E. Lucas (ed.), *Selections from the Speech Communication Teacher, 1986-1991*. New York: McGraw-Hill, 1992, pp. 58-59.

Hamlet, Janice D. "Editorial Sessions: A Different Approach to Teaching Argumentation." In Stephen E. Lucas (ed.), *Selections from the Speech Communication Teacher, 1994-1996*. New York: McGraw-Hill, 1997, p. 5.

Haze, Michael; Bloomfield, Kyla J.; and Ayres, Joe. "The Editorial Speech." In Stephen E. Lucas (ed.), *Selections from the Speech Communication Teacher, 1994-1996*. New York: McGraw-Hill, 1997, pp. 56-57.

Johnson, Craig. "Nothing to Fear but Fear . . . Or Is There?" In Stephen E. Lucas (ed.), *Selections from the Speech Communication Teacher, 1986-1991*. New York: McGraw-Hill, 1992, p. 59.

Kauffman, James. "Collecting and Evaluating Evidence." In Stephen E. Lucas (ed.), *Selections from the Speech Communication Teacher, 1991-1994*. New York: McGraw-Hill, 1995, pp. 18-19.

Langley, C. Darrell. "The Heckling Speech." In Stephen E. Lucas (ed.), *Selections from the Speech Communication Teacher, 1986-1991*. New York: McGraw-Hill, 1992, p. 67.

MacDonald, Madlyne A. "The Key to Persuasion." In Stephen E. Lucas (ed.), *Selections from the Speech Communication Teacher, 1986-1991*. New York: McGraw-Hill, 1992, pp. 59-60.

Proctor, Russell F. "Using *Swing Kids* to Teach Theories of Persuasion." In Stephen E. Lucas (ed.), *Selections from the Communication Teacher, 1999-2002*. New York: McGraw-Hill, 2004, pp. 61-62.

Ross, Charlynn. "The Challenging Audience Exercise." In Stephen E. Lucas (ed.), *Selections from the Speech Communication Teacher, 1986-1991*. New York: McGraw-Hill, 1992, p. 69.

Schreir, Howard N. "Analyzing Persuasive Tactics." In Stephen E. Lucas (ed.), *Selections from the Speech Communication Teacher, 1986-1991*. New York: McGraw-Hill, 1992, p. 61.

Schreier, Howard N. "Experiencing Persuasion and the Persuader." In Stephen E. Lucas (ed.), *Selections from the Communication Teacher, 1999-2002*. New York: McGraw-Hill, 2004, pp. 62-64.

Shelton, Michael W. "Analysis of Editorial Cartoons: An Alternative Approach to Teaching Argumentation." In Stephen E. Lucas (ed.), *Selections from the Speech Communication Teacher, 1986-1991*. New York: McGraw-Hill, 1992, pp. 5-6.

Yamasaki, Joan M. "Teaching the Recognition and Development of Appeals." In Stephen E. Lucas (ed.), *Selections from the Speech Communication Teacher, 1994-1996*. New York: McGraw-Hill, 1997, pp. 58-59.

Films and Videos

"Argumentation: The Study of Effective Reasoning." Insight Media (2001). 24 segments; 30 minutes each.

"Credibility." CRM Films (1993). 42 minutes.

"Credibility Factor: What Followers Expect from Leaders." CRM Films (1990). 22 minutes.

"Critical Thinking." Insight Media (1999). 30 minutes.

"The Language of Leadership: The Winston Churchill Method." Films for the Humanities and Sciences (1993). 60 minutes.

"The Language of Persuasion." Insight Media (1999). 20 minutes.

"Persuasion." Insight Media (1996). 26 minutes.

"Persuasion at Work." Insight Media (1998). 3 segments; 32 minutes total.

"Persuasive Language: Using and Understanding It." Insight Media (1998). 2 segments; 30 minutes total.

"Persuasive Speaking." Insight Media (1997). 30 minutes.

"Persuasive Speaking: Organization." Insight Media (1997). 30 minutes.

"Persuasive Speaking: Strategies." Insight Media (1997). 30 minutes.

"Presenting an Argument." Films for the Humanities and Sciences (1992). 20 minutes.

"Propaganda." Films for the Humanities and Sciences (2000). 29 minutes.

"Psycho-Sell: Advertising and Persuasion." Insight Media (1991). 25 minutes.

"Reasoning, Critical Thinking, and Creativity." Insight Media (1993). 60 minutes.

"The Speaker." Insight Media (1997). 30 minutes.

"Speaking with Confidence: Critical Thinking." Insight Media (1997). 30 minutes.

Chapter 17

Speaking on Special Occasions

Chapter Objectives

After reading this chapter, students should be able to:

1. Explain the guidelines for an effective speech of introduction.

2. Discuss the purpose and major themes of a speech of presentation.

3. Discuss the purpose and major themes of a speech of acceptance.

4. Indicate the fundamental purpose of a commemorative speech and explain why a successful commemorative speech depends so much on the creative use of language.

5. Explain how an after-dinner speech differs from a speech to inform or to persuade.

Chapter Outline

I. Many special occasions provide opportunities for speechmaking *(text page 464)*.
   A. Ceremonies such as weddings, funerals, and dedications often include speeches.
   B. So do retirements, graduations, award presentations, and affairs of state.
   C. Speeches are part of what makes these occasions special and memorable.
   D. The primary aim of speeches on special occasions is neither to inform nor to persuade but to fulfill the special needs of the occasion.

II.   Speeches of introduction present a speaker to an audience *(text pages 464-467)*.
    A.   A good speech of introduction achieves three goals.
        1.   It builds enthusiasm for the upcoming speaker.
        2.   It generates interest in the speaker's topic.
        3.   It establishes a welcoming climate that will boost the speaker's credibility.
    B.   There are several guidelines for speeches of introduction.
        1.   Speeches of introduction should be brief.
            a.   Long speeches of introduction irritate the audience.
            b.   Long speeches of introduction distract attention from the main speaker.
            c.   Under normal circumstances, a speech of introduction should be no more than two or three minutes in length.
        2.   Speeches of introduction should be completely accurate.
            a.   Errors in a speech of introduction embarrass both the introducer and the main speaker.
            b.   Nothing is more important in a speech of introduction than pronouncing the main speaker's name correctly.
        3.   Speeches of introduction should be adapted to the occasion.
            a.   Formal occasions require formal speeches of introduction.
            b.   Informal occasions allow for casual speeches of introduction.
        4.   Speeches of introduction should be adapted to the main speaker.
            a.   An introduction that leaves the main speaker uncomfortable has failed in part of its purpose.
            b.   Overpraising the main speaker—especially for his or her speaking skills—can be a problem.
            c.   Potentially embarrassing remarks about the main speaker's personal life are always inappropriate.
        5.   Speeches of introduction should be adapted to the audience.
            a.   If the main speaker is not well known to the audience, the speech of introduction will need to explain a bit about her or his achievements and qualifications.
            b.   If the main speaker is well known to the audience, the speech of introduction should take account of that knowledge.
        6.   Speeches of introduction should try to create a sense of anticipation and drama.
            a.   One way to achieve this is to save the main speaker's name until the last moment of the speech.
            b.   Another way is to deliver the speech of introduction skillfully with sincerity and enthusiasm.

III.   Speeches of presentation are given when someone receives a gift or an award *(text pages 467-468)*.
    A.   Speeches of presentation should usually be fairly brief.
        1.   At times, they can be only a few lines long.

2.   They can also run to four or five minutes in length.
B.   The main purpose of a speech of presentation is to explain why the recipient is receiving the award.
  1.   The speech should point out the achievements for which the recipient is receiving the award.
  2.   The speech should discuss the recipient's achievements in a way that will make them meaningful to the audience.
C.   If the recipient won the award in a competition, the speech of presentation should consider praising the other competitors as well.

IV.   Speeches of acceptance give thanks for a gift or an award *(text pages 468-469)*.
A.   A speech of acceptance should thank the people who are bestowing the gift or award.
B.   A speech of acceptance should also acknowledge the people who helped the recipient win the award.

V.   Commemorative speeches are addresses of praise or celebration *(text pages 469-472)*.
A.   Commemorative speeches pay tribute to a person, a group of people, an institution, or an idea.
  1.   Eulogies, Fourth of July speeches, testimonial addresses, and dedications are examples of commemorative speeches.
  2.   The fundamental purpose of a commemorative speech is to inspire the audience—to heighten their admiration for the person, institution, or idea being praised.
B.   Although it usually presents information about its subject, a commemorative speech is different from an informative speech.
  1.   The aim of an informative speech is to communicate information clearly and accurately.
  2.   The aim of a commemorative speech is to express feelings and arouse sentiments.
C.   Commemorative speeches depend above all on the creative and subtle use of language.
  1.   Some of the most memorable speeches in history are commemorative addresses that we continue to find meaningful because of their eloquent expression.
  2.   Two aspects of language use are especially important for commemorative speeches.
    a.   The first is avoiding clichés and trite sentiments.
    b.   The second is utilizing stylistic devices such as those discussed in Chapter 11 to enhance the imagery, rhythm, and creativity of the speech.

VI.   After-dinner speeches are a kind of speech to entertain *(text pages 472-476)*.
A.   After-dinner speeches are a long and well-established tradition.
  1.   As a formal genre, they developed in England during the early 1800s.

2. Today "after-dinner" speeches are often given at breakfast or lunch gatherings, as well as in the evening.

B. After-dinner speeches are lighter in tone than other types of speeches.

1. Almost any topic can be appropriate if the speaker approaches it in a lighthearted manner.

2. An after-dinner speech should not be technical or argumentative.

3. Supporting materials should be chosen primarily for their entertainment value rather than for their persuasive strength.

4. Listeners are looking for a good-natured talk that treats the topic imaginatively, even whimsically.

C. Although light in tone, after-dinner speeches require careful preparation.

1. They should be clearly organized around a central theme.

2. They should be adroitly delivered to produce the desired impact on the audience.

D. Humor can be an important part of after-dinner speeches.

1. Many after-dinner speeches are distinguished by their use of humor.

2. It is not necessary, however, to be a stand-up comic to be a successful after-dinner speaker.

a. The purpose of humor in an after-dinner speech is more to provoke smiles or chuckles than to convulse the audience with a string of one-liners.

b. Ideally, humor in an after-dinner speech grows naturally out of the speech materials and provides insight into the topic.

c. Many excellent after-dinner speeches contain no humor.

(1) Speakers who are not comfortable working for a laugh should not try to force humor into their speeches.

(2) If they deal with the topic creatively, select interesting supporting materials, and use language creatively, they will do just fine.

Exercises for Critical Thinking *(from text page 477)*

1. Attend a speech on campus. Pay special attention to the speech introducing the main speaker. How well does it fit the guidelines discussed in this chapter?

> **Discussion:**   If you use this exercise, you may want to have students complete an evaluation form similar to the one on page 356 of this manual.

Out-of-Class Observation
Speech of Introduction

Your name_____

Name of speaker you observed_____

Where was the speech presented?_____

Who was the speaker introducing?_____

Evaluate the speech of introduction as follows:

1. How long was the speech? Was it too long? Too short? About right? Explain.

2. As far as you can tell, was the speech accurate in its remarks about the main speaker? Explain.

3. Was the speech well adapted to the occasion? Explain.

4. Was the speech well adapted to the main speaker? Explain.

5. Was the speech well adapted to the audience? Explain.

6. Did the speech create a sense of anticipation and drama about the main speaker? Explain.

2. Observe several speeches of presentation and acceptance—at a campus awards ceremony or on a television program such as the Academy Awards, Grammy Awards, Emmy Awards, or Tony Awards. Which speeches do you find most effective? Least effective? Why?

> **Discussion:** This exercise works especially well if your class meets the day after a program such as the Academy Awards. While watching the program, each student should select his or her candidate for the best acceptance speech. After discussing all of the speeches in class, have students vote for the best acceptance speech. This often produces a spirited discussion while students defend their candidates for the best speech.

3. Analyze the commemorative speech by Keith Framnes ("The Massachusetts 54th," textbook pages 471-472). Assess the speech in light of the criteria for commemorative speaking presented in this chapter.

> **Discussion:**   An excellent commemorative speech, "The Massachusetts 54th" pays tribute to the first African-American regiment in the U.S. Civil War. In keeping with the goals of a commemorative speech, the speaker provides enough information about the Massachusetts 54th for his listeners to understand its accomplishments, but he focuses above all on engendering admiration and respect for those accomplishments. The speech also shows how students can use the stylistic devices of imagery, parallelism, and repetition to heighten the impact of their ideas. In addition to discussing this speech in class, you may want to show the videotape of it, which is available as part of the instructional supplement to *The Art of Public Speaking.* Here is a synopsis of the speech.
>
> Introduction: Paragraphs 1-2 constitute the speech's introduction. The speaker gains attention by using vivid language to create an image of the gravedigger played by Morgan Freeman in the film *Glory. He then moves quickly to reveal his topic (the Massachusetts 54th)* and its significance as the first black regiment of the Civil War. The speaker ends his introduction by previewing the three traits of the Massachusetts 54th that he will concentrate on in the body—bravery, patriotism, and courage. As with the rest of the speech, the language of the introduction is crisp, forceful, and uncluttered.
>
> Body: The body of the speech runs from paragraph 3 through paragraph 7. Paragraph 3 deals with the bravery of the Massachusetts 54th, paragraph 4 with its patriotism, and paragraphs 5-7 with its sacrifice. As the speaker develops each point, he provides concrete examples and other details that allow the audience to visualize the tribulations and triumphs of the 54th. Particularly noteworthy are his description of the

substandard equipment issued to the 54th (paragraph 3), his explanation of the lack of desertions from the 54th (paragraph 4), and his account of the assault on Fort Wagner (paragraphs 5-6). Paragraph 7 ends the body by stating that the soldiers of the 54th were buried in a mass grave which has since been covered by the "shifting tides of the Atlantic." The final sentence ("A small statue stands in Boston—a reminder of their sacrifice") is especially moving.

Throughout the body of the speech, the speaker uses the resources of language discussed in Chapter 11 to reinforce the impact of his ideas. The imagery at the end of paragraph 3 magnifies the contrast between the anti-black attitudes of most Northerners and the bravery of the Massachusetts 54th. The use of concrete language in paragraphs 5-6 to describe the 54th's heroism in the attack on Fort Wagner puts the scene vividly before the audience. The use of repetition and parallelism at the start of paragraph 7 is highly effective in reinforcing the speaker's ideas. So, too, are the transitions in paragraphs 4 and 5, both of which help listeners keep track of the speaker's main points as he moves through the body of the speech.

Conclusion: The conclusion begins in paragraph 8 by summarizing the three major traits of the Massachusetts 54th celebrated in the body of the speech—bravery, patriotism, and sacrifice—and noting how those traits helped contribute to the end of slavery in the United States. Paragraph 9 unifies the entire speech by returning to the story of the gravedigger played by Morgan Freeman in the movie *Glory*, while the closing quotation from General Truman Seymour reinforces the central idea and ends the speech on a strong note.

4.   Analyze the after-dinner speech by Julie Daggett ("The Horror of It All," textbook pages 475-476). Evaluate the speech in light of the criteria for after-dinner speaking discussed in this chapter.

Discussion: "The Horror of It All" shows how students can use humor, personal experience, vivid language, and clever phraseology to create a first-rate after-dinner speech. Although the speech produced few gales of laughter when delivered in class, it did evoke a number of knowing smiles and chuckles as students identified some of their own experiences with those of the speaker. At the same time, it indirectly made a serious point about horror films and their potential impact on children and adults alike. Here is a brief synopsis of the speech.

Introduction: The requirements of an introduction in an after-dinner speech are slightly different from those of a persuasive or informative speech. Detailed preview statements are seldom employed in after-dinner speeches. Nor is there often a need in such speeches to establish the speaker's credibility or to gain the good will of hostile listeners. The two objectives that must be accomplished in the introduction of an after-dinner speech are to gain attention and to reveal the topic. In "The Horror of It All," both objectives are achieved in paragraph 1. The opening story does an excellent job of getting the audience involved in the speech, while the last sentence states succinctly that the topic is the speaker's "love/hate relationship with horror movies."

Body: Although after-dinner speeches are often more loosely structured than other kinds of speeches, they still need to follow some discernible order rather than simply rambling from point to point. "The Horror of It All" is arranged in chronological order. After beginning the body in paragraph 2 with her "scaredy-cat tendencies" as a young child, the speaker moves to her fascination with "The Exorcist" as she was growing up and to various episodes that illustrate how the movie industry fed her "passion for terror" during "the next several years" (paragraphs 3-5) until she finally decided to give up horror films after being scared out of her wits watching television with her mother (paragraphs 6-7). Throughout the body, ideas are presented clearly and without clutter. Each episode is explained in sharp, vivid language, and the humor emerges naturally and easily from the speaker's descriptions.

Conclusion: In after-dinner speeches, there is seldom a clear break between the body and the conclusion. Nor is there a need to summarize the main points or to alert the audience with phrases such as "In closing." The primary purpose of the conclusion in an after-dinner speech is to bring the speech to a satisfying end. As in other kinds of speeches, this can be accomplished with a story, a quotation, or a clever or dramatic phrase. Also as in other kinds of speeches, it is often helpful to pull the whole speech together by referring back to the introduction.

In "The Horror of It All," the conclusion consists of the final paragraph. The repetition of the phrase "It's been two years now . . ." in the first two sentences brings the speaker up to the present and completes the chronological movement of the speech. The reference to Bette Davis recalls the opening example and gives the speech a strong sense of psychological unity. The last three sentences end the speech on an entertaining note while simultaneously reinforcing the tension about the speaker's susceptibility to horror movies that is at the heart of the speech.

Additional Exercises and Activities

1. During the final round of speeches, have each student prepare a two-minute speech of introduction for one of their classmates' speeches. The speech should conform with the guidelines for speeches of introduction presented in this chapter, and it should be delivered in class immediately before the speech it is introducing.

    > **Discussion:** This assignment gives students practice in creating and presenting a speech of introduction. Assign the speeches well enough in advance that students have a chance to interview the speakers they are introducing. Also assign the speeches of introduction so that no student is delivering both a speech of introduction and a major speech on the same day.

2. Assign a speech in which each student introduces a famous person to the class. Tell students they should imagine themselves being able to invite any well-known figure, living or dead, to speak to the class on any topic of the student's choice. The task of each student is to prepare a two-minute speech introducing his or her chosen person to the class. In their speeches, students should (a) provide some biographical information about the person and her or his contributions, (b) identify the topic of the person's speech, and (c) explain why the person's speech topic is important for this audience. Speeches should follow the guidelines for speeches of introduction discussed in the chapter.

    > **Discussion:** Like the previous activity, this assignment gives students practice in creating and presenting a speech of introduction. Unlike a speech introducing one of their classmates, however, this speech requires research so students can learn more about the person they are introducing. Indeed, one benefit of this assignment is that students can gain experience using the biographical aids available in the reference section of the library.
    >
    > When making this assignment, it is extremely important to encourage students to be creative in their speeches. Otherwise, you are likely to get a series of dull recitations summarizing information from *Who's Who*, *Current Biography*, *Notable American Women*, and the like. For the most part, though, students are enthusiastic about this assignment, which provides a nice alternative to the usual informative and persuasive speeches. Because this presentation is only two minutes long, all students should be able to deliver their speeches in a single class session.

3. Have students analyze the speech by Sajjid Zahir Chinoy in the appendix of sample speeches that follows Chapter 18 of the textbook ("Questions of Culture") in light of the criteria for commemorative speaking discussed in the chapter.

> **Discussion:** A superb commemorative address, "Questions of Culture" was presented extemporaneously, without notes, to an audience of 3,000 people at the 1996 University of Richmond commencement ceremonies and was widely reported in the press. In addition to being an outstanding student speech from a non-classroom situation, it deals with questions of cultural difference and similarity in a way that almost always provokes spirited discussion. For full analysis of the speech, see pages 261-263 of this manual. The speech is also available on the videotape of student speeches that accompanies this edition of *The Art of Public Speaking*.

4. Distribute copies of one or more of the commemorative speeches reprinted in Part Five of this manual. Have students analyze the speeches in light of the criteria for commemorative speaking discussed in the textbook.

> **Discussion:** Part Five of this manual contains four additional commemorative speeches for discussion and analysis: "James 'Cool Papa' Bell," "The Survivors," "Hail to the Heroes," and "My Grandfather." All four illustrate how students can use language to create effective—even eloquent—commemorative addresses. For texts and analyses of these speeches, see pages 495-506 of this manual.

Extra Teaching and Learning Resources

General

Burrell, Brian (ed.). *The Words We Live By: The Creeds, Mottoes, and Pledges That Have Shaped America*. New York: Free Press, 1997.

Cates, Carl. "Eulogies as a Special Occasion Speech." In Stephen E. Lucas (ed.), *Selections from the Speech Communication Teacher, 1994-1996*. New York: McGraw-Hill, 1997, pp. 85-86.

Copeland, Lewis; Lamm, Lawrence W.; and McKenna, Stephen J. (eds.). *The World's Great Speeches*, 4th ed. Mineola, NY: Dover Publications, 1999.

Ehrilch, Henry. *Writing Effective Speeches*. New York: Paragon House, 1992, Chapter 13.

Gardner, Gerald. *Speech Is Golden*. New York: St. Martin's Press, 1992, Chapter 9.

Greene, Richard (ed.). *Words That Shook the World: One Hundred Years of Unforgettable Speeches and Events*. New York: Penguin Putnam, 2002.

Johannesen, Richard L.; Allen, R.R.; Linkugel, Wil A.; and Bryan, Ferald J. *Contemporary American Speeches*, 9th ed. Dubuque, IA: Kendall/Hunt, 2000.

MacArthur, Brian (ed.). *The Penguin Book of Historic Speeches*. London: Penguin, 1995.

Nix, S. Michele. *Women at the Podium: Memorable Speeches in History*. New York: HarperCollins, 2000.

Rohler, Lloyd, and Cook, Roger (eds.). *Great Speeches for Analysis and Criticism*, 4th ed. Greenwood, IN: Alistair Press, 2001.

Safire, William (ed.). *Lend Me Your Ears: Great Speeches in History*. New York: Norton, 1992.

Smith, Peter J. (ed.). *Onward! Twenty-Five Years of Advice, Exhortation, and Inspiration from America's Best Commencement Speeches*. New York: Scribner, 2000.

Straub, Deborah Gillan (ed.). *Voices of Multicultural America: Notable Speeches Delivered by African, Asian, Hispanic, and Native Americans, 1790-1995*. Detroit, MI: Gale, 1996.

Theroux, Phyllis (ed.). *Eulogies: A Collection of Memorial Tributes, Poetry, Essays, and Letters of Condolence*. New York: Scribner, 1997.

Youra, Paula Wilson, and Koring, Heidi (eds.). *Pomp & Circumstance: Ceremonial Speaking*. Greenwood, IN: Alistair Press, 2002.

Classroom Activities and Assignments

Lamansky, Martin. "Getting to Know My Hero: The Speech of Tribute." In Stephen E. Lucas (ed.), *Selections from the Speech Communication Teacher, 1991-1994*. New York: McGraw-Hill, 1995, pp. 58-59.

Majors, Randall E. "Practical Ceremonial Speaking: Three Speech Activities." In Stephen E. Lucas (ed.), *Selections from the Speech Communication Teacher, 1986-1991*. New York: McGraw-Hill, 1992, p. 68.

Poyner, Barry Cole. "Adding a Ceremonial Touch." In Stephen E. Lucas (ed.), *Selections from the Speech Communication Teacher, 1991-1994*. New York: McGraw-Hill, 1995, p. 59.

Sikes, Shirley. "Introducing the Speaker." In Stephen E. Lucas (ed.), *Selections from the Speech Communication Teacher, 1991-1994*. New York: McGraw-Hill, 1995, pp. 59-60.

Walter, Suzanne. "Introduction of a Speaker: Multipurpose and Multicultural." In Stephen E. Lucas (ed.), *Selections from the Speech Communication Teacher, 1991-1994*. New York: McGraw-Hill, 1995, pp. 60-61.

Williams, Kathleen W. "Here's a Toast." In Stephen E. Lucas (ed.), *Selections from the Speech Communication Teacher, 1996-1999*. New York: McGraw-Hill, 2001, pp. 84-85.

Chapter 18 Speaking in Small Groups

Chapter Objectives

After reading this chapter, students should be able to:

1. Provide definitions of a small group and a problem-solving small group.

2. Identify the four kinds of leadership that may occur in a small group.

3. Distinguish among the procedural needs, task needs, and maintenance needs of a small group.

4. Explain the five major responsibilities of every participant in a small group.

5. Identify the five stages of the reflective-thinking process and discuss the major tasks of a group at each stage.

6. Explain the methods for presenting orally the findings of a small group.

Chapter Outline

I. Speaking in small groups is an important form of communication *(text pages 480-481)*.
    A. Small groups exist in virtually every area of life, including business, education, government, religion, community organizations, and volunteer associations.
    B. As its name implies, a small group has a limited number of members.
        1. The minimum number is three.

      2.   Most experts set the maximum number at eight, but some go as high as twelve.

    C.   Members of a small group assemble for a specific purpose.

    D.   This chapter deals with a particular kind of small group—the problem-solving small group.

      1.   A problem-solving small group is formed to solve a particular problem.

      2.   Speaking in a problem-solving small group involves many skills similar to those used in public speaking.

II.   To be productive, a small group needs effective leadership *(text pages 481-484)*.

    A.   There are several kinds of leadership in a small group.

      1.   In some groups, there is no specific leader.

        a.   When the need for leadership arises, any member can provide it.

        b.   At times, every member of the group will fulfill leadership functions.

      2.   In some groups, there is an implied leader.

        a.   The implied leader might have the highest rank in the group.

        b.   The implied leader may be the person with the most experience and expertise on the topic.

      3.   In some groups, there is an emergent leader.

        a.   Emergent leaders are people who, by their ability or personality, take on a leadership role.

        b.   Ideally, the emergent leader will be constructive in helping the group achieve its objectives.

      4.   Some groups have a designated leader.

        a.   A designated leader is assigned or elected when the group is formed.

        b.   Formal committees usually have a designated leader as chairperson.

    B.   Small groups have three kinds of leadership needs.

      1.   Procedural needs are the "housekeeping" requirements of the group.

        a.   They include organizing meetings, setting agendas, taking notes, preparing handouts, and the like.

        b.   Procedural needs can be met by a designated leader or can be apportioned among all group members.

      2.   Task needs are substantive actions that help the group complete its project.

        a.   Task needs include analyzing the issues facing the group, collecting information, keeping the group on task, helping the group reach consensus, and the like.

        b.   If these needs are not met, the group will not be successful in achieving its objectives.

3. Maintenance needs involve interpersonal relations within the group.
   a. They include creating a supportive environment for the group, managing conflict among group members, helping the group feel good about its accomplishments, and the like.
   b. Because interpersonal problems can interfere with a group's performance, effective leaders need to be keenly attentive to maintenance needs.

III. Regardless of a small group's leadership, every member of a group has five responsibilities *(text pages 484-490)*.
   A. Members should commit themselves to the goals of the group.
      1. For a group to succeed, members must align their personal goals with the group's goals.
      2. Hidden agendas—in which individuals put personal goals over those of the group-are especially damaging.
   B. Members should fulfill their individual assignments.
      1. Division of labor is one of the advantages of working in a small group.
      2. A group can only be effective if each member fulfills his or her specific duties.
      3. No matter what other assignments they may have, all members of a small group have one vital assignment—listening.
         a. Effective listening prevents confusion about what is happening in the group.
         b. Effective listening allows each member to evaluate the merits of other members' ideas or suggestion.
         c. Effective listening establishes a positive climate for discussion.
   C. Members should avoid interpersonal conflicts.
      1. Personal disagreements decrease a group's effectiveness.
      2. Disagreements among group members should be kept on a task level, rather than on a personal level.
   D. Members should encourage full participation in the group.
      1. One way to encourage participation is by listening attentively to other members.
      2. A second way to encourage participation is by inviting quiet members to speak.
      3. A third way to encourage participation is by offering supportive comments to other members.
   E. Members should work to keep the group's discussion on track.
      1. Members need to make sure the discussion is proceeding in an orderly fashion from one issue to another.
      2. Members also need to make sure the group does not make hasty or ill-considered decisions.

IV. The reflective-thinking method is an effective procedure for organizing discussion in a problem-solving small group *(text pages 490-495)*.

   A. The first step in the reflective-thinking method is defining the problem.

      1. Before a group can make progress, it must know precisely what problem it is trying to solve.

      2. The best way to define the problem is to phrase it as a question of policy.

      3. A group should follow four guidelines when phrasing the question for discussion.

         a. It should make the question as clear and specific as possible.

         b. It should phrase the question so as to allow for a wide variety of answers.

         c. It should avoid biased or slanted questions.

         d. It should pose only a single question.

   B. The second step in the reflective-thinking process is analyzing the problem.

      1. Too often groups try to map out solutions before they have a firm grasp of the problem.

      2. If a group analyzes the problem thoroughly, it will be in a much better position to devise a workable solution.

      3. When analyzing the problem, a group should pay special attention to two questions.

         a. How severe is the problem?

         b. What are the causes of the problem?

   C. The third step in the reflective-thinking method is establishing criteria for the solution.

      1. It is vital that a group set up criteria before discussing solutions.

      2. Setting up criteria gives the group a way to judge the appropriateness and practicality of potential solutions.

   D. The fourth step in the reflective-thinking method is generating potential solutions.

      1. At this stage, the group's goal is to come up with the widest possible range of solutions.

      2. Brainstorming is an effective way to generate potential solutions.

         a. Each member of the group lists all the possible solutions he or she can think of.

         b. The group creates a master list of all the members' potential solutions.

         c. The group then discusses the ideas, adding any new suggestions to the master list.

   E. The fifth step in the reflective-thinking method is selecting the best solution.

      1. The group should assess each potential solution in light of the criteria established for an ideal solution.

      2. In doing so, the group should try to reach consensus.

         a. A consensus decision is one that all members accept.

         b. Consensus decisions usually result in superior decisions and increased unity within the group.

V.   Once a group has reached a decision, it needs to present its recommendations clearly and convincingly *(text pages 495-497)*.
  A.   Although a group's recommendations are usually presented formally in writing, the written report is often supplemented with—or sometimes replaced by—an oral presentation.
  B.   One kind of oral presentation is an oral report.
    1.   An oral report is much the same in content as a written report.
    2.   In most cases, one member of the group delivers the oral report.
    3.   An oral report should be approached like any other speech.
  C.   A symposium is a second kind of oral presentation.
    1.   A symposium consists of a moderator and several speakers seated in front of an audience.
      a.   The moderator introduces the topic and the speakers.
      b.   Each speaker delivers a prepared speech on a single aspect of the group's work.
    2.   The speeches in a symposium should be carefully planned to cover all important aspects of the group's project.
  D.   A panel discussion is a third kind of oral presentation.
    1.   A panel discussion is essentially a conversation in front of an audience.
      a.   Panel discussions have a moderator who introduces the panelists and keeps the discussion on track.
      b.   Panelists speak briefly, informally, and impromptu.
    2.   Like other forms of speechmaking, a panel discussion requires serious preparation.
      a.   Although panelists speak impromptu, they need to study the topic and map out their ideas ahead of time.
      b.   The moderator needs to establish an agenda for the discussion and make sure all panelists get to voice their ideas.

Exercises for Critical Thinking *(from text pages 498-499)*

1.   Identify the flaw (or flaws) in each of the following questions for a problem-solving group discussion. Rewrite each question so it conforms with the criteria discussed in the chapter for effective discussion questions.

  a.   Should all students be required to take two years of a foreign language to graduate from college?

    Discussion: This question can be answered with a simple yes or no. It should be rephrased to allow for a wide variety of answers. For example: "What should be the foreign language requirements for graduation from college?"

b.   What should be done to prevent the utterly ridiculous shortage of computers for students at this school?

> **Discussion:** This question is biased or slanted. It should be rewritten more objectively. For example: "What steps should be taken to ensure that there are adequate computer facilities for students at this school?"

c.   What should be done about people running red lights?

> **Discussion:** This question is too broad and ambiguous. It should be rewritten so as to be clear and specific. For example: "What steps should our local and state governments take to prevent people from running red lights?"

d.   What should our state government do to control taxes and to combat drunk driving?

> **Discussion:**   This question poses two questions. It should be rewritten to ask a single question. For example: "What should our state government do to control taxes?" Or: "What should our state government do to combat drunk driving?"

e.   Should the federal government institute a system of standardized national tests for all schoolchildren?

> **Discussion:** This question can be answered with a simple yes or no. It should be rewritten to allow for a wide variety of answers. For example: "What should the federal government do to improve the quality of education in the United States?"

2.   If possible, arrange to observe a problem-solving small group in action. You might attend a meeting of your city council, the school board, the zoning commission, a local business, a church committee. To what extent does the discussion measure up to the criteria of effective discussion presented in this chapter? What kind of leadership does the group have, and how well does the leader (or leaders) fulfill the group's procedural needs, task needs, and maintenance needs? How do the other members meet their responsibilities? What aspects of the meeting are handled most effectively? Which are handled least effectively?

> **Discussion:** This exercise gives students the opportunity to observe a small group in action. You may want to have students write a brief paper reporting their observations. Or you may want to arrange for the entire class to observe the same group meeting, so as to provide a common basis for class discussion.

3. Identify a relatively important decision you have made in the last year or two. Try to reconstruct how you reached that decision. Now suppose you could remake the decision following the reflective-thinking method. Map out exactly what you would do at each stage of the method. Do you still reach the same decision? If not, do you believe the reflective-thinking method would have led you to a better decision in the first place?

    Discussion: This exercise requires students to sort out the steps of the reflective-thinking method and to apply them to the students' own decision making. Not only does this help familiarize students with the steps of the method, but it makes the point that the reflective-thinking method is not restricted to group discussion.

4. Attend a symposium or panel discussion on campus. Prepare a brief analysis of the proceedings. First, study the role of the moderator. How does she or he introduce the topic and participants? What role does the moderator play thereafter? Does she or he help guide and focus the panel discussion? Does she or he summarize and conclude the proceedings at the end?

    Second, observe the participants. Are the speeches in the symposium well prepared and presented? Which speaker (or speakers) do you find most effective? Least effective? Why? Do participants in the panel discussion share talking time? Does their discussion appear well planned to cover major aspects of the topic? Which panelist (or panelists) do you find most effective? Least effective? Why?

    Discussion: This can be handled much like Exercise 2. The questions in the exercise can also be used as the basis for evaluating symposia or panel discussions presented in class.

Additional Exercises and Activities

1. Have students perform the exercise "Lost on the Moon," as follows:*

    First, divide the class into groups of 4 to 6 members, and have each member complete the "Lost on the Moon" Individual Worksheet on page 371. Allow 10 minutes for this part of the exercise.

    Second, have each group discuss their individual answers and try to reach a consensus ranking of the 12 items. Each group should complete the "Lost on the Moon" Group Worksheet on page 372. Allow 25 minutes for this portion of the exercise.

    Then proceed to the third step, on pages 373-374.

    ---

    *Adapted from Jay Hall, "Decisions, Decisions, Decisions," *Psychology Today*, 5 (November 1971), 51-54, 86-88.

"Lost on the Moon" Individual Worksheet

Instructions:

Your spaceship has just crash-landed on the lighted surface of the moon. You were scheduled to rendezvous with a command ship 200 miles away, also on the lighted side of the moon, but the rough landing has ruined your ship and destroyed all the equipment on board, except for the 12 items listed below.

Your crew's survival depends on reaching the command ship, so you must choose the most critical items available for the 200-mile trip. Your task is to rank the 12 items according to their importance in allowing your crew to survive the 200-mile journey to the command ship. In the column titled "Your rank," place the number 1 by the most important item, the number 2 by the second most important item, and so on through number 12, the least important.

You have 10 minutes to complete this worksheet.

Item	Your rank	NASA rank	Difference
box of matches	_____	_____	_____
food concentrate	_____	_____	_____
50 feet of nylon rope	_____	_____	_____
parachute silk	_____	_____	_____
two .45 caliber pistols	_____	_____	_____
solar-powered portable heating unit	_____	_____	_____
two 100-pound tanks of oxygen	_____	_____	_____
map of the moon's constellation	_____	_____	_____
self-inflating life raft	_____	_____	_____
magnetic compass	_____	_____	_____
five gallons of water	_____	_____	_____
solar-powered FM receiver-transmitter	_____	_____	_____

"Lost on the Moon" Group Worksheet

Instructions:

Your task is to reach a consensus ranking of the 12 items needed to survive the journey to the command ship 200 miles away. This means that the ranking for each of the 12 items should be agreed upon by each member of the group before it becomes a part of the group's decision. Here are some guides to use in reaching consensus:

1. Don't argue stubbornly for your own point of view just because it is yours. Listen to other members of the group and be willing to change your views on the basis of reason and logic.

2. On the other hand, don't change your mind simply to avoid disagreement. Seek out differences of opinion and try to get every member involved in the decision-making process. The more information you have, the better chance you will have of making a sound decision.

3. Avoid such techniques as majority vote, averaging, flipping coins, and bargaining.

   After your group has reached consensus on how to rank the 12 items, fill in the "Group rank" column below. You have 25 minutes to complete this phase of the exercise.

Item	Group rank	NASA rank	Difference
box of matches	_____	_____	_____
food concentrate	_____	_____	_____
50 feet of nylon rope	_____	_____	_____
parachute silk	_____	_____	_____
two .45 caliber pistols	_____	_____	_____
solar-powered portable heating unit	_____	_____	_____
two 100-pound tanks of oxygen	_____	_____	_____
map of the moon's constellation	_____	_____	_____
self-inflating life raft	_____	_____	_____
magnetic compass	_____	_____	_____
five gallons of water	_____	_____	_____
solar-powered FM receiver-transmitter	_____	_____	_____

For the third step of the exercise, have students compute their individual and group scores, as follows:

a.   Provide students the correct ranking for each item, as given by NASA. Students should write this ranking in the column headed "NASA rank" on each of the two worksheets.

Item	NASA rank	NASA's rationale
box of matches	12	No oxygen on moon to sustain flame
food concentrate	4	Efficient means of supplying energy requirements
50 feet of nylon rope	6	Useful in scaling cliffs, tying injured together
parachute silk	7	Protection from sun's rays
two .45 caliber pistols	9	Possible means of self-propulsion
solar-powered portable heating unit	10	Not needed—temperature on the lighted side of the moon can exceed 100° C
two 100-pound tanks of oxygen	1	Most pressing survival need because of lack of oxygen on the moon
map of the moon's constellation	3	Primary means of navigation
self-inflating life raft	8	Some value for shelter or carrying. Also, CO_2 bottle in military raft may be used for propulsion.
magnetic compass	11	Worthless for navigation because magnetic field on the moon is not polarized
five gallons of water	2	Replacement for tremendous loss of liquid on lighted side of moon
solar-powered FM receiver-transmitter	5	For communication with command ship, but FM requires line-of-sight transmission and short ranges

b.   For each item on both worksheets students should enter the difference between their individual ranking or group ranking and the NASA ranking. It makes no difference which ranking is higher. For example, if the individual or group ranking is 12 and the NASA ranking is 8, the difference is 4. Likewise, if the individual ranking is 8 and the NASA ranking is 12, the difference is 4.

c.   The total score for each worksheet is figured by adding all the numbers in the "Difference" column on each sheet.

Fourth, have students compare their individual scores with the group score. Also have students compare the average individual score of all members of each group with the group score. In almost every case the group's score will be better—closer to NASA's rankings—than either the individual scores or the average individual score of the group's members.

Fifth, conduct a general class discussion of the results and of the decision-making procedures used in the groups.

> **Discussion:** This is an excellent exercise to acquaint students with the processes and benefits of small-group discussion. Students see how a small group can provide resources that allow it to improve upon the individual decisions of its members. Students also get firsthand experience in the difficult task of trying to reach consensus in a small group. In fact, because this exercise provokes so many questions and comments from students, you can use the general class discussion afterward to highlight any number of specific points about decision-making in small groups.

2.   Have students perform the "Hostages" exercise, as follows:[*]

First, divide the class into groups of 4 to 6 members, and have each member complete the "Hostages" Individual Worksheet on pages 375-376. Allow 10 minutes for this part of the exercise.

Second, have each group discuss their individual answers and try to reach a consensus ranking of the eight hostages. Each group should complete the "Hostages" Group Worksheet on page 377. Allow 20 minutes for this part of the exercise.

Third, have each group report its rankings to the rest of the class. Afterward, conduct a general class discussion of the results and of the decision-making procedures used in the groups.

---

[*]Adapted from Anne L. Haehl, "Adapting to Non-Traditional Students," *Speech Communication Teacher* (Winter 1988), 12-13. Used with permission of Anne L. Haehl and the National Communication Association.

"Hostages" Individual Worksheet

Instructions:

A plane has been hijacked! The hijackers offer to release four passengers to the U.S. embassy. In return for this gesture, the government of a neutral country will agree to allow the plane to land at its airport and refuel.

The captors insist, however, that U.S. authorities select the four to be released from the following list. The President has given your group the job of making the selection. If you do not select the people, the hijackers are perfectly willing to allow the plane to run out of gas and crash, killing all passengers. You must reach a decision by consensus, and you must do so within the next half hour.

You may assume the terrorists are honest about releasing those who are chosen to be released. You do not know what will happen to those who remain on the plane, but given what is known about this particular terrorist group, you expect most or all of the remaining hostages probably will die.

Quickly rank the following passengers in the order in which you would choose them to be released. In the column titled "Your rank," place the number 1 by the hostage you would save first, the number 2 by the one you would save second, and so on through number 8, the hostage you would save last.

You have 10 minutes to complete this part of the exercise, after which you will discuss the matter with your group and reach an agreement.

Hostages   **Your rank**

1. Brenda Jones, age 27, has three children by three different fathers, none of whom she has married. She loves her children, however, and has resolved to get her life together for the children's sake. Her mother is caring for them so Brenda can attend a six-week training program for women who lack job skills.   _____

2. Fr. John O'Brien, 65 years old, is in excellent health. A Roman Catholic priest, he has dedicated his life to working with the poor in an inner-city ghetto. He is taking this flight to arrange for funding and personnel that will enable him to set up a program to carry on his life's work after he becomes unable to work. Should he die at this time, the work probably will end.   _____

Hostages   **Your rank**

3.   Juan Garcia is 45. He has a history of heart trouble and might not survive the stress of a prolonged hostage situation. He is a wealthy businessman whose estate would easily provide for his wife and three young children, even if he should die in the hijacking. His business, however, which has employed and given dignity to many Hispanic people, probably would fold without his vision and drive, putting many people out of work who will not be able to find jobs.

                                                                 _____

4.   Elijah Brown is 52. He did time in jail for armed robbery. Since his release two years ago, he has worked hard, gone to school part time, and supported his invalid wife and youngest child (the only one remaining at home). There would be no money to provide for his family in the event of his death.

   _____

5.   Betsy Bates, 29, is a well-known and successful model. Married a little over a year to rock star Duke, she has just found out that she is pregnant, a discovery she views with mixed feelings.

   _____

6.   Congresswoman Jan Perkins is 47. Widowed young, when her husband died in the crash of an Air Force plane while on a diplomatic mission for the State Department, she has devoted her life to politics. She has been an effective and eloquent worker for peace and for the rights of women and minorities. Her death would be a crushing emotional blow to her elderly parents, though she has provided for them financially in her will. Perkins is widely seen as the most likely candidate for the first woman President of the United States.

   _____

7.   D. B. Calhoun is 43. Little is known about him, except that he is a very bigoted person with an unstable employment history. He reads *Soldier of Fortune* and similar magazines, and dreams about being a mercenary. It is quite possible that he will try some hostile action against the hijackers and ruin any chance of getting the remaining hostages out alive.

   _____

8.   Andrea Ohms, at 19, is already a distinguished pianist, having started performing professionally at age 8. Her performances give immense pleasure to thousands of people around the world. She is engaged to be married.

   _____

"Hostages" Group Worksheet

Instructions:

Your task is to reach a consensus ranking of the four hostages to be released by the terrorists. This means that the ranking for each of the four should be agreed upon by each member of the group before it becomes part of the group decision. Here are some guidelines to use in reaching consensus.

1. Don't argue stubbornly for your own point of view just because it is yours. Listen to other members of the group and be willing to change your views on the basis of reason and logic.

2. On the other hand, don't change your mind simply to avoid disagreement. Seek differences of opinion and try to get every member involved in the decision-making process. The more information you have, the better chance you will have of making a sound decision.

3. Avoid such techniques as majority vote, averaging, flipping coins, and bargaining.

After your group has reached consensus on how to rank the hostages, fill in the "group rank" column below. You have 20 minutes to complete this phase of the exercise.

Hostage		**Group Rank**
1.	Brenda Jones	_____
2.	Fr. John O'Brien	_____
3.	Juan Garcia	_____
4.	Elijah Brown	_____
5.	Betsy Bates	_____
6.	Jan Perkins	_____
7.	D.B. Calhoun	_____
8.	Andrea Ohms	_____

Discussion: Like "Lost on the Moon," this is an excellent exercise to acquaint students with the processes of small-group discussion. But whereas "Lost on the Moon" deals with scientific and technical matters on which there are right and wrong answers, "Hostages" revolves around subjective personal values that cannot be incontestably established as right or wrong. As a result, you should be prepared for some fairly intense discussions in the individual groups. You should also be prepared for that intensity to spill over into the general class discussion afterward. You may need to work to keep that discussion focused on the process of small-group communication rather than allowing it to turn into an extended debate on the specific decisions of each group regarding which hostages to save.

3.   Assign students the "Twelve Angry Men" group consultation project, as follows:[*]

First, divide the class into groups of 5 to 6 members. The task of each group is to view the classic film "Twelve Angry Men," which revolves around the efforts of eleven members of a jury in a murder trial to convince one member to change his "not guilty" vote to "guilty." The film dramatizes many of the aspects of small-group discussion covered in the textbook, including the kinds and functions of leadership, interpersonal conflict, hidden agendas, and the creation of consensus. Because the film is 96 minutes long, each group will have to arrange a time to view it out of class.

Second, give each group the following instructions: For this assignment, your group is to act as a consultant to the jury in the movie "Twelve Angry Men." The purpose of this assignment is for you to demonstrate your knowledge of group processes by evaluating a group's decision making. There is no single correct answer to this assignment. Your task as a group is to demonstrate that you understand and can apply the concepts of small-group discussion presented in the textbook and in class.

Third, have each group consider the following questions in its analysis:

a.   What are the strengths of the group portrayed in "Twelve Angry Men"?

b.   What are the weaknesses of the group?

c.   What kinds of leadership does the group demonstrate?

d.   What role do hidden agendas play in the deliberations of the group?

e.   If you were the leader of the group, what would you do to eliminate some of its interpersonal conflict?

---

[*]Adapted from Bruce C. McKinney, "The Group Process and 'Twelve Angry Men,'" *Speech Communication Teacher* (Winter 1990), 1-2. This article is reprinted in Stephen E. Lucas (ed.), *Selections from the Speech Communication Teacher, 1986-1991*, which is part of the instructional supplement that accompanies *The Art of Public Speaking*.

f.   Who are the most effective communicators in the group? The least effective? Why?

g.   How could the group improve its decision making and problem solving?

Fourth, conduct a general class discussion in which each group reports a summary of its deliberations and recommendations. Use the discussion to illustrate points about speaking in problem-solving small groups.

> **Discussion:**   This assignment is particularly valuable in helping students understand the dynamics of the group process. It can also be used as an alternative to the major problem-solving group discussion explained on page 38 of this manual. If so, however, it should probably be supplemented with a requirement that each student prepare either a written report or a journal of her or his group's activities—as explained in Additional Exercises/Activities 5 and 6 below.

4.   Divide the class into groups of 5 to 6 students each. The task of each group is to review the previous round of classroom speeches and provide constructive suggestions to help improve the next round. In its deliberations, each group should consider the following questions. Have each group present its thinking in a panel discussion.

a.   How well did the class as a whole perform in narrowing their topics and adapting their speeches to this audience?

- Were specific purposes sharply defined? Were they too broad? Too narrow? Too technical? Too trivial?

- Which speeches were especially well adapted to the background, knowledge, and interests of the audience? What methods of audience adaptation were used in these speeches?

- What advice would you give to the class about audience analysis and adaptation for the next round of speeches?

b.   How well did the class as a whole perform in the area of speech organization?

- Which introductions worked especially well? Why?

- Which conclusions were particularly effective? Why?

- Did speeches follow a clear method of organization? Which speeches were especially strong in this respect?

- Did speakers make effective use of connectives to help listeners follow their ideas? Which speeches stood out in this regard?

- What advice would you give to the class about organization for the next round of speeches?

c.   How well did the class as a whole use supporting materials in this round of speeches?

- Which speakers made especially good use of examples? What made their use of examples so effective?

- Which speakers made especially good use of statistics? What made their use of statistics so effective?

- Which speakers made especially good use of testimony? What made their use of testimony so effective?

- What advice would you give to the class about the use of supporting materials in the next round of speeches?

d.   How well did the class as a whole deliver this round of speeches?

- Did speakers sound fluid, confident, and conversational?

- Did speakers manage their notes effectively and establish strong eye contact with listeners?

- Did speakers avoid distracting mannerisms? Did they use gestures to help communicate their ideas?

- Did speakers use visual aids effectively? Which speeches were especially noteworthy in this respect?

- What advice would you give to the class about delivery in the next round of speeches?

Discussion: This assignment can be a helpful way to integrate group discussion into a public speaking class. Groups should be assigned before the start of the round of speeches they are to analyze. Be sure to tell the groups that this assignment will require them to meet outside of class and to reach consensus on their judgments about their classmates' speeches.

This assignment can also be used as an alternative to the major problem-solving group discussion described on page 38 of this manual. If so, however, it should probably be supplemented with a requirement that each student prepare either a written report or a journal of their group's activities—as explained in Additional Exercises/Activities 5 and 6 below.

5.   If you assign students a major group project that requires work outside of class, have them prepare a 3- to 5-page written report on the deliberations of their group. In writing their reports, students should address the following:

a.   *Leadership*. If your group has a designated leader, assess how well she or he performs. If your group does not have a designated leader, note what kind of leadership develops. Which members of the group assume leadership roles? Do you think your group would work better with a different kind of leadership?

b.   *Responsibilities of group members.* Evaluate how well each member fulfills his or her five major responsibilities. Do members commit themselves to the goals of the group and cooperate to achieve them? Do they carry out their individual assignments? Do they avoid interpersonal conflict by keeping disagreements at the task level? Do they encourage participation by other people in the group? Do they work to keep the discussion on track?

c.   *Use of reflective-thinking method.* Keep track of how your group deals with each stage in the reflective-thinking method. Does the group define the problem clearly and analyze it effectively? Does the group establish criteria for solutions and brainstorm to generate a number of possible solutions? Is the group able to reach consensus on the best solution or solutions? If not, how does the group reach its decision?

d.   *Evaluation.* Are you satisfied with the work of the group and with your role in the group? If the group were to start its project over again, what changes would you recommend to help the group work more effectively?

> **Discussion:** This assignment requires students to look closely at the communication processes in their groups. To help with this assignment, each student should be encouraged to keep a journal of his or her group's deliberations. The journal should note what happens at each meeting of the group and what developments take place over time as the group works on its project. Because this assignment requires a substantial investment of time, some teachers count it as a major part—25 percent or more—of the student's grade for the unit on group discussion. For an alternative to this assignment, see the next Additional Exercise/Activity.

6.   As in the preceding assignment, encourage students to keep a journal of their group's deliberations. The journal should note what happens at each meeting and what developments take place over time as the group works on its project. When the project is completed, have each student turn in a Group Discussion Participant Evaluation Form (page 382) assessing the work of each participant in the group other than himself or herself.

> **Discussion:** This is an alternative to the detailed evaluation called for in the preceding Additional Exercise/Activity. Because this evaluation focuses on individual group members, it usually gives a pretty clear picture of who met their responsibilities and who did not. As a result, it can be an excellent aid in assigning students individual grades for their group projects.

Group Discussion Participant Evaluation Form

Person being evaluated _____

Your name _____ Group _____

For each item, circle the number that best reflects your evaluation of the participant's contribution to the group.

poor	fair	average	good	excellent	
P	F	A	G	E	Appeared committed to the goals of the group
P	F	A	G	E	Participated frequently in group deliberations
P	F	A	G	E	Comments were clear, relevant, and helpful
P	F	A	G	E	Carried out individual assignments promptly
P	F	A	G	E	Assisted with procedural leadership functions
P	F	A	G	E	Assisted with task leadership functions
P	F	A	G	E	Assisted with maintenance leadership functions
P	F	A	G	E	Avoided interpersonal conflict with group members
P	F	A	G	E	Encouraged participation by other group members
P	F	A	G	E	Helped keep discussion on track
P	F	A	G	E	Overall contribution in comparison to other group members

Comments: (this space must be filled in)

Extra Teaching and Learning Resources

General

Adams, Katherine, and Galanes, Gloria J. *Communicating in Groups: Applications and Skills*. New York: McGraw-Hill, 2003.

Barker, Larry L.; Wahlers, Kathy J.; and Watson, Kittie W. *Groups in Process: An Introduction to Small Group Communication*, 6th ed. Boston: Allyn and Bacon, 2001.

Brilhart, John K., and Galanes, Gloria J. *Effective Group Discussion*, 10th ed. New York: McGraw-Hill, 2001.

Cathcart, Robert S.; Samovar, Larry; and Henman, Linda D. (eds.). *Small Group Communication: Theory and Practice*, 7th ed. Madison, WI: Brown and Benchmark, 1996.

Cragan, John F., and Wright, David W. *Communication in Small Group Discussions: Theory, Process, Skills*. 5th ed. Belmont: CA: Wadsworth, 1998.

Frey, Lawrence R., and Barge, J. Kevin (eds). *Managing Group Life: Communicating in Decision-Making Groups*. Boston: Houghton Mifflin, 1997.

Frey, Lawrence R.; Gouran, Dennis S.; and Poole, Marshall Scott (eds). *Handbook of Group Communication Theory and Research*. Thousand Oaks, CA: Sage, 1999.

Fujishin, Randy. *Discovering the Leader Within: Running Small Groups Successfully*. San Francisco: Acada Books, 1997.

Garside, Colleen. "Look Who's Talking: A Comparison of Lecture and Group Discussion Teaching Strategies in Developing Critical Thinking Skills." *Communication Education*, 45 (1996), 212-227.

Kelsey, Dee, and Plumb, Pam. *Great Meetings! How to Facilitate Like a Pro*. Portland, ME: Hanson Park Press, 1999.

Keyton, Joann. *Communicating in Groups: Building Relationships for Effective Decision Making*, 2nd ed. New York: McGraw-Hill, 2003.

Levine, John M., and Moreland, Richard L. "Small Groups." In Gilbert, Daniel T.; Fiske, Susan T.; and Lindzey, Gardner (eds.), *Handbook of Social Psychology*, 4th ed. New York: McGraw-Hill, 1998, Vol. II, pp. 415-469.

Northouse, Peter G. *Leadership: Theory and Practice*, 2nd ed. Thousand Oaks, CA: Sage, 2001.

Pavitt, Charles. "Does Communication Matter in Social Influence During Small Group Discussion? Five Positions." *Communication Studies*, 44 (1993), 216-227.

Pavitt, Charles, and Curtis, Ellen. *Small Group Discussion: A Theoretical Approach*, 2nd ed. Scottsdale, AZ: Gorsuch Scarisbrick, 1994.

Pavitt, Charles, and Johnson, Kelly K. "Scheidel and Crowell Revisited: A Descriptive Study of Group Proposal Sequencing." *Communication Monographs*, 69 (2002), 19-32.

Classroom Activities and Assignments

Aust, Philip Jerold. "Enhancing Group Communication Learning Through a Structured Assignment." In Stephen E. Lucas (ed.), *Selections from the Communication Teacher, 1999-2002*. New York: McGraw-Hill, 2004, pp. 48-50.

Bahti, Cynthia L. "California Dreamin'." In Stephen E. Lucas (ed.), *Selections from the Speech Communication Teacher, 1986-1991*. New York: McGraw-Hill, 1992, p. 31.

Benson, James H. "Shaping Attitudes: A Role of the Leader." In Stephen E. Lucas (ed.), *Selections from the Speech Communication Teacher, 1996-1999*. New York: McGraw-Hill, 2001, pp. 50-51.

Bourhis, John. "Video Groups." In Stephen E. Lucas (ed.), *Selections from the Speech Communication Teacher, 1991-1994*. New York: McGraw-Hill, 1995, p. 27.

Bozik, Mary. "Playing Games with the Small Group Project." In Stephen E. Lucas (ed.), *Selections from the Speech Communication Teacher, 1994-1996*. New York: McGraw-Hill, 1997, pp. 31-32.

Chaudoin, Kristin F. "The Reflective-Thinking Method and Student Empowerment." In Stephen E. Lucas (ed.), *Selections from the Speech Communication Teacher, 1996-1999*. New York: McGraw-Hill, 2001, pp. 51-52.

Chowning, James Anthony. "Decision-Making Goes Interpersonal." In Stephen E. Lucas (ed.), *Selections from the Speech Communication Teacher, 1994-1996*. New York: McGraw-Hill, 1997, pp. 32-33.

Dittus, James K. "Giving Students What They Want: A Role-Playing Exercise with True-to-Life Groups." In Stephen E. Lucas (ed.), *Selections from the Speech Communication Teacher, 1991-1994*. New York: McGraw-Hill, 1995, pp. 27-28.

Fernandes, James J. "Creative Problem Solving–From Top to Bottom." In Stephen E. Lucas (ed.), *Selections from the Speech Communication Teacher, 1996-1999*. New York: McGraw-Hill, 2001, pp. 52-53.

Foster, David E. "A Method of Comparing Follower Satisfaction with the Authoritarian, Democratic, and Laissez-Faire Styles of Leadership." In Stephen E. Lucas (ed.), *Selections from the Communication Teacher, 1999-2002*. New York: McGraw-Hill, 2004, pp. 50-52.

Hamlet, Janice D. "When Does a Group Become 'A Group'? Solving the Puzzle." In Stephen E. Lucas (ed.), *Selections from the Communication Teacher, 1999-2002*. New York: McGraw-Hill, 2004, pp. 52-54.

Johnson, Scott D. "Exploring the Influences of Culture on Small Groups." In Stephen E. Lucas (ed.), *Selections from the Speech Communication Teacher, 1994-1996*. New York: McGraw-Hill, 1997, pp. 25-26.

Kassing, Jeffrey W. "Reframing Creative Problem Solving." In Stephen E. Lucas (ed.), *Selections from the Speech Communication Teacher, 1996-1999*. New York: McGraw-Hill, 2001, pp. 53-54.

Litke, Rebecca A. "Collaborative Writing." In Stephen E. Lucas (ed.), *Selections from the Speech Communication Teacher, 1996-1999*. New York: McGraw-Hill, 2001, pp. 54-55.

Mandeville, Mary Y. "Using New Approaches in Group Discussion Projects." In Stephen E. Lucas (ed.), *Selections from the Speech Communication Teacher, 1996-1999*. New York: McGraw-Hill, 2001, pp.55-56.

Mayhew, Virginia B. "Pennies and Poems." In Stephen E. Lucas (ed.), *Selections from the Speech Communication Teacher, 1986-1991*. New York: McGraw-Hill, 1992, p. 31.

McKinney, Bruce C. "The Group Process and *12 Angry Men*." In Stephen E. Lucas (ed.), *Selections from the Speech Communication Teacher, 1986-1991*. New York: McGraw-Hill, 1992, pp. 31-32.

Miller, Ann Neville, and Hobgood, Linda Bartlett. "Invite an Administrator: Using University Administrators as an Audience for Student Presentations." In Stephen E. Lucas (ed.), *Selections from the Communication Teacher, 1999-2002*. New York: McGraw-Hill, 2004, pp. 54-55.

Mino, Mary. "Making the Basic Public Speaking Course Relevant: A Group Project." In Stephen E. Lucas (ed.), *Selections from the Speech Communication Teacher, 1986-1991*. New York: McGraw-Hill, 1992, p. 33.

Mitnick, Andrea D. "Put Your Money Where Your Mouth Is: Group Communication Classes Go Fundraising." In Stephen E. Lucas (ed.), *Selections from the Speech Communication Teacher, 1996-1999*. New York: McGraw-Hill, 2001, pp. 56-58.

Neumann, David. "Building and Destroying Groups." In Stephen E. Lucas (ed.), *Selections from the Speech Communication Teacher, 1991-1994*. New York: McGraw-Hill, 1995, pp. 28-29.

Ortiz, Joe. "Group Interaction: Processes, Problems, and Consensus." In Stephen E. Lucas (ed.), *Selections from the Speech Communication Teacher, 1986-1991*. New York: McGraw-Hill, 1992, pp. 34-35.

Rapone, Thomas M. "Using History to Teach Small Group Communication." In Stephen E. Lucas (ed.), *Selections from the Speech Communication Teacher, 1994-1996*. New York: McGraw-Hill, 1997, pp. 33-34.

Renz, Mary Ann. "Job Specific Interviews." In Stephen E. Lucas (ed.), *Selections from the Speech Communication Teacher, 1991-1994*. New York: McGraw-Hill, 1995, pp. 29-30.

Smith, Robert E. "The Outstanding Senior Award: A Realistic Small Group Decision-Making Exercise." In Stephen E. Lucas (ed.), *Selections from the Speech Communication Teacher, 1991-1994*. New York: McGraw-Hill, 1995, pp. 30-31.

Stearns, Susan A. "Small Group Activities and Student Empowerment." In Stephen E. Lucas (ed.), *Selections from the Speech Communication Teacher, 1994-1996*. New York: McGraw-Hill, 1997, pp. 34-35.

Watters, Kathleen B. "Authentic and Pseudo Small Groups." In Stephen E. Lucas (ed.), *Selections from the Speech Communication Teacher, 1996-1999*. New York: McGraw-Hill, 2001, pp. 58-59.

Films and Videos

"Effective Facilitation Tools." Insight Media (1997). Five volumes; 169 minutes.

"Group Dynamics and Communications." Insight Media (2000). 21 minutes.

"Group Dynamics: Why Good People Make Bad Decisions." Insight Media (1994). 17 minutes.

"Groups and Group Dynamics." Insight Media (1991). 30 minutes.

"Groupthink," revised edition. CRM Films (1992). 22 minutes.

"Invisible Rules: Men, Women and Teams." CRM Films (1996). 34 minutes.

"Leadership and the New Science." CRM Films (1993). 23 minutes.

"Meeting Robbers," revised edition. CRM Films (1995). 20 minutes.

"Mining Group Gold." CRM Films (1992). 22 minutes.

"The Submarine Syndrome: Workgroups Under Stress." CRM Films (1994). 17 minutes.

"Understanding Group Dynamics." Insight Media (2000). 15 minutes.

"Workteams and the Wizard of Oz." CRM Films (1993). 13 minutes.

"You Know What I Mean?" CRM Films (1990). 21 minutes.

Part Five

SPEECHES FOR ANALYSIS

AND DISCUSSION

My Eye on the World

Sakhouy Lay

---

1   Gordon Parks once said, "I choose my camera as a weapon against all the things I dislike about America—poverty, racism, discrimination." Parks, an extraordinary photographer, gives insight into my character, passions, and concerns in this one profound quotation.

2   I began photography during the fall of my freshman year in high school. After learning simple techniques of printing in the darkroom and studying the works of influential photographers, I developed an interest in this art that I have continued to pursue ever since. In addition to taking three other photo courses, I worked as a photographer and even received awards for some of my photographs.

3   My camera is therefore an effective tool that expresses my values, ambitions, and views in a literal sense. Being able to capture an idea or moment in a tangible art has always amazed me. The product that I create by the snap of a shutter greatly describes the way I see the world around me. The different angles, the way I choose to frame a photo, and my subject matter—all shed light on describing who I am as a person.

4   By photographing the world around me, I can also express my sense of beauty. This may include an abstract silhouette of the contours of a woman's body, the way the sun accents a stairwell at a certain time of day, the motion of water flowing down a channel of rocks, or the smile on a child's face.

5   My camera sheds light on my emotions and concerns as well. It can describe a feeling or an issue in a single moment—the loneliness of a stark, dreary winter day or the hunger in a homeless child's eyes.

6   So you can see photography is an outlet for my energy, my ideas, my creativity, and even my frustrations. Through the lens of a camera I can articulate my feelings and express myself to the world.

My Eye on the World   *by Sakhouy Lay*

Commentary

"My Eye on the World" is a 2-minute speech of self-introduction. In addition to having students read the speech, you can show the video of it from *Speeches for Analysis and Discussion: A Videotape Supplement to The Art of Public Speaking, Eighth Edition*. Here is a synopsis.

Specific Purpose: To introduce myself to the audience by explaining how my hobby of photography provides insight into my character, passions, and concerns.

Central Idea: Through photography, a hobby I have pursued since high school, I am able to express my character, passions, and concerns.

Method of Organization: Topical

Introduction: The introduction consists of paragraph 1, which opens with an attention-getting quotation from famous photographer Gordon Parks. The speaker then moves from this quotation to indicate how her hobby of photography reveals a great deal about her character, passions, and concerns. Although only two sentences in length, the introduction accomplishes everything it needs to in that brief compass.

Body: The body of the speech runs from paragraph 2 through paragraph 5. In paragraph 2 the speaker notes how she first became interested in photography and explains the role it has continued to play in her life. Paragraphs 3-5 focus on specific aspects of photography and what they reveal about the speaker. Rather than speaking in general terms, the speaker uses sharp imagery and concrete, descriptive language to convey her ideas. Consistent with the visual images created by a photograph, the speaker provides linguistic images for her listeners.

Conclusion: As in most introductory speeches, the conclusion is brief and succinct. Consisting of paragraph 6, it summarizes the central idea of the speech and ends with a strong final sentence.

———————————————

A Mile in My Shoes

Katherine Hillman

---

1   Someone once said, you don't really know a person until you walk a mile in their shoes. Whoever said this must have met many a person like me. Where one's shoes have been and what they have done can give you a great deal of insight into a person. I think my shoes reveal a lot about me—not only my everyday activities and hobbies, but the events that have shaped my inner self.

2   If you closely examine my shoes, you'll notice many things that connect me to what I do. I am an artist. You may see a speck of paint that fell from the brush as I worked on my latest still-life oil painting. Or you may notice a fair amount of clay, a result of my aggressive wrestling with the medium on a potter's wheel.

3   Also evident on my shoes is my major on campus. I'm a Meat and Animal Science major, and my shoes bear full documentation of my involvement in this program. The shoelaces are frayed from the sheep that chew on them while I work in the barns. The leather is marred from the hooves of animals stepping on my feet. If you're unfortunate enough, you may find something in the treads that I accidentally stepped in.

4   The exterior of my shoes can tell you a lot about what I do, but they also can provide clues to who I am and where I have been. I have always been an explorer and traveler. My father says that I was born under a wandering star. My shoes have been on my feet for many of my spiritual and physical wanderings. They've walked up into the Alps, across the cliffs of Ireland, and through 14 countries. They've been on numerous backpacking trips throughout the nation and on hikes in the northern Wisconsin woods. They've been witnesses to archeological digs and rowing regattas. They were on my feet the day I took my first hike with my fiancé and the day we took the walk that ended in his proposal.

5   So you can see my shoes have been through a lot, and they're beginning to show the wear and tear a bit. They've been witnesses to my everyday adventures and the epic journeys that have shaped my life. You could learn a lot about me by looking at my shoes, but you could learn a great deal more by walking a few miles in them.

A Mile in My Shoes   *by Katherine Hillman*

Commentary

"A Mile in My Shoes" is a speech of self-introduction based on a personal object. Clearly organized and effectively delivered, it provides a fine example of how students can approach the introductory speech creatively. The ideas of the speech are fairly ordinary, but the manner in which the speaker expresses and communicates those ideas lifts the speech well above the ordinary. Because the impact of the speech is significantly heightened by the speaker's use of her shoes as a visual aid, students will profit both from reading the speech and from viewing it on *Speeches for Analysis and Discussion: A Videotape Supplement to The Art of Public Speaking, Eighth Edition*. Here is a synopsis.

Specific Purpose: To introduce myself to my audience by explaining how my shoes reveal my everyday activities, my hobbies, and the events that have shaped my inner self.

Central Idea: My shoes reveal that I am an artist, a Meat and Animal Science major, and a wanderer and traveler.

Method of Organization: Topical

Introduction: The introduction consists of the first paragraph. The speaker gains attention by opening with the old adage about walking a mile in a person's shoes. She moves from the adage to note that one's shoes can reveal a great deal about a person. In her case, she says, one can learn about her hobbies, her everyday activities, and the events that have shaped her inner self. Crisp and concise, the introduction leaves no doubt about the topic of the speech or the major points to be covered in the body.

Body: There are three main points in the body of this speech, each of which reveals something different about the speaker. The first tells us that the speaker is an artist (paragraph 2). The second tells us that she is a Meat and Animal Science major (paragraph 3). The third tells us that she has traveled a great deal, has participated in activities from rowing regattas to archaeological digs, and is engaged to be married (paragraph 4).

   Because the speech assignment required students to use a physical object to help introduce themselves to the class, the speaker uses her shoes as a visual aid in paragraphs 2-3. The major reason for this is that. But even if this had not been the assignment, using the shoes would have been an excellent idea. Not only do they make the speech more interesting, but they give the speaker something to do other than worry about her nervousness. She does an excellent job of using the shoes to reinforce her ideas; her words are perfectly coordinated with her actions; and she maintains strong eye contact with the audience every step of the way.

Conclusion: The speaker concludes in paragraph 5, in which she summarizes the major themes of the speech and provides a sense of psychological unity by

Conclusion: The speaker concludes in paragraph 5, in which she summarizes the major themes of the speech and provides a sense of psychological unity by referring back to her opening line. Here, as elsewhere, she chooses her words carefully and communicates them extemporaneously.

_____

Kiyomi and Me

Gurpreet (Priya) Paul

---

1   Her name was Kiyomi. She was a mysterious Japanese dancer. Last autumn I got to meet her. How, you ask. Well, actually, she was a character in a play. I met her the day I became her. That day was one of the happiest days of my life. I wanted that part so desperately it was all I could think about. Being Kiyomi was one of the most memorable experiences of my life.

2   When I first read the script for the play *A Wind of a Thousand Tales*, I couldn't believe it. The description of the character Kiyomi was perfect. She was everything I ever wanted to be in life. She was beautiful, humble, shy, loving, loved, and, most of all, she was graceful. To me, she was the ideal woman. So, obviously, I tried out for the part.

3   I had to wait an entire weekend to find out if I got the part or not. Now I know that doesn't seem like a long time, but to me it felt like an eternity. So when I found out I got the part that Monday, I was so excited that I memorized all my lines that night.

4   Yet it wasn't getting the part that made so much of a difference in my life. The most important experience came after all the rehearsals, when it was finally time to perform the play. I was performing on stage, when gradually I forgot who I was. I said all the lines and performed all the actions—but not as Priya acting as Kiyomi, but as Kiyomi herself. It was the strangest experience of my life. I had become a completely different person. Even after the play was over, it took me a good five minutes to snap out of it.

5   After finding myself again, I realized why I had this strange experience. I needed this experience to appreciate who I was. I realized that I should be myself and not long to be someone else. So what if I'm not the most graceful or feminine person? So what if I don't possess all the wonderful characteristics of Kiyomi? I am still me—not a character in a play. Yet by playing that character, I learned one of the most important lessons of my life. I learned that by becoming a woman who never was, I became proud of who I am.

Kiyomi and Me   *by Gurpreet (Priya) Paul*

Commentary

A narrative speech of self-introduction, "Kiyomi and Me" is clearly organized and creatively developed. In addition to being reprinted in this manual, it is available on the videotape of student speeches that accompanies the 7th edition of *The Art of Public Speaking*. Here is a synopsis.

Specific Purpose: To introduce myself to the audience.

Central Idea: Playing the role of Kiyomi in *A Wind of a Thousand Tales* was one of the most memorable experiences of my life.

Method of Organization: Chronological

Introduction: The introduction consists of paragraph 1 and provides an excellent example of how students can gain the audience's attention by arousing curiosity about the speech topic. After beginning with the opening words, "Her name was Kiyomi," the speaker gradually reveals the identity of Kiyomi as a character in a play. She ends the introduction by making clear that the rest of the speech will explain why playing the role of Kiyomi was one of the most memorable experiences of the speaker's life.

Body: Running from paragraph 2 through paragraph 4, the body of this speech is organized chronologically and presents a narrative about the speaker's experience playing Kiyomi. In paragraph 2 the speaker begins her narrative by recalling the day she read the script of *A Wind of a Thousand Tales* and how captivated she was by the character of Kiyomi. In paragraph 3 the speaker describes waiting for the results of her audition and her excitement when she learned that she was chosen to play Kiyomi. In paragraph 4 she explains how she found herself so absorbed by the role of Kiyomi during the play that she became "a completely different person." It was, she says, "the strangest experience of my life." As with most good narratives, this one is clearly structured and communicated. The speaker uses vivid, descriptive language and provides enough details for the audience to understand what occurred, but not so many as to make the speech run over the time limit.

Conclusion: Consisting of paragraph 5, the conclusion is especially effective. Having presented her narrative in the body of the speech, the speaker now explains why her experience playing Kiyomi was so significant. In doing so, she makes a larger point about the importance of being true to one's self. The final two sentences end the speech on a dramatic and thought-provoking note.

As is evident from the videotape, the speaker presents her ideas vibrantly and with excellent eye contact. However, in keeping with her training as an actor, she chose to memorize the speech, rather than to deliver it extemporaneously. Although her classmates liked the speech, most felt it would have been even better if it had not sounded memorized. If you show the videotape to your students, you can use it to highlight both the excellent content and structure of this speech and the importance of conversational delivery.

A Family Tradition

Kristin Berg

---

1   Drawers pulled open. Clothes scattered all over the floor. A little girl with white blonde curls is digging through her father's chest of drawers. "At last," she exclaims, "I found you." She pulls the expensive European cigars out from the drawer and holds them triumphantly to the sun. Little Reva was not going to let her father ruin his health. Without hesitation, she hoists the cigars out the open window and skips out of the room.

2   Reva's parents were not sure what to make of their five-year-old daughter and her precocious antics. Thirteen years later, Reva, your classmate, continues to astound her parents. She likes to meet new people; she loves to party; and she left her home state of Indiana to come here to the University of Wisconsin. They attribute her daring to the American culture. But I contend that, more than anything, she embodies the values of her family.

3   Reva's parents were born in a small backwater town in the Netherlands, just 10 miles from the German border. Both parents were raised in traditional Dutch Catholic families where 10 to 12 children were the norm. However, Reva's parents turned out to be anything but traditional. They renounced both Catholicism and traditional Dutch life. Reva's mother had never seen an orange, a person of color, or even a Protestant, yet she decided she was going to America. Knowing little English, the young couple set off to build a new life in a new land.

4   Surrounded by a new people, a new language, and a new culture, the young couple struggled to make their growing family belong. Reva remembers her father's daring and sometimes dangerous stunts to give her an authentic American childhood. One Christmas Eve, Reva was snuggling under her covers, waiting for the night to pass, when, all of a sudden, a rapid stomping shook the ceiling above. The children screamed as the roof rumbled and roared. They went scurrying down the stairs only to watch as large, dusty bundles dropped down the chimney into the fireplace. Meanwhile, Reva's father was wrestling wind and ice atop the roof, losing several toys and nearly his life in his struggle to give his children a genuine "Santa and Reindeer" Christmas.

5   Today, Reva's family is fully comfortable in American life and society. Her father travels the country in his work as an engineering specialist. Her oldest sister, Amy, attends Washington University Medical School in St. Louis, while her other sister is a junior at MIT. Clearly, Reva's family has accomplished a great deal.

6   How many of us can imagine leaving our families and everything we own to travel thousands of miles across the ocean to a land where we have no guarantee of success? Furthermore, a land where we don't even speak the language. And yet, once here, Reva's family was able to carve out an extremely successful lifestyle.

7   This is why I think Reva's daring nature is not simply a result of an American life. Rather, I would contend that Reva's parents passed on to her their own adventurous spirit, which allowed them to break tradition; their own courage, which enabled them to leave their homeland; and their own creativity, which they used to weave their traditions into the fabric of American society. If, as it's been said, one is inevitably the product of one's own family, then Reva is truly blessed indeed.

A Family Tradition   *by Kristin Berg*

Commentary

Marked by expressive language and dynamic delivery, "A Family Tradition" is a fine example of an ice-breaker speech introducing a classmate. In addition to being printed in this manual, it is available on the videotape of student speeches that accompanies the 7th edition of *The Art of Public Speaking*. Here is a synopsis of the speech.

Specific Purpose: To introduce my classmate Reva to the audience.

Central Idea: Reva's daring nature is attributable primarily to the values of her family.

Method of Organization: Chronological

Introduction: The introduction consists of paragraphs 1-2. It opens in paragraph 1 with a story about the speaker's classmate Reva as a little girl. Featuring colorful, descriptive language and sharply etched details, the story does an excellent job of gaining the audience's attention. Paragraph 2 moves from Reva's childhood into her current interests as a student at the University of Wisconsin. It also introduces the main theme of the speech—that Reva's daring nature is attributable above all to the values of her family.

Body: Running from paragraph 3 through paragraph 6, the body focuses on several aspects of Reva's family that reveal her adventurous spirit and willingness to break with tradition. Paragraph 3 explains how Reva's parents boldly decided to leave the Netherlands and emigrate to the United States. Paragraph 4 situates Reva and her family in the U.S. and discusses her parents' efforts to provide their children a "genuine" American childhood. Paragraph 5 brings the sketch of Reva's family up to the moment, while paragraph 6 reinforces the family's achievements by asking the audience to imagine whether they could succeed under the same conditions.

Conclusion: The speech concludes in paragraph 7 by reemphasizing the extent to which Reva's parents passed on to her their courage, creativity, and adventurous spirit. The final sentence brings the entire speech together and adds a touch of eloquence.

Throughout "A Family Tradition," the impact of the speaker's words is enhanced by her vibrant delivery. She has excellent vocal variety, maintains strong eye contact, and uses gestures to reinforce key ideas. Most notable in this regard are paragraphs 1 and 4, both of which relate engaging stories about Reva and her family. If you show the videotape of this speech in class, try playing a minute or so of it without sound. Ask students to concentrate on the speaker's physical actions. It is very clear from those actions that she is engrossed in the speech and is intent on communicating directly with her listeners.

Feng Shui

Liz Elegant

---

1   It's move-in day. While most everyone is rushing about carrying boxes, computers, TVs, and stereos to make their dorm rooms feel a little more like home, my mom is carrying—wind chimes. Don't wind chimes belong outside? In a garden? On a patio? Anywhere but a dorm room? My mom had strategically placed them so that each time I opened the door, it would swing into them. It was all because of feng shui.

2   According to Simon Brown, author of the book *Practical Feng Shui*, feng shui, which literally means wind and water, "is the art of designing your home to promote success in life, health, wealth and happiness." Feng shui originated in China over 4,000 years ago and is still practiced throughout the world today.

3   While it may seem like only ancient Chinese philosophers can master this art, even college students like us can learn simple techniques for improving the flow of energy in our dorm rooms, homes, or apartments. With my mom's enthusiasm behind me, I decided to research this topic some more on my own. First I'll explain a bit more about what feng shui is and then give you some tips on putting this ancient art into practice.

4   As I mentioned in my introduction, the ancient Chinese art of feng shui is a method of maximizing energy flow by manipulating your environment. Pam Kai Tollefson, director of Feng Shui Design, believes that feng shui changes and harmonizes the environment. There are many components of feng shui, the most important of which is chi. According to Sarah Rossbach, author of the book *Feng Shui: The Chinese Art of Placement,* chi is defined as the energy flow that connects all things, and it has a profound impact on our lives. Simon Brown describes chi as carrying thoughts, ideas, emotions, dreams, and energy from the environment. Practitioners of feng sui maintain that chi can move through air, people, buildings, windows, and doors. The flow of chi is the basis of feng shui.

5   The aim of feng shui is to improve your chi, which is accomplished by altering your surroundings. There is good and bad chi that flows throughout buildings such as this one. For example, the sharp corners on this lectern create negative chi because sharp corners cause chi to swirl, creating confusion or illness. Another problem in this room is that there are no windows. Sunlight is crucial because it's the main medium that keeps chi moving.

6   According to its followers, feng shui has many benefits once a home or office is arranged according to the principles of feng shui. Decreased stress and a better night's sleep are one advantage of feng shui. Improved health, motivation, relaxation, love, and romance can even occur. Feng shui helps create more harmonious family relationships. Overall, it can help you feel more in control and might even win you fame and respect.

7   Nancilee Wydra, author of the book *Feng Shui: 150 Simple Solutions for Health and Happiness in Your Home or Office*, believes that feng shui is beneficial in the workplace as well. Balanced chi creates a good start to a new career and a growing business, while evenly circulated chi throughout the body can help you become more assertive in the workplace.

8   Now that we've taken a look at what feng shui is, let's put this newfound knowledge into practice. To illustrate, we'll look at how feng shui works in a typical dorm room. Since we don't have control over the actual structure of our dorm rooms, we're forced to work with what we have.

9   Let's start with the ideal floor covering. Winifred Gallagher, in *The Power of Place*, says that soft materials slow chi energy and create a relaxing atmosphere. Few dorm rooms are carpeted, so make sure to cover your floor with a soft, fitted carpet.

10   Next, we'll look at the placement of your bed in your dorm room. In *Practical Feng Shui*, Simon Brown claims that "the direction you sleep in affects your whole life as well as how well you sleep." Feng shui recommends having the head of the bed face east because it's good for career building, ambition, getting things done, and ideal for growth. Or, if you're having trouble sleeping, try having the head of the bed face the north. This will enhance feelings of peace, tranquility, and spirituality. No matter what direction the head of your bed faces, make sure you can see the door and the window from your bed.

11   Once it's located in the ideal position, make sure to cover your bed with cotton, linen, or silk sheets to create a harmonious flow. Synthetic materials have a negative effect on chi. Finally, keep your curtains tightly closed at night to slow the flow of chi energy through your window.

12   Now that we've looked at the possibilities with what's already in your dorm room, let's see what we can add to enhance the already flowing chi.

13   For starters, try adding a wide mirror on one end of your dorm room to reflect the energy across the entire room. Most dorms provide harsh, electric lighting. To soften this light, bring in lamps with shades on them.

14   You can also add simple elements to enhance the flow of chi. Plants are always a good addition to a room because of their soothing effect. As my mom insisted, try placing wind chimes next to your door so they sound every time you open it. Lurrae Lupone, author of *Feng Shui: Therapy for the New Millennium*, says that wind chimes cleanse and purify the chi energy already in your room.

15   In addition to hanging wind chimes near your door, you can hang crystals such as this one in a window. The crystals bring energy from the outside environment into your dorm room. Adding water, such as a bowl of water or a fish tank, can also bring fresh chi energy into the room. If you place a bowl of water in your room, place it in the east or the southeast and refill it every day. According to advocates of feng shui, the water element can help you attain your goals and might even help you study for those midterms.

16   Finally, for those of you who tend to be a bit messy, beware. Untidiness slows the flow of chi energy. Make sure to store everything in cupboards or storage areas, and remember to stay organized.

17   In conclusion, we have taken a look at one of China's most time-honored traditions. We've seen what feng shui is and then put this ancient art into practice. Although we looked at how feng shui works in a typical dorm room, you can apply the principles of feng shui to your home, office, or apartment.

18   Now as I walk into my dorm room, I no longer cringe at those wind chimes' loud clanging or avoid touching them at all costs. Instead, I swing the door right into them and smile. It may be noisy, but it sure is good chi.

Feng Shui   *by Liz Elegant*

Commentary

An outstanding informative speech, "Feng Shui" is well researched, clearly organized, and adroitly tailored to the audience. In addition to having students read the speech, you can show the video of it from *Speeches for Analysis and Discussion: A Videotape Supplement to The Art of Public Speaking, Eighth Edition.* Here is a synopsis of the speech.

Specific Purpose: To inform my audience about the principles of Feng Shui.

Central Idea: The aim of Feng Shui is to improve the flow of positive energy by the harmonious arrangement of one's physical surroundings.

Method of Organization: Topical

Introduction: The introduction of "Feng Shui" consists of paragraphs 1-3. The speaker begins in paragraph 1 with a brief story about her mother helping her move into her dorm room. Although this would not have been a good attention-getter for an audience of older students, it was perfectly suited to the speaker's classmates, almost all of whom were 18- to 19-year-old first-semester students. In paragraph 2 the speaker defines feng shui and takes note of its 4,000-year-old tradition. Because few of her listeners were familiar with feng shui, the speaker used an overhead transparency to show how the term is spelled and to help her classmates remember it.

In paragraph 3 the speaker again relates the topic to her audience and then establishes her credibility by mentioning her research on the topic. (The extent of that research will become evident in the number and variety of sources she cites as the speech progresses.) The introduction ends with a concise preview of the main points to be discussed in the body.

Body: The body of this speech provides a superb example of how to organize ideas for effective communication. The first main point runs from paragraph 4 through paragraph 7 and explicates the philosophy of feng shui. It deals with the role of chi as the major component of feng shui (paragraph 4), the manner in which feng shui seeks to improve the flow of chi by altering one's surroundings (paragraph 5), and the benefits of feng shui in both the home and the workplace (paragraphs 6-7).

A transition at the start of paragraph 8 marks the speaker's move to her second main point, in which she illustrates the principles of feng shui by showing how they can be applied in a typical dorm room (paragraphs 8-16). Given the fact that almost all her classmates were living in the dorms, this was an excellent way for the speaker to make her ideas more applicable to her audience. As in her first main point, the subpoints are clearly organized and explained. First the speaker discusses floor coverings, bed placement, and bed coverings (paragraphs 9-11). After a transition in paragraph 12, she turns to items that can be added to a dorm room: mirrors, lamps, plants, wind chimes, crystals, and water (paragraphs 13-15).

She ends the second main point by discussing the need for tidiness to maintain the flow of chi (paragraph 16).

The speech is also noteworthy for its use of testimony to support the speaker's ideas. Because the speaker is not an expert on feng shui, she repeatedly refers to the opinions of experts. All told, she cites six different books. These citations boost the speaker's credibility and make clear that she has done her research. Also noteworthy is the way the speaker relates her ideas to the audience. Not only does she illustrate the principles of feng shui by applying them to a college dorm room, but she repeatedly addresses the audience directly by using "you" and "your."

Conclusion: Consisting of paragraphs 17-18, the conclusion is concise and effective. Paragraph 17 reminds listeners of the significance of the topic and summarizes the main points. Paragraph 18 provides a sense of psychological unity by referring to the story told in the introduction. As with the rest of the speech, the conclusion is delivered conversationally and with superb eye contact.

———————————————

Sign Language

Leah Pogoriler

---

1   [The speaker begins by using Signed English to express the words, "You are my friend."] Do you know what I just told you? The message I communicated probably escaped most of you. Communication through hand motions is something we do all the time without even thinking about it. For most of us, it's a supplement to spoken language. But for many deaf and hearing-impaired people, sign language isn't just a supplement, it's a primary mode of communication.

2   I'm not an expert in sign language, but I've been interested in it for several years. My father is the treasurer for a group of deaf and hearing-impaired people, and I've attended some functions with that group. At those times, I had a chance to learn bits and pieces of sign language. I also had the chance to learn more in researching for this speech.

3   In the speech, I'd like to first give you a bit of background about sign language. Then I'd like to teach you how to sign one important sentence, the one I started with: "You are my friend." By sharing this sentence with you, I hope to help you realize that sign language is just as expressive as spoken language. Let's start with a little background.

4   There are two broad categories of sign language used in America. One is Signed English, and the other is American Sign Language. Both use most of the same hand gestures. Signed English usually uses one hand gesture for each spoken word and presents the signs in the same order as the spoken words. On the other hand, American Sign Language—also called ASL—doesn't always have exactly one sign for each spoken word, and might present them in a different order. This distinction will become clear during the demonstration.

5   No one knows exactly how many people use sign language as their primary language today. The National Center for Health Statistics estimates that about 20 million Americans have some sort of hearing impairment. Depending on the exact definition of "deafness," about half a million to 2 million of these people are deaf. Most sources agree that American Sign Language is the fourth most used language in the United States today, after English, Spanish, and French.

6   Some people think that sign language is a primitive substitute for spoken language, but in fact sign language is just as rich and expressive as spoken language. For example, Karen Nakamura states in the online *Deaf Resources Library* that American Sign Language "should not be considered in any way to be a broken, mimed, or gestural form of English." According to Nakamura, ASL is a complex, full, and natural language in its own right, with "its own beautiful grammar."

7   Keeping these points in mind about sign language, let's return to the sentence I started with and see if we can learn the signs for "You are my friend." [At this point, the speaker begins her demonstration of how to sign, "You are my friend." Each of the signs she discusses in paragraphs 7-13 is accompanied by a demonstration that explains the steps in making the sign.]

8   First, make the sign for "you" with your right hand. Extend your index finger and point at a classmate.

9   The word "are" is interesting because it starts with the letter "R." To make the sign for the letter "R," extend your index finger and wrap your next finger around it. This is the sign for the letter "R." Now we're going to make the word "are." Just put your fingertips under your chin and arc outward.

10   "My" is easy. It's just an open right hand. Put your palm inward on your chest.

11   "Friend" is a little trickier. It takes both hands. Extend your index finger on each hand, with your fingers folded down. And now bend each index finger. Now you're going to hook them together, hanging the back and knuckles of your right hand outward from your left hand. And now reverse, with the back and knuckles of your left hand hanging outward from your right hand.

12   Now please tell a classmate these four signs slowly: "You are my friend." And now try to sign the whole sentence quickly: "You are my friend."

13   What you just learned was Signed English. In American Sign Language, the word "are" is generally implied, so you wouldn't need to use it. The sentence in ASL would usually just be "You're my friend."

14   In closing, I hope you learned that sign language is just as expressive as spoken language. Think back to the way we signed "friend." That sign isn't an arbitrary combination of empty symbols. It's a visual depiction of the way friends really are—interdependent, interlocked. In addition to learning how to sign the sentence "You are my friend," I hope you'll also take away from this speech a new appreciation for the complexities of sign language.

Sign Language   *by Leah Pogoriler*

Commentary

A first-rate informative speech, "Sign Language" illustrates how a speaker can use a demonstration, as well as audience participation, to communicate ideas and to get listeners involved in the speech. Because so much of this speech revolves around the speaker's demonstration of how to sign the phrase "You are my friend," its impact can only be gauged by viewing the speech, which is available on *Speeches for Analysis and Discussion: A Videotape Supplement to The Art of Public Speaking, Eighth Edition.* Here is a synopsis.

Specific Purpose: To inform my audience about the richness of sign language and the steps involved in signing a simple sentence.

Central Idea: By learning how to sign a simple sentence, we can see that sign language is just as expressive as spoken language.

Method of Organization: Topical

Introduction: The introduction consists of the first three paragraphs. The speaker gains the audience's attention in paragraph 1 by making a series of gestures while she remains silent. Doing so arouses the curiosity of the audience, a move that the speaker reinforces by asking, "Do you know what I just told you?" After noting that, for most people, gestural communication is a supplement to spoken language, the speaker ends paragraph 1 by revealing that the topic of her speech is the use of sign language by deaf and hearing-impaired people.

Paragraph 2 provides an excellent example of how classroom speakers can establish their credibility. After acknowledging that she is not an expert on sign language, the speaker explains that she has long been interested in the topic as a result of her interaction with a group of deaf and hearing-impaired people, that she learned some sign language from this group, and that she has done further research on the topic. The fact that she cares about the subject and seems qualified to talk about it further boosts audience interest at this early stage of the speech.

Paragraph 3 begins with a concise preview statement of the two main points to be discussed in the body of the speech. The speaker then states her central idea: that sign language is just as expressive as spoken speech. She will reinforce this idea by restating it again in the body of the speech and in the conclusion. An excellent signpost—"Let's start with a little background"—completes the introduction and provides a bridge to the body of the speech.

Body: The first main point in the body provides background information about the two types of sign language used in the United States. In paragraph 4 the speaker identifies those types as Signed English and American Sign Language. In paragraph 5 she uses figures from the National Center for Health Statistics to show the number of Americans with hearing impairments and to document the fact that American Sign Language is the fourth most used language in the United States. In paragraph 6 she uses expert testimony to emphasize the richness and complexity of sign language. In keeping with the guidelines for using supporting materials, she identifies the source of her testimony (Karen Nakamura) and where the testimony was obtained (the online *Deaf Resources Library*).

In her second main point, the speaker demonstrates how to sign the sentence "You are my friend" (paragraphs 7-13). To make sure the audience can see her clearly, she steps away from the lectern, thereby facilitating a more conversational delivery that enhances direct communication with the audience. Although the speaker's explanation is clear from the transcript of the speech, the full effect of her presentation can only be gauged from the videotape. At each stage of her demonstration, the speaker times her actions perfectly with her words. When going through the steps of signing "You are my friend," she has a slow and easy pace that allows the audience to understand everything she is saying and to practice the gestures themselves.

Because of the speaker's demonstration, this speech is also highly instructive for illustrating the interaction of language and physical action. Based on words alone, the speaker's explanation in paragraphs 7-13 is as clear as it can be. But the effectiveness of the explanation increases dramatically once the speaker's physical demonstration is added to her words. If you show the videotape of the speech to students, have them read the text of the speech first so they can more fully appreciate the importance of the speaker's demonstration to the communication of her ideas.

Conclusion: The speaker concludes in paragraph 14. She begins by re-emphasizing her central idea that sign language is just as expressive as spoken English. Once again, she supplements her verbal message with physical action—this time when showing the manner in which the sign for "friends" depicts visually the interlocked and interdependent nature of true friends. She ends by noting that she hopes her audience has gained a fuller appreciation of the complexities of sign language in addition to learning how to sign "You are my friend." Here, as elsewhere, the speaker does an excellent job of connecting her specific demonstration to a larger set of ideas about the nature and importance of sign language.

CPR

Margaret Fugate

---

1   Imagine this: You're at home enjoying dinner with your family when you glance around the table and notice that your uncle suddenly has a painful and terrified look in his eyes. He grabs his chest and moments later falls to the floor, unconscious. Would you know how to handle the situation while everyone around you was panicking? Would you know that your uncle was probably suffering from a heart attack and needed cardiopulmonary resuscitation, or CPR?

2   As a lifeguard, I was required to become certified in CPR, and I have been certified for four years. In an emergency, it is not your job to treat the illness, but you are to keep the victim alive until trained medical professionals can come and take over for you. Tonight I want to explain to you the lifesaving process of surveying an emergency, contacting an emergency medical service, and starting CPR if needed. Let's start with the first step of surveying an emergency.

3   According to the American Red Cross, the first step in any emergency is to survey the scene. The most important thing to remember in administering first aid is to make sure you and the victim are safe—you don't want to put yourself or the victim in any more danger. If it is safe to proceed, and the victim is not moving, check the victim for responsiveness. Call the victim's name if you know it. Shake him or her and ask if he or she is okay. Then call for help.

4   Now that you have checked out the scene and know that the victim is unconscious, the second step in any emergency is to contact an emergency medical service. An emergency medical service can be any number of contacts. If the service is offered in your area, call 911. If 911 isn't offered in your area, call the hospital or the police directly. And if you do not have those numbers, you can always call the operator and he or she will connect you with the correct officials right away.

5   Designate one person to contact EMS. If there is no one around, you must call the emergency medical service yourself. Give them your name, address, the victim's name, condition, and the aid being given. It's particularly important to remember to let the dispatcher hang up first so you know that he or she has no more questions and that an ambulance can be sent right away.

6   After the EMS has been called, return to the victim and perform CPR. First, position the victim. Move the victim into the correct position, trying to keep the person's body as stable as possible, protecting the head and the back in case there has been any injury to the backbone or to the spinal cord.

7   Then place yourself next to the victim's shoulders and check the ABC's: Open the airway, check the breathing, and check the circulation or the pulse. First, open the airway. Take the hand that's closest to the victim's head and put it on his or her forehead. Next, take two fingers of the other hand and put it on the bony part of the victim's chin. Tilt back.

8   Next, check for breathing. Look, listen, and feel for the breath. Look for the chest rising and falling; listen for the breath in your ear; and feel the breath on your cheek. Do that for about five seconds. If there is no breathing, you must give two full breaths right away. Take two fingers of the hand that's on the victim's forehead and pinch the nose shut. Then take your mouth and seal the victim's mouth, giving two full breaths so that no air escapes while you're trying to breathe.

9   Then check the circulation or check the pulse. Take two fingers and put them on the center of the victim's throat and slide them into the groove that's next to the throat. Do this for about five seconds. If there is no pulse, chest compressions must be started right away.

10   Position your hands on the victim's chest. Take two fingers of your hand that's closest to the victim's feet and slide your hand up the bottom of the rib cage until you reach the notch that is directly beneath the breastbone. Then take your other hand and place it right next to your two fingers. Weave your fingers inside your other hand. According to the American Red Cross, while keeping the correct hand position, straighten your arms and lock your elbows so that your shoulders are directly over your hands. While in this position, enough pressure will be created to compress the chest one and a half to two inches for an adult. Do this fifteen times, counting out loud, "One and two and three and four and five and six and . . . "

11   Continue the cycle of breathing and compressions four times. After the fourth time, check the victim's pulse again, and if there is still no pulse, continue these cycles until the victim breathes again or until trained medical professionals arrive and can take over for you.

12   In conclusion, this short speech has shown you the importance of surveying an emergency, contacting an emergency medical service, and starting CPR. If you take the Red Cross course, you will learn more about the details of administering CPR.

13   Now let's go back to the emergency I mentioned at the beginning of my speech. Because of your knowledge of the three steps in administering CPR, you can be that vital link in an emergency and you can help save a life.

CPR   *by Margaret Fugate*

Commentary

As with most informative speeches about processes, "CPR" depends heavily upon its organization, delivery, and use of visual aids. It is especially effective in illustrating how a speaker can use a model—in this case a life-size dummy of a human torso borrowed from the Red Cross—to demonstrate how to perform the steps of a process. In addition to being reprinted in this manual, the speech is available on *Speeches for Analysis and Discussion: A Videotape Supplement to the Art of Public Speaking, Sixth Edition.* Here is a synopsis.

Specific Purpose: To inform my audience of the three steps to take when responding to a medical emergency.

Central Idea: When responding to a medical emergency you should take three main steps: survey the scene, contact emergency medical services, and start CPR.

Method of Organization: Chronological

Introduction: The introduction consists of the first two paragraphs. After gaining attention in paragraph 1 with a hypothetical example that relates the topic directly to her audience, the speaker reveals her topic in paragraph 2 and establishes her credibility by explaining that she has been certified to administer CPR for the past four years. She then completes the introduction by previewing the main points to be discussed in the body.

Body: Arranged in chronological order, the body takes listeners step by step through the process of responding to a medical emergency. By grouping the steps into three main points—surveying the scene (paragraph 3), calling emergency medical services (paragraphs 4-5), and administering CPR (paragraphs 6-11)—the speaker limits the number of main points so they are distinct and easy to recall. Although the third main point is developed in much more detail than the other two, it is the most important and complex step in the process of responding to a medical emergency. Rather than being problematic, the weight given to the third main point seems to be an accurate reflection of the process being explained in the speech.

As the speaker develops each main point, she explains her ideas clearly and straightforwardly. She avoids jargon and other technical language, and she uses plenty of connectives—especially signposts—to help listeners follow her from idea to idea. Most important, she uses her visual aid with great effectiveness. By practicing with the aid while rehearsing the speech, she was able to integrate it smoothly into the final presentation without breaking eye contact or stumbling in her delivery. Especially notable is the way she moves effortlessly between explaining her ideas, demonstrating those ideas by reference to the visual aid, and, at times, using her own body as a visual aid to help clarify key points.

Conclusion: The conclusion consists of paragraphs 12-13. After restating her main points, the speaker provides a sense of closure by briefly mentioning the example with which she opened the speech. The final sentence reinforces the importance of the topic and provides a somewhat dramatic closing line.

Mother of Love

Mei Chu

---

1   Imagine you are a small child lying on the dirt roads of Calcutta, India. You are severely dehydrated because no one you ask will offer you some of their water. You are weak and malnourished because you have not eaten for days. You are hysterically and painfully coughing from your tuberculosis. You have no family, no friends, and, it seems, no future.

2   As you begin to shut your eyes, gentle but strong arms reach out and pick you up off the dirt road. You regain enough strength to focus your eyes on the face before you. Her face is wrinkled with age and love and is like a ray of light in your dark world.

3   This is a familiar story for the many poor and needy of India that were touched by Mother Teresa. Her death in September of 1997 touched the nation and the world almost as much as her life had. I chose to speak about Mother Teresa today, because, like many people, I was moved by her compassion for the poor and her devotion to the needy. Through my research I have learned more about her outstanding character. In my speech, I would like to focus on her mission in life to serve humanity, the amazing work she accomplished, and the vision and hope she left behind. Let's begin with her mission in life.

4   Mother Teresa always felt a calling from God to serve in the world. She was born to an Albanian building contractor and his wife in 1910. In her quest to serve the needy, she joined the Sisters of Loretto at the age of eighteen. They were a community of Irish nuns who ran schools in India. Even there, she felt that her work was too limited, and she soon left her religious order to work in the slums of Calcutta. It was there that she established her goal in life. In her own words, she wanted to minister to the "unwanted, unloved, and uncared for."

5   With a small group of nuns at her side, she ran a makeshift clinic where the poor and dying could come to die in peace. She led this group, known as the Missionaries of Charity, to live out a simple life and to devote themselves entirely to the poorest of the poor. She and her sisters lived in poverty with only a single change of clothes and minimal possessions.

6   Her mission did not seek fame or wealth. It sought only comfort for the dying, the abandoned, and the outcast. When given a white Lincoln Continental from Pope Paul VI, she immediately auctioned it off to build a leper colony. Her only ambition, as biographer Srinivasa Murthy has written, was "responding to the human need, hour by hour, day by day, whether the need" was "for food, for love, for prayer, or for medicine."

7   In fulfilling her mission, Mother Teresa became known all over the world as a living saint because of her abundant good works. In Calcutta, she established homes for the dying and orphanages for abandoned children. In Bengal, she built a leper colony where she could aid the frail and the sick. In war-torn Beirut in 1982, she stopped a siege so she could rescue handicapped orphans from a nearby hospital.

8   Everywhere her calling took her, she was a savior in desperate times. Although she was a small woman, barely five feet tall, she was, to quote biographer Kathryn Spink, "strong-willed, resolute, determined and totally fearless, because God was on her side."

9   In 1979 she was awarded the Nobel Peace Prize. She, of course, skipped the lavish dinner and asked that her monetary prize of $190,000 be donated to the poor. In 1985 she was awarded the Presidential Medal of Freedom. Five years later, her health began to fade, but her compassion never did. Even after two heart attacks, she was reelected by her sisters to head the Missionaries of Charity. On September 5, 1997, at the age of 87, Mother Teresa passed away. Her funeral was attended by over 200 foreign delegates from 23 countries and was broadcast live on television across the world.

10   Although no longer able to carry on her work personally, Mother Teresa left behind a vision—a bright light that continues to inspire compassion for the poor and needy. In this light, AIDS victims feel love from an otherwise indifferent society. In this light, battered women are given a place to feel safe from the horrors of their lives. In this light, drug addicts find hope in an otherwise bleak future. As she stated, "Right here in the United States, I'm sure you know better than I do, there are many poor people that need love and compassion, that need your hands to serve them, that need your hearts to love them."

11   Since her death, Mother Teresa's compassion for the needy has continued to flow into the hearts of others who have decided to be a part of her mission. The original charity begun by Mother Teresa in 1950 now numbers more than 4,500 sisters in 126 countries around the world. The lasting appeal of her mission was stated well by biographer Anne Sebba, who wrote, shortly before Mother Teresa's death, that "She is, so transparently, someone who eschews the values of our age where success in life is measured by the number of trappings acquired, and in doing so she offers us hope that spirituality, not materialism, will triumph, hope that there are higher standards we can aspire to, and hope that maybe one day all the children in the world will be fed."

12   In conclusion, Mother Teresa followed a long road from her birth in Albania to her position as one of the most recognizable and beloved people on the globe. In her memorable life, she amazed the world with countless acts of mercy and compassion. To paupers, to lepers, to orphans, she was the mother of love. In the words of one of her biographers, she was "a spiritual giant . . . in a world torn with greed, selfishness, and oppression."

13 Mother Teresa once said of herself, "By blood and origin I am Albanian. My citizenship is Indian. I am a Catholic nun. As to my calling, I belong to the world. As to my heart, I belong entirely to the heart of Jesus."

Mother of Love   *by Mei Chu*

Commentary

"Mother of Love" provides a good example of an informative speech about a person and is also available on the videotape of student speeches that accompanies this edition of *The Art of Public Speaking*. Here is a synopsis of it.

Specific Purpose: To inform my audience about the life of Mother Teresa.

Central Idea: In addition to the many good works she accomplished during her life, Mother Teresa left behind a vision that continues to inspire others to help the poor and needy.

Method of Organization: Topical

Introduction: The vivid scenario in the opening two paragraphs relates the topic directly to the audience and gets them involved in the speech. Paragraph 3 reveals the topic, establishes the speaker's credibility, and provides a clear preview of the main points to be covered in the body. In all respects, this is an outstanding introduction.

Body: Organized in topical order, the body contains three main points. The first summarizes the development of Mother Teresa's mission in life (paragraphs 4-6). The second focuses on the good works Mother Teresa achieved in fulfilling that mission (paragraphs 7-9). The third explains how Mother Teresa's vision has inspired others, after her death, to continue the work of her mission (paragraphs 10-11).

In developing these points, the speaker uses a blend of historical facts, revealing anecdotes, and well-chosen quotations. Rather than recounting names, dates, and places as if she were writing an encyclopedia article, she highlights major aspects of Mother Teresa's life and achievements and explains those aspects clearly and engagingly.

Conclusion: The conclusion consists of paragraphs 11-12. Paragraph 11 provides an excellent summary of the speaker's main points, while paragraph 12 brings the speech to an end with a strong quotation from Mother Teresa herself.

Dandelions: The Uncommon Weed

Susan R. Hirsch

---

1. What starts out yellow and ends up as a fluffy white ball? If I told you it was *Taraxacum officinale*, would that ring a bell? What if I told you it was of the family *Compositae*—would that excite your senses?

2 If you haven't figured it out by now, the subject of which I am speaking is none other than the common, ordinary dandelion. Yes, those bright, yellow flowers which we all, as kids, eagerly snapped off the stems while chanting the words, "Mama had a baby and its head popped off!" I'm sure all of us remember having blown the fluffy white tufts into the air above.

3 Although we have these pleasant memories from our childhoods, most home-owners consider the dandelion as the most irritating and troublesome of all the weeds—partly because their deep root system makes them almost impossible to get rid of. However, from a botany class, I learned that the dandelion, in reality, is a very useful plant. From further research, I discovered that the dandelion has both wide medical and culinary uses. Today, I will explain these uses to you. We'll start by looking at the dandelion's medicinal value.

4 The scientific name of the dandelion, *Taraxacum officinale*, testifies to its value as a medicine. According to Edward Spencer, in his book *All About Dandelions*, *Taraxacum* refers to medical properties of a plant found in Persia. *Officinale*, the species name, when given to any plant, indicates that it is used by druggists and pharmacists.

5 Throughout history, dandelions have been used to help cure various medical ailments. Dandelions were reportedly used by the ancient Egyptians to treat kidney and stomach disorders. The dandelion's many cures were recorded by Arabian physicians in the tenth century. And in sixteenth-century England, dandelion waters were used in the treatment of illness among the nobility.

6 Today, scientists know as a fact that the dandelion has great medicinal value. According to Mea Allan, in her book *Weeds*, the plant contains chemicals that stimulate blood circulation, the liver, digestive organs, and especially the kidneys and bladder—which has gained the dandelion fame as a so-called "potty herb." Audrey Hatfield, in her book *How to Enjoy Your Weeds*, says that a tea made from dandelion roots or leaves is helpful in relieving many conditions. It helps relieve liver and lung disorders, and it helps treat anemia. In addition, it serves as a mild laxative and is helpful in aiding digestion. Hatfield also suggests that dandelion tea is highly effective in cases of eczema, scurvy, and similar skin conditions. So valuable is the dandelion in treating medical ailments that 100,000 pounds are imported into the United States each year for this purpose.

7   If you have no interest in using dandelions for your health, you can still find them of use in the kitchen. Historically, dandelions have been used as food for thousands of years. According to an article in *National Wildlife* magazine, they were among the original bitter herbs of Passover, a Jewish holiday which commemorates the Hebrews' liberation from slavery in Egypt. The English have been using dandelions in salads since the Middle Ages. And currently, many ethnic groups in the United States—such as Greeks, Poles, French, Italians, and even the Amish—all eat dandelions.

8   All parts of the dandelion can be utilized to make a variety of delicious foods. Its bitter leaves, if picked before the yellow flowers appear, can be added to a salad. The leaves are usually mixed with other vegetables to vary their flavor. The dandelion's roots may be roasted in an oven, then ground and used as a caffeine-free coffee substitute. The golden yellow flowers can be steeped in water and then used to produce a delicious wine. And the entire dandelion plant may be used to make beer.

9   In addition to being tasty, dandelions are extremely nutritious. According to Peter Gail, a professor of economic botany at Cleveland State University, "The dandelion's nutrient qualities read almost like a One-a-Day vitamin." Dandelion greens have 50 percent more vitamin C than tomatoes, twice as much protein as eggplant, and double the fiber of asparagus. They have as much iron as spinach and more potassium than bananas.

10   All of this may sound strange to you, but not to the people of Vineland, New Jersey, the official Dandelion Capital of the World. In Vineland, the dandelion has grown from being a $68,000 crop in 1977 to almost a half-million-dollar crop today. At the beginning of the season, dandelions sell for as much as $1.25 a pound. Most of Vineland's dandelion crop ends up in restaurants and markets in Baltimore, Philadelphia, and New York City.

11   Every March the town hosts its annual seven-course dandelion dinner. The menu consists of dandelion soup, dandelion salad, dandelion sausage, dandelions and vegetables, dandelion beef roulade, dandelion sweet cup, and dandelion wine. Tickets for the dinner sell for $25 apiece, with people coming from as far away as Ohio. Former Vineland mayor Patrick Fiorilli has humorously summed up Vineland's position in the dandelion world: "In your yard, you go out and pull the dandelions out of the grass. Our farmers pull the grass out of the dandelions."

12   As we have seen, then, the dandelion is a greatly misunderstood plant. Despite its reputation as an irritating weed, in reality it is a very useful plant. Having various medical and culinary uses, the dandelion stands as one of the most underrated and least appreciated plants in the world. Hopefully, in the future, more people will come to recognize the usefulness of the dandelion, thereby reestablishing this "common" weed as a truly uncommon plant.

Dandelions: The Uncommon Weed   *by Susan R. Hirsch*

Commentary

Creative, crisply organized, and packed with fascinating supporting materials, "Dandelions: The Uncommon Weed" is a fine example of how to produce a captivating informative speech on a seemingly ordinary topic. For the convenience of instructors, the speech is also available on *Speeches for Analysis and Discussion: A Videotape Supplement to The Art of Public Speaking, Sixth Edition*. Here is a synopsis of it.

Specific Purpose: To inform my audience about the medical and culinary uses of dandelions.

Central Idea: Despite its reputation as an irritating weed, the dandelion's medical and culinary properties make it a very useful plant.

Method of Organization: Topical

Introduction: The speaker opens with a series of three rhetorical questions that capture attention by arousing the audience's curiosity. She follows, in paragraph 2, by revealing the subject of her speech and by relating it directly to the audience. In paragraph 3 she establishes her credibility and previews the main points to be discussed in the body. All in all, this is an excellent example of an introduction for a speech to inform.

Body: Organized in topical order, the body of this speech contains two main points. The first, running from paragraph 4 through paragraph 6, explores the medical uses of dandelions. After explaining that the scientific name of the dandelion, *Taraxacum officinale*, indicates that the plant is used by druggists and pharmacists (paragraph 4), the speaker notes some of the ways it has been employed throughout history to cure medical ailments (paragraph 5). In paragraph 6 she relates what modern medical science knows about the medical value of dandelions. Because she is not a medical expert, she is careful to identify the sources of her information.

In paragraph 7 the speaker turns to her second main point, which continues through paragraph 11. This point deals with the culinary uses of dandelions and, like the first main point, is brought to life with a variety of intriguing supporting materials. In paragraph 7 the speaker provides historical facts about some of the ways different cultures have used dandelions as food through the years. In paragraph 8 she notes how dandelions can be used in salads, as the basis for a caffeine-free coffee substitute, and to produce wine or beer. In paragraph 9 she cites Peter Gail, a professor of economic botany at Cleveland State University, to establish the nutritional value of dandelions.

Paragraphs 10-11 present the story of Vineland, New Jersey, "Dandelion Capital of the World." Entertaining as well as informative, the story brings the speaker's ideas to life and gives them human interest. Its details about the size of Vineland's dandelion crop, the price per pound of dandelions, and the seven-course dandelion dinner are crucial. One way to communicate this to students is to have them imagine how much less effective the speech would have been if the speaker had merely said, "Dandelions are very important to the people of Vineland, New Jersey."

It is also worth noting how clearly the body of the speech is organized and how the speaker uses ample connectives to help listeners keep track of her ideas. Equally important, those ideas are presented in straightforward, nontechnical language. Finally, if you show the speech on videotape, be sure to have students note how effectively the speaker presents her visual aids and integrates them smoothly with the rest of her speech.

Conclusion: The conclusion consists of paragraph 12 and is short and to the point. The phrase "As we have seen" cues listeners that the speech is coming to an end. The speaker then summarizes her main points and ends by restating her central idea—that, despite its negative reputation, the dandelion is a very useful plant.

———————————————

The Thrilling World of Roller Coasters

Brian Dombkowski

---

1   What primordial urge sends us racing groundward at speeds that would be illegal on the interstate? No one knows. But roller coasters certainly satisfy it magnificently. People across America are lining up to ride these increasingly bizarre contraptions. Made of steel and wood, each one is calculated to be taller, faster, steeper, and, above all, scarier than anything you've ever seen before.

2   I'm a roller coaster enthusiast who has ridden some of the fastest and most exotic coasters in existence. I've also done a considerable amount of research on this thrilling topic. Today I would like to discuss America's addiction to the thrill of roller coaster riding and then present to you the past, present, and future of the roller coaster, allowing you to experience, through the use of videotape, what waits for you at today's top amusement parks.

3   Why are today's coasters so popular? Probably because the moment you step off one and regain your composure, you hesitate and then you get right back in line to do it again. Amusement parks and their marketing teams know this. The $4-billion amusement park industry is responding to this demand. Exit polls show that what brings customers back to parks are thrill rides, and nothing can possibly compare to a new roller coaster.

4   According to *Smithsonian* magazine, Cedar Point, Ohio, home to the Magnum XL-200, has attracted 3 million people just four times in the past twenty years—three of those times were after opening a new roller coaster. The market for riders is huge, boasting an estimated 214 million riders every year. The competition for these thrill-seekers is fierce, and consequently a sort of coaster war has erupted between parks.

5   What fuels all this excitement? University of Wisconsin psychologist Frank Farley, a leading researcher on the thrill-seeking personality, explains that sometimes the normal individual needs "a three-minute burst of stimuli to remind us that sitting at home in front of the television and waiting for one's pension isn't what it's really all about."

6   However, thrill-seeker or not, the question most of us ask ourselves as we are nearing the top of a coaster's incline is, "Who would ever build such a contraption?" The short answer is, "The Russians." The Russians built ice slides as early as the fifteenth century in St. Petersburg. Consequently, coasters were deemed "Russian mountains" for the next four centuries.

7   The first American coaster was built in 1884 by Lamarcus Thompson. Thompson's attendants would push a railroad car up an incline and it would coast down the

422 SPEECHES FOR ANALYSIS AND DISCUSSION

other side at 6 miles per hour over 450 feet of track. After that the coaster trade took off, and by the time the Depression hit, the U.S. had over 1,500 roller coasters—so many in fact that the Soviet Union began calling them "American mountains."

8 Unfortunately, the coaster declined greatly in popularity during the Depression. But now, for the first time since the 1920s, the number of coasters in this country is on the rise. According to the same *Smithsonian* article cited earlier, coasters numbered 147 in 1979. Today, however, over 170 of these momentum machines terrify riders—and wait until you see what you've been missing. Let's take a look at some of today's hottest rides.

9 We'll begin with a trip to Busch Gardens in Florida for a ride on the Loch Ness Monster. Nessie is thirteen stories tall and travels at 60 miles per hour. Riders must face an initial drop of 114 feet followed by a second 52-foot drop. It puts riders two and three quarters times through its famous 60-foot interlocking loops. Here riders experience 7 Gs— which means a 150-pound person would feel like he or she weighed in excess of 1,000 pounds.

10 Next we travel to Six Flags Great America outside Chicago to ride the Shockwave. When it was built in 1988, it was the world's tallest and fastest looping coaster. Boasting a 155-foot banked drop, riders accelerate to 65 miles per hour, only to enter a 130-foot teardrop loop. Passengers must endure two boomerang turns and two corkscrew loops. The Shockwave changes elevation sixteen times and turns riders upside down seven times. As you can see, it gives you quite a ride.

11 Now we venture off to the distant land of Six Flags Magic Mountain in California to ride the Ninja. This is an example of the suspended roller coaster. The track above suspends the coaster as the terrified riders swing below like a pendulum at up to 110 degrees to the vertical axis. Traveling at 55 miles per hour, the Ninja inflicts 4 G's on riders. There are only two suspended roller coasters in the United States, and this is the only one on the west coast.

12 Finally, we have the Magnum XL-200 in Cedar Point, Ohio. Welcome aboard the world's tallest and fastest roller coaster. This roller coaster is 30 feet higher than any other coaster in the world. The initial drop of 201 feet is taller than the space shuttle *Discovery* and propels riders at a record-breaking 72 miles per hour. Keep in mind that you are traveling at speeds illegal on the interstate.

13 So far we have seen that the normal individual's need for a three-minute burst of stimuli has, in part, produced a growing demand for thrill rides and has helped launch a coaster war between parks. Then we looked at the roller coaster's past and present. Now I'd like to show you what's in store for us in the future.

14 For the roller coaster, power and prestige comes from technology. The latest design on the drawing board is the pipeline coaster. It merits the name because instead of rolling on top of the tracks, like a train, it will be suspended between them in a sort of pipeline. In this manner, the roller coaster can simulate an airplane's capabilities and do such things as snap rolls. As one designer put it, "Your heart moves forward as your body rotates around it." If you have trouble convincing yourself to ride today's roller coasters, tomorrow's will certainly not be any tamer.

15   In conclusion, you can see how one can easily become addicted to the thrill of roller-coaster riding, in part because the rides keep getting more elaborate. If you still don't want to ride roller coasters, you're not alone. The leading designer of roller coasters, a 59-year-old former rocket scientist, suffers from motion sickness and won't ride his own contraptions because, he says, "My rides have gotten too wild and crazy for me." But it's these too wild rides that bring 200 million riders every year into amusement parks and have helped rekindle the popularity of the roller coaster.

16   Thank you, and I hope you enjoyed your ride through the thrilling world of roller coasters.

The Thrilling World of Roller Coasters   *by Brian Dombkowski*

Commentary

"The Thrilling World of Roller Coasters" is an outstanding informative speech. Not only is it well-researched and effectively delivered, but it provides a fine model of how to use videotape as a visual aid. In addition to having students read the speech, you can show the video of it from *Speeches for Analysis and Discussion: A Videotape Supplement to The Art of Public Speaking, Sixth Edition.* Here is a synopsis.

Specific Purpose: To inform my audience about the past, present, and future of roller coasters.

Central Idea: Americans love roller coasters, which have had an up-and-down history, currently offer a wide range of rides, and will become even more daring in the future.

Method of Organization: Topical

Introduction: The introduction consists of paragraphs 1-2. After opening with a question to gain attention, the speaker reveals his topic, establishes his credibility, and provides a succinct preview statement. He could have improved the introduction by relating the topic more directly to his listeners—by noting, for example, that roller coasters are extremely popular among college students.

Body: The body is arranged topically and contains four main points. After explaining the attraction of roller coasters (paragraphs 3-5), the speaker discusses their history (paragraphs 6-8), the major kinds of rides available today (paragraphs 9-12), and the future of roller coaster technology (paragraphs 13-14). The subpoints are clearly presented, and the speaker uses a combination of transitions, signposts, and internal summaries to help his listeners move with him from point to point.

The most striking feature of the body of the speech is its use of videotape as a visual aid in main point three (paragraphs 9-12). As part of his research, the speaker sent away for a twelve-minute promotional tape from Arrow Dynamics, the world's largest manufacturer of roller coasters. He then edited excerpts from that tape (minus the sound) onto a second tape, which he timed to fit precisely with his words. By using a remote control during the speech, he was able to start and stop the tape exactly when he wanted, so it meshed flawlessly with the rest of his speech.

One of the difficulties students encounter when using videotape is making sure it functions as an adjunct to the speaker's words rather than becoming a substitute for the speaker. This is not a problem in "The Thrilling World of Roller Coasters." Even though the speaker shows almost two minutes of videotape, he continues to speak the entire time, and the tape is perfectly integrated with his verbal message. All in all, this is an outstanding example of how videotape can be used in classroom speeches.

It is also worth noting how well the speaker supports and explains his ideas throughout the body of the speech. In addition to using video clips to demonstrate the major kinds of roller-coaster rides, he uses an excellent blend of statistics, examples, and testimony. Had he simply shown the videotape without fully researching and developing his ideas, the speech would have been much less effective.

Conclusion: The conclusion consists of the last two paragraphs. Although the speaker does not summarize his main points, he clearly signals the end of the speech and provides an effective sense of closure. His final words—"I hope you enjoyed your ride through the thrilling world of roller coasters"—are perfectly suited to the content of his speech and end his presentation on a strong, upbeat note.

Edible Insects

Chinaka Steady

---

1   As the days of summer descend upon us, we await lazy days, beach parties, deep suntans, and, of course, insects. We may look forward to seeing grasshoppers jump through meadows and admiring backyard butterflies fluttering through flowers, yet we dread being stung by those yellow and black villains. But the future may bring insects an extra step closer to us—not so much for their stings, but for their food value.

2   I realize this idea of consuming those small, creepy and sometimes hairy creatures might turn one's stomach and boggle the mind. However the idea may not seem too unusual once we understand what it involves.

3   As a biology major, I have been enrolled in a course entitled "Insects as Food" in which I learned about edible insects people can and do consume. Today I'd like to share some of this information with you by first exposing the presence of insects in our everyday foods. Then we'll consider a history of edible insects. Next their nutritional value. Finally we'll see what the possibilities are for making insects a more prevalent part of our diet.

4   To begin, we must realize that while the idea of eating insects may be a new one, we unconsciously consume them with our everyday foods. Ronald Taylor's *Butterflies in My Stomach* informs us that lettuce, bread, corn, peanut butter, tomato sauces, and fruit juices contain insects or insect fragments. However, these small defects or, if you will, bugs in the food system should probably not be considered as dangerous as chicken salmonella or other food poisoning. As entomologist Gene DeFoliart, head of the food insect research division program here on campus, explains, "Unlike the dangerous chemicals in our foods, sometimes the insects in food are more nutritious than the food they are in."

5   In fact, our ancestors relied on insects for mere survival. Taylor describes a time—one and a quarter million years ago—when we were supposedly apes in the African continent, surviving by eating insects during droughts. More recently, the 1855 Dakota and Utah settlers survived by consuming the very grasshoppers that had plagued their crops. And today Dr. DeFoliart indicates that in some of the world's tropical areas, people consume insects as part of their daily diet. For example, insects comprise 40 percent of the protein intake in southern Zaire, caterpillars are an inexpensive agricultural alternative in China, and the University of Mexico documents 270 insects consumed regularly among rich and poor alike in that country. These and at least 60 other countries use insects in their diets.

6   The insects' taste and nutritional value make them an excellent food source. Their nutritional value is supported by figures from the consumer and food economic research division. As you can see on this chart, if we take 100 grams or a quarter pound or a hamburger size portion of cooked meats such as chicken, perch, ham, and beef, the average protein content is 23 grams and the energy content is 240 calories. If we take an equivalent serving portion of cooked caterpillars, termites, and weevils, the average protein content is 15 grams higher and the energy content is nearly double that of our usual meats.

7   What is more striking is that, except for niacin, these insects also surpass the traditional meats in mineral content. In our usual meats, the mineral content might be a few or up to a couple dozen milligrams, whereas in these insects, it may be several or even hundreds of milligrams.

8   However, this idea of using insects for their nutritional value is only that—an idea—unless a market is created. Dr. DeFoliart, who in the next few years plans to introduce edible insects to the American market, realizes the stomach-turning nature of such topics. Indeed, while individuals who sampled edible insects accepted their taste, the fact that they looked like insects was the major complaint.

9   Therefore, to his team of twenty-five scientific advisors, DeFoliart has added food engineers who can pellet and flake insects into more desirable looking snack foods. Some of his candidates include dried acheta crickets, the honey bee pupae, and the *galleria* larvae, a small caterpillar which tastes like bacon. He will probably also emphasize to the health-minded population that unlike potato chips and french fries, which contain saturated fats, these insects contain the healthier unsaturated fats.

10   Most important, Dr. DeFoliart strategically intends to introduce edible insects not only to the general public but to those upper echelons who can afford other odd foods like escargot and caviar, which are no more than snails and fish eggs. The belief is that this approach will cause people to treat edible insects as a status food as opposed to denouncing them as pet food. Edible insects might also be legitimized by books such as Ronald Taylor and Barbara Carter's *Entertaining with Insects*, which includes 95 recipes for hors d'oeuvres, entrées, and other uses of insects.

11   In conclusion, I'll admit that the idea may indeed bother some people. Yet we should bear in mind that insects are consumed unconsciously with our everyday foods, historically they ensured the survival of some of our most distant ancestors, and currently they nourish many people in various parts of the world.

12   In the future, the possibility of expanding insects as a food source might not receive an available space at every single dinner table. But when we sit down and consider options for feeding the world's hungry, insects are likely to be on the table. Given these possibilities, the animal kingdom might eventually experience sibling rivalry between dogs and insects over who really is humanity's best friend.

Edible Insects   *by Chinaka Steady*

Commentary

Superbly researched, crisply organized, and engagingly delivered, "Edible Insects" is an exceptional informative speech. In addition to having students read the text of the speech, you can also show them the videotape, which is available on *Speeches for Analysis and Discussion: A Videotape Supplement to The Art of Public Speaking, Sixth Edition*. Here is a synopsis of the speech.

Specific Purpose: To inform my audience about the history, current use, nutritional value, and future of insects as a human food source.

Central Idea: Edible insects have long been consumed by people in various parts of the world, are high in nutritional value, and may one day find their way onto our own dinner plates.

Method of Organization: Topical

Introduction: Running through paragraph 3, the introduction begins in a fairly leisurely fashion as the speaker arouses curiosity about his topic by discussing the upcoming days of summer. After revealing his topic at the end of paragraph 1, he uses paragraph 2 to calm the queasiness some listeners might feel about the prospect of using insects as a food source. In paragraph 3 he establishes his credibility by referring to the class he is taking on "Insects as Food." He also provides an excellent preview statement that lets the audience know exactly what to listen for in the body of the speech.

Body: "Edible Insects" contains four main points. The first, developed in paragraph 4, explains that we unconsciously consume insects with our everyday foods—especially in items such as lettuce, bread, corn, peanut butter, tomato sauces, and fruit juices. Recognizing that this might be disturbing to some listeners, the speaker notes that the presence of insects in our food is far less problematic than such things as chicken salmonella and food poisoning. The quotation at the end of the paragraph provides a bit of wry humor and is consistent with the light touch the speaker employs throughout the speech.

In paragraph 5 the speaker turns to his second main point, in which he shows that humans have long used insects as a food source. The series of brief examples at the end of the paragraph is especially effective because it demonstrates that many people in the world today consciously consume insects as part of their daily diet. It is also worth noting how the speaker takes care, here and elsewhere, to document the sources of his information.

The speaker's third main point is that the nutritional value of insects makes them an excellent food source (paragraphs 6-7). Using figures he had found in his research, he shows that many insects are higher in protein and energy content than are beef, fish, and poultry. He also shows that insects are higher in minerals such as zinc, magnesium, and calcium. As can be seen from the videotape of the speech, the speaker uses a chart in this section to help communicate his ideas. Although some listeners though the chart was a bit small, the speaker does an excellent job of explaining its meaning.

In his fourth main point, the speaker explores current efforts to develop a market for edible insects in the United States (paragraphs 8-10). His primary source here is Dr. Gene DeFoliart, the speaker's biology professor and an internationally recognized expert on the subject of edible insects. In addition to taking Dr. DeFoliart's course on "Insects as Food," the speaker interviewed him outside of class. Indeed, this speech provides a fine example of how students can use information gained from classes and interviews in their speeches—as long as they augment that information with additional research.

Conclusion: The speaker begins his conclusion in paragraph 11 with a concise summary of his main points. In paragraph 12 he reinforces the central idea and brings the speech to an end with a clever closing line.

———————————————

The Hidden World of Perfumes

Kyle Knoeck

---

1   Few would dispute the importance of petroleum to the world economy. In fact, some argue that in 1991 the United States and its allies fought a war in the Persian Gulf over this liquid that, at current prices, costs less than half a cent per fluid ounce and doesn't even smell all that good.

2   Imagine the lengths one might go to protect access to a liquid that, in some cases, costs over $100 per ounce—20,000 times the cost of crude petroleum. Wars may be fought again—advertising wars—this time to claim a portion of the international perfume market, which, according to *Smithsonian* magazine, has sales of $10 billion each year.

3   Ever since the ancient Mesopotamians first used perfume in burial rites over 4,000 years ago, humankind has developed an obsession with scent and is willing to pay amazingly high prices for something as intangible as a smell.

4   Puzzled by my own inexplicable fondness for aftershave, I've spent some time researching our culture's partiality to perfume. Even if you're someone who doesn't especially like to dabble Chanel or Polo behind your ears, you probably smell someone else's fragrance every day. Or maybe you use a product made with perfumes—such as soap, facial tissue, insecticides, or even cattle feed.

5   With that in mind, we'll first discuss the ingredients of perfume and then we'll examine some of the new commercial applications of perfume. Let's start with the ingredients.

6   Quite likely, you think of perfume only as a smelly liquid. But many connoisseurs of the stuff would disagree. In fact, perfume is a complex mixture of many ingredients.

7   The most important ingredients of any perfume are a variety of aromatic oils, usually called essential oils. According to Edwin Morris in his book *Fragrance*, essential oils have two important properties—they easily evaporate and become gas at room temperature, and they are detectable to us as fragrance in unimaginably minute quantities. The essential oil of the vanilla bean, for example, can be detected as a fragrance when present in the air at amounts of just two parts per million.

8   Some essential oils are found in animal products. According to Diane Ackerman in her book *A Natural History of the Senses*, the best known of these may be musk, a red, jelly-like secretion found in the gut of an East Asian deer.

9   As *Smithsonian* magazine reports, however, most essential oils are extracted from one of 2,000 different species of flowering plants. These plants may be as exotic as the fragrant ylang-ylang tree that grows on the Comoro Islands, or as common as the rose.

10   But even oils from common plants may be difficult to come by. The finest rose oil in the world can only be found in roses grown near the town of Kazanlâk in Bulgaria. It takes nearly 800 pounds of jasmine flowers to produce just one pound of the oil found in its petals. And oils can be expensive. Iris absolute, an essential oil tortuously extracted from the root of the iris, costs nearly $437 per ounce.

11   Not all perfume ingredients come from natural sources. Synthetic ingredients can imitate or enhance the smells of natural essential oils and can greatly reduce the cost of a perfume. In the case of the perfume classic Chanel No. 5, an artificial aldehyde provides the perfume with its signature scent. But Chanel may be the exception that proves the rule. Synthetic ingredients rarely compare in quality to natural ingredients. As French perfumer Françoise Martin explains, "It's like silk against polyester. You cannot replace the touch of nature."

12   When creating a new fragrance, a perfumer will usually draw upon the scents of between 30 and 50, and sometimes up to 500, different oils, hoping to find the perfect blend of smells. Of course, the perfume or cologne you buy in the store isn't just a bottle of essential oils. When marketed, the oils are dissolved in alcohol. A high-quality perfume will contain up to 25 percent essential oils and 75 percent alcohol; an inexpensive *eau de toilette*, just 2 to 4 percent essential oils. If the perfume is to be used in a product other than a cosmetic fragrance, the oils may be dissolved in something other than alcohol, but these fragrant oils remain the key ingredient in any manufactured scent.

13   Having explored the ingredients that go into creating these pricey odors called perfume, it's important to remember that perfumes are found in more places than wrists and ears. Researchers are learning how perfumes can affect human behavior, and we will now examine the new commercial applications of perfume that this research is bringing.

14   Doctors William Dember and Joel Warm at the University of Cincinnati have found that people who receive regular puffs of perfume can perform much better at tasks that require sustained attention. The scents of peppermint and muguet can spark alertness, and *New Scientist* magazine reports that applications of this research could find the best use in jobs like air-traffic control, quality-control inspections, and long-distance truck-driving, where a lapse of concentration would prove fatal.

15   Don't let it be said that any enterprising businessperson would let this opportunity slide by. The *Los Angeles Times* reveals that some companies in Japan are already delivering small doses of perfume via the air-conditioning ducts to improve worker productivity. Tokyo's Kajima Corporation uses a lemon scent in the morning to wake workers up, rose to calm them during lunch, and tree-trunk oil to perk them up in the afternoon.

16   Businesses may also one day use perfume to complement Muzak. As last January's issue of *American Demographics* reports, one shopping mall in Minneapolis has experimented with the idea of using perfume in the air to increase sales, and an experiment at a Philadelphia jewelry counter found that a floral scent in the air seemed to make prospective customers linger longer.

17   The new commercial applications of perfume do raise some thorny issues, however. *American Demographics* points out that workers and customers may not like the idea of being subconsciously influenced by smell. Other issues arise because, in some people, perfumes can trigger allergic reactions. According to the national Center for Environmental health Strategies, the Food and Drug Administration has acknowledged that perfumes can cause reactions, including headaches, sore throats, confusion, and dizziness.

18   The issue is starting to come to public attention. *The Wall Street Journal* reports a movement afoot in Los Angeles to ban perfume from certain public places. Perfume wearers are learning that they have to consider those around them who might suffer from reactions to their fragrance. This issue is sure to be one with which businesses will have to contend as well if they decide to use perfume in their air systems.

19   As we have seen, perfume is much more than a smelly liquid. These complex mixtures of aromatic oils may make us work harder and spend harder, if they don't trigger an allergic reaction first. Today we have explored perfume's pungent ingredients and some new uses for these fragrant creations.

20   It seems almost absurd to think that perfume is thousands of times more expensive than a precious energy resource like petroleum. But on the other hand, no matter how far you can drive your car on petroleum, oil is not the kind of fragrance you would want in your cologne, hair spray, room deodorizer, or even, I suppose, in your cattle feed.

The Hidden World of Perfumes   *by Kyle Knoeck*

Commentary

Clear, entertaining, and sharply organized, "The Hidden World of Perfumes" is a superior informative speech that illustrates many of the principles discussed in the textbook. It is also available on *Speeches for Analysis and Discussion: A Videotape Supplement to The Art of Public Speaking, Fifth Edition.* Here is a brief synopsis.

Specific Purpose: To inform my audience about the production and uses of perfumes in today's world.

Central Idea: A complex blend of many ingredients, the most important of which are essential oils, perfumes are being put to a number of new uses in today's commercial world.

Method of Organization: Topical

Introduction: The introduction consists of paragraphs 1-5. In addition to gaining attention, the comparison in paragraphs 1-2 between the cost of petroleum and the cost of perfume indicates the importance of the topic. So too does the statement in paragraph 3 that perfumes have been used by humankind for at least 4,000 years. In paragraph 4 the speaker uses a touch of humor to establish his credibility and to relate the subject directly to his listeners. The droll tone of this paragraph is appropriate for the topic and crops up again in several places throughout the speech. Paragraph 5 provides a succinct preview statement and a strong lead-in to the body of the speech.

Body: Arranged in topical order, the body contains two main points, the first of which deals with the ingredients of perfumes (paragraphs 6-12). After explaining the nature of essential oils, the key ingredients in any perfume (paragraph 7), the speaker distinguishes among three kinds of essential oils—those that come from animal products (paragraph 8), those that come from flowering plants (paragraphs 9-10), and those that come from synthetic ingredients (paragraph 11). The speaker then completes his first main point by relating how essential oils are combined with other ingredients-usually alcohol—to produce the final product (paragraph 12).

An excellent transition in paragraph 13 moves the speaker into his second main point, which deals with the new commercial applications of perfumes generated by research on the links between perfume and human behavior (paragraphs 14-18). The speaker begins by summarizing some of the major findings of that research (paragraph 14). He then explains how businesses are experimenting with perfumes to improve customer sales and worker productivity (paragraphs 15-16). He brings the body of the speech to a close by examining some of the ethical and health issues raised by the new commercial applications of perfume (paragraphs 17-18).

Although a speech on the topic of perfumes could easily become either too technical or too trivial for a classroom presentation, the speaker steers between both of these potential pitfalls. With few exceptions, he avoids technical language and explains his ideas in clear, familiar, everyday terms. He provides a wealth of fascinating supporting materials from reliable sources, and he consistently identifies his sources for the audience. Nor does he make the mistake of overestimating his audience's knowledge of the topic. Throughout the body of the speech, he explains ideas clearly, fully, and credibly.

Conclusion: The conclusion consists of the last two paragraphs. After a quick summary of his main points in paragraph 19, the speaker adroitly ties the entire speech together in paragraph 20 by referring back to ideas he had broached in the introduction about the cost of perfume and its use in a wide range of commercial products. The closing words—about the use of perfumes in cattle feed—ends the speech on a clever note.

Nothing to Sneeze At

Jeffrey Moran

---

1   You feel it welling up inside you, this delicate tingling, as if your every nerve were firing at once. You want to grope for the newspaper, your homework—anything—but you no longer control your body.

2   These seconds of helpless anticipation seem like an eternity, but then the spell is broken. You crash forward, your muscles contracting like a fist, and you can't even see that people are running away from you because something has forced your eyes shut.

3   And then it's over. You relax. Your head is clear, your body under control.

4   I'm talking, of course, about sneezing. I come from a long line of sneezers. My father sneezed, and his father and his father's father before him were all men for whom a blast from the nose was every bit as bracing as a plunge into the snow following a sauna.

5   This involuntary reflex known as the sneeze is not one of the burning mysteries of our time, but I'd like to tell you about some superstitions that have sprung up around sneezing and also let you know what's actually happening when you sneeze. Finally, in the interests of social harmony, I'll tell you how to sneeze safely and politely.

6   Sneezing is old. Citizens of the Roman Empire sneezed, but they were only following the tradition of the ancient Greeks, among them Aristotle, who considered the sneeze a favorable omen.

7   A sneeze worked wonders for Xenophon, the Greek historian and general. According to the *Concise Dictionary of Ancient History*, in 400 B.C. Xenophon, while still a mere foot-soldier, marched with the Greek army deep into hostile Persia, where the enemy slew all the Greek leaders and threatened to do the same to the confused troops when nightfall postponed the slaughter.

8   The desperate Greeks spent the night debating who should lead them in battle the next day. Xenophon rose to give a dramatic oration exhorting the men to follow him to liberty or to death. He spoke for an hour in the flickering firelight until a soldier to his right seconded his conclusion with a sneeze. Thinking this sneeze a favorable sign from the gods, the Greeks made Xenophon general, and when the sun rose the next morning, they marched to safety 10,000 strong behind their new leader.

9   Sneezing is seldom this dramatic, but many cultures echo the Greeks in their praise of the nose's most conspicuous function. Indeed, the *Encyclopedia of Occult Sciences*,

Superstitions, and Folklore devotes eleven tightly spaced, oversized pages to the subject. For example, a Zulu who has just sneezed proclaims, "I am now blessed; the ancestral spirit is with me. It has come to me. Let me salute it, for it is he who causes me to sneeze."

10   Sneezing in India provokes a shorter, but no less salutary, response. If you were walking down the dusty streets of Karim Nagar, for instance, and you sneezed, bystanders would shout, "Live!" and you, as a polite tourist, must reply, "Live with you!" Most Indians consider sneezing healthy, if not supernatural; it is the inability to sneeze that is cause for alarm. *Science* magazine reports Indian scientists have labeled this malady "asneezia" and are currently researching ways to artificially induce the healthy sneeze.

11   In the West, despite the cheerful, almost compulsive blessing we give anyone experiencing spontaneous nasal expulsion, the sneeze has long been regarded with suspicion. Some people, my grandmother among them, believe we say "Bless you" because the heart skips a beat when you sneeze. It's true your eyes must close when you sneeze, but the heartbeat remains steady. I used to think we say "Bless you" because of the superstition that when you sneeze the soul exits through your nostrils. If no one blesses you, evil beings with a penchant for nasal drip will snatch your spiritual essence. Natives of Motlan and Mota in the South Pacific believe this, but our European blessing has a grimmer origin.

12   The Black Death of 590 A.D. left one half of Europe's population dead. The bubonic plague responsible for this holocaust didn't kill its victims without warning. Instead, it signified its presence by rosy rashes, swelling, and, as any medical student can tell you, telltale fits of sneezing. Since death so frequently followed sneezing, people began to say "Bless you"—a final blessing.

13   However differently a sneeze is reacted to throughout the world, its cause is generally the same: nasal irritation. Pollens from grass, trees, house dust, and a dozen other sources are basically harmless, but when they irritate the nose your body responds as if they were rampaging predators. In a case of mistaken identity and overkill, you inhale sharply and exhale with explosive force—up to 104 miles per hour.

14   Pollen is not the only culprit, though. The nose mistakes strong odors, sudden chills, and even bright lights for more dangerous parasites, and it tries to defend itself by banishing the intruders with a sneeze.

15   In addition to its physical causes, the *New York Times* reports a sneeze can also be brought on by psychological and emotional factors. If a man lunged at you with a knife, fear might make you sneeze. Once he left, your anguish and frustration over losing your valuables could cause you to sneeze again. If you decide to chase the criminal, bring along some tissues—the excitement could give you another sneezing fit.

16   In each of these cases, sneezing is assisting the nose in reaching equilibrium. Strong emotions can cause your nasal membranes to shrink or expand, and a sneeze brings you back to normal quickly and forcefully.

17   Occasionally, someone is blessed with an overly active equilibriating mechanism. In 1966 June Clark had a fit in which she sneezed every twelve seconds for 174 days. Before she finally stopped, doctors had tried tranquilizers, narcotics, x-rays, muscle relaxants, shock treatment, and even hypnosis, which almost worked until she sneezed and broke the trance.

18   Sneezing will probably never give you the trouble it gave June Clark, but the odds are that sooner or later you'll have to sneeze in a social setting. This can be especially uncomfortable given that no one carries a handkerchief any more—at least not in my social circle. Nevertheless, when you're in a crowded room, don't try to stifle or abort your sneeze in the interests of social propriety—you don't want to stop a force going over 100 miles per hour. With the air pressure that builds up from a stifled sneeze, people have been known to get nosebleeds, pop blood vessels, or even go blind.

19   Instead, open your mouth while you sneeze so your nose doesn't take all your force. Most important, cover your nose. Jane Brody writes in the *New York Times* that "An unimpeded sneeze sends two to five thousand bacteria-filled droplets into the air." With a single sneeze, any one of us could raise this room's bacterial count for the next forty-five minutes. Understandably, every etiquette theorist from Lord Chesterfield and Amy Vanderbilt to Eleanor Roosevelt and Miss Manners advocates being a quick draw with a handkerchief. Failing this, hold the hankie over your nose after the sneeze—it shows good faith.

20   Whatever the cause and whichever country you're sneezing in, with practice and luck you'll be able to cover your sneeze quickly and effectively. Then you can sit back and relax, waiting for someone to bless you, wish you *gesundheit*, or, if you're in the right place at the right time, appoint you to high military command.

Nothing to Sneeze At   *by Jeffrey Moran*

Commentary

"Nothing To Sneeze At" is a top-notch informative speech. It is interesting, clearly organized, fits well with the guidelines discussed in Chapter 14 of the textbook, and is short enough to be discussed in a single class session. Here is a synopsis of the speech.

Specific Purpose: To inform my audience about the superstitions associated with sneezing, the causes of sneezing, and the proper way to sneeze.

Central Idea: Sneezing has long been the subject of superstition, has a number of causes from pollen to strong emotions, and should be done safely and politely.

Method of Organization: Topical

Introduction: The introduction consists of paragraphs 1-5. After cleverly arousing curiosity and relating the topic to the audience in paragraphs 1-3, the speaker reveals his topic in paragraph 4 and previews the body of the speech in paragraph 5. His tongue-in-cheek approach to establishing credibility in paragraph 4 is consistent with the overall tone of the speech, but some listeners felt it should have been supplemented by a brief reference to the speaker's research.

Body: The body is arranged topically and contains three main points, the first of which deals with superstitions that have sprung up around sneezing (paragraphs 6-12). This point is particularly effective because it casts new and interesting light on what would appear to be a mundane subject. The story about Xenophon (paragraphs 7-8) is a model of clear explanation. Rather than assuming the audience knew about Xenophon before the speech, the speaker provides all the necessary details. Yet he does so in a way that does not oversimplify the story for someone already familiar with it.

The statement in paragraph 9 that "the Encyclopedia of Occult Sciences, Superstitions, and Folklore devotes eleven tightly-spaced, oversized pages to the subject" of sneezing not only identifies the speaker's source, but reinforces the importance of the subject. The final example of this section—about sneezing and the bubonic plague (paragraph 12)—is highly effective. Notice especially the dramatic impact of the final sentence: "Since death so frequently followed sneezing, people began to say, 'Bless you'—a final blessing."

The second main point in the body deals with the causes of sneezing (paragraphs 13-17). While the information about pollen is fairly ordinary, the speaker brings it alive through his use of colorful language. He follows this with the interesting observation that sneezing can also be caused by psychological and emotional factors. Rather than getting overly technical, however, he explains with a hypothetical example that personalizes the subject for his listeners (paragraph 15). The story of June Clark (paragraph 17) ends this section on a strong note.

It should also be noted how well the speaker uses connectives here (and throughout the speech) to help listeners keep track of his ideas. At the beginning of paragraph 13 he introduces the second main point with an excellent transition ("However differently a sneeze is reacted to throughout the world, its cause is generally the same: nasal irritation"). He then has a signpost ("Pollen is not the only culprit, though") at the start of paragraph 14. Another transition at the start of paragraph 15 leads listeners from the physical causes of sneezing to its psychological and emotional causes.

The third main point explains how to sneeze politely and safely in a social setting (paragraphs 18-19). Its first observation—that stifling a sneeze can cause nosebleeds, popped blood vessels, even blindness (paragraph 18)—is an important bit of information that was new to most members of the audience. Indeed, it was so new that some thought the speaker should have presented a source here. Although the second observation—that a person should cover his or her nose when sneezing (paragraph 19)—is commonplace, it could not have been left out of the speech. Fortunately, rather than just saying, "You should cover your nose when you sneeze," the speaker provides a wealth of colorful information that keeps the audience's attention.

Conclusion: The conclusion consists of only two sentences (paragraph 20). The first sentence subtly reminds the audience of the main points discussed in the body. A good question for discussion is whether the speaker should have provided a more detailed summary here. One point of view holds that he did not need such a summary because the body of the speech was sufficiently clear and nontechnical. Another point of view holds that a summary is always helpful in the conclusion of an informative speech because it helps the audience remember what the speaker has said. Whatever one's position on this question, there can be no doubt that the final sentence of the speech brings everything together and concludes on a spirited, upbeat note that gives the speech a sense of psychological unity.

It is also important to note that the conclusion—like so much of the speech—is related directly to the audience. One of the strongest features of this speech is that the speaker consistently personalizes his ideas. Rather than talking in abstract terms, he gets the audience involved by employing the terms "you" and "your." Particularly effective examples of this occur in paragraphs 1-3, 10-11, 15, and 18-20. Indeed, by my count, the words "you" or "your" occur sixty times in the full speech. In addition, there are a number of references to "us," "we," and "our"—all of which reinforce the personal tone of the speech.

The Heimlich Maneuver

Kelly Marti

---

1   Imagine this scene. You are sitting with a friend at dinner. You tell a joke and your friend bursts out laughing. Then, suddenly, he isn't laughing any more, or making any sound at all. His eyes seem about to pop out of his head; his face turns pale and then blue. Finally, he collapses over his plate. You rush to his side, trying to figure out what is wrong. Could it be a heart attack? Then you realize what has happened. Your friend has choked on a piece of food that "went down the wrong way." You start to pound him on the back, try to help in any way you can. But it is too late. Five minutes have passed, and your friend is dead.

2   This story is imaginary, but it could be real. Incidents like this one happen every day—in restaurants, in the home, in dormitory cafeterias. According to a report from the National Safety Council, choking causes 3,900 deaths per year, which makes choking the sixth leading cause of accidental death in the United States. This statistic is even more tragic because 95 percent of these deaths could be prevented—more than 3,700 lives could be saved each year—if someone near the choking victim knew of a simple technique called the Heimlich maneuver.

3   The Heimlich maneuver was developed by Dr. Henry Heimlich, a professor of clinical sciences at Xavier University in Cincinnati, and it is so easy to learn that even a child can perform it. I learned the maneuver from my mother, who is a nurse, and I have read several articles about it. Today I would like to teach it to you.

4   The effectiveness of the Heimlich maneuver depends on two factors—knowing the symptoms of a choking victim, and knowing how to perform the maneuver to save the victim. First I will explain the symptoms. Then I will demonstrate the maneuver.

5   If you are to use the Heimlich maneuver, you must be able to recognize when a person has a piece of food or some other object caught in the windpipe. You may be surprised to know that until Dr. Heimlich offered a clear list of symptoms, not even doctors were sure how to diagnose a choking victim. There is a famous story of a medical convention in Washington, D.C., at which a large group of doctors had gathered for a dinner meeting. All at once a member of the group began to choke on a piece of food. A hundred doctors sat by helplessly while the man choked to death, because the doctors didn't know what was wrong and didn't know what to do.

6   Fortunately, Dr. Heimlich has since provided a reliable list of symptoms. First, the choking victim is unable to breathe or to speak. Then, because not enough oxygen is reaching the brain, the victim becomes pale, turns blue, and falls unconscious. Of these symptoms, the most important is the victim's inability to speak. There are other conditions that might cause someone to have difficulty breathing and to pass out—a heart attack, for example. But when a conscious person cannot speak—or make any utterance whatever—it is usually because something is lodged in the air passage. In most cases, blockage of the airway is so complete that the choking victim is not able to make any sound at all.

7   It is important that you, as an observer, learn to recognize these symptoms and to act quickly. There is no time to waste. Within about four minutes the victim will suffer permanent brain damage. Within about five minutes the victim will be dead. Four to five minutes—that is just a minute or so longer than the amount of time that has passed since I began this speech.

8   Now that you know how to recognize when a person has something caught in the air passage, you are ready to apply the Heimlich maneuver. When applied properly, it is the most effective way to save the life of a choking victim. The principle behind the maneuver is quite simple. Even when a foreign object is lodged in the windpipe, there is still enough air left in the lungs to dislodge the object if the air is forced upward suddenly. The purpose of the Heimlich maneuver is to create a strong enough burst of air from the lungs to free whatever is stuck in the windpipe.

9   You can apply the maneuver in any of three positions—while a victim is standing, sitting, or lying on the floor. Let me demonstrate with each position.

10   If possible, hold the victim up in a standing position to perform the Heimlich maneuver. This is the most effective way to dislodge whatever is caught in the air passage. Stand behind the victim and put both your arms around his waist. Let his head, arms, and upper torso hang forward. Make a fist with one hand and place it thumb side in against the victim's abdomen—slightly above the navel but below the rib cage. Then cover the first with your other hand and press into the abdomen with a quick upward thrust, bending your arms at the elbows. [Here the speaker gently demonstrated the procedure on a volunteer.] Repeat this action as many times as necessary until the food pops out.

11   If the victim is sitting down and you cannot get him up, kneel behind him, put your arms around both him and the chair, and perform the maneuver in the same way. [Demonstration by the speaker.] Again, continue the upward thrusts until the food pops out.

12   If the victim is already prostrate and you cannot get him up, you may have to perform the Heimlich maneuver with the victim lying down. In this event, lay the person flat on his back, with his face turned upward (not to the side). Kneel straddling the victim. Do not try to perform the maneuver from the side, because you could rupture the victim's liver or spleen. Place the heel of one hand against the choking victim's abdomen, above the navel but below the ribs. Put your other hand on top of the first one and press into the victim's abdomen with a quick upward thrust. [Demonstration by the speaker.]

13   As you can see, the Heimlich maneuver is easy to learn and easy to perform. Thousands of people, from children to senior citizens, have saved lives by using it. So if you are ever in a situation like the one I described at the start of this speech, remember what you have heard today: If your dinner companion suddenly can neither breathe nor speak, he or she has a foreign object stuck in the air passage. By applying the Heimlich maneuver, you can expel the object and save your companion's life.

The Heimlich Maneuver   *by Kelly Marti*

Commentary

"The Heimlich Maneuver" illustrates many of the principles of effective informative speaking. Students should pay special attention to how crisply the speech is organized, how the speaker adapts the topic directly to her audience, how she clarifies her ideas with concrete language and vivid description, and how she uses examples to personalize the speech and give it dramatic impact. Here is a synopsis of the speech.

Specific Purpose: To inform my audience how to perform the Heimlich maneuver.

Central Idea: The effectiveness of the Heimlich maneuver depends on two factors—knowing the symptoms of a choking victim and knowing how to perform the maneuver to save the victim.

Method of Organization: Topical

Introduction: The introduction is superb and consists of paragraphs 1-4. Vivid, dramatic, and realistic in its details, the hypothetical example in paragraph 1 relates the topic directly to the audience and gets them involved in the speech. In paragraph 2 the speaker uses statistics to show that the example is not far-fetched and that thousands of lives can be saved each year if people know how to perform the Heimlich maneuver. Paragraph 3 establishes the speaker's credibility, while paragraph 4 states the central idea and previews the main points to be discussed in the body.

Body: The body of the speech develops two main points, the first of which begins in paragraph 5 and explains the symptoms of a choking victim. The story of the medical convention in paragraph 5 dramatically illustrates the importance of being able to recognize when a person has a piece of food or some other object caught in the windpipe. Here, as elsewhere, the speaker is adept at working human interest factors into her speech. Paragraph 6 explains the key symptom of a choking victim—the inability to produce sound—while paragraph 7 emphasizes the importance of acting quickly to remove the obstruction. The speaker does an excellent job in paragraph 7 of relating "four or five minutes"—the amount of time it takes a choking victim to suffer permanent brain damage—to the immediate experience of her audience.

A transition at the beginning of paragraph 8 moves the speaker into her second main point, in which she explains how to apply the Heimlich maneuver. After stating the principle behind the maneuver (paragraph 8), the speaker provides an excellent internal preview of the three positions in which the maneuver can be performed (paragraph 9). She then explains how to perform the maneuver when the victim is in a standing position (paragraph 10), when the victim is sitting (paragraph 11), and when the victim is lying down (paragraph 12). In each case the speaker demonstrates the steps of the Heimlich maneuver on a volunteer from the class. She had arranged for the volunteer well ahead of time, and the volunteer participated in the speaker's final practice session. As a result, the volunteer knew exactly what to expect, and the speaker could get the timing of her demonstration just right.

Two other aspects of paragraphs 10-12 deserve mention. First, even though the speaker demonstrates the Heimlich maneuver, she also provides a clear step-by-step verbal explanation of it. This is important because a visual aid is usually no more effective than the quality of the explanation that accompanies it. Second, the speaker adopts a very personal tone throughout her demonstration of the Heimlich maneuver. Rather than talking about how an abstract "someone" might perform the maneuver, she talks in terms of "you." This strengthens the speaker's rapport with her listeners and helps keep them interested.

Conclusion: The conclusion, which consists of paragraph 13, is short and to the point. By referring to the introduction, the speaker again relates the topic directly to her audience, cues listeners that the speech is nearing an end, and enhances the unity of the entire speech. The final sentences reinforce the central idea and summarize the main points of the speech.

To Save a Child

Dawn Follendorf

---

1   For every morning that you wake up and eat breakfast, there are 840 million people beginning their daily struggle with chronic, persistent hunger. For every morning that you have the privilege of going to class, 250 million children head off to work where many will make less than $1 a day. And for every day that this vicious cycle continues, there are 24,000 fewer people in our world.

2   Millions of children living in developing countries cannot depend on their parents to support them. Rather, they live each day with little more than the hope that someone more fortunate than them might take compassion on them. By sponsoring a child for two years through an organization called Compassion International, I have seen the difference that $28 a month can make in a child's life.

3   Today, I'd like to encourage you to become involved with Compassion International. First, I will look at the desperate help children worldwide need. Second, I want to explain Compassion International and what it is they are doing to help meet the needs of these children. And finally, I will show you that Compassion International is an upstanding, legitimate organization that will put your money to work saving the lives of children. Let's start by looking at the need for this organization.

4   The demand for organizations such as Compassion International in developing countries is so great because of two main reasons: poverty and poor education. According to the World Bank website, it is poverty that causes 250 million children to work full- or part-time jobs while they should be receiving an education. In Thailand, for example, the typical 11- to 15-year-old boy or girl is forced to work an average of 50 hours every week. Similarly, in Bangladesh, children who do not attend school work as long, if not longer, hours than adults by the time they reach just 13 years of age.

5   According to a brochure sent to me by Compassion International, the average family income in Central America is $50 per month. Unfortunately, the cost of food in Central America is the same as in the United States. Because so few families can afford the cost of groceries, half of all children living in Central America are malnourished. Twenty percent of them are so severely malnourished that improved diet alone will not cure them.

6   Of course the problem isn't limited to Central America. The Hunger Project website claims that worldwide "about 24,000 people die from hunger or hunger-related causes every day, and three-fourths of them are children under the age of five." To put this in perspective, 24,000 deaths is equivalent to more than half the students on this campus dying every day. To think of it another way, it means that more children lose their lives to hunger every week than the number of Americans that lose their lives to cancer in an entire year.

7 According to the Hunger Project, "the best way to reduce hunger is through education because the educated are best able to break out of the cycle of poverty that causes hunger." Once again, let's look at Central America. Most of the children in Central America are not required to go to school. And if they do go, it is rare that they ever make it past the 6th grade because even public education is too expensive. This cycle is never-ending. If children do not become educated, they will never be able to make enough money to break out of the cycle of poverty. However, this vicious cycle can be broken with the help of Compassion International.

8 Compassion International was founded in 1952 by the Reverend Everett Swanson as a result of working with orphans in Korea. Swanson established a program through which people could sponsor needy Korean children for a few dollars a month. Those children would receive benefits that included food, clothing, education, shelter, and health care. Since then, Compassion International has expanded to 22 countries and has assisted more than 500,000 children across the globe.

9 Compassion International works in this way: In each community where they sponsor children, there is a place called the project. This is where the children go to receive nutritious meals and additional schooling. The projects are small, usually 150 children, and the local staff works hard to become personally acquainted with each sponsored child and his or her individual needs. Through providing them with an education now, Compassion is helping children to support themselves and their families in the future.

10 When you sponsor a child, it is usually for several years until the child is either 18 or has completed their schooling. You can sponsor a child for just $28 a month and even have the option of paying several months to a year in advance. Compassion International understands that there may be a time when you can't support your child. This is why there is no obligation to continue your sponsorship. Compassion International claims that they will immediately look for a new sponsor for your child and he or she will have continued support without interruption.

11 I have been sponsoring a little boy named Jose Francisco for two years. He lives in Ecuador with a family of seven and is ten years old. I get about three letters a year from Jose, and it's clear from those letters that he has had new opportunities to learn and grow—both physically and mentally. Being Jose's sponsor has been incredibly rewarding and is something that every one of us has the opportunity to do.

12 At this point, most of you are probably thinking, "How much of my money actually goes to helping my child?" Any true skeptic would feel the same way. From my class survey, more than 50 percent of you thought that less than half of your money would go directly to your child. And I, too, was reluctant to sponsor a child at first for the same reason.

13   Because of this, I read a report on Compassion conducted by the Better Business Bureau. This report shows that 78 percent of your money goes directly to your child. Of the rest of your money, 9 percent goes toward fund-raising. The other 13 percent is for administration purposes and includes the increase in net assets.

14   Another reassuring factor for me was that when I went to Compassion International's website, I discovered that they are audited both internally on a periodical basis and externally every year. Both of these audits help to ensure that funds are properly received, tracked, and managed for each child. From this evidence it's clear that Compassion International is an upstanding organization and is deserving of its rank from *Smart Money* magazine as "one of the top ten charitable organizations in the entire country."

15   So today I'd like to encourage you to sponsor a child of your own through Compassion International. When you consider that $28 a month amounts to less than one dollar a day, is this really too much to give to provide a child with an education, food, and health care that will help break the cycle of poverty? If $28 a month, every month, is still too much, I encourage you to provide a child with a one-time gift of $28.

16   Your $28, whether you give it just once or every month, can help save a child's life and fill them with hope for the future. This is why the time to start thinking about sponsoring a child is right now, and the time to take action is today. If you are interested in sponsoring a child or want to find out more information, I'll be distributing brochures for Compassion International after my speech.

17   May your compassion for the well being of the world's children encourage you to open your heart and maybe even your checkbook. Because as Compassion International states, "while we cannot individually change the world, we can change the world for one child."

To Save a Child   *by Dawn Follendorf*

Commentary

A persuasive speech seeking immediate action, "To Save a Child" is an excellent example of how to use Monroe's motivated sequence. In addition to having students read the speech, you can show the video of it from *Speeches for Analysis and Discussion: A Videotape Supplement to The Art of Public Speaking, Eighth Edition*. Here is a synopsis of the speech.

Specific Purpose: To persuade my audience to help children worldwide by contributing to Compassion International.

Central Idea: Contributing to an organization such as Compassion International can help break the cycle of poverty that affects millions of children.

Method of Organization: Monroe's motivated sequence

Introduction: The introduction consists of paragraphs 1-3. In paragraph 1 the speaker accomplishes the attention step of Monroe's motivated sequence by relating the plight of millions of impoverished children around the world to the daily activities of her audience. Paragraph 2 introduces the topic of the speech and establishes the speaker's credibility by noting that she has sponsored a child through Compassion International for the past two years. The introduction ends in paragraph 3 with a detailed preview statement that provides an excellent lead-in to the body.

Body: In the first main point of the body, the speaker demonstrates the need to help impoverished children around the world (paragraphs 4-7). Drawing on sources such as the World Bank and the Hunger Project, she uses statistics and testimony to argue that poverty, hunger, and poor education create a need for charitable organizations such as Compassion International. The speaker does a fine job translating statistics into terms that can be readily understood by her classmates when she states that the 24,000 hunger-related deaths that occur in the world every day are equivalent to half the students on her campus dying every day. She also draws a comparison between the number of daily hunger-related deaths and the number of Americans who die of cancer every year.

After providing a brief transition at the end of paragraph 7, the speaker moves to the satisfaction step of Monroe's motivated sequence, which constitutes the second main point in the body of her speech. Paragraph 8 provides information about the founding and growth of Compassion International. Paragraph 9 provides details about the activities of Compassion International in the communities where it sponsors children. Paragraph 10 explains the options for donating to Compassion International, with special emphasis upon a monthly gift of $28. Paragraph 11 concludes the satisfaction step of Monroe's motivated sequence with the speaker explaining her personal involvement in Compassion International. The content of this paragraph, combined with the sincerity of the speaker's delivery, significantly enhances her credibility and strengthens the persuasive appeal of her message.

In paragraphs 12-14 the speaker moves to the visualization step of Monroe's motivated sequence. Knowing from her class survey that many of her classmates were skeptical about the extent to which money donated to charitable organizations actually goes to the people it is intended to help, the speaker provides evidence to document the financial integrity of Compassion International. In paragraph 13 she cites figures from the Better Business Bureau to show that 78 percent of the money donated to Compassion International goes directly to helping needy children. In paragraph 14 she explains how Compassion International is audited on a regular basis to help ensure that its funds are properly received, tracked, and managed. She ends paragraph 14 with a quotation from *Smart Money* magazine indicating that Compassion International is one of the top 10 charitable organizations in the United States. All in all, paragraphs 12-14 provide an excellent example of how to develop the visualization step when using Monroe's motivated sequence.

Conclusion: Consisting of paragraphs 15-17, the conclusion presents the action step in the motivated sequence. In paragraph 15 the speaker asks listeners to donate $28 a month. If they can't afford that, she encourages them to make a one-time gift of $28. In paragraph 16 she calls for immediate action and explains that she will distribute brochures from Compassion International after her speech. Paragraph 17 reinforces the call for action and ends the speech with a moving quotation about the manner in which each individual can make a difference in the life of a child.

———————————————

Universal Health Care

Alice Pearson

---

1   Suppose you come down with a serious, but treatable, illness. You are too sick to go to class, too sick to work. What do you do? You go to the doctor, right? What if, when you got to the doctor, you were turned away because you couldn't pay and were sent home to suffer alone?

2   Most of us have difficulty imagining this, but for many people this is not just a hypothetical situation. The current health care system in our country is based on your ability to pay. The more money you can pay, the better medical treatment you can receive. Of course, there's health insurance and some government programs to help people get medical care, but there are millions of uninsured people, people who have inadequate insurance, and people who don't fit the stipulations of the government programs.

3   If you are like me, you may never have given an enormous amount of thought to the topic of health care until very recently. According to my class survey, every one of us in this room has some type of health insurance, whether it be from the government, our parents and their employers, or our current employer. Because of this, most of us have never had to worry about getting medical treatment when needed. However, even if this issue doesn't directly affect you or your immediate family, I am asking you to look at it from the perspective of the 43.4 million people in our country who do not have health insurance.

4   I have learned about the plight of these people through my research and from firsthand accounts, including that of my mother, who is a public health nurse and is able to see the problem on a daily basis. Today I am here to propose that our country adopt a universal health care program. This would be a program in which everyone would receive free and equal access to health care. I will first explain the problems with health care in our country today. Then, by using Canada as a model, I will propose one possible solution and explain the advantages of it. Let's begin with the health care system in the United States.

5   Although our country is experiencing a time of economic prosperity, the number of Americans without health insurance is steadily increasing. According to Dr. David Himmelstein of Harvard University, "These may be the best of times for the economy, but they're the worst of times for health care." The "worst of times" that Dr. Himmelstein is referring to is best exemplified by the fact that an average of one out of every six Americans does not have health insurance.

6   This number is increasing every year, with children and members of working families suffering the brunt of it. According to former governor and presidential candidate Michael Dukakis in a recent article published in *America* magazine, the number of uninsured children is rising twice as fast as uninsured adults. The article also states that nearly 90 percent of people without insurance come from families where at least one of the adults is working. This is partly a result of welfare reform, which in many cases is forcing people to take low-income jobs that do not provide insurance. If the person's job does happen to provide insurance, oftentimes the premiums are so high that they are simply not affordable.

7   Because of the lack of insurance in our country, people are not getting proper health care. Dr. Bob LeBow of the Physicians for a National Health Program states, "We see terrible consequences of patients lacking insurance in my clinic every day." One of these consequences is the putting off of visits to the doctor, in which case the person's ailment often becomes much worse. Recent studies done by the National Center for Health Statistics show that children without insurance receive less than half the visits to the doctor's office than children with insurance do. These studies also show that these uninsured children are four times less likely to receive medical and surgical care when they need it, and also four times less likely to receive prescription medicine when needed. These are all prime examples of what medical ethicist Larry Churchill of the Florida House of Representatives calls rationing of health care, and he states that "Access to health care is mainly contingent on having a way to pay for it."

8   It is ironic that the big issue in our country over universal health care seems to be the cost; yet statistics show that our current system is hardly cost efficient. According to the same article in *America* magazine mentioned earlier, we spend more money per person on health care in our country than in any other country in the world, and two times as much as any other industrialized country. Yet we are one of only two other industrialized countries that doesn't provide our citizens with universal health care, and about 20 percent of our population goes without adequate health insurance or health care.

9   It is time for the United States to make the same commitment to health care for all Americans that other countries have made to care for their citizens. The plan that I advocate is based on the system used by our neighbor Canada. As opposed to our country's system that leaves so many people uncared for, Canada's government provides all of its citizens with free universal health care. Of course, the Canadian system doesn't cover such things as cosmetic surgery, so some physicians do have private practices for those types of procedures, but the majority of doctors are paid a set salary depending on the service they provide.

10   What this means is that in Canada, if you get sick or hurt, you can go to any hospital or doctor's office and receive free basic medical treatment. In Canada, according to an article in *Public Health Reports*, "Health care is viewed as a right, and nobody is denied medical or surgical care because they are unable to pay."

11   As far as the health of Canadians goes, this system is working extremely well. An article in the *Washington Monthly* states that in Canada compared to the United States, the infant mortality rate is lower, the maternal mortality rate is lower, and the life expectancy is higher. Canadians can receive treatment from the doctor of their choice in a timely fashion without having to wait for approval from insurance companies.

12   Canada's health care system is financed through a combination of revenues—including federal grants, income taxes, and "sin" taxes on things like cigarettes and alcohol. You may be wondering if a system funded in this way is more expensive for Canadian citizens. According to *Canadian Public Health Reports*, Canadians pay about 55 percent less per person on health care than we do in the United States.

13   The main difference in the cost of health care in the United States compared to that in Canada is the difference in administration. Because Canadian patients are not billed individually, and because there is no insurance paperwork or eligibility determination for government programs, the cost of administration in Canada is significantly less than in the United States. As stated in an article from *In Health* magazine, in Canada the average citizen pays about $18 each year toward administration, while in the United States that cost is about $95 a year.

14   Not only does the Canadian system provide excellent health care, as we have seen, but public opinion polls show that Americans and Canadians alike find it to be superior to the U.S. system. According to a poll published in *In Health* magazine, 72 percent of United States citizens would rather have the Canadian system, while only 3 percent of Canadians said they'd prefer the U.S. health care system. Clearly it is time for the United States to meet the health care needs of its citizens by adopting a program similar to that used in Canada.

15   So in conclusion, we have seen that there are definite problems with the equality and economics of the health care system in the United States, which are affecting our citizens and our nation as a whole. I have shown you a viable solution that our entire country would benefit from. Using Canada's system, or one similar to it, would ensure that a much greater percentage of the population receives the health care they need. Now it is time for our country, considered to be the most advanced in the world, to stop lagging behind other countries in caring for its citizens and begin setting an example of how a country can truly prosper under a universal health care plan.

Universal Health Care   *by Alice Pearson*

Commentary

"Universal Health Care" is a persuasive speech on a question of policy. Have students pay special attention to how the speaker deals with three basic issues of need, plan, and practicality, as well as to how she supports her claims with strong, credible evidence. Here is a synopsis of the speech.

Specific Purpose: To persuade my audience that the United States should adopt a program of national health insurance.

Central Idea: The problem of inadequate health care faced by more than 40 million Americans can be solved by adopting a national health insurance program similar to that in Canada.

Method of Organization: Problem-Solution

Introduction: The speaker begins by asking her listeners to imagine themselves being unable to receive health care when they need it. In paragraph 2 she explains that this is precisely the situation faced by millions of people in the United States. Paragraph 3 brings the topic home to the speaker's classmates by referring to the results of her audience-analysis questionnaire and by asking her classmates to see the issue from the perspective of those Americans who do not have adequate health care. In paragraph 4 the speaker establishes her credibility and provides an excellent preview of the main points to be discussed in the body.

Body: The first main point in the body demonstrates that there is a serious problem with the U.S. health care system (paragraphs 5-8). In paragraph 5 testimony from Harvard professor David Himmelstein points out the irony of poor health care in times of economic prosperity and establishes the fact that one in six Americans lacks health insurance. Paragraph 6 explains that the number of Americans without health insurance is growing every year, while paragraph 7 shows that the lack of insurance is preventing many people from getting proper health care. Paragraph 8 addresses the issue of cost by noting that the current system of U.S. health care is much less cost-efficient than that of most other countries. As in other parts of the speech, the speaker supports her claims in paragraphs 5-8 with evidence from credible sources and identifies those sources for the audience.

The second main point in the body presents the speaker's solution to the problem (paragraphs 9-14). After sketching the basic elements of the plan in paragraphs 9-10, she devotes paragraphs 11-14 to demonstrating its practicality. Paragraph 11 draws from a *Washington Monthly* article documenting the fact that Canada has lower rates of infant mortality and higher life expectancies than the U.S. Paragraph 12 presents figures from *Canadian Health Reports* indicating that Canadians pay significantly less per person on health care than do people in the U.S. Paragraph 13 explains that this cost difference is due largely to the lower administrative costs associated with the Canadian system, while paragraph 14 cites a poll from *In Health* magazine showing that 72 percent of Americans would prefer the Canadian system to the current U.S. system. Although the speaker could have provided more information about the size and composition of the polling sample, for the most part, she does an outstanding job of addressing the practicality issue.

Conclusion: Presented in paragraph 15, the conclusion begins by summarizing the main points presented in the body. Because of the complexity of the topic, the summary is fairly detailed, and it does a fine job of reinforcing the central idea. The speaker then ends with a final plea for the United States to catch up to other nations by establishing a universal health care plan.

———————————————

The Dangers of Chewing Tobacco

Catherine Twohig

---

1   On March 30, Tom, a twenty-three-year-old man from northern Wisconsin, went in for his yearly dental checkup. As far as he could tell, there were no real problems except maybe the one or two usual cavities that the dentist always seems to find. The dentist began poking around at Tom's teeth, but soon became more interested in tom's lower lip and gums. The dentist noticed an unusual growth on Tom's lower lip and asked if Tom was a regular user of chewing tobacco. Tom answered yes.

2   After a series of tests, Tom was diagnosed as having a deadly type of oral cancer. Just one week after Tom's dental checkup, he had surgery to remove the cancer. This photograph shows Tom after his surgery. As you can see, a large portion of Tom's lower lip was removed and the area was drawn together by stitches. The surgery left Tom disfigured and looking quite grotesque, but it was not the worst part. Tom died just one month later. Chewing tobacco caused Tom's death.

3   Due to the fact that I am currently studying to be a dentist, and because my father is a dentist and I have worked for him as an assistant for over four years, I have actually seen cases similar to Tom's which result from chewing tobacco. I have also attended a number of seminars on this topic, and today I'd like to persuade each of you to feel as strongly as I do about the dangers of chewing tobacco.

4   In my speech, I'd like to show you the many problems that can result from chewing tobacco. Then I'd like to persuade each of you to take action and help change the lenient laws governing the use of chewing tobacco in our society. Let's begin by looking at how widespread the problem of chewing tobacco really is.

5   Chewing tobacco is more common than you may think. According to the American Cancer Society, one in every twelve Americans is a regular user of chewing tobacco. The average age of first use is just ten years old, which means that many children are chewing tobacco when they are in fourth grade. The American Cancer Society also reports that 40 percent of high-school boys have tried chewing tobacco—and, what's worse, 21 percent of kindergartners have tried it. Children are using chewing tobacco before they can even read the warning labels!

6   Now you know that chewing tobacco is widespread, but you may wonder what could possibly happen when a person uses chewing tobacco. Well, smokeless tobacco has multiple dangers according to the American Dental Association and the American Cancer Society. First, tooth decay and tooth loss can occur. Chewing tobacco contains grit and sand, which wear away at the teeth. It also contains added sugars to improve the taste—but they also wear away at the teeth, leading to cavities and tooth loss.

7 Another effect of chewing tobacco is gum disease. Regular use of chewing tobacco causes visual gum damage in less than two to three months. According to the American Dental Association, about half of all teenage users have some type of gum problem. But what's wrong with gum disease? Well, it causes the gums to pull away from the teeth, which further increases the risk of tooth decay and loss.

8 Gum disease and tooth loss are serious enough, but as we saw at the beginning in the story about Tom, chewing tobacco can have most serious consequences. According to the American Dental Association, those who use chewing tobacco just once in a while have four times the risk of developing oral cancer than do nonusers. And if that isn't bad enough, those who use chewing tobacco three or more times a week for over a year have fifty times the risk of developing cancer than do nonusers. This risk is even greater than that of smoking cigarettes. But unlike smoking cigarettes, where cancer develops slowly over time, chewing tobacco can cause cancer in teens and young adults.

9 For example, Sean Marsee, a nineteen-year-old high-school student from Oklahoma, was one of the most well-liked students in his senior class. Sean used chewing tobacco from age twelve to age eighteen, when he was diagnosed as having oral cancer during his senior year in high school. As a result, Sean had to have a series of disfiguring operations. First three-fourths of his tongue was removed. Then all the muscles and lymph nodes on the right side of Sean's face and neck were removed. And lastly his jawbone was removed from her to here. As you can imagine, Sean was left looking quite grotesque. But this was not the worst part. As extreme as the surgery was, it could not stop Sean's cancer from spreading, and he died just one year later. There can be no doubt that chewing tobacco caused Sean's death.

10 I know this is a terrible thought, but the point I'm trying to make is an important one. You must be aware of the terrible consequences of chewing tobacco because next time it could happen to you or to someone you love.

11 Let's look, then, at what can be done to diminish the use of chewing tobacco. First, the laws in Wisconsin pertaining to the age at which chewing tobacco can be bought must be strengthened. The law in Wisconsin states that chewing tobacco can be purchased at age eighteen, but according to the Department of Law Enforcement, the laws on chewing tobacco sales have been ineffective. To be effective, the laws must be enforced and have adequate penalties.

12 A number of other states, including California, set the fine for selling chewing tobacco to minors at $1,500 for the first offense and $6,000 for the second offense. According to the American Dental Association, this law has cut the use of chewing tobacco by minors by almost 60 percent. I would like you to help pass a law resembling this in Wisconsin. You must help stop people from selling cancer to our children. You can make a difference. You can write to our legislators urging that a bill like this be created here in Wisconsin.

13   Second, use of chewing tobacco during all professional sporting events should be banned. According to the American Dental Association, the primary reason children develop an interest in chewing tobacco is because they see their role models doing it. These role models include parents, relatives, and friends, but more importantly, they include sports stars. Children see athletes as role models. Children think if it's all right for athletes to use chewing tobacco, it must be all right for me to do it too. If these role models would stand up and say chewing is wrong, many of our children would change their minds about the drug.

14   What we need, then, is a ban on chewing tobacco use during professional sporting events. You may think this is impractical, but already one baseball team, the Kansas City Royals, has taken a stand. They have switched from chewing tobacco to bubble gum. You can help influence other teams to do the same. I urge you to write to your favorite team or to your favorite athlete urging them, individually or as a team, to take a stand against chewing tobacco as the Royals did.

15   In conclusion, then, I am pleading with each of you to take action against the use of chewing tobacco. When you think of this subject, remember the problems of chewing tobacco. Remember Tom—and remember Sean. By adopting the measures I have discussed today, you can help stop what happened to Tom and Sean from happening to others.

The Dangers of Chewing Tobacco   *by Catherine Twohig*

Commentary

"The Dangers of Chewing Tobacco" is an excellent persuasive speech that illustrates how students can make effective use of all the methods of persuasion discussed in Chapter 16 of the textbook. In addition to having students analyze the text of the speech, you may want to show the videotape of it, which is available on *Speeches for Analysis and Discussion: A Videotape Supplement to The Art of Public Speaking, Sixth Edition*. Here is a synopsis that focuses on how the speaker employs the methods of persuasion presented in Chapter 16.

Specific Purpose: To persuade my audience that the laws governing the sale of chewing tobacco should be strengthened and that professional athletes should refrain from using chewing tobacco during games in order to reduce the problem of chewing tobacco use among young adults.

Central Idea: The dangers of chewing tobacco pose a serious problem that can be curbed by state legislation and by banning the use of chewing tobacco during professional sporting events.

Method of Organization: Problem-Solution

Introduction: The introduction consists of paragraphs 1-4. The speaker begins with an extended example that does an excellent job pulling the audience into the speech (paragraphs 1-2). A color photograph enlarged to 11 x 17 inches and mounted on posterboard adds to the story's drama and impact. In paragraph 3 the speaker establishes her credibility, and in paragraph 4 she provides a clear preview statement that lets the audience know what to listen for in the body of the speech.

Body: There are two main points in the body. The first demonstrates that the use of chewing tobacco is a serious problem in the United States (paragraphs 5-10). After showing how widespread that use is, the speaker demonstrates that chewing tobacco poses a number of dangers, including tooth decay and tooth loss, gum disease, and, most deadly, oral cancer. The speaker then turns to her second main point, in which she presents a two-part solution to the problem (paragraphs 11-14). The first part deals with the laws governing the sale of chewing tobacco to minors (paragraph 11-12). Because the speaker is a student at the University of Wisconsin, she focuses on the laws in that state. The second part of the speaker's plan calls for banning chewing tobacco in all professional sports events (paragraphs 13-14).

Conclusion: Brief and hard-hitting, the conclusion is presented in paragraph 15. After restating the need for action against chewing tobacco, the speaker ends by referring back to the two extended examples presented earlier in the speech. This helps reinforce the central idea and ends the speech on a strong note.

Credibility: Paragraph 3, in which the speaker explains her professional training and personal experience on the topic, provides an excellent model of how students can establish their credibility in classroom speeches. In addition, as the speech progresses, the speaker's command of the topic and her obvious sincerity reinforce the audience's perception of her competence and good will.

Evidence: The speaker does an excellent job of using evidence to persuade her listeners. The extended examples of Tom in paragraphs 1-2 and of Sean Marsee in paragraph 9 dramatize the speaker's claim about the dangers of chewing tobacco. Both examples are vivid and richly textured, and both deal with people in the same age group as most members of the speaker's audience. These examples alone make up almost 25 percent of the speech, and they are crucial to its impact. In addition, the speaker uses brief examples to good effect in paragraphs 12 and 14 to demonstrate the practicality of her plan.

The speaker's use of examples is complemented by her use of statistics in paragraphs 5, 7, 8, and 12. In each case, the speaker employs statistics from credible sources and identifies those sources for her audience. She also does an excellent job of translating her statistics into human terms. The most dramatic instance of this is the extended example of Sean Marsee in paragraph 9 that gives a personal dimension to the statistics cited in paragraph 8. Less dramatic, but equally effective, is the speaker's method in paragraph 5. After stating that the average age of first use of chewing tobacco is "just ten years old," she explains that this means "many children are chewing tobacco when they are in fourth grade." Then, after noting that 21 percent of kindergartners have tried chewing tobacco, she exclaims, "Children are using chewing tobacco before they can even read the warning labels!"

Testimony plays less of a role in this speech than do examples and statistics. The speaker uses testimony in three places. In paragraph 6 she cites the American Dental Society and the American Cancer Society on the multiple dangers of chewing tobacco. In paragraph 11 she cites the Department of Law Enforcement to note that laws regulating the sale of chewing tobacco in Wisconsin have been ineffective. In paragraph 13 she cites a statement from the American Dental Association that the use of chewing tobacco by role models is the primary reason children develop an interest in it. In all three cases, the speaker uses credible sources and identifies them in the speech.

Reasoning: The speaker relies primarily on causal reasoning and analogical reasoning. She uses causal reasoning in paragraphs 6-9, where she argues that chewing tobacco is a cause of tooth decay, tooth loss, gum disease, and oral cancer. She does not claim that chewing tobacco is the sole cause of these conditions, only that it is an important contributing factor. In each case, she supports her claim with credible evidence of a causal connection. The speaker also uses causal reasoning in paragraphs 13-14, when she claims that many children start chewing tobacco because they see athletes chewing. If the athletes stopped chewing in games, she reasons, then children would be less likely to chew themselves.

The speaker employs analogical reasoning in paragraph 12. Her argument there is that because tougher laws against selling chewing tobacco have worked in California and other states, similar laws would work in the speaker's state of Wisconsin. Analogical reasoning is often used in this way by speakers to demonstrate the practicality of their proposed policy.

Emotional Appeal: For the most part, the speaker allows her emotional appeal to grow naturally out of her speech content. Vivid and richly detailed, the extended examples of Tom (paragraph 1) and Sean Marsee (paragraph 9) help to encourage a strong emotional reaction against chewing tobacco. When the speaker delivered the speech, she used a visual aid to show what Tom's face looked like after his surgery. The visual aid was an oversized color photograph, 11 inches by 17 inches that had been enlarged for the speaker at a local copy service. To enhance the visibility of the photograph, the speaker mounted it on a large piece of white poster board. The effect was quite dramatic—as can be seen from the videotape of the speech—and powerfully reinforced the emotional impact of the speaker's words.

The speaker also does a fine job in paragraphs 10 and 15 of relating the examples of Tom and Sean to her listeners and of appealing to the fear that they, or someone they love, could be victimized by chewing tobacco. Finally, if you view the speech on videotape, you will see how forcefully the speaker's own emotion and intensity regarding the topic come across. In the last analysis, here—as in other speeches—the sincerity and conviction of the speaker are the strongest source of emotional appeal.

Boxing: The Most Dangerous Sport

Rob Goeckel

---

1   "I killed a man. Afterward, they told me that it wasn't my fault, and that anyway it was nothing new. It had happened before. It has happened since. And, believe me, it will happen again."

2   This quote was uttered by boxer Roger Donoghue after he fought fellow boxer George Flores. During the fight, Donoghue punched Flores so mercilessly and with such force that shortly after the bout was over, Flores went into a coma. He never woke up again.

3   This horrifying scenario, the sight of one man literally beating another man's brains out, is what boxing is all about. What's even more frightening is that many, many other fighters have suffered the same fate as George Flores. In fact, as *Time* magazine reported, in the last decade over seventy boxers have died from boxing-related causes. Moreover, at least 15 percent of all boxers, even if they don't die, incur irreversible brain damage.

4   Growing up, like most of you, I watched boxing, and sometimes I even enjoyed it. But as I recently watched Mike Tyson pummel Frank Bruno into submission in a heavyweight championship fight, I began to wonder what possessed one man to beat another with such force and without remorse.

5   In answering my audience analysis questionnaire, most of you said the sport of boxing was violent but that the decision to fight should be left up to the individual. However, I'm here to show you that the choice cannot be left up to the individual, who probably has been swayed by the chance for fame and fortune. The evidence against boxing is shocking and overwhelming, and tonight I hope to convince you that all states should ban the sport of boxing because it damages its participants and our society.

6   For decades, experts have warned us about the dangers of boxing. As long ago as 1928, Dr. Harrison Martland published the first article regarding the dangers of fighting in the *Journal of the American Medical Association*. Today the American Medical Association argues that "The principal purpose of a boxing match is for one opponent to render the other injured, defenseless, incapacitated, and unconscious. Boxing, as a throwback to uncivilized man, should not be sanctioned by any civilized society."

7   Even heavyweight champion Mike Tyson says, "This is a hurt business. When you see guys like Trump, Kennedy, and Rockefeller come to a fight, regardless of what they may represent, they come to see someone get hurt, and my objective is to inflict as much punishment as possible."

8　But why all the warnings? Because boxing can cause irreparable physical damage to its participants. A punch thrown by a heavyweight can land with a force exceeding 1,000 pounds, which causes the head to snap back or twist violently, forcing the soft brain to be rammed into the rigid skull like a yolk slammed into the side of an egg. The nerve cells and blood vessels in the brain are then twisted, ruptured, and stretched, which causes swelling and results in the brain pressing against the inside of the skull. A blow to the head so that consciousness is lost causes minute or larger hemorrhages, contusions at the base of the brain, and a tearing of nerve fibers that cannot be easily identified. These symptoms are not detectable by the victim of the beating.

9　Neurologist MacDonald Critchley states that a boxer's chances of suffering brain damage increase in proportion with the number of bouts fought. Another neurologist, Dr. Jan Corsellis, examined the brains of fifteen boxers who died of natural causes. He observed a pattern of abnormal cerebral changes not present in non-boxers.

10　Subsequent studies have shown that boxers are also far more likely to suffer from another type of brain damage called *cavum septi pellucidi*, which occurs when a boxer receives a blow to the brain and a cave or space develops between the two membranes that divide the brain. Many boxers who have this ailment suffer permanently with symptoms similar to the brain disorder Parkinson's disease. This disease develops when the brain ceases to produce sufficient amounts of dopamine, a substance that helps in the transmission of nerve impulses involved in motor control.

11　Perhaps the most poignant example, because he was so admired for his once-strong body, is the case of Muhammad Ali. In his prime, Ali was glamorized, but now he suffers from a severe case of Parkinson's disease. Ali's side effects are impaired hand-eye coordination, slurred, unintelligible speech, reduced muscle strength, and chronic fatigue. Ironically, Ali became a victim of the sport he once saved. Ali, once the unbeatable heavyweight champion, the force who claimed that "boxing never scarred his pretty face," has been reduced to a mere shell of a man, a shaking, silent reminder of the brutality of boxing, a brutality which does not discriminate on the basis of race, creed, or religion.

12　Not only is boxing dangerous to its participants, but it can hurt our society as well. Boxing influences how violent some spectators become. According to David Phillips, a sociologist at the University of California, homicides increase dramatically after every nationally televised broadcast fight.

13　Sadly, inner-city minority teens are the real victims who learn that the way to success is to emulate the violence condoned by boxing. According to the *Saturday Evening Post*, kids even drop out of school to become professional fighters. What awaits them is a future filled with punishment and abuse, while only a handful of fighters go on to make the millions of dollars that are so glorified by our society.

14   Of all athletes to emulate, the last ones should be boxers, who get rich without an education and achieve heroic status through violence. Of all sports to emulate, why boxing, where the object is to move your opponent closer to death?

15   You've heard how boxing causes physical and mental damage to its participants, and about the negative effects it has on our society, so now let's take a look at the solutions.

16   The best solution is to ban the sport of boxing. All fifty states should pass resolutions to abolish this barbaric sport. Granted, there is a lot of money invested in the sport, but can we put a price on human life?

17   The American Medical Association strongly supports this proposal and has attempted time and again to eliminate boxing. AMA President Dr. Joseph Boyle called their resolution to abolish the sport "a statement that's about as strong as it can get."

18   Elsewhere, people have also recognized the need to eliminate this dangerous sport. In 1969 Sweden banned pro boxing, but the U.S. has done nothing despite all the evidence that has been levied against boxing. Just as Sweden has survived without it, so can we.

19   Even world-renowned sportscaster Dick Enberg, who has spent his career watching sporting events of all kinds, couldn't think of a reason to continue boxing. In fact, in a speech given last week here on campus, Enberg said that while the goal in other sports is to defeat the opponent by scoring more points, the goal in boxing is to hurt, knock out, and incapacitate the other competitor. Though he professed admiration for the fighters, Enberg felt there was no justification for the sport.

20   For the sake of fighters, and for the sake of our society, it's important for us to take a stand against this brutal activity.

21   So in conclusion, boxing is unquestionably a dangerous and often deadly sport and must be banned. The goal of a boxer is to destroy another human being. How many more fighters must be rendered permanently injured to killed in the ring before we put an end to this deadly sport?

22   The next time you turn on the television or read the paper, you just might hear of someone suffering the same tragic fate as George Flores. But unlike the other deaths we read about, this one will have been different. It will have been endorsed by our society, and thousands of people will have cheered for the killer and paid big money to watch the killing happen—all in the name of sports entertainment.

23   As we've seen, in boxing there are no winners. Let's stop the madness before someone else loses. Let's ban boxing before someone else dies.

Boxing: The Most Dangerous Sport   *by Rob Goeckel*

Commentary

"Boxing: The Most Dangerous Sport" is a persuasive speech on a question of policy. In addition to illustrating many of the principles discussed in Chapters 15-16 of the textbook, it provides a useful speech for discussion because of its use of supporting materials. Most members of the audience opposed the speaker's position, and he knew he would have to provide persuasive evidence if he were to have any hope of getting people to reassess their attitudes on the topic.

This speech is also available on *Speeches for Analysis and Discussion: A Videotape Supplement* to *The Art of Public Speaking, Sixth Edition*. If you show the tape, you should be aware that the speaker has a cleft palate, which at times affects his articulation, though not to the point that it hampers communication with the audience. Here is a synopsis of the speech.

Specific Purpose: To persuade my audience that professional boxing should be banned in the United States.

Central Idea: Professional boxing should be banned in the United States because it is harmful to society and causes irreparable physical damage to its participants.

Method of Organization: Problem-Solution

Introduction: The introduction consists of paragraphs 1-3. It begins with an attention-getting quotation from boxer Roger Donoghue about a fight in which he killed fellow boxer George Flores. Although the quotation was uttered in 1951, the speaker presents statistics in paragraph 3 to show that boxing remains a deadly sport to this day. Although the speaker seeks to establish his credibility and good will in paragraph 4 by stating that his opinions about boxing have changed over time, he could have done a better job if he had mentioned the great amount of research he put into researching the speech. In paragraph 5 he refers to his audience-analysis questionnaires and provides a clear preview statement of the ideas to be developed in the body of the speech.

Body: The body of this speech contains two main points. The first, which explains the need to abolish professional boxing, runs from paragraph 6 through paragraph 14. In these paragraphs, the speaker devotes most of his attention to showing that boxing causes irreparable physical damage to its participants (paragraphs 6-11). He also argues that it harms society in general (paragraphs 12-14). After an excellent transition in paragraph 15, the speaker moves into his second main point (paragraphs 16-20), in which he presents his plan that all fifty states should pass legislation banning the sport of boxing.

Conclusion: The conclusion consists of paragraphs 21-23 and does an excellent job of strengthening the speaker's central idea. After ending paragraph 21 with a pointed rhetorical question, in paragraph 22 the speaker returns to the opening story of George Flores to reinforce the brutal nature of boxing. He ends in paragraph 23 with a series of sharp, dramatic sentences.

Supporting Materials: The speaker uses two extended examples. The first is that of boxer George Flores, who was killed in a fight with Roger Donoghue. This example, accompanied by testimony from Donoghue, is developed in paragraphs 1-2 and is mentioned again in the conclusion. Although there are many other examples of fighters dying in the ring, the speaker had time to develop only this one. To show that the example is not unrepresentative, in paragraph 3 the speaker presents statistics from Time magazine on the number of fighters who have died from boxing-related causes in the past decade.

The speaker's second extended example is that of Muhammad Ali, who suffers from Parkinson's disease as a result of his boxing career (paragraph 11). This example is especially well-chosen because Ali is a well-known figure even to people who are not boxing fans. The effectiveness of the example is heightened by the speaker's vivid portrayal of Ali as "a mere shell of a man, a shaking, silent reminder of the brutality of boxing, a brutality which does not discriminate on the basis of race, creed, or religion."

In addition to these extended examples, the speaker presents a brief example in paragraph 18 to support the practicality of his plan. He notes that Sweden eliminated pro boxing in 1969 and has survived just fine. Arguing analogically, he infers that the U.S. would also do just fine without boxing.

Unlike some topics for persuasive speeches, this one does not lend itself to heavy use of statistics. In contrast to issues such as gun control or drunk driving, there are not so many professional boxers in the U.S. as to produce thousands of deaths or serious injuries every year. Although the speaker seeks, in paragraph 3, to quantify the seriousness of the number of deaths caused by boxing, he could have strengthened his argument by adding a few more statistics. He might also have strengthened his argument by saying something like, "Although the number of professional boxers is small compared to some sports, we should not tolerate any sport that produces such a high proportion of deaths and brain injuries among its participants. Certainly, we would not find it acceptable if a comparable number of players in professional baseball or professional football were killed each year."

The only figures in the body of the speech occur in paragraphs 8 and 9. In paragraph 8 the speaker states that a punch thrown by a heavyweight boxer can land with a force exceeding 1,000 pounds. Although it is debatable whether this is a statistic in the strict sense of the term, many students will identify it as such. Many will also note that the speaker does not identify the source of the figure. He could have avoided this problem by preceding the figure with a statement such as "According to Sports Illustrated, a punch thrown by a heavyweight . . . ." On the positive side, the speaker's use of vivid language to explain the impact of a 1,000-pound force when applied to the human skull is highly effective. If not for this explanation, the 1,000-pound figure would have had little meaning for the audience.

In paragraph 9 the speaker cites the research of neurologist Jan Corsellis, who detected a pattern of abnormal cerebral changes in the brains of fifteen boxers who died of natural causes. Unlike the figure in paragraph 8, however, this one is neither explained fully nor related to the audience.

Given all the testimony that has been advanced against boxing over the years, it is not surprising that the speaker relies above all on this form of supporting material. In addition to the quotation from Roger Donoghue in paragraph 1, he presents testimony from the American Medical Association (paragraph 6), boxer Mike Tyson (paragraph 7), neurologist MacDonald Critchley (paragraph 9), sociologist David Phillips (paragraph 12), the *Saturday Evening Post* (paragraph 13), AMA president Joseph Boyle (paragraph 17), and sportscaster Dick Enberg (paragraph 19). All of these are credible sources, and all are identified in the speech.

Seatbelts: A Habit That Can Save Your Life

Andrew Kinney

1   As you may have noticed, I was on crutches for two months this semester. I had already been on crutches for three months before that, and last year I was on them for seven months. You see, I've had hip surgery three times in the last year and a half.

2   It all started when I experienced my first serious car accident. I swerved off the road to avoid a head-on collision with another car. My car rolled over and struck a large tree. I was not wearing a seatbelt. In the process of being thrown back and forth across the car, I chipped a tooth, cut the back of my head, broke my hip, and cracked three ribs, which resulted in a punctured lung and massive internal bleeding. When they got me to the hospital, my blood pressure was down from a normal 120-over-70 to 50-over-30 as a result of all the internal and external bleeding and as a result of shock. The doctors waited more than twenty-four hours to do surgery to repair my hip because they didn't think I was going to survive all of my other injuries.

3   Somehow I survived, and now a year and a half later I am finally walking normally, though I will be walking around for the rest of my life with a piece of metal this long in my hip, and I'm not allowed to do any athletic activities that require running.

4   All that pain and suffering could have been avoided if only I had been in the habit of wearing a seatbelt. But I wasn't in that habit, and I know from my class survey that 40 percent of you do not usually wear a seatbelt, and 75 percent of you do not always wear one. Yet the National Highway Traffic Safety Administration tells us that each person stands a one-in-three chance of being in a serious car accident at some time in his or her life. So we can possibly predict that one-third of you will be in a serious accident at some point. And it may sound corny, but I mean it, so I'm going to say it—I don't want what happened to me to happen to any of you.

5   So I want to talk to you about wearing seatbelts. First I'm going to tell you to what extent you will be protected by wearing a seatbelt. Then I'm going to look at some of the reasons why people don't wear seatbelts and point out the problems with those reasons. And after I've given you the evidence, I am going to ask you all to make a habit of wearing seatbelts.

6   So first, to what extent will you be protected by wearing a seatbelt? Well, the Wisconsin Department of Transportation says if you are in an accident and are not wearing a seatbelt, you are four times more likely to be killed than if you are wearing one. Furthermore, consider this—there are 35,000 deaths each year in the United States as a result of traffic accidents. The National Highway Traffic Safety Administration, the National Child Passenger Safety Association, and the Wisconsin Department of Transportation all estimate that traffic deaths would decrease from 35,000 to around 17,000 annually if everyone wore seatbelts.

7   So our most knowledgeable and reliable sources of information on seatbelts have all come to the same conclusion—that we would cut traffic deaths in half if everyone wore seatbelts, and that we would save 18,000 lives each year. Now let me put that number into perspective—18,000 people, or the equivalent of more than half the undergraduates on this campus, are needlessly killed every year because they do not wear seatbelts.

8   But why is this true? What does a seatbelt do to protect you? Well, in a head-on collision, which is usually the worst type, your body will be thrown forward into the steering wheel, into the dashboard, or through the windshield with incredible force. Imagine falling headfirst from the top of a three-story building. The force with which you would land on the ground is equal to the force with which you would be thrown forward in only a 30 mile-per-hour collision. But a seatbelt will absorb that force and prevent you from slamming into the interior of the car.

9   In my own experience there is little doubt that a seatbelt would have minimized my injuries. I looked at pictures of the car after my accident. The car was totaled, and it was an ugly mess, but the two front seats and the entire driving compartment were completely intact. I have to believe that if I had been strapped into that seat, I would have walked away from my accident with minor bruises. But remember I used the word "if"—if I had worn a safety belt.

10   So the evidence is strongly in favor of wearing seatbelts. That brings me to the next question—why don't people wear seatbelts?

11   People often say that in an accident they would rather be thrown free of the car, or at least be able to get out of the car in case of fire or submersion in water. Well, according to the Wisconsin Department of Transportation, accidents involving fire and submersion make up less than one out of every 200 auto accidents. Furthermore, you are actually more likely to be able to get out of the car if you are wearing a seatbelt, because you are more likely to be conscious and not seriously injured. And with regard to being thrown free of the car, the Wisconsin Department of Transportation says you are 25 times more likely to be killed if you are thrown out of the car, because you can be thrown onto hard pavement, thrown into stationary objects, or struck by other cars. Clearly you are safer being strapped in than being thrown around.

12   The other major reason why people don't wear seatbelts is that seatbelts are uncomfortable and restrict movement. Now, if this is your reason for not wearing a seatbelt, let me ask you to do something right now. Imagine in your mind a two-sided scale. On one side of the scale, put the value that you place on being completely comfortable while driving. And on the other side of the scale, put the value that you place on your life and your health. Which side is heavier? If your life and your health mean more to you than a little bit of extra comfort while driving, then it only makes sense to wear a seatbelt.

13   So I'm here today to ask all of you to make a habit of wearing seatbelts. The statistics are simple—chances are that about one-third of you will be in a serious auto accident at some time in your life. It could happen fifty years from now, and it could happen tomorrow. And if you are in an accident, you are four times more likely to be killed if you are not wearing a seatbelt than if you are wearing one.

14   So if you think you are safer not wearing a seatbelt, you're betting against heavy odds. And if you still won't wear a seatbelt, because a seatbelt is uncomfortable and inconvenient, then you're placing your momentary comfort ahead of your life and your health. So tell yourself that you are going to make a habit of wearing seatbelts. Then do it.

15   There is nothing I can do about my accident now, and I don't plan to go around for the rest of my life kicking myself because I didn't wear a seatbelt that day. What's important is that I learned something from the experience. I've made a habit of wearing seatbelts when I ride in a car, and I'm hoping that each of you will do the same if you haven't already.

16   I will never be able to play basketball or go downhill skiing again, but at least I'm here and at least I can walk. I was a lot luckier than 35,000 other Americans that year.

Seatbelts: A Habit That Can Save Your Life   *by Andrew Kinney*

Commentary

A persuasive speech on a question of policy, "Seatbelts: A Habit That Could Save Your Life" is notable for its sharp organization, for the manner in which the speaker establishes his credibility by drawing on his personal experience, and for the way he relates the topic directly to his classmates throughout the speech. The speech is also superbly delivered, and it is available on *Speeches for Analysis and Discussion: A Videotape Supplement to The Art of Public Speaking, Sixth Edition.* Here is a synopsis.

Specific Purpose: To persuade my audience to use seatbelts every time they drive or ride in an automobile.

Central Idea: Because seatbelts are proven lifesavers and there are no good reasons not to wear seatbelts, everyone should get in the habit of wearing seatbelts whenever they drive or ride in an automobile.

Method of Organization: Topical

Introduction: The introduction consists of paragraphs 1-5 and does a superb job of fulfilling the functions of a speech introduction. Paragraphs 1-3 gain attention with a dramatic story based on the speaker's personal experience. The story is especially effective because of its specific details about the speaker's injuries and how close he came to dying. In contrast, imagine if the speaker had merely said, "A year and a half ago I was in a serious automobile accident." This would not have had nearly the same impact. Nor would it have done as much to establish the speaker's credibility and good will.

In paragraph 4 the speaker moves from his opening story to reveal the topic of his speech and to relate it directly to his audience. The final sentence of this paragraph—in which the speaker says, "I don't want what happened to me to happen to any of you"—had a strong emotional impact when delivered in class. In paragraph 5 the speaker ends his introduction by previewing the main points to be discussed in the body. Although it is longer than usual, the introduction of this speech is extremely effective in preparing the audience for the persuasive appeals that follow.

Body: The body of the speech runs from paragraph 6 through paragraph 14 and has three main points. The first main point, developed in paragraphs 6-9, is that seatbelts are a proven way to reduce the chances of injury and death in an automobile accident. In paragraph 6 the speaker presents statistics to show that traffic deaths in the U.S. would be reduced from 35,000 per year to 17,000 per year if everyone wore seatbelts. In paragraph 7 he adroitly translates those statistics into terms that relate directly to his audience.

The speaker continues with his first main point in paragraph 8 by explaining why seatbelts are so valuable in helping to prevent injuries. He compares the force of a 30-mile-per-hour collision to falling headfirst from a three-story building. In paragraph 9 he draws on his own experience to reinforce his point about the value of wearing a seatbelt. The final sentence of this paragraph is especially effective.

After a transition in paragraph 10, the speaker moves into his second main point, which consists of paragraphs 11-12. These paragraphs are extremely important, for they answer the audience's two major objections to wearing seatbelts. Had the speaker ignored these objections, his speech would have been much less effective. In paragraph 11 he supports his position with statistics from the Wisconsin Department of Transportation. While this would not have been the best source of statistics for a speaker in another state, it was an excellent source for this speech, which was presented to a class at the University of Wisconsin.

In paragraph 12 the speaker deals with the fact that many people find seatbelts uncomfortable by asking his audience to imagine a two-sided scale on which they weigh the value of personal comfort versus their lives and health. Which do you value more, he asks, your life and health or "a little bit of extra comfort"? If you value your life and health more, he notes, it only makes sense to wear a seatbelt.

Paragraphs 13-14 develop the speaker's third main point, in which he calls for the audience to make a habit of wearing seatbelts. He begins the point in paragraph 13 by reiterating key statistics from earlier in the speech. This is an excellent technique. Rather than overwhelming listeners with a barrage of figures, the speaker uses a few well-chosen statistics to drive home his message. In paragraph 14 the speaker makes a direct call for action. Here, as elsewhere, his appeal is enhanced by his clear, forceful language.

It is also important to note that the speaker's appeal throughout the body of the speech is strengthened by his use of the words "you" and "your" to relate the topic directly to his listeners. In addition to increasing audience involvement, this gives the speech a strong conversational quality. As you will observe if you view the speech on videotape, the speaker comes across as talking with the audience, not at them. This comes both from his personal tone and from his use of pauses, vocal variety, and eye contact to communicate directly with his listeners.

Conclusion: The speaker begins his conclusion in paragraph 15 by referring to the accident he had discussed in the introduction and by reiterating his call for action. Paragraph 16 ends the speech on a strong emotional note. The speaker's sincerity here and throughout the speech did much to strengthen his credibility and persuasiveness.

Family Medical Histories: A Proven Lifesaver

Steven Harris

---

1   Actress-comedian Gilda Radner, alias Roseann Roseanna Danna as she's well known to long-time *Saturday Night Live* fans, gave us laughter and enjoyment for decades before her death at the age of forty-two from ovarian cancer. She suffered through a year of intense pain before her doctors finally diagnosed the problem. If detected early, the survival rate for ovarian cancer is 85 percent, but that drops to 15 to 20 percent if the cancer spreads. Doctors and Radner's husband, Gene Wilder, believe she died a premature death that could have been prevented had she known that her grandmother, aunt, and a first cousin all suffered from the same disease.

2   The importance of knowing your family's medical history is becoming increasingly urgent, as more and more diseases are found to have genetic links. Researchers at the National Institutes of Health are working to isolate all of the body's 50,000 to 100,000 genes and match them to specific diseases, a project they hope to complete by the year 2004. It may be only a matter of time before scientists locate the genes that cause such common illnesses as diabetes and high blood pressure. But unfortunately, time is not on our side. Hereditary diseases are a crisis potentially affecting everyone in this room.

3   In order to better understand this, we'll discuss the scope of this threat, the medical community's reaction or inaction, and finally indicate an easy solution to help you deal with the threat of hereditary diseases.

4   First we'll look at the problem hereditary diseases pose to all of us. The number of diseases with a genetic link is staggering, and these are only the diseases scientists know have a hereditary component. *U.S. News and World Report* states that if a member of your family had ovarian cancer, your risk of contracting the disease increases by 20 to 40 percent. If a family member had breast cancer, your risk increases by up to 50 percent. And if lung cancer runs in your family, your risk increases by 300 percent.

5   The *U.S. News and World Report* article gives several examples of diseases found to have genetic links—diabetes, stroke, mental illness, alcoholism, allergies, arthritis, sickle-cell anemia, and high blood pressure. Even birth defects and a predisposition for miscarriages can be inherited. Researchers at the University of Utah found that men under age forty in families with histories of heart attack had twelve times the risk of early heart disease, while women from such families had eight times higher risk.

6   Now you may be thinking that your doctor is your best chance of early detection, but unfortunately the medical community has put us at even greater risk, accentuating the problem.

7   The problem lies not only with the severity of the diseases themselves, but also with an historic belief by the medical community that family history is of minimal importance. Doctors have traditionally taken meager medical histories, failing to recognize their importance. Ask yourself if your doctor updated your family history during your last physical. Most likely he or she did not. This leaves a gaping hole in your diagnosis.

8   The *New York State Journal of Medicine* describes a recent study in New York City designed to determine if data on the family history of cancer patients were being recorded by hospitals. They found that only four of sixty-four hospitals indicated familial recurrence of cancer on medical charts, and no hospital accrediting agency required that this information be recorded.

9   Another study by the same researchers investigated 200 cancer patients undergoing treatment in an oncology clinic. These cases showed numerous examples of hereditary cancer syndromes, but their clinical charts demonstrated that the family history of cancer had either been completely omitted or reported as "negative," despite substantial evidence to the contrary. There are doctors, of course, who do take into account hereditary factors, but unfortunately they are still a small minority, as reported by the Hereditary Cancer Institute at Creighton University.

10   Having heard the problems, we must now look at some solutions. Obviously, one step is for doctors to take better account of medical history in order to ensure that we receive quick treatment and proper diagnoses. But what I want to focus on is what we as individuals can do.

11   You can help your doctor and yourself by making a medical family tree. To assist you in making a medical family tree, *U.S. News and World Report* offers this chart as a guide. List all medical conditions contracted by close relatives—especially parents, siblings, grandparents, aunts and uncles, and cousins. Include important information about each relative in the space provided, such as age, height, weight, personal habits, and any medical conditions they have contracted.

12   In addition, list the age when each relative contracted that condition; this will inform your doctor of the best time to begin testing for a disease or to begin preventive medicine. Don't hesitate to overelaborate your medical family tree. Trained physicians may see patterns that you cannot.

13   Getting this information is not that difficult. Simply speak to your relatives and include every medical condition they recall having. Not only heart disease and high blood pressure, but even such things as migraines and allergies should be included. Even if you think your family is in good health, a little probing may uncover hidden problems. Consider the few hours required to make a detailed medical family tree as an investment in your health future.

14   Today we learned what an important issue and just how big a threat hereditary diseases are and how you can protect yourself by making a medical family tree. The first item mentioned in the UCLA School of Public Health's book *50 Simple Things You Can Do to Save Your Life* is to know your family history. Had Gilda Radner and her doctor known her family's medical history, she might be alive today. The knowledge you gain by investigating your family's medical history may help you fend off future problems and possibly save your life.

Family Medical Histories: A Proven Lifesaver   *by Steven Harris*

Commentary

A persuasive speech on a question of policy, "Family Medical Histories: A Proven Lifesaver" illustrates many of the principles discussed in Chapters 15-16 of the textbook. It is also interesting because of the effectiveness of, and the occasional flaws in, its use of supporting materials. Below is a synopsis of the speech, including special discussion of its use of examples, statistics, and testimony. The speech is also available on *Speeches for Analysis and Discussion: A Videotape Supplement to The Art of Public Speaking, Fifth Edition.*

Specific Purpose: To persuade my audience that they should make a family medical history.

Central Idea: Because so many diseases have genetic origins, a family medical history is often of vital importance in helping to ensure proper medical diagnosis and treatment.

Method of Organization: Problem-Solution

Introduction: The introduction consists of paragraphs 1-3. The story of Gilda Radner in paragraph 1 is an excellent attention-getter and provides a striking illustration of why a person should know her or his family medical history. In paragraph 2 the speaker indicates the importance of the topic and relates it to his audience. Paragraph 3 provides a clear preview statement of the main points to be covered in the body of the speech. All in all, this is a fine introduction except for its lack of a statement establishing the speaker's credibility. Although it is clear from the rest of the speech that the speaker has done a thorough job of research, he should have made reference to his research in the introduction.

Body: There are two main points in the body of this speech. The first deals with the need for family medical histories and is developed in paragraphs 4-9. The speaker begins by showing the large number of diseases with genetic links (paragraphs 4-5). He then explains that the medical community has not placed as much importance as it should on family history in diagnosing and treating patients (paragraphs 6-9).

The second main point presents the speaker's solution and runs from paragraph 10 through paragraph 13. After an excellent transition, the speaker notes that he will focus in his solution on what individuals can do to help doctors provide accurate diagnoses of genetically based medical conditions. He then explains, in paragraphs 11-13, how to create a family medical history. His explanation is clear, specific, and detailed enough to give the audience a good sense of exactly what is involved. The speaker also used a striking visual aid in this section of the speech so his listeners could see what a family medical tree might look like.

Conclusion: The conclusion consists of paragraph 14, in which the speaker summarizes his main points and reinforces the central idea by referring to the

UCLA School of Public Health's *50 Simple Things You Can Do to Save Your Life*. He then gives the speech a sense of psychological unity by alluding back to his opening example of Gilda Radner. The closing line is somewhat dramatic and ends the speech by once again relating the topic directly to the audience.

Supporting Materials: The speaker uses one extended example—the story of Gilda Radner in paragraph 1, which introduces the topic and dramatizes the need to know one's family medical history. The story of Radner's tragic death hangs over the entire speech and is mentioned again by the speaker in his conclusion.

Unfortunately, the speaker did not have time to present a second extended example—this time of someone whose life had been saved by creating a family medical history. Although this would have been very helpful in demonstrating the practicality of the speaker's solution, it was more important that he include the opening example. If a speaker has time for only one extended example, as is frequently the case in classroom speeches, he or she can usually get the greatest rhetorical mileage out of the example by presenting it in the introduction.

The speaker uses statistics more than any other kind of supporting material. In paragraph 1 he mentions the survival rates for ovarian cancer as part of the Gilda Radner story. In paragraphs 4-5 he gives figures from U.S. News and World Report and researchers at the University of Utah to support his point that hereditary factors play an important role in many diseases. In paragraphs 8-9 he presents the results of two studies published in the New York State Journal of Medicine to illustrate the fact that doctors often do not include family history as part of their patients' medical records.

The only instance of testimony occurs at the end of paragraph 9, where the speaker quickly cites the Hereditary Cancer Institute at Creighton University in support of his claim that only a small minority of doctors take hereditary factors into account when diagnosing and treating patients. Not only would a stronger citation have been more effective here, but the speech as a whole would have been improved if the speaker had included more testimony in support of his position. Although he uses a fair number of statistics, he should have provided at least a couple quotations from highly qualified medical experts to bolster his view of the problem and of the practicality of his solution.

———————————————

A Friend in Need

Sandy Hefty

---

1   Loretta Olson sometimes gets confused and does some pretty bizarre things. For instance, sometimes she puts her ice cream in the refrigerator instead of the freezer, and sometimes she feeds her cat chocolate chips instead of cat food. You see, Loretta is an 85-year-old woman who suffers from Alzheimer's disease. She was preceded in death by her husband and only child and now is trying to live on her own the best that she can. You may be wondering how somebody as confused as Loretta could possibly keep living on her own, but she does.

2   During my freshman year, I volunteered six hours a week to help Loretta remain independent in her home. Due to the forgetfulness associated with Alzheimer's disease, my main duty as a volunteer was to help Loretta with her cooking and house cleaning, which she often forgot to finish on her own.

3   Since I started volunteering time with Loretta, I've learned that there are millions of elderly Americans who need help to remain independent in their homes. According to the United States Census Bureau, our elderly population is the fastest growing segment in the nation. This trend is even seen in my class survey, in which all but two of you said you have living grandparents and seven of you said you have grandparents living alone.

4   Although the elderly are no longer the poorest segment of American society, according to the Poverty and Wealth Branch of the United States Census Bureau, 1.8 million Americans in the 75-plus age group fall below the poverty line. One point eight million—that's roughly the populations of Seattle, Indianapolis, and Boston combined.

5   Today, I would like to persuade each of you to help solve the problems facing more advanced and less fortunate elderly Americans by volunteering time to help them remain independent in their homes. Let's begin by addressing the problems that can occur among this group of people.

6   There are two problems that can occur when elderly people living alone do not get the companionship and care they need. The first problem is that elderly people may not be able to meet all of their physical needs. Before I met Loretta, I was a caregiver for an 87-year-old woman who suffered from arthritis. This woman often needed help buttoning her blouse and tying her shoes, as well as needing help cutting vegetables for meals and doing light house cleaning. This is not unusual for many people of advanced age. Like Loretta, they can continue living at home, but need help with certain physical tasks such as house cleaning, food preparation, and transportation.

7   Not only is there the problem of elderly people not meeting all of their physical needs, but there is a second, more tragic problem that can occur. That second problem is suicide. According to the National Center for Vital Statistics, persons age 75 and older have the highest rate of suicide compared to all other age groups. Anthony Boxwell, author of the article entitled "Geriatric Suicide: The Preventable Death," says that suicide among the elderly stems from three main causes—helplessness, hopelessness and haplessness. Helplessness describes the feelings of impotence some elderly people feel after retirement or upon realizing they're losing their physical and mental vigor. Hopelessness is associated with depression caused by the realization of the onset of old age. And haplessness refers to a series of repeated losses, such as loss of earnings, friends, and family.

8   Now that we have talked about the two major problems facing elderly people who do not get the companionship and care they need, let's talk about what we can do to help solve these problems.

9   We as individuals can't do everything, of course. Some responsibility lies with families, government, and charitable agencies. But there is something we can do, and that is get involved with a volunteer program that assists elderly people who need help living at home. Here in Wisconsin, we have a Community Options Program, which is an individually tailored financial assistance method to help keep the elderly and people with disabilities out of nursing homes. Right here in Madison, Independent Living has a Friendly Visiting Program in which volunteers provide companionship and household assistance for elderly people who live at home. You can contact Independent Living by calling the number on this handout, which I will be giving you after my speech.

10   Now I'm sure you have some questions about this kind of work. For instance, how much time does it take? It takes as much time as you want to put into it. You can volunteer as little as one to two hours a week or as many as forty hours a week. You decide how much time you want to volunteer based on your own schedule. But no matter how much time you spend, you will certainly experience great personal gratification. I know I have. I have been a volunteer for six years, and volunteering time with people who are less fortunate than I makes me feel good about myself. Volunteering time with the elderly has also taught me unique ethnic traditions, as well as American history.

11   You should also know that this kind of volunteer work can have benefits for you beyond feelings of personal gratification. Some volunteer organizations such as the state-run Community Options Program and the federally funded Title 19 Program offer financial assistance to people who participate. This can run from reimbursement of your travel expenses to an actual salary for certain kinds of work.

12   In closing, I am urging you to volunteer time to help needy elderly people remain independent in their homes. Remember that spending time with elderly people living alone can help them meet their physical and emotional needs. You can adjust the time spent to fit your needs, you can get great personal gratification, and you can even receive monetary benefits as well. But most important, Loretta Olson—and millions like her—will be forever thankful for your efforts.

A Friend in Need   *by Sandy Hefty*

Commentary

"A Friend in Need" is a persuasive speech on a question of policy. In addition to illustrating many of the methods of persuasion discussed in the textbook, it provides a helpful model of how students can use Monroe's motivated sequence to organize persuasive speeches that seek immediate action. Here is a synopsis of it.

Specific Purpose: To persuade my audience to volunteer time to help needy elderly people remain independent in their homes.

Central Idea: By participating in a volunteer program, college students can help needy elderly people continue to live independently in their homes.

Method of Organization: Monroe's motivated sequence

Introduction: The introduction consists of paragraphs 1-5. The opening story about Loretta Olson gets the audience's attention and also contains a gentle trace of humor. When the speech was delivered in class, several members of the audience chuckled as they identified Loretta Olson's forgetfulness with the memory lapses experienced by some of their elderly relatives. In paragraph 2 the speaker explains her personal involvement with the topic and, at the same time, establishes her credibility and good will.

In paragraphs 3 and 4 the speaker uses statistics from the U.S. Census Bureau to establish the importance of the topic. Her comparison, in paragraph 4, between the 1.8 million Americans in the 75-plus age group who fall below the poverty line and the combined populations of Seattle, Boston, and Indianapolis is an excellent illustration of how speakers can translate large numbers into figures that are more meaningful to the audience. It is also worth noting how, in paragraph 3, the speaker relates the topic to her audience by mentioning the results of her class survey, which showed that almost all of her classmates had living grandparents. Paragraph 5 ends the introduction by stating the speaker's central idea and providing a clear lead-in to the body of the speech.

Body: After getting the attention of her audience in the introduction, the speaker begins the body of her speech in paragraphs 6 and 7 with the second step in Monroe's motivated sequence—showing the need for a new course of action. In paragraph 6 the speaker explains that many elderly people cannot meet all of their physical needs, and she illustrates the point with an example of an 87-year-old woman whom she helped as a caregiver. Had she had more time, she could have provided more support for this point, but, as in most classroom speeches, she had to develop her points crisply and concisely.

In paragraph 7 the speaker continues with the need step of Monroe's motivated sequence by discussing the tragic problem of suicide among the elderly. After presenting figures from the National Center for Vital Statistics showing that persons age 75 and older have the highest suicide rate in the U.S., she provides testimony from Anthony Boxwell about the causes of suicide among the elderly. As in other parts of the speech, the speaker uses credible evidence and identifies her sources for the audience.

After an excellent transition in paragraph 8, the speaker moves to the satisfaction step of the motivated sequence by explaining, in paragraph 9, how students can participate in volunteer programs to help the elderly. Rather than talking in abstract terms, the speaker relates her plan to her classmates at the University of Wisconsin by focusing on state and local programs in which they can get involved. After the speech, she provided her audience a handout identifying volunteer agencies they could contact.

Of course, getting an audience to agree that something should be done and getting an audience to do something are two different matters. In paragraphs 10 and 11, therefore, the speaker turns to the visualization step of the motivated sequence by showing the audience the practicality of getting involved in a volunteer program to help the elderly. She explains that students can readily adapt their volunteer work to their personal schedules, that they will experience substantial personal gratification from volunteering, and even that they might be able to receive financial assistance for their efforts. Had the speaker failed to address these issues, her speech would have been much less effective.

Conclusion: The speaker concludes with the final step in Monroe's motivated sequence—an appeal to the audience to take action. After quickly summarizing her main points, she closes with the poignant statement that "Loretta Olson—and millions like her—will be forever thankful for your efforts." The emotional appeal of this line, in combination with the sense of psychological unity gained by referring back to the opening example, closes the speech on a strong note.

A Reel Doctor's Advice to Some Real Doctors

Alan Alda

---

1   Ever since it was announced that a nondoctor, in fact an actor, had been invited to give the commencement address at one of the most prestigious medical schools in the country, people have been wondering—why get someone who only *pretends* to be a doctor when you could get a real one?

2   Some people have suggested that this school had done everything it could to show you how to *be* doctors and in a moment of desperation had brought in someone who could show you how to act like one.

3   It's certainly true that I'm not a doctor. I have a long list of non-qualifications. In the first place I'm not a great fan of blood. I don't mind people having it, I just don't enjoy seeing them wear it. I have yet to see a real operation because the mere smell of a hospital reminds me of a previous appointment. And my knowledge of anatomy resides in the clear understanding that the hip bone is connected to the leg bone.

4   I am not a doctor. But you have asked me, and all in all, I think you made a wonderful choice.

5   I say that because I probably first came to the attention of this graduating class through a character on television that I've played and helped write for the past seven years—a surgeon called Hawkeye Pierce. He's a remarkable person, this Hawkeye, and if you have chosen somehow to associate his character with your own graduation from medical school, then I find that very heartening. Because I think it means that you are reaching out toward a very human kind of doctoring—and a very real kind of doctor.

6   We didn't make him up. He really lived as several doctors who struggled to preserve life 25 years ago during the Korean War. In fact, it's because he's based on real doctors that there is something especially engaging about him.

7   He has a sense of humor, and yet he's serious. He's impertinent, and yet he has feeling. He's human enough to make mistakes, and yet he hates death enough to push himself past his own limits to save lives. In many ways he's the doctor patients want to have and doctors want to be.

8   But he's not an idealization. Finding himself in a war, he's sometimes angry, sometimes cynical, sometimes a little nuts. He's not a magician who can come up with an instant cure for a rare disease without sweating and ruining his make-up. He knows he might fail. Not a god, he walks gingerly on the edge of disaster—alive to his own mortality.

9   If this image of that very human, very caring doctor is attractive to you—if it's ever touched you for a moment as something to reach for in your own life—then I'm here to cheer you on. Do it. Go for it. Be skilled, be learned, be aware of the dignity of your calling—but please, don't ever lose sight of your own simple humanity.

10   Unfortunately, that may not be so easy. You're entering a special place in our society. People will be awed by your expertise. You'll be placed in a position of privilege. You'll live well. People will defer to you, call you by your title—and it may be hard to remember that the word "doctor" is not actually your first name.

11   I know what this is like to some extent because in some ways you and I *are* alike. We both study the human being. And we both try to offer relief—you through medicine, I through laughter; we both try to reduce suffering. We've both learned difficult disciplines that have taken years to master, and we've both dedicated ourselves to years of hard work. And we both charge a lot.

12   We live in a society that has decided to reward my profession and yours, when we succeed in them, very highly. It can sometimes be easy to forget that the cab driver also works 14 or 15 hours a day and is also drained of energy when he's through. It's easy to think that because our society grants us privilege we're entitled to it.

13   Privilege feels good, but it can be intoxicating. As good doctors, I hope you'll be able to keep yourselves free of toxins.

14   It's no wonder, though, that people will hold you in awe. I know I do.

15   You've spent years in a grueling effort to know the structure and process of human life. I can't imagine a more difficult task. It has required the understanding of complexities within complexities, and there has been more pressure placed on you in four years than most people would be willing to take in a lifetime. I stand here in utter amazement at what you've accomplished. And I congratulate you.

16   I only ask one thing of you: Possess your skills, but don't be possessed by them.

17   Certainly your training has encouraged you to see the human side of your work, and you've examined the doctor-patient relationship. But still, the enormity of your task has required you to focus to such an extent on technique and data that you may not have had time enough to face your feelings along the way.

18   You've had to toughen yourself to death. From your first autopsy, when you may have been sick, or cried, or just been numb, you've had to inure yourself to death in order to be useful to the living. But I hope in the process you haven't done too good a job of burying that part of you that hurts and is afraid.

19   I know what it's like to be absorbed in technique. When I write for *M*A*S*H* I'm always writing about people in crisis with what I hope is compassion and feeling. And yet one day I found myself talking to someone who was in a real crisis and real pain—and I remember thinking, "This would make a *great* story."

20   Both of these things—becoming set apart and becoming your skill—can make it tough to be a compassionate person.

21   All right, that's my diagnosis of the problem. Here's my prescription.

22   I'd like to suggest to you, just in case you haven't done it lately, that this would be a very good time to give some thought to exactly what your values are, and then to figure out how you're going to live by them. Knowing what you care about and then devoting yourself to it is just about the only way you can pick your way through the minefield of existence and come out in one piece.

23   It can be a startling experience when you try to rank your values, though. Just ask yourself what's the most important thing in the world to you. Your work? Your family? Your money? Your country? Getting to heaven? Sex? Alcohol? What? (I don't need a show of hands on this!)

24   Then, when you get the answer to that, ask yourself how much time you actually spend on your number-one value—and how much time you spend on what you thought was number five, or number ten. What in fact is the thing you value most?

25   It may not be easy to decide. We live in a time that seems to be split about its values. In fact it seems to be schizophrenic.

26   For instance, if you pick up a magazine like *Psychology Today*, you're liable to see an article like "White Collar Crime: It's More Widespread Than You Think." Then in the back of the magazine they'll print an advertisement that says, "We'll write your doctoral thesis for 25 bucks." You see how values are eroding? I mean a doctoral thesis ought to go for at least a C-note.

27   The question is, *where* are their values? *What* do they value? Unfortunately, the people we look to for leadership seem to be providing it by negative example.

28   All across the country this month commencement speakers are saying to graduating classes, "We look to you for tomorrow's leaders." That's because today's leaders are all in jail.

29   Maybe we can afford to let politicians operate in a moral vacuum, but we can't afford to let doctors operate under those conditions.

30   You know how we're feeling these days, as the power and fuel monopoly has its way with us. Well, you people graduating today are entering a very select group. You have a monopoly on medical care. Please be careful not to abuse this power that you have over the rest of us.

31   You need to know what you care about most and what you care about least. And you need to know now. You will be making life-and-death decisions, and you will often be making them under stress and with great speed. The time to make your tender choices is not in the heat of the moment.

32   When you're making your list, let me urge you to put people first. And I include in that not just people, but that which exists *between* people.

33   I suggest to you that what makes people know they're alive—and in some cases keeps them alive—is not merely the interaction of the parts of their bodies, but the interaction of their selves with other selves. Not just people, but what goes on between people.

34   Let me challenge you. With all your study, you can name all the bones in my body. You can read my x-rays like a telegram. But can you read my involuntary muscles? Can you see the fear and uncertainty in my face?

35   If I tell you where it hurts, can you hear in my voice where I ache? I show you my body, but I bring you my person. Can you see me through your reading glasses?

36   Will you tell what you're doing, and in words I can understand? Will you tell me when you don't know what to do? Can you face your own fear, your own uncertainty? When in doubt, can you call in help?

37   These are things to consider even if you don't deal directly with patients. If you're in research, administration, if you write—no matter what you do—eventually there is always going to be a patient at the other end of your decisions.

38   Now, of course, everyone is for this in principle. Who's against people? But it gets harder when you get specific.

39   Will you be the kind of doctor who cares more about the *case* than the *person*? ("Nurse, call the gastric ulcer and have him come in at three." "How's the fractured femur in Room 208?") You'll know you're in trouble if you find yourself wishing they would mail you their liver in a plain brown envelope.

40   Where does money come on your list? Will it be the sole standard against which you reckon your success? How much will it guide you in relating to your patients? Do patients in a clinic need less of your attention than private patients? Are they, for instance, less in need of having things explained to them?

41   Where will your family come on your list? How many days and nights, weeks and months, will you separate yourself from them, buried in your work, before you realize that you've removed yourself from an important part of your life?

42   And if you're a male doctor, how will you relate to women? Women as patients, as nurses, as fellow doctors—and later as students. Will you be able to respect your patient's right to know and make decisions about her own body? Will you see nurses as colleagues—or as handmaidens? And if the day comes when you are teaching, what can young women medical students expect from you?

43   Questionnaires filled out by women at 41 medical schools around the country have revealed a distressing pattern. The women were often either ignored in class or simply not taken seriously as students. They were told that they were only there to find a husband and that they were taking the places of men who would then have to go out and become chiropractors. (Logic is not the strong point of sexism.)

44   They were often told that women just didn't belong in medicine. And at times they were told this by the very professors who were grading them. They would be shown slides of *Playboy* nudes during anatomy lectures—to the accompaniment of catcalls and wisecracks from male students. And in place of discussions about their work, they would often hear a discussion of their appearance. These are reports from 41 different medical schools.

45   I'm dwelling on this because it seems to me that the male-female relationship is still the most personal and intense test of humane behavior. It is a crucible for decency.

46   I hope you men will work to grant the same dignity to your female colleagues that you yourselves enjoy.

47   And if you're a female doctor, I hope you'll be aware that you didn't get where you are all by yourself. You've had to work hard, of course. But you're sitting where you are right now in part because way back in 1848, in Seneca Falls, women you never knew began insisting you had a right to sit there. Just as they helped a generation they would never see, I urge you to work for the day when your daughters and their daughters will be called not "A woman doctor," or "My doctor, who's a woman," but simply "My doctor."

48   It may seem strange to rank the things you care about. But when you think about it, there isn't an area of your work that won't be affected by what you decide to place a high value on and what you decide doesn't count.

49   Decide now.

50   Well, that's my prescription. I've given you kind of a big pill to swallow, but I think it'll make you feel better. And if not—well, look, I'm only human.

51   I congratulate you, and please let me thank you for taking on the enormous responsibility that you have—and for having the strength to have made it to this day. I don't know how you've managed to learn it all.

52   But there is one more thing you can learn about the body that only a nondoctor would tell you—and I hope you'll always remember this: The head bone is connected to the heart bone, and don't let them come apart.

A Reel Doctor's Advice to Some Real Doctors   *by Alan Alda*

Commentary

An actor giving a commencement speech at a medical school? Many people must have asked themselves this question when it was announced that Alan Alda would address the 210th graduating class of New York's Columbia College of Physicians and Surgeons in May 1979.

Alda, of course, is not just any actor. At the time the speech was delivered, he played Army surgeon Captain Hawkeye Pierce in the classic television series M*A*S*H. Over the course of the series, he won Emmy awards as an actor, writer, and director. *Time* magazine once called him "perhaps America's favorite doctor."

Still, the idea of an actor offering advice to doctors is so unusual that Alda needed to take special steps to establish his credibility and to adapt his message to the audience. Alda accomplished both of these tasks with consummate skill, and even though his speech was delivered more than two decades ago, it remains a model of rhetorical excellence. For people who are familiar with Alda's voice, it is possible to get a fuller sense of the speech by "hearing" him deliver it.

The speech was greeted enthusiastically by Alda's listeners and received much favorable comment in the press. It is reprinted with permission from the Columbia College of Physicians and Surgeons. Here is a synopsis of it.

Specific Purpose: To persuade the graduates of the Columbia College of Physicians and Surgeons to analyze the values they will follow in their careers as doctors.

Central Idea: Be skilled, be learned, be aware of the dignity of your calling—but please don't ever lose sight of your own simple humanity.

Method of Organization: Problem-Solution

Introduction: The introduction runs through paragraph 9. Alda's main task here is to establish his credibility as an actor advising an audience of medical doctors. He begins by confronting the question directly: "Why get someone who only pretends to be a doctor when you could get a real one?" He uses humor to make clear that he has no pretensions of being a doctor, and he spends paragraphs 5-8 discussing Hawkeye Pierce, the television character for which he is famous. In addition to reinforcing Alda's credibility, these paragraphs introduce the kind of doctor Alda will urge his audience to be. Paragraph 9 brings the introduction to an end by announcing the central idea of the speech: "Be skilled, be learned, be aware of the dignity of your calling—but please don't ever lose sight of your own simple humanity."

Body: The body of Alda's speech contains two main points. The first begins in paragraph 10 and deals with the problems that keep doctors from being as humane and as compassionate as they should be. Alda finishes discussing this main point with the internal summary in paragraph 20. Paragraph 21 is a transition into the second main point, which begins in paragraph 22. Having defined the problem in main point I, Alda gives a solution in main point II. The solution is to decide "exactly what your values are, and then to figure out how you're going to live by them" (paragraph 22). Alda continues to discuss the solution through paragraph 49.

Conclusion: The conclusion, which is quite effective, begins in paragraph 50. Notice especially the last paragraph, which poignantly reinforces the central idea.

Audience Adaptation: Alda uses a number of methods to build his credibility and to establish common ground with his audience. They include expressions of humility (paragraphs 1-3, 50); humor (paragraphs 2-3, 11, 23, 26, 28, 39); expressions of confidence in himself (paragraph 4); drawing on the audience's positive attitudes toward Hawkeye Pierce (paragraph 5); noting the similarities between actors and doctors (paragraphs 11-12, 19); and complimenting the audience (paragraphs 14-15, 51). It is worth noting that most of these appear in the first half of the speech, before Alda concentrates on giving advice to his audience.

Ghosts

Ken Lonnquist

---

1   There are ghosts in this room. We cannot see them, but they are here. They have come to us from a far off place—some billowing up out of the pages of history books, others returning to us after only a short absence. Some are large; some are old; some are very young; and some are very, very small. Some are the ghosts of men and women who more than a century ago trod upon the same ground which we are treading today. Some are spirits which look to us for justice—tiny spirits that look to us for retribution for an act of wrong that was committed against them. And then there are the other ghosts—ourselves, the ghosts which we, ourselves, have become—puppets in a judgment play which is being dusted off and reenacted by history after centuries.

2   I first became aware of these ghosts when I announced to you the nature of my discourse for today. Those who were hostile in their reaction to my subject—those who said to me, "Our minds cannot be changed," those who said in effect, "We will not listen"—made me think: "What kind of a people are we? What kind of a people have we become when we will no longer listen to one another?"

3   In that moment, I was haunted by visions of a bygone era—a time in which abolitionists were afforded much the same treatment as I had just been. For, you see, they too were involved in a titanic, moral struggle—a grave moral crisis. They were speaking out against a notion that was deeply imbedded in the minds of nineteenth-century men and women—the notion that black men and black women were not human. They were speaking out against slavery—that wicked by-product of prejudice. At times they were ignored by indifferent masses. At times they were tarred and feathered and run out of town. At times they were murdered. Never were they listened to, because the men and the women of the nineteenth century who favored human bondage had decided that their minds could not be changed on the matter. They had decided that they would not listen.

4   Now I have come here today, as you all know, to speak for life—human life and human rights. And there is something—something about my subject which seems strangely reminiscent—reminiscent of, and haunted by, the days, the people, and the events of the nineteenth century. It is more than just a parallel between the treatment that was accorded abolitionist speakers and the treatment that is accorded antiabortionist speakers today. It is deeper than that. It rests in the very heart of the issue—in the very heart of each moral struggle.

5   You see, in the 1840s it was argued by proslavery forces that their rights as citizens of the United States were being subverted by abolitionists who were working to eradicate slavery. "The abolitionists," they argued, "are denying us our constitutional right to hold property." They could not see that their rights of property could not supersede the rights of black men and black women to life, liberty, and the pursuit of happiness. They could not see, because they did not regard black men or black women to be of human life. They were blinded by the prejudice of their age.

6   And today a similar logic has been evolved by the proponents of abortion. They argue that their rights of self-determination are being infringed upon by those who would take away the option of terminating a pregnancy. They do not recognize that they are determining the course of not one life, but two. They cannot see because they do not recognize a human life in its earliest stages to be human.

7   Now there are many kinds of life, and what we have to ask ourselves is, "What is life? What is human life? What are the values we attach to human life? What are the rights we grant to those whom we say possess human life?" These are the questions which I believe must be asked when dealing with the matter of abortion. These are the questions over which this whole controversy rages.

8   The concept of life is not so difficult to understand. We look at a stone and we say, "It does not live." We look at a flower and we say, "It lives." We may crush the flower, it dies. A biological process has been halted, and the mysterious thing that we call life has been taken away.

9   As I said before, there are many kinds of life. And each is distinct from all the rest. The kind of life that we possess is human life. We all recognize this to be true. But down through the course of the centuries there have been those who, for reasons of fulfilling their own ends, have attempted to qualify the definition of human life. For centuries slaveholders claimed that blacks were not human. For them, color was the key element in defining the humanity of an individual. Today there are many who claim that a human being in its earliest states is not a human being—and that the life it possesses as a biologically functioning entity is not a human life. In their mentality, age becomes the key element in determining the humanity of an individual.

10   Once there was a color line. Today there is an age line. But an age-line definition of humanity is no more just—is just as fallacious, and just as evil, as was the color line which existed in the past.

11   Even in the textbook *The Essentials of Human Embryology*, it says, "The fertilized egg is the beginning of a new individual." It cannot be denied. The fertilized egg is, itself, a human being in its earliest stages. It is not a zebra; it is not a monkey. It is human. Whether or not it is a fully developed human is not the issue. The issue is humanity. And a fertilized egg is human life.

12   Look around you at the other members of this class. Just look for a moment and ask yourselves, "Was there ever a time in the existence of any of us here in which we were nonhuman?" I do not believe so.

13   Now we have laws. We do not have any laws which govern the lives of plants. We have but one law which governs the life of an animal. That animal is man. The law has been written and rewritten down through the course of the centuries—in stone, on leather, on parchment, on paper, in languages that have been lost and long forgotten. But the law has remained the same. No man, it states, may take the life of another man. Perhaps you would recognize it this way: "We hold these truths to be self-evident—that all men are created equal and are endowed by their Creator with certain unalienable rights—that among these rights are life." Or this way, quite simply stated, in another book: "Thou shalt not kill."

14   Whatever their form, the laws are there. And there were no qualifications written into these laws on the basis of race, on the basis of color, on the basis of creed, on the basis of sex—nor were there any qualifications written into these laws on the basis of age. What the whole matter boils down to is this: A human life has been determined by us, for centuries, millennia, to be sacred, and we have determined that it cannot be taken away. And a fertilized egg is human life.

15   Now for any violations of these laws to occur, especially on a grand scale as is happening today, a mentality has to have been developed through which those who are going to commit a wrong can justify their actions and can appease the guilt that they might feel—the guilt that they might feel if they had to admit that they were killing a living human entity. And this is what we have done. This is what we are doing. We have learned to call a flower a stone. Why? And how?

16   You see, we are blinded. Just as Americans of another generation were blinded by prejudice, we are blinded by violence. We live in a violent society, in which the killing of a young human being means no more to us than the holding in bondage of black men and black women meant to another generation of Americans. Said E. Z. Freidenburg on this matter, "Not only do most people accept violence if it is perpetrated by legitimate authority—they also regard violence against certain kinds of people as inherently legitimate, no matter who commits it." An abolitionist once was speaking about this condition, and he said, "You might call it paralysis of the nerves about the heart, in a people constantly given over to selfish aims." We have become selfish. And in our selfishness, have become heartless.

17   We say that it is our right to control our bodies, and this is true. But there is a distinction that needs to be made, and that distinction is this: Preventing a pregnancy is controlling a body—controlling your body. But preventing the continuance of a human life that is not your own is murder. If you attempt to control the body of another in that fashion, you become as a slave master was—controlling the lives and the bodies of his slaves, chopping off their feet when they ran away, or murdering them if it pleased him. This was not his right; it is not our right.

18   Abortion is often argued for in terms of its beneficiality. It is better, some say, that these young human beings do not come into the world. It is better for them; it is better for the parents; it is better for society at large. And they may be right. It may be more beneficial.

19   But what we are arguing is not beneficiality. We are not arguing pragmatism. We are not arguing convenience. We are arguing right and wrong. It was more convenient for slaveholders to maintain a system of slavery, but it was wrong. A matter of principle cannot be compromised for a matter of convenience. It cannot be done.

20   Now I'd like to say something more about the whole matter. I'd like to say something particularly to the women in the room, who I think should understand more clearly what I have to say now than the men.

21   For thousands of years women have been deprived of their rights. They have been second-class citizens and have been, in the eyes of many, something less than human themselves. For thousands of years they have been controlled, physically and mentally, by men. They have been controlled through physical power and physical coercion. But in this age of enlightenment—in this age of feminism—it has rightly been determined that might does not make right. The fact that males might be able to physically dominate females did not make their doing so just, and it did not mean that females were not deserving of protection under the law so that they might pursue the course of their choice.

22   But today, after tens of thousands of years, the tables are turning. Today men and women (who more than any man should understand the shamefulness and the unjustness and the inhumanity involved in control through physical power) have been determining not the roles that another segment of humanity will have in life, but whether or not this segment of humanity will have life at all. Under the pretext of controlling their own bodies, they are setting out on a course of controlling the bodies of others. After tens of thousands of years, they are transferring the shackles in which they themselves have languished, and against which they have struggled, onto a new segment of humanity—only with a difference. The shackles have been transformed into a guillotine.

23   Why? It has happened because no one will do anything about it. No one will stop it. We are all like ghosts in the fire. We are all involved. Although we do not hold the knife in our hand, neither do we stay the hand that does hold the knife.

24   History is repeating itself. Abraham Lincoln once said that the eyes of history were upon us and that we would be remembered in spite of ourselves. He also said, "We are engaged in a cause, a struggle, not just for today, but for all the ensuing generations."

25   And so are we. Ghosts are crowding around us, and looking, and watching what we do. Frederick Douglass once said, in speaking of black bondage, "I hear the mournful wail of millions." Today there are the ghosts of the past, the ghosts of the present, and the ghosts of all the ensuing generations watching us, and watching the struggle that is being repeated—the struggle of human life. I, too, hear the mournful wail of millions.

Ghosts   *by Ken Lonnquist*

Commentary

"Ghosts" is particularly interesting because it provides an example of a classroom speech delivered to an audience made up almost entirely of people opposed to the speaker's point of view. It is reprinted here with permission from Wil A. Linkugel, R. R. Allen, and Richard L. Johannesen (eds.), *Contemporary American Speeches*, 4th ed. (Dubuque, Iowa: Kendall/Hunt, 1978). Here is a synopsis.

Specific Purpose: To persuade my audience that abortion is morally wrong.

Central Idea: Abortion is morally wrong because it is the taking of a human life.

Method of Organization: Topical

Introduction: The introduction is long (paragraphs 1-7), complex, and in some ways quite artful. Its major function, in addition to the usual functions of an introduction, is to get the audience to listen to the speaker even though they disagree with him. The opening paragraph does an excellent job of gaining attention with its suspenseful images of "ghosts in this room." In paragraphs 2-4 the speaker chastises listeners who say their minds "cannot be changed" and tries to build his credibility by identifying his position with that of nineteenth-century abolitionists. Paragraphs 5-6 introduce the central idea of the speech by claiming that the stand of people who favor legalized abortion today is analogous to that of pro-slavery forces in the 1840s. Paragraph 7 completes the introduction by previewing some of the major questions to be pursued in the body.

When delivered in class, this introduction worked very effectively. Many students who read it, however, find it troublesome. The initial paragraph, they say, is confusing because it suggests that the speech is actually about ghosts or some other paranatural phenomenon. Moreover, they feel that the comparisons among proabortionists, antiabortionists, and slave owners are dragged out much longer than necessary. Finally, they claim that the topic of the speech is never clearly announced in the introduction. When this speech is discussed in class, a keen debate usually develops among students over the merits of the introduction.

Body: The body of the speech can be divided into five main sections. The first section starts in paragraph 8 and develops the speaker's view that "a fertilized egg is human life"—just like other forms of human life. The second section begins in paragraph 13 and claims that it is wrong to take any form of human life, regardless of its color, creed, age, or sex. The third section begins in paragraph 15 and argues that the violence of our time has blinded many people from seeing the wrongness of abortion. The fourth section begins in paragraph 17 and deals with the counterarguments that women have a right to control their own bodies and that abortion is socially beneficial. The fifth section begins in paragraph 20 and is addressed specifically to the women in the audience.

Conclusion: The conclusion consists of paragraphs 23-25. The speaker seeks to reinvigorate feelings of guilt and personal responsibility for abortion. He turns again to the ghost imagery used in the introduction, and he invokes once more the analogy between abortion and slavery. The final paragraph is particularly effective in bringing the speech full circle and reinforcing its emotional appeal.

Reasoning: This speech is dominated by reasoning from analogy. The speaker develops a series of analogies in which the undeveloped fetus is compared with black slaves before the Civil War, proabortionists with slave owners, and antiabortionists with abolitionists. Just as the slaves had a right to freedom, the speaker claims, so the fetus has a right to life. Just as slave owners were wrong in claiming that their rights of property superseded the rights of black men and women to freedom, so proabortionists are wrong in claiming that the right of women to control their own bodies supersedes the right of the fetus to life. And just as abolitionists were right in fighting to free the slaves, so antiabortionists are right in fighting to save the lives of unborn children. These analogies run throughout the speech and can be found, explicitly or implicitly, in paragraphs 1-6, 9-10, 16-17, 19, and 24-25.

There is another major analogy in paragraphs 21-22. Here the speaker claims that the powerless state of women historically is similar to the powerless state of the undeveloped fetus today. Just as it was wrong for men to use their power to deprive women of their rights, so it is wrong for women to use their power to deprive "another segment of humanity" of its right to life.

These analogies focus attention on the questions of value involved in the abortion controversy. Yet in many ways the persuasiveness of this speech to a hostile audience may depend more on a question of fact than on a question of value. In essence, the speech can be seen as advancing an argument from principle:

General Principle: The killing of human beings is wrong.

Minor Premise: The fertilized egg is a human being.

Conclusion: Therefore, the killing of fertilized eggs is wrong.

The first premise, a question of value, is supported in paragraphs 13-14. Most listeners, regardless of their views on abortion, are likely to accept this premise. The second premise, essentially a question of fact, is supported in paragraphs 11-12. This is the crucial premise for listeners who favor abortion. Yet the speaker backs it up with only one piece of evidence. He says, "Even in the textbook, which is called *The Essentials of Human Life*, it says 'the fertilized egg is the beginning of a new individual'" (paragraph 11). But this quotation does not explicitly support the speaker's view. Moreover, even if it did, one brief quotation from a textbook whose author is not identified would probably not be strong enough evidence to persuade a listener who opposes the speaker's position. Given the opposition of his listeners, the speaker should have done a more thorough job of supporting his second premise.

James "Cool Papa" Bell

Ryan Saurer

---

1   In 1946 one of the greatest baseball players of all time retired after almost twenty-five years as a pro. No, it wasn't Babe Ruth, Joe DiMaggio, or any other star you've probably heard of. The man was James "Cool Papa" Bell, star of the Pittsburgh Crawfords of the Negro League.

2   The Negro League was the name of the league where black players were forced to play until 1947, when major league baseball became integrated. The Negro League had some of the best players never to be appreciated, and Cool Papa Bell headed that list.

3   Many say that Bell was the fastest player ever to play the game. This could very well be true. He led the league in stolen bases almost every year he played until he retired at age forty-one. Satchel Paige, a former teammate of his, said Cool Papa was so fast he could flip the switch and be in bed before the lights went out.

4   In fact, Jesse Owens, the Olympic sprinter who was known as the fastest man in the world, said he would race and beat anyone around the bases as long as that person wasn't Cool Papa Bell. At five feet, eleven inches tall and only 135 pounds, Bell was thin as a rail. But no one made fun of his slender size as he swiftly and smoothly stole second or scored from first on a single.

5   And Cool Papa was smooth. In his first game as a pro, the seventeen-year-old, then known as James, came into the game in the bottom of the ninth inning and struck out one of the league's best hitters on three straight pitches. Pretty smooth for a guy who wasn't even a pitcher. For playing with the savvy of a seasoned veteran even though he was only a kid, his manager called him "Cool Papa."

6   But to say that Cool Papa had style would be an injustice to him. Cool Papa *was* style. Whether in his baseball uniform or his Sunday best, Cool Papa had a flair all his own. Some of you may have seen flip-down sunglasses, a necessity and fashion statement for many major league players today. Flip-down sunglasses weren't unknown to Cool Papa. After all, he invented them.

7   But despite all of Cool Papa's baseball feats and the style with which he accomplished them, his greatest achievement was that he played at all. You see, James "Cool Papa" Bell was the victim of a disease known as racism—racism that kept him from playing in the same league as white players, racism that kept him from being in the same record books as white players, racism that kept him from earning the same money as white players. In fact, to make ends meet, Cool Papa would race home after each game just so he could change clothes and get to his second job as a nighttime security guard. This kind of thing would be unheard of for players today.

8   But despite the inequalities he faced, Cool Papa kept on playing the game he loved. He helped pave the way for Jackie Robinson, the first African American in the major leagues, and others who followed him. Cool Papa did this by fighting racism the same way he played baseball—stylishly but effectively. Despite knowing that he would never reach his dream of playing in the major leagues just because of his color, Cool Papa Bell, and many others for that matter, played on, hoping that someday there would be only one league—a league of professional baseball players, regardless of race.

9   So let's take a few moments, which is longer than it would take Cool Papa to steal second base, to appreciate James "Cool Papa" Bell—the speedy baseball star, the stylish innovator, the man who fought racism just by going to work every day.

James "Cool Papa" Bell   *by Ryan Saurer*

Commentary

"James 'Cool Papa' Bell" is a commemorative speech that deals with one of the greatest baseball players in the old Negro League, to which black players were relegated before the integration of major league baseball in 1947. The topic will probably be appreciated most by students who are baseball fans, but the speech transcends sports to focus on the larger issue of racism in U.S. society and the refusal of "Cool Papa" Bell to be ground down by it. The speech also illustrates the differences between a commemorative speech and an informative speech. Although the speaker provides information about Bell, he does not present a full view of Bell's life or even of his career as a baseball player. Rather, he focuses on Bell's most praiseworthy qualities and seeks to enhance his listeners' appreciation of those qualities. The speech is also available on *Speeches for Analysis and Discussion: A Videotape Supplement to The Art of Public Speaking, Fifth Edition.* Here is a synopsis.

Introduction: The introduction consists of paragraphs 1-2. The speaker begins by arousing curiosity about the topic of his speech. He then reveals that his subject is James "Cool Papa" Bell, who played his entire baseball career in the Negro League because the major leagues were still segregated. The last sentence of paragraph 2 identifies Bell as the finest player in the Negro League and provides a deft lead-in to the body of the speech.

Body: Composed of paragraphs 3-8, the body of the speech develops three main points. The first is that Bell was the fastest baseball player of all time (paragraphs 3-4). The second is that Bell played the game with a style all his own (paragraphs 5-6). The third—and most important—is that Bell was a pioneer who helped pave the way for Jackie Robinson and other African Americans who would later play Major League Baseball (paragraphs 7-8).

Throughout the body of the speech, the speaker provides well-chosen supporting materials to illustrate Bell's athleticism and character. The speaker also makes effective use of the resources of language discussed in Chapter 11 to elevate and polish the style of the speech. At the end of paragraph 4, for example, he employs alliteration in the sentence, "But no one made fun of his slender size as he swiftly and smoothly stole second or scored from first on a single."

In paragraph 8 the speaker uses repetition and parallelism to emphasize the extent to which Bell was victimized by racism—"racism that kept him from playing in the same league as white players, racism that kept him from being in the same record book as white players, racism that kept him from earning the same money as white players." The dexterity of this passage, in combination with its sharp message about the evils of racism, gives the speaker's words special force.

Conclusion: The conclusion consists of the final paragraph. After subtly announcing that the speech is coming to an end by saying, "So let's take a few moments . . . ," the speaker closes by reminding the audience of Bell's accomplishments as "the speedy baseball star, the stylish innovator, the man who fought racism just by going to work every day." The parallel structure of these phrases enhances the cadence of the speaker's delivery, while the final words—"the man who fought racism just by going to work every day"—provide a sense of drama and reinforce what the speaker sees as Bell's most important attainment.

The Survivors

Andrea Besikoff

---

1   "Work! Harder. Faster. Shovel! Don't just stand there. Shovel!"

2   And so he shoveled with all of his energy and all of his might. Hour after hour, he shoveled until his body could not shovel any more. Finally, he stopped working, leaned over on his shovel, and let his body limply rest, as his eyes stared at the ground.

3   The commander looked his way and hollered in a low and penetrating voice, "Shovel!" But the man did not move. The commander lifted his gun, loaded it with ammunition, and shot him. The man released his hands from the shovel and fell to the ground. He murmured his last words, "How could this happen?" The Nazi walked over, lifted his heel, and kicked the man into the mass grave, which he had been digging.

4   One more Jew was removed from this world. He was one of 6 million who was brought to his death by the Nazi policy to annihilate the Jewish race. The Nazis collected the Jews in the ghettos; they transported the Jews to the death camps; they worked the Jews until they could not work any more. Then they killed them—by gun and by gas, by starvation and sickness, by torture and terror.

5   Millions of Jews died in the death camps of Dachau, Buchenwald, Auschwitz, and Treblinka. It seems unfathomable that people could have survived the Nazis' wartime atrocities. Yet, by the grace of God, there were survivors. The survivors were the young and the strong, not the old and the meek. The survivors were the lucky and the few.

6   My grandparents are Holocaust survivors. They are each the only survivors in their families. They witnessed the deaths of their mothers and fathers, sisters and brothers, friends and neighbors. They witnessed the destruction of their lives and homes, towns and country, shops and synagogues. They lived through the ghettos. They lived through the death camps. They lived through the excruciating work. They lived to see liberation.

7   Since I was a little girl, my grandparents have told me about their lives during the Holocaust. They have told me about the persecution, the intolerance, and the injustice so that I could appreciate my freedom, my liberty, and my independence. It has always amazed me that my grandparents don't have spite or malice. After all they suffered, they have only hope and love. They don't want to hate any more.

8   During World War II, my grandparents were victims of anti-Semitism. Fifty years later, they are victims no longer. Today they fight against the "isms" which plague our communities, our states, our nation, and our world. They tell their story so that we, the younger generation, will understand the horrific force which anti-Semitism was in their lives. They relate their experiences to the struggles which so many people grapple with today. They will tell their story, and they will not rest until all people can live without fear and without denial—until all people can live with pride and with dignity.

9   And when my grandparents are gone, I will continue to tell their story. I will tell my children about the men and women who were murdered for no cause. I will tell my children about the heroism of the Jews in the Warsaw ghetto who fought strength for strength against the Nazi militia. I will tell these stories to all who will listen.

10   And I hope that you, too, will tell stories. As the Holocaust survivor and writer Elie Wiesel, once said, "Not to transmit an experience is to betray it."

11   To the millions who died in the Holocaust, lie peacefully in your graves, for you have not been forgotten.

The Survivors   *by Andrea Besikoff*

Commentary

An excellent commemorative speech, "The Survivors" functions at several levels. At one level, it pays tribute to the speaker's grandparents, who lived through Hitler's concentration camps in World War II. At another level, it honors those Jews who lost their lives in the camps. At yet another level, it is a celebration of human pride, freedom, and dignity in the face of tyranny and oppression. The speech also illustrates the differences between a commemorative speech and an informative speech. Although the speaker provides information about the Holocaust and her grandparents, she does not go into historical detail about either. Rather, she deals with her grandparents' experiences at a very general level and relates those experiences to larger issues of freedom and tolerance. In addition to discussing this speech in class, you may also want to show the videotape of it, which is available as part of the instructional supplement to *The Art of Public Speaking*. Here is a synopsis of the speech.

Introduction: As in many commemorative speeches, there is no visible break between the introduction and the body of "The Survivors." The best way to parse the introduction of this speech is to see it as running through paragraph 5. This is an unusually long introduction, but it works well to get the audience involved in the speech. After opening with a story about a Jewish prisoner who is murdered by a Nazi guard (paragraphs 1-3), the speaker expands briefly upon the millions of Jews killed during the Holocaust (paragraph 4). Then, in paragraph 5, she shifts attention to "the lucky and the few" who survived the Holocaust. Had the speaker made this shift sooner, it would not have had the same effect. She needed to spend time discussing the victims of the Holocaust before mentioning its survivors.

Body: The body of the speech (paragraphs 6-10) focuses on the speaker's grandparents. In paragraph 6 she discusses her grandparents' experiences during the war. In paragraphs 7-8 she relates her grandparents' story to "the struggles which so many people grapple with today." In paragraph 9 she notes that she will continue to tell her grandparents' story so people will not forget the horrors of the Holocaust or the heroism of its victims. In paragraph 10 she ends the body with the oft-quoted statement of Elie Wiesel that "Not to transmit an experience is to betray it."

Throughout the body of the speech, the speaker uses repetition and parallelism with great effectiveness. Paragraph 6, for example, proceeds through seven consecutive sentences that begin with the word "They." The last four sentences are especially powerful: "They lived through the ghettos. They lived through the death camps. They lived through the excruciating work. They lived to see liberation." Also note the last three sentences of paragraph 9, which begin with "I will tell . . ." The restatement of these words in parallel structure reinforces the speaker's ideas and strengthens the rhythm of her speech.

Conclusion: The conclusion is made up of the last three paragraphs, the first two of which continue the speaker's use of repetition and parallelism and restate her tribute to the victims of the Holocaust. The final sentence gives a sense of unity to the entire speech by reiterating the dying words of the man in the opening story. It also ends the speech on a powerful note by reinforcing the speaker's opposition to tyranny wherever it might occur around the globe.

Hail to the Heroes

James Davis

---

1   There are many great sporting events in the world and there are many great athletes, but no sporting event nor athlete better exemplifies the definition of courage, determination, and stamina than the Tour de France bicycle race and its magnificent racers.

2   Over a 2,400-mile course through the French countryside they race. Across endless flatlands and over demoralizing mountains they endure—nay, they conquer. To win the race outright is no more than a pipe dream for all but a select few. The real victory is to finish the race. It becomes not a competition against the other racers, but a competition against one's self. The capacity to transcend relentless pain is an earmark of any great athlete, but the racers of the Tour de France deserve special credit.

3   Courage—the quality of being brave. They show me this. Prim and trim, dressed in racing tights that reflect a kaleidoscope of colors, they gather at the starting line. But the flash and glimmer of the starting line is fleeting. At the sound of the gun, the battle begins, and as in all battles, there will be casualties. I remember one racer who suffered a broken nose and still continued. I've heard of many a racer who had dinner-plate sized patches of flesh torn away by sixty-mile-per-hour crashes and still continued. I recall another racer who suffered a broken arm and had a team doctor set it on the spot so he could continue. For courage like that, I say hail to the heroes.

4   Determination—a firm intention. They show me this. Only by failing to finish the race, say the bikers, is one truly defeated. So with this in mind, they grit their teeth and pedal on. Through blinding downpours, they wipe their glasses dry and pedal on. Suffering from freezing cold on mountain tops and sweltering heat in valleys, they pedal on. Enduring the voice within that cries for rest and relief, they pedal on. Suffering from agonizing backaches and a never-ending barrage of leg cramps, they pedal on. For determination like that, I say hail to the heroes.

5   Stamina—staunch resistance to fatigue. They show me this. For twenty-two days they race. Each day brings a new level of exhaustion that must be endured and overcome. When watching the bikers go by, one can almost read their facial expressions: "I want to stop, but I can't. Push, push, push." "My chest is exploding, I can hardly breathe, but I can't stop. Push, push, push." "One more climb. I can't make it. Yes, I can. Push, push, push." For this special brand of stamina, I say hail to the heroes.

6   In the morning light I often climb aboard my own bike. I push myself up hills and race down the other side. But not like they do. I pace myself on flatlands and straight-aways. But not like they do. I have courage, determination, and stamina. But not like they do. So during the Tour de France, I climb off my bike and become one in a throng and watch them as they pedal by and silently say to myself, hail to the heroes.

Hail to the Heroes   *by James Davis*

Commentary

"Hail to the Heroes" is a splendid commemorative speech. Rather than reciting a history of the Tour de France, the speaker focuses on what he regards as the most praiseworthy aspects of the racers who participate in it. The speech also illustrates how students can use the resources of language discussed in Chapter 11 to express their ideas vividly, even eloquently. Here is a synopsis of the speech.

Introduction: The introduction consists of paragraphs 1 and 2. In paragraph 1 the speaker announces his central idea—that "no sporting event nor athlete better exemplifies the definition of courage, determination, and stamina than the Tour de France bicycle race and its magnificent racers." In paragraph 2 he gives background information on the Tour for listeners who may not be familiar with it. The last sentence of paragraph 2 focuses attention back on the racers and provides a smooth lead-in to the body of the speech.

Body: The body of the speech consists of paragraphs 3-5, in which the speaker develops three main points. The first deals with the courage of the Tour de France racers (paragraph 3), the second with their determination (paragraph 4), and the third with their stamina (paragraph 5). The parallel wording at the start of each main point clarifies the structure of the speech and reinforces the speaker's ideas. So, too, does the parallel structure and the repetition of "hail to the heroes" at the end of each main point.

Throughout the body of the speech, the speaker brings his ideas to life with a variety of stylistic devices. In paragraph 3 he uses vivid, colorful language in combination with a series of brief examples to illustrate the courage of bikers who race on despite their injuries. In paragraph 4 he employs sharp imagery that captures the torturous physical conditions the bikers must endure. He also repeats "they pedal on" at the end of five successive sentences to reinforce the racers' determination in the face of those conditions. In paragraph 5 the speaker uses imaginary dialogue to give voice to the bikers' internal feelings as they endure fatigue and exhaustion. The impact of the dialogue is strengthened by its parallel structure and by the restatement of "Push, push, push" at the end of each sentence.

Conclusion: The conclusion consists of the final paragraph. By bringing himself into the speech at this point, the speaker not only reinforces the praiseworthy traits of the racers, but relates those traits to ordinary bikers such as himself. Once again he uses repetition and parallel structure to reinforce his ideas and to give them artistic unity. The final sentence provides a perfect ending for the speech—especially the repetition of "hail to the heroes" as the closing words.

My Grandfather

Kim Lacina

---

1   Every day people are born and people die. Human beings come into this world and leave it—most without their names being immortalized in any history books. Millions of people have lived and worked and loved and died without making any great claims to fame or fortune.

2   But they aren't forgotten—not by their friends, not by their families. And some of these people, some very special people, are not forgotten even by those who hardly knew them. My grandfather was one of these very special people.

3   What made him so special? Why is he remembered not only by friends and family but even by casual acquaintances? Very simply, because he was the essence of love. More than that, he was the essence of what I think of as "active" love. Just as his heart was not empty, his words were not empty.

4   He didn't just speak of compassion. During the Great Depression he took homeless people off the street into his home when they needed a place to sleep. He gave them food when they needed something to eat. And though he wasn't a rich man by any means, he gave them money when they had none. Those people off the street will remember the man who had enough love in his heart to share with them all that he had.

5   He didn't just speak of tolerance. During the 1960s, when his peers were condemning those "long-haired hippies," I can remember riding in the car with my grandfather, picking up dozens and dozens of those "long-haired hippies" who were hitchhiking, and going miles out of our way to give them a ride somewhere. Those men and women will remember the man who had enough love in his heart to bridge the gap between his world and theirs and to practice the spirit of brotherhood.

6   And he didn't just speak of courage. He proved his courage time and time again. He proved it to a little girl who was trapped in the basement of a burning building. He pulled her out of the flames and gave her back her life. And that little girl, now a grown woman, will remember the man who had enough love in his heart to risk his life for a person he didn't even know.

7   He also proved his courage, in a more personal way, to his family. In 1966 he was told he had leukemia and only a year to live. He immediately started chemotherapy treatment, and I don't know which is worse—the effects of the disease or the effects of those treatments. In the ensuing year we saw his hair fall out, we saw his skin turn a pasty shade of gray, and we saw him lose so much weight that he seemed to shrivel up into half the size he had been. We didn't want to see him go out that way.

8   And we didn't. He fought that disease with all his strength and all his courage. And despite the pain he endured, he never complained. I think about him when I catch myself complaining about my "tons of homework" or a "terrible headache," and suddenly that homework or that headache doesn't seem so terrible after all.

9   He lived through that first year, and he lived through eight more. And that disease never stopped him from working, and it never stopped him from caring. All through those years of suffering, he continued to show compassion and tolerance and courage.

10   He died in 1975. And though he left this world without ever making the pages of a history book, he still left the world a great deal. He left to the people who knew him a spirit to exemplify life—a spirit of unconditional, selfless, and truly inspiring love.

My Grandfather   *by Kim Lacina*

Commentary

Presented in an introductory public speaking class, "My Grandfather" illustrates how a commemorative speech should focus on the essence of its subject. Rather than presenting a biography that simply recounts the facts of her grandfather's life, the speaker deals with what she believes to be his most praiseworthy qualities. The speech also shows how students can use clear, simple language to convey meaning and to arouse emotion. Here is a synopsis of the speech:

Introduction: The introduction consists of paragraphs 1-3. Because many previous speakers had dealt with famous people, paragraphs 1-2 were especially effective in capturing the attention of the audience. At the end of paragraph 2 the speaker announces the exact topic of the speech, and in paragraph 3 she presents the central idea—that her grandfather was the essence of "active love." The last sentence of paragraph 3 helps to clarify what the speaker means by "active love" and provides a smooth bridge to the body of the speech.

Body: The body of the speech begins in paragraph 4 and runs through the next-to-last paragraph. Three main points are developed: "He didn't just speak of compassion" (paragraph 4); "He didn't just speak of tolerance" (paragraph 5); "He didn't just speak of courage" (paragraphs 6-9). The parallel wording of each main point reinforces the speaker's ideas and gives coherence to the body. So, too, does the repetition and parallelism in the last sentences of paragraphs 4-6. Throughout, the speaker gives her ideas life with specific examples that illustrate her grandfather's "active love." The language of the speech is clear, familiar, and concrete. Most of the words consist of one or two syllables, and there are few wasted words. The speech moves crisply from idea to idea. When delivered in class, it also picked up considerable emotional power as it proceeded.

Conclusion: The conclusion consists of the last paragraph. By stating that her grandfather "left this world without ever making the pages of a history book," the speaker relates back to her introduction. This gives the speech a sense of unity and signals that the speaker is about to conclude. The final sentence ties the entire speech together by rephrasing the central idea clearly and vividly.

Capital Punishment

Lee Hawkins, Jr.

---

1   Imagine being ready to die. On January 7, 1988, at 3:19 a.m., Texas began to execute convicted murderer Robert Streetland by pumping lethal drugs into his veins. Before he was pronounced dead seven minutes later, the telephone rang in the death chamber. The governor's office had received word that the United States Supreme Court was ready to consider a new motion of appeal. In the words of a prison spokesman, "The Supreme Court wanted to know where we were in the process, but by then it was too late."

2   I stand before you today to discuss the issue of capital punishment. Should the death penalty be administered to those who are deemed guilty of murder in a court of law? Based upon your answers to my class survey, if this decision were left up to this class, 75 percent of you would sentence the guilty defendant to death by way of lethal gas, lethal injection, hanging, or electrocution.

3   In my speech, I want to persuade you to reassess your view of capital punishment. My arguments will address the following issues relative to capital punishment: the injustice of capital punishment, the immorality of capital punishment, and capital punishment as a deterrent to crime. First of all, allow me to discuss the injustice of capital punishment.

4   Evidence shows that capital punishment is a discriminatory means of punishment. Some refer to capital punishment as the poor man's justice. In other words, those without the capital get the punishment. As criminologist Hugo Adam Bedeau has stated, often people are sentenced to death and executed not because they have been found to be uncontrollably violent, but because they are too poor to purchase a first-rate lawyer to defend them. To quote Bedeau, "People who have been executed for capital crimes have historically been the losers in an arbitrary lottery, the victims of the disadvantages that almost always come with poverty."

5   This discrimination is not only economic, but is also racial. As Supreme Court Justice William Brennan has stated, "Race casts a lot of shadows on the capital sentencing process." The most compelling evidence of this comes from a study conducted by Professor David Baldus of the University of Iowa. After studying nearly 2,500 murders in Georgia, Baldus concluded that no matter whether the killer be black or white, when it came to sentencing, the victim's race held firm as a primary determinant of life or death. People convicted of murdering whites, Baldus concluded, were eleven times more likely to be sentenced to death row than people convicted of killing blacks. This tends to confirm the analysis of Welsh White, of the University of Pittsburgh Law School, that it is built into the system that those in the predominant race will be more concerned about crime victims of their own race. Justice? I think not.

6   In addition to being discriminatory, capital punishment is also immoral. In fact, one reason why capital punishment is immoral is because it is discriminatory. This was stated especially well by Daniel Hoye, General Secretary of the United States Catholic Conference. "The system under which criminals are sentenced," he says, "is such that race often plays a prominent role in determining whether they will live or die. The fact that capital punishment is applied in a racially discriminatory way has been one of the reasons for our continued opposition on moral grounds to the application of the death penalty."

7   The immorality of capital punishment is not a matter of statistics or hard scientific fact. Instead, it is a matter of belief. The Bible says, "Thou shalt not kill." The Bible does not say, "Thou shalt not kill except in cases of murder, treason or capital crimes." It simply says, "Thou shalt not kill."

8   Proponents of the death penalty maintain that anyone who is lowly enough to commit murder deserves to die. But I ask you, how can we show that killing is wrong by killing someone ourselves? When we execute people, we are telling the rest of the world, and our children, that murder is acceptable. How can we maintain that murder is wrong if we are committing the same act that we allegedly denounce? In other words, two wrongs don't constitute a right. I agree with Dr. Rupert Theobald, a criminologist and statistician from the Wisconsin Legislative Reference Bureau, who stated that the message that capital punishment sends is that vengeance is acceptable. Morality? I think not.

9   But there is yet a third issue that we must confront, and that is whether capital punishment is an effective deterrent to crime. And this is a very controversial point with strong opinions on both sides. In truth, the small number of executions in the United States in recent years makes it hard to judge the value of capital punishment as a deterrent. It may be that the death penalty deters crime, but there is no clear-cut evidence which proves that it does. As the National Academy of Science concluded in its analysis of the death penalty, and I quote, "Available studies provide no useful evidence on the deterrent effect of capital punishment."

10   Indeed, there is at least one strong reason to believe that capital punishment does not work as a deterrent. As the Wisconsin Legislative Reference Bureau recently reported in its report on capital punishment, a major problem with the concept of deterrence is that it requires the would-be murderer to contemplate the consequences of his or her crime. In other words, if the murderer is not likely to think about the prospect of capital punishment before committing a crime, or is not able to think about it, then capital punishment cannot logically work as a deterrent to the commission of that crime. As the *Columbia Law Review* reports, "Many people who commit murder may not be able because of mental illness, mental retardation, or excessive emotion to realistically accept the danger of being caught, convicted, and executed. It is very unlikely that capital punishment would deter many of the people who are committing capital crimes." Deterrent? I think not.

11 In conclusion, we must realize that capital punishment is discriminatory. We must realize that capital punishment is immoral. And finally, we must realize that capital punishment is not an effective deterrent to crime. I would urge all of you who support capital punishment to reassess your views and to see its injustice, its immorality, and its ineffectiveness as a deterrent to crime.

Capital Punishment   *by Lee Hawkins, Jr.*

Commentary

A thoughtful speech on a highly controversial topic, "Capital Punishment" illustrates many of the principles of effective persuasion and is especially notable for the speaker's audience analysis and adaptation. Knowing from his class questionnaires that most of his listeners opposed his position, he takes care to address their objections and to answer them with evidence. He also does an excellent job of organizing the speech and uses plenty of transitions and signposts to help listeners grasp the connections among his ideas. This speech is also available on *Speeches for Analysis and Discussion: A Videotape Supplement* to *The Art of Public Speaking, Sixth Edition*. Here is a synopsis of it.

Specific Purpose: To persuade my audience that capital punishment should be abolished.

Central Idea: Capital punishment should be abolished because it is unjust, immoral, and ineffective as a deterrent to crime.

Method of Organization: Topical

Introduction: Although the speaker does not establish his credibility on the topic of capital punishment, his introduction is exemplary in all other respects. The opening sentence commands attention and leads into the story about the execution of convicted murderer Robert Streetman. After relating this story, the speaker announces his topic, relates it to his listeners by referring to their responses to his class survey, and ends the introduction with a concise preview of the main points to be discussed in the body.

Body: Organized in topical order, the body of this speech contains three main points, each of which takes up a major issue relative to capital punishment. The first, developed in paragraphs 4-5, argues that capital punishment is economically and racially discriminatory. The speaker's statement in paragraph 4 that "those without the capital get the punishment" is especially compelling and is followed by a quotation from criminologist Hugo Adam Bedeau that points to the fact that having the financial resources to hire a first-rate defense lawyer is a critical factor in avoiding capital punishment. The claim of racial discrimination, presented in paragraph 5, is supported with a brief quotation from Supreme Court Justice William Brennan, with statistical evidence from University of Iowa professor David Baldus, and with testimony from University of Pittsburgh Law School professor Welsh White. Main point one ends with the biting statement: "Justice? I think not."

An excellent transition at the start of paragraph 6 introduces main point two, which deals with the immorality of capital punishment. The speaker advances three subpoints. First, he states that capital punishment is immoral because it is discriminatory, a claim he supports with a quotation from Daniel Hoye of the U.S. Catholic Conference (paragraph 6). Second, the speaker contends that there are no limitations on the Biblical injunction,

"Thou shalt not kill" (paragraph 7). Third, he holds that killing someone through capital punishment is just as wrong as killing someone through murder (paragraph 8). The last words of paragraph 8—"Morality? I think not"—parallel the end of main point one and end the second main point on a powerful note.

The third main point addresses the value of capital punishment as a deterrent to crime (paragraphs 9-10). After noting that this is a difficult issue to assess because of the limited number of executions in recent years, the speaker quotes the National Academy of Science's judgment that there is "no useful evidence on the deterrent effect of capital punishment." He then turns to a report from the Wisconsin Legislative Reference Bureau to explain that there are logical reasons to believe that, in many cases, capital punishment is not likely to deter people from committing murder. As in other parts of the speech, the speaker's evidence here does not prove that he is right in an absolute sense—capital punishment is too complex and contentious an issue to admit of perfect proof on either side—but it does enhance both the credibility and potential persuasiveness of his arguments. The final words of main point three—"Deterrence? I think not"—reinforce the speaker's position and lend artistic unity to the speech by echoing the language used to end both of the preceding main points.

Conclusion: Brief and hard-hitting, the conclusion (paragraph 11) succinctly signals the end of the speech and reinforces the central idea.

Responsible Drinking

Joveta Dixon

---

1   "This Bud's for you." "Buy that man a Miller." "It's the right beer now." The message you get from beer companies is that you deserve that ice-cold beer when you're having a good time.

2   On the other hand, you hear, "Drinking and driving can kill a friendship" and "Friends don't let friends drive drunk." You easily get the impression that it's no problem to drink to excess as long as you don't drive. But I've seen students who didn't drive get carried out of parties on stretchers because they drank until they passed out. I've had to put friends in cabs or have them stay over at my home because they drank too much to be able to make it home safely.

3   As a student at this and another university, I've seen firsthand that drinking too much is a problem and my research shows that it's a growing problem on college campuses. Tonight, I will tell you of the serious problem of excessive drinking by college students. I'll discuss some causes and I'll propose a solution.

4   Let's first examine the problem when college students drink to excess. From my in-class survey, I learned that eleven of you agree that excessive drinking by college students causes serious problems for the university community, while only four of you are either undecided or disagree. We're probably all aware of the dangers of drinking and driving, and we're becoming increasingly aware of the role of alcohol in acquaintance rape, but let's turn to some problems you may not have thought about.

5   First, students may use a community's medical resources if they drink too much. According to an article published in *Newsweek*, the number of students from Boston University hospitalized for alcohol-related illnesses doubled this year. Hospitals and police are valuable community resources being used by students who drink too much.

6   In addition to causing problems for the community, students may cause problems for themselves if they drink too much. A student may skip class, work, or studying due to a hangover. Now you might be thinking, what's a skipped class here and there? Well, it adds up. According to the Office for Substance Abuse Prevention in Washington, D. C., alcohol is a factor in 21 percent of all college dropouts.

7   Next, students who drink to excess sometimes injure themselves or others. I found from my in-class survey that eight of you have had an alcohol-related injury or you know someone who has had an alcohol-related injury. Much more tragic are student deaths caused by alcohol. In February of this year, a student at Princeton University climbed on top of a train that was stopped at the station. This student was electrocuted when he touched the train's live wire, and he had been drinking heavily at a campus party.

8   According to the Office for Substance Abuse Prevention, alcohol is the leading cause of death among young adults. Furthermore, of college students currently enrolled in the United States, more than 240,000 will eventually lose their lives to alcohol. Two hundred and forty thousand—that's the current student population of this university, six times over.

9   Now that we've seen how drinking too much is a serious problem for students and their communities, let's look at some causes. Of course, there are many general causes—from the glorification of drinking that we see in the media, to the tradition of drinking heavily as a rite of passage. But I'd like to discuss some causes that are more specific to college life. I'll tell you how alcohol-centered activities and social pressure can lead to excessive student drinking.

10   Now, college has many activities that are alcohol-centered. Many parties may have drinking as a main event or feature drinking games, and we all know that the purpose of a bar located within walking distance of a campus is for people to purchase and to consume alcohol. If alcohol is the thrust of the activity, then most people who attend that activity will drink, and no one is setting limits as to how much they should drink. All around the country, Spring Break has become such an alcohol-centered activity that the Surgeon General said, "Spring Break used to be where the boys are, now, it's where the booze is."

11   In addition to alcohol-centered activities, social pressure is a cause. I remember well my initiation into an eating club at Princeton University back in 1984. Most of my friends were getting initiated that night as well, and we got the message clearly—from each other and from the club—that if we wanted to make it into the club that night, we would have to drink, and drink heavily. Everyone I knew drank a great deal that night. Many of you have also experienced social pressure, because I found from my survey that nine of you feel that social pressure has an impact on the amount you drink.

12   Now that we've seen how social pressure and alcohol-centered activities can lead to excessive student drinking, I'd like to discuss solutions that address these causes. These are simple solutions that are within your power to use right away.

13   First, you can choose fun activities that are not alcohol-centered. For a friend's twenty-first birthday, rather than just taking them out for drinks, take them shopping for a special gift. You can go for walks, go to sporting events, or go for bicycle rides to see the view of the city rather than just the view from the bar. You can choose parties and clubs that are alcohol-free. You may say, "Nobody wants to go to activities that don't involve alcohol," but this year the Wisconsin Union Directorate offered students a chance to help the poor in Florida, North Carolina, and Texas as an alternative to Spring Break. There were only 40 positions available, but over 120 people applied.

14   Choosing activities is important, but the choice not to drink too much is equally important. So if you attend activities that do involve alcohol, make a decision before the event that you will not drink too much. You can use the buddy system and say to a friend, "Tonight at the party I've decided only to have three drinks. If you help me maintain my limit, I'll help you maintain your limit."

15   In social situations where there is a lot of pressure to constantly have a drink in your hand, you can alternate an alcoholic drink with a non-alcoholic drink. For instance, I like to drink rum and coke, so what I'll do is I'll have one rum and coke and then for my next drink I'll ask the bartender to fill that same glass with just Coca-Cola. I can easily maintain my limit, and no one else at the party needs to know that I'm not always consuming alcohol. If we recognize that social pressure is a factor in our drinking, we can use it to our advantage to help us drink responsibly.

16   Tonight we have learned about the serious problem of excessive drinking by college students and some of its causes, and I do hope you realize that solutions are within your power. Please don't think I'm against alcohol, but I am advocating responsible use of the drug—and we must recognize alcohol's power as a drug.

17   Let's go beyond "Friends don't let friends drive drunk" to "Friends don't let friends get drunk." Be a good friend to the most important person of all—yourself—and if you choose to drink, please don't drink to excess.

Responsible Drinking   *by Joveta Dixon*

Commentary

Presented in an introductory public speaking class at the University of Wisconsin, "Responsible Drinking" is a persuasive speech on a question of policy. Although students have heard so much about the problem of excessive drinking on college campuses that they often tune out part way through speeches on the subject, in this case everyone listened intently. A returning student, the speaker presents her ideas clearly and forcefully, but without sounding morally superior to her classmates. As can be seen from the videotape of the speech, which is available on *Speeches for Analysis and Discussion: A Videotape Supplement to The Art of Public Speaking, Sixth Edition*, the impact of the speech is also enhanced by the speaker's delivery, which is measured and serious yet still conversational and highly personal in tone. Here is a synopsis of the speech.

Specific Purpose: To persuade my audience that, if they choose to drink, they should take action to drink responsibly.

Central Idea: Excessive drinking among college students is a serious problem that can be combated by choosing social activities that are not alcohol-centered and by overcoming social pressure for excessive drinking.

Method of Organization: Problem-Cause-Solution

Introduction: Consisting of paragraphs 1-3, the introduction captures attention with a series of well-known slogans from beer companies. After presenting the slogans, the speaker suggests that the problem of drinking on college campuses involves much more than drunk driving—a theme she will develop in detail as the speech progresses. She also establishes her credibility and provides a succinct preview of the main points to be discussed in the body.

Body: This speech provides an excellent example of problem-cause-solution order. Main point one (paragraphs 4-8) deals with the problem of excessive drinking by college students. Rather than focusing on such familiar issues as drunk driving and the role of alcohol in acquaintance rape, the speaker mentions these in passing and spends the bulk of her time discussing equally important but less publicized aspects of student drinking. Main point two (paragraphs 9-11) focuses on two major causes of the problem unique to college life: the large number of alcohol-centered activities on and around campus and the social pressure on students to drink to excess. Main point three (paragraphs 12-15) presents solutions to the problem.

It is important, when using problem-cause-solution order, to make sure the solution deals directly with what the speaker identifies as the cause of the problem. In this case, the first part of the speaker's solution, choosing social activities that are not alcohol-centered (paragraph 13), addresses the first of the causes she had discussed in main point two. The second part of her solution, coping with the social pressure to drink excessively (paragraphs 14-15), addresses the second cause she had mentioned in main point two. Here, as throughout the body, the impact of the speech is strengthened by the excellent use of transitions and signposts to ensure that the audience can follow the speaker's reasoning and progression of ideas.

Conclusion: The conclusion consists of paragraphs 16-17. After summarizing her main points in paragraph 16, the speaker ties the whole speech together in paragraph 17 by referring back to the quotations she had used in the introduction. The closing line reinforces the central idea and ends the speech with a final appeal for individual action.

———————————————

Making Campus Accessible for Disabled Students

Diane Bright

1   I'd like to ask you to use your imaginations and think how it would feel if you'd spent an evening studying for an exam. You get up in the morning all set to go to classes, you go down, you get to your door, and it won't open. You think, "Oh, I can just use my back door." But you go to your back door, and that won't open either.

2   It would be pretty frustrating, wouldn't it? That's the kind of frustration handicapped students feel when they can't get to class because of the snow. And that's the same kind of frustration I found when I tried to get my scooter through the snow and it short-circuited because it got so wet from the snow.

3   Now there are many reasons that campuses could be inaccessible, but what I would like to address today is the inaccessibility of this campus due to the uncleared snow. You may think, "This is never going to affect me," but sadly it could. By accident or illness, it could become a problem for you.

4   As you can see, I use a scooter to get around campus, and I have found that this campus is inaccessible due to the uncleared snow. I'd like to share that problem with you and then share my solution. Let's start with the problem.

5   As I see it, the problem faced by handicapped students has two components: the uncleared snow and the violation of the Americans with Disabilities Act. The first component is the inaccessibility of this campus due to the uncleared snow that creates a barrier for wheelchairs and scooters to pass through. Here in Wisconsin, we get an average of 43 inches of snow in any winter and an average of thirteen days of snowfall over one inch or more. As you can see, that would create a significant barrier for those of us who have to use scooters or wheelchairs to get around.

6   A fellow handicapped student shared his story with me. He is a quadriplegic; he has no use of his arms or his legs. He directs his scooter with a wand by his chin. He tried to get through the snow this winter, and he tipped over and was hurt. This is unfair, and it's dangerous. Why should he have to jeopardize his life just to try to get to class? And why is it fair for him to be kept out of class when he has paid for classes out of his pocket just like you and just like me? I've heard the same kinds of horror stories from several handicapped students. The fact remains that the snow creates a barrier that we just cannot pass through, and that barrier really creates a significant problem for us.

7   The second component of this problem is that the Americans with Disabilities Act, a civil rights act that was passed by Congress and signed by President Bush in 1990, prohibits discrimination and requires that barrier-free access to any public accommodation be given to the handicapped students. The university is in violation of this act. Let me read part of it for you: "People with disabilities have the right to full and equal access to any facility or accommodation of any public place. They have the right to make a request for acceptable services by that public accommodation." I believe that language is clear: "Full and equal access." And we're not getting that. That's why I believe the university is violating the Americans with Disabilities Act.

8   Now that we have a clear understanding of the problem, let me share my solution with you. An effective solution could have three components. The first component is that the university should adopt a policy of snow removal similar to the ordinance that the city of Madison has. That ordinance reads: "Sidewalks must be cleared of all ice and snow whenever it accumulates to one-half inch or more and the walks must be cleared by noon the day following the snowfall." I think the university should adopt this as a campus policy.

9   Second, the university should set priorities to the areas that the handicapped students need. In an interview with Gene Turk of the Grounds Department, I learned of the university's priorities. He says that first the stairs and the hills are taken care of. Then the parking lots and the sidewalks are cleared by the plows. There was never any mention of the ramps or the curb cutaways that we handicapped students need. We're not getting a fair deal here. That's why I think the university is violating the Americans with Disabilities Act. The university needs to set as priorities the areas that we need—the ramps and the curb cutaways.

10   The third component of my solution would address the lack of personnel in the Grounds Department. The university should hire a staff member who could focus on those areas that handicapped individuals need to get around. Some of you may be wondering, "How much would this cost?" A forty-hour week, at eight dollars an hour, would be $15,000 dollars a year, plus benefits. The official published university budget is $1 billion. Surely, they can find, in a budget that big, funding for $15,000 to hire someone who could make this campus accessible to all of us.

11   In closing, I really believe this is a workable solution. If the university were to go ahead and adopt this policy, it would fulfill the requirements of the Americans with Disabilities Act and make this campus accessible, providing full and equal enjoyment for those of us who are the handicapped students. Won't you help me effectuate this change? Please consider signing a petition that would encourage this university to change its snow removal plan. I will have those petitions in the back of the room when this speech is finished.

12   To end, let me share with you a quote out of the book *Access: The Guide to a Better Life for Disabled Americans*: "The disabled minority is not a closed society. While nobody would ever change skin color, anyone can join this minority by accident or by illness." Disability does not respect age, sex, religion or social status. Every American should see himself or herself as an ally for the disabled person who is just seeking a fair deal. Thank you.

Making Campus Accessible for Disabled Students   *by Diane Bright*

Commentary

"Making Campus Accessible for Disabled Students" shows how students can construct speeches on matters of local concern. As can be seen from the videotape of the speech (available on *Speeches for Analysis and Discussion to Accompany The Art of Public Speaking, Sixth Edition*), the speaker, who suffers from multiple sclerosis, addresses the audience while seated in her scooter. Her delivery is fairly subdued—partly because she is naturally soft-spoken, partly because her illness can sap her strength even in the course of presenting a speech. Yet she speaks conversationally, maintains consistent eye contact, and establishes a strong bond with her listeners. Here is a synopsis of the speech, with special attention to how it utilizes the methods of persuasion discussed in Chapter 16 of the textbook.

Specific Purpose: To persuade my audience that the University of Wisconsin-Madison should change its snow removal policy to make campus more accessible to handicapped students.

Central Idea: The University of Wisconsin should change its snow removal policies to solve the problem of inaccessibility to handicapped students.

Method of Organization: Problem-Solution

Introduction: Consisting of paragraphs 1-4, the introduction begins with a hypothetical scenario that allows students who are not disabled to imagine themselves in a situation akin to that of a handicapped student who cannot get to class because of the snow. The speaker then tells her audience: "You might think this never is going to affect you, but, sadly, it could. By accident or illness, it could become a problem for you." She ends the introduction by previewing the main points she will discuss in the body.

The introduction also plays a crucial role in establishing the speaker's credibility. The fact that she suffers from multiple sclerosis and has to get around campus in a scooter gives her high initial credibility. She reinforces that credibility by noting that she, like other handicapped students, has experienced problems getting to class because of the university's failure to clear snow in a timely fashion. Moreover, as the speech progresses, she continues to build her credibility by exhibiting sincerity and good will and by delivering the speech with genuine conviction.

Body: Organized in problem-solution order, the body of this speech contains two main points. The first details the problem of inaccessibility to campus for handicapped students because of the uncleared snow (paragraphs 5-7). The second presents the speaker's solution to the problem (paragraphs 8-10).

Both points are amply supported with evidence. In the problem section, the speaker uses statistics and examples to demonstrate that there is a need to change the university's snow removal priorities. In the solution section, she uses testimony from a member of the Grounds Department to reinforce her claim that ramps and curb cutaways are not currently a priority for snow removal on campus. She also presents statistics to show that the university can afford to hire additional personnel to clear snow from ramps, curb cutaways, and other areas needed by handicapped students. This is important because a potential objection to the speaker's plan is that it might be too costly. Anticipating the objection and answering it with evidence makes her position more persuasive.

The speaker also makes effective use of reasoning in both main points. In the first, she reasons from principle in arguing that the university is violating the Americans with Disabilities Act. Her reasoning is as follows:

a.   The Americans with Disabilities Act requires equal access to all public facilities for people with physical disabilities.

b.   The university's policy of snow removal does not provide equal access for students with physical disabilities.

c.   Therefore, the university's policy of snow removal violates the Americans with Disabilities Act.

In her second main point, the speaker reasons from analogy by contending that the city of Madison's snow removal policy is also appropriate for the university. If that policy works in the city, she suggests, it should be workable on campus as well.

Although the speaker does not employ a great deal of emotional language, her personal involvement with the topic, the sincerity and conviction of her delivery, and her examples of handicapped students who have had trouble getting around campus because of the snow all combine to give her speech a degree of emotional appeal and to enhance its persuasiveness.

Conclusion: The conclusion consists of paragraphs 11-12. Paragraph 11 summarizes the main points and calls upon listeners to sign the petition that the speaker will have available after the speech. The closing paragraph reemphasizes the fact that anyone can become disabled at any time and encourages all members of the audience to see themselves as allies for the disabled.

_____